NORTHERN IRELAND: THE ORIGINS OF THE TROUBLES

NORTHERN IRELAND: THE ORIGINS OF THE TROUBLES

THOMAS HENNESSEY

Gill & Macmillan

Published by Gill & Macmillan Ltd
Hume Avenue, Park West, Dublin 12, Ireland
with associated companies throughout the world
www.gillmacmillan.ie

© Thomas Hennessey 2005
0 7171 3382 6
Index by Cover to Cover
Type design by Make Communication
Typesetting and print origination by Carrigboy Typesetting Services, Co. Cork
Printed by MPG Books, Cornwall

The paper used in this book is made from the wood pulp
of managed forests. For every tree felled, at least one tree
is planted, thereby renewing natural resources.

A catalogue record is available for this book
from the British Library.

5 4 3 2 1

For
Nicholas Vincent
Bene Facis

CONTENTS

NOTE ON TERMINOLOGY   VIII

INTRODUCTION   IX

1   Protestant Ulster   1

2   O'Neill and the Enemy Within:
the Unionist Party   36

3   Catholics in the Six Counties   67

4   The Gathering Storm   107

5   London Intervenes: British Policy and
Westminster–Stormont Relations
October 1968–February 1969   145

6   Towards Disaster: Northern Ireland
February–August 1969   190

7   August 1969   237

8   Cold War: September 1969–May 1970   286

9   Resurrection: the Irish State and Origins of the
Republican War   337

CONCLUSION   377

NOTES   396

BIBLIOGRAPHY   422

INDEX   431

NOTE ON TERMINOLOGY

In the text the terms 'Unionist', 'Nationalist' and 'Republican' are capitalised to denote the parties or organisations to which they refer; in the lower case they refer to supporters in the wider community. Terms such as 'Ulster', the 'North' and the 'six counties' are generally employed in the context that Unionists or Nationalists use them. 'Londonderry' or 'Derry' is used interchangeably by the author.

INTRODUCTION

The Troubles in Northern Ireland are the tragedy of modern Irish history. Now, for the first time, the archives have been opened and we have the opportunity to examine the decisions made in London, Dublin and Belfast that helped shape the origins of the Troubles. As a result it has become possible to correlate the decisions of high politics with events on the ground. This is what this book does and what makes it different to all other major works on this subject so far. But I am under no illusions as to the influence such a work will have on the popular perceptions held of the origins of the conflict, particularly in the North. Already new myths are being formed legitimising the roles played by some of the prominent actors in the events of the last three decades. What the book attempts to do is to answer the following questions: Why did the Troubles occur when they did and why did the people of Northern Ireland have to be condemned to such a trauma?

One of the problems with a study of the origins of the Troubles is deciding when to begin the project. Depending on one's view of history the study could start in 1169 with the arrival of Strongbow, or with the Plantation in the seventeenth century, or with the partition of Ireland in 1920. Theoretically one could start with the arrival of the Celts in Ireland and the consequent dislocation of Ireland's first inhabitants. Such reductionism, in the end, teaches us nothing: for example, but for the First World War there would have been no Easter Rising and it is quite conceivable that all of Ireland would have remained within the United Kingdom to this day; this is but one illustration of how it is important to look at a sequence of events in detail and over a limited period, rather than looking over a vast canvas to locate causation. I have chosen to begin with the premiership of Captain Terence O'Neill in 1963. Why? Partly because O'Neill challenged some of the basic assumptions of what Northern Ireland actually stood for. To set the scene for this journey we have to remind ourselves of certain characteristics of the Northern Ireland 'problem'.

One of the main things that spring out at an observer of the Troubles is that none of the main protagonists agree about who or what was instrumental in causing them. The Nationalist view of Ireland's history essentially has, at its core, two propositions: that the geographic island of Ireland equates with the political Irish nation, and that it is English, and later British, interference that has contributed—and some argue still contributes—to the divisions in Ireland. The first position is, for all Nationalists, non-negotiable while the latter has been modified over time to take account of Unionist opposition to a united Ireland. The Unionist view is that there are two peoples in Ireland and if only everyone would accept this—and leave the Unionists alone to get on with their existence—everything would be all right. Because of this basic cleavage the politics of Northern Ireland has been dominated by partition. Aside from Nationalists and Unionists in Ireland the other key actor is the British government. Northern Ireland's problem embodied the following: the clash between the right of British sovereignty in Ireland and the claim to Irish national self-determination, the clash of British and Irish national identities within Northern Ireland, and the clash between Protestant and Catholic ethno-religious identities and theologies. In addition to this was the controversy surrounding the distribution of state resources and the economic disparity between the two communities in the Province.

The Government of Ireland Act 1920, which partitioned Ireland, created a 'Northern Ireland' consisting of six of the nine counties of the province of Ulster: Antrim, Armagh, Down, Londonderry, Fermanagh and Tyrone. In the last two counties there were Catholic majorities. The remaining twenty-six Irish counties eventually seceded from the United Kingdom in 1922, first as the Irish Free State within the British Commonwealth and later as Eire, a sovereign independent republic. Northern Ireland was granted its own Parliament, eventually based at Stormont in Belfast. Northern Ireland remained within the UK returning MPs to its own subordinate Parliament and to the UK Parliament at Westminster which, according to Section 75 of the 1920 Act, remained sovereign over all things in Northern Ireland. The UK, or Imperial, Parliament devolved certain powers to Belfast but retained control of taxes, customs and excise, the Crown and external affairs. Financially, Stormont remained heavily dependent on British subsidies. The British Government did not envisage partition as a permanent settlement: a Council of Ireland, which never met but was to consist of representatives from the two Irish Parliaments established by the 1920 Act, was designed, by mutual consent, to create a united Ireland under one all-Ireland legislature if that was its wish. The Northern Ireland Parliament itself was elected by the first-past-the-post system. With roughly two-thirds of the population Protestant—and Unionist—this ensured one-party government committed to the Union with Great Britain. The Ulster Unionist Party—and therefore Protestants—were in power for over fifty years.

The Protestant population in Northern Ireland exhibited a siege mentality, fearing an enemy within and outside its borders. Northern Ireland had been born in sectarian violence in 1920–22, with the Irish Republican Army also seeking to destabilise the new statelet with assistance and encouragement from Michael Collins in the Free State Government of the time. Later, Eire laid claim to Northern Ireland. Its 1937 constitution, Bunreacht na hÉireann, declared in Article 2 that: 'The national territory consists of the whole island of Ireland, its islands and the territorial seas.' Article 3 stated that pending the 're-integration of the national territory', the Irish parliament and government had the right to exercise juris-diction over the whole of the island, although it chose, voluntarily, not to apply this to Northern Ireland, which was occupied by a foreign power—Britain. This was a territorial claim. According to the Irish Constitution, Northern Ireland was a part of both the Irish nation and the independent Irish state—it was not part of the United Kingdom. According to the Acts of Union 1800, however, Northern Ireland was part of the United Kingdom. Thus the Irish state formally challenged the right of British sovereignty in Northern Ireland. The Unionist Government in Northern Ireland was outraged. The outbreak of war in 1939 drove the two parts of Ireland further apart. Northern Ireland, as part of the United Kingdom, took its part in the Allied war effort. Eire remained neutral. The final parting of the ways was Eire's formal declaration of a republic in 1948.

As a response Attlee's Labour Government passed the Ireland Act a year later: the key clause stated that Northern Ireland would remain part of His Majesty's Dominions unless the Northern Ireland Parliament voted to leave the United Kingdom.[1] For the first time Northern Ireland's constitutional destiny had been transferred from Westminster to Belfast. This outraged Nationalists, North and South, for they considered this the creation of an artificial Unionist veto in the path of Irish unity: Britain had partitioned Ireland so she could, and should, end partition unilaterally. Northern Nationalists in particular were bitterly disappointed: they had expected the Labour Government to be pro-active in ending partition. Instead, the Labour Government was conscious of Britain's debt to Northern Ireland arising from the War. After the War, Nationalist energies had been channelled into an Anti-Partition League in a vain attempt to influence British political opinion in favour of Irish unity. But by 1951 this was visibly fragmenting. The Irish Republican Army filled the vacuum. In 1955, its political wing, Sinn Féin, won two seats in the Westminster general election. This was followed in 1956 by the launching of an IRA border campaign, which lasted until 1962. It proved unsuccessful mainly because of a lack of popular support from the Catholic population. The campaign ended with recognition of this by the IRA and an order to its Volunteers to dump arms.[2]

Despite their rejection of violence, Catholics within Northern Ireland retained a reservoir of grievances that they felt had never been remedied since the creation of Northern Ireland—particularly by Westminster which seemed to have washed its hands of any involvement in the six counties following the paralysis that Ireland appeared, periodically, to exert on British politics. In terms of law and order, the armed police force, the Royal Ulster Constabulary, was overwhelmingly Protestant; even more Protestant were the personnel of the part-time Ulster Special Constabulary or B-Specials—especially distrusted by the minority as an unprofessional sectarian force. Catholics, on the other hand, had steadfastly refused to enlist within the RUC despite 1,000 places out of 3,000 being set aside for them at its inception. In terms of legislation the Civil Authorities (Special Powers) Act, the first in a series of such legislation introduced in 1922, gave the Minister of Home Affairs in the Northern Ireland Government the power to make new regulations 'for making further provision for the preservation of the peace and maintenance of order'. The 'civil authority' was to have 'power, in respect of persons, matters and things within the jurisdiction of the Government of Northern Ireland, to take all such steps and issue all such orders as may be necessary for preserving the peace and maintaining order, according to and in the execution of the Act and the regulations'. The civil authority, that is the Minister of Home Affairs, might 'delegate, either unconditionally or subject to such conditions as he thinks fit all or any of his powers under this Act to any officer of police, and any such officer of police shall, to the extent of such delegation, be the civil authority as respects any part of Northern Ireland specified in such delegation'. The Special Powers Acts amounted to the civil equivalent of the statutory imposition of martial law.[3] Further Public Order Acts gave additional powers to the authorities. In terms of cultural identity the Flags and Emblems (Display) Act (NI), 1954 provided for the removal by the RUC of any emblem the display of which seemed likely to lead to disturbance. Basically this meant the Irish Tricolour.

The Unionist Government's decision to abolish proportional representation (PR) in local and then parliamentary elections aroused bitter controversy between Nationalists and Unionists. It was abolished in 1929. Unionist representation on elective public boards increased at the expense of all other parties. In Belfast, official Unionist representation increased from eight in 1925 to eleven in 1929, at the expense of Labour and independent Unionist candidates. Under PR, Nationalists secured thirty-three per cent of the parliamentary representation outside Belfast and Queen's University; after 1929 they secured at most 28.1 per cent. But on balance, in Parliamentary elections, Nationalists lost only one MP through the abolition of PR. However, Unionist representation on, and their control of, local bodies was increased by the abolition of PR in local elections. In Fermanagh, under PR, Nationalists had returned sixty-three members to the Unionists' fifty-seven. This fell to forty-three after PR's abolition, while the Unionists' number of representatives increased to seventy-four. Catholics in Fermanagh, comprising fifty-six per cent of the population, obtained only 36.75 per cent of the representation on public bodies.[4]

What made the abolition of PR so controversial was the consequent redrawing of electoral boundaries. Nationalists were convinced that the Unionist Government had deliberately decided to gerrymander all constituencies to its advantage. In the example of Omagh Rural District Council the electoral units were so arranged that large Nationalist-Catholic majorities were lumped together and given the same representation as the smaller Unionist majorities. In this way, it was claimed, 5,381 'unionist' electors were assured of twenty-one seats at the next election, compared with eighteen seats for the 8,459 'nationalists', with the average number of votes required to elect a member in the Nationalist units 463, compared with 228 in the Unionist units.[5] The greatest outcry was over Londonderry, Northern Ireland's second city. Under PR, Nationalists had controlled Londonderry Corporation, with 6,868 Nationalist electors returning twenty-one councillors and 6,340 Unionists returning nineteen. The abolition of PR and redistribution returned the Corporation to Unionist hands. Unionist control was achieved by dividing the city into five wards, with three of the wards having Unionist majorities, and the other two Nationalist majorities, the Nationalist wards being significantly larger than the Unionist. In the 1930s the Derry electorate was again redistributed, this time into three wards, into one of which the majority of Nationalist electors was placed. Two wards contained safe Unionist majorities. Therefore 9,961 Nationalist electors returned eight councillors, while 7,444 Unionist voters returned twelve councillors.[6]

Catholics also claimed that they were discriminated against in terms of employment. Sir James Craig, Northern Ireland's first Prime Minister, declared that he was an Orangeman first and a politician and Member of the Northern Irish Parliament afterwards. In a reply to a Nationalist MP he asked MPs to 'remember that in the South they boasted of a Catholic State. They still boast of Southern Ireland being a Catholic State. All I boast of is that we are a Protestant Parliament and a Protestant State.' The Prime Minister urged 'the public to employ only loyalists – I say only loyalists. I do not care what their religion may be. I say that as long as they are loyal people we will engage them and give them every chance.'[7] His colleague and successor but one, Sir Basil Brooke (later Viscount Brookeborough), was not so discerning for in 1932 he told an Orange audience: 'There was a great number of Protestants and Orangemen who employed Roman Catholics. He felt he could speak freely on this subject as he had not a Roman Catholic about his own place. He appreciated the great difficulty experienced by some of them in procuring suitable Protestant labour but he would point out that Roman Catholics were endeavouring to get in everywhere. He would appeal to Loyalists therefore, wherever possible, to employ good Protestant lads and lassies.'[8]

With Brooke as Prime Minister from 1943 to 1963 and the Nationalist Party opposing him, it seemed that, since the 1920s, nothing had changed much in Northern Ireland by the time the Beatles began creating upheavals in popular music. But this was going to change with the coming to power of Captain Terence O'Neill. O'Neill was typical of the 'Big House' type of politician who dominated Unionist politics: aristocratic, Eton-educated (in Earl Onslow's description the original comprehensive as the school didn't care how stupid a child was so long as their parents had the money), service in the Irish Guards during the Second World War and a bit of the amateur about him in an age of players. But things in Northern Ireland were about to change.

Chapter 1 ∾

PROTESTANT ULSTER

THE SOUL OF PROTESTANT ULSTER

One of the most striking features of Northern Ireland in the 1960s was just how mono-cultural it was. Its dominant cultural identity was British and Protestant. In a way this was not surprising. The majority of Northern Ireland's population—roughly two-thirds—were Protestant and, according to every survey, overwhelmingly Unionist. And nothing demonstrated the Protestant ethos of the Province more than the perennial debate between Protestants over the sanctity of the Sabbath. This usually revolved around the use of children's swings, and occasionally the opening of cinemas or swimming pools, on a Sunday, the day of rest. Whenever a Unionist council permitted such relaxations the fundamentalists were outraged and campaigned for a reversal of the decision. This in itself would not necessarily be of much relevance beyond a certain curiosity to those from outside Northern Ireland but for one thing: the Roman Catholics. The inherent instability of Northern Ireland was that one-third of its population was Catholic and, on the whole, Nationalist. The problem was how to accommodate them within the entity of Northern Ireland; an entity from which, politically and culturally, they had been excluded and from which, if they were honest, they had excluded themselves. This was something which concerned Captain Terence O'Neill, the Prime Minister of Northern Ireland. He took the view that in the long-term Northern Ireland's position rested on assimilating Catholics into Unionism. All the indications are that O'Neill saw this as a long process to be achieved incrementally. This did not necessarily mean reform to alleviate Nationalist grievances—gerrymandering, the local government franchise and so on—rather a reaching out to Catholics and making them feel that Northern Ireland could belong to them as much as to Protestants. This would be secured through a general rise in the whole community's prosperity achieved through economic reform. Time would take care of the rest. What O'Neill did was to embark on a series of symbolic gestures which from outside Northern Ireland, both at the time and from the perspective of temporal distance, seemed small, but which from within the Province of the 1960s were quasi-revolutionary. For example, in June 1963 O'Neill offered a public condolence to Cardinal William Conway, the Roman Catholic Primate of All Ireland, on the death of Pope John XXIII. The Prime Minister broke with tradition when he decided that the message of sympathy on the Pope's death should be sent by him on behalf of the Northern Ireland Government.[1] In his message to Conway O'Neill acknowledged that the late Pope had 'won acclaim throughout the world because of his qualities of kindness and humanity'.[2]

This and subsequent gestures produced a storm of protest from the supporters of fundamental Protestantism. Their most vocal advocate was the Reverend Ian Paisley. The Moderator of the Free Presbyterian Church did not represent the majority of those Protestants who felt concern with O'Neill's gestures, but he did represent a general concern that the very cultural ethos of the Northern Irish state was being undermined. This was often summed up in the phrase 'traditional Unionism'. In essence this meant that Northern Ireland was the Protestant and British part of Ireland; that the function of the Northern Irish state was to preserve that heritage in opposition to internal and external threats from the Irish and world manifestations of the Roman Catholic Church; that Unionist govern- ments had to show determination in resisting the imperial ambitions of the Republic of Ireland to annex Northern Ireland; and that the state had to be prepared at all times to defeat any internal threat from a disloyal Catholic minority which was equated with Irish Nationalism and wanted union with Southern Ireland. Traditional Unionism was based upon an interpretation of what the legacy of Carson, Craigavon and Brookeborough was—that there could be no compromise with an enemy that sought to destroy you.

In assessing these influences it is well to bear a number of points in mind. The first is that these threats had some substance. When O'Neill came to power in 1963 it had been less than a year since the IRA called off its Border Campaign. It would only be six years from the ending of that campaign to the beginning of the Troubles in 1968. The IRA had not dismantled its structure, surrendered its weapons or renounced violence. If one might borrow a phrase from the future: it hadn't gone away, you know. Alongside the IRA threat there was a fear among Ulster Protestants that they would be absorbed into a Gaelic-Republican-Catholic Ireland. Ulster Protestants did not, nor did they show any desire to, speak Irish (a trait it seemed they shared with the vast majority of their Southern neighbours) which they regarded as an artificial attempt to make the Irish different from the English, Scots and Welsh. It is well to remember that Unionists retained a strong and positive sense of Irishness. They were Irish—but British too. Many even wanted to see a united Ireland—under the Crown. Republicanism was alien to them. For them it had not been the Unionists who had been responsible for partition—it had been the Republicans who had partitioned the British Isles. And the Republic of Ireland was a Catholic country. The Protestant population had declined there through the strict Catholic rules regarding inter-marriage; its population was overwhelmingly Catholic; its leaders were Catholic. This was the context in which Ulster Protestant Unionists of all variations often regarded their world. Northern Ireland was the last bastion of Protestantism in Ireland. It was theirs to be defended against the hereditary enemy. This was the general background to Protestant fears. For Protestant fundamentalists the 1960s produced another threat: the ecumenical movement. The controversy surrounding this movement is often mentioned but rarely analysed in any depth with regard to the political rise of Ian Paisley. Yet it is central to any understanding, not only of Paisley, but of the whole ethos of Protestant Ulster. For within this debate—primarily between Protestants—lies not only an understanding of the strength of the resistance to O'Neill's détente with the Catholic minority but also the strength of support which also existed among Protestants for such policies. It was a battle for the soul of—Protestant—Ulster.

Nothing worked up Paisley and his supporters more than the ecumenical movement and the—apparently—closer ties developing between the Roman Catholic Church and the Protestant churches in Ireland, Britain and beyond. The touchstone for the movement was the World Council of Churches. Its origins lay in August 1948 when the delegates of 147 member churches gathered for their inaugural service in the Nieuwe Kerk in Amsterdam. Some of the oldest churches in the world, such as the Church of Ethiopia and the Syrian Church of Malabar in India, were represented alongside some of the newest, such as the Presbyterian Church of Korea. The Roman Catholic Church and the Russian Church were not represented, though the Eastern Orthodox Church was. The Russian Church was later admitted in 1961. This wideness was both its strength and its weakness. It meant that authority was conferred on the Council but it also meant that any collective excursions into theology had to be kept at the most general level. The first article in the constitution stated that the Council 'is a fellowship of Churches which accept our Lord Jesus Christ as God and Saviour'. Thereafter were listed the objects of the new body. These were the facilitation of common action by the churches, the promotion of co-operation in study and of ecumenical consciousness, the making of contact with other denominational federations and ecumenical movements, the holding of world conferences and the support of the churches in ecumenicalism. At no point was there any commitment to unity.[3]

Paisley, however, saw in the ecumenical movement a move towards eventual unity with Rome. There was some reasoning behind this fear as certain Anglican clerics appeared more eager than most to push the Communion in this direction. Paisley, alarmed by such suggestions, argued that the sooner Ulster Protestants got back to the viewpoint that their fathers held concerning the Church of Rome the better for the welfare and safety of the Province. The thirty-nine Articles of the Prayer Book (Anglican), the Westminster Confession of Faith (Presbyterian) and the Notes of John Wesley (Methodist) on the New Testament were the basic standards of the three principal Protestant denominations in Ulster and set out Reformation teaching in a clear manner. Paisley believed that the campaign by the World Council of Churches to discredit the Reformation and 'apologise for our fore-fathers' stand for truth is in reality a conspiracy to betray us to our enemies'.[4] Paisley took his campaign against ecumenicalism onto the streets. In 1964 Paisley announced the picketing of two Protestant meetings to be addressed by Roman Catholic priests. He argued that the 'time has come in Ulster for a demonstration of loyalty to Bible Protestantism so that all . . . [Protestant] ministers will know that unity with Rome will not be tolerated here'.[5] Occurrences of this kind led one Methodist paper to call Paisley's methods a 'kind of "Protestant Fascism"' which were 'meat and drink to the enemies and critics of Northern Ireland. They make its friends despair.'[6] There were more noisy scenes in Hillsborough when Paisley tried to deliver a letter of protest to the Governor concerning the Archbishop of Canterbury's visit to Northern Ireland. It protested against the 'Romanising actions' of Dr Ramsey.[7] And just as dangerous as the ecumenicalists in the religious field where those in the political field who had abandoned 'traditional Unionism'. Any hint of a departure from the basic principle of a Protestant parliament for a Protestant people was seen as a threat to Northern Ireland's position within the United Kingdom and a sell-out. And top of Paisley's hit list was the Prime Minister.

On 24 April 1964 O'Neill visited the Lady of Lourdes Intermediate School, the first Roman Catholic school he had visited on his tours of provincial towns. After taking the opportunity of sampling some school cooking the Prime Minister saw a gym display by the senior girls, heard the girls' choir and watched a hurling match between two school teams arranged for his benefit.[8] This simple act was enough to provoke disapproval from Paisleyites. Prior to the visit a faded Union Jack was removed by police from the railings of the Lady of Lourdes Roman Catholic Church near the school.[9] The Reverend John Wylie, Minister of Ballymoney Free Presbyterian Church, made a personal protest to the Prime Minister about the visit. As O'Neill was being introduced to local councillors in the town hall, Wylie, also a member of the urban council, took him aside: 'I said I was very surprised after his statement to the Young Unionist Association in Enniskillen about Roman Catholics practising segregation, that he should come here to meet the priests of this district who are the enemies of liberty.' The Prime Minister thanked Wylie for his comments and moved on quickly. As a consequence Wylie planned to organise a Protestant rally 'dealing particularly with the Church of Rome and with the Prime Minister's attitude'.[10] When Wylie held his rally—Paisley was there too—he accused the Prime Minister of not being an Orangeman or a Protestant. 'It is time the Orange people were catching themselves on and calling for his resignation,' he declared. Wylie was also worried about the 'danger of mixed marriages' arising from Presbyterians allowing Catholic youth to play badminton in their halls. Catholics, he noted, had also opened their doors and invited Presbyterians in to play ping-pong.[11] When Paisley commented on the school visit he 'deplored' the publication of a picture of O'Neill beside a Roman Catholic crucifix: 'Whether willingly or unwillingly, Capt. O'Neill, by countenancing this Roman idol, has given food to the Roman propagandists.'[12]

By this stage Paisley was convinced that he and his supporters were getting a bad press from the liberal Unionist media, in particular the *Belfast Telegraph*. He concluded that an Ulster Protestant weekly newspaper was needed to 'oppose and expose Roman Catholicism'. He accused the Belfast press of discrimination against Protestants and claimed that Catholics received more attention from local newspapers than Protestants could ever hope to gain.[13] Hence the birth of the *Protestant Telegraph* which, for those unacquainted with the strength of some Protestant feeling in Northern Ireland (particularly the average secular English reader), often left them confused as to what century the paper was published in. In it and on the streets Paisley took every opportunity to highlight the threat posed by ecumenicalism and the Roman Church. For example it was headline news when the Pope flew over Northern Ireland on his way to the United Nations Organisation (UNO) in New York. The Queen and the Pope exchanged messages of goodwill. But for Paisley this amounted to an unwarranted infringement of Protestant Ulster's airspace: the Return to the Reformed Faith Council of Great Britain and Ireland cabled U Thant, Secretary General of the UNO, protesting at the Pope's visit. One of the signatories was Paisley. The cable stated: 'Adherents of the reformed faith refuse to recognise the validity of the Pope's right to be an advocate of peace. The past alliance of the Vatican with the Fascist dictators Hitler and Mussolini, and its present alliance with France indicate the true nature of the Papacy. Pope Paul's appearance at the UNO is a contradiction of its charter that the UNO is an association of peace-loving states.'[14] The contents of the message should not be dismissed arbitrarily: the Vatican's role in the Second World War, its relationship with the axis powers and its silence on the fate of the Jews remains a controversial one.

The protests continued through 1965 and 1966. During 1965 Paisley protested at an invitation to the Catholic chaplain of the Belfast Hospital Management Committee to dedicate a new fifty-bed wing of the Royal Victoria Hospital. Paisley said the invitation had been a mistake since the Roman Catholic Church was against many of the things that would happen in the hospital with regard to the saving of the life of the mother or the child. He added that while his job was a full-time one at the moment, if there might come a time when it was reckoned that he was the only man to represent the Protestant position he would be willing to stand for parliament.[15] A year later Paisley sent another telegram to the Queen complaining about the proposal that a Catholic priest should speak at Westminster Abbey during a prayer week for Christian unity because: 'The visit constitutes a grave violation of the terms of your Coronation oath, is contrary to the Bill of Rights and the articles and is an insult to the martyrs whom Rome burned. As Protestants we reaffirm that the Pope of Rome has no jurisdiction in this realm.'[16]

Paisley's was not a lone voice—merely the loudest in the Province—in expressing such concerns with ecumenicalism. There was evidence of Protestant concern wherever one looked. At the General Assembly of 1962 the Presbyterian Church decided to co-operate with the World Council of Churches; while there were a number of objections the vote was carried. However, by April 1964 the Presbyterian Church in Belfast was seeking signatures to a letter objecting to the Assembly's policy of co-operation.[17] Of 580 ministers, ordained assistants and retired clergy of the Presbyterian Church who were circularised, sixty-nine signed a statement expressing 'deep concern' over the trend of the ecumenical movement. The signatories found that in order to attain an outward unity, the great Scriptural doctrines reasserted at the Reformation were being compromised or dismissed as of minor importance. They were bound by conscience to expose these dangers. The matter would now come up for discussion at the next General Assembly.[18] In May the General Synod of the Church of Ireland asked the House of Bishops to initiate talks on church unity with the Methodist and Presbyterian Churches.[19] The Presbyterian Church immediately gave a welcome to the proposal.[20]

The Reverend Carlisle Patterson, co-convenor of the Committee on Inter-Church Relations, stressed that union between the Presbyterian Church and the Roman Catholic Church was 'not even within the area of consideration'. There could be no question of seeking to unite with Rome 'so long as that church holds to those beliefs and practices which our church has consistently regarded as erroneous'. This, however, did not mean that Presbyterians should not show the hand of friendship towards Catholics. Patterson acknowledged that it had always been necessary for some members of the Presbyterian Church who lived in predominately Catholic areas to engage in 'certain relationships' with their Catholic neighbours. 'Many of us in the north who in the past have had few dealings with Roman Catholics are finding a new openness to contacts of various kinds.' In this situation there were two things that Patterson believed the Presbyterian Church was called on to do. One was to work in every way open to Presbyterians for the removal of injustice, intolerance and discrimination throughout the land wherever and by whomever these things were practised. Their second obligation was to help Presbyterians to see the situation as an opportunity of witnessing to the reformed faith even though 'They knew that the Church of Rome had not even begun to amend its basic doctrinal position.' To attempt to build barricades against their Roman Catholic neighbours would be evidence of the most lamentable 'ghetto-mentality' and a confession of a disastrous failure of nerve on their part as Protestants.[21] The General Assembly accepted and passed a resolution that recognised that the official doctrine of the Roman Catholic Church was unchanged but welcomed indications of a desire for reform on the part of that Church.[22]

But any mention of closer contacts with Catholics had the potential to cause trouble. There were threats of splinter groups breaking away from the Irish Methodist Church as a result of a decision—taken, it should be noted, by an overwhelming majority at the Methodist Conference of June 1964—to welcome reciprocal discussions between Methodist groups and Roman Catholics on questions of social and religious concern. Fears were expressed that such meetings might lead to an increase in 'the terrible problem of mixed marriages'. One of the longest and most controversial debates of the entire conference took place when the Memorials Committee recommended a resolution concerning relations with Catholics. The Enniskillen Synod's resolution deplored 'in the strongest possible terms the action of inviting Roman Catholic priests to address gatherings of Methodist ministers and people' urging Conference to forbid the recurrence of such events. The progressive element fought back. Reverend John Stewart of Monaghan warned that 'there has arisen, I believe, a monster, which changes in shape from time to time. At one time it is a form of McCarthyism and next a sort of John Birch Society of extremism . . . Very often a man can be smeared as leading to Rome . . . We are criticising our own people if we cannot trust them to talk intelligently with others. We might as well ban talks with Buddhists or Moslems and cut off all communication with the outside world.'[23]

There was further controversy at the 1965 General Assembly after Presbyterians were urged in a resolution to ask for forgiveness for attitudes and actions towards Roman Catholics unworthy of followers of Jesus Christ. This led to some heated debate as the Reverend W. W. Porter of Killead said that Presbyterians were being asked to indulge in a form of 'verbal flagellation'. Such a resolution would be an affront to the whole body of the Presbyterian Church. An amended resolution humbly begged pardon of God 'and of our separated brethren, just as we forgive them that trespass against us'.[24] Twenty-two Presbyterian ministers recorded their dissent when the General Assembly accepted agreed statements on the Scriptures, the Creed and the Confessions between the Presbyterian, Methodist and Congregational Churches as a basis for further conversations. The leader of the objectors, Reverend Martin Smyth of Alexandra in Belfast, said that nowhere in the statements was there an explicit declaration that the Scriptures were the word of God and he asked for further clarification of the attitude towards the truth and the authority of the Creeds and Confessions.[25]

A former ally of Paisley, Norman Porter, Director of the Evangelical Protestant Society, criticised this as a trend towards Christian unity. He told Orangemen: 'If some of the Protestant clergy feel they have been uncharitable towards the Roman Catholic Church let them speak for themselves and not in the name of their denominations or their people. They have no right to involve the Protestant people of Ulster, who do not feel that they, nor their forefathers, have been unchristian. This bending over backwards is utter folly and a definite betrayal of our Protestant heritage.' Policies of appeasement were being adopted towards Romanism and the 'New Morality' by many Protestant clergy. It was clearly evident that this appalling situation was the outcome of a steady departure from the historic Christian faith as reaffirmed at the Protestant Reformation and as contained in the doctrinal statements of the major Protestant churches. Protestants were considered unchristian if they would not join in the craze for closer unity with Romanism. 'God forbid that we should ever engage in such diabolical exercises and thus trample underfoot the blood of the Protestant martyrs. We urgently need a revival of true religion. We need to return to the basic principles of our Protestant reformed faith.'[26] For men like Porter and Paisley there seemed to be evidence in all the major churches of a move away from established Protestant rejection of idolatry; for example in 1964, and by an overwhelming majority, the Church of Ireland Synod repealed the ninety-three-year-old canon which prohibited the placing of the cross on or over the communion table.[27] As the Reverend Edwin Hastings, Rector of Trillick, preaching at the Relief of Derry service in St Columb's Cathedral, said, he felt that Protestants were dishonouring the memory and sacrifice of the men of Derry and those who died at the stake: 'We are continually talking about Christian unity. The whole thought and action [is] to please Rome in every way, and our leaders are quite well aware that there will be no unity with Rome except according to her conditions.' As they looked back on those days of 1688–90 Hastings suggested everyone ask of themselves: 'Has their sacrifice been all in vain?'[28]

But it is necessary to note that even 'progressive' clergymen had their limits which highlighted a fundamental schism between all the Protestant churches and the Roman Catholic Church. The Bishop of Clogher, Dr Alan Buchanan, presiding at a special meeting of Clogher Diocesan Synod across the border at Clones in County Monaghan, called for tolerance while at the same time pointing out that this part of the 'geographical province of Ulster' had remained a 'divided community ever since the time of the Plantation of James I'. Accusations of intolerance— particularly with external references to the reluctance for mixed marriages— ignored how 'It is a serious step for anyone to sign away the spiritual guiding of his unborn children.'[29] Buchanan was highlighting the enormous impact that the Roman Catholic Church's insistence on the offspring of a mixed marriage being brought up as Catholic had on the psyche of Ulster Protestants. This was a practical example of a potentially devastating Catholic doctrine on Protestants. Ulster Protestants only had to look across the border to see how devastating this doctrine could be: while the 1961 census data from the Republic revealed no increase in the percentage of Roman Catholics it did show a fall in the percentage of all other Christian denominations with the exception of Baptists. Out of a population of 2,818,347, Catholics numbered 2,786,033 at the previous census in 1946; Church of Ireland members numbered 104,016 in 1961 against 124,829 in 1946, a drop from 4.2 per cent to 3.7 per cent of the population; Presbyterians numbered 18,953 in the Republic in 1961 against 23,870 in 1946, and were now 0.7 per cent of the population compared against 0.8 per cent; and the number of Methodists had fallen from 8,355 to 6,676 and now constituted 0.2 per cent of the population against 0.3 per cent in 1946.[30]

The Republic of Ireland was *de facto* a Catholic country. The overwhelming majority of its citizens were Catholic and a large percentage of them were practising. This had important consequences for how the South was viewed from the North and the influence of the Catholic Church in the Republic and on Catholics in the North. In March 1967 Cardinal Conway pointed out that while there was much in the Roman Catholic Church that could change, there was an inner core that could not change because it came from God. The Church's role was to proclaim God's message and interpret it to the world. The Church, he said, had no power to change it. It was part of the essence of the Catholic faith that God had promised to preserve His Church from error in interpreting the message of the Gospel. Once the Church, in a *de fide* or equivalent way, put the final seal of approval on a particular truth as part of God's message to the world, then that affirmation was free from error. That applied to all the *de fide* affirmations in the past or in the future. Conway added: 'Being a Catholic involves accepting this position. No one who declines to accept that position can say that he is a Catholic.'[31]

Catholics had to accept the Papal infallibility of Rome in religious matters. There was no room for dissent. This was what revolted God-fearing Protestants. For them no one man such as the Pope had a monopoly of Christian truth. The democratic nature of Protestantism meant that, at the end of day, if one disagreed with the teaching of a particular clergyman then one could get direct access to the teachings of God by picking up the Bible. For Ulster Protestants the effect of the Catholic Church's influence was plain to see: if Northern Ireland was a 'cold place' for Catholics then it was also true that the Republic of Ireland was a cold place for Southern Protestants. This is perhaps the great untold story of the background to the Troubles. Economically Southern Protestants did well but culturally—in a Gaelic, Catholic and Republican Ireland—their historic links with Britain were effectively ignored. From the Ulster-Protestant perspective the Catholic Church seemed to poke its nose in everywhere in the Republic. For example even though Trinity College, Dublin was considered a last bastion of Protestantism in the South in reality a majority of its students were Catholic; but this did not stop the Roman Catholic Archbishop of Dublin insisting that the Church's ban on Catholics attending there remain in force. In his 1967 Lenten regulations for Dublin Diocese Dr McQuaid confirmed that the relevant canon law passed by all the bishops of Ireland and confirmed by the Holy See 'has not been changed or relaxed'.[32] Ulster Protestants resented and feared what they regarded as the interference of the Catholic Church beyond religious matters and into the social world. It was the Catholic Church's insistence that its canon law overrode civil law, that it claimed to hold ultimate sway over the souls of Catholics, that there was no right of dissension against the doctrinal teaching of the Church, combined with the insistence that all offspring of mixed marriages should be brought up as Catholics which meant that Ulster Protestants *knew* what fate awaited them in a united—Catholic dominated—Ireland.

This is why ecumenicalism produced such a reaction among a significant number of Protestants in Northern Ireland. There was a tremendous fuss in early

1967 when the Bishop of Ripon, Dr John Moorman, was invited by the Church of Ireland to deliver a public meeting at St Anne's Cathedral, Belfast. Moorman was an enthusiastic ecumenicalist, particularly with regards to Rome. He had been the leader of an Anglican delegation that had recently had conversations with Roman Catholic theologians in Northern Italy. Such was the negative reaction in Northern Ireland to his invitation that Moorman declined to speak to a private meeting of the Irish Church Association and then went on to cancel his entire visit because of what he described as 'local opposition'. St Anne's Cathedral had already been withdrawn as the venue for the public meeting by the Dean of Belfast, the Very Reverend C. I. Peacocke, following protests from Protestant sects and the Orange Order.[33] In particular the County Grand Lodge of Belfast had objected to Moorman's utterances relating to union with Rome under the 'chairmanship' of the Pope. All of this was occurring as Pope Paul VI reiterated the concept of infallibility within Romanism. To emphasise their objection to union with Rome the Orange Order announced that services would be held in the near future to reaffirm Protestant faith and dedication.[34]

The Grand Master, Sir George Clark, defended the position taken by the Orange Order and claimed that there was no conflict with the Order's allegiance to civil and religious liberty and the views of the County Grand Lodge on the cancelled visit: 'What we resented was the fact that the meeting was to have been held in the cathedral.' Clark would have no objection to the visit if it had been held in a public hall.[35] What is revealing about this episode is that ecumenicalists refused to take this lying down. The reaction from many quarters of the Protestant churches revealed that liberal Protestantism was alive and well. A counter-attack began with the executive committee of the Irish Council of Churches' passing a resolution stating that civil and religious liberty could never be equated with 'blatant attempts to suppress free speech and the search for information'. It noted that protests against Moorman's visit had begun in advance of the announcement that the meeting would take place in the cathedral.[36] The bitter controversy soon became the subject of sermons in many churches throughout the Province. The secretary of the Irish Church Association, the Reverend E. J. Moore, hit out at the Orange Order for trying to dictate to the Church of Ireland: the Church, he said, 'would not bear its distinctive witness within the straitjacket of extreme Protestantism'. Reverend Robert Nelson of the Methodist Church warned that there was a 'spirit of fear' abroad in Ulster's life, while Reverend Eric Gallagher described the issue at stake as 'the soul of Ulster and its place in the modern world'.[37] The Venerable John Mercier, Archdeacon of Connor and Deputy Grand Chaplin of Ireland, described the decision by the Orange Order to hold Reformation services in all churches as 'further evidence of arrogance and a dictatorial attitude which all loyal church members—clergy and laity—must reject' since it was only the bishops and clergy who could make such a decision.[38] By March 1967 the reaffirmation services were not being associated overtly with the Ripon controversy but canvassed as a means of making Orangemen who were irregular church attendees more conscious of their religious obligations.[39] When the services did take place, in April, members of the Sandy Row No. 5 District were in for a shock when Reverend J. A. Fair of the Church of Ireland (and himself an Orangeman) delivered his sermon. Fair, of St Comgall's Parish Church, Rathcoole, said he had come to 'bury the Orange Order not to praise it' and hit out at the 'insane banging of drums as Orangemen pass Roman Catholic chapels'. The Orangemen sat in stunned silence.[40] Other reaffirmation sermons were more traditional in their sentiments.

What all this does is put Paisleyism in context. It demonstrates the tensions within Protestantism. For every example of a Protestant fundamentalist position taken one can find a more liberal one among Protestants. This extended through-out Northern Irish society. Those who opposed closer contacts with Catholics did not represent a majority but they did represent a powerful and vocal constituency. For example, again in 1967, Protestant members of a church indoor bowling club moved out of the church hall where they played their matches because they had been refused permission to entertain a Catholic team. The Kirk Session of First Ballymena Presbyterian Church decided by a small majority that their club could not meet bowlers from Ballymena All Saints Roman Catholic Church for a friendly match. In protest the Protestant bowling club secured new premises and changed its name from First Ballymena Presbyterian Indoor Bowling Club to First Ballymena Bowling Club. A club official explained that this would remove the club from the jurisdiction of the church and allow them to arrange matches against teams of their own choice.[41] A second bowling controversy emerged in the town when another Ballymena Presbyterian church advised its bowling team not to play the same Catholic team.[42]

Two years earlier the Mayor of Ballymena Borough Council had decided not to attend the Catholic service in All Saints Church to mark the beginning of the town's Civic Week programme after he received a protest letter from the local Gospel Tabernacle which declared the service would be 'another betrayal of reformation principles and doctrines and a further step towards appeasement of Rome'. It was signed by the Reverend J. K. Paisley, father of Ian, and R. J. Beggs. Previously it had been announced that the Mayor, Alderman J. D. Henry and members of the Council would attend.[43] In the event some Protestant members of the borough and county councils, as well as the Deputy Lord Mayor of Belfast, did attend in their capacity as private individuals.[44] The Evangelical Protestant Society passed a resolution 'viewing with grave concern the recent incidents involving Protestant representatives and the Roman Catholic Church'. Their attendance was 'even more deplorable for it involves countenancing the blasphemy and idolatrous practice of the Roman Catholic Church'. Norman Porter believed that people who had been put in positions of authority by Protestant votes would do well to respect the wishes of the Protestant community whom they represented.[45]

Another example of what, to outside observers, seemed to be an intolerant attitude, was provided in 1966 when a Belfast woman claimed she was forced to resign from the Women's Orange Order because she wanted to go to Rome: she wanted to watch the ordination to the priesthood of a young German whose father had saved her brother's life during the war. Mrs Thomas Watson recalled that when she told her fellow members of the Margaret Craig Memorial Women's Lodge of her intentions there was uproar: 'I was told in no uncertain terms to "get out or be thrown out"', she said. 'So I have decided to hand in my resignation.' In 1943 her brother, Edward Law, was at the point of death after being wounded in battle. His life was saved by a German surgeon, Dr Franz Kreuter, after nearly twenty operations, in one of which the wounded man's arm was amputated. Another operation was to his hip, and it was feared at the time that he would never be able to walk again. Some years later Dr Kreuter, who was anxious to learn if his former patient could walk again after the operations, managed to trace him to Belfast. They corresponded frequently and when Law learned that Dr Kreuter's eighteen-year-old son, Franz, was coming to Britain for a holiday, he took the opportunity to invite him to Belfast. They kept in contact.

In August 1966 young Franz invited Mrs Watson over to Rome in October for his ordination into the priesthood. The visit would include an audience with the Pope the following day: 'I was thrilled about it. I thought it was a wonderful thing that I, a Protestant, in this so-called bigoted country, could be invited to such a ceremony. Then I told my Orange Order colleagues . . . and was brought down to earth with a bump. Only one woman sided with me. She said she was sure when the doctor was attending my brother's wounds he did not ask if he was a Protestant or a Roman Catholic.' However as Mrs Margaret Drennan, Grand Mistress of the Association of Loyal Orangewomen of Ireland, explained: 'The lady took on an obligation when she was initiated in regard to attendance at Roman Catholic ceremonies. It would have been discreet for her to resign before going to this service. There was no uproar. It is very clear in our book of rules and obligations.'[46]

Was this an example of bigotry or simply an example of applying the rules of an organisation to an individual who must clearly have understood what those rules were when she joined? Perhaps what made such examples so offensive to many Catholics was the suggestion that all contact with Catholic services—and in some case Catholics themselves—needed to be avoided in order to prevent Protestants being seduced by the Roman faith. It demonstrated a certain lack of confidence. In terms of politics it had a further consequence: the belief among Catholics and their representatives that the tentacles of the Orange Order extended into the heart of government. Many Catholic-Nationalist politicians genuinely believed that the Order could dictate to the Northern Ireland Government rather like some Conservatives in Britain saw the relationship between trade union barons and the Labour Party. While many members of the Order, particularly on Orange platforms, denied that the institution was a political body (it merely operated in the field of the religious), Brian Faulkner, one of the rising stars of Unionist politics, consistently argued for its continued involvement in the sphere of politics. As he told the Blackmen in 1964, the Black Institution and the Orange Order 'owe it to themselves and to the community as a whole to take their place in local government and central government and to bring with them the courage of those Christian principles upon which these institutions are founded'. While it had been claimed from time to time that members of the Orange and Black institutions should not concern themselves with politics because these were primarily religious institutions, Faulkner had 'said before and I say again it is not possible nor is it desirable to separate politics from the day to day business of living'.[47]

Catholics had their prejudices confirmed in mid-July 1967 when Phelim O'Neill, the Unionist MP, and Colonel Henry Cramsie, Deputy Lieutenant for the County, were expelled by the County Antrim Grand Orange Lodge from membership of the Order because they attended Catholic services during Ballymoney Civic Week. Nat Minford, MP for Antrim, pleaded that he had attended a Catholic service on the occasion of the opening of a new school in Andersontown in his constituency. No action was taken by the Lodge in this case although the rules of the Order stipulated that an Orangeman 'should oppose fatal errors and doctrines of the Church of Rome and scrupulously avoid countenancing by presence or otherwise any act or ceremony of Popish worship'. Here, for Nationalist politicians, was the confirmation that, as Harry Diamond of Republican Labour claimed, the Unionist Government was dominated by the Order.[48]

Eddie McAteer, the leader of the Nationalist Party, hit out at the close ties between the Orange Order and the Unionist Party. He had no hostility to the members of the Order so long as they remained in their own bailiwick. Indeed, he thought that the Northern Ireland scene, particularly tourism, would not prosper so much if this 'colourful asset' was removed. 'But it is far from a joking matter,' he said, 'when you have the sorry spectacle of a whole Government apparently in thraldom to a few surly men crouched around some table in an Orange hall.' It was essential, before anything like normality could come to Northern Ireland, that the Government broke away from the shackles that bound it to the Order. McAteer believed that there was the curious position that in negotiations which were attempted with the Government there was always an uneasy feeling that those with whom they were speaking were really unaccredited spokesmen whose every word and action must be referred back for approval. This, concluded McAteer, produced a 'thoroughly diseased state of political affairs' that needed to be 'cured'.[49] For Catholics the Order reeked of hypocrisy as when the Republican Labour MP, Gerry Fitt, pointed out that during the annual Twelfth celebrations there was an unscheduled stop by the Prince Albert Orange Lodge outside Belfast Prison to convey fraternal greetings to prisoners, including two convicted murderers. One of the Lodge outside the prison was John McQuade, the Unionist

MP for Woodvale. Fitt contrasted how, recently, 'honourable men' had been expelled from the Order for attending Catholic services and weddings yet people convicted of the most heinous crime in the calendar were still members of that Order. He and other opposition MPs called on the Prime Minister and the cabinet to resign from the Order;[50] the fact that ministers such as Faulkner condemned the 'deplorable' incident outside the prison[51] left the opposition unimpressed.

Catholic-Nationalist convictions were reinforced in June 1968 when Phelim O'Neill was formally expelled from the Orange Order. Once again Fitt condemned the 'ridiculous pressure' that the Order wielded in the 'Northern Ireland political scene'[52] and vowed to make known at Westminster (to which he had been elected in 1966) his concern at the Order's 'unhealthy influence' over the Northern Ireland Government.[53] O'Neill reacted to his expulsion by declaring that the Order had 'far too much political power as a pressure group'.[54] He stressed that he had only been trying to further good community relations by his attendance at a Catholic service: it was now time for the Order to decide whether it was a religious institution or 'an extreme political organisation masquerading under the cloak of religion'.[55] Austin Currie, a rising star of the Nationalist Party in Stormont, felt that it was now essential for the Prime Minister to demonstrate the sincerity of his convictions regarding community relations by leaving the 'sectarian' Order.[56] Forced on this occasion onto the back foot, Faulkner revealed an interesting insight into the psychology of the siege mentality when he attempted to argue that only a 'tiny and misguided minority' were 'bigoted and intolerant men who discriminate against their Roman Catholic and Nationalist fellow-countrymen'. The press and the opposition parties, he argued, ought to be fairer to the Unionist Party whose members, condemning extremism and seeking to improve community relations, 'are tacitly being forced into endorsing the criticisms of our predecessors and of Unionist policies, and allegations of unfair treatment towards the nationalist minority'.[57] He also believed that Northern Ireland generally did not deserve the image of an intolerant society. Unionists were in a difficult position for, by repudiating extremists, they seemed tacitly to endorse opposition criticism.[58]

Evidence of this defensiveness was seen some years earlier when it was decided that an investigation into religious discrimination throughout Ireland was to be carried out by the Presbyterian Church's Committee on National and International Problems. In 1965 Reverend G. B. G. McConnell of Donore, Dublin, and the convenor of the committee, announced that he personally felt it was high time they faced this question. As a Church they were pledged to uphold religious liberty and they must therefore give some answer to the charges: 'If the charges are false, then we should refute them; if any of them are true we should admit them and see what we as Christians can do to right what is wrong.'[59] But when the report emerged it had a stormy passage before being accepted in principle by the General Assembly of the Presbyterian Church in Belfast in 1966. A resolution that the report be received and the Assembly declare itself opposed in principle to all unfair religious discrimination was adopted. But it was also agreed that the report be referred back to the committee which prepared it for revision in the light of comments from presbyteries and that it be presented to the Assembly again the following year. The first amendment that the report be referred back for revision came from Robert Rodgers of Abbots Cross, who said he took great exception to the observations on church life and mixed marriages. He took exception to the claim that even without Ne Temere the problem of mixed marriages would remain: the Ne Temere decree, he said, was one of the 'most Hellish' decrees there had been.[60] If there was discrimination it had to be understood in a wider context. Protestants generally were angered at being accused of being the sole perpetrators of sectarianism.

It is clear from the above that the concerns articulated by Paisley were present throughout Protestant society in Northern Ireland. Paisley was seen as a destabilising force for Captain O'Neill as he led a campaign that 'O'Neill Must Go'— also a famous headline from his *Protestant Telegraph*. But this did not translate into electoral success for him or his Protestant Unionist Party. That Paisley was also aware of his limited electoral appeal was demonstrated by his reluctance to put himself forward as a candidate. His electoral campaigns made some, but limited, progress. Their main focus revolved around the appeal of Protestantism. In April 1964 Paisley made the lowering of the Union Jack to half-mast when Pope John died an election issue in Belfast's municipal elections. Protestant Unionist candidates were to contest the Duncairn ward in which the Lord Mayor, William Jenkins, was one of the Ulster Unionist Party (UUP) representatives.[61]

In Windsor Ward Protestant Unionists issued a pamphlet to the electors which stated that Sir Martin Wallace had authorised Alderman Sir Cecil McKee, the sitting Independent Unionist, to state on his behalf 'that he agreed with the Lord Mayor and that he also would have pulled down the Union Jack'. McKee protested that Wallace did not authorise him to use any such language and 'nor did I do so'. What Wallace actually said was that 'we would have lowered the flag at the City Hall'. McKee wanted to know why Paisley felt it necessary to substitute the 'untruthful' words in his pamphlet. As Paisley maintained that he was fighting a similar battle to that of the Ulster Volunteer Force to keep the Union Jack flying over Ulster, McKee pointed out that 'As ex-servicemen Sir Martin Wallace and myself proved beyond dispute our allegiance to the Union Jack. Perhaps Ian K. Paisley would state for the enlightenment of the voters in Windsor Ward exactly what part he played in the last war to keep the Union Jack flying over Ulster.'[62] Mrs Eileen Paisley, who was in fact the Protestant Unionist candidate for Windsor, stood by everything in the pamphlet and pointed out that her husband was just thirteen years of age when the war broke out[63] (which nicely side-stepped the fact that her husband was of martial age by the end of the war). The UUP MP Sam Magowan—'As one who served my country in the First World War'— congratulated McKee on exposing Paisleyite tactics. He had known 'for a long time how hollow Ian Paisley's assertions often are' and protested that 'Our generation, which sacrificed many noble sons on the fields of Flanders and elsewhere, know to our cost what loyalty really meant.'[64] It was the suggestion from Paisley and his followers that those who had donned the King's uniform and fought for their King and country were not true loyalists which really angered men such as McKee and Magowan. For Protestant Unionists it was Protestantism rather than any demonstration of practical patriotism which counted the most; hence in 1966 the disgust of Stratton Mills, the Unionist MP for North Belfast, with regard to the 'campaign of anti-Semitism' employed as a tactic of Protestant Unionists in the Duncairn by-election for the City Council. Mills, who had made several speeches in support of the official Unionist candidate, Harold Smith, a former naval officer, criticised leaflets and remarks made over car loudspeakers by Protestant Unionists. The leaflets declared:

> Remember—The Unionist Party's candidate is not a Protestant. The Unionist Party are boasting that he is a Jew. As a Jew he rejects our Lord Jesus Christ, the New Testament, Protestant principles, the glorious Reformation and the sanctity of the Lord's Day.
>
> Mr Smith is actually an anti-Protestant for in his election address he calls Protestantism 'sectarian bias'.
>
> Mr Smith is not and cannot be a traditional Unionist. The Protestant Throne and the Protestant constitution are nothing to him. No wonder he denounces faithful Protestants as extremists.
>
> The choice of this non-Protestant by the Unionist Party is a move on the part of Captain Terence O'Neill to destroy Protestant representation in historic Duncairn. You have only one vote. Strike a blow to save your Protestant heritage.

Mills attacked 'this attempt to introduce anti-Semitism' into democratic elections: 'If a man is prepared to fight for his country in time of war then he is equally entitled to offer himself to the electorate on behalf of the Unionist Party.'[65] Smith won the by-election beating Mrs Paisley by 1,902 votes.[66] The most significant aspect of the election was the relative electoral weakness of the Protestant Unionists. Paisley himself was not a candidate: 'I have no political ambitions,' he said in the 1964 election.[67] In that election a total of seventy-three candidates stood in the Belfast City Council elections with the Unionist Party returned to City Hall with forty seats—a reduction of two. Yet what was clear was that the Unionist Party remained dominant over all its rivals. To become a significant electoral force in Northern Ireland, Paisley needed a real political crisis involving the legitimacy of the state rather than the narrow crisis of ecumenicalism. Part of Paisley's problem was that what made him so popular with one section of Protestants repelled many other Protestants. A spell in jail in 1966 for the non-payment of a fine made him a martyr to his supporters but embarrassed 'respectable' Protestants; as Dr Alfred Martin, Moderator of the General Assembly, complained, the good name of Presbyterianism had been 'stolen' and those guilty of the theft were 'masquerading in our name'. As a visitor from England said to him: 'So your Moderator is in jail.'[68] To Martin, Paisley gave all Presbyterians a bad name. But another problem was that there was not necessarily a need for such a vivid demonstration of anti-Catholicism, because it was already quietly institutionalised within the Unionist Party. This brings us to a discussion of the relationship between the UUP and Catholics in general.

It was the Prime Minister's hope that in the long term Catholics could be weeded away from Nationalism and towards Unionism. And there was some evidence to support this hope. According to the 1967 National Opinion Polls poll more than eighty per cent of all voters in Northern Ireland favoured some form of political link with Britain. Half of those supported the present constitutional position—the Union with Britain—but half again wanted to see a united Ireland linked to Britain. A majority of the electorate, including forty-one per cent of Unionists, thought the border would eventually disappear. Of those who held this view, sixty per cent believed it would come about within twenty-five years. Among Nationalists, around sixty-three per cent supported a British connection of some sort and only about thirty-eight per cent favoured an independent all-Ireland republic. Only two per cent of Unionists favoured an independent united Ireland. But thirty-eight per cent of Unionists supported a united Ireland connected to Britain. Of these, forty-five per cent were from the Church of Ireland and forty-one per cent were Presbyterians. Yet a surprisingly low thirty-eight per cent of Nationalists and thirty per cent of Catholics regarded an independent united Ireland as the best arrangement for Ireland. Forty-seven per cent of Nationalists and fifty per cent of Catholics were willing to support a united Ireland linked to Britain.[69]

For O'Neill the most surprising fact disclosed in the poll was that the pursuit of a united Ireland 'in the old sense is dying'. He had always thought that the economic realities of the situation would produce this in time 'but quite frankly I am surprised that the trend is already so marked'. O'Neill pointed out that the poll did not show that Unionist voters preferred an independent united Ireland linked to Britain: Carson and Craig did not fight for the creation of a border but for the continuance of Ireland's political unity with Britain and they accepted the 1920 settlement as the only means by which part at least of Ireland could maintain that link. Unionists who favoured a united Ireland were in sympathy with this early broader Unionist doctrine of the United Kingdom of Great Britain and Ireland as it existed before 1920. Alternatively they might simply consider that economic realities would force the Republic to rethink their policies and attitudes of the last half-century towards separation from Great Britain. O'Neill regarded the eighty-six per cent of all voters who wanted a political link with Britain as the really significant figure. To O'Neill this seemed to be a clear indication of how the

'Unionist way of thought' in its positive and broadest sense was spreading to a majority of the people of Ulster: 'If, and only if, the South came back into the United Kingdom, Ireland would then be united in the sense of having a single allegiance. We would in fact be returning to something like the 1920 Act settlement which the North accepted and the South rejected.'[70] There were certainly Catholic Unionists—the evidence is of far more of them than Protestant Nationalists—but the issue was how to accommodate them in what was essentially a Protestant state: as one Catholic wrote in May 1964: 'Unionists must recognise that all Catholics are not Nationalists, and they must treat us better as equal citizens in British Ulster, for they can not hope to survive unless they win us over to their side. Therefore, I refute the suggestion that Catholics are synonymous with Nationalists, for it is utterly false and misleading, and I look forward to an Ireland united under the British crown.'[71] And a Catholic student wrote:

> All Catholics need not be Nationalists. A great many Catholics prefer the material advantages of union with Britain to the empty coffin of Nationalism.
>   I am a Catholic, yet I am a Unionist for I can see that Ulster being British is to my advantage, to the advantage of my family, and to the advantage of all Ulstermen.[72]

But there was a basic problem: where were these Catholic Unionists supposed to go? O'Neill's Unionist Party did not seem particularly welcoming. While at one level many senior Unionists thought it desirable that Catholics should be encouraged to join the Unionist Party there were a number of obstacles: one was good old-fashioned hostility to Catholics (particularly at grassroots level); and the other was, even with the best will in the world, a stereotype that Catholics as a group were the victims of their own social, economic and religious background which hampered their advancement. In 1965 Captain L. P. S. Orr, the Imperial Grand Master of the Orange Order and Leader of the Ulster Unionists at Westminster, pronounced that admission to the Unionist Party depended not merely upon loyalty to the Crown but upon a willingness to co-operate in the perseverance of the Protestant religion, for that was the object of the Order and *ipso facto* of the Unionist Party. A columnist in the *Church of Ireland Gazette* observed how by this standard 'it is hard to see how a Roman Catholic could ever become a member [of the Unionist Party]. He would be debarred by definition.' It seemed to the writer that this was a broad definition of 'Protestantism' encompassing all shades of the term so that it simply meant anyone who was not a Roman Catholic. That being so the impossibility of a Catholic being accepted in the Unionist Party 'is complete'.[73]

The problem of Catholics and the Unionist Party was not a new one. One solution put forward by Senator Nelson Elder, Secretary of the Unionist Trade Unionist Alliance, was to suggest the formation of a 'Catholic Unionist' society which would give Catholic Unionists the opportunity of putting forward their views rather than being embarrassed by the 'rantings of their power-crazy fanatics' who portrayed them as a down-trodden persecuted minority which they themselves knew to be false. Senator Elder observed: 'Does it not seem strange to see no hordes of Roman Catholics fleeing South in order to escape the so-called tyranny of Unionism? There is no wall around the border, no barbed wire entanglement, nor is it necessary to tunnel underground to escape. This Opposition propaganda fools nobody.'[74] There were many Unionists who wanted to see Catholics admitted to the Unionist Party. One of O'Neill's senior ministers, William Craig, wished to see the demise of Nationalism in Northern Ireland: in 1966 he called for 'Every effort we can command . . . [to] be summoned up to combat and defeat Nationalism and if possible to eradicate it from our society. It is a poison in our community and not anything that is to be found in Unionism.'[75]

But this was not a call to deny Catholics their political rights: rather Craig publicly stated that support from Roman Catholics would be welcomed by the Unionist Party. Claiming that the Nationalist Party was not in a position to speak for the whole Catholic minority, he recalled how Eddie McAteer had said that he would rather 'have his people' unemployed than working on a British naval base such as HMS *Sea Eagle* in Derry, and described this as 'ridiculous coming from a responsible leader of a party. My complaint against the Nationalist Party is that it refuses the minority of the people of Northern Ireland the right to decide it for themselves.' Craig wanted Catholics to express themselves through a constructive party which was interested in the welfare of the people and not a party spending all its time and energy on a destructive policy.[76] He hoped more and more Catholics would identify with the Unionist Party. For example there was no barrier, he said, to a Roman Catholic becoming a member of a Unionist cabinet.[77]

Except perhaps the Unionist Party. It was easy to recall how the question of admitting Catholics to membership of the Unionist Party had created a storm at a Young Unionist conference in 1959: then Sir George Clark, Grand Master of the Orange Order, declared that the admittance of Catholics to the Party would not be countenanced by the Orange Order. The Grand Lodge subsequently passed a vote of confidence in Clark and Lord Brookeborough, the Prime Minister, made it clear that the matter would be best left alone. The issue did not exist and probably would not arise, he said. Since then it had been left to individual Unionist associations to decide on whether or not to admit Catholics. The official view was that there was no religious test for membership. But as Nat Minford, the Unionist MP for Antrim, now pointed out in response to Craig's remarks, while a number of people in the party leaned to the view that there should be no barrier to membership and he knew of Catholics who worked for the Unionists in election time: 'the idea that a Roman Catholic could be a Unionist MP or a cabinet member is wishful thinking at this time' for 'He would have to get nomination and he would have as good a chance as a Protestant at a Nationalist convention.'[78] Effectively, given the virtual autonomy of the member associations in the UUP's structure, the power of vetoing Catholic admittance rested with the grassroots. And just how prevalent anti-Catholic views were within the UUP was evident in January 1966 when an awkward moment arose for the Prime Minister as he addressed a meeting of the Antrim Unionist Association. The president of the Association, Robert Erwin, said he could not see how Roman Catholics could join the Unionist Party 'because they would never be loyal to the Queen'. O'Neill was on the party platform when Erwin referred to a 'lot of talk' about Catholics joining their Unionist associations. 'I can't see how that is going to happen,' said Erwin. 'I never knew a Roman Catholic that would recognise our flag or be loyal to the Queen.' By now he was obviously on a roll and added: 'They will take the Queen's money and sickness benefit and everything else, but never be loyal to the Queen.' The Prime Minister, who spoke after Erwin, made no reference to the president's comments. Afterwards Erwin explained that he was simply questioning the suggestion that a Catholic could ever be loyal to the Party or the Queen. 'But I'm not saying they must not be admitted,' he stressed. 'I made it clear that I had no quarrel with the Roman Catholics, but they have their beliefs and we have ours.'[79]

A month later Edmund Curran, Chairman of the Queen's University Unionist Association, was forced to apologise for saying, in the course of an interview with *The Gown*, a student magazine, that any person who was a Catholic Unionist 'is most probably masquerading as a Catholic and is not a practising one'. Curran, a twenty-one-year-old student teacher, later accepted that his was a 'scurrilous' statement; it did not represent his true viewpoint, it was inappropriate and without foundation. The incident was particularly embarrassing since there were two Catholics on the Queen's Association's committee.[80] That there were tensions within the Queen's Association became clear in November when the only remaining Catholic member of the Queen's Association was expelled by the Executive Committee. Neill Oliver, the chairman, denied the move had been taken on religious grounds. Louis Boyle, the Catholic member concerned, claimed he had been expelled on the grounds that he had been engaged in 'grave misconduct' and that this rested on an allegation that he was planning to bring into the Association 'undesirable elements' with the sole object of having himself elected Chairman of the Association at the next annual meeting. 'I am convinced that Mr Oliver had no other real motive than the fear on his part that I, as a Catholic, would obtain the chair next year and that the only way he could prevent me doing this was by expelling me.' Robert Porter, the Unionist candidate in the forth-coming Queen's by-election, intervened in the matter.[81] Boyle was quickly reinstated. Oliver apologised for the inconvenience and embarrassment caused to all concerned and to Boyle in particular.[82]

In the same month a row erupted within another Unionist Association amid more allegations of sectarianism. It began when more than 200 people in the Lisburn Road area of Belfast signed a petition protesting at the possibility of a Roman Catholic church being built on the site of the Regal Cinema. The petition stated that there should not be a Roman Catholic church there because it was 'a predominately Protestant area' and the Catholic population was 'so relatively small in numbers that the church would in fact be serving the needs of other overcrowded parishes outside the area'.[83] This sparked a discussion in the press. One correspondent described the 'real concern' that the Protestant community on the Lisburn Road had as the fear that a new Roman Catholic church would see Catholics moving into the district at such a rate that within a few years, instead of being a Unionist district, the area would become an extension of Catholic west Belfast.[84] The row escalated after Belfast Corporation's town planning chairman, John Allen, claimed he had not been re-selected by Victoria Unionist Association as a candidate for the May local elections because his committee approved the conversion of the Regal into the Catholic church. This was denied by the chairman of the Victoria Association, J. D. Morrison, who was 'satisfied that the cinema controversy had nothing to do with it'. The issue had not even been mentioned while the controversy was running in the press.[85] Some members of the Association claimed that opposition to Allen was in fact due to his occupation as a bookmaker.[86]

Apart from the explicit sectarianism of some Unionist Party members it is virtually impossible to state at which point some disputes were the result of bigotry or the outcome of genuine non-sectarian concerns. But it is obvious that the ambience of 'Protestant Ulster' seeped throughout Northern Irish society. Governing many of the attitudes held by Protestants towards Catholics was the belief that the Roman Catholic Church exercised control over its flock. Desmond Boal, the Unionist MP for the Shankill, touched on this when, in the aftermath of Craig's comments on Catholics and the Unionist Party, he said that there was no reason why people who subscribed to 'the basis of Unionist beliefs' should not be accepted into the Party; but he then qualified this:

It is not just enough that we say of Roman Catholics that all they have got to do is accept the basic principles of Unionism before membership. I say there is one other thing we ought to observe—and that is, we ought to remember the history of Roman Catholicism in this country.

We will learn readily that the Roman Catholic Church in this country is traditionally and historically allied with the Nationalist Party which is opposed to our own. We are not being intolerant or exercising discrimination.

All we are doing is acting on bitter experience and history. The real fear Unionists have had for time immemorial is domination by Roman Catholicism.

Is that fear irrational? All one has to do is look at history and the country south of the border to see it—to look at Spain and what the Vatican Council has failed to say any more than what it has said.[87]

Underlying assumptions such as these were shared by the Prime Minister. How else is one to explain an episode in May 1967 in which O'Neill allowed Protestant stereotypes of Catholics and their Church to cloud his judgment? On this occasion, just before rising to speak at the dispatch box, O'Neill was passed a letter by the Leader of the House, Major James Chichester-Clark, purporting to come from a 'loyal Irish Roman Catholic'.[88] The letter alleged that a priest had told his congregation not to employ Protestants nor to buy from a Protestant shop unless it was run by a Catholic. Instead of taking time out to consider its contents O'Neill made the mistake of reading it to the House there and then. Immediately Gerry Fitt accused the premier of knowing that he would inflame opinion in Northern Ireland; Fitt believed it was calculated to assist the Unionist Party in a forthcoming local government election. When he realised what he'd done O'Neill made a fumbling apology claiming that he had been 'lightly provoked' by opposition MPs and acknowledging that it was an 'unwise' thing to do.[89] But the matter did not rest there. A senior Roman Catholic cleric, Bishop Philbin, entered the fray with a public attack on the Prime Minister: in his experience nobody in a position of responsibility accepted a damaging accusation of this sort without asking for the exact facts about the place and date of the occurrence and above all the name of the person charged. Philbin felt that the Prime Minister must have known that many would read his attitude as 'confirming their belief that Catholic people are instigated by their priests to bigoted and un-Christian practices, that we are in fact the real cause of disharmony and bitterness in Northern Ireland'. The Catholic clergy who, said Philbin, had been working so patiently and so effectively in allying resentments to many recent events were deeply hurt that they should be regarded as agents of ill-will.[90] At Stormont a humbled O'Neill was forced to accept unreservedly the complete denial 'from responsible quarters' of the substance of the allegations made in the letter.[91] The significance of the episode was that it revealed the underlying assumption about the relationship between Catholics and their Church; how else can one explain O'Neill's actions except by recognising his pre-existing world-view of Roman Catholicism that convinced him of the genuineness of the letter?

SHOUTING AT THE NEIGHBOUR

The most dramatic evidence of O'Neill's 'New Ulster' would come not in the internal relations of Protestant and Catholic in Northern Ireland but between the Province and its southern neighbour. It was all the more dramatic because, according to Articles 2 and 3 of the Irish Constitution, the Republic of Ireland claimed that Northern Ireland—and all its inhabitants—were not part of the United Kingdom but part of the Irish state and nation instead. On the whole Unionist governments had recoiled from detailed co-operation with Dublin because of the South's territorial claim to the North although there had been some co-operation over the years. As long as the Republic laid claim to the North it had been a cornerstone of Unionist policy that the heads of government on the island should not meet face to face. O'Neill abandoned this principle. The process which would lead to a thawing of North–South relations arose out of an exchange of views on the Ulster question between O'Neill and the Taoiseach, Sean Lemass. This exchange began with a round of megaphone diplomacy. It is worth exploring because it set out the respective world-views of Dublin and Belfast to the 'problem' of Northern Ireland.

Lemass kicked off the exchange at a Fianna Fáil dinner in July 1963 at Tralee. He announced that the Irish Government recognised that the Stormont Government and Parliament 'exist with the support of the majority of the people' in Northern Ireland. In order to attract Unionists to his treasured goal of national unity he offered an autonomous Northern Irish statelet within a unitary Irish state; the Irish Government saw the Northern Ireland Government and Parliament continuing to function within its current powers and was 'prepared to stand over the proposal made by the united Republican cabinet of 1921 that they could continue to function these powers, within an all-Ireland Constitution' for as long as it desired to have them. 'Recognition of the realities of the situation had never been a problem for us.' Lemass complained that efforts which appeared to be developing spontaneously for North–South contact and discussion 'are now being countered by a new gimmick called "constitutional recognition"'. This he considered an excuse for inaction. What it meant was never made clear. Sometimes it was presented as meaning that the six north-eastern Irish counties were a part of Britain, which was an 'absurdity'. Sometimes it meant some formal abandonment of hopes for Irish unity which was an impossibility. It was Eire's wish to end partition by an agreement made in Ireland between Irishmen—a 'family reunion'—in which the memory of past dissensions would be forgotten.

Lemass believed that the forces making for division were growing weaker, although they were still strong, and while misunderstandings still persisted, it was with less conviction than before. He pointed out that Dublin had never failed to recognise the genuineness of the fears which had influenced the 'religious minority in the North' (by which he meant the Protestants who were a majority in Northern Ireland but a minority on the island of Ireland) or to understand that assurances which had been given in this respect down the years by all national leaders were not regarded as sufficient. He accepted that more positive and binding safeguards would be needed for a long time before full confidence would be established. 'We have in effect said to our separated countrymen: "What safeguards do you need in a reunited Ireland? Whatever you may in reason ask we are prepared to give."'[92] As Lemass had admitted this was not a departure in Dublin's thinking: while he recognised the *de facto* existence of the Northern Ireland Government and Parliament, he still held to the belief that Northern Protestants constituted a religious minority within the Irish nation. Lemass was asking Northern Unionists to state what civil and religious safeguards were required of the Irish state to encourage reunification. And even the term 'reunification' carried the implication that Ireland had once been a united political and cultural entity before its division by the British.

O'Neill chose not to respond to Lemass' speech immediately. Instead he waited until September before commenting because, he said, he doubted the value of off-the-cuff remarks. When he did respond he took the view that after four decades of stable government 'our constitution is an established fact and not a subject for continuing debate'. He told Lemass bluntly that 'The Constitution of Northern Ireland is not—I repeat, not—open to negotiation.' There were still many die-hard elements in the Irish Republic who were far from pleased to be reminded that modern living demanded more of a people than a sentimental recollection of ancient struggles. To this extent Lemass deserved his reputation for realism. His remarks were not without courage, said O'Neill. However O'Neill saw little trace of that realism in the reference to Northern Ireland. It was after all hardly a new approach to say that 'we are prepared to stand over the proposal made by the united Republican cabinet of 1921'. The recognition of Northern Ireland's constitution demanded more than an acceptance that the Government and Parliament of Northern Ireland existed with the support of the majority in the six-county area. Lemass had asked for the term 'constitutional recognition' to be clarified. O'Neill obliged: 'It means no more and no less than a full unequivocal acceptance not merely of the existence of our Government and Parliament, but of our indisputable right to remain—by our own clear choice—part of the United Kingdom.' O'Neill pointed out that it was the Taoiseach's predecessors who turned their backs first on the United Kingdom and then on the Commonwealth. He added: 'We have no wish to set upon that road.'

The Prime Minister was afraid that the word from the South betokened a new sophistication of approach rather than a genuine change of heart. While welcoming the flavour of realism which was creeping into Southern speeches this did not mean that 'they have recognised our constitution, as we have for many years accepted theirs'. And he warned that 'As long as there is talk of "the national territory" and a suggestion that Ulster will soon be ruled either directly or indirectly from Dublin, so long will Northern Unionists be wary of accepting the good faith of Southern Nationalists whatever their party label.'[93] In his reply Lemass adopted a non-confrontational approach by choosing to focus on the practical benefits of North–South co-operation. He spoke of the 'many possibilities which were well worth discussing' and argued that the rate of prosperity in the North and the South could be accelerated by co-operation in matters relating to industrial, agricultural and tourist development. This enabled O'Neill to thank Lemass for the 'succinct and courteous nature of his remarks'. But O'Neill emphasised that hopes for improved relations in the future would largely depend on two factors: a demonstration of Dublin's will, intention and ability to control the activities of the Irish Republican Army (IRA) and such organisations; and a recognition that the main barriers to co-operation were those erected by the Irish Republic against Northern Ireland and other parts of the United Kingdom. Nevertheless the Prime Minister pointed out that it had been demonstrated in the past that there was no bar to specific co-operative measures provided these were of clear mutual benefit, had no political or constitutional undertones and could be carried out within 'our limited powers'.[94]

But prospects for co-operation appeared poor particularly once Lemass arrived in the United States a month later, in October 1963. North America had traditionally been a stage where visiting Irish dignitaries (of the Nationalist variety) had been expected to deliver explicit statements of principle for their hosts who yearned for the old country (despite many of them being second or third generation Americans). To the disappointment of O'Neill, the Taoiseach used the dreaded 'reunification' word. Lemass told civic and political leaders in Chicago that the reunification of Ireland remained the supreme objective of Eire's national endeavour. The problem was never absent from their minds or hearts. The Taoiseach explained: 'We intend to solve it in the way that Wolfe Tone and the United Irishmen hoped the unity of Ireland would be achieved—by establishing between ourselves and our fellow countrymen in the North a community of interest and a union of hearts between Irishmen of every religious persuasion.' Ireland, he said, had changed: 'The Ireland of the mists on the bogs is gone for ever. The bogs have been drained and the mists have been replaced by power plants which produce electricity from the peat.'[95]

The Taoiseach followed this with another speech in Washington during which he called on the British Government to make a statement that there would be no British interest in maintaining partition when Irishmen wanted to be rid of it. This had not been said yet. Lemass believed that Britain's acceptance of 'winds of change' in Africa and Asia should be applied to encourage Irish unity.[96] There was nothing in Lemass' remarks that would have surprised any Unionists back in Ireland. But they were a disappointment for O'Neill who expressed his surprise and regret at Lemass' remarks after the 'civil exchanges' of the past few months had seemed to reveal some understanding of Northern Ireland's position. In his earlier exchanges O'Neill had defined what he meant by 'constitutional recognition'. Now it seemed necessary to define what he understood by co-operation: 'Co-operation certainly does not stem from derogatory speeches in another country . . . I suggest that the true meaning of co-operation is to be found in internal helpfulness—not in external hectoring.' O'Neill wondered where the Tralee speech was now? Where were all those reasonable sentiments? Were they only for London's consumption?[97]

Back in New York Lemass held no quarter. He told a press conference that he believed the partition of Ireland was under review in Britain (which it wasn't). He rejected the notion of Unionist consent to unity, arguing instead that any plebiscite in the North would be unnecessary 'if Capt. O'Neill and I could come to an agreement'. But he emphasised that the Republic's view on partition was changing and moving away from her former position of relying on a reiteration of her rights and a majority all-Ireland decision. Contacts had to be increased and

Ireland had to look at the basic causes used as a justification for partition. His Government was trying to develop a dialogue with Northern Ireland. At present the dialogue was at a 'very long range'. But it had just started and Lemass hoped to take it a little further in the coming months. The first step would be the elimination of barriers of suspicion and hostility which were deep in Irish history. The 'rest would follow automatically'. To guard against Northern fears of discrimination on political or religious grounds in a reunited Ireland, Lemass again promised that the present Government and Parliament of Northern Ireland would be retained while a central Irish government would take over the function now exercised by Britain.[98] But the Prime Minister of Northern Ireland pronounced himself disappointed once again: O'Neill concluded that, after forty years of folklore, even astute and gifted politicians in Eire were unable to distinguish the truth about Northern Ireland and the myth which surrounded it. 'Thus we have Mr Lemass, basically I believe a reasonable and sensible man', recognising at Tralee that the Government and Parliament of Northern Ireland existed with the support of the majority but proclaiming in the United States that Britain should abandon the partition of Ireland. 'Only in Eire could the same person make both these remarks and see nothing inconsistent in them.'

Yet the Prime Minister did not want to see an end to the process and declared that he would like to take the initiative in the dialogue. He suggested that the first step should be an end to statements, either in Ireland or abroad, about the 'ultimate reunification of our country', the 'evils of partition', and the 'Six County area' (which denied legitimacy to 'Northern Ireland' as an entity) and similar subjects. O'Neill did not suppose that Lemass or his colleagues would change their personal opinions overnight; but they, equally, must realise that he did not intend to change his. Only in mutual respect, an absence of recriminations and an atmosphere of true friendliness could any real progress be made: 'Talk will not of itself change things—there is more to the "wind of change" than hot air.'[99] By the time Lemass returned to Ireland it was the party conference season. Now he once more adopted a conciliatory approach. The Taoiseach told the Fianna Fáil conference that he hoped for a new atmosphere between North and South in which 'old problems will be re-examined and old divisions seen with increasing clarity to be anachronistic'. 'It is because' said Lemass 'we think of all the Irish people as one people, and their welfare—no matter where in Ireland they live or what their religious beliefs or political convictions—as our concern, that we want to build the unity we desire from the bottom up. We are not thinking in terms of imposing our will or winning victories, but of clearing away the accumulated rubble of centuries of misunderstanding and opening a new road on which no men of goodwill can refuse to meet us. We dream of a day when all the Irish people will have finally buried the memory of their past dissensions and will be able to present an example to the world of how a Christian people can resolve their problems and work in unison for the most worthy purposes which can inspire men everywhere.'[100] He avoided the 'r' word.

This was the pattern of the exchanges. The core issue of partition for Unionists was so raw that any reference by Lemass to ending it was likely to produce a stinging rebuke from O'Neill: in March 1964, for example, as the Prime Minister travelled to North America, he was prepared to admit that much of the bitterness which existed between Northern Ireland and Eire was abating. 'Time is a great healer,' he said, and since de Valera had passed from the scene (as Taoiseach that is, but resurrected as President of Ireland) new leaders had improved the outlook.[101] But only a few days later when Lemass had again reiterated a traditional stance on partition, O'Neill described the comments as the biggest disappointment of his first year in office. At the same time he believed that realism would emerge again. The 'rising generation was bored with these ancient obsessions'. He also believed that the 'thinking members' of the minority were tiring of old-style political Nationalism with its selection of thirty-year-old quotations and its outdated jargon.[102] In November, when Lemass was due to visit Queen's University to take part in a debate, O'Neill declined to extend the usual courtesies paid by the Government to distinguished visitors and meet the Taoiseach on the grounds that courtesy had to be reciprocal: Lemass had not encouraged a meeting by stating that his ultimate purpose in such a meeting would be to improve the prospects of ending partition.[103] O'Neill had already felt compelled to respond to the core Nationalist claim of Ireland a nation with the core Unionist answer—the geographical entity of the island of Ireland did not equate with the political Irish nation. In March he had dismissed the fundamental argument of Nationalists as simplistic:

> There are tidy-minded people who look at the map of Ireland and cannot understand why there is a frontier across such a small tract of territory ... They fail to understand that the existence of peoples is not governed solely by considerations of geographical convenience. I suppose ... the tidy thing, if that were the case, would be to lump the Iberian and Scandinavian peninsulas into one! Nor is it governed by language differences; if it were ... [Canada] would have been absorbed by the United States long ago, and Switzerland would have been parcelled out between France, Italy and Germany. In my view, the existence of a people depends alone upon its collective will to survive and to preserve its identity. And as long as that will exists it gives to communal life a meaning it would not otherwise have. Our collective will in Northern Ireland is, has been, and will continue to be to remain a part of the United Kingdom.[104]

TALKING TO THE NEIGHBOUR

If, by the beginning of 1965, O'Neill's liberal star was beginning to lose some of its shine in some Catholic quarters he dramatically restored it with a bold stroke of North–South diplomacy. By the new year O'Neill had been in office for twenty-one months. He now felt sufficiently secure to take some bold initiative, as he later put it, 'in order to try and break Northern Ireland out of the chains of fear which had bound her for forty-three years'. One evening in January, O'Neill summoned his advisors to his official residence and gave it as his considered view that he should ask Sean Lemass to lunch at Stormont in a few days' time. After a lengthy discussion it was finally agreed that on balance it was the right thing to do. O'Neill and his private secretary, Jim Malley, already knew Ken Whitaker, the civil service head of the Ministry of Finance in Dublin, from various World Bank meetings. Malley rang up Whitaker and arranged to have lunch with him at the Shelbourne Hotel in Dublin. Shortly before Malley left O'Neill had a last-minute idea and told him that if possible Malley should see the Taoiseach himself. During the Dublin lunch Malley made it plain that he wanted to see Lemass personally. This was arranged and when they met Malley 'popped the question'. The Taoiseach asked for time to think about the proposal and to consult his colleagues. But he accepted in principle.

No one within O'Neill's cabinet was informed of the secret contacts; only on the day before Lemass' visit North did the Prime Minister inform the Minister of Finance, the most senior member of the Government after himself. The Governor of Northern Ireland, Lord Erskine, already knew and approved. On the morning of the visit the remaining members of the cabinet were informed by telephone, as was the chairman of the Unionist Party.[105] The news was released to the press at 1 p.m. the moment Lemass arrived at Stormont. When Lemass arrived by car, having been driven from Dublin, he lunched with O'Neill before being introduced to the cabinet.[106] O'Neill only informed London of the visit as the Taoiseach was en route to Stormont.[107] Upon his return to Dublin, Lemass told reporters that 'things can never be the same again'. He stressed, however, that he had no desire to exaggerate the importance of the breakthrough in North–South relations. The next step would be to consider ideas for further discussions covering matters, for example, of trade and tourism.[108] The visit had been a dramatic event. Northern and Southern premiers had not met since Craig and Cosgrave in 1925, but given the circumstances since that last meeting—particularly the enactment of the territorial claim—the drama was more akin to the Craig–Collins meetings of 1922.

If the cabinet was surprised this was nothing to the surprise felt by the Orange Order which was shocked into paralysis and decided not to make an immediate response.[109] The move had a distinct air of an attempt to pacify troubled waters. Unsurprisingly the most vocal opposition from within the Unionist community came from Ian Paisley. He and three of his supporters drove to Stormont in a Union Jack-bedecked car to deliver a protest letter to O'Neill. The letter pointed out that, only the previous April, O'Neill had pledged that he would not 'have anything to do with Mr Lemass so long as he continued his refusal to recognise our constitution and the sovereignty of our Parliament'. A similar attitude was to be adopted as long as Lemass continued with his stance on partition. But: 'Yesterday in a veil of secrecy you [O'Neill] succeeded in smuggling this IRA man

into Stormont.' This was a grave departure from the stand of O'Neill's predecessors in office. The visit of Lemass demonstrated this and 'also adds insult to the
memory of the British forces whom Mr Lemass and his friends murdered in the
1916 rebellion'. Protestant Unionists 'were not prepared to sit idly by and have our
heritage bartered by you or anyone else. We declare that we will yield not one iota
of our heritage but will act as the Ulster Volunteers acted to defend our rights.'[110]
For good measure Paisley accused O'Neill of 'treason': he had 'forfeited the right
to be our Prime Minister'. He argued that if O'Neill was so confident that he had
the people behind him then he should test this at the polls. He promised that
every Unionist MP who supported the meeting would have 'Protestant' candidates
against them at the next Stormont general election. It was not just a question of two
men coming together to shake hands: 'It was not even mere politics. It is a matter
of our faith and our heritage.' And it was the Irish Constitution that O'Neill was
building bridges to: 'He is a bridge builder he tells us. A traitor and a bridge are
very much alike for they both go over to the other side. It was the bloody hand of
a traitor that he (Captain O'Neill) held.' Ulster was married to the United
Kingdom 'and Mr Lemass and Mr O'Neill will never break the ties which bind us
to the UK'.[111]

Paisley was a *force majeure*—but one operating from outside the Unionist Party.
What might be a little more worrying for O'Neill was the initial level of unease
inside that party. One early critic of O'Neill was Desmond Boal. Boal expressed a
sense of unease which many of the grassroots felt with the new direction the Party
seemed to be taking. He was fiercely critical of the Party's quest for a 'new image'. He
thought that this made it difficult to know at any given moment what the policy of
the Unionist Party was. The phrase 'new image' was used too much by prominent
Unionists and far too much by the Prime Minister. 'What is wrong with the old
image?' asked Boal. He suggested that it was in the field of industry and technology that a new approach and a new image were required—not in questions of
fundamental beliefs and principles. 'People were sometimes afraid to use the word
"Protestant", as if it was a dirty word. If one expresses his opinion dogmatically he
is immediately labelled an extremist or bigot. But if someone on the other side
states their case strongly—that is not bigotry because that is their belief and their
faith. In some queer way we accept that.'

One dictionary definition of 'image', noted Boal, was 'imitation of the real
thing'. Boal warned that 'If we clothe ourselves in a new image, as we are
encouraged to do by our own Prime Minister, we would have to change our moral
attitude. Then we will end up a pale imitation of the real thing.'[112] Specifically,
Boal 'deprecated the meeting greatly'. Unionists had been told again and again
'until we are sick of hearing it' that their Prime Minister would have nothing to do
with Lemass until he recognised Northern Ireland's constitution first. Boal
understood that O'Neill was just as firm in this regard as Lord Brookeborough.
But: 'Not only was this meeting secret, but it was sinister. If it was a good thing,

why was it not stated beforehand.' It was 'suddenly and secretly thrown upon us'. Boal complained that he had not been given an opportunity to form an opinion. Even if there was a change of mind on Lemass' part 'the secrecy of the whole thing indicates that there is a guilty conscience in someone's mind about the meeting'.[113] He returned to this at Stormont when he quoted from a reply that the Prime Minister gave to Patrick Gormley in April 1963, in which O'Neill had stated that the failure of the Eire Government to recognise the constitutional position of Northern Ireland was an obstacle to meetings between the Northern and Southern heads of government. O'Neill was explicit that it was his primary duty to safe-guard the constitution. Thus, said Boal, the Prime Minister had made the matter a constitutional issue and when the meeting took place despite this obstacle, people were led to believe that the constitution did not matter. Whether he wanted it or not O'Neill had brought the constitution into disrepute in the minds of the people. No doubt the Prime Minister was motivated by a sense of goodwill but not by proper principles. Boal thought it was a good thing that such a meeting take place as long as it took place within a proper framework. At this point O'Neill intervened to say that it was all very well for members to make speeches in the House which they thought would be popular in their constituencies but 'make things awkward for people who are doing what they consider to be right, but it isn't very estimable.'[114]

Nevertheless Boal had struck a chord. His unease was shared by others. The vice-chairman of the Ulster Unionist Council (UUC), Lieutenant Colonel Liddle, stated that no one objected to co-operation for the good of both parts of Ireland but added: 'We are not going to sell our birthright for any member of Parliament or leader.' Unionists he said, could not weaken their determination to remain under the British flag and in the Commonwealth in spite of whether it suited Lemass or others in the South. James Kilfedder, Unionist MP for West Belfast, was prepared to give the Prime Minister the benefit of the doubt: he believed that Lemass' visit 'must mean that he gives de facto recognition to Ulster'. But the next stage would have to be an unequivocal declaration from the Eire Government that it accepted the constitution and sovereignty of Northern Ireland. That was the only way to prove the sincerity of its friendship and co-operation with Ulster. Until that happened 'we should remain as much on our guard as before'.[115] But a month later Kilfedder backtracked from his earlier support for the Lemass meeting. He declared that a policy of 'not an inch' in constitutional matters was 'just as essential and relevant to-day as ever before'. Overnight a vital plank in the Unionist platform had been changed and changed not by the vote of the people, not by party conference, not even by the cabinet, but changed by the sole decision of the Prime Minister. The only benefit this had brought was the 'doubtful congratulations of our opponents'. Any trade benefit could have been secured by a Government minister meeting his opposite number in the Eire Government. Instead 'Mr Lemass has benefited from the Stormont tea party. He has given nothing away. He has given a new impetus to the anti-partition movement . . . What could not be achieved in former times by guns and threats will now be attempted by soft insidious words.'[116]

Kilfedder denied that he was calling for the Prime Minister to resign; he was merely stressing his strong disagreement with him about the summit meeting and the way it came about: the last thing Ulster could afford was to have a suggestion of a split in Unionist ranks.[117] From outside the Party strong criticism of the meeting came from Norman Porter, Director of the Evangelical Protestant Society. He declared that it was utterly impossible to separate religion from politics under present conditions, in either the North or South of Ireland. Consequently it was always the concern of both Protestants and Roman Catholics when issues concerning the border were raised on any level: 'When the Prime Minister of Northern Ireland is involved in such a matter it immediately becomes the concern of the majority of Protestants' and caused 'much concern among those who are desirous of keeping Ulster both Protestant and British'. Porter explained that if the secrecy attached to the visit was for security reasons 'then we do not complain'. But owing to the lack of information on this matter 'we cannot help but have justified suspicions'. The major objection of most Protestants was the fact that O'Neill 'led the people to believe that he held the same view as his predecessor, Lord Brookeborough'. The Prime Minister had given his assurance to Orangemen. It was in view of this that many were alarmed: 'Men of conviction on matters of such importance do not usually retrace their steps easily and without first of all some warning or indication of a change of policy. Our Prime Minister has thrust this new position on the people of Northern Ireland without any explanation.' Therefore Porter concluded that the remarks made by Boal appeared to be justified.[118]

Back in Stormont O'Neill defended his actions. He called for a 'spirit of friendship' to be established between Northern Ireland and the Republic. If this could be done, he believed that those 'sterile forces of hatred and violence which have flourished for so long will at last be crushed by the weight of public opinion'. This statement was in response to a request from Nat Minford, the Unionist MP for Antrim, and was received with enthusiasm on both sides of the House drawing immediate praise from Eddie McAteer and the Labour leader, Tom Boyd. As he continued O'Neill argued that Northern Ireland was, after forty years, strong enough to shed any traces of a defensive attitude: 'Our constitutional position is not in doubt; why should we continue to behave as if it were?' It seemed to O'Neill that it was in the spirit of the times to treat the border as nothing more than an ordinary frontier. Across virtually all the frontiers of the world friendly co-operative exchanges took place without any loss of prestige or sovereignty: 'Why should we be the exception?'

The Prime Minister went on to say that he believed Lemass to be a realist. In the past he might have said things to which they had taken exception in Northern Ireland 'but he seemed to be a man who would accept things as they were'. O'Neill thought Lemass had showed not only realism but courage in accepting his invitation to come to Stormont 'which is, after all, the very symbol of the separate existence of Northern Ireland'.[119] Defending himself against his two sternest Unionist critics at Stormont—the former Attorney-General, Edmund Warnock, had emerged along-side Boal—O'Neill said the decision was one of those occasions when a leader had to judge the temper of the times and take a step forward on his own authority: 'If he has judged aright the sentiments of the country, Parliament will endorse his action. That is the nature of leadership.' He had kept the meeting secret not because he feared the reaction of the great mass of the people but because he wanted no untoward incident by a tiny and irresponsible minority to tarnish an occasion from which much good might come. O'Neill was determined that the IRA were not going to have the opportunity to cut down trees between Dublin and Newry 'and a certain gentleman was not going to be at Stormont's gates with banners'. The picture he wanted painted of Northern Ireland was one of reasonable people meeting and discussing problems, not of bloodshed and strife. When the people of Ireland saw their leaders behaving in a civilised way, instead of hurling insults at each other, the time would eventually come when the extremist policies of organisations such as the IRA would cease to hold a place in the community.[120]

Such, by this stage, was the goodwill emanating from the opposition benches that Rory O'Connor, the Nationalist MP for West Tyrone, had already criticised Warnock for his 'violent attack on the youthful and popular Prime Minister'[121] (whether such praise was more damaging than bolstering to O'Neill is difficult to judge). But it should be noted that O'Neill was not without support from his own side. The strength of support among Unionist backbenchers for the summit talks was indicated by the number of MPs who backed a Commons motion congratulating the Prime Minister for his action. A total of eleven added their signatures. Of the remaining seven backbenchers, some were absent while Boal had already voiced his disapproval.[122] The Executive Committee of the UUC followed suite and 'enthusiastically' supported the 'statesman-like' action of the Prime Minister. The motion was seconded by Lieutenant Colonel Liddle who had earlier voiced concerns. By this stage Lord Brookeborough had let it be known that if O'Neill considered that Lemass had accepted the constitution of Northern Ireland then 'it was all right to have talks'. Such talks were 'good' provided they did not weaken the constitutional position of Northern Ireland. In fact Brookeborough revealed how, during his premiership, such a meeting had been considered but ruled out of the question with so much IRA activity all around the border.[123] In similar conditions as those in which the current Prime Minister now found himself: 'I should have no hesitation in doing what Captain O'Neill has done.' Brookeborough confirmed that if he had been in the country at the time, he too would have signed the parliamentary motion supporting O'Neill.[124]

With these political endorsements it was possible to move on to the next stage of practical North–South co-operation. Brian Faulkner, as Minister of Commerce, drove to Dublin for talks with his opposite numbers Jack Lynch, Minister for Industry and Commerce and Erskine Childers, Minister for Transport and Power. The talks covered the possibility of co-operation in the economic field, particularly trade, industrial research, tourism and power.[125] On 9 February O'Neill, accompanied by Mrs O'Neill, paid a return trip to Dublin and had lunch with Mr and Mrs Lemass. It was the first visit by a Northern Ireland prime minister since 1921.[126] On his return O'Neill announced that any future meetings between the heads of government would remain secret as long as the IRA adopted a hostile attitude.[127] This was followed by the confirmation that Harry West, Minister of Agriculture, would be meeting his opposite number in Dublin, Charles Haughey, for informal talks on the eve of the Ireland–England rugger international on 12 February.[128] On 10 March Faulkner announced that, as a result of his discussions with Childers, a joint North–South committee was to be set up to investigate the possibilities of cross-border co-operation in the field of electricity. The committee was to be composed of five nominees from Childers and two from Faulkner.[129] Faulkner also praised the co-operation in tourism that was now occurring between North and South, arguing that all sections of the population 'in geographical Ireland' had nothing to lose and much to gain from the well-ordered and properly controlled development of tourism 'in the country as a whole'.[130] Prospects for building a Belfast–Dublin motorway were discussed at Stormont when Bill Craig, Minister of Development and his Southern counterpart, Neil Blaney, Minister for Local Government, met.[131]

Eventually—more than a month after the Lemass meeting—even the Orange Order was on board as the Grand Lodge of Ireland passed a unanimous vote of confidence in the Prime Minister after a three-and-a-half-hour debate. Sir George Clark announced: 'We are firmer behind the Prime Minister than ever before.'[132] This was reflected in the resolutions submitted for the Twelfth which were 'conscious of the efforts the Prime Minister and the Government are making for a better understanding between the peoples of Ireland'. While welcoming this the resolution went on to reassure any faint hearts that 'we are also aware of the continuing assault on our constitutional position. This we will resolutely resist, never yielding in our resolve to uphold our position under the Queen and within the framework of the United Kingdom and the British Commonwealth.'[133]

At the same time, however, O'Neill wasn't exactly helped when Faulkner stated that while he explicitly backed the Prime Minister, he was obliged to point out that those who believed that Lemass had tacitly recognised the right of the Ulster people to govern themselves were deceiving themselves.[134] This was clearly the opposite of what O'Neill was arguing. In strictly constitutional terms Faulkner was right. And the rumblings from within the Unionist Party continued. Three leading members of the Young Unionists—Edward Gibson, Elizabeth Ewing and Robert Cooper—resigned from the movement with the summit controversy acting as a catalyst. Cooper claimed that the Young Unionists were 'becoming more and more of a right-wing extremist group while the rest of the party is becoming more moderate and progressive'. For example the Young Unionists had twice discussed sending a congratulatory telegram to the Prime Minister on his talks with Lemass but could not reach a decision.[135] The most prominent critic remained Boal. In a speech to Cormac Unionists Boal was listened to in silence until he said that O'Neill 'had made a liar of himself, a laughing stock of his cabinet, and wee boys of us including myself'. At this point Councillor Marjorie Sinclair interrupted: 'That is what you are. How dare you talk like that of our Prime Minister. You are most disloyal. The Prime Minister has done a lot for us.' Mrs Sinclair was cheered by many in the audience. Others began to talk. Boal, when he was able to continue, managed to begin: 'This lady says the Prime Minister has done a lot for us . . .' but at this point was interrupted again:

> Mrs Sinclair—Everything for us.
> Mr Boal—I don't know what sort of religious awe she regards him: I am prepared to use my head and examine what the Prime Minister does, and judge him against his own words. Just because he is the Prime Minister doesn't mean that he is not to be judged by human standards, standards of frankness, truth and commonsense. (Applause).

Boal stressed that he was not suggesting that O'Neill was prepared to 'sell us down the river, but I do say he has moved unwarily and stupidly against the principles of truth and I think he has done enormous harm'. He added: 'If you are happy to leave your destiny with him I am not.' The policy of the Eire Government had not changed. It was still dedicated to the 'problem of the unification of Ireland'. There might be many people who thought that there was nothing to this meeting beyond the clasping of two hands, but Boal's view was that 'there is an awful lot more to it than that. If we have the welfare of the Unionist Party and the ultimate welfare of Ulster at heart then we will have to ponder long and well before we allow a situation to develop in which the constitutional destiny can depend upon the thought or the whim of one man without reference to Parliament or the Cabinet.'[136]

  If O'Neill had his critics within the Party then Paisley, from outside, wasn't letting up either. He and his supporters were engaged on a policy of harassment of the Prime Minister. This often meant turning up at engagements where O'Neill was a guest or venues where they knew he would be. For example, on the evening of 25 February hundreds of Paisley's flag-waving supporters marched through the streets of Belfast. They were addressed by the Big Man who told them: 'We will stand where our fathers stood. We are the people who have a great and glorious heritage. We will not be moved.' Placard-carrying teenagers and mothers pushing prams danced and sang to the beat of 'No Surrender' and other party tunes. The placards stated: 'O'Neill welcomed in Dublin by Ulster's would-be destroyers', 'No welcome in Sandy Row' and 'King William crossed the Boyne to save us—O'Neill crossed it to sell us.' The marchers arrived at the UUP's headquarters in Glengall Street to voice their protest at O'Neill but missed him by twenty minutes.[137]

Given all this fuss it is perhaps here that we should try and assess the impact of the summit, and subsequent contacts, upon O'Neill's position. Certainly O'Neill was of the opinion that it was the events of 1966 and not 1965 when things started to go wrong during his premiership.[138] A National Opinion Polls survey in 1967 seemed to bear out the view that North–South relations were not a major problem for O'Neill. It revealed that there was a widespread feeling that the Government should endeavour to improve North–South relations. But it was noticeably less strong among Unionists than the rest of the electorate. Overall seventy-four per cent of those surveyed thought relations should be improved and of these ninety-two per cent of Nationalists agreed compared to sixty-three per cent of Unionists. Denominationally, ninety-five per cent of those calling themselves Catholic agreed compared to sixty-seven per cent of Church of Ireland members and sixty-seven per cent of Presbyterians: a significant minority of Church of Ireland members—thirty-one per cent—and Presbyterians—twenty-nine per cent—believed there should not be an effort to improve North–South relations. Defined in terms of Unionists opposed to such contacts the figure panned out at thirty-one per cent. Specifically, more than three-quarters of the entire electorate believed that O'Neill was right to meet Lemass with ninety-eight per cent of Nationalists and ninety-seven per cent of those describing themselves as Catholics taking this position. Among Unionists this support was lower—sixty-nine per cent—but still strong. This broke down as seventy-one per cent of Church of Ireland members and seventy per cent of Presbyterians. But significantly, twenty-five per cent of Unionists—one in four—thought O'Neill was wrong to meet Lemass. Twenty-six per cent of Church of Ireland members and twenty-three per cent of Presbyterians took this position. What this meant was that there was a hard-core of Unionists who felt distinctly uncomfortable with the position adopted by O'Neill: one in four Unionists believed O'Neill was wrong to meet Lemass and an equal number were opposed to talks with his successor Jack Lynch. Close to one-third felt the Stormont Government should not try to improve cross-border relations.[139] Yet O'Neill retained high support from both Unionists and Nationalists on the issue of North–South dialogue. By itself the issue was not enough to damage his leadership. And given time it might become accepted policy by more of his Unionist opponents. But that required stability.

Chapter 2 ⌒

O'NEILL AND THE ENEMY WITHIN: THE UNIONIST PARTY

OUT OF THE WEST

Catholics complained that the Unionist Government discriminated against them 'west of Bann'. The accusation was that government decisions concentrated development in the east and neglected the west, even though the west needed more development. The suspicion was that the east was favoured because it was mainly Protestant, while in the west Catholics were a slight majority. Among the more controversial decisions made were, in 1963, the Benson Report on railways, leading to the removal of the west's only railway line, cutting off Derry from Strabane, Omagh and Dungannon; in 1964, the Matthew Report siting Northern Ireland's 'new town' at Craigavon in the east; in 1965, the Lockwood Report rejecting Derry's claim for Northern Ireland's second university despite the existence of a university college in the city; in 1965, the Wilson Plan which designated growth areas for Northern Ireland, concentrating them heavily in the east; and in 1966, the closure of Derry's naval base.

Each of these decisions could be justified individually. The naval closures were part of a general cutback in British naval defence expenditure from which Northern Ireland could not expect to remain immune. Railways in Northern Ireland were losing money and, as in Britain and the Republic, the Government was obliged to close lines to limit losses. In fact the Benson Report had recommended the closure of both lines to Derry. The Matthew Report was not a regional plan for Northern Ireland as a whole, but as one of the civil servants involved explained, a means of circumventing a long-running dispute between Belfast Corporation and the Ministry of Health and Local Government over the rehousing of Belfast's surplus population: the new city grew out of the need to solve this problem. The Lockwood Committee produced reasoned arguments for concluding that the Coleraine area best fulfilled the requirements of a site for a new university, among them being the availability of an area large enough to allow for expansion, a criterion which the existing university college in Derry could not meet. Finally, Stormont could point to sound practical reasons why entrepreneurs preferred to settle in the east of the province. That was where skilled labour, docks and communications were most concentrated.[1] However, while these points are more than enough to undermine the Catholic claims of discrimination in regional development, there is a further factor that lends support to the view that the Unionist Government did not consciously discriminate against the west. This is the mayhem that the issue of regional development caused in the Unionist Party west of the Bann. Given that one of the overriding goals of O'Neill and his predecessors had been to maintain the unity of the Unionist Party, the issue of regional development—or the alleged lack of it—proved to be a significant factor in undermining confidence in the Unionist Government among the Unionist grassroots. It was not a decisive factor but when further complications arose for O'Neill's Government it had already had a corrosive effect. For any government to have actively sought to alienate its supporters in the west—and it is well to remember the cultural significance which Derry held in the Protestant psyche—would be political folly. To perpetuate any such folly would be just plain dumb. But there remained a fear, summed up perfectly by Labour's David Bleakley, that the problems of the west were leading to the emergence of a 'three-county state for all practical purposes'.[2]

The reaction of the Protestant west was anger to the changes announced by the Unionist Government. Not only was Craig, as the relevant minister, closing rail links to Derry but he also considered, in 1963, the closure of the Belfast–Dublin line. The Benson Report had suggested that the line should be streamlined and treated as a prestige service. Craig's view was that prestige in itself was not sufficient grounds for keeping a railway open.[3] This was not discrimination but a fixation with 'modernisation' and reflected the feeling in many quarters that the future belonged to the car. For example, another Unionist MP, Phelim O'Neill, concluded that in the near future the entire railway system would come to an end.[4] Such actions and intentions drew criticism from across the Unionist Party: the Windsor Young Unionists Association in Belfast was just one group from within the party that added their criticism to the closure of Derry's rail links.[5] At the Unionist Party conference in May 1964, a North Londonderry Unionist Association motion on transport calling on the Government to take all possible steps to retain the railways and improve their efficiency was accepted. Craig had stated that Derry would not be isolated but John Hamill, the proposer, asked 'will Derry feel isolated?' By isolating Derry 'will you not be giving a wonderful weapon to the other side? Will they not be able to say "Now you see your real place is over here with us [in the Irish Republic]."' E. T. R. Herdman of North Tyrone told delegates that a feeling was growing in the country that the Government 'does not care what happens to us'. Someone in Londonderry had told him recently that: 'It is not Lundy we are burning in Derry this year. It is somebody else we are going to burn.'[6] It was unclear whether this referred to O'Neill or, more likely, Craig, who was gaining a reputation for being unmoveable once he had made a decision.

This was the prelude to a drama the following year that convinced many Nationalists *and* Unionists that there was a deliberate policy to run down the west. An accusation that 'nameless, faceless men from Londonderry' had gone to Stormont and advised against the siting of the second university in the city or the settling of industrial development there was made by Dr Robert Nixon, a maverick Unionist MP. Speaking at the annual meeting of the Londonderry Middle Liberties Young Unionist Association, he told his audience: 'Your present danger is a political line of thinking that could relinquish Derry to the Nationalists. You can't win wars by running away from your forward positions, or because there are Unionists who see Derry as a Papist city and say that it must be allowed to run down.' Nixon claimed that men from Londonderry went to Stormont 'and said under no circumstances must industrial development come to the Derry area. And on both these counts your men of Derry are indicted—those men who are supposed to represent you.' Then, saying that he would let the Young Unionists into a secret, Nixon described how, after Sir John Lockwood had produced the site at Coleraine, he was aghast that Derry should have been passed over: 'I went to a Cabinet Minister—not Faulkner nor Ivan Neill—and I said "Tell me, were you surprised at Lockwood recommending Coleraine as a site for a university?" He looked at me and said "How could I be when we directed Lockwood to site the university at Coleraine?"' Nixon said that wild horses would not drag the name of the cabinet minister from him. He also used the occasion to denounce the lack of democracy in the UUP, complaining that Craig, when he had been Chief Whip, had accepted Brookeborough's recommendation of O'Neill for Prime Minister without consulting anybody else.[7]

This was powerful stuff. O'Neill immediately denied that the cabinet ever issued any such directive,[8] as did Lockwood from his hospital bed (it transpired that he was terminally ill) in London: 'I have worked for a number of Governments and I have never on any occasion allowed my views to be influenced or dictated by any of them.' His committee had been appointed as an independent body made up of independent-minded people. Having followed the controversy in the press, Lockwood concluded that many people in Northern Ireland were 'very imaginative'[9] (he didn't know the half of it). Back in Derry the story was given further credence by both sides of the communal divide despite the Government's denials. Alderman Campbell Austin, of the Corporation, confirmed that Nixon's accusations were a repetition of what had been said by many people for some time: 'My only regret is that the worthy doctor could not have named the "nameless ones".' He found other suggestions by Nixon that a similar process may have gone on with regard to the new city 'rather terrifying. To think that any would-be government could be so influenced behind the scenes makes me wonder if, in fact, there is any hope for this area.'[10] Patrick Gormley, the Nationalist, declared: 'What Dr Nixon has said is the truth. There are five men in Derry who did use this influence. I know their names and later on I will name them.' Gormley also claimed there was written evidence of this. What Nixon said was accepted by the vast majority of people in the north-west as true. There was supposed to be a democratic parliament but 'they were run by the Civil Service' and it was through the Civil Service that all these suggestions were made. Lockwood would be right in saying that he was not directly primed but the Civil Service 'set everything up and he had to finish in Coleraine'.[11] Gormley subsequently listed seven members of the council of the City and Foyle Unionist Association as leading the campaign against Derry acquiring the new university. In fact as Major Glover, the president of the association, could demonstrate, the records showed that in 1962 the council decided to support public opinion and devote the full weight of the Unionist organisation in the area to a campaign to secure the raising of Magee University College in Derry to full university status. The association supported the motion at the Ulster Unionist Council (UUC) and had been part of a delegation to the Prime Minister and Minister of Education supporting Magee's case. Glover considered that of all the past Nationalist attempts to discredit Unionists 'never has an attempt been so futile and so helplessly inaccurate' as that made by Gormley.[12] Robin Chichester-Clark, the Unionist MP for Londonderry at Westminster, was another of those named by Gormley. Chichester-Clark repudiated the allegations and pointed out that his attitude had been one of strict neutrality on the siting of the university given that it would involve his taking the part of one half of his constituency against the other.[13]

Gormley's claims did at least have the short-term effect of uniting the Unionist Party in the face of the hereditary enemy. Alderman Austin had been one of four prominent Unionists who signed a petition calling for a public inquiry into Nixon's allegations but now withdrew their names in the fallout over Gormley's intervention. Instead, a meeting of the Unionist Council attacked Gormley for setting back the spirit of co-operation that had been encouraged by both O'Neill and Lemass and 'up till now had been put into practice on the university issue'. The seven members of the Unionist Association identified by Gormley denied any of the Nationalist MP's accusations.[14] Magee's future was eventually secured as a constituent part of the new university in May 1965.[15] Eddie McAteer, the leader of the Nationalist Party, dismissed the outcome as 'merely ointment on the deep wound inflicted on the North-West as a whole'.[16]

As for Nixon, he was hauled before a meeting of Unionist MPs at Stormont on 18 May, where he withdrew his allegations concerning the Lockwood Committee. It was agreed that no disciplinary action would be taken against him. According to the Chief Whip, Major James Chichester-Clark, Nixon agreed that he would refrain 'at all times' from further personal attacks on the Prime Minister; agreed that 'Because he could not substantiate' the allegations that a cabinet minister had stated that the Government had directed the Lockwood Committee 'he unreservedly withdrew it'; and agreed to withdraw similar claims regarding the Matthew Committee. He also agreed to refrain from attacking the Prime Minister in the current and the following Parliaments.[17] But no sooner had he withdrawn his allegations at the meeting than he publicly denied having withdrawn them with regard to the new city and implied considerable reservations with regard to the university question. Chichester-Clark felt he was left with no choice but to withdraw the whip from him. Nixon, however, still considered himself a loyal party man and 'still the official Unionist member for North Down' who would vote for or against the Government as he saw fit. He then went on to reveal that he had been 'most unhappy' since Jack Andrews, the former Minister of Finance and now Leader of the Senate, was 'sacked' early in O'Neill's premiership. For the past two years there had been a serious difference between his conception of a Unionist Government and what was the fact. Alongside the Drainage Act, which had put a third rate on valuations in North Down, there had been issues of town planning, the new city, new industries and the refusal of the Government to permit a public inquiry into planning which had led Nixon to 'believe that Captain O'Neill was progressing rapidly to a dictatorship . . . All they have done now is to put the jackboot on.' As for the nameless and faceless men: 'Everyone agreed that these gentlemen existed, but it would be impolite to say so.'[18] Nixon was publicly reprimanded by his Unionist Association for his attacks on the Prime Minister although he was allowed to remain the sitting MP for North Down. During his thirty-four-page speech to the Association, Nixon added yet another allegation—that the Prime Minister had personally told him and others that leading Unionist citizens in Derry were against new industries and the new university coming to the city.[19] There was in fact no evidence for any of Nixon's accusations. What the episode illustrated more than anything was how a specific issue acted as a lightening conductor for a kaleidoscope of other grievances.

In the west the university controversy had only added insult to injury. The Matthew Report of 1964, recommending the creation of the new city east of the Bann, had already upset Unionists and Nationalists in the west. While Londonderry was outside the terms of reference for the Belfast Regional Plan it had been considered in a survey of the whole of Northern Ireland. Sir Robert Matthew gave four reasons for selecting Lurgan and Portadown as the site of the new city planned to rise in population from 36,000 in 1964 to 100,000 in 1981. The first was that their location beyond the head of the Lagan Valley was the natural direction of development into the hinterland and close enough to Belfast to attract industrial enterprise. Second, they had good rail communications with Belfast and the South and could easily be linked by road to the proposed Belfast–Dungannon motorway. Their proximity to Lough Neagh could take advantage of water transport, should it develop, on the largest stretch of inland water in the British Isles. Third, the configuration of the land was well suited for building. It was not of first-class agricultural quality but had a ready availability of utility services such as water and electricity. And fourth, the existing urban centres had established populations and reasonable existing social and commercial facilities that would make a sound basis for expansion.[20]

After accepting the Report, Craig, as the new Minister of Development, Transport and Local Government, faced a renewed challenge to the Government's planning policy based on it. In August 1964 Geoffrey Copcutt, the former head of the design team for the new city, condemned in a 7,000-word statement the concept of the new city for County Armagh and declared that Londonderry should be redeveloped as Northern Ireland's second city. Once again it was not just Nationalists, generally, or Unionists from the west, specifically, who cried foul: Belfast's Unionist Lord Mayor, William Jenkins, regarded Copcutt's repudiation of Matthew as justification for the city's opposition to it.[21] The university controversy merely compounded the earlier concerns relating to the new city. In May 1965, by 147 votes to 124, the UUC carried a resolution from Belfast's St Anne's Association condemning the dictatorial manner and outlook of recent Government planning proposals. Dr N. D. Laird, who proposed the motion, said the handling of the Lockwood Report was a complete negation of democracy. He accused the Government of being very much out of touch with public opinion and claimed no Ulster government before had alienated so many people.[22] A month later the North Tyrone Unionist Association adopted a resolution asking for a solemn assurance from the Prime Minister that the counties of Tyrone and Fermanagh and the city of Londonderry would remain, and continue to remain, an inviolate and integral part of Northern Ireland within the United Kingdom. Furthermore the Association wanted reassurances that steps would be taken to ensure that the said counties would enjoy equal rights and parity with other parts of the UK in terms of amenities, transport and social services. This followed the closing of the railway line between Portadown and Londonderry. W. S. Moody, who proposed the motion, explained how 'everybody' in Tyrone was very disturbed by the Government's 'arbitrary' action. The circumstances of the closure were a gigantic confidence swindle. Tyrone, said Moody, had become one of the biggest railway deserts in the UK. 'There is a suggestion' he added, 'that we in Tyrone and Fermanagh may be cast off tomorrow, and land up in the Free State. This is a serious threat . . . It seems to me the people of Tyrone and Fermanagh are cut out for abandonment.' Supporting the motion was William Rankin who warned that unless something was done 'we are going to lose not only North Tyrone; we are going to lose the city of Derry. I have only to go round my own townland and count the people who have left for Canada, Australia and New Zealand, and they won't be back. They are all Unionists. Others are content to sit there and draw National Assistance, and live there and rear their families; but the best of our people are not content to do that . . . There is nothing for them to do in their own country, and it could have serious repercussions in the days to come.'[23]

The Unionist Government, of course, rejected these claims from its own supporters. O'Neill declared that the Government recognised no distinction between Ulstermen. The Ministry of Commerce was doing its best to 'push' industrialists as far from Belfast as possible but in the final analysis it was the industrialist who had the final say as to where he wanted to go.[24] He described suggestions that the Government was abandoning the western counties as 'a complete misunderstanding of the basic constitutional beliefs of the Unionist Party'. He had even heard this from supporters who should know better. They had been lending themselves far too readily to an insidious campaign mounted by political opponents. He emphasised that: 'Neither at this time nor at any time in the future will we value one inch of our territory less than another.'[25] No one within the Government was more angered by such accusations than Brian Faulkner who, as Minister of Commerce, had done an immense amount of globe-trotting to persuade businesses to come to Northern Ireland. He 'bitterly resented' charges of neglect towards the west[26] and pointed out that, since 1945, twenty-eight Government-sponsored industries had been established in Coleraine, Londonderry, Strabane, Omagh and Enniskillen. Twenty of these were still in production employing 6,435 people. The total employment for Londonderry was 2,859; for Coleraine, 1809; and for Strabane, Omagh and Enniskillen together, 1,767. This, however, made no impression on the Government's critics. Eddie McAteer focused on Coleraine as the 'most favoured darling' of Faulkner: it got preferences not only in the new university, but also in the siting of industries.[27] The Government was thus assailed from both sides—by supporters and opponents—on the issue of regional policy. It was undermined on two counts: by alienating its traditional support amid allegations of dictatorial policies, and by the skilful usage of the issue by opponents who used it as yet another example of discrimination. On this issue the Government was in a no-win situation.

ELECTION

Yet O'Neill's troubles within the Party have to be placed in context: it would be a mistake to assume that it was all bad news for the Prime Minister. He remained confident in his own abilities and the appeal of his modernising agenda. His success in the Stormont election of 1965 reinforced this. Up to the election O'Neill had been unproven and for him to survive as Prime Minister his primary aim was to demonstrate that he could ensure that the electoral hegemony of the Unionist Party would remain intact. The most serious threat to the Party's position came not from the Nationalist Party, but from the Northern Ireland Labour Party (NILP). In the Westminster election of October 1964 the NILP had polled 103,000 votes, though it won no seats. This unnerved many activists within the UUP. O'Neill had to produce an effective formula to counter the NILP's electoral threat. The answer was to take the NILP head on with regard to social and economic policies. The Northern Ireland Parliament was dissolved in November 1965. When the Unionist Party's manifesto was published—the Stalinist-sounding 'Forward Ulster to Target 1970'—O'Neill declared that he would fight on the Government's economic record. He would make no mention of the IRA in election speeches. But then he really he didn't need to. There was already an IRA scare story doing the rounds following the arrest of five young men wearing semi-military combat tunics. They were detained by a police patrol in the Glen Road district near Belfast on the night of 17 November. There had been a greater security presence since masked men burst in on an army recruiting film show at St Gabriel's Roman Catholic School in October. The IRA claimed responsibility. Subsequently cabinet ministers were given special armed guards.[28] The five arrested men, apparently led by Joe McCann, an eighteen-year-old labourer, refused to recognise the court and were sentenced to one year's imprisonment for having offensive weapons in their possession. The weapons were bayonets. They also possessed a map showing the location of the residence of the General Officer Commanding Northern Ireland (GOC NI).[29] And despite O'Neill's personal pledge not to mention the IRA, he could not commit Party candidates to avoiding traditional rallying cries. For example, the dissent in the west saw the Attorney-General, E. W. Jones, an unopposed Unionist MP for thirteen years, having to face the first serious election campaigning of his political career as he squared up to the Liberal candidate, Claude Wilton. The problem for Jones was summed up by one leading Unionist who stated: 'I am going to vote, not against the Unionist Party, but against the anti-university Protestant element in the city. I hope to see the Unionist Party purified and rooting for Derry.' The Attorney-General, who lived in Belfast but journeyed to Derry once a week, was forced to deny allegations that he was not a Derryman by turning to a traditionalist stance: 'One of my ancestors was Bishop of Derry in 1610; another took part in the siege, and one was killed at the Boyne.'[30] Jones said he was 'all for unity' but the minimum he required was unity under the Crown and under the Union Jack: 'When we get to that stage with the Liberals then we can start talking about other material matters.'[31]

A basic problem for O'Neill was that, for all his commitment to modernising Ulster, the fact was that nothing got the juices flowing like a good old-fashioned appeal to the blood and thunder of traditional Unionist dogma. And why shouldn't it? This is what Unionist voters had been used to for decades. Added to this was O'Neill's persona. Dennis Kennedy of the *Belfast Telegraph* joined O'Neill on the streets where he witnessed some of the personal and ideological barriers that the premier had yet to overcome. He observed how, while there was no doubt that the Prime Minister had enjoyed these strolls, 'he is much more the PM meeting his people than the politician with the common touch, winning votes'; for in this campaign it was becoming apparent that while O'Neill 'can certainly charm, he finds it more difficult to inspire. The charm is evident in the personal encounter, the lack of inspiration in the election meeting.' Kennedy reflected how the 'Eton drawl' might go down well after dinner, 'but it is something of a liability in an overcrowded church hall in Crossgar'. Nor was the content of his speeches the sort of thing which Orange and church halls had come to expect from their Unionist politicians. 'For in turning away from the blood and thunder of the Old Ulster, Capt. O'Neill has substituted a challenging which is a good deal less intoxicating.' Having stuck to his promise not to fight on the old slogans the Prime Minister found himself at Crossgar following Basil Kelly who had told the electors of East Down that he was, and they should be, Unionist because his father had fought off Sinn Féin attacks on his small farm in Monaghan half a century ago. Worse, not better, was to follow. Introducing the Prime Minister, the chairman remarked that there was some doubt as to who the National Democratic Party (a new and small left-of-centre Nationalist outfit) were: he had a story—one farmer asked another: 'What is a National Democrat?' 'I'll tell you. It's another name for the Papishes.' With that Captain O'Neill got up to make a solid speech on shipyard redundancies and labour retraining. Kennedy commented how the torpor of the audience was as unmistakable as the apathy of the electorate at large during the campaign and largely stemmed from the same cause: 'Basically, pure economics is not a controversial issue.' There was too much agreement between all parties on this. Bridge-building, on the other hand, had not been preached in the election—the plank with real potential for broadening the Unionist platform. 'Perhaps the truth is that at the hustings the finest goods are not the most saleable,' reflected Kennedy.[32]

Despite this the election proved to be a victory for O'Neill and the UUP. When the results were declared the state of the parties was: Unionists 36, Nationalists 9, Labour 2, Republican Labour 2, Liberals 1, National Democrats 1 and Independents 1. As for the voting in contested constituencies (twenty-three seats were uncontested) the sums were: Unionists 101,696, Nationalists 26,748, Liberals 12,618, National Democrats 15,166 and others 11,798.[33] It was clearly a personal triumph for the Prime Minister. In contrast to the NILP's advances in 1958, because of economic uncertainty and rising unemployment, the Unionist Party had stolen the NILP's clothes with a comprehensive social and economic programme. Tom Boyd, the Labour leader, had his majority halved. The one substantial Unionist setback was in Dock (Belfast) where Gerry Fitt more than doubled his majority despite a lower poll. Newly elected Unionists were Roy Bradford, an experienced London property developer who made a triumphant entry into Victoria (Belfast) after three times failing to get the nomination for Westminster seats, and John Taylor, a twenty-eight-year-old engineer and a former leading Young Unionist.[34]

1966 AND ALL THAT

While across the water 1966 would be remembered for England's glorious triumph over West Germany in the World Cup (alas both Irish football teams failed to qualify for the tournament; and it is perplexing how the Northern Irish complain how often the English keep referring to this triumph no matter how distant it now is, but somehow miss the irony when they refer to 1690, 1798, 1912, 1916 etc.), in Northern Ireland the year would be remembered for the political turmoil that engulfed O'Neill and the Unionist Party. At the centre of this was Paisley who must have thought he had the perfect opportunity to embarrass

O'Neill following the controversy surrounding the naming of a new bridge over the Lagan in February 1966. What might appear a relatively minor issue in fact illustrated the charged nature of symbols in Northern Ireland. The controversy was sparked off by the dramatic intervention of the Governor in February. Intervening to avoid embarrassment to the Queen, Lord Erskine prevailed on Belfast Corporation's Improvement Committee not to give the name 'Carson' to the new Lagan bridge. The Governor's message, sent through the town clerk, reflected a widespread feeling that the Unionist caucus in the city hall had committed a blunder. A majority of councillors had voted for 'Carson' as the new name closely followed by 'Somme'. The Queen was to officially open the new £4-million bridge when she visited Belfast in July. 'Queen Elizabeth' was proposed as the new name for the bridge by Alderman Sir Cecil McKee, the Independent Unionist, and seconded by Councillor Thomas Fitzpatrick of Republican Labour. Fitzpatrick thought 'Queen Elizabeth' was the lesser of two evils. This was unanimously accepted.[35]

But resentment remained in Unionist circles that Erskine had butted into council business. As Unionist Party chiefs in the city hall agreed at a specially-called meeting to approve the choice of the name 'Queen Elizabeth Bridge' they also criticised the 'unconstitutional manner' in which the Governor's views were expressed. Lord Brookeborough also regretted the interference: Lord Carson was without doubt one of the greatest men of their times and he felt that in these matters they gave way too easily to the 'opposition'. However, as an old soldier, he thought the 'Somme' was the right name for the new bridge.[36] Paisley soon waded into the fray, declaring that the Governor should mind his own business and not interfere with the Protestant rights and liberties of the Ulster people.[37] He then appeared to pull a master-stroke when he involved the younger son of Lord Carson, the Honourable Edward Carson, in the controversy. Carson accused the Governor of 'running rough-shod over public opinion' in Ulster. This had been done against the wishes of the majority of the Unionist Party. Carson asked: 'Why would Her Majesty be embarrassed by the use of my father's name? He was one of the most loyal subjects that ever served the Crown.' And while no loyal subject of the Crown—and 'the Ulsterman is the most loyal in the world'—could object to the name of 'our beloved Queen' being used, 'I feel that the Governor has run rough-shod over public opinion.'[38]

For critics of O'Neill the issue was being turned into more than the naming of a bridge: it was further evidence of a dictatorial style of government evolving in the Province. The political drama unfolded on 21 February as a rash of incidents revealed heightened levels of tension in and around Belfast. In the early morning a petrol bomb was thrown into the grounds of St John's Roman Catholic Church on the Falls Road. Later in the day, some eighteen miles away in Crumlin, St Joseph's Roman Catholic Primary School was broken into and set alight. Political slogans were daubed on St Gerard's Roman Catholic Church on the Antrim Road in Belfast. The slogans, painted in red, were: 'Remember 1690' and 'Remember

Carson' with an unprintable reference to the Pope. Later in the evening a window in premises owned by the Free Presbyterian Church at Albertbridge Road, Belfast was broken.[39] As politicians of all persuasions condemned the incidents, the IRA denied all involvement and instead blamed the Unionist Party for deliberately heightening tensions amid claims that Republicans were involved in an alleged plot to kidnap the senior British military commander in the Province—the General Officer Commanding—and about to initiate a new violent campaign. It was the view of the Republican movement that this was an attempt to make the observance of the forthcoming Easter Rising jubilee in the 'occupied area' impossible.[40] Faulkner, for one, accepted that the incidents were not contrived.[41]

By now Carson was sharing a platform with Paisley calling on the Governor: 'Go. For God's sake, go.' Paisley challenged the Prime Minister to 'clear up the lingering suspicion' that the Government might have advised Lord Erskine to take the action that he did. He reminded O'Neill that when the Prime Minister next sought loyalist votes (with a UK general election pending): 'Let him tell Ulster whether he is against Carson or for Carson.' Extra police were on duty at the Ulster Hall where thousands of people who were unable to get into the building heard the speeches through loudspeakers. Police were also on duty along the routes taken by four large groups of marchers on their way home. A gang of about twenty-five youths who were walking ahead of the Shankill Road procession attempted to lead the parade into the Old Lodge Road which had a large Catholic population. The youths were turned back by two young police constables.[42] O'Neill, for the record, denied tendering any advice to the Governor.[43]

Carson then announced that he would be standing in North Belfast as an unofficial Unionist candidate in any forthcoming election. He understood that his campaign would be financed by Paisley's Ulster Constitution Defence Committee (UCDC). Carson now began to express some of his views on the Province. For example, on the religious problem in Northern Ireland, Carson said he didn't want a 'Nazi state' with privileges withdrawn from Catholics: 'But I can't say I like Roman Catholics very much. Loyalty to the Crown usually goes by religion.' His arrival on Northern Ireland's political scene allowed Ulster people to get a closer look at him. They found that Carson, who was forty-six, had been the youngest MP when elected as the Conservative member for the Isle of Thanet in 1945. He had gone straight into politics after war service with the Life Guards 'which', in his own words, 'was probably a mistake'. He retired in 1953 for financial reasons as well as ill heath. Keeping up two jobs—he was a MP and in business at the same time—meant he became run down. This, apparently, was the reason for his brief disappearance in 1952 when he had a complete blackout after leaving the Commons and was traced to Inverness after a forty-eight-hour search. Since giving up his business interests in London—he sold steel scrap abroad until the UK Government stopped the licenses for this—he had become an articled clerk in a friend's solicitor's office in Windsor. He now stood in North Belfast against

Stratton Mills, because he wanted Ulster loyalists to be given the opportunity 'to declare whether they are for or against my father's principles'. The present leaders of the Northern Ireland Government, declared Carson, were pursuing a policy which could only lead to the destruction of Ulster's hard-won constitution and liberties. His appearance created turmoil within Unionist circles. Captain Orr, an old personal friend of Carson and his wife, appealed to him not to split 'the great Unionist Party of which his father was the adored leader'. No one would gain from this except Ulster's enemies.[44] Initially this fell on deaf ears, as did a telephone call to Carson from Brookeborough[45] and a last-minute plea to his mother, Lady Carson,[46] who continued to back her son. But then, as suddenly as Carson arrived on Northern Ireland's political scene, he departed with the dramatic announcement that he was pulling out of the election and returning to England. He blamed the inability to get a fair hearing in the local press and the fear that he could split the Unionist vote to the advantage of the Labour candidate as the reasons for his decision;[47] subsequently he admitted that the latter factor was driven home to him by 'people close to Glengall Street and Stormont'.[48] Paisley's great opportunity to strike a blow at the Unionist Party's hegemony had been thwarted.

The Westminster or 'Imperial' General Election, as it was still called, was announced soon afterwards at the end of March. At first sight it seemed that, overall, the Unionist Party was in a strong position with the Westminster contest, coming as it did after the Party's recent successes in the Stormont election. In the Westminster election of 1964, out of the twelve contests, there were three majorities over 30,000, two over 20,000, four over 10,000 and of the remaining three, West Belfast was the lowest with 6,659 for James Kilfedder. The last was the real battleground in this election. Kilfedder's winning margin in West Belfast was deceptive. The previous election had been a four-cornered contest in the constituency with the opposition split three ways, yet the Unionists had polled well under half the total votes cast: 41.2 per cent to be precise. Now the opposition produced one candidate instead of three. The unknown factor in the election was the 12,500 votes cast for Labour, which could swing the contest. More so than other constituencies West Belfast was a uniformly working-class district of small houses, small streets and—as one correspondent suggested—some said small minds. Standing against Kilfedder was Gerry Fitt of Republican Labour. Fitt's tactics seemed clear enough: to play down the 'Republican' side of his banner: 'I'm a Labour man, first, last and always.' Kilfedder, on the other hand, emphasised the constitutional factor, regarding the election as a referendum on the link with Britain. But the odds-on bet was that Fitt would win it. Were he to do so he would be fulfilling a fifteen-year-old ambition when he was Jack Beattie's twenty-four-year-old election agent: 'I said to myself when I saw Jack elected that I would get there someday—and I meant it.'[49] As the campaign unfolded, apart from West Belfast, the key question was whether or not the Unionist Party's vote would hold up.

The tone of the election was set by Paisleyites who dogged O'Neill wherever he went. There was a disturbance at a Unionist election meeting in Coleraine after a Free Presbyterian Minister shouted: 'I very much doubt that I can look on our Prime Minister as a Protestant.' Captain O'Neill was on the platform when a familiar 'friend', Reverend John Wylie of Coleraine, called out during the singing of the National Anthem: 'God save the Prime Minister' and 'All we get from the Prime Minister is a smile.' After the interruption Wylie asked if he could put a question. From the platform he was told he could if it was relevant to election issues. Wylie said that Unionist headquarters at Glengall Street had made it clear that they did not want the vote of extreme Protestants. 'I would like the Prime Minister to clear this statement,' he said. 'What is an extreme Protestant? I am Protestant. You are either a Protestant or not.' Wylie felt that the Unionist Party had not made very clear its position concerning the border and 'I am very much in doubt that I can look on our Prime Minister as Protestant.' Lemass was entertained to lunch at Stormont but when the son of Edward Carson came to Ulster 'they sent down the head gardener to meet him'. O'Neill didn't respond but in a hard-hitting reply from the platform Robin Chichester-Clark reiterated what he had said at the beginning of his campaign: he did not want help from anyone who was of a sectarian nature. He argued that the Prime Minister had visited places which were not in the UK but which had brought more credit to the UK than 'the visits abroad of some people I know'.[50] This was a reference to the Free Presbyterian protest the previous week concerning the Archbishop of Canterbury's visit to Rome for an audience with the Pope; Wylie and Paisley were refused entry into Italy.

While there was little evidence that the Unionist Party's hegemony was in any real danger it was nevertheless the case that when the results were in the Unionist Party was alarmed to find that their majorities were down in all constituencies except South Down. The Ulster Liberals polled well in North Antrim and South Down but Republicans suffered crushing defeats in Derry and North Antrim. The exception was Tom Mitchell in Mid-Ulster who picked up all the Nationalist votes and reduced the Unionist majority by 4,500 to 2,500. House-bound (because of a serious car accident) Paddy Gormley of the Nationalist Party scored a notable victory in Derry polling 22,000 votes and cutting the Unionist majority by 4,000. He netted practically all the votes that had gone to the Republicans in 1964. But the big inquest was into the fall of the Unionist vote in Belfast. There was a uniform heavy swing to Labour that reflected a national trend as the Labour Government swept to a large majority in Britain. In the four contests where there were straight fights between Unionist and Labour the swing averaged seven per cent—well above the national average and in complete contrast to the Stormont election.[51] But, most spectacularly, the Unionists lost West Belfast as Fitt 'won the West' defeating Kilfedder with a majority of 2,011. He was the first non-Unionist to hold the seat since 1955.[52] The results were all the more disappointing for the Unionist Party following the optimism generated by the Stormont results a year before. Yet while this suggests that the success in that election should add a cautionary note when assessing the security of O'Neill's position, it should also be borne in mind that it was the Stormont elections that mattered most. And there O'Neill had proved a success.

In the aftermath of the election Paisley upped the ante when he announced to a rally of 700 men and women in Lisburn Town Hall that divisions of Ulster Protestant Volunteers (UPV) would be formed in every parliamentary constituency so that where there was a 'Lundy' politician 'then we are going to challenge him in the polls'. 'We have decided to organise Protestants in Ulster,' he declared. 'We are looking for volunteers, men who are prepared to stand together in this day of crisis and in this evil age.' The UPV would be under the control of the UCDC and would be constitutional, democratic and legal. His meeting, he noted, had caused a 'flutter in the Stormont dovecotes'. People there were worried about it. 'They say Thompson machine-guns will be handed out tonight. I don't see any machine-guns,' said Paisley. On the other hand he did see that 'We have Protestants who are selling our constitution bit by bit and inch by inch. It is time we came to a serious fight. That is why we are organising a division in every constituency.'[53] The UPV was open only to those who were born Protestants and not to Catholics or members of the Royal Ulster Constabulary (RUC), except for the almost exclusively Protestant B-Specials. The UCDC constitution declared that it and the UPV were one united society of 'Protestant patriots pledged by all lawful methods to uphold and maintain the Constitution of Northern Ireland as an integral part of the United Kingdom as long as the United Kingdom maintains a Protestant monarchy and the terms of the Revolution Settlement'. The UCDC, which had a committee of twelve originally called together by Paisley, was also the governing body of the UPV. The rules of the UCDC declared that 'No one who has ever been a Roman Catholic is eligible for membership. Only those who have been born Protestants are eligible for membership.' Each meeting of the UCDC and UPV had to be opened with a reading from the Authorised version of the Bible. Each member had to be prepared to pledge his first loyalty to the society, even when its operations were at variance with any political party to which the member belonged. Any member associated with, or giving support to, any subversive or lawless activities, would be expelled from the body. The UCDC and UPV pledged to 'maintain the Constitution at all costs. When the authorities act contrary to the Constitution the body will take whatever steps it thinks fit to expose such unconstitutional acts.'[54]

Paisley found willing volunteers for his new organisation as, with Easter approaching and the fiftieth anniversary of the Rising of 1916 with it, the political temperature within Northern Ireland began to rise once more. On 1 March police in the Dungannon area investigated reports that a County Tyrone unit of the Ulster Volunteer Force (UVF) was being re-formed. A man who called the *Belfast Telegraph* anonymously stated that a declaration would be drawn up and sent to the Government later in the week. He said the UVF were being re-formed because of dissatisfaction with the way the Government was handling the situation created by preparations for the Easter Rising celebrations. Protestants 'were not going to be trampled by these Sinn Féiners,' said the caller. 'We will oppose the demonstration with force of arms if necessary.'[55] The closer the Easter Rising commemoration came the higher rose the collective Protestant blood pressure. In late February the Republican National Commemoration Committee had announced that, in addition to Belfast, there were to be 1916 parades in Derry, Dungiven, Loup, Armagh, Lurgan, Maghery, Castlewellan, Kinawley, Antrim, Coalisland and Newry.[56] In the South the approach of the anniversary inspired Republican attacks on British symbols and personnel there. In Dublin there was a fire at the British Legion Club. Raiders planted two petrol bombs. The same thing had happened at the Legion's Cork branch the week before.[57] A week later a fire severely damaged the kitchen at the house of the British Military Attaché, Brigadier Thicknesse, in Dublin. A petrol can was found in the kitchen.[58] A few days after this an early-morning explosion demolished Nelson's Pillar in the heart of Dublin.[59] Yet overall the Republic was a country at ease with the forthcoming anniversary. In contrast to the controversy of the Lagan bridge episode the Irish Government announced that the three main Dublin stations and twelve throughout the country were to be renamed after the executed leaders of Easter Week.[60] Given the divisions of the Civil War the commemoration allowed the pro- and anti-Treatyites to agree at least on the glory of 1916; unless of course you might be a Southern Protestant who was more likely to feel uncomfortable with the State's act of remembrance. The commemoration presented the Church of Ireland with a dilemma: when the bishops of the Church met in Dublin in January 1966 they were unable to reach any formal decision on what part, if any, it should take on the fiftieth anniversary of the Rising. The difficulty was for the Church to recognise that this was a great state occasion without offending many of its own members for whom 1916 still had unhappy memories.[61] Eventually the Church decided to participate—which in turn disgusted some Northern Unionists. One 'Loyalist' wrote to the *Belfast Telegraph* to complain that if the Protestant churches in Dublin intended to hold a religious service to commemorate the Rising 'then let it be a service of remembrance for the 103 members of the Army and 17 members of the police force who were killed on this occasion'. The writer also thought that those members of the services who lost their lives in the years following the rebellion should also be remembered.[62]

In the North there was widespread Protestant concern at what the Easter commemorations might entail. There were rumours, fuelled by Paisley, that up to 30,000 people would travel up from the Republic to Belfast, amounting to an 'invasion' of the North. This would not merely be a physical incursion but, just as importantly, a psychological violation. Northern Ireland was British, Protestant and had been loyal to the Crown, sacrificing her sons at the Somme—also to be remembered in 1966—as Catholic rebel Ireland was betraying Britain. It was one thing to celebrate the Rising in the South, quite another to celebrate it in the loyal North. Thus Paisley attacked plans for the celebration of 'a Papal plot to stab England in the back while she was at war with Germany'. It was an insult to the constitution that people should be allowed to flaunt the Tricolour and celebrate what was a great act of treachery against the Crown 'on our own doorstep'. As proof of his accusation of Papal involvement in the rebellion he quoted from an editorial in the *Irish Press* of May 1933, which described how, prior to the Rising, Pope Benedict XV received a mission from Count Plunkett who disclosed to him the decision to rebel and the date and 'received from him his Apostolic Benediction for the men who were facing death for Ireland's liberty'. Paisley said the document bearing the Pope's blessing was hung up in the GPO in Dublin when the fight began. 'It is a disgrace that this rebellion is to be commemorated in Ulster,' he declared.[63] Referring to the claims that about 30,000 people would be travelling to Belfast from Dublin for the commemoration of the Easter Rising, Paisley warned: 'Let me say that they had better stay at home on this Sunday. We mean business; we are not going to be hammered into the ground by these people.'[64]

Paisley had plugged into a widespread concern that the Government was going soft in allowing these celebrations as letters to the press ably demonstrate: 'This part of Ireland remained steadfastly by the side of Great Britain in her hour of need and had no connection whatsoever with events in Dublin in Easter Week,' wrote one. The very idea of 'freedom trains' running from Dublin to Belfast was laughable if it was not so serious: 'Let these people stay at home and celebrate freedom where, incidentally, there is little freedom—not even to plan one's own family; and let the authorities encourage them to do so by banning all these celebrations before the loyal Ulster people are pushed too far.'[65] 'Peace-Lover' was also of the opinion that the celebrations should be banned: 'Why should we allow this murderous rising to be commemorated here with IRA sympathisers carrying their rebel flag' aided by large numbers of people from Southern Ireland. If a few people from Northern Ireland wanted to take part in these celebrations 'let them go south of the border to celebrate'.[66]

By April, with the 1916 celebration imminent, posters issued by Paisley's UCDC began appearing in centres where commemorations were planned, declaring that the 'loyalists of Ulster have no intention of sitting idly by while you revile their constitution, insult their flag and gloat over their murdered kith and kin'. Paisley denied that the posters were provocative: they were only provocative to those that wanted to insult the flag. He also denied that the posters were his doing; instead they were the work of the UCDC which, although he was chairman, represented 'every' loyalist in Northern Ireland.[67] By now the Government was becoming increasingly worried as the commemoration approached. A four-man Ministerial Security Committee had been formed under O'Neill in the new year to assess and counter any renewed IRA threat. The RUC Reserve was reactivated to operate at strategic points; police stations were strengthened and reinforced in border areas;

and the USC as a whole was placed on patrol duty with some on full-time mobili-sation.[68] McConnell, at Home Affairs, banned the Republican demonstration at Loup, County Derry on the grounds that it 'would undoubtedly lead to serious public disorder'.[69]

In the event the commemorations passed off peacefully. But the damage had been done. Tensions had been heightened considerably. On 6 June Paisley led a parade through Cormac Square, a Catholic area in the Markets, where local residents tried to block the road and were cleared by the police after a riot; he then went on to the Presbyterian General Assembly where the marchers tried to attack the Governor of Northern Ireland.[70] Cormac Square was the scene of renewed tension on the evening of 7 June. Two petrol bombs were thrown at a police car passing through the area. They missed their target. About twenty minutes later three missiles, one of which contained an explosive charge, were flung at a RUC Land-Rover in nearby Hamilton Street. They too caused no damage or injuries.[71] In the aftermath of the riot, and aware of the growing influence of Paisleyism, Sir George Clark warned Orangemen that there could be a considerable split in the Order if they continued to be misled by militancy. But while appealing to Orangemen to stand on good sense and common sense, he admitted: 'I would be extremely dumb if I did not realize that there is a feeling that there is not enough militant people at the head of the institution today.' At the same meeting Lord Brookebourgh, Grand Master of Fermanagh Grand Orange Lodge, continued to adopt a less-than-enthusiastic attitude towards the improvement in community relations. He would only say: 'I believe in neighbourliness and there I stop.' Having referred to 'various conferences which are going on' he added: 'Other Churches have their own methods of worship and we have ours. Don't let us mix the two.'[72]

It was left to the current Prime Minister to tackle head on what he perceived to be the menace to public order and the improved state of community relations. A public exchange developed between O'Neill and Paisley as the Prime Minister went on the offensive and the Moderator of the Free Presbyterian Church, in turn, defended his position. O'Neill told the Commons that he had no doubt that the attacks on the police in Cormac Square required careful preparation before-hand. In offering insults to the Queen's representatives 'these people' were abusing the Crown itself. They called themselves 'loyalists', but to what were they loyal? To the Queen whose personal representative they reviled? To the United Kingdom in which their fellow citizens viewed their conduct with a mixture of ridicule and contempt? To Protestantism, many of whose leaders they had personally abused? 'I am not prepared to accept lectures from such a source,' declared O'Neill:

> My family has been practically wiped out fighting for the Flag. Some of us are
> so proud of the Union Jack that we would not choose to thrall it through areas
> in which it may not be properly venerated, especially when it is accompanied
> by placards insulting other people's religions . . . Now I understand Members

of this House are being threatened with personal violence if they dare to raise their voices. Respectable citizens lift their telephone receivers and are forced to listen to a torrent of disgusting language followed by threats of violence, or that they cannot sleep. These are not the activities of a political party seeking the support of the electorate, but the sordid techniques of gangsterism.

To those of us who remember the Thirties the pattern is horribly familiar. The contempt for established authority; the crude and unthinking intolerance; the emphasis upon monster processions and rallies; the appeal to a perverted form of patriotism: each and every one of these things has its parallel in the rise of the Nazis to power. A minority movement was able in the end to work its will, simply because most people were too apathetic or too intimidated to speak out. History must not be allowed to repeat itself in this small corner of the British Commonwealth.[73]

Paisley was outraged by this attack. He responded by telling more than 600 people at a rally in Ballymoney Town Hall that his voice would not be silenced by all the commands of the Prime Minister. The premier had referred to him and those who supported him as gangsters, Fascists and Nazis; but as Ulstermen they resented these baseless accusations and were determined, come what may, to keep the thoroughfares open for the Union Jack. In regard to the trouble at Cormac Square and other parts of the city, he alleged that it was the Catholic Church and the 'Romanists' who started it. So far as the General Assembly disturbance was concerned, Paisley warned that he would return with 10,000 or 20,000 next time.[74]

When Paisley took to the streets there was often the possibility of trouble. A pattern was developing where he pushed freedom of association to the limit. Cormac Square had not been the first such instance. In the autumn of 1964 he had been the catalyst for disturbances in west Belfast. A Tricolour was displayed in the window of Sinn Féin's election office at the bottom of Divis Street. Under the Flags and Emblems Act such displays were deemed illegal only if the police considered they were likely to create a breach of the peace. To one of Paisley's supporters, Noel Doherty, 'It was like flying the swastika in London during the Second World War. It represented something that was anathema to every Ulsterman.' Paisley announced a march and vowed to 'remove it myself'. Faced with the threat of a Paisley-led march into Nationalist west Belfast, the police removed the flag. Fighting erupted between Republicans and the RUC. Three days later the Tricolour was back in the window. The RUC moved in, smashed the window and removed the flag. Fierce rioting broke out; petrol bombs were thrown and guns were used by the IRA. It was the worst rioting in Belfast since the 1930s. Paisley had no regrets: 'It was an act of defiance and the IRA made it clear they were defying the law and thumbing their nose at the authorities . . . It was the only way you could move the jellyfish who were in government. It wasn't as if I was a lone voice crying in the wilderness. I was voicing the strong resentment of the Ulster people at the time.'[75]

Paisley never sanctioned violence. But he created the conditions in which it might thrive. Only when one has heard the passion and power of Paisley's voice and understood its effect on people can one grasp the true power of oratory. He inspired his supporters yet articulated their deepest fears. This in itself was enough to push some towards illegality. Noel Doherty was one such. He had been drawn to Paisley in the mid-1950s when he was a pupil at high school and involved in intense debates on the true nature of the Bible: 'As a young man I was religious and having trouble with my class-mates about the Creation story and the Virgin Birth. Paisley explained them in his sermons and did so with conviction. His fundamentalism appealed to me . . . I saw him as a true disciple of Christ. He thundered the message forth in a way that brought joy to my heart and I was spellbound by his oratory. I felt he was going places and I wanted to go with him . . . I felt ecumenism had to be destroyed and Paisley was the man to do it . . . One likes to be led. There was power with Paisley—power in his mannerisms and power in his preaching . . . I saw him as a great Ulsterman and a second Carson.' Doherty joined the B-Specials because he saw them as an arm of the Protestant religion. He also joined Paisley's Free Presbyterian Church.[76]

It was Doherty's idea to set up the UPV: 'The idea was to have cells all over Ulster—in every hamlet, every town and every major city . . . If we needed a demonstration, the support was already organized and sitting there. We could do it at the toss of a coin. The "Bishop" [Paisley] liked the idea.' But Doherty also had other plans and set about organising a 'secret cell structure' within the existing UPV cells which he proposed to arm. 'My idea was to have the [secret] cell made up mainly of "Specials" so that at the snap of a finger or a secret code word we could have a private army just like Carson did with the signing of the Covenant. So Paisley would have had his own private army and he'd have been a second Lord Carson.' Paisley was never told of this because 'he had to be protected'. Paisley 'was our saviour, our Moses, our champion prepared to resist to the death, to oppose the Roman Catholic Church and ecumenism. O'Neill spelled the end of the Ulster we all knew. In a "doomsday" situation, we felt that in some mystical way, the UPV was going to save Ulster.' Doherty helped the reconstituted UVF acquire gelignite. Unfortunately for Doherty the police found out and he was sentenced to two years' imprisonment. Paisley disowned him.[77]

Thus Paisley's sectarian message, in its broadest sense, appealed to members of the UPV. But it would be wrong to try and place all the blame at Paisley's door as the inspiration for paramilitary revivals. There was indeed some overlap between the UPV and the UVF. But many unattracted by Paisleyism were drawn to the extremes by their concerns with O'Neillism. The revamped UVF was not an overnight creation. It was the outcome of a socialisation process as the experience of its legendary leader demonstrates. Gusty Spence was born in the Shankill Road area in 1933. His father, Ned, had been a member of Carson's Ulster Volunteer Force and had gone on to fight in the Great War.[78] Young Gusty attended the

Church Lads Brigade where he paraded with dummy rifles: 'Always in the back of my mind were the First World War, the Somme and the men of the UVF. We were brought up with the sound of the drum and the flute. Old soldiers sat on a bench outside Stewart's barbers, covered in a sea of blue smoke from pipe tobacco. They talked about the trauma of the Somme and the men who died. My own Da fought from 1915 to 1918 and had only 27 days' leave but at least he came back.' He learnt his politics from his mother: 'My Ma told me about the Prods and the Taigs ambushing the cops . . . during the 1932 hunger riots.'[79] He joined the Junior Orange Lodge. Remembering the Belfast Blitz of 1941 he recalled there were rumours that Catholics had kept their lights on during the blackout to guide the German bombers into Protestant areas: 'The famous rumour at the time was that the Catholics were burning newspapers and ringing the place with flames to guide the bombers. A lot of nonsense of course, but you'd be surprised how many people actually believed that, including myself.'[80] When boys from the Shankill went to the baths on the Falls Road they remained vigilant. Spence recalled tales of Protestant boys being asked to recite the Hail Mary. If they couldn't repeat it 'they got their pans knocked in'.[81] Eventually he followed in his father's footsteps and joined the Army—the Royal Ulster Rifles. There he mixed with Catholics, Southern Irishmen and Republicans: 'St Patrick's Day was a big day in the Ulster Rifles. We marched to two tunes: an Orange song, "The Sash my Father Wore", and a republican song, "Kelly the Boy from Killan", representing both traditions in a cultural sense. Then on Rifles Day we commemorated the Somme. The Slainte [toast in Irish] was given, and the pipe major drank the last drains of Irish whiskey. The dress of the Royal Ulster Rifles included the standard saffron kilt. We had Tara brooches, the shamrock and the Maid of Erin harp. All those things awakened in me the feeling that we're Irish. We're British, of course, but we're also Irish.'[82]

In 1965, according to Spence, two people, one a UUP politician, approached him and told him the UVF was being reformed and that he was to be responsible for the Shankill: 'The way the story was put to me was that there was incipient rebellion and I had taken an oath to Her Majesty the Queen to defend her . . . against enemies foreign and domestic. I saw my service in the UVF as a continuation of my British army service.' He joined not for sectarian reasons but 'purely for patriotic reasons'. Spence was sworn in at a ceremony outside Pomeroy, County Tyrone where he took a secret oath. Formal and informal meetings of the Shankill UVF took place throughout the winter of 1965–6. They consisted of a small group of no more than twelve people. £8,000 was acquired through a bank robbery. Arms were acquired from those who had hidden them in the 1920s. With the fiftieth anniversary of the Easter Rising approaching the UVF was armed and on duty at interface areas. A UVF volunteer threw a petrol bomb through the window of what he thought was a Catholic-owned pub on 27 March 1966. It was the wrong address. Matilda Gould, a Protestant, burned to death. For Spence the UVF was not reconstituted merely to deal with a renewed IRA threat, it was also to 'oppose or be used as a bargaining counter against some of the things O'Neill had brought into debate. People do not realize how heavy the opposition was to O'Neill ... Probably he was only trying to keep the wolf from the door, but there was great concern within the Unionist Party that he was going too far, especially when he brought Lemass to the North. His overthrow was to take the shape of violent incidents in Belfast and Northern Ireland to hype up communal and political tensions.' There were emotional reactions as well to the approaching 1916 celebrations: 'All the Catholic streets were decorated and we saw barricades at the end of the streets.'[83] On 21 May 'Captain William Johnston' of the 1st Battalion the UVF issued a statement to the press announcing: 'from this day on we declare war against the IRA and its splinter groups. Known IRA men will be executed mercilessly and without hesitation ... we solemnly warn the authorities to make no more speeches of appeasement. We are heavily armed Protestants dedicated to the cause.'[84]

In June the Shankill UVF met in the back room of the Standard Bar where a decision was made to kill a leading Republican, Leo Martin. Four men were dispatched to the Clonard area, just off the Falls Road, to perform the assassination. They failed to find him. Instead the UVF men came upon John Patrick Scullion. He was drunk and apparently singing Republican songs. They shot him dead. So inept was the police and forensic investigation that, when his body was found, it was thought that Scullion had fallen over drunk, injured himself and subsequently died. Only when, three weeks later, the UVF contacted the press to claim the killing was it found, after the victim's body was exhumed, that this was a murder case. On Saturday 25 June another—unsuccessful—attempt was made to locate and kill Martin. Gusty Spence and some other UVF men went on to the Malvern Arms on the Shankill Road. That night three young Catholic barmen— Peter Ward, Richard Leppington and Liam Doyle—had been working late in Belfast city centre at the International Hotel. Andrew Kelly, their manager and also a Catholic, suggested a drink after a long Saturday night. The only pub he knew that would be open was the Malvern Arms off the Shankill Road. Catholics drinking on the Shankill or Protestants on the Falls were not an unusual occurrence then: 'I'd been drinking there before without any problems,' recalled Kelly. One of the UVF men with Spence was Hugh McClean according to whom Spence went to the bar beside the four Catholics to buy a drink. He said: 'I've been listening to their conversations and they are four IRA men ... they will have to go.'

The four young men left the Arms about 1.45 a.m. Kelly remembered seeing flashes and hearing the sound of gunfire: 'Peter Ward was hit first ... He was dead before he hit the ground. I was shot too and dropped down but they kept on shooting at me.' Leppington and Doyle were also hit and seriously wounded. Kelly reflected: 'I don't know why they did it. We were ordinary working people with no IRA connections. We were shot just because we were Catholics.' Peter Ward's mother, Mary, was sitting at home waiting for her son to come home. She was worried because it was so late. A priest knocked at the door. He said he had 'bad news' about Peter and gradually explained that he had been shot. Mary Ward was devastated and never recovered from her sense of loss: 'They shot at Peter and Peter fell. It was the UVF that killed him and he was shot for nothing, just because he was a Roman Catholic . . . I never go anywhere or never look to go anywhere because Peter's always there.' Mary Ward was speaking more than thirty years after her son's death. Spence, McClean and Robert Williamson, another UVF man, were arrested. During his police interview McClean was 'asked did I agree with Paisley and was I prepared to follow him. I said that I was.' After being charged he was alleged to have said: 'I am terribly sorry I ever heard of that man Paisley or decided to follow him.' Paisley announced that he deplored the killing. Meanwhile Spence was charged and convicted of the murder of Ward. He always denied he was at the scene of the shooting. He served eighteen years.[85]

The killings sent a tremor through Northern Ireland. It was a clear and ugly manifestation of the often respectable sectarianism that flowed through the veins of Protestant society. Addressing a packed House of Commons at Stormont on 28 June, O'Neill announced that two men had been charged with the murder of Peter Ward and three men with the murder of Patrick Scullion. That morning the Minister of Home Affairs had declared the UVF an unlawful association under the provisions of the Special Powers Act. The Prime Minister had flown back from France where he had been honouring the sacrifice of the men of the 36th (Ulster) Division, many of whom had been members of the 'authentic' UVF: 'Let no one imagine that there is any connection whatever between the two bodies: between men who were ready to die for their country on the Fields of France and a sordid conspiracy of criminals prepared to take up arms against unprotected fellow-citizens.' O'Neill warned: 'We stand at the crossroads.' He baulked at the prospect of reprisals and counter-reprisals, the consequences of which 'could be very grave indeed for us all'.[86]

Although O'Neill had made no explicit connection between Paisley and the UVF, there was an implied connection between the atmosphere of intolerance he associated with Paisley and the manifestation of intolerance on the streets, first in street disorders and now murder. Paisley himself denied any such connection declaring that he 'did not know what the Ulster Volunteer Force is, or who its leaders are, or what its intentions are, but evidently Captain O'Neil does'. He also said that he had never been associated with, or had anything to do with the UVF. But O'Neill had an ace up his sleeve when he gave his reply, which contradicted Paisley's denial of any knowledge of the UVF. He had received from the police a verbatim report of a speech made by Paisley at the Ulster Hall on 16 June. The Prime Minister quoted the relevant extract to Parliament. Paisley, who had said earlier that he was well aware that the police were present, had stated:

Let me tell you this friends, there are many ex-Servicemen at this meeting, they are the defenders of the Flag of Ulster. I have a resolution here from some of them, the ex-Servicemen of both World Wars, now comprising four divisions of the Ulster Volunteer Force. 'We are solidly behind Rev. Paisley and repudiate the dirty slur and the classifying of those who fought the menace of Nazism as Republican inspired and we give him our entire support.'

O'Neill considered it a slur on the body of ex-Servicemen of Ulster to suggest that any considerable number of them would lend support to 'this sordid organisation'. Going back to 17 April, O'Neill recalled that, at the Ulster Hall, Paisley thanked all those who had come along and marched that day 'and he specifically mentioned by name the Ulster Volunteer Force'. The RUC had also informed the Prime Minister that a leading member of the UVF was an important official of the UCDC of which Paisley was the publicly-acknowledged chairman. O'Neill asked the House of Commons to judge for themselves the extent to which 'Mr Paisley can properly claim ignorance of the activities of the Ulster Volunteer Force. He is no doubt anxious to wash his hands of them now; but the record clearly shows that he has hitherto received and welcomed their support'.[87]

The practical political impact of this was to marginalise Paisley further. Even when the heightening of tension within the Protestant community is taken into account there was no evidence of a Paisley breakthrough in politics. But the absence of a breakthrough did not mean the absence of support. This is backed up by the evidence of the National Opinion Polls data which revealed over-whelming opposition to Paisley among the electorate. He certainly had an image problem: seventy per cent of all voters usually disagreed with what he said; sixty-five per cent thought that he deliberately tried to stir up bad feeling between Protestants and Catholics; and when asked to choose between O'Neill and Paisley as Prime Minister, ninety-five per cent of all voters picked the former. However, a word of caution here: thirty-four per cent of Unionists—thirty-two per cent Church of Ireland and thirty-one per cent of Presbyterians—agreed with what Paisley said compared to fifty-six per cent of Unionists, of which there was greater opposition to him among Church of Ireland members—sixty-three per cent—compared to Presbyterians—fifty-eight per cent. There was a discrepancy between Belfast and the rest of Northern Ireland: thirty-seven per cent of those in Belfast agreed with Paisley compared to sixteen per cent in the rest of the Province as a whole. While fifty per cent of Unionists (fifty-eight per cent Church of Ireland and fifty-two per cent of Presbyterians) thought Paisley deliberately stirred up trouble between Protestants and Catholics, forty-four per cent of Unionists (thirty-six per cent Church of Ireland and forty-one per cent of Presbyterians) thought that he did not. Not surprisingly, ninety-eight per cent of Nationalists and ninety-one per cent of Catholics thought Paisley did stir up trouble. Eighty-four per cent of Unionists and 100 per cent of Nationalists preferred O'Neill as Prime Minister rather than Paisley. Paisley, however, noted that thirty-seven per cent of the people of Belfast agreed with what he was doing: 'That is over half of the Protestant people and that figure itself is significant.' It certainly was. He also pointed out that he was not in the running for the premiership 'and this is a ridiculous question to ask anybody. Why did they not ask anybody how many people were for Eddie McAteer . . . ?' It was quite evident, claimed Paisley, that 'the Protestant people who support me also support the traditional Protestant position'.[88] What this reveals is that, just as with the opposition to North–South dialogue, there was a hard-core of Unionists who, if not wholly supportive of Paisley, were at least sympathetic. His greatest problem was that the tactics that had propelled him into the political limelight were just as likely to prevent him from attaining mainstream political respectability within Unionism. For O'Neill it wasn't so much Paisley that was his problem as the tensions within the Unionist Party. It was the impact of Paisley on the Party activist grassroots (always more unrepresentative compared to the 'average' Unionist voter) in terms of the fears he articulated, rather than the electoral prowess of Protestant Unionists, that created problems for O'Neill. Nowhere was this more evident than in the 'plot' to overthrow the Prime Minister in 1966.

PLOT

By late September it was clear that all was not well within the Unionist Party. A 'Back the Government' group of senior Unionists and backbench MPs held two meetings in an effort to promote unity in the Party's ranks. The decision to convene these informal meetings reflected the anxiety among Unionist leaders regarding the Party's public image.[89] These fears seemed to have some basis in fact as rumours began circulating of a petition criticising O'Neill's leadership having been signed by a dozen or more backbenchers.[90] But it seemed that the revolt was over almost as soon as it had begun. None of the rebel MPs would go public while several constituency association spokesmen threw their weight behind the Prime Minister.[91] When he became aware of the rumours O'Neill came out fighting against the 'conspiracy' which had been plotted against him: 'I fought for my country in time of war. I have fought to maintain our constitution in time of peace. There will be no surrender now.' He was aided by Brookeborough who supported O'Neill in this 'moment of great unease for every Ulster man and woman'. Although 'many of us do not . . . like the ways things have been going of late' he warned against a Party split. Faulkner, on the other hand, declined to make any comment 'at this stage' while other cabinet ministers, such as Craig and Chichester-Clark, pledged their support.[92] Brookeborough announced that he had been approached and asked to head a caretaker government but had turned down the proposal because 'I've had 20 years of it, and I'm not interested.' The seventy-eight-year-old described himself as 'too old and too square'.[93] He might have used the same phrase to describe any stage of his career without any sense of irony.

By now it was becoming clear that the 'revolt' was far from over. It emerged that one of the leading spokesmen for the rebels was O'Neill's old critic, Edmond

Warnock, representing St Anne's. Others who declared against the Prime Minister were John Taylor, South Tyrone, and Austin Ardill, Carrick. Warnock asserted that the revolt was now stronger than it had ever been. While he claimed to have the greatest regard for the Prime Minister personally, Warnock thought he was misguided in his actions. 'When Captain O'Neill succeeded Lord Brookeborough the Parliamentary Party was united and at peace, and the constituency associations were working happily together, and the Orange Order was quietly doing its job. Today the Unionist Party is split, the constituency associations are disturbed, and the Orange Order seriously dismayed . . . I don't want to see the Unionist Party destroyed, or the Orange Order destroyed—or damn near it—but I am very much afraid that this may happen unless there is an immediate change.' Warnock believed that in Faulkner there was a man 'very acceptable' to every shade of Unionist opinion: 'Moreover if we had a more acceptable Prime Minister the extremist movement which has been so troublesome would have little to feed on and would subside.'[94]

The crisis split some branches of Unionist associations. A resolution calling for the resignation of the Prime Minister and the Ministers of Development and Home Affairs was unanimously passed at a meeting of the Bush division of East Tyrone Unionist Association. The terms of the resolution also stated that the division was dissatisfied with recent policies. On the other hand, Carrick Unionist Association —Ardill's—sent a telegram to the Prime Minister assuring him of loyal and continued support. But the Killyman branch of the Association decided to support the revolt. Almost simultaneously the Aughnacloy branch was voicing its support for the premier.[95] Since the revolt was so sudden—and in the recess— there was little or no cultivation of grassroots opinion. This meant the crucial battleground would be the Parliamentary Party. It would decide the Prime Minister's fate. O'Neill saw in the challenge a fear of Paisley. He warned that he had no intention of having his or his Government's polices dictated by people whose activities had ended in street scenes that damaged the image of Northern Ireland. 'It would be a denial of Government if we were to be dictated to by the mob in this way.' If he stood aside he would be giving encouragement to 'a certain gentleman who has been carrying certain suggestions on his banner'. O'Neill believed that his successor would then be open to blackmail in the form of 'Remember what happened to O'Neill'. His policies were designed to reduce unemployment and generally to bring Northern Ireland into line with the requirements of the modern world. The constitutional position was better defended by modern rather than outdated methods.[96]

O'Neill's resolute stand forced at least one breach in the rebels' ranks. As the UUP Parliamentary Party met to decide the Prime Minister's future on 27 September, one of the rebels, Walter Scott, the MP for Bloomfield, abandoned the cause, as he put it, to avoid misinterpretation of his actions. Scott emphasised that his proposed action was never a suggestion of a move towards Paisleyism—he condemned that movement and would regret anything that would encourage its growth. He stressed that by joining the revolt he had hoped to achieve better unity within the Party. Scott now hoped that the Prime Minister would be more aware of the steps necessary to allay unease in the Party. He also revealed how the revolt—the suggestion of a 'conspiracy' was 'ridiculous'—came about: it had evolved when, with the House in recess, a group of MPs decided to call a Parliamentary Party meeting of the House of Commons Party and 'present certain suggestions' to the Prime Minister at that meeting.[97] As the revolt began to melt away in the face of O'Neill's resolute stand and a lack of grassroots support, the House of Commons Parliamentary Unionist Party unanimously passed a motion of confidence in the Prime Minister. A similar motion was passed separately by the Senate although with one abstention.[98] Smiling broadly after the meeting, O'Neill gave an immediate assurance to reporters that his policies would not be changed as a result of the leadership struggle. The criticisms, he said, had not materialised to any great extent. They were 'local problems'. As for what was to blame for the crisis, the Prime Minister thought 'Possibly the long summer recess'. He found it difficult to assess if Paisley carried any great influence in the Unionist Party. People had been worried about the Easter celebrations but Belfast had got through them. Asked if the crisis had given Paisleyism anything to feed on, O'Neill replied: 'No, not after tonight's meeting.' The 'O'Neill Must Go' campaign had, indeed, been killed.[99] O'Neill responded with a point-blank 'No' when asked if the suppression of the revolt meant the end of 'O'Neill the liberal'. Assessing his achievements in office, O'Neill felt that there was now a feeling that Ulster was 'with it' and forging ahead into the '70s. That feeling possibly did not exist before.[100]

Even the rebels appeared in a good mood. Leaving the meeting John Taylor pronounced himself 'very happy with the result'. Austin Ardill stated: 'There were no rebels. There was no conspiracy. The party is now stronger than ever before. The Prime Minister gave a very frank statement which cleared the air.'[101] In the aftermath Chichester-Clark, as Chief Whip, tried to make sense of the crisis. He accepted that there was a lack of communication between the Government and the back bench and the Party in general. The Prime Minister had made some suggestions and as such there would be closer liaison between the Government and the Party and therefore more discussion. Referring to the rebel MPs who spoke, Chichester-Clark thought that they did not seem to agree on any particular issue. They all had individual points that they wanted to put across. Only one of the speakers had called for the Prime Minister's resignation. There was criticism of individual ministers although no calls for any resignations. Chichester-Clark admitted that Paisley had been mentioned on a number of occasions and it was very plain that many people were very worried about his release following his short imprisonment for refusing to pay a fine relating to the Cormac Square disturbances. 'But nothing definite was decided': the Prime Minister didn't prescribe any course of action. As to what points of criticism had been raised, Chichester-Clark listed the Lemass meeting, the Easter Rising celebrations, the closing of the railways in Tyrone, the new city and planning.[102] Apparently there was no point of focus, no coherence, to the revolt.

Although there had not been any calls for ministerial resignations, the criticisms voiced ensured that the Prime Minister had a clear idea of what was needed to defuse the criticisms raised by backbenchers. For example, in the run-up to the Glengall Street meeting Dr Robert Simpson, the MP for Mid-Antrim, had refused to state his position on the Prime Minister's future. This, he explained to his local association, was because he felt that he could only support O'Neill in certain circumstances, one of which was that the Minister of Home Affairs, Brian McConnell, 'would have to go'. Following the Glengall Street meeting Simpson felt confident that these reservations 'have now completely gone'. After seven hours of discussion he declared, 'we offer him [O'Neill] blind allegiance whatever difficulties may arise'.[103] And sure enough, O'Neill followed up the meeting with a cabinet reshuffle with two of the ministers who had received criticism being moved. Craig was shifted from Development back to his old job at Home Affairs. McConnell was clearly demoted as he lost Home Affairs and, although retaining his cabinet seat, became Minister of State in Development (suffering a £750 drop in salary in the process). Overall O'Neill added two ministers to the cabinet and appointed two new joint Whips increasing the Government's representation in the Commons to fourteen out of a total party strength of thirty-six. For the first time the Commons had a Leader of the House—Chichester-Clark—traditionally a post held by the Minister of Finance although recently under the Deputy Prime Minister—Faulkner—at Commerce. Chichester-Clark, who retained control of the Whips, had two new assistants: Roy Bradford representing Victoria and Sam Magowan representing Iveagh. William Fitzsimmons became Minister of Development while Captain William Long became Minister of Education.[104] As part of the attempt to improve liaison between MPs and the Government a new committee of backbench Unionist MPs had its first meeting on 11 October. It was modelled on the 1922 Committee of Tory backbenchers at Westminster. There had been one previous attempt to set up a backbench committee at Stormont but this had collapsed in 1958 after only two years.[105] The new body became known as the '66 Committee.

O'Neill now appeared more secure than ever. This was deceptive. There was a reservoir of discontent within the Party that, though lacking a central issue, did not bode well for the future. On the other hand it seemed that Faulkner—O'Neill's nearest rival—appeared to have suffered a notable setback in his ambitions to become premier. In the run-up to the Glengall Street meeting O'Neill had received qualified support from the man some of the rebels had placed their hopes on. Faulkner had declared that he would not be a member of the Government if he did not support the policies of the Government and pronounced himself 'tired' of having his name banded about in the affair; but he did not rule out becoming leader if there was a crisis to such an extent that the Party was not prepared to give its support to the leader of the day. He made a point of observing that there was serious discontent in the Party and that this had been growing over recent months.[106] On the day of the Glengall Street meeting all the cabinet had spoken in favour of O'Neill except Faulkner who was in the United States. When asked about Faulkner's first trip to the States, O'Neill revealed that he himself should have been the one in Chicago but for the fact that 'I thought it would be a nice thing for Mr Faulkner to do, so I passed it on to him.'[107]

HOW TO ALIENATE PEOPLE AND MAKE ENEMIES

If O'Neill had to look over his shoulder with regard to the darling of the rebels— Faulkner—what he didn't need was to create enemies of any other powerful members of his cabinet. But this is precisely what happened in April 1967 when he sacked his Minister of Agriculture, Harry West. West was popular and, politically, a big hitter within the Party. In the inward-looking, client politics of rural Ulster, alienating West meant alienating the Fermanagh Unionists whom he represented. Yet the fault for West's losing his job was that of the Minister and nobody else. He was sacked because of a property deal involving ninety-nine acres of land that were part of 260 acres purchased by him from a cousin for £24,250 in 1964. In 1967 West was awarded £13,450 for ninety-nine of those acres that were then acquired by Fermanagh County Council. As it was known for quite a while that the Council wanted this land it created the impression of a potential conflict of interest. What forced O'Neill into dismissing West was that, almost three years previously, the Prime Minister had outlined, for the first time, the terms of a code of principles to govern the private activities of ministers; a code designed to prevent a conflict or the *appearance* of conflict between the private and official interests of ministers.

In May 1964, West had urged that that an inter-departmental meeting be convened to discuss the various issues involved in a proposal to bring St Angelo Airport back into regular use. In the course of a subsequent inter-departmental discussion, in which the Attorney-General participated, it was concluded that Fermanagh County Council would have the power to operate the airport. When West subsequently met with O'Neill he gave no indication that his cousin, Victor West, had approached him to buy a farm which included a substantial portion of the airport runways or that he was giving serious consideration to buying the land. However, on two later occasions when West indicated to the then Secretary of the Cabinet that he was contemplating buying the farm, the Cabinet Secretary strongly advised West not to proceed with such a purchase. He did so not because any such transaction could in any way be regarded as improper in itself but because of the knowledge that a public authority—the Council—might well wish to acquire the land for a purpose which West himself had advocated. Such a purchase, decided O'Neill, would be likely to expose the Minister to a misunderstanding of a kind that ought to be avoided.[108] West decided to ignore this advice so O'Neill felt he had no choice but to sack him. The Prime Minister had concluded that, however innocent the motives of such a transaction, the mere fact that a minister of the Crown appeared to have pre-empted a public authority was sufficient to provoke criticism, particularly where public funds might be involved: ministers should as far as possible stand wholly above criticism in their private affairs. It was not necessarily improper for a minister to become involved in a land transaction with a public authority: 'But is it right for a minister to acquire public property in the knowledge that it may in the reasonably near future be required for a public purpose?' asked O'Neill.[109]

For O'Neill the facts he had to consider were that the land was bought against strong advice to the contrary in August 1964; that the county council had already decided to buy the property on which the airfield land was situated just three weeks earlier, so there was no doubt that they wanted the land; and accordingly, West's purchase appeared to have pre-empted the County Council. The Prime Minister had only heard of the purchase in the press. He had never been informed about it by West despite the pervious warnings not to buy. The Attorney-General had then strongly advised West that he must offer the required land to the County Council at a controlled price; West accepted this advice. But then, early in 1965, West twice pressed the Attorney-General to release him from this commitment but did not tell the Attorney-General that he was in fact taking action to get out of it at that very time himself. Since at that time West had two letters from the Attorney-General telling him in unmistakable terms that he must not vary his offer in any way, O'Neill took the view that West could not have been in the slightest doubt that what he was doing was wrong. It was only in early 1967 that it emerged that West's offer to the Council had been withdrawn over two years before. O'Neill was left with 'the most unpleasant decision I have had to make as Prime Minister. Some people have called it a harsh decision, but you know there really is no purpose in having a code of principles unless it is observed in the letter and the spirit.' O'Neill noted that the course he had been forced to take had no advantages for him. He had lost a likeable and useful colleague and was faced with widespread misunderstanding of what was involved.[110]

In West's defence no one accused him of any sort of dishonesty. The property in question had been in the ownership of a near relative who had fallen on hard times and who would be compelled to sell the estate. The relative had visited West many times during the eighteen months before it went for public auction inviting him to buy it because he wanted it to remain within the family. West already had a strong sentimental attachment to the estate long before the County Council had shown any interest in it. He wanted to buy it for a home and indeed that was what it ultimately became for West. It was after acquiring the land that he agreed with the Attorney-General to sell part of it to the Council at a price set by the

Government's own valuers. However, he then received a counter-offer from the Council that he considered—confirmed by the independent Lands Tribunal—inadequate. But the Attorney-General insisted West accept this offer[111] so as to avoid any appearance of a conflict of interest. Yet he ignored this and was sacked.

He blamed O'Neill. When West had his opportunity to make his personal statement to the House of Commons he accused O'Neill and the Attorney-General of a plot 'to get rid of him'. West said Harry Diamond was not far wrong when he suggested that the former Minister was paying the price for taking the wrong side in the leadership crisis the previous August. He told the House that when his resignation was sought by the Prime Minister, the thought flashed through his mind that he was there 'as a lamb prepared for the slaughter by a carefully prepared plot'. The Attorney-General, however, in his response, detailed the case for West's dismissal and described it as not a case of someone blundering into error but a case of someone who went into it with his 'eyes wide open'.[112] The Party appeared to back O'Neill. He secured the support of the '66 Committee of Unionist backbenchers: they issued a statement supporting the Prime Minister. Sixteen members of the Committee, while agreeing with the Prime Minister's course in asking West to resign 'by a narrow majority' wished to add that, in its opinion, the latter was guilty of an error of judgment but not guilty of any dishonesty.[113]

The incident was noticeable not merely for the alienation of West and his supporters from O'Neill but also for the position adopted by Faulkner: his apparent hesitation in supporting the Prime Minister's decision fuelled speculation of a leadership challenge. As the Unionist Party gathered for the annual UUC meeting (this was before West had had his opportunity to state his version of events in the Commons) most of the delegates gave the Prime Minister a minute-long standing ovation; but twenty delegates at the front of the hall, some of them from Fermanagh, remained seated. It was also noted that Faulkner and William Morgan, the Minister of Health and Social Services, were both absent from the platform during the Prime Minister's speech, despite being present earlier in the proceedings. When pressed Faulkner denied that his position in the Government was untenable. He remained content to hear what West had to say before passing judgment on whether or not the dismissal was justified.[114] Such was the speculation surrounding Faulkner that he issued a statement two days later denying there was a crisis of leadership in the Unionist Party. He had not been approached by anyone suggesting he take over the reigns of office. Faulkner added that under no consideration would he allow his name to be linked 'at this time' with any attempt to usurp the leadership of the Party. In fact it had been Faulkner who seemed to have generated much of the press speculation—which spilled over into the British press as well—when he gave a BBC interview two days after West's sacking in which he described the former Minister's position as 'absolutely blameless'; then Faulkner's absence from the platform was noticed; which in turn was followed by intense press speculation that Faulkner might resign from the Government.[115] Faulkner's ambivalence was fooling nobody. Robert Porter, the Unionist MP for Queen's University, asked if Faulkner did not appreciate that the use of the phrase 'at this time' seemed to be 'most peculiar for anyone who wishes to produce solidarity'.[116] Faulkner, however, declined to give a declaration of 100 per cent support for the Prime Minister. Earlier, Chichester-Clark, the Chief Whip, had called for an unreserved and unequivocal declaration of support for the premier. Faulkner refused citing a wish 'to get away from personalities and back to policies'. In fact he found the Chief Whip's call 'ridiculous. The situation is getting like a farce. I am absolutely amazed by what the Chief Whip has said.' While behind the Prime Minister's policies '100 per cent' following Chichester-Clark's advice would mean that all that was left for him to do would be to pledge support to O'Neill on every issue 'that will ever arise in this country right or wrong. That pledge I would not give to the Archangel Gabriel himself were he to become Prime Minister . . . For goodness sake let us get rid of personalities and stick to policies.'[117]

Chapter 3 ~

CATHOLICS IN
THE SIX COUNTIES

SECOND CLASS CITIZENS?

In Northern Ireland Catholics believed themselves to be the victims of systematic discrimination by the Unionist regime. And the view that discrimination was an underlying factor in Catholic violence against the state in 1968–9 has enjoyed widespread currency. The allegations of discrimination were usually in a number of forms: the gerrymandering of local government boundaries to favour the Unionist Party; the retention of multiple voting in the local government franchise to the benefit of Unionist candidates; the unfair allocation of public services—particularly housing—to the benefit of Protestants and at the expense of Catholics; unfair employment practices in private and public employment; and a bias in regional policy towards Protestant areas at the expense of Catholic areas, put crudely as favouring the area east of the River Bann (Protestant) rather than west of the Bann (Catholic). Added to these might be the sense that emergency legislation, such as the Special Powers Acts, was directed against one part of the community only and enforced by an overwhelmingly Protestant security apparatus. Perhaps the most difficult to quantify was discrimination in employment. From 1971 census data, and cross-tabulated by religion and occupation, Edmund Aunger, a Canadian political scientist, found that Catholics were disadvantaged in three ways. Firstly, they were somewhat more likely than Protestants to be low in the socio-economic scale. Protestants were over-represented in the three highest classes while Catholics were over-represented in the two lowest. Secondly, within each class there was a tendency for Catholics to cluster in the lower reaches, Protestants in the higher ones: 'While a clerk may be a Catholic, it is more likely that the office manager will be a Protestant; while a skilled craftsman may be a Catholic, it is more likely that the supervisor will be a Protestant; and while a nurse may be a Catholic, it is more likely that the doctor will be a Protestant.' Thirdly, Catholics were more likely to be found in industries with lower status and more unemployment, such as construction, while Protestants tended to be found in industries such as engineering that ranked higher in pay and prestige. The cumulative effect of these differences was to produce 'a noteworthy congruence between the class cleavage and the religious cleavage in Northern Ireland'.[1] The 1971 census also revealed that Catholic males were 2.62 times more likely than Protestant males to be unemployed.[2]

The Campaign for Social Justice (CSJ), a predominately middle class Catholic pressure group, pointed out that if all grades in public employment were lumped together there appeared to be little if any under-representation of Catholics. In 1951, of 3,476 local authority workers of all kinds, 1,096, or 31.5 per cent were 'Nationalist', by which was meant Catholic. This was close to the proportion of Catholics in the adult population. Richard Rose, in a 1968 survey, found that sixteen per cent of Protestants and thirteen per cent of Catholics reported that they or someone in their family was, or had been, publicly employed. However, the moment one distinguished lower grades from higher ones, marked discrepancies appeared. In 1951 just over forty per cent of manual labourers were 'Nationalists'; but of the 1,095 senior posts only 130, or 11.8 per cent, were held by 'Nationalists'. The Cameron Commission, which was set up to investigate the causes of the 1968 disturbances, was satisfied that the Unionist-controlled councils it investigated had used their power to make appointments in a way which benefited Protestants. For example, in October 1968 only thirty per cent of Londonderry Corporation's administrative, clerical and technical employees were Catholics, and in County Fermanagh no senior council posts and relatively few others were held by Catholics.

Similar figures were found for the Northern Ireland Civil Service. The only Catholic to reach the rank of Permanent Secretary was Bonaparte Wyse. After his retirement no other reached the same rank until Patrick Shea in 1969. The CSJ reported that of 319 officers down to the rank of Deputy Principal, twenty-three, or 7.2 per cent, were Catholics. Catholics were also under-represented on statutory bodies, and among the highest ranks of the employees of such bodies. The CSJ listed twenty-two public bodies with a total membership of 332, of whom forty-nine, or fifteen per cent, were Catholics. In the publicly-owned gas, electricity and water industries, the imbalance against Catholics seemed to have reached down through all levels. The census of 1971 showed that of 8,122 people employed in those industries only 1,952, or 15.4 per cent, recorded themselves as Catholics. An overall working figure shows that in 1971 of 1,383 senior government officials, including ministers, MPs, senior government officials and senior officers in local authorities, eleven per cent reported themselves as Catholic compared with 31.4 per cent of the census as a whole declaring themselves Catholic. To some extent this very low representation of Catholics in the higher grades of public employment may have been connected with a difference in educational qualifications between Protestants and Catholics. Three-quarters of the grammar school and university population was Protestant, so that it would be reasonable to expect at least a proportion of Protestants among higher post holders.[3] Against this, however, the proportion of Catholics with higher educational qualifications was much greater than the proportion in senior positions. It has been argued that the discrepancy arose not because of discrimination, but because Catholics who decided not to apply for senior public appointment would have been making a rational decision, since there is evidence that had they applied they would have faced discrimination. This was derived from public statements by certain government ministers.[4]

It may also have been true that Catholics were unwilling to serve or were discouraged by their co-religionists from serving. Patrick Shea recorded that Catholic civil servants were viewed with suspicion by other Catholics because 'we had joined the enemy; we were lost souls'. A Southern Catholic journalist, Desmond Fennell, met a prominent Nationalist who told how a friend had remarked to him that 'it was a bad day for the Nationalists when a Catholic was appointed a Supreme Court judge—it had sounded good to be able to say that the Supreme Court hadn't a single Catholic judge!'[5] Yet even when taking account of these factors, it seems evident that some discrimination did occur. Captain O'Neill recalled that when he was Minister of Finance in the 1950s he had to face a campaign against him in the cabinet because it was believed that since he had taken up office Catholics were being encouraged to join the Civil Service. Patrick Shea was held for many years, into the 1950s, at the rank of Principal Officer, and his Permanent Secretary finally told him that 'because you are a Roman Catholic you may never get any further promotion. I'm sorry.' Shea eventually received promotion, but only several years later and after a change of department.[6] The picture is further complicated by the fact that Richard Rose's Loyalty Survey found in 1967 that only five per cent of the total population thought religion was a barrier to getting a job. The Survey found a Catholic concern with collective well-being, that is the well-being of the Catholic community. Catholics offered economic benefits by the Unionist regime readily accepted them but would not give allegiance in return because they believed that there remained *other* Catholics who were discriminated against or suffered unemployment because of the Unionist regime.[7]

So it was the *collective* perception of Catholics that Catholics were discriminated against rather than their *individual*, actual experience that convinced them that the Unionist state discriminated against them. And there were plenty of opportunities for Catholics to have this perception renewed. In January 1964 Senator J. E. N. Barnhill told a meeting of the Londonderry Upper Liberties Unionist Association that Unionist employers should only employ 'Unionists'. David McCelland, Chairman of the Unionist Party Executive, was forced to deny that the Senator's comments reflected the views of the Party. R. N. L. Moore, Secretary of the Association, rather sheepishly added that Barnhill did not suggest that 'nationalists' employed by 'unionists' should be discharged.[8] Alderman Glover, President of the City of Londonderry and Foyle Unionist Association, sprung to the defence of Barnhill, calling on Nationalists to tell the 'whole story'. It seemed to Glover that Barnhill's message to his audience had been: if they had employment to give they should not forget their fellow political travellers. Glover argued: 'We as Unionists are trying to preserve for our people British citizenship and if we employ persons who have the same aims as ourselves surely we can expect a higher degree of loyalty from them than we can expect from persons whose aims are exactly opposite and completely opposed to ours.'[9] There was some evidence for this: the Loyalty Survey found that a majority of Catholics, even those in public employment, rejected the constitutional settlement. Economic benefits, whether higher income or the receipt of welfare from the state, had a limited or non-existent impact in securing Catholic allegiance to the state.[10] Just a month after Barnhill's comments there was further controversy when members of the Derry Trades Council were told that workers seeking jobs with a new industrial concern starting in the area were to be asked to state their religion in an application form for employment. The company, Cyril Lord Carpets Ltd, denied that the question was a form of discrimination: 'The information is very useful at holiday time. For example, if we have to operate shifts over the Twelfth of July period, we know exactly who would be prepared to work and who would not. And if an individual takes seriously ill at work we would like to know if we should call the priest or the vicar.' The company, it said, employed people of all denominations in its existing factories. Seamus Quinn, Branch Secretary of the Irish Transport and General Workers Union, thought the forms 'repugnant' adding 'I cannot understand how a person's religion has anything to do with his or her ability as a stitcher.'[11]

In 1966 the Catholic Church became publicly involved in such controversies when the large Sirocco Engineering Works in Belfast was accused of discrimination against Catholics by the Bishop of Down and Connor, Dr William Philbin. Philbin said that the firm had been regarded by generations of Catholics in the area around the plant as a 'symbol and concrete evidence of the economic and social injustice they have had to suffer for many generations in this city'. These comments were made in an exchange of correspondence with Sirocco's chairman, E. D. MaGuire. Philbin claimed 'There is a tradition here of "no Catholics need apply."' The Bishop had begun the correspondence by stating how he had been told that out of the 1,500 workforce at the factory there were scarcely any Catholics: he had heard figures ranging from one to three or four. MaGuire replied that the fact that there were few Catholics employed in the firm 'is not a matter of management policy, but arises largely due to location and environment'. In the 'not-too-distant past' Sirocco had had a Catholic director. In 'very recent months' the applicants for a senior executive position were whittled down to two candidates. One was from the Church of England and the other was a Catholic: 'That the former was ultimately selected had nothing to do with religion, merely his better technical qualifications,' stated MaGuire. He had no idea of the exact number of Catholics employed on the staff 'as I do not make a point of inquiring into their religious beliefs'. There were very few Catholics because in the earliest days of the company the Protestant element from the Memel Street and Newtownards Road areas provided the bulk of its workers and large numbers were now in the third or fourth generation of the original families. And he added: 'Catholics probably do not feel at home in a Protestant atmosphere.' MaGuire argued that this preponderance of Protestant employees would presumably change when large numbers of Catholics came to live in these areas 'and when religious tolerance comes to be more widely accepted by the public at large'. The crux of the problem was 'therefore an external one and not an internal one'.

In reply Philbin pointed out that MaGuire had not contradicted his estimate about the numbers of Catholics employed by the firm. A distortion of this proportion in a city twenty-five to thirty per cent Catholic 'can only be a result of a deliberate policy'. And Philbin pointed out that the district immediately beside the factory on the Seaforde Street side contained around 2,000 Catholic adults. Far from there being any prospect of Catholics coming to live in this area there had in fact been the removal of 500 Catholics in recent years. MaGuire's reference to Catholics feeling uneasy in a Protestant atmosphere was 'a frank assertion that the atmosphere of your firm is sectarian'. Philbin asked MaGuire if he 'seriously suggested' that the non-employment of Catholics in his firm was due to reluctance on their part to be employed by him. 'Can anyone believe that Catholics in this city have ever been able to afford the luxury of choosing employment where the atmosphere is congenial to them? You know that in conditions of permanent underemployment such as have obtained here it is the employer, not the employee, who is in a position to choose. You must be aware that in Belfast, Catholics have always worked wherever they could find work.' Philbin found that MaGuire's implication that he could do nothing to correct the 'extreme form of religious discrimination for which your company is responsible a matter of grave concern'.[12]

Taking all of the above points it is still almost impossible to qualify the level of discrimination in private employment. Sirocco is a case in point. Was it that Catholics did not apply for positions there because they knew they would not get them as a result of a deliberate policy of discrimination on the part of the company; or because—and this was not uncommon throughout the British Isles—informal employment networks reproduced themselves in successive generations via employees passing on to family members information relating to forthcoming employment opportunities? This would make employment in such a concern sectarian by convention rather than design. In Sirocco's case it would become part of the local ether that Catholics were not employed. On the other hand it is equally clear that calls for employment discrimination usually came from Protestants. It was based on the familiar assumption that all Catholics were Nationalists and therefore disloyal to the state and committed to its ultimate demise. All of which had a coherent logic to it. Except that it ignored the fact that not all Catholics were inherently hostile to the state or that those Catholics that were hostile to the state might be supplanted generationally by Catholics who were less hostile if they were given a stake in the continuance of the state. Or indeed that it was morally indefensible to discriminate on the grounds of political or religious belief. And there was clearly a tendency for Protestants to publicly proclaim in favour of sectarian employment practices. Ian Paisley was one who was in the forefront of advocating discriminatory practices: when the Sirocco correspondence became public he intervened to declare that a Protestant employer had a perfect right to employ 'his own sort'. There was nothing unscriptural or unloving about an employer saying that he was going to employ people who were loyal to the constitution and believed in their country. 'You would think to-day he had no right,' he said. Paisley considered that Philbin's 'dictation' meant that Sirocco, and all other employers, should always employ thirty-three per cent Catholics.[13] But although Protestants tended to be more 'honest' on this issue it did not mean that Catholics were not using similar employment practices. The Unionist MP, John Taylor, touched a raw nerve in 1966 when he claimed that the chairman of the Nationalist Party, who was a leading Nationalist politician in Derry, employed almost sixty people, not one of whom was a Protestant. Nationalists could not deny the allegation and the best Eddie McAteer, the leader of the Nationalist Party, could come up with by way of a reply was to ask: 'What would be the position if Catholics were not to be employed by Protestants and also not to be employed by Catholics? They would be stateless people altogether, and we must have an outlet somewhere.'[14] Such evidence undermined the Catholic case relating to discrimination. In this instance it wasn't so important because it did not receive attention across the water. But in 1967 Gerry Fitt, the Republican Labour MP, was outraged at an advert in a local paper seeking the employment of a Catholic because the piece was sent to Labour MPs in London. At Stormont, and with parliamentary privilege, he accused a Ballymena man, Oliver Brady, a former Catholic who had appeared on platforms with Paisley, of being the author of the allegedly forged advertisement. Brady claimed he was innocent of the charge.[15]

   A clear-cut example of discrimination was the example of the related issues of gerrymandering of electoral boundaries and housing allocation; however, even here the issue was complicated. A widely held impression from outside Northern Ireland was that such discrimination was Province-wide: it was not, being instead concentrated (although not exclusively) in the western half of Northern Ireland where Protestants were a minority. Here the most obvious example of gerrymandering was in Londonderry. As the CSJ pointed out, in Derry the electoral wards were gerrymandered with a majority of Catholics in one large ward alongside two smaller wards composed of Protestants. Thus despite the fact there were 19,870 Roman Catholic adults over the age of twenty-one, compared to 10,673 Protestants, a Unionist majority was produced on Londonderry Corporation because of the ethnic composition of the three electoral wards.[16] Catholics also believed that the local (not the Stormont or Westminster Parliamentary) franchise was weighted in favour of Protestants. In local government elections several categories of adults, amounting to over a quarter of the parliamentary electorate in 1961, had no vote, and a small number of property owners had more than one vote. However, the evidence suggests that they made only a slight difference to election results.[17] Nevertheless the perception among Catholics was that it benefited Unionists at the expense of Nationalists and even if it did not there was clearly a perception among many Protestants that it did. So even though it didn't affect the outcome of local elections it proved a powerful rallying cry for Nationalists throughout Ireland and for those in Britain concerned with the situation in Northern Ireland. The cry of 'One man, one vote' was erroneously taken by many in Britain to mean that no Catholics had the vote in Ulster. As a result of gerrymandering—not the local government franchise—Unionists in the west of the Province often dominated in areas where they were a minority. By the 1960s what made this such an explosive issue was that the control of local government had a much greater impact on the distribution of scarce resources such as public employment and, most controversially, public housing. The issue of public housing had scarcely surfaced before the 1950s: there had been few allegations of discrimination in the allocation of public housing because there was little public housing to allocate. But this had begun to change after 1945 when a large-scale public housing drive was launched. By 1961 twenty-one per cent of all housing in the Province was publicly rented; by 1971 the proportion was thirty-five per cent. As public housing became more plentiful so complaints about its allocation multiplied. The Housing Trust, set up in 1945, funded by the Northern Ireland Government and headed by an independent body of part-time members, selected tenants not just on the basis of need, but on their ability to pay. The Housing Trust has been generally exonerated from a conscious desire to discriminate. This was not the case with regard to local authorities.

In Fermanagh, where Catholics were a slight majority of the population, it was claimed that of 1,589 post-war council houses, 568 were let to Catholics and 1,021 to Protestants. The Cameron Commission concluded that there were many cases where councils had withheld planning permission or caused needless delays when they believed a housing project would be to their electoral disadvantage. The Commission concluded that in Unionist-controlled areas it was fairly frequent for housing policy to operate so that houses allocated to Catholics tended, as in Dungannon Urban District, to go to rehouse slum dwellers, whereas Protestant allocations tended to go more frequently to new families. Thus the total numbers allocated were in rough correspondence to the proportion of Protestants and Catholics in the community; the principal criterion in such cases, however, was not the actual need but the maintenance of the current political preponderance in the local government area, that is to preserve the established pattern of gerry-mandering. The areas where allegations of discrimination in public housing persisted were without exception those west of the River Bann. Against the majority of councils in Northern Ireland there were no complaints. The veteran Nationalist, Cahir Healy, even praised local authorities in Belfast, Antrim and Down, as well as the Housing Trust, for their fair play to needful ends. Belfast Corporation, for example, was the largest local authority in the Province. In those areas which did attract criticism, the objection was not that Catholics were refused houses but that they were confined to those wards where they were already a majority, so as not to disturb the electoral balance. The Cameron Commission pointed out that, in Londonderry, Catholics were rehoused almost exclusively in the South Ward, and in Omagh and Dungannon almost exclusively in the West Wards. But it also remarked that in several of the areas the actual total of new housing had been substantial.

Survey data by Richard Rose to test allegations of discrimination in housing found that thirty-five per cent of his Catholic respondents, as against thirty per cent of his Protestant ones, lived in public housing. Taking account of income size he found that in all but one income category the proportion of Catholics in subsidised housing was slightly higher than that of Protestants. Breaking down his figures by county and county borough, he found that the generally fair pattern remained. In four out of the eight counties and county boroughs—Belfast, Derry City, Armagh and Tyrone—a majority of respondents in public housing were Catholics. The only evidence he found of bias against Catholics came when he tested for family size and found that among the very largest families (six children or more) there was a twelve per cent difference against Catholics in the proportion assigned public housing. This indicated that housing policies in individual areas such as Fermanagh or Dungannon could be very unfair, but that in many parts of Northern Ireland it was very fair.[18] The impression created by the Cameron Commission was that Unionist councils across the Province discriminated against Catholics. But Cameron based its findings on seven areas only. By the time Rose carried out his survey in 1968 it seemed that the proportion of Catholics in public housing was higher than that of Protestants even when the comparison was made within income categories. This supported the view that there were 'famous abuses by certain councils, rather than a pattern of widespread discrimination'.[19]

In effect, then, the entire Unionist state lay damned by the actions of a minority of Unionist councils west of the Bann. For example, there was outrage among Catholics when in December 1963 the Unionist Chairman of the Enniskillen Housing Committee stated that council houses would be let on 'party lines'. Alderman George Elliott said the Council would build houses for letting to the 'right people' and make no apology for it. William Morgan, Minister of Health and Local Government, publicly attacked Elliott, deploring such an attitude and stating that the allocation of housing should be on the basis of need. However, he defended the principle that the allocation of housing should remain with local authorities and the Housing Trust. He ruled out interference by his Ministry without detailed knowledge of individual cases as an interference with local rights and duties. Morgan concluded that the attitude expressed by Elliott could not be regarded as a policy statement on behalf of Enniskillen Borough Council.[20] The area's local Unionist MP defended the Council's record and denied that there was actual discrimination in housing allocation, citing 311 houses allotted to 'Nationalists' and 311 to 'Unionists'. Cahir Healy, who welcomed the Minister's comments, disputed this.[21] Morgan wrote to the Mayor of Enniskillen, Alderman W. F. Bryson, asking him about the Council's attitude to housing allocation but received no reply.[22] The Minister then declined to formally intervene on the grounds that he lacked the detailed local knowledge he would require in order to do so.[23] In an effort to repair some of the damage to community relations, Mayor Bryson called on all church leaders in Enniskillen to meet him 'in an effort to restore friendliness and co-operation'. The Mayor was replying to the Roman Catholic Bishop of Clogher, Dr Eugene O'Callaghan, who appealed for an end to housing discrimination in the town.[24] The controversy, however, smouldered on.

In November 1964 the *Belfast Telegraph*'s Dennis Kennedy decided to investigate the housing situation in Enniskillen. Catholics constituted a majority of the population in Enniskillen. But there were two Unionist electoral wards to one Nationalist thereby returning a majority of Unionists to the Council. From the October 1964 minutes of the Enniskillen Town Improvement Committee, Kennedy found that Unionists had put forward twenty-seven names for housing allocation and the Nationalists twenty-seven also. The Unionist majority voted in twenty-seven Protestants. Almost the only houses that Enniskillen Borough Council built in 1963 were in the Unionist wards. Nationalists claimed that since the War the Council had allocated 252 houses—232 to Protestants and twenty to Catholics. Unionists' estimates differed—'Nationalist' allocated houses were not above thirty-five. Kennedy noted that 'At this point the Nationalist case rests, and Unionist blood pressure rises. What about the Housing Trust, they cry' which the latter cited as the organisation that looked after Nationalists.

Kennedy reported how, shortly after the War, the Council bought land at Cornnagrade in the Nationalist North Ward of the town. The intention was to build Nationalist houses—'houses, like everything else, are either Nationalist or Unionist in Enniskillen'—for Catholics to be moved into from the slum areas of the town. The Council was advised by the Government to allow the newly formed Housing Trust to take over the development. Between 1950 and 1955 the Housing Trust built 340 houses on the site. Since then another sixty or so houses and thirty maisonettes and flats had been added. Although, said Unionists, the estate was seventy-five per cent Catholic the Council was paying £7 per subsidy on 100 houses in the estate. Furthermore in 1962 the Council had decided to build houses for Nationalists—333 of them at Kilmacormick to the north of the town, just outside the boundary, but inevitably in the Nationalist North Ward if the boundary was extended. At the beginning of 1964 some 148 were under construction. The scheme was in two parts: 161 in the first batch now out to contract, 172 in the second lot for which the contract had not yet been placed. Most of the 333 new houses, claimed the Unionists, would go to Catholics ('And they should know,' commented Kennedy). In addition the Trust was putting up another sixty maisonettes and Catholics would get their share of these—more than fifty per cent. When the present building programme was completed there would a grand total of 661 minus the Unionist tally and there would be 482 for Nationalists. In other words Nationalists would have their fair share. Kennedy commented: 'Quod erat demonstrandum. Discrimination case dismissed. Or is it?'[25]

From this it can be seen that if Catholics were not getting a fair share of council houses from the Unionist-dominated Council then they were still being allocated houses thanks to the Northern Ireland Housing Trust. This led Kennedy to define discrimination, in the political or religious sense, as treating a person or group of persons in an exceptional way because of their political or religious beliefs. And in Enniskillen houses were, without doubt, allocated with the tenants' religion very much in mind. The present occupancy of houses in the town would prove it if anyone denied it. Ninety-five houses in the Derrchara estate and not one Catholic in sight; seventy houses already occupied in Coleshill, all by Protestants. But Kennedy found that Unionist councillors from the Mayor down took it for granted, as a normal fact of life, that houses in the East and South Wards were for Unionists and those in the North Ward were for Nationalists. 'Everyone in Enniskillen is either Unionist or Nationalist. All Protestants are Unionists, all Catholics are Nationalists according to the local politicians, that is. (Atheists have to fend for themselves.)' Unionists in the area argued that by 1970 everyone who needed a house would be housed and this was backed up by a comparison of the waiting list with houses planned. But Kennedy found some Catholics were not appreciative of the Council's generosity. Twenty-seven at least—the twenty-seven who did not get the houses allocated in October 1964. These people certainly saw the simple explanation of their predicament—'they do not get houses because they are Catholics'. Kennedy was quick to point out that this did not mean that the Unionists of the Town Improvement Committee were hard-hearted ogres with horns and forked tails. They did occasionally breathe fire and brimstone 'but it would be wrong to suppose that they callously condemn Catholic mothers and children to inferior housing'. They acted according to the peculiar logic that existed in Enniskillen and in other parts of the Province, 'that a council is a Unionist (or Nationalist) Council and not a Town Council. That it has a first duty to its own supporters, and that it would be the height of folly to allocate houses in a way that might upset voting at elections . . . It could happen that a Catholic might vote Unionist. The Unionists are not banking on it, however.'[26] Kennedy's conclusion, after looking at similar practices by Lisnaskea

Rural District Council, was that: 'By denying a fair share of housing to Catholics the Unionists are in fact ensuring that Catholics remain Nationalists.'[27]

This was discrimination by any definition of the term. But not discrimination which meant that Protestants received houses while Catholics did not: merely that the Unionist council looked after housing for Protestants and, more often than one might think, Catholics provided they were built in the correct electoral district while the Housing Trust looked after any other slack in Catholic housing. Whatever the situation in the early years of Northern Ireland's existence there now appeared to be an almost benevolent discrimination, in that fair quotas of housing were being allocated across the religious divide. The problem was that, as Kennedy pointed out, councils did not behave neutrally in the allocation of homes. Yet bizarrely, in some places this discrimination had been conducted with the co-operation of Catholics.

Take the example of Lurgan Borough Council. The Council was a target for the opposition in terms of jobs and gerrymandering. In 1967 Harry Diamond of Republican Labour complained that no Catholic was employed on the salaried staff of the local authority and none was employed locally in the electricity or gas undertakings. Furthermore, not one of the three post offices in the town was located in the area where the 'religious minority' resided.[28] Out of a population of 21,000—'roughly half and half'—the borough council consisted entirely of fifteen members of the Unionist Party. When Fitzsimmons, the Minister responsible, replied that this was a matter for the local authority, Dr Robert Nixon, a fellow Unionist MP, criticised him for the 'defence of the indefensible'.[29] However, it was also the case that Unionist-controlled Lurgan Borough Council was, in Nationalist eyes, far from being the worst offender in so far as the record of its 'treatment of the "nationally-minded" section' in the allocation of houses was concerned. The Unionist mayor, James Carson, stressed that although the entire Council was Unionist, the members had no personal grievances against their political opponents: 'We get on very happily together,' he said. In October 1967 Hugh News and H. P. McConville became the first Catholics to be invited to join the management committee of Lurgan Technical College. Jack Kelly, a former councillor, praised the good community relations in Lurgan and praised the Council for its fair allocation of houses: 300 houses were being built at Drumnamoe, about a mile outside the town, for 'allocation to Nationalists'. But Kelly disapproved of the continuation of the 'ghetto system'. Nationalists in Lurgan were now asking the Council to give a lead to other Unionist councils by ending housing segregation in the borough.

Yet ten years earlier the Council had experimented with mixing Catholics and Protestants in two estates at Kilwilke and Avenue Road. But after a period of time the people there began to seek exchanges to estates dominated by their co-religionists. Local Nationalist politicians recognised this factor and agreed that community relations were not as good then as they were now: but they still asked the Council to again try to give all sides of the community the chance to try to live together. However, it was also the case that matters were complicated by the fact that, years before, the then parish priest of Lurgan, the Right Reverend Dean O'Hagan—in consultation with the Unionist-controlled Council—approved the grouping of Catholics together because it would make easier the problem of planning the requirements of the parish as far as schools and churches were concerned. The priest had been concerned about the possible financial threat to Church plans for new churches and schools if the Catholic population was too scattered. Local Nationalists were annoyed when Mayor Carson reminded them of this on television.[30]

BRIDGE-BUILDING

Despite their sense of being second-class citizens, the Catholics of Northern Ireland looked forward with a sense of cautious optimism following the end of Lord Brookeborough's premiership when Captain O'Neill became Prime Minister of Northern Ireland 'at about 6 p.m.' on 25 March 1963.[31] On 5 April he attended the annual meeting of the Ulster Unionist Party's governing body, the UUC, at which the new Prime Minister stated that the Unionist Government's task was to transform the face of Ulster. This was greeted with cheers and O'Neill received a standing ovation. But as he later reflected: 'How often have I heard the clergy in Ulster preaching in favour of toleration. So long as it is kept in general terms then everyone is happy. If however, they actually say something specific about welcoming their Catholic neighbours into homes or their church halls to play bowls, then the trouble really starts.' O'Neill noted how, in the twenty years that his predecessor Lord Brookeborough was Prime Minister, he never crossed the border, never visited a Catholic school and never received or sought a civic reception from a Catholic town: 'As I see it the tragedy of his premiership was that he did not use his tremendous charm, and his deep Orange roots to try and persuade his devoted followers to accept some reforms.'[32]

What O'Neill meant by transforming the face of Ulster had, in fact, been hinted at in a speech delivered to Young Unionists at Portrush a few weeks before the UUC meeting. Then he had declared: 'In the past our Unionism may have been somewhat negative or at best neutral. We have been united against our enemies—united for the maintenance of the constitutional position. To-day we must have a Unionism prepared to move forward into new positions. The time for a defensive attitude is over.' In an interview later in the year the Prime Minister explained that by 'negative Unionism' he meant how, in the past, there had been times when Unionist political thinking had been concerned only with the 'No Surrender' and 'Not an Inch' theme. 'To-day we have to persuade the people of Northern Ireland that we have forward-looking policies which will improve social conditions. This is positive Unionism—something which young people can support.' O'Neill identified the social sphere as an area in which there was a great

deal to be accomplished. He wanted 'all sections of the community to feel committed to the task'. It was important to convince more and more people that the
Government was working for the good of all in Northern Ireland 'and not only
those who vote Unionist'.[33]

For many Catholics O'Neill seemed like a breath of fresh air after the stale, stag-
nant premiership of Brookeborough. In some quarters there was an undercurrent of
hope that there might be changes of attitude in both communities. As early as
October 1963 Ivan Neill, Minister of Education, had noted that there was a greater
interest in activity on the part of Nationalist members at Stormont. He predicted
that if they could agree amongst themselves, the Nationalists would gradually take
over the role of official opposition for the first time in Northern Ireland's
history.[34] This was but one of a number of indicators that Catholics might be
ready for greater participation in the body politic of Northern Ireland. At a
conference of Catholic organisations held in Belfast, also in October 1963, a
prominent lay Catholic, Gerald B. Newe, Secretary of the Northern Ireland
Council of Social Service, urged his Catholic co-religionists to abandon their
policy of non-co-operation with the Northern Irish state and to take public office
where possible. In a paper entitled 'The Catholic in our Community' Newe
observed that 'We Irish, north and south, seem to suffer a proneness to be "agin
the government"'. This had led some, especially in Northern Ireland, to show their
disapproval and dislike in ways which 'let us admit it frankly, has earned the
disgust, not to say the disapprobation, of all Christian men and women'. Newe
acknowledged that while 'we Catholics' might, of course, allege that the Northern
Ireland Government tended to discriminate against Catholics, 'I feel this
allegation cannot be made against the Government itself to the same degree as it
might have been made twenty-five or forty years ago.' In one way or another
Newe had had contact with ministers and Government departments for over
thirty years and 'I can say, with all sincerity, that the climate has, in that period,
changed greatly.' Many of the ministers and senior civil servants he had known,
and 'know today', were men of goodwill, of the highest character and integrity,
most of whom were 'really guided by Christian ethics'. However, he was not so
satisfied that government at local level was above criticism. Despite this last
misgiving Newe urged fellow Catholics to examine their consciences. He believed
that they would be forced to admit that their attitude towards the Northern
Ireland Government had been, generally speaking, anything but in keeping with
the precept of charity, or indeed with many of the other precepts governing their
duties and responsibilities as Catholic citizens. It would be argued that Catholics,
as such, had had much provocation, 'but so have non-Catholics. The provocation
had not all been on the one side.' Catholics must now show a readiness to serve—
to take public office where they could, to serve on public committees, to work for
and with many organisations which were non-denominational in character and
whose objects were good in themselves or could be turned to good. For example,

time and time again Newe had been asked to suggest names of Catholics for public committees but he found the greatest difficulty in getting names.[35]

The paper caused something of a stir but, on the whole, other leading lay members of the Catholic community responded positively to Newe's call. Patrick Gormley, Nationalist MP for Mid-Derry, 'agreed absolutely' with Newe's views. J. J. Campbell, Principal Lecturer at St Mary's Training College, Belfast, predicted that the reception to the paper would be very different from similar sentiments expressed by Catholics at Garron Tower in the late 1950s. It was not so fashionable now to oppose the idea of co-operation: 'I think since Garron Tower we Catholics have given sufficient intimation of our willingness to co-operate and that the time has come for the Government in its turn to give some sign that it welcomes this.' Frank Benner of Fruithill Park, Belfast believed that the effort to build bridges in the community had to be lifted out of the realm of politics. He looked forward to seeing Catholic students being trained to take part in public life. Ronnie McBride of the Belfast Chamber of Trade accepted that the idea of a society of complete toleration and mutual respect would appeal to all people of goodwill. But he thought Newe had oversimplified the problem: 'I think that it cannot be expected that the climate of thought and opinion will be changed quickly. It is contrary to human nature in these parts.'[36]

Reflecting on the previous attempts to shift Catholic attitudes and their failure, Campbell considered that there was nothing new in the views expressed at Garron Tower; what was significant lay in two factors. One was that it gave expression to an opinion widely held among Catholics about the need for co-operation with the community as a whole in all matters concerning the common good and the consequent need to break down the barriers of apartheid that divided Protestants and Catholics in the community. The other was that in the public examination of their position in the community, Catholics had invited a Protestant to tell them freely and frankly what she thought of their shortcomings. But this positive programme had attracted criticism. Eddie McAteer had referred to the 'genteel tinkling of intellectual teacups' and the 'supercilious chatter about co-operation'. Brian Faulkner had rejected the implied hand of friendship for the reason that it came from Catholic laymen and women and not from the Catholic hierarchy. William Douglas, Secretary of the Unionist Party, had been even less subtle: he was satisfied with things as they were, being able to cope with Nationalist politicians ('the devil he knew'); this co-operation business was, he said, a 'Trojan horse'.

However, Campbell had noted how there was now more and more dialogue between individuals and groups and an increasing tendency to find points of agreement on fundamental issues in the social life of the community and a greater willingness to credit the other fellow with sincerity in his beliefs and convictions and recognise his right to them. Campbell identified the ecumenical movement as a major impetus in the trend towards reconciliation. Various 'mixed' conferences showed how much common ground there was—not least a starting point being common Christian values. The grievances of the minority assumed a new importance in this context. Many who had dismissed them were now willing to take them seriously. A book by two social anthropologists, Carter and Barritt, had recently created a stir by highlighting the sources of sectarian tension in the community. No one was found even to attempt to controvert the factual material addressed in support of the grievances. And the opinion had gained strength among Protestant fellow-citizens that they merited investigation. In this context, suggested Campbell, Newe's paper represented a kind of stocktaking of the position. But while the movement towards co-operation was now seen to be stronger than ever, it was clear that it was attended by a considerable degree of Catholic impatience with the attitude of the Unionist Government —as distinct from that of many individual Protestants. There was a strong Catholic conviction that there was, in high places, a cynical indifference to the minority's efforts to assume its full responsibilities in the community. Thus some sign of goodwill on the part of the Government was being asked for. The fact that Catholics were excluded—by the 'apartheid' of the Orange Order—even from membership of the party which ruled and was likely to rule Northern Ireland for some time was a situation 'surely without parallel in democratic communities'. This, argued Campbell, made it all the more incumbent on the Government to show some notable sign that it accepted the co-operation of Catholics.[37]

Such reactions, however, were far from universal in the Catholic community. Gerry Fitt, the Republican Labour MP at Stormont, acknowledged that Newe had shown 'tremendous courage' in making his appeal. But it might be very well for someone in Newe's position to make such a call. There was a certain 'Malone Road [middle class] Catholic' type who were acceptable to the Unionist Government and who met with members of other religions at golf clubs on a Sunday afternoon. It was the type of person Fitt represented—the unemployed labourer, the man with a big family—who felt the real brunt of political divisions in Belfast. The Prime Minister and his colleagues had done nothing whatsoever in recent times to heal these divisions—divisions that had to be healed before there could be any real industrial prosperity. Fitt challenged O'Neill to make some gesture to the Catholics of Northern Ireland, some indication that if they co-operated with the Government that co-operation would be accepted.[38] This debate rumbled on through the remainder of 1963 and into 1964. If anything it was Fitt's sentiments—which Campbell had touched on—that struck a chord in the Catholic community: it was up to the Unionist Government to demonstrate that it was committed to reconciliation. For example, Thomas McLaughlin, a member of Armagh City Council, accepted that there was some truth in the statements about Catholics not accepting responsibility and playing their proper role; but 'before anybody can play their part they must be permitted to do so by the majority'. He felt that it was up to Unionists to 'divorce politics and religion'. The 'community' also had certain obligations: to give fair treatment in regard to employment, housing and so forth. This the community was not doing. But 'If the community had an obligation to me, then I in turn have an obligation to that community.'[39]

And Catholic perceptions of Unionist bigotry appeared to be confirmed when Bill Craig, Minister of Home Affairs, offered his thoughts on community relations to Orange brethren. He argued that the onus was on the Catholic community, not the Government, to make a gesture to the community in which they lived. 'We are ready, all of us, to help and assist as becomes a democracy,' said Craig. 'We are ready to be good neighbours and good citizens to all provided that we receive in turn the same respect and understanding that we should accord to all and sundry.' The Catholic community had remained aloof from the society and—this was the key point—the constitution within which they lived. So far so good as Craig had just stuck to a good old-fashioned diatribe against the minority. But then turning to what he described as the 'lack of family planning' amongst the Catholic community, Craig observed that large families in themselves were not to be decried but they became a 'social evil' when they were brought into the world with inadequate resources to cater for them let alone provide for greater opportunity. Because of the economic burden the Catholic family carried by virtue of its size, these children would be ill equipped to take their place in a modern society. It was no accident, either in Ulster or the Republic, that these boys and girls had had to leave their native shores and take employment in foreign climates; and employment of the lowest order. This, Craig explained, was a social problem that Ulster had to face. It could not be faced or a solution found for it if the people concerned ran away from the realities of the problem and sought to cover it up with false charges of discrimination.[40] The response to these comments was swift. The Bishop of Down and Connor, Dr William Philbin, attacked Craig's comments as 'calculated to injure the standing and the prospects of people of our faith'. On *a priori* grounds it cast on Catholics a stigma of inferiority that was an offence against truth and justice. It was a reflection on Catholic homes, schools and their entire way of life. And it tended to keep alive group prejudices 'at a time when enlightened people everywhere are trying to eliminate them'.[41] Nationalist MPs followed this up with a demand for Craig's resignation for the latest in a series of blundering statements.[42]

Given the 'respectability' of such views in mainstream Unionism it is perhaps easy to see why O'Neill was reluctant, if not unable, to make any more dramatic gestures towards Catholics. In April 1964 some of the frustration among Catholics became apparent when two leading members of that community published the text of two letters to O'Neill—because they had received no reply to either of them—in which they gave an assurance that representatives of the minority were prepared ('if given the opportunity') to play a more active role in public affairs. The letters were from J. J. Campbell and Brian McGuigan, a solicitor. The first letter was sent to O'Neill in August 1963, prompted by the absence of any Catholic among those invited to serve on the Government-appointed Economic Council. Another was forwarded at the beginning of March 1964 indicating an intention to disclose the terms of the correspondence and a third—to the Cabinet Secretary, Cecil Bateman—confirming this. In the letter of August 1963 Campbell and McGuigan stated that, with regard to the composition of the Economic Council, the minority 'has a right to feel that it is not wanted in this drive for prosperity'. In the selection of the Council there had been, at the very least, an indifference to the minority's feelings 'and feelings matter a great deal in motivating co-operation and support'. The two men called upon O'Neill and the Minister of Commerce— Faulkner—to make a gesture that would eliminate what the two men considered to be a valid grievance of their fellow co-religionists. Campbell and McGuigan emphasised that they had been at the forefront of the movement for integrating Catholics into Northern Ireland:

> in spite of the sneers and opposition of politicians on both sides . . . There are some Catholics who maintain that it is futile, that we are not wanted. There are Government spokesmen who reject it as a 'Trojan horse'. We have personally risked misunderstanding; have incurred the charge of toadying, of being quislings, of meekly bowing to snubs and rejection, etc . . . We have persistently attacked attempts to denigrate Northern Ireland; we have tried to give credit where credit is due . . . We are deeply disappointed. If our fellow-Catholic critics are proved to be right, then we shall be forced to reconsider whether there are other means within the constitution and the rule of law by which our rights as citizens are to be won.

In the second letter to O'Neill, on 5 March 1964, Campbell and McGuigan referred to the address made by Craig regarding co-operation in community relations. Campbell and McGuigan felt it was open to two interpretations: a sign that the Government was prepared to inaugurate a new era of community effort which would deliberately include and seek the co-operation of the minority; or a repetition of a standard Unionist reply based on a supposed unwillingness of the minority to co-operate and seeking to justify party policy accordingly. If the second interpretation was correct then Campbell and McGuigan invoked the significance of their first letter to O'Neill. They did not disagree with Craig's charge that, in the past, the Catholic attitude was marked by aloofness 'but it must now be clear to everyone that this is no longer the case'. Finally on 26 March Campbell and McGuigan wrote to the Cabinet Secretary in response to an interview O'Neill had with Roy Lilley, the political correspondent of the *Belfast Telegraph*. In the course of the interview O'Neill recounted how he had called on the minority to abandon its historic separatist outlook and to co-operate fully in furthering the prosperity of the community. A real improvement in community relations had to stem from the grassroots: O'Neill believed this process was underway and that 'thinking members' of the minority were tiring of old-style political Nationalism with its selection of thirty-year-old quotations and its outdated jargon. But for Campbell and McGuigan this appeared to be a repetition of a stock Unionist reply based on the alleged unwillingness of the Catholic minority to participate in the furtherance of the community's prosperity. In fact since they had last written to the Prime Minister, yet another statutory body—the Lockwood Committee—had been set up without a single Catholic member. This prompted the question: 'How does one co-operate if one is not offered the opportunity?'[43]

The publication of the letters forced O'Neill to respond. He told a Young Unionist rally in Enniskillen that: 'We have bent over backwards to be fair.' He laid the blame for poor community relations at the door of a favourite theme of his: the separate Catholic education system which for forty years 'has continuously and deliberately fostered a sense of separate identity. Yet it is WE who are being told that any move must come from US. We are being asked to open doors which have never been closed.' The present situation under which some institutions were adopted and others shunned was 'totally illogical'.[44] But even some Unionists were unconvinced by O'Neill's rhetoric. Robert Cooper, a prominent—and liberal— Young Unionist, criticised the 'leaders of Ulster' for failing to lead and mould public opinion. There had been a few straws in the wind but Unionism's leaders had not come out into the open and said that Catholics were not second class citizens and that they wanted to see them playing their full part in the community. The duty of a Prime Minister, said Cooper, was to lead.[45] Cooper suggested—to the UUP conference no less—that allegations by the Nationalist Party that Catholics were discriminated against should be examined.[46] There was no chance of that.

This in turn produced frustration among the Catholic minority. There was no recourse through the Stormont system. During 1964 any attempts by the Nationalist Party to seek a remedy against alleged local government discrimination ran into the sands, as they had done on every previous occasion. The Nationalists tabled new motions at Stormont on the allocation of houses and appointments by local authorities.[47] When a bill aimed at changes in local government reached the committee stage at Stormont, Eddie McAteer tabled an amendment to bar members of the Orange Order from serving on local authorities. Brian McConnell, Parliamentary Secretary to the Ministry of Health and Local Government, rejected the amendment on the grounds that the Order was a religious body and Section 5 of the Government of Ireland Act 1920 laid down that no person could be penalised on the grounds of religious belief. The Order, he said, stood in high regard in the community and it would be 'absurd' to agree to McAteer's amend-ment.[48] Yet there was some Unionist concern. So concerned was Captain Orr MP, President of the Imperial Grand Lodge of the World, that he told the Grand Lodge of Ireland that Orangemen had to get rid of their image as 'a narrow-minded, bigoted fanatical lot'. They had got to show where they stood—not against things but for things.[49]

The Nationalists next introduced a Diminution of Discord (Improvement of Community Relations) Bill which sought to transfer all local housing authority powers to a reconstituted Housing Trust, set up a local appointments commission to carry out competitive exams for all public posts and institute an immediate review of the constitutions of all state and semi-state boards to ensure adequate representation of minority interests.[50] But William Morgan, Minister of Health and Local Government, rejected the bill on the grounds that it would wreck local government and the work of statutory bodies.[51] This reflected a deep distrust on the part of the Government as to the real motives of the—still unofficial—opposition: O'Neill, for example, was wary of McAteer whom he described as someone who had preached a philosophy very close to civil disobedience but now tried to surround himself with an 'aura of sweet reason'.[52]

The problem for the Nationalist Party was, with no joy to be had at Stormont, there was little mileage at Westminster either. When, at the beginning of 1964, they sent a delegation to London, only the leader of the Liberal Party, Joe Grimond, was prepared to receive them. The Labour leader, Harold Wilson, refused an interview because 'as an Opposition this is not something on which we are in a position to take any action'. He did, however, offer the possibility of the appropriate ministers' receiving representations on discrimination should Labour form the next government. Unsurprisingly the Prime Minister (and leader of the Conservative and Unionist Party), Sir Alec Douglas-Home, turned down a request for a meeting on the grounds that 'these matters are within the responsibility of the Parliament and Government of Northern Ireland'. In their reply to the Prime Minister the Nationalists expressed regret that a 'sincere and earnest effort has evoked a reply along the lines wearily familiar'. While there was no real surprise here, the Nationalists were genuinely disappointed by Wilson's response. They had entertained great hopes that he would not deem it necessary to follow the 'ostrich-like' attitude of Douglas-Home.[53] The Nationalists did receive some support from Fenner Brockway, Labour MP for Eton and Slough, who issued invitations to 300 MPs to meet the delegation. He did this with regard to his concern over religious discrimination rather than any affinity with the Nationalists' political goals.[54] The result of all this was the tabling of a motion by Brockway, signed by fifty-three MPs, calling on the British Government to appoint a royal commission to inquire into allegations of religious discrimination in Northern Ireland.[55] But these were Labour MPs and for the moment Labour was in opposition.

Back at Stormont there remained, of course, no meeting of minds. The Unionist Government rejected all Nationalist proposals for reform. In December 1964 the Nationalist Party demanded the appointment of an ombudsman. James O'Reilly, MP for Mourne, claimed that it was no coincidence that the heads and secretaries of the departments in the six county councils were all of the one religious persuasion and supported the one political party.[56] Brian McConnell, now Minister for Home Affairs, refused to accept the motion, instead arguing that each individual had access to his MP and a man who knew the area and the people in it was better qualified to deal with complaints than a stranger appointed by the Government. Furthermore, members of the community had access to the courts if they felt aggrieved. McConnell congratulated the Nationalists on their ingenuity in being able to raise old topics—discrimination and gerrymandering —under a new heading. The Nationalists, though, had support from one unlikely quarter: a Unionist MP. Dr Robert Nixon supported the appointment of an ombudsman; what saddened him was that he felt that the motion was 'immediately slipping off the tracks and going into the reiteration of old complaints and bitterness'.[57] Next Morgan rejected a Nationalist motion calling for all clerical appointments to local authorities to be filled by competitive examinations. He submitted that the practical difficulties would be such as to make it impossible to operate any fair system of centrally-run competitive exams to suit all the needs of all local authorities. Academic qualifications in themselves were not the sole criteria that any prudent employer would apply when making appointments to his staff. Joseph Connellan, the Nationalist MP for South Down, replied that public bodies were brazenly turning down highly qualified candidates because of their religion. For example, James O'Reilly claimed that a town clerk of Belfast had been dismissed because it was discovered after his appointment that his wife was a Catholic. Once again it was Robert Nixon who swam against the tide: he was impressed by the general Nationalist argument on this occasion and advocated the integration of local government employees into the Civil Service. Nixon told Morgan that if he ran away from the examination argument 'he must be afraid that our boys and our girls are not able to defeat their boys and their girls'.[58] This was followed by a Nationalist motion that claimed that the allocation of houses by some councils amounted to a 'travesty of justice': it was described by Morgan as 'a biased and unwarranted attack on local authorities'. The motion, which called for direct Government intervention where it was apparent the claims of the needy were not given proper consideration, was defeated by twenty-six votes to fifteen. Walter Scott, the Unionist MP for Bloomfield, dismissed the motion as the 'usual Tuesday activity' of Nationalists to claim discrimination and unfairness on the part of the Government.[59]

The attitude taken by nearly all Unionists towards Nationalist claims of discrimination was simply to deny that any discrimination occurred—or if it did then it was practised by both communities. For example, Faulkner, interviewed for British television by Robert Kee of *This Week*, did not subscribe to the view that there was discrimination against Catholics in housing. He pointed out that the reason politics was inclined to run on religious lines was that the Roman Catholic Church took a very strong Nationalist line: 'I don't quarrel with them. They have a perfect right to do so. Because of that it is inevitable that the people of their Church should normally line up as Nationalists. I think it is a little unfortunate.'[60] This negative influence and attitude of the Catholic Church was a recurring theme in Unionist responses. Brookeborough's son, Captain John Brooke, Chairman of Fermanagh County Council—an authority that Nationalists reserved a particular ire for on account of its alleged practices—denied there was any religious discrimination by Protestants in Northern Ireland. While Unionists had no interest in the other man's beliefs at all, Brooke felt that the Roman Catholic Church was exercising its discipline in an area that did not concern them. The hierarchy, he added, had never recognised Northern Ireland and were determined to destroy it: 'The leopard does not change its spots. The Roman Catholic Church demands loyalty to the Church, which modifies loyalty to the State. We are portrayed as being bigots and they are portrayed as liberals and free thinkers. Our discrimination is not against Roman Catholics. We are trying to prevent the Roman Catholic Church in its determination to destroy Ulster.' The Orange Order was held up as an 'Aunt Sally' but there was never a word of its Catholic counterparts.[61]

Yet whenever there was a denial of discrimination from a Unionist source, Nationalists could rely on some dyed-in-the-wool Unionist backwoodsman to make a discriminatory statement and hole the no-discrimination line. In June 1964 Nationalists unsuccessfully tried to have a Justice of the Peace's name removed from the Commission of Peace at Stormont. Stanley Revels was alleged to have advised his local Orange Lodge to see that all key positions in a new meat factory at Newry should go to members of the Order. Revels was also a member of the Special Constabulary. However, William Fitzsimmons, Parliamentary Secretary to the Ministry of Home Affairs, denied that Revels had advocated discrimination: 'He did no more than probably any member of the House would do in suggesting that members of the lodge should help their unemployed brethren.' It was only for 'very grave and scandalous conduct' that JPs were removed from office. Only two had been removed since the creation of Northern Ireland.[62] That such remarks were embarrassing for some Unionists was demonstrated by Phelim O'Neill, the Unionist MP for North Antrim, who criticised Revels' remarks on the grounds that they 'certainly smacked of discrimination'. While it was true that the Government was not responsible for what any individual said outside Parliament he was concerned that Fitzsimmons had given the impression that he was trying to defend what was quite indefensible. If he thought that the majority of people in his constituency really agreed with Revels, O'Neill said he would leave public life: 'I would ask my constituents to find themselves a bigot and an imbecile—because the two go hand-in-hand—to represent them. I would not do it.' Observing that the General Assembly of the Presbyterian Church had just stood up to extremists, O'Neill asked: 'Why can't we do it?' This sparked off an exchange with Desmond Boal who remarked: 'Always assuming that your interpretation is correct'. Boal asked MPs to look at the Revels affair in its proper perspective. Mr Revels was a 'minor citizen' and it was unreasonable for MPs to have the temerity and the effrontery to expect ministers either to accept or reject random statements by private individuals.[63]

What eased, but didn't end, Catholic criticism of the Unionist Government was the Prime Minister's startling summit with Lemass in early 1965. Its almost revolutionary nature had a tremendous impact on Nationalists in the short term. In the North it was on the Catholic side of the political river bank that the most positive impact of the summit was felt. Harry Diamond of Republican Labour welcomed the meeting as a 'breaking of the ice and in a sense unprecedented in 40 years. It is the beginning of wisdom.' Eddie McAteer described the meeting as a 'significant step forward . . . The inevitable has happened a few months earlier than was expected.' It could bring 'nothing but good'.[64] The day after the summit—15 January—Lemass met with McAteer in Dublin to explain why the latter had been left out of the loop as the arrangements were made for the visit North. McAteer asked the Taoiseach for advice on a role the Nationalist Party was considering: that of official opposition in Stormont. The main obstacle, explained McAteer, was 'ceremonial and formal occasions, i.e. flags and toasts'. Lemass advised him that 'non-acceptance need not mean political ineffectiveness' even though he would not accept these himself. Later Frank Aiken, Lemass' Minister of External Affairs, cautioned the Taoiseach against opening a formal channel between Dublin and the Nationalist Party for fear of weakening O'Neill's hand: 'naturally no Government wishes another Government with which it is negotiating to be in regular consultation with its own opposition in Parliament'. He also came out against a federal solution to Irish unity fearing 'we might well be faced with a demand for equal representation of the six counties and the 26 counties in the all Ireland parliament. An all Ireland constitution of this kind with a built in veto would render normal government impossible—as happened in the recent tragic case of Cyprus.'[65] Sometimes the practicalities of a united Ireland didn't always look quite so attractive from Dublin.

Having secured Lemass' blessing for his idea McAteer set about persuading the Nationalist Party to adopt the role of official opposition. By the end of January 1965 the Party, meeting at Stormont, was taking longer than expected to be convinced that it should take over the role. McAteer, who had expected a short meeting to endorse the new role, found it turning into a two-hour one instead. It looked as if the inscription over the door of the Nationalist's room—'Official Opposition'—might remain as it was, with the first word covered by a brown paper sticker.[66] In the end it was a further week before McAteer was able to write to the Speaker confirming that the Party would take up the role of official opposition.[67]

In March the Nationalist members of Londonderry Corporation demonstrated their support for the new policy when they decided to attend a Guildhall reception as the Governor, Lord Erskine, accompanied by Lady Erskine, paid his first official visit to the city. It also proved to be the first occasion for many years that the Nationalist aldermen and councillors had taken part in a civic function of this kind. The seven Nationalists were presented to the Governor in the council chamber. But they did not attend a luncheon that followed in the Assembly Hall where a royal toast was to be honoured. While this might seem a mild gesture at first sight it should be remembered what had transpired the last time: when the Governor's predecessor, Lord Wakehurst, paid his first official visit to Derry in 1953 the Nationalist members of the council had staged a protest at the luncheon in his honour. They refused to eat, remained seated while the loyal toast was drunk and Eddie McAteer, who was then a member of the council, rose to make a protest as the Governor was speaking.[68] This was the first in a series of steps that illustrated an improvement in Nationalist–Unionist political relations and community relations in general. For the first time in twenty-two years a Nationalist occupied the chair in the Senate, on 15 June 1965, and received the twelve members successfully elected to the Upper House. J. C. Drennan, Chairman of the UUC, proposed Patrick McGill, the Omagh newspaper proprietor, for the office of Deputy Speaker.[69] Often, though, this process of readjustment was fraught, combining one step forward with one step back: again in June 1965, for the first time since early in the century, Nationalist members of Derry Corporation attended a reception given by The Honourable The Irish Society—the London-based body which owned considerable lands and properties in the north-west of the Province from the time of the Plantation and was seen as a historic symbol of Protestant domination.[70] Then in October—for the first time ever—it was announced that a Nationalist member of Derry Corporation was to attend the annual dinner of the Society in London. Alderman James Hegarty and the Corporation's Finance Committee had been invited to represent the city whereas, previously, only the Mayor and the town clerk had been asked to attend. After a 'heart-rending search' Hegarty agreed to attend 'to see if it will do anything to better or ease the relations and tensions' that had existed between Nationalists and Unionists on the council.[71] But only a few months later opposition MPs were calling for the abolition of the Society. McAteer called it a 'curious body' born under a 'dark charter' 350 years ago. To add insult to injury the Society was controlled by the City of London and 'the mere Irish', either the new or the old, were not given any voice in the spending of the money being extracted from them.[72]

Symbols, then, were a real problem for Nationalists. One of the greatest criticisms levelled at Nationalists by Unionists was their apparent discourtesy towards symbols of Britishness. In June 1967 Thomas Gormley, Nationalist MP for Mid-Tyrone, broke with tradition and became the first Nationalist to attend a Royal Garden Party at Hillsborough in honour of Princess Margaret and her husband, Lord Snowden, who were on a three-day visit to Northern Ireland.[73] But the very next day in Newry there were protests against the visit of a British Army recruiting unit to the town in connection with a Civic Week, and the organisers of a round-the-houses cycle race cancelled the event.[74] To try and defuse the situation the Army unit called off their visit after a request from the Civic Week executive committee; a Royal Ulster Rifles band, however, would play as planned because the committee failed to secure any local bands in time.[75] The Army, of course, was a symbol of British occupation in the North; yet at the same time it was a source of employment for many working class Catholics who had a long and distinguished service in its ranks (Northern Ireland's only recipient of the Victoria Cross in the Second World War was a Belfast Catholic). Yet few Catholics—and certainly no Nationalist politicians—attended the remembrance day services recalling the fallen in Britain's wars, a significant proportion of whom were Catholics. As a result these services became *de facto* Protestant services. So, for example, when in 1964 some 520 members of the British Legion from all over Ireland joined in a unique ceremony at Newry, as the old standard of the local branch was laid up and a new one dedicated, there was no representative of the local Catholic Church to officiate. The only one willing to participate was Father Joseph Murphy from Dublin, an ex-chaplain of the Irish Guards. It therefore took on the character of a British and Protestant ceremony with Catholic tokenism.[76]

As we have seen, a big area of contention was the use of the royal toast at official functions. Nothing seemed to get up Nationalist noses more than this while nothing seemed to get up Unionist noses more than the Nationalist attitudes to the toast. It is difficult to exaggerate how contentious this was; hence in 1964 the rift that developed between McAteer and Patrick Gormley arising out of comments made by the latter that he was 'not unduly troubled' about standing for the British National Anthem or drinking the royal toast. McAteer replied that he welcomed and encouraged co-operation but 'not at the expense of national principles. No concession to Unionist attitudes has yet been made and I cannot understand why we must surrender any ground.'[77] It was McAteer and not Gormley who represented the view of most Catholics. For example, in 1967 the unexpected playing of 'God Save the Queen', at the first all-denominational festival of carols for schoolchildren near Lurgan, angered Catholic teachers and the parents of the children who were participating in it. The teachers told the local education committee that their Catholic schools would not take part in any future festival without a guarantee that the anthem would not be played. Following the protests a special meeting of the Armagh Education Committee was held where it was decided that the national anthem must be played at functions held in county schools under the Committee's control. In view of this decision, Catholic teachers in Lurgan decided to inform the Committee that they would not take part in any future functions held in county schools.[78]

For Catholics such symbols were rubbing their noses in it. Any acquiescence in such symbolism might be mistaken for an acceptance of the state, partition and British sovereignty in Ireland. In 1964 McAteer had called for an all-out effort at all levels and in all sections of the community to end what he described as the 'feudin' and fightin' image' which had won such damaging notoriety for Derry. In particular he highlighted flags, toasts and anthems as the usual flashpoints. If these 'tension-packed' occasions could be reduced it would be to the benefit of all. He therefore suggested that a serious attempt be made to politically neutralise as many functions as possible under civic, sporting and professional auspices. No one was being asked to desert his flag but just to avoid shoving it down the throat of a fellow guest: 'If we can dine in peace there is a very good chance that we can learn to live and work in peace.'[79] For Unionists this was unacceptable. The Mayor of Londonderry, Councillor A. W. Anderson, criticised McAteer: 'He simply says that Unionists should not honour the flag of this country and should not have the loyal toast at luncheons and civic functions. This we cannot agree to.' The fundamental fact was that 'Mr McAteer refuses to recognise Northern Ireland as a separate entity' from the rest of Ireland.[80] So for Unionists this refusal to acknowledge the legitimacy of Northern Ireland, as represented through its British symbols, was abhorrent. In 1967 a private member's motion in Stormont, in the name of Nat Minford, called on the Government to take immediate steps to have the Union Flag flown at all country schools during teaching days. The motion failed but not before Nationalist MPs absented themselves from the chamber as soon as Minford rose to speak; as they left McAteer called to Minford: 'You ought to be ashamed of yourself.' Minford obviously wasn't and went on to argue that the Union Jack was the flag of 'their' country and sought an assurance from the Education Minister, William Long, that 'this emblem of our loyalty' should fly freely and proudly at all country schools. Joseph Burns, seconding the motion, said he would have heartily supported the motion if it had also applied to all schools—not only country schools. In the United States, he pointed out, there was a ceremony at the beginning and the end of school with the children standing to attention when the flag was run up and taken down. The same thing should apply in Northern Ireland because there was 'a subversive element who said their flag was the Tricolour and not the Union Jack. The children should be taught to respect the flag which supplied them with education, transport, free milk and many other things.' Long preferred to see the matter handled voluntarily by the schools rather than by legislation; he did, however, feel compelled to reassure MPs that the Government 'was loyal to the flag.'[81]

While the Prime Minister would not have been foolish enough to ever try and implement such an unenforceable policy his gut instinct would have been to be sympathetic with the spirit of it. Giving, in 1966, an address on 'The Ulster Community' to open a joint Protestant–Catholic conference at the Corrymeela Centre, Ballycastle, O'Neill outlined his views on the subject. He described the 'Ulster Community' as 'a place where two traditions meet, the Irish Catholic tradition and the British Protestant tradition. In India the place where two great rivers join together is often considered to have a particular sanctity, but it is often a place of turbulence, as the currents from different directions swirl around each other.' By and large these religious traditions had also been synonymous with political views. This correspondence of religion and politics had, in the past, created 'certain peculiar frictions in our public affairs' and prevented a united effort to surmount other social and economic problems. O'Neill highlighted the *de facto* segregation of education along religious lines. He also noted that political divisions 'become unusually sharp when the argument is not means, but the ends'. Thus:

in most countries, political parties differ merely about the methods to be used for the achievement of certain accepted national goals—economic stability and prosperity, higher standards of living and so on.

Disagreements of this kind admit the possibility of compromise. While the extreme positions, for instance, may be of untrammelled private enterprise or complete state control, what in fact has emerged in the UK under governments of different complexion is a mixed economy.

Here in Northern Ireland, however, disagreement has been centred not around the activities of the State, but around its very existence . . . I must say clearly that the constitutional position of Northern Ireland is a matter on which there can be no compromise now or in the future, and I must say too, that I believe we have a right to call upon all our citizens to support the Constitution.

The whole basis of constitutional government would be debased if the State were not to expect of its citizens at any rate the minimum duty of allegiance.[82]

But to Catholics this sounded more like a request to sit back and accept a position as second-class citizens without any evidence of reform. McAteer commented that 'It has all been said before, only with more sincerity.' He noted that 'Unquestioning Catholic allegiance to an Orange government seems to be Capt. O'Neill's brilliant idea of statesmanship. These long range salvoes of goodwill are less effective than one hour of head-to-head discussion on practical measures.' The Government had not yet made any move to show the basis of their fears, and this proved that strict one-party rule was still their idea of democracy. 'Neither can I help noticing that all the gun barrels are trained on our side while Orange nose-thumbing goes unrebuked.' Gerry Fitt was equally dismissive: 'These statements could be seen as demonstrating a very enlightened attitude, but taken with the actions of the Government one suspects that they are only paper talk.'[83]

Yet, despite these divisions, beneath the surface there seemed to be some evidence of flexibility on the part of Catholics. The findings of the National Opinion Poll in 1967 had revealed that only thirty-eight per cent of Nationalists supported an independent all-Ireland republic. McAteer's response was: 'I am not at all startled . . . It must be a right few years ago since I said that the final Irish paradox that total independence would mean an instant marriage of the two islands. The feeling among Unionists for a united Ireland of some sort is simply a recognition that modern transport and communications mock at our parochial senses. "Terence take heart" is the message I read.'[84] In his old—political—age McAteer seemed to be mellowing somewhat. By 1965 McAteer had come to the conclusion that the political situation in the North was 'not so tightly deadlocked' as it had been. There was still the traditional conflict of opinion as to whether 'the priority' should be political union with Britain or 'natural re-union' with the rest of Ireland; but 'exciting glimpses' of a larger European unity indicated that 'our local choice is simply one of priority. The final paradox of the Irish story may well be that Irish freedom will be swiftly followed by true partnership with the neighbouring island.'[85] McAteer told Nationalists that they must open their eyes and acknowledge that the Stormont Government had, through the passage of time, 'almost acquired a right to recognition as an Irish-based institution'. Nationalists would have to adapt themselves to the idea that the local parliament would survive for a 'fairly long time' to give security to those who feared incorporation in a wider Irish national and, indeed, European community. He emphasised that he was not suggesting that Nationalism had been watered down to the acceptance of British lordship of any part of Ireland. 'But we do recognise that we are now faced with nearly a half century of legislative and administrative growth which cannot be uprooted overnight.' He added that: 'Since this area forms a physical part of the national territory we must bestow on it and its people the same love that we bear for our country as a whole.'[86]

But any hope that such flexibility in Nationalist thinking, such as the acceptance of a Northern Irish patriotism, would develop further depended on the Unionist Government treating Catholics fairly. As the national secretary of the Ancient Order of Hibernians, Francis Matthews, had stated in 1964, he welcomed how many Unionists now recognised their obligations to the Catholic population. If Unionist promises of friendship were made a reality 'our Orange neighbours will find that their proffered hand of friendship is not scorned by us'. But Matthews also stressed that: 'In taking our hand the Unionists must remember one thing. We are nationalists in our deepest conviction. They must cease calling us subversive for that, just as we must cease calling them bigots for what they believe.' Senator James Lennon agreed that while Northern Nationalists 'ardently desire to make a bonfire of the mistrust, intolerance and bigotry of the past' they could not 'be expected to forswear our allegiance to our native land or admit the right of England to impose and maintain partition in Ireland'. Matthews added that the 'answer to the fundamental division between us lies in the realm of time'.[87] Rather like O'Neill's hope for a long-term integration of Catholics into Unionism, Matthews and McAteer looked to the long-term integration of Northern Protestants into Nationalism. Things could change. McAteer held to the view that Nationalism was non-sectarian. As one of his colleagues, Joseph Connellan MP, put it: 'We will not accept the dictum that Roman Catholics are born to be Nationalists or that all Protestants are born to be Unionists. Our aim is to provide a common ground of action in which such absurd distinctions will disappear.' Connellan echoed McAteer with the thought that in a fast-changing world those 'who were slaves to the Unionist machine' should see the wisdom of exercising 'at long last the rights of free men'.[88]

There was just one problem with this view of a non-sectarian Nationalism: while the rhetoric and vision of Nationalism was non-sectarian it was *de facto* Catholic. The idea that the later civil rights movement was, essentially, Nationalist rather than reformist has been a controversial one because of the implication that this gives sustenance to Unionist opposition to it on the grounds that it was an anti-partitionist conspiracy. It should not. But the simple truth is that those prominent in civil rights reveal that they were socialised, through family, school and Church, into a Nationalist political environment and perception of the world. For example, Paddy Doherty, a key figure in Derry during the civil rights period, recalled from his youth that Bogsiders only rarely discussed politics. Nevertheless they considered the 1921 Treaty to have been 'an abomination; a united Ireland was the holy grail. My introduction to Anglo–Irish relations came at the dinner table, when it was announced on the radio that the Right Honourable Lloyd George had been admitted to hospital. My father slowly put down his knife and fork and said, in a voice quavering with emotion, "Hell will never be full until the Welsh bastard is in it."'[89]

For Doherty his period of association with the Catholic Church was a formative time: 'I never met an Irish Catholic priest who did not despise the Northern Ireland establishment' although very few of them had any time for the Republican Movement either—Doherty thought this was because they were perceived by the clergy to be working to a socialist agenda. He found his loyalty to the Church tested at election time when priests would drive around the area with the name of the Nationalist candidate displayed on their car windows. Doherty's father, however, always voted for the Republican candidate and 'In any contest between my father and the Church, I backed my father.'[90] Doherty also noted the role played by the Church in perpetuating sectarian divisions. He recalled the close watch the nuns kept on the young as one aspect of the tight hold the Church had on the Catholic community in Derry: 'It forbade us to mix socially with other Christians.' No one, for example, ever suspected that a member of one well-known Republican family would challenge the taboos. 'She was sparkling company, petite, dark and very beautiful, and had set many hearts aflutter.' But she caused a great stir when she married a Protestant. 'The rigorous sanctions employed against Catholics who married outside the Church were brought to bear on the teenager, who had answered the call of her heart. At each mass on Sunday, her name was read out and that most awful punishment—excommunication—was pronounced. I heard the terse statement which severed the limb from the body of the Church. It wasn't the sharp, clean cut of the guillotine, but a blow from a blunt, rusted axe, which mutilated a follower of Christ.'[91] How far apart Catholics and Protestants really were became clear to him during the funeral of John Eakin, the Protestant founder of a company for which Doherty worked. All of the company's workers attended the funeral. Eakin's had a mixed workforce, but while the Protestants filed into the church 'the Catholics stood outside, stamping their feet in the light covering of snow that had fallen during the night. For them to enter the building would have been to recognise that those who had left the Church during the Reformation had had some right on their side.' As the funeral cortege slowly made its way to the cemetery, the Christians mixed once again, only to separate once more when they arrived at the open grave. Breaking ranks from his co-religionists and taking courage from a fellow Catholic who stood beside the Protestant minister, Doherty left his workmates and 'stepped across the few yards of earth which divided the two groups, separating Protestant prayers from Catholic ears.'[92]

Such experiences are fundamental to understanding Catholic perceptions which were deeply embedded in the Catholic-Nationalist psyche. Yet it was undeniable that there had been an improvement in community relations. This was measured in 1967 by Richard Rose. He found that most Catholics and Protestants, sixty-five per cent and fifty-six per cent respectively, believed that community relations had improved since O'Neill became Prime Minister, although, crucially, this did not necessarily change their political outlook. While a majority of Catholics, even those in public employment, rejected the constitutional settlement, only five per cent of the total population thought religion was a barrier to getting a job. However, Rose's Loyalty Survey refuted O'Neill's theory that Catholic allegiance to the state could be bought with economic benefits and found that an increase in Catholic support and compliance, resulting from higher income or the receipt of welfare, was limited or non-existent.[93] Furthermore a large majority of Catholics described themselves as 'Irish' (seventy-six per cent) compared to a small number (fifteen per cent) who described themselves as 'British'.[94] The upshot of this was that, at the end of the day, Catholics possessed a group mentality based on their experience as Catholics in a Protestant state and as Irish Nationalists in British Ireland. The significance was that, whether or not Catholics wanted greater participation in Northern Ireland's life, should there be any perceived attack on that community it was more than likely that this would be perceived in traditional Nationalist terms. In this sense whether the civil rights movement was reformist or anti-partitionist was irrelevant: those participating in it were Catholics who had been socialised into a Nationalist interpretation of the Northern Ireland state. If this view was dormant it would not take much to reawaken it.

THE IRA

There remains one key actor within the Nationalist camp to which our attention needs to be turned: the Irish Republican Army. The IRA had been defeated in the Border Campaign of 1956–62. Lacking support from the Catholic population and unable to deliver any significant military blows against the North's security forces, a major rethink of its strategy began within the higher command of the IRA. But who constituted the IRA and how was it structured? A 'Review of Unlawful and Allied Organisations' by the Commissioner of the Garda Síochána in 1966 gives a unique insight into the personnel and structure of the pre-Troubles IRA. It was estimated that the strength of the IRA on 31 October 1966 was a total of 1,039 members. Since the cessation of the Border Campaign in February 1962, the strength of the organisation had varied as follows:

31 December 1962   –   657
31 December 1963   –   763
31 December 1964   –   807
31 December 1965   –   923

The strengths of the organisation in divisions in the country indicated that the Dublin Metropolitan Area had 306 members; Cork East Riding had 164 members; Cavan/Monaghan had eighty-one members; Limerick had fifty-nine members; and Louth/Meath and Waterford/Kilkenny had the next highest membership, with a total of forty-nine and forty-eight respectively. It was manifestly a Southern-dominated movement. The basic Unit of the IRA was a Section, which normally totalled from five to seven men. This group organised, trained and worked together. The Section was under the charge of a Section Leader and Section Instructor, but in many cases these two ranks were combined. Local control of the Sections was administered by the Unit Officer Commanding (OC) and Unit Officers, and all came under the jurisdiction of a Command Staff, which in practice was a miniature replica of the General Headquarters Staff of the IRA. IRA Headquarters Staff dealt only with the Command Staffs who in turn dealt with the local Unit Officers. IRA Headquarters appointed the OC and the Intelligence Officer (IO) of each Command Area and the Command OC appointed the other Command Staff Officers, namely the Adjutant, Quartermaster, Training Officer, Finance Officer and a new rank which was known as a Political Education Officer. Members of the Command Staff visited each Unit in the area once a month mainly to ensure that co-operation existed between all Unit activities, including organisation and training. In addition to the Command Staff, each Command Area operated a Command Council, which consisted of the Command Staff together with the Officer Commanding each Unit in the area. The Command Council was supposed to meet once a month. In 1966 the IRA General Army Convention, which was held every two years, was convened at a secret rendezvous in the country during the weekend of 15–16 October. It was attended by approximately fifty-five delegates. The following were elected to IRA controlling bodies:

Executive

1) Rory BRADY, Roscommon
2) Michael A. MEADE, Skerries, Co. Dublin
3) Cathal GOULDING, Rathfarnham, Co. Dublin
4) Séamus COSTELLO, Foxrock, Co. Dublin
5) Seán GARLAND, Walkinstown, Dublin
6) Seán STEPHENSON, Knockumber, Navan, Co. Meath
7) Frank DRIVER, Ballymore Eustace, Co. Kildare

8) Laurence GROGAN, Drogheda, Co. Louth
9) Roy JOHNSTON, Rathmines, Dublin
10) Thomas GILL, Mount Merrion, Dublin
11) Denis FOLEY, Rathmines, Dublin
12) Thomas MITCHELL, Fairview, Dublin

Army Council

1) Thomas GILL
2) Seán STEPHENSON
3) Cathal GOULDING
4) Rory BRADY
5) Séamus COSTELLO
6) Seán GARLAND
7) B. QUINN, Co. Tyrone

Headquarters Staff

Chief of Staff	– Cathal GOULDING
Adjutant General	– Séamus COSTELLO
Asst. Adjutant General	– Larry BATESON, Dublin
QMG	– Malachy McGURRAN, Rathgar, Dublin
Director of Training	– Denis FOLEY, Rathmines, Dublin
Director of Finance	– Thomas MITCHELL, Fairview, Dublin
Director of Intelligence	– Liam NOLAN, Crumlin, Dublin
Assistant Director of Intelligence	– Thomas BRADY, Whitehall, Dublin
Director of Publicity	– Seán BRADY, Glenageary, Co. Dublin
Director of Political Education	– Roy JOHNSTON
Liaison Officer for the Six Counties	– Larry BATESON, Dublin

It was decided at the Convention that GHQ would concentrate more on training the 'Army' for a military campaign and that only men who were prepared to carry out this policy be elected to the Army Executive. Following the holding of the General Army Convention in 1963, the IRA had been reorganised on a Command Area system throughout the country and, for this purpose, the thirty-two-county area was divided into eighteen Command Areas. IRA General Headquarters issued a directive to all Command and Unit OCs to ensure, as far as possible, that the new Command Area system in operation should not be generally known to the public and that Volunteers in the organisation were not to know the composition of the Command, the area covered or the Units under its charge. It had also directed that all changes in the Command must be ratified by the General Headquarters Staff. The area which comprised each Command, together with the OC appointed by IRA General Headquarters, were as follows:

Command Areas	OCs
No. 1 Command (Cork & South Kerry)	— William E. WILLIAMS, Cork
No. 2 Command (Limerick, Clare & North Kerry)	— Patrick MULCAHY, Singland, Limerick
No. 3 Command (Tipperary)	— Patrick HAYES, Birr, Co. Offaly
No.4 Command (Carlow, Kilkenny, Wexford & Waterford)	— Lorcan BERGIN, Kilkenny
No. 5 Command (Dublin, Wicklow & South Meath)	— Peter PRINGLE, Chapelizod, Dublin
No. 6 Command (Leix, Offaly & Kildare)	— Terence S. O'TOOLE, Portlaoise, Co. Leix
No. 7 Command (Galway)	— Rory BRADY, Roscommon
No. 8 Command (Mayo)	— do.
No. 9 Command (Longford, Roscommon & Westmeath)	— do.
No. 10 Command (Sligo & Leitrim)	— John J. McGIRL Ballinamore, Co. Leitrim
No. 11 Command (Donegal)	— Patrick DAWSON, Letterkenny, Co. Donegal
No. 12 Command (Louth & North Meath)	— Peter DUFFY, Dundalk, Co. Louth
No. 13 Command (Monaghan)	— George POYNTZ, Castleblayney, Co. Monaghan
No. 14 Command (Down & Armagh)	— J. B. O'HAGAN
No. 15 Command (Antrim)	— Billy McKNIGHT
No. 16 Command (Derry)	— John McCLUSKEY

No. 17 Command   – Joe O'CONNOR
(Tyrone & Fermanagh)

No. 18 Command   – Philip MURRAY, Cavan
(Cavan)

The Army Council was the supreme authority of the IRA when a General Army Convention was not in session. The Council was elected by the Army Executive within forty-eight hours of the termination of the General IRA Army Convention. It was supposed to meet once a month. The Army Executive was elected by ballot of delegates in attendance at the General Army Convention. At least eight of its members had to be delegates to the General Convention, but the remaining members might be active Volunteers who were not delegates. Substitutes to fill vacancies on the Executive were also elected by the General Convention. This Executive was scheduled to meet at least once every six months. According to the Constitution of Óglaigh na hÉireann, the only functions of the Army Executive were:

1) To elect an Army Council within forty-eight hours after the holding of the General Army Convention.
2) To meet every six months and to advise the Army Council on all matters concerning the Army.
3) The Executive shall have the power by a majority vote to summon an Extraordinary General Army Convention.

Meetings of OCs of Command Areas in the country were held at infrequent intervals and were generally presided over by the Chief of Staff or the Adjutant General. Matters discussed covered activities of the respective Command Area Staffs concerning organisation, training and so on. Following the ending of the Border Campaign, a controversial decision was made to alter the strategy of the Republican Movement and shift it in a leftwards direction with the result that many of the traditionalists within the IRA became disillusioned and left the organisation. At the Army Convention of 1966 a clear indication of this shift in the policy and programme of the organisation was signalled with the following motion:

That this Convention instruct the incoming Army Council that the Movement shall adapt itself, if necessary by organisational changes, to increase its influence in all organisations of which their objectives do not conflict with the national interest, especially in the 6 Counties, through the Trade Union movement on the issue of civil rights and discrimination in jobs, etc., as well as in job security and wages, fostering especially such few areas and actions as involve both Catholics and Protestants with a view to undermining the basis of support for Unionism among the Protestant population, keeping intact however the basic principle of training of key people in the Movement in the use of weapons so that when the time comes the Movement will be prepared to back up its political and economic advances with such force and popular support as will ensure rapid and complete victory.

The Convention instructed the incoming Army Council to draw up and implement an educational course for all ranks explaining 'Economic Resistance' theory; and how to implement it and its benefits to the Army and the Nation. This course would also explain the logical sequence of events towards successful revolution, that is: (i) economic resistance followed by (ii) political action which in turn was followed by (iii) military action. Following this educational course an all-out effort was to be made to organise and maintain an effective nationwide economic resistance campaign. If and when necessary, militant and punitive action as part of this campaign would be taken when popular support was developed to the necessary degree by the foregoing phases and at the discretion of the Army Council. The plan of political action was to be implemented as soon as possible after the development of the Economic Resistance Campaign. The educational course, the economic resistance and political action would not replace but supplement ordinary unit activities and training programmes. The argument put forward in support of these new policies was that, following the obvious failure of the IRA to draw support from the population at large, these measures were 'necessary to bring about a successful military confrontation with the British Government and its forces of occupation on the National issue'. In addition a long discussion took place at the Convention on the feasibility of an early resumption of Border activities until, finally, it was agreed to leave the matter entirely in the hands of the incoming Army Council. A decision on the contesting of Dáil Éireann and Westminster elections was left to the incoming Army Council and the Sinn Féin Árd-Chomhairle.

On 3 November 1966 a meeting of the Army Council discussed a number of resolutions referred to it by the General Convention. A resolution that organised help from the six counties be forthcoming for twenty-six-county elections, and that as soon as feasible at least eighty seats be contested in the twenty-six counties with a view to forming a government, was passed by the Army Council. At a meeting of the IRA Army Council held in August 1966 a draft of proposed 'political' action by IRA/Sinn Féin groups in regard to a radical, social and economic programme had been discussed. A copy of a draft of this plan, together with a draft of a proposed 'military' plan, was found on Seán Garland, the Chief of Staff of the IRA, when he was intercepted and arrested by Gardaí at Portlaoise on 7 September 1966. The Army Council decided at the meeting to formulate such a programme and to have this circulated to members of the Council as early as possible. The following programme was approved at the meeting:

1) That the 'Movement' needs an organisation of representatives in the Trade Union Movement whose function it would be to examine Trade Union Law

and Structure with a view to making the Trade Unions more revolutionary and to draw up directives for Volunteers on the subject of Trade Unionism.

This organisation should be in the form of a 'staff', not necessarily a branch of GHQ, but under the control and direction of the Chief of Staff.

2) To make the fullest use of experts to lecture to Republicans on Trade Union, Economic and other subjects. It was decided that formal committees should be set up to cover various fields and to work for short-term limited objectives. These committees will have terms of reference and will be under the direction of the 'Army Department'. They will deal with such matters as Housing, Free Trade, Co-operatives, etc., and will work with other radical-minded groups such as Trade Unionists, etc. These committees will have such an organisation structure to enable them to mobilise the mass of the membership of the 'Movement' in any agitation.

3) That the committees should work with other radical-minded groups such as the Labour Party people, Trade Union people, etc.

4) That the committees mentioned will have as their task the education of Sinn Féin people and Sinn Féin people will be involved on the committees. It was expected that the committees, by educating the Sinn Féin people at local level, would rejuvenate Sinn Féin. It was decided to refer the whole question of an Educational Programme back to a special committee for a further report.

5) That if the minds of the Irish people are to be influenced in any significant numbers towards national objectives, it is going to be necessary to reform the structure of the 'Movement' in order to reach them. This alteration will be effected through the committees which have been mentioned in previous paragraphs.

The meeting decided that the social and economic objectives of the movement would receive all possible publicity in future, but that they would not take precedence over military objectives. It was also decided to re-draft the present recruit course in order to place proper emphasis on the social, economic and cultural objectives of the movement. It was felt that the present high turnover in membership was caused by the recruit, having seen an emphasis laid on military activity, not being prepared for the political activity which must precede it. It was decided that 'The Army' would retain its own organisational structure and would function within the revolutionary organisation as a backbone. Army recruits would be chosen from the best and most conscientious members of the organisation, but, in special cases, recruits would come direct into the Army. It was also decided that the Army Convention would continue as the main policy-making body. The proposal that the Constitution be drafted in such a way as to allow for affiliation of friendly organisations such as the Wolfe Tone Society, Felons Clubs, Trade Unions, etc., was approved, but it was decided that any organisation which recognised either Irish Parliament would not be allowed to affiliate. Parliamentary elections were to be avoided until it was considered that the organisation was strong enough to win a large number of seats, but there would be no compromise on taking an oath. The proposal that the elected representatives of the people, North and South, would meet and set up a national parliament was also approved. A proposal that MPs and TDs meet nationally at a central place during parliamentary recess and proceed to legislate for the whole country, starting with laws which could be enforced by social pressures and proceeding to pass laws which would bring the two state structures into head-on conflict, thus enabling the takeover to be completed by military action, was approved in principle. A summary of the draft 'military' plan which was found on Garland was divided into four stages:

1) Anti-agent campaign (start immediately)
2) Large stunt-type operations
3) Final phase (agricultural and industrial sabotage)
4) Kidnapping of prominent members of British Government (publicity)

Stage One of the operation was to be done quietly and to be phased in such a way as not to excite maximum retaliation from the enemy. The idea was to prepare the way for a campaign to 'harden our people and organisation' to police pressure and 'to get our people psychologically prepared for further killing'. The victims were to include ordinary policemen 'who are active as agents against us. THIS STAGE IS ESSENTIAL.' In Stage Two, Units composed of specialised sections were to be formed, ('e.g. Thompson Section from Dublin; Rifle Section from Dundalk; Bren Section from Cork; Engineers from Limerick, etc.') This would avoid concentration of an elite in an area and circumvent the danger of a split. The danger of police observation would be obviated to a degree. Assuming a Unit consisted of sixty men, the withdrawal from their different areas for an operation would not draw the attention of the police as would the absence of sixty men from Dublin. The selection of men for Special Units would be made after an intensive three-week course in military skills and requirements. Weapon training would consist of: Bren, Thompson, Rifle, Grenade and Short Arms. A detailed training schedule should be drawn up and given to carefully selected Units in the twenty-six-county area. So that a Special Unit may be assembled at the earliest possible moment the programme should be on a staggered system. On completion of two weeks of the programme, Unit A would be joined by the pre-selected staff of the Special Unit who would take part in the final week of training during which they would select the men deemed most suitable for further specialist training. By the end of the three-week period with Unit A, Unit B would have reached the third week and would be joined by the Staff, and so on until the selection process was finished. It was concluded that due to the limited area of operation, vast array of police and military and hostility of population, classic guerrilla-type operations could not be successful in the six counties. 'We must learn from the Cypriots and engage in terror tactics only. We must therefore expect the Police to torture a captured Republican. The type of operation should be of an anti-personnel and sabotage nature. The basic unit will consist of not more than 4 men. Anyone breaking under Police interrogation could then only squeal on 3 men.' Suitable areas should have a number of such Units so one could be in action and the others on reserve, for instance four such Units in each Postal District in Belfast, thirty-two Units of four men in each, one man in charge of each District. Each District leader was to be responsible to the GHQ Agent in Belfast. Organisations would take the following form:

Six Counties—Secret Small Units.
26 Counties—Shock Units for special operations of a purely military character.

ASSASSINATIONS: Open Assassinations to be performed in situations such as Divis Street Riots [of 1966]. Informers also to be assassinated openly. Quiet assassinations for Police. Silencers, poison darts can be used with effect.

SPECTACULAR: To be used to secure Hostages in the event of execution of Republicans.

EASTER: If North creates another Divis Street, retaliatory action to be taken against selected R.U.C. men. Military action against the British should also be considered.

FULL-TIME MEN: Unknown men to be maintained in fighting areas to carry out squad type jobs.

This military plan still had to be approved by the Army Council. The delay was partly because elements of the leadership deemed it necessary for the people to be prepared for the coming conflict. Hence the significance of appointing men such as the academic Roy Johnston to the Department of Political Education, IRA Headquarters, early in 1965. He was a member of the Irish Workers' Party and had been associated with left-wing groups for the past sixteen years, including the Irish Workers' League, the World Union of Students, the Connolly Association (London), the Dublin University Fabian Society and the Socialist Youth Movement. He had also been active in the Anti-Apartheid Movement. The appointment of Johnston was a complete departure from former IRA policy not to have any association with communist or left-wing groups. The Department of Political Education was established by IRA Headquarters at the time of Johnston's appointment in early 1965. All Commands and Units were circularised by the Director of Political Education to the effect that a series of lectures, discussions and debates would be held in Dublin on 7 March 1965. The programme was given as follows:

11.00 a.m. Political Education—the need for it and plans.

11.20 a.m. Economic Resistance—a lecture by an expert.

12.30 p.m. The meeting will break into Discussion Groups. All those attending will have an opportunity of making their views on Economic Resistance known during these discussions.

1.00 p.m. Lunch.

2.00 p.m. The Co-Operative Movement—the part the Army can play in this— how to do it, etc. Lecture by one of the accepted leaders and live wires of this Movement.

3.30 p.m. Discussion Groups will discuss how this Movement can be organised in various areas.

4.00 p.m. Break for tea or drink.

4.45 p.m. Trade Unionism—a short talk on what part the Army can play in this sphere. This talk will serve as an introduction to a full-day series of lectures and discussions on Army attitude and plans in Trade Unionism, which will be held in the near future.

The circular stressed the fact that Political Education Officers and other Command and Unit Officers should attend the meeting, because they would learn the reasons for the existence of the Department and get an idea of the work which they would be expected to do. The meeting took place at the La Cabena Ballroom, Howth Summit, and was attended by at least twenty people. Subsequent to this conference, IRA Headquarters directed that an intensive course of lectures on Political Education be given in each Command Area. For this purpose, officers of the Political Education Department visited some Command Areas and held discussions on the Political Education programme with Command Area Political Education Officers. Literature was also distributed to all such Officers. In November 1965 a circular was sent by the Political Education Department of IRA Headquarters to Command OCs, certain members of the IRA, and other branches of the Republican Movement throughout the country inviting them to participate in an Educational Conference in Dublin on the weekend of 18–19 December. The first session was presided over by Thomas Gill whose subject was 'Social and Cultural Objectives'. Other speakers spoke on 'Housing and Urban Property', 'Social Problems in Rural Areas' as well as more traditional subjects such the language movement. The second session was presided over by Roy Johnston who was also the principal speaker. He spoke on the subject 'Industrial and Financial Objectives —in particular the impact of the proposed Free Trade Agreement' which had just been signed between Ireland and Britain. Others spoke on 'Moves Against Free Trade', 'Credit Unions as a Potential Independence Co-operative Financial System',

'Trade Unions and Industrial Co-operation' and 'How to Fight Industrial Closures'. In Johnston's address he advised all persons present to infiltrate into trade unions and other organisations where opposition could be organised against free trade. The third session dealt with:

1) Co-operation in Agriculture and Fisheries.
2) Co-operation as a Unifying 32-County Force.
3) Ireland's Fishing Rights.
4) Initial Problems in Agricultural Co-operative Formation.
5) Producers' Co-operatives and how they can Influence the Market.
6) Co-operation as a Social Force: Glencolumbkille.
7) Fishing Co-operatives and the State.

Since its inception the Political Education Department had spearheaded the organisation's agitational, economic, social and political policy through groups such as the Wolfe Tone Society, the Dublin Housing Action Group and Republican Clubs. The most important of these in terms of generating ideas was the Wolfe Tone Society which consisted mainly of graduates and professional people who were working towards the idea of a united, independent Ireland. It regarded itself as part of the traditional Republican Movement and was accepted by the latter; it was, however, not bound by tradition and was in the process of evolving a new approach to 'national problems'. This new approach consisted in the forging of links between the Movement and organisations such as the trade union movement in urban areas, and the co-operative movement in rural and urban areas. For example, the Adjutant General, IRA Headquarters, issued a directive in October 1965 to Command OCs to instruct all Volunteers and sympathisers of the organisation to get themselves involved in the National Farmers Association (NFA) campaign for the withholding of rates and to create as much agitation as possible. At a meeting of the Army Council held in October 1966 it was decided that every effort should be made to involve the IRA in the NFA agitation. As a result of this decision each Command OC was instructed by IRA Headquarters to do whatever possible at local level to enable members of the organisation to infiltrate the ranks of the NFA.[95]

Overall, the main effect of all this agitation on the Irish population was marginal and at the cost of alienating a lot of good old-fashioned IRA gunmen. But the Republican Movement did produce one idea that had an impact on the national question: the creation of a civil rights movement in Northern Ireland. The idea for a civil rights campaign originated from a conference of Wolfe Tone societies. The intellectual leaders of the societies were Johnston and another Dublin academic, Anthony Coughlan. Like many other Nationalists they believed that Unionism was built on discrimination and the artificial division of Protestant and Catholic workers, who would no longer oppose each other if the machinery of discrimination—the Northern Ireland state—was destroyed. According to this thesis, Unionism could not possibly survive 'when Protestant and Catholic are no longer at each other's throats'. Securing the utmost degree of civil liberties possible would put 'an end to the bitterness of social life and divisions among the people fostered by the Unionists' and permanently weaken the basis of Unionism. To achieve this the aim of a civil rights movement would be to 'Force O'Neill to CONCEDE MORE THAN HE WANTS TO OR THAN HE CAN DARE GIVE without risking overthrow by the more reactionary elements among the Unionists. Demand more than may be demanded by the comprising elements that exist among the Catholic leadership. Seek to associate as wide a section of the community as possible with these demands, in particular the well-intentioned people in the Protestant population and the trade union movement.'[96] The basic problem with this thesis was that it was sheer fantasy. Rather than exorcise the demons of sectarianism it would unleash them.

Chapter 4 ∿

THE GATHERING
STORM

CATHOLIC FRUSTRATION

The problems that O'Neill had encountered within his own Party were to
have a longer-term significance for both him and the Unionist Party. A key
element in the emergence of the Troubles was the continuing internal
dissension we encountered earlier within Northern Ireland's ruling political party.
For, alongside the personal animosities which would dog the Party, there was also
the fact that the Unionist Party was too broad a church: as the attempts to
preserve party unity became more and more desperate the incompatibility of the
strands of Unionism contained within that party produced constant tension
between the leadership on the one hand and prominent backbenchers and
elements of the grassroots on the other. But this was in the not-too-distant future.
An immediate problem for O'Neill and the Unionist Government he led was the
challenge set it by the proactive strategy of Catholic pressure groups and
Nationalist politicians. This raised the possibility of intervention in Northern
Ireland on the part of the United Kingdom Government—the ultimate authority
with regard to Northern Ireland. The O'Neill–Lemass summit had improved the
Prime Minister's standing among Catholics generally; indeed the growing
frustration with the lack of reform never quite undermined his relative popularity
with the minority. But it was politicians and groups representative of the minority
that, combined with the tensions within the Unionist Party, squeezed O'Neill
from both ends of the political spectrum. One of these was the Campaign for
Social Justice. The CSJ was launched in Belfast on 17 January 1964. It focused its
efforts at British political opinion. The CSJ grew out of the Dungannon-based
Homeless Citizens' League in May 1963, which had been led by two middle-class
Catholics, Conn and Patricia McCluskey; they also helped form the CSJ. Dungannon
was one of those councils to which Catholics pointed as a blatant example of
gerrymandering. In terms of population it was evenly balanced between Protestants
and Catholics; but control of the Council was in Unionist hands. The East Ward
was predominately Protestant and the West Ward predominately Catholic; the

Central Ward, with half the population of the other two wards, returned the same number of councillors but had a majority of Protestants. The result was that fourteen Unionists were returned against seven 'anti-Unionists' as the CSJ and others linked to them liked to call themselves—avoiding the equating of 'Nationalist' and 'Catholic' despite being what were, in reality, collections of mainly Nationalists and Catholics. Although its membership was confined to thirteen professional people, and despite its avowal that it was non-sectarian, the CSJ was entirely Catholic.

What was different about the CSJ was that it focused the bulk of its efforts on Westminster but avoided nationalistic rhetoric. It had faith in the intrinsic fair play of, if not the Conservative Government that had been in power since 1951, then at least in Harold Wilson's Labour Party that would soon come to power. Another factor was the hopelessness of waiting for any reform to come from Stormont. Patricia McCluskey explained how the demand for social justice shifted to Westminster because: 'We cannot, for example, remember, a time in their forty-odd years of rule when the Unionists conceded anything of consequence which the opposition in Stormont asked for. Thus we decided that all our resources should be given over to publicity outside Ireland.'[1] Efforts were also directed to Westminster because the CSJ identified—although 'stumbled upon' might be a better description—how the British Parliament, as the supreme authority in the United Kingdom, could intervene in Northern Ireland. This emerged from a correspondence with the Conservative Prime Minister, Sir Alec Douglas-Home. The Government of Ireland Act's Section 5, which outlawed religious discrimination in Northern Ireland, was clearly not working while every attempt to have the grievances of the minority discussed at Westminster was defeated by the existence of a convention which prevented discussion of matters which were within the competence of the Parliament of Northern Ireland.[2] This convention arose from the tradition that once a subordinate parliament had been established by Westminster—as was the case with early Dominion legislatures—matters devolved to it could no longer be raised in the supreme legislature in London. This all seemed perfectly acceptable as the British Empire evolved into the British Commonwealth of Nations and *de facto* independence was made a fact of political life by the Statute of Westminster in 1931. But to those in Britain who were concerned with the situation in Northern Ireland, the convention seemed a little odd when applied to a region of the United Kingdom in the 1960s when the British Empire had virtually ceased to exist. The key point was that although, by convention, the United Kingdom *Government* did not interfere in matters devolved to the Northern Ireland Parliament and therefore within the ambit of the Northern Ireland Government, ultimately the United Kingdom *Parliament* could intervene because that body was the sovereign power. This was expressed explicitly in Section 75 of the Government of Ireland Act 1920 which stated that the Westminster Parliament was supreme over all matters in Northern Ireland. In reality, given the intertwining of executive power with the need for a parliamentary majority this meant that all a British Government lacked for intervention was the will to intervene. The problem was that one of the key ideas behind devolution for Northern Ireland was to get Irish politics out of British politics given the paralysis that the Irish Question seemed, periodically, to exert over Westminster before partition. The problem for the CSJ was how to get over the hurdle of British reluctance to intervene in Ulster. The CSJ believed that British Government intervention was necessary because it considered that Section 5 of the 1920 Act, which provided against religious discrimination in enactments of the Northern Ireland *Parliament*, did not apply to religious discrimination in the exercise of executive powers granted to the Northern Ireland *Government*; did not appear to prevent discrimination in the exercise by others of powers or duties imposed by Acts of the Northern Ireland Parliament; and in particular did not give any redress against discriminatory acts by local authorities in the exercise of their duties. Therefore Section 5 was useless.[3]

But the realisation that under the terms of the Government of Ireland Act 1920 the Westminster Parliament retained supreme authority over Northern Ireland affairs spurred the CSJ on. A 'new situation has been created'.[4] The new focus of hope in 1964 was that Harold Wilson's incoming Labour Government would reverse decades of Westminster neglect. This optimism was spurred on, as Patricia McCluskey noted, in letters to the CSJ from the new Prime Minister who had been 'so sympathetic, and has given us such heart that it is impossible to assess the amount of good will already generated here towards the new Labour Government at Westminster'.[5] This, however, proved over-optimistic. Some hint of Wilson's reluctance to embroil the Labour Party in the mire of Ulster politics had been indicated in the run-up to the 1964 general election when he wrote to McCluskey to caution how, before steady progress could be made in solving Northern Ireland's problems, there had to be changes in the parliamentary representation of Northern Ireland, both at Westminster and at Stormont. Wilson, pointing out that the NILP was opposed to discrimination, suggested that this was the most immediate way of furthering the CSJ's cause, and called upon it to give active support to NILP candidates in the forthcoming general election of 1964.[6]

Furthermore, Wilson's first Home Secretary, Sir Frank Soskice, appeared to set the tone when he declined to apply the Race Relations Bill to Northern Ireland on the basis of the constitutional convention that the Parliament at Westminster did not legislate in respect of matters within the competence of the Northern Ireland Parliament except at the request and with the agreement of the Government of Northern Ireland. And in the case of this bill, that agreement was not forth-coming.[7] At Stormont, Brian McConnell, Minister of Home Affairs at the time, stated that the Unionist Government had asked for Northern Ireland's exclusion on the basis that there was no need for hypothetical legislation to deal with racial discrimination that did not exist in the Province. Nationalists, such as Austin

Currie, suggested that if the Minister studied the bill he would find that it was relevant to Northern Ireland with regard to slogans—anti-Catholic, anti-Christian and sometimes obscene—that decorated many of the region's walls and bridges.[8] McConnell disagreed.

But Wilsonian intervention of a sort was provoked not by events in Northern Ireland but by the behaviour of the Ulster Unionist MPs at Westminster. The UUP MPs were essentially Tories. Regardless of the fact that Unionism was a pan-class constitutional movement that, rather like different strains of Nationalism or Republicanism, could accommodate right and left leanings, the Unionist members in the Imperial Parliament were conservative by nature and Conservative by politics. They allied themselves with the Conservative and Unionist Party (as they had done since the Home Rule crisis) that now found itself in the unaccustomed position of opposition. The position taken by the Ulster MPs was of critical importance since the Labour Government had a majority of only four (and soon to be reduced to three). And nothing got up Wilson's nose more than the fact that the Ulster members could vote on matters affecting Great Britain but the convention prevented London sticking its nose into Northern Ireland. Consequently, in May 1965 there were heated exchanges in the Commons at Westminster when Wilson answered a question about the representation of Northern Ireland there. The Prime Minster stated in a reply that his Government had no plans with respect to altering the terms of Northern Ireland's representation at Westminster (to prevent Ulster members voting on British matters). He did, however, point out the anomalous situation in which Ulster MPs could vote on housing discrimination in London but English, Scottish and Welsh MPs could not express their views about housing conditions in Belfast.

But it was in response to a question from Captain Orr, the Unionist leader at Westminster, that Wilson vented his anger. He recognised that Ulster MPs had great duties to do at Westminster in the sense of foreign affairs, defence and matters affecting Northern Ireland. 'What was not so obvious in 1920,' said Wilson, 'was that those who came here to represent Northern Ireland interests should become just hack supporters of the English Tory Party.'[9] Instead of taking the hint, Orr saw in the exchanges a confirmation of how important it was that Northern Ireland should rely on her 'friends' in the Conservative Party. Stratton Mills, the MP for North Belfast, expressed his concern at seeing the support 'anti-Ulster' elements received on the Labour benches. 'There was row upon row spitting hatred,' he said. 'And I was also concerned to see that Mr George Brown [Secretary of State for Economic Affairs] and Mr James Callaghan [Chancellor of the Exchequer], sitting beside the Prime Minister, were apparently mouthing gibes at the Ulster Unionists sitting opposite.'[10] It didn't occur to them that this was mischief of their own making.

Antagonising Wilson was a dangerous game to play. It was well known that his constituency had a significant immigrant Irish population and, as his subsequent actions would show, his sympathies were more with the Catholic minority than with the Protestant majority. That, however, did not mean that he wanted to embroil his Government—committed to using the 'white heat of technology' to transform Britain—in the ancient and unfathomable hatreds of Ireland. As far as many in Westminster were concerned it was almost as if Northern Ireland were in a political quarantine. Ireland was the graveyard of many politicians and parties: for example it had split the Liberal Party under Gladstone, brought the country to the verge of civil war before the Great War, and the 'Troubles' of post-war/pre-independent Ireland were within the living memory of many of the politicians and civil servants in London. This was the basic problem the Nationalist Party and the CSJ had in highlighting Catholic grievances in Northern Ireland and attracting some interest from London.

What kept up its momentum was the election of Gerry Fitt to Westminster in the 1966 general election. The drawback was that the election also gave Wilson a majority of nearly 100 and so reduced the antagonism engendered by the Ulster Unionist MPs. But Fitt, through the sheer exuberance of his personality, kept Northern Ireland on the Westminster agenda. In particular, he acted as a lightning conductor for those Labour backbenchers concerned with the situation prevailing in Northern Ireland. Fitt organised several trips to Northern Ireland for sympathetic Labour MPs, notably on the occasion of the Londonderry riots of 5 October 1968. His socialism made him a natural supporter of the Labour Party in London. And Fitt, while discounting rumours that he might apply for the Labour Whip, emphasised that, as a socialist, he admired Wilson's Government and would support its social and progressive legislation. He maintained his stand on the twin pillars of national unity and social and economic justice for the common man in Ireland. Soon after his election Fitt was visited by Paul Rose, the Member for the Blackley division of Manchester, who was holidaying in Ireland at the time. Fitt boasted how he was 'on the friendliest terms with at least sixty members of the new Labour Government. They regard my victory in West Belfast as a signal breakthrough and feel I can now propagate the case they have been advocating.'[11]

Contacts between Rose and Fitt were significant for, however reluctant Wilson was to intervene in Northern Ireland's internal government, he could not escape from the mounting pressure for him to do something. This took shape in the formation of the Campaign for Democracy in Ulster (CDU) in June 1965. Rose was a key member. The CDU had its origins among a group of Irish exiles in Britain, created by rank and file members of the Labour Party, mainly of Irish extraction. Among its aims were to secure a full and impartial inquiry into the administration of government in Northern Ireland and into allegations of discrimination in the field of housing and employment. It also wanted to bring electoral law in Northern Ireland into line with that in the rest of the United Kingdom, and to examine electoral boundaries with a view to providing fair representation for all sections of the community. One of the methods that the

CDU thought might be used to eliminate discrimination was by extending the Race Relations Act to include Northern Ireland, albeit amended to include religious discrimination and incitement.[12] The aim of the CDU was to introduce reform in Northern Ireland, not to reopen the question of the partition of Ireland. Lord Brockway, the president, told its inaugural meeting at Westminster on 2 June 1965 that its aim was to secure social justice in Northern Ireland—the border question did not concern the campaign committee. About twenty-five Labour MPs attended the meeting. One of them was Paul Rose. He explained that it would be the function of MPs to act as sounding boards in obtaining and giving information about Northern Ireland on the floor of the House. He, like Brockway, wanted the Race Relations Bill extended to Northern Ireland: 'But we cannot legislate for Northern Ireland without the agreement at [sic] Stormont. Now is the time to break with this confinement.'[13] Patricia McCluskey also attended the meeting, which she told: 'So far we feel the Labour Government has done nothing to help us.' She begged the Government to act quickly, resolutely and comprehensively. For forty-five years they had been asking for equal rights while successive governments had repeatedly ignored them. But this was the first time that MPs had become really interested in the welfare of people who were only one hour's flying time away. She spoke of discrimination in housing, electoral laws, and the provision of industry.[14]

From the beginning the CDU was sponsored by over one hundred Labour MPs and peers in Westminster. Fitt, after his election, provided all the information— and eye-witness evidence in the Commons—that the CDU required. The CSJ were also impressed with Fitt's work at Westminster, Patricia McCluskey describing him to the National Council for Civil Liberties in London as 'fearless' and unlikely to run out of material for his speeches for a 'very long time'. She did 'not think that a very heavy hand will be necessary' to encourage reforms. The CSJ knew that there were thousands of Protestants who were heartily ashamed of much that was being done in their name. The CSJ was looking to the Labour Government to 'prod the Stormont Government into making reasonable changes'. But at this stage there was disappointment that the assurances given by Wilson in 1964 that a Labour Government would do everything in its power to see that infringements of justice would be 'effectively dealt with' had not been implemented. McCluskey asked that Wilson, who had used the word 'compassion' no less than three times in his last television address before the election, apply some of it to one of the few places under his control where this quality was needed more than most.[15]

Here it is perhaps apt to ask just what would have satisfied Catholics. In April 1966, Nationalists, meeting in Belfast, set out their stall. They called on O'Neill to take the necessary measures to introduce democratic procedures into all matters under the Unionist Government's control. If O'Neill really wanted to sink differences then the first step, said James O'Reilly, was in the electoral laws. This

would be followed by the abolition of discrimination in local government appointments and the introduction of competitive examinations, legislation for bringing
equal opportunities for all citizens and a substantial increase in voluntary school
grants—because the Nationalist people were being 'bled dry' trying to find thirty-
five per cent of the costs of the building and upkeep of Catholic schools while
there were 'Protestant schools for Protestant people'.[16] In May McAteer hinted that
the Nationalist Parliamentary Party would have to, at some time, review their
position as the official opposition. The Government remained reluctant to accept
any ideas that arose from outside the narrow limits of their own front bench.[17]
The problem with dealing with these grievances, however justified they might be,
was that no Unionist Prime Minister could possibly force these reforms through
the Unionist Party, at least not in the short-term (taken here to mean years). Only
external pressure might move the Northern Ireland Government. But Wilson
rejected Fitt's suggestion to set up a royal commission to investigate the workings
of the Government of Ireland Act in so far as it affected matters within the
responsibility of the British Government. The Prime Minister was unaware of any
issue in which an inquiry was needed. But Wilson acknowledged that many MPs
were disturbed about 'things that go on' in Northern Ireland; he was not taking
sides because there were allegations and counter-allegations from both camps.
Wilson believed that the right thing to do would be for the Home Secretary and
himself to have informal talks with the Prime Minister of Northern Ireland 'to see
if some of the difficulties all of us recognise exist may be overcome in an informal
way'. The immediate reaction of McAteer to this statement from Wilson was to
demand a place at any conference arranged. Wilson's comments obviously delighted
him as he declared: 'Now there will be light in the darkness' although he qualified
this with a warning against over-optimism: 'A centuries old disease is not likely to
be cured overnight. But now at least there is hope and we are grateful to Mr
Wilson for that.' As Joseph Connellan, MP for South Down, pointed out: 'This is
the first occasion that any expression of this kind has been made by a British
statesman of the standing of Mr Wilson.'[18]

Wilson had already had informal talks with O'Neill the year before and wanted
to continue this format in 1966. Roy Jenkins and O'Neill had a brief discussion on
7 June about the projected talks between the two prime ministers. O'Neill had
welcomed the proposed talks, but had nevertheless stressed the difficulties he
would face in Northern Ireland if he moved too far ahead of public opinion.
Specifically he warned that an attempt to advance too rapidly could even lead to
violence in Ulster. Jenkins passed this information on to his Prime Minister.[19]
Wilson eventually entertained O'Neill to lunch at No. 10 Downing Street on
Friday 5 August 1966. The main discussion was concerned with the political
situation in Northern Ireland and the effect this had on relations with the United
Kingdom Government. O'Neill explained that the latent politico-religious feelings
in Northern Ireland were still very strong, particularly among the 'poorer

members' of the community. His Government had made considerable progress towards greater internal tolerance and better relations with the Irish Republic during the past three years but this progress itself, plus the passionate celebrations of the fiftieth anniversary of the Easter Rebellion, had led to a 'backlash' of ultra-Protestant feeling. The main manifestation of this was the movement which had grown up about Paisley. Matters had now reached a dangerous point and he thought no other course was now open to him but to call a halt to progress for a period of six months or so. Any early movement towards reconciliation either internally or with the Republic would endanger him politically and could lead to his replacement by a more intransigent figure, or event to a return to a '1912' situation. The Paisley movement and the events which had led to it had 'blown him off course' and he could only get back on course after leaving time for passions to cool.

Wilson and Jenkins expressed understanding of the position in which O'Neill found himself but nevertheless explored various lines along which further progress might be achieved. Ideas canvassed included an inquiry into the operation of the franchise for Northern Ireland seats at Westminster (on which O'Neill said that there were faults on both sides which probably balanced out in the event); a revision of the franchise for Stormont and in local elections (O'Neill said this was a highly explosive issue which, moreover, probably had little or no impact on the allocation of seats in these bodies. Indeed the end product might worsen the situation by, for example, removing the two liberals who sat for University seats in Stormont and increasing rather than diminishing Protestant representation in and around Belfast); and the introduction of an ombudsman for Northern Ireland (which O'Neill said would inflame rather than quieten the situation without producing any impact on the basic attitudes which were at the root of the problem). Wilson undertook to do his best to restrain those numerous members of the House of Commons who felt that action should be taken to end discrimination in Northern Ireland. He emphasised, however, that while he might succeed in doing this for a time he could not, nor would he seek to, restrain these members throughout the whole of the present Parliament. Progress must be made if the position was to be held. O'Neill ended by regretting that it had not been possible for Her Majesty the Queen to make some suitable remarks during her recent visit to Northern Ireland approving the progress which had been made in recent years: the Queen had a very special place in the lives of Ulster Protestants and an open expression of her support for religious tolerance and for non-discrimination could have a major impact. Wilson and O'Neill agreed to meet again later in the year to continue their discussions.[20]

The two prime ministers met again on 12 January 1967. Wilson, accompanied by the Home Secretary and the Minister of State at the Home Office, Alice Bacon, entertained O'Neill, Faulkner and Craig to lunch at Downing Street. O'Neill was in a position to offer some minor reforms as evidence of his continuing commitment to progressive policies. Opening the discussion Wilson emphasised that the Northern

Ireland political situation continued to arouse strong feelings on the Government benches at Westminster and he and his colleagues had faced, and would continue to face, much questioning and probing on this issue. It must be recognised that the many new members of the Government back benches were of an irreverent turn of mind and it would no longer suffice to say that the present arrangements were the result of an agreement reached forty years before. He knew that the minds of some of these members were turning towards the possibility of action in the fields where the United Kingdom Parliament did have an effective voice in Northern Ireland, particularly in the matter of the provision of funds to the Northern Ireland Government. In the circumstances there must be movement and, while he had been most encouraged by reforms of the Stormont franchise—abolishing university seats for example—just heralded by the Queen's Speech in Northern Ireland, it must be accepted realistically that the removal of causes of complaint in one field would merely concentrate greater attention on others—in particular on the conduct of local government affairs in Northern Ireland.

In response O'Neill and his colleagues pointed out the reforms of the Stormont franchise had yet to be carried on the floor of the Northern Ireland House of Commons. They did not, therefore, represent a base from which further advance could be immediately undertaken but were a stage of development which had yet to be completed. Other steps were, however, in prospect. The abolition of the university seats in the Northern Ireland Parliament would mean a re-drawing of boundaries in Belfast. They proposed to ask the British Parliament Boundary Commission to undertake this task on behalf of Stormont so as to ensure the independent nature of the re-distribution. Thereafter they proposed to set up an independent boundary commission to look at all Stormont boundaries. As for local government in Northern Ireland it had three distinguishing features. There were many very small local authorities; their powers were much more limited than similar authorities in Britain because, inevitably, Stormont fulfilled many of the functions which would be undertaken by a major local authority in Britain; and the franchise for local authority elections rested, as it had in Great Britain before 1947, on a property qualification. The restricted franchise was a source of criticism but could be defended on the grounds that services provided by the local authorities were closely related to property. The situation was of course changing somewhat as local authorities moved further into the welfare and social fields but the issue was not in their opinion one of great importance. The truth was that allegations of discrimination really arose from the small size of local government units which gave rise to a situation where family ties or personal connections could be, or might be thought to be, of significance in the running of local affairs. They claimed that if discrimination occurred it arose mainly from the effects of life in small communities rather than from political or religious motives as such.

The Northern Ireland Government had it in mind to greatly reduce the number of local authorities in Northern Ireland—perhaps to nine or twelve from the present seventy-four—and were working on a 'statement of aims' for local government which would set out their guidelines in this field. The production of this statement and the subsequent re-organisation of local government would, they thought, go a long way to 'de-personalise' local government and thereby remove many of the suspicions which were the basis of present dissatisfaction. As an interim measure they had already introduced legislation which would enable local authorities to amalgamate by consent and a voluntary amalgamation of this kind had already taken place in County Fermanagh. They would be studying the outcome with interest. Following this discussion Wilson explained that, as he saw it, the pressures for reform could not be resisted within the framework of the present arrangements between Great Britain and Northern Ireland—nor indeed would he think that they should be resisted. His assessment was that within a period of about three years one of two things must happen. Either (1) the Westminster Parliament would insist on interfering more and more with the internal affairs of Northern Ireland with the inevitable erosion of the 'division of powers' which formed the basis of the present arrangements, or (2) an agreement would be reached whereby the British Parliament and Government would refrain from interfering at all in Northern Ireland affairs provided that Northern Irish members of the Westminster Parliament observed the same discretion in voting on matters appertaining to Britain. Under such an arrangement members of all parts of the United Kingdom would of course be able to vote on those matters of common concern such as defence and foreign policy.[21] The inference, though, was that it was the former that was more likely. Yet O'Neill could be satisfied that his package of reforms had bought him more time. Wilson accepted his warning of the consequences of pushing him too far too fast. Wilson was prepared to give O'Neill more time—up to three years—to see movement on the local government franchise. Although he did not know it O'Neill had less than two.

But at this stage it was still possible to remain optimistic. At the beginning of 1967 McAteer remained adopting an optimistic and conciliatory tone towards O'Neill and the Unionist Government. If the 'Derry problem' could be settled it would mean that a long-standing stain on the whole of the North would have been removed: 'If there was true democracy well established in Derry it would be an inspiration to men of good will on both sides.'[22] But if he and other Catholics were hoping that some white smoke might emerge from either Stormont or London they were to be disappointed. The CSJ felt let down by the recent Queen's Speech at Westminster because, said Patricia McCluskey, 'we were entitled to expect that Mr Wilson's promises would have been reflected in it.'[23] There was no word of Northern Ireland in it. She was now doubtful, however, that—even with the maximum pressure from Wilson—the Northern Ireland Government would accede to all the demands that had been made for administrative reform in the North. If any change for the better were to come about it would mean that the Government of Ireland Act would have to be changed.[24]

So the campaign went on: during a discussion between Fitt and a number of Labour backbenchers, it was suggested that a delegation from Westminster should visit the North. The backbenchers were confident that Wilson would force the Stormont Government into changes; as Fitt put it: 'After all he cannot talk about the absence of democracy in Rhodesia and at the same time ignore an even worse state of affairs on his own doorstep.'[25] By early spring it seemed that the pressure on London to force reform was becoming a little listless. Then opposition politicians in the North were handed an issue with which to batter the Unionist Government and engage British sensibilities. On 7 March Craig, as Minister of Home Affairs, announced a complete ban on all Easter processions specifically linked to the forthcoming centenary of the Fenian Rising of 1867. He had made an Order under the Public Order Act of 1951 prohibiting for a month the holding of all public processions and meetings other than those for which the organisers obtained specific permission from the RUC. Craig explained that he did not want to interfere with the 'customary practice' of Easter celebrations—which meant the parade to Milltown Cemetery commemorating the Easter Rising or the Junior Orangemen's parades. But proposals to commemorate the Fenian Rising were 'blatantly provocative and likely to endanger the peace'. Just as controversially he also announced an Order under the Special Powers Act proscribing Republican Clubs—of which there were about forty—a substantial proportion of whose members were associated with the IRA and Sinn Féin.[26]

Craig explained that his chief concern was the preservation of peace. He added that he did not think there was another community in the world where minorities took every opportunity to celebrate rebellions. He hoped 'this sort of thing' would not be repeated because he presumed that if people wanted they could find all sorts of events to celebrate every month of the year and every day of the month. He had decided to ban the parades before he had become aware of any planned counter-demonstrations (by Paisley). Explaining his ban on the Republican Clubs, Craig said that he was satisfied that these were really illegal Sinn Féin clubs under another name. While it was true that Sinn Féin was a political party it was also true that 'it was more than that'. It was an organisation pledged to sustain a movement of violence in support of the IRA. If it was right, as Nationalists believed, to take the gun out of politics, was it not right to condemn and remove an organisation that was being used as a recruiting ground for Sinn Féin and the IRA?[27] He pointed out that the Republican Clubs had been established after the Sinn Féin annual meeting in 1964 for the sole purpose of circumventing the ban on Sinn Féin. Craig was satisfied 'beyond all doubt' that almost half the members of the Clubs were members of the IRA. He hoped that the IRA would never again reach the stage where it would be considered a threat but 'it was still there'.[28] Craig had received a report from the RUC on the Clubs (for some reason also informing the Commons that 'at the time I had mumps') and concluded that the history of IRA activity over the last few years made James Bond look like an anaemic thriller.[29]

Predictably this was not welcomed by the opposition. The ban provided a rallying call. Currie believed that this showed that the 'real ruler in Northern Ireland was the Rev. Ian Paisley'. He warned that the ban was a threat to free association that should be stopped, otherwise what had happened to Republicans could happen to his Nationalist Party as well. It was a damnable state when a minister, on a 'whim' and without giving solid reasons, could ban these 'legitimate' organisations. The Special Powers Act was capable of being used to change democracy into dictatorship. Fitt commented that Craig would have to ban the Fourth of July celebrations in the American Consul's office in Belfast because that country had thrown off the yoke of British imperialism. The Minister was throwing down the gauntlet to the nationally-minded people of the North, for his actions were a complete surrender to an extremist organisation which even the British Prime Minister had described as quasi-Fascist[30] (again a reference to Paisley).

The Northern Directory of the Republican Clubs announced that it would hold a meeting in Belfast to defy the unjust ban.[31] The RUC detained four men after the meeting on 19 March,[32] while others were later arrested in Armagh and Tyrone. Fitt promptly put down a series of questions at Westminster.[33] Eighty-two Labour MPs signed the motion tabled by Fitt regretting the convention preventing members questioning the Home Secretary on the Republican Clubs.[34] At Queen's University more than sixty students decided to form a Republican Club in defiance of the Government.[35] For Nationalists, Craig was rapidly becoming the bogeyman of the Unionist Government. It has to be said that the Minister continued to display an alarming capacity—perhaps somewhat refreshing in a politician but not always the most constructive contribution in Northern Ireland—to actually say what he thought rather than to let some time elapse between the two processes. For example, at the same time as the banning controversy Craig managed to send the House of Commons into uproar when he alleged that MPs had tried to 'blackmail me into a course of action, based on friendship rather than on the merits of the case . . . You are all guilty of it on the basis of the old pals act.' Opposition benches were outraged although Austin Currie, grinning, called out: 'You are in trouble again, boy.'[36] Craig later withdrew the remarks unreservedly.[37] Perhaps the mumps had taken more out of him than he had first realised.

Having said that, a reasonable case could be made for Craig's actions with regard to the Republican Clubs. The Clubs were a cover for Sinn Féin, a proscribed organisation that was the political wing of the IRA. From information exchanged between the RUC and the Gardaí, Craig would have been well aware of some of the proposals being made by the Republican Movement for combining military operations with greater subversive activities in politics. And Craig had to bear in mind how the 1916 commemoration the year before had led to a dangerous deterioration in community relations, leading to Protestant extremists taking up arms. At the same time the banning orders had given anti-Unionists another—and contemporary as opposed to old—grievance with which to attack the Unionist Government. There is no reason to doubt the opposition was genuine in their outrage at what they perceived as another example of a Unionist abuse of power. But this fails to understand Unionist perceptions: for them the IRA-Sinn Féin-Republican Clubs were subversive terrorists who wished to overthrow the state by fair means or foul (sometimes the latter). The entire Unionist experience of the Republican Movement had not, exactly, been a positive one. In 1967 it was only five years since the Border Campaign had ended. For Unionists the IRA's greater involvement in politics was merely old wine in a new bottle with the old bottle ready to break over the Unionist head just in case no one bought the new bottle. Yet for Catholics who opposed violence the IRA weren't faceless enemies, rather misguided members of the Nationalist family. They were neighbours, relatives (Eddie McAteer's brother Hugh was a former IRA Chief of Staff) and friends who, faced with discrimination and the immoral (from their perspective) mutilation of the country, had taken the ill-judged route of armed struggle. But they weren't irredeemable.

The controversy helped spark a marked increase in anti-Unionist activity in Northern Ireland. Some of this was generated internally, some externally. The NILP conference instructed its Executive Committee to 'take all possible steps to publicise the Northern Ireland situation and the necessity for such an inquiry in Britain and especially in the British Labour Movement'. Conference was also instructed to support and closely co-operate with the CDU. The Nationalist Party and Fitt were delighted by the decision.[38] The National Council for Civil Liberties (NCCL) called for a royal commission 'or some other tribunal of enquiry' to investigate the working of the Government of Ireland Act, the repeal of the Special Powers Act, and the restoration of democratic principles to the electoral system in Northern Ireland. The NCCL took the view that Stormont was denying free speech in the face of extremist threats: the ban on Republican Clubs was 'even more serious' than 'other' allegations.[39] On 7 April the British Society of Labour Lawyers announced that it was to conduct an inquiry into affairs in Northern Ireland. The five-man team, consisting of Samuel Silkin MP, Peter Archer MP, Ivor Richard MP, Lord Gifford and Cedric Thornberry (a London School of Economics lecturer), invited a number of political organisations in the North to submit written evidence to it. As the Society's committee of investigation was a private venture and its results could not be placed before the Westminster Parliament, some, such as Eddie McAteer, were less than enthused by the project; he thought it would be simpler for 'Mr O'Neill to perform an act of real statesmanship and invite representatives of the minority to sit around a table and hammer out a solution to our problems. We know them better than any visitor, however well intentioned.'[40]

Despite McAteer's misgivings the Labour Lawyers' intervention can be seen as yet another part of a growing momentum for Westminster to intervene in Ulster. Fitt organised a two-day fact-finding mission for three British Labour MPs to the

Province. Paul Rose, now Chairman of the CDU, Stanley Orme, MP for South Salford and Dr Maurice Miller, MP for Kelvin Grove, Glasgow addressed meetings in Coalisland, Dungannon and Strabane before going to Derry over the weekend of 15–16 April. In for the Derry leg of the visit was John Hume, a teacher and rising star in the politics of Derry, who took charge of the arrangements. The group went to the city walls where they were shown the political boundaries by McAteer. Dr Miller, observing that he and his wife had recently visited India, concluded that 'With all its problems and difficulties there is more democratic right in India than in Northern Ireland.' Rose, recalling his visit to Dungannon, 'saw segregated housing estates which would have done credit to South Africa'. Noting that Unionist MPs were worried by the visit, Rose warned: 'They have every reason to worry, for we are going turn the spotlight on Northern Ireland and its affairs at Westminster.' John Taylor dismissed 'the Labour members' participation in an anti-Partitionist rally in Coalisland, with bands etc, [which] shows clearly that they are biased'.[41] The visitors decided upon their return to the mainland that they would send an account of their visit to Wilson and Roy Jenkins.[42] The 1000-word report was delivered on 25 April.[43]

Just as, if not more, annoying for the Unionist Government was the decision of a Conservative bastion, *The Times*, to investigate allegations of discrimination in Northern Ireland. In a 2,500-word article headlined 'Ulster's Second-class Citizens' *The Times* found that there was 'overwhelming evidence' that the electoral system in some local elections was deliberately weighted against the Catholic minority; that segregation, amounting to discrimination, was widely prevalent in the allocation of council housing by local authorities, although not by the Housing Trust; and that Catholics were discriminated against either deliberately or, more often, by the prevailing system in many senior government appointments and many private firms. The newspaper's investigative team had toured Northern Ireland, visiting Derry, Strabane and Dungannon, interviewed Government and local authority officials and checked out specific instances of discrimination.[44] O'Neill, who was in Leeds for the opening of a promotional 'Ulster Week', was forced to respond. He found the report 'facile'[45] and felt that the findings seemed to be a mere repetition of the 'so-called Campaign for Social Justice in Northern Ireland' whose publications were 'highly tendentious and often inaccurate'. Captain Orr was 'astonished' that *The Times* should have departed from 'its usual high standard of impartial and balanced reporting' while J. O. Ballie, Secretary of the UUC, claimed that 'these allegations are part of an attempt to force Northern Ireland into an Irish Republic' although 'this aspect is conveniently left alone when allegations are recklessly thrown about'.[46] McAteer, who was delighted at the report, called on O'Neill to admit that discrimination existed in Northern Ireland and take immediate steps to remedy the situation. If he did so, McAteer suggested, the Prime Minister would gain in stature and would give an immense fillip in removing this cause of criticism.[47]

Back at Westminster, Wilson entered the fray, confessing that there had been 'widespread concern' about certain acts which had happened in Northern Ireland, and, 'without departing from convention', he thought it right to embark upon more talks with O'Neill. He rejected a royal commission as inappropriate but noted that some of his honourable friends—the Labour MPs who had just returned from Northern Ireland—had recently set up their own commission and he hoped their findings would be made available. While paying tribute to the advances made in O'Neill's premiership, Wilson said it was a fact that there was acute concern about many questions affecting the functioning of democracy in Northern Ireland. Yet he thought that progress would be made not by talking about sweeping changes but in the sort of progress they hoped to make in his discussions with O'Neill. There was 'still a long way to go'.[48] Ulster Unionists reacted with increasing anger to these intrusions. Rafton Pounder, the Westminster MP for South Belfast, warned that the ultimate objective of the 'anti-Ulster' wing of the Labour Party was to achieve a climate in which partition could be abolished. 'This is their goal,' he declared. 'Anyone who believes it to be otherwise is deceiving himself. There are some who feel that the enemies of Ulster in the Labour Party are amenable to reasoned argument. This is not so.' Once the convention prohibiting discussion of Ulster affairs at Westminster was breached then it was only a short step before the powers of Stormont were similarly assailed. He warned that the tenacity and determination of the Ulster loyalist was best seen in times of adversity.[49] A blunter warning that the Unionist Party would resist to the full any attempt at Westminster to interfere with or limit the rights of the Northern Ireland Parliament was issued by Craig. He hit out at speculation that Treasury finance might be applied as political pressure to Northern Ireland because unless some British Government was prepared to act illegally and unjustly 'this is also so much rubbish'. He dismissed ideas that Section 75 of the Government of Ireland Act 1920 was a section subtracting from or entitling any interference with the Parliament or Government of Northern Ireland; instead he declared: 'Let me sound a note of warning: That Ulster will fight and Ulster will be right, and that this sort of attack and interference would mobilise Ulster loyalists in the same way as attacks by bomb and bullet.' Any suggestion to override a democratically elected Parliament in the name of democracy 'is the absurdity of absurdities'. Ulster's constitution was settled and sacrosanct, inviolate and unalterable without the consent of the Northern Ireland Parliament. While 'in theory' any Act of the UK Parliament could be amended or repealed in practice 'a code of democracy—a code of constitutional propriety' imposed limits. The Northern Ireland Parliament was a sovereign body except where its powers were limited.[50]

Given the evident concern in Unionist circles, O'Neill was stung into a robust defence of the status quo in Northern Ireland. In the course of a speech to the UUC the Prime Minister singled out Paul Rose for particular criticism. O'Neill defended the local government franchise arguing that, by and large, local government had only one independent source of tax revenue—the rates. And, just as the large institutional shareholder in a major public company had greater voting power than the individual holder of a few shares 'it is reasonable that the larger ratepayer, upon whom a major part of the local government burden fall, should have some weight in the voting system'. In any case, local government in Northern Ireland, as elsewhere, was in the melting pot. Its functions, structure and finance were all under examination. On the question of appointments to legal and civil service positions the Prime Minister declared that he did not know, nor did he propose to inquire, the religious affiliations of persons holding such appointments. People were chosen according to their fitness to perform the duties of an office and for no other reason. Civil Service appointments were the same in Northern Ireland as those for the British Civil Service. Most of the people who now held senior rank came in as new entrants before the War. During that period it was 'unfortunate' that the Catholic community adopted an attitude to 'our institutions ranging from aloofness to outright hostility'. O'Neill believed that things had changed since then 'and I hope I have played my part in making such a change possible, but one cannot abolish overnight the legacy of earlier detachment and mistrust'. The Prime Minister denied that Catholics were discriminated against in the legal profession, that the Government deprived areas west of the Bann of regional development or that it had put pressure on Sir John Lockwood to avoid recommending Derry for the site of the new university. He also defended the Orange Order, of which he was a member himself, whose basic purpose was the protection of civil and religious liberty: 'The Order is a religious and social brotherhood with much less of a political slant than (say) the trade unions to which some members of the United Kingdom Government belong. In any case, I would like to make it perfectly clear that I do not allow myself to be influenced in the performance of my official duties by any outside affiliation.' Then, referring to the Government's ban on the Fenian centenary celebrations, O'Neill argued that:

> The provocative glorification of this half a century after the events, was abhorrent to a great many people who are not extremists, except in the sense of being extremely loyal to Mr Rose's country and mine. Nevertheless, these demonstrations were allowed to proceed almost wholly without interference. But it really was asking too much of the patience of our people to expect them to stomach a repetition of these demonstrations for a second year, this time under the pretext of commemorating the abortive and insignificant Fenian Rising of 1867.
>
> So many attempts have been made to overthrow British rule in Ireland that it would probably be possible to find some excuse for celebrating a separate incident or movement each year. Such celebrations are not organised by responsible and moderate Nationalist elements; they are merely a device used by extreme Republicans to create trouble which they can then exploit. These are the men who refuse to renounce the gun as a legitimate weapon in Irish politics.

The primary duty of any government, explained O'Neill, was to preserve peace and public order: this they would continue to do.[51] Rose, replying in this instance to a follow-up attack by the Prime Minister, dismissed claims that he had an anti-partitionist agenda. He had always argued that his main priority was with social justice, not the border. He accused O'Neill of 'mud-slinging' which was unworthy of his office. He denied that he ever appeared on 'anti-partition' platforms: the future of Ireland was for the Irish to decide, not him. 'All I have demanded,' he explained, 'is the same rights and privileges for the citizens of Derry as exist in Doncaster, for the citizens of Strabane as for the citizens of Salford. If people share this aim, then whether they are Labour, Unionist, Nationalist or Republican Labour, I will share the platform with them for our common humanitarian aim.' He was particularly disappointed with some of O'Neill's comments because he believed that the Prime Minister 'would like to take Northern Ireland into the 20th century and rid it of the medieval bigotry and mutual hatred which is its curse'. Rose could only conclude that the more intelligent and liberal Unionists were imprisoned by their extremist supporters on whom they relied for votes. O'Neill's attempts to brand the CDU as agents of Dublin was a libel Rose utterly rejected. Partition was not even an issue. Rose warned that it was O'Neill, by his refusal to adopt Westminster's standards, 'who feeds the flame of Republicanism. It is we who wish to see a reconciliation between Dublin, Belfast and Westminster which could gradually overcome animosities of the past and allow Englishmen and Irishmen of all denominations to work in closer harmony for the benefit of all who live in these two islands. The Irish people will in time decide their own development for themselves.'[52]

O'Neill's actions at this juncture can be seen as an attempt to bolster his position and reassure the faithful. He was trying to steady nerves because he took the fairly radical view for a Unionist leader that Northern Ireland no longer faced any constitutional threat, at least not in the traditional sense; for he warned that Ulster must retain the sympathy and support of as large an element as possible of the British people: 'We are British or we are nothing,' he declared. He felt it was his duty to bring home to the people of Ulster what was at risk in any weakening of ties with Britain: 'People tend not to appreciate what they have until they have lost it. A man can gamble away his father's inheritance in the hope of great gain only to realise at the end of the day how fortunate he was before he ever started on his ill-advised activities. The whole basis of our standard of living, the whole structure of our Welfare State, the whole impetus of our economic development depend upon our place in the United Kingdom.' Yet it also went without saying that 'our beliefs mean so much to us that we would be prepared to give up some degree of material prosperity to preserve them'. But Ulster alone would be Ulster weak, friendless and threatened—Ulster, for the first time, in danger of falling into the lap of the Irish Republic: 'What we must do is to argue patiently, reasonably and with judgment for what we believe to be right. We cannot go around saying that a Westminster MP has no right to come here. If, however, he behaves foolishly and speaks biased nonsense, we must point this out to him and to others in no uncertain terms. We cannot go around saying that Westminster does not have supreme legislative authority in Northern Ireland because quite patently it does. But we should continue to argue that soundly-based conventions of non-interference in the work of a responsible Government and Parliament should not be lightly set aside.' The Prime Minister emphasised that Northern Ireland retained its position in the United Kingdom by the will of the people of Ulster *and* the people of Britain, and in the long run, the will of the people of Ulster must come to rest upon the support of all sections of their community. Their constitutional status was too important to be allowed to rest upon the imponderable factors of birth-rates and emigration figures. If they believed that Ulster was British they would have to be certain that their children, like themselves, would continue to enjoy the 'fantastic' benefits of the British connection. And every day it was borne in upon O'Neill, more and more, that people from a tradition long opposed to his were now starting to question some of the traditions in which they were reared and were trying to play a more responsible role in the state in which they lived.[53]

But while O'Neill emphasised the constitutional security which underpinned Northern Ireland's position within the UK, Faulkner contradicted him. Like his Prime Minister, Faulkner believed that the 'traditional allegiance' of the Catholic community in the North to Nationalism was weakening: 'Eventually the day may come when the vast majority of the people of Northern Ireland will work for the good of the Province within the framework of the Constitution. I believe this will be a source of great strength to us all.' The participation of the Catholic community in the affairs of the North ought to be encouraged and welcomed. But, emphasised Faulkner, this was change, not transformation, evolution not revolution. This represented a slow growth, assimilating two strong religious faiths, two historic traditions, two political loyalties. To be strong and enduring this interrogation had to be built upon mutual respect and tolerance and the self-interest in personal prosperity which was common to all. Faulkner denied that the Unionist Party was surrendering any of its principles in promoting such progress. It was at this point that Faulkner departed from O'Neill and joined Craig. Vital to all this was the constitutional position of Ulster within the United Kingdom: 'It is nonsense to suggest this is no longer threatened. To do so is a disservice to all sections of the population, for co-operation and trust must be built upon realities. It is also a disservice to the Unionist Party because it confirms the fears of those who maintain that the Party and the Northern Ireland Government are blind to the political facts of life.' The Government of the Irish Republic, and all the parties there, made no secret of their determination to work for a United Ireland. While each year that passed made their claims more unreal 'we have a long way to go before we can enjoy security of tenure'. Faulkner believed that, on the whole, the

'Protestant Unionists' of Northern Ireland—by which he meant the Unionist community generally—looked on the aspirations and loyalties of their fellow Irishmen in the Republic with a tolerance that was not reciprocated. Just as important as his difference with O'Neill over the security of the constitution was Faulkner's interpretation of British policy. Where the Prime Minister had warned that the Union depended on the goodwill of Britain as much as the desire of Ulster to remain within it, Faulkner believed that Northern Ireland had much more room for manoeuvre. The Government of Northern Ireland, he pointed out, was created in 1920 to solve the Irish problem that had bedevilled British politics for generations. Faulkner did not accept, 'for one moment', the suggestion that the British Government would be moved by its Labour supporters, activated by the surfeit of adverse publicity from which Northern Ireland had been suffering, to 'put the clock back'. Nor was he aware of any hint from Whitehall that Northern Ireland might be subjected to economic pressures 'to act in any way contrary to our own convictions'.[54]

In the longer run it was O'Neill, not Faulkner nor Craig, who was to be proved correct. But in 1967 it was easy to take the latter view; the Labour Government was not exactly rushing towards involvement in Northern Ireland. Yet it was also clear that Northern Ireland remained on the political agenda in Britain. When McAteer visited London to meet Roy Jenkins and the new Liberal leader, Jeremy Thorpe,[55] he could not but contrast the interest shown by the latter compared to previous visits to Liberal leaders. The Liberal Party, at its conference in Blackpool, saw its delegates pass a four-part resolution calling for electoral reform, the introduction of the single transferable vote, the repeal of the Special Powers Acts and the passing of a human rights bill in Northern Ireland.[56] Soon afterwards the anti-Unionist opposition had more material to send to interested parties in Britain following a police raid on a Gaelic cultural club, the Sean McGaughey Club in Oldpark, Belfast which brought protests from the indignant parents of children attending an 'Irish language class'.[57] Fitt promised to report the incident to the Labour Lawyers' inquiry and addressed a strongly-worded letter to the Home Secretary. The incident, said Fitt, recalled the 'bad old days of police raids on Catholic homes in the city' and would again create the feeling of tension which prevailed in the past. It was 'monstrous' behaviour and the explanation that the hall was being used as a lottery 'ludicrous'.[58] But Craig countered that the young women were drawn up in military formation and responding to military commands. Among the women known to the police were members of Cumann na mBan, the women's branch of the IRA. The lottery funds were suspected of going to an illegal organisation. The hall was adorned with a Tricolour four feet by two feet pinned to a wall. Below the flag were a number of photographs of deceased Republicans who had lost their lives in the cause of the IRA. There were no text books, no instructor nor any teaching material.[59] The problem for Unionists was that, to the outside world, it appeared like another abuse of minority rights. Unionists would become increasingly exasperated by what they regarded as wishy-washy liberal values in Britain which failed to understand the real nature of the subversive threat in Northern Ireland, which Unionists believed they had learned through bitter experience.

This was confirmed when Jeremy Thorpe visited Northern Ireland in the same month. He made a scathing attack on the Unionist Government to the Queen's University Liberal Association: 'In many ways Northern Ireland is to the United Kingdom what the Southern Sates are to the USA. It is not as bad as Mississippi, but it is not much better than Georgia.' He paid tribute to Fitt who had 'contributed his own brand of fireworks' at Westminster and attacked the Conservatives for failing to show some sign of concern for the position in Northern Ireland.[60] The Unionist Party replied to the attack in the form of a resolution passed by officers of the fifteen Unionist Associations in Belfast. It stated:

1   One of the principal reasons why the Liberals are today merely the rump of a once-great party is their record of injudicious intervention in Irish affairs.
2   When comparisons between Ulster and the Southern States may please those who are amused by a facile type of political propaganda, they are totally inapposite for many reasons.
3   There has never been a time in which any citizen of Northern Ireland has known anything but equality before the law and equality in the eyes of the state.
4   From the outset, guarantees of such equality have been written into the constitution of Northern Ireland—the 1920 Act.
5   In Northern Ireland any lack of integration of the community cannot be held at the majority's door.
6   Not since the [American] Civil War had there been in America any organised attempt to subvert the Constitution whereas such attempts have repeatedly been made in Northern Ireland up to quite recent times.
7   Northern Ireland is one part of the United Kingdom in which the problem of race relations as experienced in Great Britain is non-existent.[61]

Currie described some of the Unionist arguments as 'utter rubbish' while McAteer commented that it was possible now to see the three faces of Unionism. In the first instance the Unionists had flatly denied the existence of any problem such as gerrymandering or discrimination. Secondly, they admitted that discrimination did exist but that it was practised by both sides. And finally, they were now putting forward the argument that it was all the sole fault of the minority. McAteer pronounced himself fearful of this 'Hitler-like' thinking on the part of the Unionist Party.[62] He wrote to Roy Jenkins asking him to chair joint talks between himself and O'Neill to see if there was any common ground between them.[63] Unionists were clearly on the back foot but the deliveries were still playable because, crucially, this still did not translate itself into overt action by the one actor which mattered most: the Labour Government. Patricia McCluskey found Wilson's inertia perplexing given the mood of Labour's rank and file. She had received letters from many Labour people in Britain asking why progress had been so slow in even approaching the point where Westminster could be seen to be exerting tangible pressure for reform on Stormont. Rank-and-file party members felt that in the past they had been deprived of an opportunity to show their sympathy with the fight for social justice in Northern Ireland because of the absence of a resolution at the conference: McCluskey asked 'perhaps 1967 will see this trend reversed?'[64] It didn't: at the Labour Party conference in Scarborough, a motion on discrimination in Northern Ireland, to have been proposed by Croydon Constituency Labour Party, did not go before the delegates on account of time; it was, instead, passed onto the National Executive Committee.[65] Although this put it on the back burner, Roy Jenkins, replying in a parliamentary debate on Northern Ireland, continued to emphasise the 'concern' that both he and the Prime Minister shared with regard to the Province.[66]

In retrospect the failure of the Labour Government to intervene directly in Northern Ireland and force through reforms appears a strategic error. But is this fair? Why did it not do so? In theory the Secretary of State for the Home Department was responsible for Northern Ireland. In reality, however, the staff at the Home Office engaged on Northern Ireland was extremely small. Indeed, Northern Ireland was crammed into what was called the General Department, which was responsible for anything which did not fit into any of the major departments of the Home Office. It covered such matters as ceremonial functions, British Summer Time, London taxi-cabs, liquor licensing, the administration of state-owned pubs in Carlisle and the protection of animals and birds. One division also dealt with the Channel Islands, the Isle of Man, the Charity Commission and Northern Ireland and this group of subjects was under the control of a staff of seven, of whom one was a member of what was called the administrative class. The day-to-day work and responsibility for Northern Ireland affairs was in the hands of Lord Stonham, first Parliamentary Under-Secretary and later Minister of State at the Home Office.[67] Even by June 1968—so close to the first outbreak of disorder—Stonham, on a visit to Northern Ireland, was pledging that Westminster would not 'interfere in matters which are domestic to Northern Ireland'. He expressed the hope that 'some things here which are not satisfactory will change' but indicated that, judging from his communication with political leaders on both sides of the community, the process of change had already begun.[68] He expressed the hope that the Northern Ireland Government could be persuaded of the wisdom of reform[69] but stressed that O'Neill was not being pressurised although Westminster desired fairly rapid change to remove what 'appeared to be legitimate grievances'. He asked Stormont to treat the official opposition with respect by the Unionist Government although 'this was a two-way business and an Opposition should not look for some dark and dirty meaning behind every meaning.'[70] After meeting him McAteer described Stonham as 'frank' but expressed surprise at the Minister's remark that Westminster interference in Northern Ireland would be as much resented by McAteer as by O'Neill. McAteer felt that such intervention would 'speed up Captain O'Neill's lagging footsteps'.[71]

So, it is clear from this that there had been no change in Labour's policy since Jenkins left the Home Office to be replaced by James Callaghan in December 1967. But why should there be? There was no suggestion of any imminent outbreak of disorder. Northern Ireland just wasn't an immediate problem. Upon becoming Home Secretary, Callaghan asked his Private Secretary for a series of documents on the problems that he thought would concern him most during his early weeks and months. When he opened the box it contained books and papers about the future of the prison service, the fire service, problems on race relations, a number of questions about the police, children in care and their future and the reform of the House of Lords—but not a word about Northern Ireland, although it was the concern of the Home Office. Callaghan was not surprised by this omission for the subject rarely, if ever, came before the cabinet and its concerns had fallen into a settled routine in the Home Office itself. Callaghan found that Stonham was on very good personal terms with Northern Ireland Ministers and opposition MPs and the Northern Ireland Civil Service: 'There seemed to me at that time no reason to disturb the arrangement that I found on arrival. Besides, there were many other things to preoccupy me,' he recorded.

First there was the legislation on race relations to which Callaghan's predecessor had committed the Government. None of the main principles or details had been decided by the cabinet and one of Callaghan's first tasks was to shape this legislation and take it through the various committees. Another interest of his was the care of children, of which he had learned from his wife's activities in the field. It seemed to Callaghan that reform was long overdue. Another question which took up much time was the reform of the House of Lords, while a bill to control betting and gambling was at an advanced stage. During the winter of 1967–8 Callaghan also had the problem of the Kenyan Asians who had been emigrating to the UK in large numbers for several months. Callaghan came under heavy criticism for introducing legislation to control the flow. Quite apart from these matters there were the day-to-day problems which forced themselves on the attention of the Home Secretary. All questions concerned with the relationship between the citizen and the law, or problems of civil rights, aroused intense concerns among the public and the press and the Home Secretary's own personal attention was frequently needed for an individual case. The question might concern a jail escape, or the problem of a child who had been treated badly at an approved school, or it might be a matter of young people and drugs or allegations of corruption against a policeman: 'these issues,' insisted Callaghan, 'demand great care and often take up a lot of time'. He found them absorbing and vital in his attempts to strike the right balance between the individual and the state. 'So with all of this I had no occasion to seek more work or to go out and look at the problems of Northern Ireland, unless they forced themselves upon me.'[72]

It is also well to remember that this was the Labour Government that—even when re-elected with an overall majority of ninety-seven in 1966—reeled from crisis to crisis: it inherited a poor economic legacy from the previous Tory Government; there was the humiliation of devaluation (which cost Callaghan his job as Chancellor of the Exchequer); conflict with the unions; and the Rhodesian unilateral declaration of independence. The last thing this Government needed was to go looking for more trouble in Ireland. And yet this was the most interventionist British Government in Northern Ireland since the 1920s, even before the outbreak of the Troubles in October 1968. This is often forgotten by critics who chastise the Labour Government for not intervening. The question as to whether earlier intervention would have made a difference is usually asked without any reference to the problems facing the Government—and assuming that it would have made a difference. Anyway, Callaghan and the Labour Government were about to have Northern Ireland forced upon them very soon.

THE STORM BREAKS

Which brings us back to the beginning of this study for it was the IRA's concept of a civil rights movement which changed everything. The Northern Ireland Civil Rights Association (NICRA) was formed on 29 January 1967. A thirteen-man steering committee was set up with, among its members, representatives from the CSJ, the Communist Party of Northern Ireland, the Belfast Wolfe Tone Society, the Belfast Trades Council, the Republican Clubs, the Ulster Liberal Party and the NILP; even Robert Cole of the Young Unionists and Chairman of Queen's University Conservative and Unionist Association was subsequently co-opted onto the committee. How it was possible for a Unionist to be part of what would ultimately become an anti-Government movement can be understand through an examination of NICRA's constitution: it laid out its objectives as the defence of the basic freedoms of all citizens; the protection of the rights of the individual; the highlighting of all possible abuses of power; the demanding of guarantees for freedom of speech, assembly and association; and the informing of the public of their lawful rights.[73] All of this was non-specific allowing all political persuasions to sign up. It lost moderate Unionist support when it identified itself with specific Catholic-Nationalist grievances and became the umbrella organisation that would co-ordinate a Catholic rebellion against the Protestant state. The road to this point began with a shift in Catholic political thinking away from parliamentary action and towards direct action.

Austin Currie was a key figure in this shift. In September 1967 he lamented the apparent lack of concern shown by many within the community at the plight of those discriminated against. He knew, from his own experience of speaking to constituents, that it was 'almost impossible' for a young married couple to obtain a council house unless they had the right 'pull' or were the 'right colour'. He believed that in Northern Ireland there were all the ingredients for a social and economic revolution and that in any other country that was what would happen. The people of Britain would not tolerate it so 'Why do we?' asked Currie. The answer, he believed, was that a large section of the population of the state had become so used to injustice—political, social and economic—that it now accepted it as a part of life, natural and inevitable; while others, who ought to know better, remained silent: many professional and business people adopted an 'I'm all right Jack' attitude. Currie, on the other hand, could understand the attitude of the Unionists: 'Unionism is after all the party of privilege, the party of the haves, using sectarianism to distract the attention of the ordinary people from their real problems, and thus enable a small clique to keep their heels on the throats of the have-nots.' Currie asked if it was not time for a union of all those people who really cared about the wrongs being inflicted on their fellow man irrespective of political, social or religious background.[74]

But how could this be done? Gerry Fitt thought he might have an answer. He called for a more aggressive response on the part of Northern Catholics (although he began his appeal with a demand for stronger action to end partition on the part of the Irish Government). Fitt argued that while bigotry was breaking down at the lower levels of Northern society, discrimination was still used as a Government 'policy weapon'. He believed that O'Neill was hoping for the defeat of the Labour Government 'for he fully realized that if this happened there would be little danger of reform'. To counter this Fitt called on the Catholic minority to embark on a campaign of extra-parliamentary methods to bring their plight to Westminster. What he advocated was relatively modest: for example, a vigorous protest by Derry Corporation's Nationalist councillors, perhaps to the point of ejection from the council chamber and a consequent court case. As an immediate measure he suggested that a demonstration could be staged at Westminster when Northern Ireland was debated there. Fitt emphasised that the spotlight of public opinion must be focused on the undemocratic practices in Northern Ireland. He was confident that the British working class would, however belatedly, rally in support.[75]

What was important here was the advocacy of civil disobedience. How this would manifest itself was unclear. As it turned out housing was to be the catalyst for direct action. On 18 October Currie called, at Stormont, for a Government inquiry into the allocation of houses in the Dungannon rural area, with particular reference to lettings in Caledon. He raised the question of two Catholic families who were in dire need of accommodation and had taken over new houses in Caledon as squatters, after they had failed to get homes there through the local council. He condemned the system of individual councillors allocating houses in their area and said that of fifteen new houses in Caledon only one was given to a Catholic family. In this case, Councillor W. H. Scott, a Unionist, 'seemed to represent the entire housing committee and his word seemed to be final'. Currie asked if the houses were legally allocated. There was no proposal, no resolution, no debate. Councillor Scott merely handed in a slip of paper at a meeting of Dungannon Rural District Council on which there were fifteen names and next day a list was issued showing that these people had been allocated the houses. Currie pointed out that such a system, whether operated by a Unionist or a Nationalist councillor, was open to abuse and various pressures. The obvious solution was a points system for all allocations. There were many people who had been by-passed. Yet, alleged Currie, a widower with only one child, a person who had returned from England only a month before and another who had been allocated two other houses within a year were offered the tenancies in this case. Another successful applicant was a man who had sold his house for £3,500 a fortnight previously. The two Catholic families became squatters because they felt they were being unjustly treated and others in less need than themselves had been given priority over them. They also felt that they had no other way of obtaining houses under the present system. They were not prepared to be treated as second-class citizens. Currie also claimed that Councillor Scott had admitted that he allocated houses according to religious proportion in the area, and not need. He warned:

> There cannot be any compromise with injustice and unless action is taken the Government will find that these growing injustices will cause trouble. Unless the Government is prepared to take action to prevent what is taking place in Caledon and elsewhere and join in the ranks of those fighting injustice, then the Government must take responsibility for anything that might happen ... These things inevitably boil up and what I am concerned about—and I admit I am afraid—is that in the conditions in Northern Ireland at present where no action is taken, the people will resort to other activity.[76]

A few days later Currie followed up with his analysis on 'O'Neillism' to a meeting of the Economic and Political Studies Society at Magee University College, Derry. In it he set out the exasperation he and others felt with the Prime Minister: no politician in the history of the state had aroused hopes and expectations to the same extent as O'Neill. For the first time they seemed to have a Prime Minister who could shake off the shackles of the past and look to the future. He became Prime Minister at a time when the liberal conscience of the community, so long muted, was again beginning to make itself heard. There was an overpowering desire to be optimistic, to look forward with hope, to give the new Prime Minister a chance. Opposition politicians were prepared to refuse opportunities for making political capital rather than force his hand or push him into the arms of the backwoodsmen. Men of goodwill in all spheres of society looked to him to harness the potential for good in the community. When he met Lemass it seemed as if the great expectations were to be realised.

'What has happened since then?' asked Currie. 'Has the O'Neill car burned out its battery since the historic meeting with Sean Lemass? The public speeches continue to be liberal; they continue to PROMISE but ACTION has not followed the WORDS. Our 19th-Century electoral system continues to make a farce of democratic claims; the Special Powers Act is still the envy of dictators everywhere, even in South Africa.' Despite the expression of pious hopes and well-intentioned phrases, many of his supporters continued to carry on in the traditional way as if the Prime Minister had not mentioned liberalism, tolerance or injustice. 'Down in the grassroots nothing stirs.' Currie pointed out that only that month appointments to public boards showed that nothing had changed: two Catholic representatives out of thirty-three to the Youth Committee, two out of twenty-two to the Hospitals Authority and two out of twenty-four to the General Heath Services Board:

> So much for pleas for the minority to play their full part in the affairs of this state. So much for words, not followed up by action!
>
> If Terence O'Neill was a circus performer and not a Prime Minister his performances would merit a five-star rating. The handshake with a nun in Newry is balanced by the public reading of a scurrilous anonymous letter. Corrymeela is balanced by different speeches in Orange halls 'down the country'. The promises of reform to Harold Wilson are balanced by a failure to do anything at home.
>
> The anti-Paisley speeches are balanced by a failure to take effective action against those who think like him in Constituency Associations, local authorities and even in Parliament itself.
>
> What effect has O'Neill's failure to live up to his promises had on this community? The hopes roused and then dashed have led to greater frustration and anger. People disappointed and frustrated with the apparent failure of constitutionalism and parliamentary action to remove their grievances tend to try and solve their own problems in their own way. Discrimination—and the fear of possible discrimination—has its effect in preventing minority participation in the affairs of the community ... if he [O'Neill] does not take action quickly—certainly within the next 12 months—the ever-growing frustration and anger to which I have already referred must make a real impact on politics in this area. I foresee a growing militancy. There will be more squatting, more acts of civil disobedience, more emphasis on 'other means' and less on traditional parliamentary methods. And Terence O'Neill and his Government must carry the responsibility.
>
> If the Prime Minister refuses to take action which is necessary he will be recognised as the political confidence trickster and stuntman of this generation. 'O'Neillism' will be a new word in our language signifying a shabby myth and a showy sham.[77]

O'Neill hit back. He claimed that Currie had taken his cue from Fitt: 'It is simply not convincing for these men to declare, with an air of great innocence, that they are not inciting irresponsible behaviour, but merely prophesying that it may happen. This just will not wash. They know as well as I do that the peace of this country has not at all times been secure and that there are always people ready—with the slightest encouragement—to take the short-cut to political power by way of violence.' Ulster's Government would be decided by votes not threats: 'We will not be influenced in any way by the bombastic threats of a paste-board politician, too dazzled by his own eloquence to care for the damage his words may do.' The Prime Minister described Fitt as 'the man who seems to believe that myth can be converted into truth by constant repetition'. His speeches at Westminster 'shy away from truth like a frightened horse. Either he is completely and woefully ignorant about the simplest facts, or he is wilfully and deceitfully closing his eyes to them.'[78]

By now the squatting situation in Caledon had become a media event. The two Catholic families, the McKennas and the Goodfellows, had begun squatting in two newly-built houses in Kinnard Park on 13 October. The families moved into the empty houses after claiming that Dungannon Rural Council had allocated them unfairly. John Taylor demanded that the Council remove the 'trespassers' forthwith as they were duty-bound to do. He was satisfied that the houses had been allocated fairly.[79] A few days later, just as the Council decided to take legal action to evict the families, the problem of squatting spread to Dungannon itself. At 1.30 on the morning of 19 October, Matthew McKenna, a father of six, broke a window and entered one of Dungannon Urban Council's new houses at Fairmount Park. McKenna, who owned the house he had been living in, said that his name had been on the Council housing list for five years and that in 1964 he had reapplied for a house. He complained of living in cramped conditions with only two small bedrooms, no bathroom, no indoor toilet and no water supply.[80]

As the situation drew more and more attention, Mrs Elizabeth McQuaid, the only Catholic allocated a tenancy out of the fifteen houses at Caledon, and Brian McKenna, who was one of those squatting in the estate, received threatening letters warning: 'Now that the long winter nights are here if you hear a knock at the door you will know that we have called.'[81] At Stormont Currie asked the Prime Minister whether, in view of the fact that he had publicly identified himself with efforts to improve community relations, he would intervene to prevent communal strife in Caledon resulting from the decision of the local council to allocate a house to a nineteen-year-old unmarried girl while next door a family which included three young children was threatened with eviction.[82] The young Protestant girl allocated the house—and drawing unwanted attention—was Emily Beattie. Eventually, in June 1968, the Goodfellow family was evicted from the house where, by now, it had been squatting for eight months. During the proceedings force was used. As a result Currie claimed that 'feeling was running very high in the Dungannon district' and described the eviction 'as the most outrageous scandal that had ever been perpetrated by any local authority in the country'.[83] It was 'bad enough for a family not to be able to get a house but when they could see no other reason for them not getting a house other than their religion or politics, then the feelings of that family were much worse.'[84] It was now that the Northern Ireland Civil Rights Association came of age. It announced plans for 'an emphatic protest' against the eviction. It could only conclude that the principles on which Dungannon Council made its allocations 'are neither those of Christian charity, nor the plain humanity of the Declaration of Human Rights'.[85]

When the issue was debated at Stormont, Currie was expelled from the Commons chamber after accusing John Taylor of lying about the circumstances surrounding the allocation of the house to Emily Beattie. Taylor accused Currie of causing the trouble and of damaging community relations; he refuted accusations of partiality by the council.[86] Fitzsimmons, the Minister of Development, claimed that extending special treatment to the Goodfellow family would merely set an undesirable precedent showing that squatting could be a successful tactic. He agreed, however, that the scenes at the eviction were 'deplorable' but they were the results of the actions taken by people illegally in possession of property. Taylor described the whole affair as a 'political stunt' of which many Catholics disapproved.[87] It seemed that only Mrs Goodfellow could draw something positive from the proceedings: she recalled that her family was shunned on their initial arrival in Caledon—'more because we had taken the stand we did than because we're Catholics'—but found that the family had come to be accepted by local people once they came to realise the difficulty of the Goodfellows' position.[88]

The charity of Mrs Goodfellow and her Protestant neighbours was notably absent in the wider ethnic schism of Northern Irish politics. The political temperature had been raised. There was a sense of fluidity. Currie and two other men now began to squat in Emily Beattie's house. This was condemned as unjustifiable by Fitzsimmons.[89] All three men were soon ejected from the house. As Fitt announced that he proposed to send a dossier on the Caledon affair to Westminster, Joe McCann of the National Democratic Party suggested that Nationalists should re-think their strategy and consider civil disobedience.[90] McAteer spoke of his frustration, and that of Nationalists generally, that the opposition was never paid much heed at Stormont: 'it makes me wonder whether there is any bloody sense in coming here at all'. Fitzsimmons, he said, was failing to resist the 'local powers of darkness'. McAteer 'had been searching the horizon to find out from where the torch could come to ignite the dry heather. What might now be taking place in Caledon might very well be the prelude to another period of turmoil and strife.' He warned that it could set back community relations by years.[91]

The squattings and the evictions, combined with the widespread attention given to them, gave a sense of momentum to events. In Londonderry, the Derry Housing Action Committee (DHAC) moved a caravan onto a busy road in protest at the general housing condition in the city. The Chairman of the DHAC, Matt O'Leary, claimed that 'this is the beginning of a series of such incidents because it is obvious that the normal channels are of no avail'.[92] The East Tyrone branch of the Nationalist Party expressed its disillusionment with the pace of change and called for a programme of non-violent civil disobedience 'to wreck a system which had as its basis a deliberate policy of denying equal treatment and equal opportunity for all'. The Executive of the Party was to consider the request. Currie contended that civil disobedience would constitute a 'safety valve against the possibility of violence'; violence which, while he disapproved of it, he felt was likely to occur as tensions built up. Normal channels for redress had failed: 'if we cannot have justice we must make a government based on injustice unworkable'.[93] However, to Currie's disappointment, the party conference voted to consider the implications of a policy of non-violent civil disobedience rather than declare support for it immediately. The conference called on the Party to introduce a bill for the reform of local government without waiting for its reorganisation by the Government.[94] The Nationalist Party, however, was being left behind by events on the ground as NICRA fixed 24 July as the date for a protest march into the centre of Dungannon.

Two thousand protesters assembled in Coalisland, accompanied by Nationalist bands, to be faced by 1,500 loyalist counter-demonstrators, led by Paisley. The Dungannon meeting was attended by Currie, Fitt, McAteer and Patricia McCluskey. Currie told the gathering that the fight for social justice would continue and would use all the 'many weapons in the arsenal of non-violence and civil disobedience'. The situation in Northern Ireland was the same as that in the southern states of the United States or that in South Africa: the sole difference was that discrimination in Northern Ireland was based on religion rather than colour. Good community relations were desirable but these could only be established on the basis of justice and equal treatment for all sections of the community.[95] Currie emphasised that a policy of 'non-violent civil disobedience' was worthy of support since it would publicise injustice and force the Government to act. But, he repeated, 'If we do not have justice we will make a government system based on injustice unworkable.'[96]

It was clear that a defining moment had been reached—a decision to commence a co-ordinated campaign of civil disobedience. And acting as the co-ordinating umbrella body would be the Northern Ireland Civil Rights Association. As Fred Heatley, Chairman of NICRA, spoke out in favour of civil disobedience, he accepted this meant the abandonment of the Association's 'neutrality' policy. Prominent in the proceedings were well-known Republicans such as the solicitor Kevin Agnew: he voiced the opinion that, since Nationalists paid taxes and were 'condemned to live under the Union Jack', they should join Currie in demanding their due from the state.[97] IRA men acted as stewards for the march. The meeting was a success—it upset Unionists and was noticed in London: when Currie returned to the Commons chamber Unionist backbenchers walked out;[98] but the

CDU sent a letter to Currie praising his recent actions and urging him to 'persevere in your efforts to achieve civil rights for all the people of Ulster'. His was a 'courageous stand against discrimination'.[99] However, there was a sting in the tail: once NICRA became associated with specific Catholic grievances, advocated civil disobedience and combined this with the prominent role of Republicans within the Movement, Protestants saw it as a challenge to the state. It had been born of Republicanism, was marshalled by Republicans and Republicans formed part of its leadership. To Protestants it was easy to misinterpret the level of Republican influence within NICRA—they did not control the organisation, which was dominated by moderates. But it was naïve of the non-Republican leadership of NICRA to underestimate the impact of this on Protestant perceptions. Partly this was because Republicans and Nationalists of all varieties—overwhelmingly Catholic and making the Civil Rights Movement *de facto* a Catholic organisation—shared the same assumptions of Unionism: that it was not based on a sense of Britishness or (for some Protestants at least) a rational fear of the power of Catholicism in an all-Ireland environment, but solely on discrimination and the maintenance of a Protestant ascendancy. Get rid of that and the rationale for two states in Ireland would vanish. This was a fantasy. And upon that ideological foundation the hopes for a non-sectarian mass civil rights movement was dead in the water, regardless of the legitimate grievances of the minority.

The next key event was the Civil Rights march in Dungannon on 24 August. This occurred because of the feelings aroused by the Caledon incident and was intended mainly as a protest against housing policy in the area. Currie persuaded members of the CSJ to organise a march from Coalisland to Dungannon. Through Conn McCluskey a meeting with the NICRA Executive was arranged. This was held on 27 July at Maghera. The Civil Rights Association had doubts about getting involved in housing agitation and mass processions, but eventually agreed to a march. When the march had been announced at the end of July the police originally raised no objection in principle. However, there was soon a move in extreme Unionist circles to oppose the march, on the grounds that Market Square was Unionist territory. Senator Stewart (Chairman of the Urban District Council and a prominent resident) told the police that there would be trouble if the march entered the Square and proposed a re-route by Quarry Lane to Anne Street. John Taylor also told the police that there would be trouble if the procession entered the Square. Faced with these representations the police decided that the threat of counter-demonstration should be taken seriously, the more so as the Ulster Protestant Volunteers advertised a public meeting to be held in the Market Square on the evening of 24 August. Late on 23 August the march was re-routed, and arrangements were made to halt it near Quarry Lane at Thomas Street, Dungannon, and divert it to Anne Street.

The march took place on the evening of 24 August as arranged, but halted at the police barrier. At least 2,500 people marched from Coalisland and a much larger number gathered at Thomas Street. Beyond the police was a miscellaneous crowd of at least 1,500 people, some of whom were potential counter-demonstrators. Opponents noted the presence of several prominent Republicans among the marchers. The police calculated that about seventy of the stewards were Republicans, and of these some ten were members of the IRA. On the other hand the organisers prevented the public display of any banners except the Civil Rights banner. Betty Sinclair of NICRA closed the proceedings by leading those present in singing 'We Shall Overcome'. The marchers thereafter dispersed.[100]

PANDORA'S BOX: DERRY

After the march in Dungannon a left-wing group in Derry had decided to press for a Civil Rights march in the city. The initial steps were taken by the Derry Housing Action Committee, in which Eamonn McCann and Eamonn Melaugh were prominent. This group had been organising protests, sit downs and demonstrations, mainly against Londonderry Corporation's housing policy, but had not obtained much publicity for their efforts. At their invitation seven or eight members of the NICRA Executive attended a meeting in Londonderry on 31 August to discuss the proposal. A further meeting between NICRA representatives and the Derry activists was held on 7 September in the City Hotel there. It was decided to set up an 'October 5th Ad Hoc Committee'—the date of the proposed march. Administrative responsibility for the march devolved largely on McCann. He was not in fact a member of the Ad Hoc Committee, but he became prominent in the absence of any other central or local direction.

The route proposed on behalf of the Civil Rights Association was one commonly followed by 'Protestant' and 'Loyalist' marches in Londonderry. It was to start from the Waterside Railway Station, east of the River Foyle, cross the river along Craigavon Bridge and proceed to the Diamond, the central point of the city. This route traversed certain Protestant districts, and ended within the city's ancient walls, which had major significance in Orange tradition because of the successful defence of Londonderry against James II. The proposal to follow this route was designed to symbolise the claim of the Civil Rights Association to be non-sectarian, and neither Unionist nor Nationalist.

The local Unionist headquarters objected to the march as offensive to a great majority of the citizens residing on the route, and also to any meeting near the war memorial or any place closely associated with the siege of Londonderry. There was also a threat of counter-demonstration by the Middle Liberties Young Unionist Association. A third, written protest, came from the General Committee of the Apprentice Boys of Derry. It was dated 30 September and argued that the march was objectionable, since it was alleged that Civil Rights was only a cover for a parade of the Republican and Nationalist movements, and that it would show no respect for the war memorial in the Diamond. On 1 October the same organisation served notice of an 'Annual Initiation Ceremony', whose participants would march in procession on the afternoon of 5 October from the Waterside Railway Station via the Diamond to the Apprentice Boys Memorial Hall. Such a procession would have taken place at virtually the same time as the advertised march of the Civil Rights Association. In the event no march by Apprentice Boys took place. The local police intimated to Bill Craig that if all processions were banned on 5 October the Apprentice Boys would hold their ceremony in private. In general, they favoured a ban because they feared trouble from Unionists or 'Loyalists' if the Civil Rights march followed its proposed route. On 3 October Craig prohibited all processions either in the Waterside ward (that is, east of the river) or within the city's walls.[101]

Eddie McAteer phoned Craig to protest strongly at the decision. Craig told him that he regarded the march as a 'Nationalist-Republican parade'. He protested that the Nationalist Party had nothing to do with it and told Craig that his ban was harking back to the bad old days of 1933 when a ban was put on a proposed meeting at Newtownbutler on the pretext—the first time this now 'wellworn tactic was used'—of a counter-demonstration at the same place and at the same time. Craig answered that he was acting in the interests of peace. The Apprentice Boys' parade was a traditional event, yet it was being banned also. The message that McAteer took from this conversation was that there was no room in the North of Ireland for anyone except the 'official Orange Order party'. Even if the anti-Unionist majority in Derry City became ninety-nine per cent instead of the present seventy per cent, it seemed that the majority would still be dictated to by the one per cent.[102] Lord Cameron's inquiry into the resulting disturbances subsequently found that: 'The effect of the ministerial order was to transform the situation. It guaranteed the attendance of a large number of citizens of Londonderry who actively resented what appeared to them to be a totally unwarranted interference by the Minister . . . and we have good reason to believe also that during the six weeks since the Coalisland–Dungannon march certain left wing activists had decided that their campaign would benefit from violent conflict with the authorities. The decision to prohibit the march on 5th October from part of its proposed route gave them the opportunity to prove their point.'[103]

The activists in Derry were now determined that it should proceed as planned. Representatives of the Civil Rights Association at first disagreed. A meeting was held at the City Hotel on the evening of 4 October at which the whole subject was discussed. Those present included representatives of the Civil Rights Association and of the Derry organisations involved in the march. The discussion was prolonged, and eventually other local people, who were also permitted to be present but had no title to attend, took an active part in the debate. The ultimate decision of the meeting was that the march should take place as originally planned.[104]

For the marchers the timing of the demonstration—and its ban—could not have been better: the Labour Party Conference was in session in Blackpool. Attending were Gerry Fitt and Paddy Devlin, chairman of the NILP. In his speech to delegates, Fitt echoed the words of Harold Wilson: 'It is the dignity of man we are fighting for. We are the Party of human rights.' Fitt suggested that the Prime Minister include the people of Northern Ireland within this philosophy; he asked for no more and would accept no less. He also announced, with reference to the march in Derry, that he was inviting six Labour MPs to be present 'to witness what can happen in an integral part of the UK'. After being 'exposed' to 'police brutality' in Dungannon, the Civil Rights marchers were intending to make another stand for their rights in Derry, the symbol of all that was inherent in Unionist philosophy. Fitt was in no doubt that they would once again be subjected to police interference. While he realised that the Labour administration was beset with difficulties such as Rhodesia, Vietnam, the economic crisis and the balance of payments situation, he impressed on the Government the urgency of the situation. The inaction of the British Government, allied to the attitudes of the Unionist Party, had brought about a situation where the oppressed minority in Northern Ireland were now prepared to take steps to remedy the situation. The British Government could no longer say that it had not been warned.[105] Paddy Devlin suggested that O'Neill was stalling for time in the hope that the Labour Government would suffer electoral defeat before he was forced to fulfil the promises made.[106] At Blackpool there was a mood of anger among CDU MPs, some of whom hoped that the ban would trigger action by the Labour Government to become more involved in Northern Ireland affairs.[107]

In Derry on the afternoon of 5 October the marchers gathered at the Waterside Railway Station. Members of the IRA were present and represented among the stewards. However, the crowd, which grew to over 2,000, also included a number of prominent and moderate members of the Nationalist Party, including Eddie McAteer and members of the NILP and the Liberal Party; also present were John Hume, Ivan Cooper and Gerry Fitt who had brought three English Westminster MPs. In Lord Cameron's view the NICRA organisers wished to make a protest in a city whose administration was unrepresentative and partisan, and were not in any way seeking a violent confrontation with the police, while Fitt 'sought publicity for himself and his political views, and must clearly have envisaged the possibility of a violent clash with the police as providing the publicity he so ardently sought. His conduct in our judgement was reckless and wholly irresponsible in a person occupying his public positions. The extremists of the left were anxious to ensure that there was a violent "confrontation" with the police, and to organise opposition in the city on class lines. Since these extremists had been principally responsible for the detailed organisation of the march it is not surprising that there were no serious plans to control it, or to ensure that it went off peacefully. The chief marshal notified to the police appears to have been inexperienced and relatively ineffective.'

The police, for their part, certainly expected trouble. Only sixty police were normally available, but altogether about 130 men were assembled on the morning of 5 October. This included two platoons of the Reserve Force, known popularly as the 'Riot Police'. Two water wagons were also brought into Londonderry. The local County Inspector was on leave and the County Inspector in charge of the Special Branch of the RUC was sent to Londonderry to take his place.[108] The march had been arranged to start at 3.30 p.m. At first there was a confused group of people at the Waterside Railway Station. The police had blocked the normal traffic routes to Craigavon Bridge at Simpson's Brae and Distillery Brae, and the County Inspector in charge outlined the scope of the Minister's order by loudhailer, warning that women and children should not remain. The chief marshal then decided to march up Duke Street towards Craigavon Bridge. The local organisers insisted that Eddie McAteer, Austin Currie and Gerry Fitt lead the march. The marchers moved off along Duke Street and the police hurriedly moved a Reserve Force platoon, who were at Distillery Brae, to positions on Duke Street about fifty yards from the Bridge. Two large police tenders were placed across the road behind them. This was contrary to the plan which the police intended to carry out, which would have placed the cordon of police behind and not in front of the tenders. But, because of the short time in which the unexpected change of position had to be made the line of police was stationed in front instead of behind the tenders. The procession marched straight up to the police, and according to Cameron, 'it appears to us established on the evidence that at this stage batons were used by certain police officers without explicit order, although this is denied by the police. We regret to say that we have no doubt that both Mr. Fitt and Mr. McAteer were batoned by the police, at a time when no order to draw batons had been given and in circumstances in which the use of batons on these gentlemen was wholly without justification or excuse.' Fitt was at this point removed to hospital with a minor head injury which he ascribed to a blow from a baton, and McAteer also sustained a minor injury.

Very few of the marchers realised what had happened, but the march halted and there was considerable confusion. The stewards succeeded in moving the marchers back a yard or two from the police. At that point—about 4 p.m.—Betty Sinclair arrived from Belfast and reached the head of the march. No effective plans had been made to meet the situation which had arisen but Sinclair obtained a chair from the police and started a meeting. Her remarks amounted to a plea for the right of non-violent procession. Currie and McCann 'gave what could be interpreted as more or less guarded encouragement to the use of violence to break the police barrier'. After about half an hour the meeting was ended by Sinclair, who requested those present to disperse. Others made the same request, using the police loudhailer. The crowd was noisy and ill-organised and the extent to which the words of the speakers were heard among the bulk of the marchers was doubtful. What happened at the next stage 'is a matter of controversy. It appears however that certain of the left wing extremists who were in the van of the procession and were members of the body known as the "Young Socialists

Alliance" (most if not all of whom had come from Belfast and had taken up positions at or near the head of the procession) threw their placards and banners at the police, and that some stones were thrown at the police from the crowd.' After about five minutes many of the police, having drawn their batons individually, were ordered by the County Inspector to disperse the march. On the evidence presented, Cameron concluded: 'we think that nothing resembling a baton charge took place but that the police broke ranks and used their batons indiscriminately on people in Duke Street'. This situation was made worse by the fact that the other end of Duke Street (nearer the Waterside Station) was blocked by the party of police which had originally been stationed at Simpson's Brae but had moved down in rear of the march. This party had not been informed that the march was to disperse and their choice of position had the effect that the marchers felt themselves to be trapped. No specific orders were given to their party to let the marchers through and when a number of marchers hurried towards them some violence was almost inevitable. 'There is a body of evidence, which we accept, that these police also used their batons indiscriminately, and that the District Inspector in charge used his blackthorn with needless violence.' Rapid dispersal of the crowd was also assisted by the use of water wagons which were moved along Duke Street and then along Craigavon Bridge. There was 'no real doubt that they sprayed the dispersing marchers indiscriminately, especially on the bridge, where there were a good many members of the general public who had taken no part in the march. There was no justification for use of the water wagons on the bridge, while the evidence which we heard and saw on film did not convince us of the necessity of their use in Duke Street.' By about 5 p.m. Duke Street was cleared.

This did not end the violence. A flare-up occurred a little later at the Diamond, within the walls. This arose out of the forcible removal by police officers of a political banner from some marchers in the vicinity of the war memorial in the Diamond. This led to a clash with the police in which a number of 'hooligan elements' rapidly joined and in the 'inflamed state' of public feeling this led to serious rioting in the Diamond and its vicinity. Ultimately the police drove these rioters, who were not themselves marchers, down to the Catholic Bogside. Stones were thrown and the police had to use their riot equipment, including long batons. Violence continued that night and broke out again during the afternoon and evening of Sunday 6 October, when very few police were available. The County Inspector in charge on 5 October had by then returned to Belfast. On 6 October the County Inspector in charge of County Fermanagh was sent to Londonderry and took temporary charge of the police force there. A good deal of damage and looting of shops took place before the County Inspector was able to organise the dispersal of the young hooligans involved, by the use of units of the Reserve Force using Land-Rovers. Casualty figures showed that eleven policemen were injured on 5 and 6 October, four at Duke Street and seven during the later rioting. Total civilian casualties on 5 and 6 October were seventy-seven of whom the great majority had bruises and lacerations (mainly of their heads). Four of those injured, including two policemen, were admitted to hospital; the remainder were sent home after treatment. In Lord Cameron's view the course which events took on those days arose out of the following immediate circumstances:

(1) The Northern Ireland Civil Rights Association did not directly plan or control the march which was left to a local and purely *ad hoc* Committee.

(2) No properly thought out alternative plans of action were available if the march was stopped by the police.

(3) Stewarding was ineffective and no adequate communication system was available.

(4) Some of the marchers were determined to defy the Minister's order. They accepted the risk that some degree of violence would occur, believing that this would achieve publicity for the Civil Rights cause, especially in Great Britain.

(5) A section of extremists actively wished to provoke violence, or at least a confrontation with the police without regard to consequences.

(6) The police were determined that the Minister's order should be made effective on this occasion and by a display, and, if necessary, use, of force to deter future demonstrators from defying ministerial bans.

(7) Hooligan elements wholly unassociated with the Civil Rights demonstrators later took advantage of a minor clash in the Diamond to cause a serious riot with looting and damage to property—wholly unassociated with the Civil Rights demonstration itself or the clash in the Waterside.

(8) The police handling of the situation in the Waterside was ill coordinated and ill conducted. The marchers' change of direction apparently took the police by surprise. The time available to take up a new blocking position in Duke Street was too short to permit the same disposition of police and tenders to be effected as that originally planned. The use of batons was probably unnecessary and in any event premature, as the major part of the demonstrators were obeying their leaders' advice to disperse quietly. The baton charge was lacking in proper control and degenerated into a series of individual scuffles, while the failure to inform the party of police moving down from Simpson's Brae, of the action being taken by the majority of the demonstrators in dispersing, led to the demonstrators being caught between two fires and to a flare up of further unnecessary violence.

(9) The Minister's order had already caused irritation and resentment in Londonderry, and swelled the number of demonstrators, and was no doubt a subsidiary cause of the trouble which occurred.

One of the consequences of the break-up of the demonstration in Duke Street was that press and television reports ensured that some very damaging pictures of police violence were seen throughout the United Kingdom and abroad. This produced a violent reaction of feeling in many places and led directly to the formation at Queen's University, Belfast of a protest movement which subsequently became the People's Democracy.[109] Just as damaging from the Unionist Government's point of view was the presence of Labour MPs at the march: Annie Kerr was, more than anything, shocked at the impression she got that the police were 'looking pleased' at what they had to do. 'I saw some of them grinning. It was appalling,' she said. Another Labour MP, John Ryan, told the BBC that he had seen an elderly woman have her spectacles removed by a policeman before being struck by a baton. He also saw the police hitting men they caught on the testicles with batons, contrary to all police procedures in Britain. He declined to compare the RUC with those he had recently witnessed in Chicago, but he added that the two police forces were 'in the same league'. He described the action of London police at the recent Grosvenor Square riots—outside the US Embassy and in protest of the Vietnam War—as like being at a Buckingham Palace garden party when compared with those of the police in Derry.[110] Harold Wilson could no longer put Northern Ireland on the long burner: London was once more embroiled in Ireland's ancient conflict. From the events at Caledon evolved the tragedy of modern Irish history. For more than thirty years it has been a legacy that Austin Currie has had to live with:

Had I known the consequences of what I intended to do later that day, at Caledon, would I have proceeded with it? I have asked myself that question many, many times over the years. Would I have gone ahead had I known, or even suspected, that the action I was about to take would initiate a process that would lead to the loss of nearly four thousand lives? Would I have gone ahead had I known that my intended action and other actions stemming from it would transform the political scene in Northern Ireland and destroy a political regime which, at that time, appeared permanent and unchangeable; would I have proceeded? These are some of the questions I have wrestled with for more than thirty years, particularly in the aftermath of barbarous events, such as occurred at Enniskillen and Omagh, McGurk's bar, Greysteel and Bloody Sunday, or when people personally known to me, such as Jim and Gertie Devlin, were murdered in cold blood.

The answer is 'No', I would not have proceeded if I had had knowledge of these things. The injustices suffered by the Catholic population of Northern Ireland were great and caused much suffering to individuals. And the initial injustice of a nation divided by a foreign country against the wishes of a great majority of its inhabitants was also great. But none of these injustices justified the loss of a single life, never mind close to four thousand.

What occurred over the following three decades was not inevitable. The deaths resulted from the decisions and actions of individuals, organisations and governments. The men, women and children who lost their lives in the Troubles did so because of hundreds of decisions, some intentional, others unintentional, which resulted in their deaths. Among the many decisions were my own—taken in good faith, with all the available information at the time and always, I can honestly say, with a desire to put right the wrongs that proliferated in Northern Ireland, and yet, not all correct, not all productive, not all to be proud of. It was not inevitable, I have repeated to myself so many times over the years.[111]

Chapter 5

LONDON INTERVENES: BRITISH POLICY AND WESTMINSTER–STORMONT RELATIONS
OCTOBER 1968–FEBRUARY 1969

DERRY: THE AFTERMATH

The events of 5 October altered everything. It proved a disaster for the Northern Ireland Government. From this point on intervention by the British Government was inevitable. Television had transformed the situation. Unlike the troubles of the 1920s and 1930s, the troubles of the 1960s could not be relegated to column inches in national newspapers. They were beamed into the living rooms of Britain. And into those of Labour backbenchers. From now on Wilson would have to be proactive rather than merely encouraging. The pressure would be on O'Neill to deliver reform. On 7 October Wilson and Callaghan met to discuss the disturbances. Callaghan's initial response was to establish a constitutional commission to discuss Northern Ireland's problems. Possible candidates for the chairmanship of the commission were discussed with both Wilson and Callaghan, who were inclined to think that he should be a senior privy councillor and former minister[1] (there was some suggestion that the Duke of Edinburgh might be a suitable candidate for chairman but fortunately this was not proceeded with as Northern Ireland had enough problems already). While no final decision was made on whether to proceed with this strategy it was easier to make a more obvious one: O'Neill was invited to talks in London. This was well received by Labour backbenchers. Wilson thought the meeting should take place as soon as possible after the opening of the new session of Parliament. He decided that the line to be taken with O'Neill should be that the present situation could not be allowed to continue, for two reasons. Firstly, because of growing pressure in the House of Commons for the British Government to take action in a situation where they had responsibility without power; and secondly, the increasing difficulty of reconciling the situation in Northern Ireland with the United Kingdom's international obligations on human rights[2]—specifically this referred to the fact that the United Kingdom had to derogate from the European Convention on Human Rights because of the Special Powers Acts.

Back in Belfast O'Neill tried to bring home to his cabinet colleagues the gravity of the situation facing the Northern Ireland Government. On 14 October he set out his thoughts in a memorandum. He began by recalling that at their previous meeting they had agreed to issue a statement supporting in a firm way the decisions of the Minister for Home Affairs and the actions of the police in Londonderry. They had also decided to ask Parliament to support the Government in this. The Prime Minister was sure that the cabinet were right in these decisions because 'our people resent the way some of these issues have been presented in the Press and TV, and look to us to stand firmly behind the forces of law and order. We all feel, I think, that firmness must be an essential aspect of our posture at this time.' But there were wider ramifications here that the Government could not ignore. There had been two meetings now with Harold Wilson. The Ministers of Commerce (Faulkner) and Home Affairs (Craig) knew from personal experience the pressure the Government was under to justify some of Northern Ireland's practices. The cabinet was also aware that a strong section of left-wing opinion had been pressing Wilson very hard to take some positive step. Up to now he had fobbed off this pressure and, from the Northern Ireland Government's point of view, very well. With his many other headaches, Northern Ireland's affairs had not been high up on his agenda. With Northern Ireland calm, and a general feeling that slow but steady progress was under way, he could contain the situation by references to the inter-governmental talks—though not without a veiled threat on occasions. However O'Neill felt that he would be failing in his duty if he did not make it clear to the cabinet that, in his view, Londonderry had 'dramatically altered this situation to our great disadvantage. Whether the Press and TV coverage was fair is immaterial. We have now become a focus of world opinion.' Within the next month or so the Government would have to face Wilson again.

O'Neill asked his colleagues to be realistic about the situation the Northern Ireland Government was likely, indeed in his view certain, to face in London: 'We shall be told that unless we can give a definite undertaking that we will introduce further reforms, H.M.G. will no longer be able to stand aloof from the situation.' He asked ministers to consider what they could expect if they were unable, or unwilling, to give such an assurance. At their last meeting the Prime Minister had itemised a number of the ways in which Stormont was heavily dependent upon economic and financial support. Many of these—the Social Services Agreement, agricultural support, National Insurance arrangements, etc.—had a statutory basis, and could not be easily or swiftly set aside. But, he warned, in many other cases Her Majesty's Government in London had a degree of discretion which they could easily use to Northern Ireland's detriment: 'For let's face the fact—H.M.G. do not have to do something openly spectacular to make us feel the pinch; they merely have to be unwilling in the future to do any more exceptional things for us.'

For example in 1969 Northern Ireland was to receive from London £10 million in subsidies out of £11.3 million in total expenditure. It would be easy to take a different and much less generous decision the next year. Economic and financial stringency could be invoked as a reason. Or again, the future of Shorts was once more in the melting pot. London could easily take a hard-nosed view. Again, the Minister of Agriculture was, the Prime Minister knew, worried about the burden of the cost of imported feed-stuffs upon the Ulster farmer, and was seeking special aid for this. That request could be turned down without any trouble. These were just examples to show how Whitehall controlled a number of levers which it could pull without any great fuss or bother. O'Neill asked: 'what if it is made clear that—in the absence of a promise of some movement here—sanctions such as these would follow?' Some would say 'we'll just have to tighten our belts and suffer it for the sake of our independence'. But this was not the real choice. The Prime Minister did not believe that London was prepared to cut Northern Ireland adrift financially and concern itself no more. On the contrary, in this situation he believed Northern Ireland would face at once such highly dangerous possibilities as a royal commission or proposals to amend the 1920 Act. In any case, as he had made clear before, such an action was a large step towards a UDI attitude, which was wholly absurd in view of Ulster's geographical, military and economic position. Ulster had said for years: 'Ulster is British.' If the decision now was to turn their backs on Britain and go their own way, it would be one difficult to defend as being in Northern Ireland's true interests.

This was the external position. But, internally too, O'Neill believed that the Government had to be seen to temper firmness with fairness. Of course there were anti-partition agitators prominently at work, but could any ministers truthfully say in the confines of the cabinet room that the minority had no grievance calling for a remedy? The Prime Minister added: 'Believe me, I realise the appalling political difficulties we face. The first reaction of our own people to the antics of Fitt and Currie and the abuse of the world's press is to retreat into old hard-line attitudes. But if this is all we can offer, we face a period when we govern Ulster by police power alone against a background of mounting disorder. Are we ready, and would we be wise, to face up to this?' While the Government would never set at risk the basic constitutional integrity of Northern Ireland, the greatest threat to this was any tinkering with the 1920 Act—and to avert this, concessions in other directions could well be the wisest course. The Government would have a very hard job to sell such concessions to 'our people'; but in this critical moment might this not be its duty? Things like the multiple vote at local government elections 'are not essential to maintain our position. And we may even in time have to make a bitter choice between losing Londonderry and losing Ulster.' O'Neill felt that he could not urge too strongly upon his colleagues the seriousness with which he viewed this situation. If they took the wrong turning now they might well risk rising disorder, encourage a UDI mentality, or bring nearer a dreadfully dangerous review of Ulster's whole constitutional position. So the time had come for them as a cabinet to make up their minds to start thinking seriously about these matters, and to weigh carefully the consequences of continuing on what he believed to be a collision course with the British Government.[3]

When the cabinet convened on 15 October to consider O'Neill's memorandum, there was general agreement that the retention of multiple voting was difficult to justify; but Craig pointed out the basic problem for the Government: he had publicly stated it would be premature to consider any element of the local government franchise in advance of general local government reform.[4] The Government could not easily row back from this position without its being obvious that such a political retreat was being forced on it by London. This still left the problem of a possible intervention by London. And with a meeting now arranged with Wilson in London, Basil Kelly, the Attorney-General, supported O'Neill's stance when the cabinet met again on 23 October. He pointed out that Westminster retained full legal powers to legislate for Northern Ireland, even in relation to transferred matters, and that the convention of non-interference without the Northern Ireland Government's consent might not hold if it came to be widely felt that responsibility for 'peace, order and good government'—the basic task for the Northern Ireland Government and Parliament as laid down in the Government of Ireland Act—was not being discharged in an acceptable way.

Herbie Kirk, Minister of Finance, expressed alarm about the evident hardening of attitudes towards Northern Ireland at Westminster; but Faulkner and Craig dissented, thinking it unlikely that London would proceed to any extreme course that would be wholly unacceptable to majority opinion in Northern Ireland. Craig warned that in the present circumstances a proposed change on the franchise could have disastrous political repercussions, and proposed to hold to his consistent public position that local government reform must precede any examination of the franchise. Faulkner suggested that Wilson might be told that the Northern Ireland Government had no dogmatic view on the franchise; evidently it could not be changed in the short term, but for himself he did not share the reservations which, he understood, some members of the Party felt about changing it in the longer term. Kelly added that he was not at all sure that the UUP as a whole would oppose a change, if given a clear lead by the cabinet. As a possible bridge between the Northern Irish and British positions, Faulkner advocated that a time limit should be set for the reform of local government, although Ivor Neill, the Minister of Development, doubted the feasibility of this given the intense difficulty of finding any generally acceptable pattern. Craig, however, was clear on one point: he could not agree that Wilson should be allowed to tell them how to act. Although they should go to the London meeting in a co-operative spirit, clearly they must be responsible to their own electorate and Wilson could be relied upon to appreciate this. Intervention would provoke a constitutional crisis and a 'massive uprising' of the loyalist community. Faulkner agreed that any attempt to impose a solution by way of a royal commission or otherwise would lead to wholesale chaos and virtual civil war. Devolutionary government could not be conducted if they were to consider these serious issues under a threat of duress which he did not believe would materialise. The basic issues were jobs and houses. When John Andrews, the Minister in the Senate, asked what was the present view on the Special Powers Acts, Craig replied that he had been actively considering the possibility of putting such powers into 'cold storage' in the next session; but clearly this would be inopportune in the present atmosphere.[5]

So, unable to carry his cabinet with him, O'Neill joined Craig and Faulkner as they met UUP backbenchers the next day. The backbenchers were seeking an assurance that at no time would the Government propose any change in the local government franchise. O'Neill and his colleagues warned them that such an undertaking, which would inevitably become widely known, could not be given; but, on the other hand, they emphasised that there had been no change in the position as publicly announced in Parliament by Craig on several occasions: the question of the franchise could only be reviewed in a general re-organisation of local government. This explanation appeared to satisfy the backbench deputation, allowing, in O'Neill's view, for all members of the Party—including candidates or prospective candidates—to adopt a consistent line. When this was reported back to the cabinet, Kirk commented that it would be difficult to justify the present basis of the local government franchise at another general election, and particularly the retention of multiple voting. He asked if it was not the fact that abolition of the company vote would make no practical political difference. Craig agreed that this was so; but in spite of this, soundings had revealed some intense opposition to abolition. Faulkner added that while he accepted the need to hold the present line on the local government franchise as a whole, he agreed that the company vote was difficult to justify, and he felt that a short bill for the abolition of multiple voting should be prepared for reasonably early introduction once a calmer atmosphere prevailed. Craig, however, argued that such a bill would place him in an impossible position, and would inevitably provoke a major debate on the local government franchise as a whole. On the other hand, it might be possible to consider the question at the time of the next stage of local government review, which he understood was likely to take the form of a white paper on functions, finance and representation. Ivor Neill stated that this stage might be reached within six months.[6]

Before the next cabinet meeting O'Neill tried once more to convince his colleagues of the need to alter their position by stating again—'however unpalatable it may be to us'—that Westminster had many sanctions which could be brought to bear on Northern Ireland. In the last resort 'we would either have to bow to such pressures or take a course of a "UDI" character'. He believed that no responsible minister would contemplate the latter alternative for a moment. So, in O'Neill's view, the clear logic of the situation was that the Northern Ireland Government should go to Downing Street, empowered by the cabinet as a whole, to tell Wilson that they would be moving forward with a steady programme of realistic reforms. It was not weakness but common sense to go into the conference chamber with 'some weapons in our own hands, rather than to be placed entirely on the defensive'. Taking suggestions which had been floated during recent cabinet discussions, O'Neill identified specific proposals:

(i)   Some form of New Town or Development Commission for Londonderry;
(ii) Early action to remove present obstacles in the way of Londonderry Area housing;
(iii) A clear commitment to local government re-structuring by a specific date;
(iv) Legislation within the next few months to abolish the company vote at local government elections.

O'Neill proposed that the cabinet examine these suggestions—and any others—with a view to reaching definite commitments on at least some of them. He repeated that 'if we are not prepared to show a willingness to cope with these problems ourselves, we are inviting intervention by others, and ... to imagine we can prevent such intervention without grave damage to Ulster is a delusion'.[7] Basically O'Neill was stressing to his colleagues that he had to have something to offer Wilson if there was to be no reform of the local government franchise.

When the cabinet considered O'Neill's latest suggestions on 31 October, Craig offered no resistance on the question of abolishing the company vote—although he preferred deferring abolition for another six months when he could present his white paper on local government finance and functions. Faulkner was concerned about the timing of the change: it was all-important. To make it now would give the appearance of a concession wrung out of the Government by violence; it would be greeted with suspicion by Unionists and with derision by the opposition. In this situation it would be better not to enter into any definite commitment at Downing Street. Basil Kelly supported this line of argument and suggested that the matter should be reconsidered after the Downing Street meeting. O'Neill agreed.

As for local government reform, Faulkner again argued that the Government's position would be greatly strengthened in London if a definite date could be given for the completion of the re-structuring process. He suggested that a reasonable date would be in three years; this was strongly supported by O'Neill who pointed out that by 1971 the next Parliament would probably be entering its second year. But Ivor Neill expressed serious doubts about the wisdom of setting any definite date, particularly one as close as three years; more time might be needed and he pointed out that the Welsh reform scheme had been under consideration for seven or eight years. Chichester-Clark, the Minister for Agriculture, suggested that it would be more prudent to declare a target date and went on to urge the early submission of detailed proposals from Craig. In the end the cabinet agreed that, at Downing Street, Craig would indicate that it was the Government's 'intention' to have the re-structuring process completed in 'about' three years' time.[8] O'Neill had thus shifted the cabinet from a position of no proposals to at least offering a promise of reform. But of course, all of this meant that, as things stood, O'Neill would still be travelling to London without any substantial movement by the Northern Ireland Government on the core issue—the local government franchise.

The inter-governmental meeting took place on 4 November at Downing Street. On the United Kingdom side were Wilson and Callaghan; on the Northern Ireland side were O'Neill, Faulkner and Craig. After welcoming O'Neill and his colleagues Wilson expressed the deep concern felt on all sides of the House of Commons both about the disturbances in Londonderry and particularly the causes underlying them. The formal position was that these matters lay within the competence of the Parliament and Government of Northern Ireland but that the Imperial Parliament—Westminster—retained the right to legislate under Section 75 of the Government of Ireland Act 1920. Wilson preferred to deal with the situation informally by seeking agreement on measures to resolve the difficulties but he had been forced to recognise the feeling in the Commons that the time had come for Westminster to intervene. He appreciated the efforts that O'Neill had made to introduce a more liberal regime and remove sectarian bitterness. But if events retarded the progress of liberalisation the position of the UK Government would become untenable and some 'more radical solution' might become necessary, perhaps involving a reconsideration of the financial arrangements or even a change in the constitutional relationship between the two countries.

Callaghan emphasised the political realities of the situation. The demand for action to safeguard civil liberties in Northern Ireland was pressing and the situation was not helped by the feeling in some quarters that the Northern Ireland Government was seeking to delay the introduction of reform in the hope of a change of administration after the next election. He wished to make it clear that in all this the United Kingdom Government was not concerned with the issue of partition. When this issue had been raised by the Taoiseach, Jack Lynch, Wilson had made the position of the United Kingdom Government clear and had repeated his confirmation of the pledge given by Attlee in 1948 and 1949. The political problems involving the risk of violence in Northern Ireland were fully appreciated but this made the problem even more urgent; violence would grow if legitimate demands were not met. He referred also to the very generous financial treatment that had been ungrudgingly accorded the Northern Ireland Government since 1964 when Labour came to power. The local government franchise—the plural company vote and the property qualification—was a most emotive issue on which he would be glad to learn what progress was contemplated by the Northern Ireland Government. Callaghan finally raised the issue of the appointment of a parliamentary commissioner for administration for Northern Ireland, or an ombudsman. The mere fact that the Unionist Party had secured an over-riding majority in the Northern Ireland Parliament for the whole period of its existence emphasised their special responsibility to be seen to be taking every step to protect the interests of the minority. They would be in a stronger position to reply to accusations of discrimination if there were in existence a system similar to that in Great Britain whereby the grievances could be examined by someone independent of that Government.

Replying, O'Neill explained that from the time he had assumed office as Prime Minister of Northern Ireland he had set himself the task of breaking down the animosities that existed between the communities in Northern Ireland. He had, for example, refused police protection in order to demonstrate that there was no need for him to be guarded against minority action; he had paid visits to areas of the country from which his predecessors had been excluded and had been received with a 'Kennedy-like' reception in Nationalist towns like Newry. Recent threats of assassination on the part of extreme Protestant organisations had forced him, much to his annoyance, to accept police protection; but he would not be deflected from his purpose of breaking down the communal bitterness that existed as a relic of past history. At the same time he pointed out that passions arose in Northern Ireland in a way that they did not in Great Britain.

Supporting his Prime Minister, Faulkner emphasised that the aim of the opposition remained the abolition of the border and it was unavoidable that any proposal for change should be hotly contested since the Stormont Government's supporters regarded any concession to the opposition as undermining the constitution. Craig then argued that the local electoral law could only be examined once the new structure for local authorities was known. The plural company vote was of no numerical significance and as more houses were provided the issue of 'one man, one vote' would follow the allocation of houses. The Government did not intend to delay their examination of the re-organisation of local government and it could be expected that a white paper dealing with the functions of local authorities and the financing of local government services would be published within six months. Their aim was to put themselves in a position to push through a comprehensive reorganisation at the beginning of the next parliament and to complete the operation within two to three years.

After hearing this Wilson and Callaghan expressed their great disappointment. They saw no reason why the reform of the local authority franchise should wait upon the reform of local government generally. In particular, they did not agree with Craig's suggestion that a reduction in the responsibilities of local authorities made the demand for 'one man, one vote' any the less important. Callaghan had noted that O'Neill had already invited housing authorities in Northern Ireland to adopt a points system. He thought that the Northern Ireland Government should bring pressure to bear upon the housing authorities to adopt a system similar to that used in Great Britain. Whatever the shortcomings of the points system, it not only helped to ensure that those in greatest need were re-housed first but also provided a system whereby those responsible for the allocation of houses were able to defend themselves against charges of discrimination in the way in which they carried out their duties. Wilson agreed, pointing out that the points system was the best protection against nepotism and suggested that the Northern Ireland authorities might consider a system under which different committees of local authorities were responsible for building houses and for their allocation.

When the discussion turned to the possibility of appointing a parliamentary commissioner for administration, or ombudsman, in Northern Ireland, Craig recalled that the Northern Ireland Parliament had already debated on two occasions the desirability of such an appointment and that it had concluded that circumstances in Northern Ireland were very different from those in Great Britain, so there was no need to make an appointment of this kind. The allegations of discrimination that had been made were directed against local authorities and not against Stormont, where the parliamentary commissioner's investigative responsibilities would lie. He thought that any further discussion of the appointment of a commissioner should await the outcome of the examination of local government structure and in particular the re-distribution of the functions between local and central government. Callaghan, however, disagreed and again urged that further consideration should be given by the Northern Ireland Government to the appointment of a parliamentary commissioner, if for no other reason than that the existence of a parliamentary commissioner would enable the allegations of discrimination to be investigated independently and so provide a means of clearing the authorities of the charges brought against them.

On the question of what was to happen with the Special Powers Acts, Craig explained that it had been the hope of the Northern Ireland Government that many of the regulations at present in force under the Acts could have been put into cold storage, say, at the time when the present Northern Ireland Parliament came to an end. They were, however, disappointed in this expectation by the grave situation now facing Northern Ireland and the serious risk of a recrudescence of IRA activity. The IRA had been extensively infiltrated by Communists and were concerned to intervene in trade and industrial disputes and to exploit any cause of social unrest. He gave instances of action taken by the IRA in the Irish Republic and said that the Northern Ireland Government had justifiable grounds for believing that a new campaign of violence was about to be instituted. He added that the Dublin Government were equally anxious about current developments in the IRA. Craig was satisfied that the IRA had played a big part in the origins of the Civil Rights Association; at the first meeting the Director of Education of the IRA and the Area Commander of the Belfast IRA, together with thirty sympathisers, were amongst the seventy persons present. These Republican sympathisers advocated protest meetings at flash-points of communal tension, two of which had now been seen in Dungannon and Londonderry. In these circumstances the powers contained in the Special Powers Acts were indispensable to the security of the state. They were seldom used but were essential as a deterrent against the IRA and could only be dispensed with if peace and quiet prevailed over a long period.

Craig went on to suggest, however, that it might be possible to devise means whereby powers of this kind were available to the Northern Ireland Government in a way that avoided weakening the authority of the United Kingdom in connection with the Human Rights Convention. He suggested that talks should be undertaken at official level to see whether some system such as at present obtained in the Republic of Ireland whereby similar powers were available on proclamation of an emergency, could be adopted for Northern Ireland. Wilson at last had something to welcome from the Northern Ireland delegation. He expressed the hope that the Northern Ireland Government would put its proposals into writing in order that they might be considered in discussions between officials. But in concluding this part of the discussion both Wilson and Callaghan again expressed their disappointment that the Northern Ireland Government not only had no present proposals for the reform of the local government franchise or the appointment of a parliamentary commissioner, but could not even see their way to publishing such proposals along with the white paper on the reorganisation of local government which they expected to publish in six months' time. They recognised that these matters were to some extent linked with local government reform, but could see no reason why progress should not be made much more quickly than contemplated by the Northern Ireland Government. They were also anxious to see prompt action taken to secure the adoption of a points system for the allocation of houses.

The final part of the discussion turned to the disturbances in Londonderry. Wilson informed O'Neill and his colleagues of the very great concern that had been expressed on all sides in Great Britain over the handling of the Civil Rights demonstration, stemming from the very full news coverage on television, radio and in the press. He recognised that under Northern Ireland's constitution the responsibility for law and order rested with the Northern Ireland Government but, in the absence of some impartial enquiry, he would be in a poor position to defend the present position. Moreover if the Northern Ireland Government was so confident that no undue violence had been used on this occasion there was no reason why an impartial enquiry should not be ordered. O'Neill pointed out that the film shown on the BBC had come from Irish television. Craig gave a detailed account of the events of 5 October, emphasising that the demonstration had been banned from this particular area and that the RUC were faced with the most difficult position of having to enforce the law against men who were determined on breaking it. In circumstances in which extremists of either party were prepared to provoke the police in the way in which the Londonderry demonstrators had done, the Northern Ireland Government had to demonstrate its complete confidence in the police force. No enquiry, therefore, should be ordered unless there were justifiable cause for ordering such an enquiry; an enquiry ordered as a result of political pressure could only undermine the confidence of the police and shake the authority of the Northern Ireland Government in its task of maintaining law and order. Indeed, Craig's examination of the events had given him no cause to regret his confidence in the RUC. The police had resisted severe provocation before taking action to clear the streets using batons and water cannon, and the hospital authority had stated that no cases of injury had been dealt with which indicated an undue use of violence. The use of petrol bombs later that evening had shown the degree of premeditation on the part of the demonstrators and he was satisfied that, had it not been for the efficiency of the RUC, violence would have continued in Londonderry for many days. Craig felt that it must be made clear to extremists on both sides that the law was to be enforced, otherwise they would take the law into their own hands.

In his response Wilson repeated that if the Northern Ireland Government were satisfied that no undue violence was used there seemed to be no reason why an enquiry should not be held to demonstrate the confidence of that Government. He acknowledged that the five main topics they had discussed—the local electoral franchise, the allocation of housing, the appointment of a parliamentary commissioner for administration, the Special Powers Act and the Londonderry riots— were all matters within the competence of the Northern Ireland Government and Parliament according to the 'present Northern Ireland constitution'. But that was not to say that these matters could be shrugged off by the UK Government, particularly having regard to the reservation of supreme authority to the Westminster Parliament by Section 75 of the 1920 Act. Wilson reminded the Stormont delegation that the UK Government had shown great generosity in their financial treatment of the special economic and social problems of the Province, but it could not be expected that this generosity would continue if Northern Ireland refused to accept the obligations that fell upon it as part of the United Kingdom. He remained of the opinion that the public interest at large would be served better by action taken by the Northern Ireland Government to remedy these grievances, but if the Northern Ireland Government failed to take such action a 'more radical solution' would have to be found.[9]

The Downing Street meeting left the Northern Ireland Government in an exposed position. Implicit in Wilson's final comments was the threat of direct intervention in Northern Ireland's affairs by Westminster. This could take a number of forms, such as financial sanctions or legislation at Westminster on the local government franchise. Ultimately, though, it could mean the suspension of the Northern Ireland Government and Parliament and the imposition of direct rule by London. The onus was on the Northern Ireland Government to demonstrate that it was committed to reform. In mid-November, as an attempt to demonstrate this, Chichester-Clark proposed a 'package' of measures to the cabinet that Stormont could put to Wilson and Callaghan. Some of the proposals were original while others built on previous cabinet discussions (three of them were those originally suggested by O'Neill).

The first proposal was a 'Committee to consider grievances'. Chichester-Clark made it clear that what he had in mind was a terminable committee to investigate the matter in depth. If the cabinet were to proceed with changes in other matters it was unlikely that the report of such a committee would be too damaging.[10] When the cabinet discussed this proposal the feeling was that, on the one hand, such a commission could gain valuable time, ensure a presentation of both sides of the case and make it easier to carry out necessary reforms on the basis of its report; on the other hand, there was an expression of concern that such a committee would be seen as an act of procrastination and evasion of responsibility by the Government. No decision was reached as a consequence.[11]

Chichester-Clark's second proposal was for a 'democratic decision on the local government franchise'. This revolved around whether or not an electoral mandate should be sought either through a general election or a referendum to alter the franchise. It was widely felt by the cabinet, however, that an election in the current circumstances could be confused and indeterminate, and while there was a degree of support for a referendum as an objective method of determining the issue, substantial doubts were expressed that there would really be a clear-cut decision. Moreover, if the Government were to adopt a neutral stance, hard-line MPs would certainly campaign fiercely against change. While the cabinet avoided any decision on this, Chichester-Clark's third proposal, relating to the company vote, was straightforward for his colleagues: it should be abolished subject to a further consideration of timing.[12] As to the timetable for local government reform the cabinet confirmed that three years would be a reasonable period within which to complete the restructuring process.[13]

On housing—Chichester-Clark's fourth point—the cabinet agreed that the Government would urge all local authorities to adopt a points system for the allocation of houses[14] with Faulkner being tasked to consider what sanctions might be used with recalcitrant authorities.[15] Chichester-Clark's fifth proposal related to the settlement of the financial relations between the Catholic Mater Hospital (which was disadvantaged in terms of financial support from Stormont because it refused to become part of National Health Service administration) and the Government; a long-standing problem the resolution of which, it was hoped, would have a profound impact on moderate Catholic opinion. The sixth proposal concerned an ombudsman. For the first time a majority of the cabinet took the view that the appointment of a local ombudsman for central government services was a concession which might be made without undue embarrassment.[16] Stormont officials were duly dispatched to the Home Office to meet with Sir Edmund Compton, the Parliamentary Commissioner in Great Britain, who explained his role and the functions of his office.[17] The final proposal was for a commission for Londonderry. The cabinet authorised the establishment of a special unelected development commission to replace the Corporation and promised full backing for the Minister of Development in resisting the pressures which would be generated by such a move.[18]

The cabinet had hoped that its discussions and subsequent decisions on Chichester-Clark's proposals would give them a package which they could present to Wilson before he next contacted them. Unfortunately Wilson was quicker off the mark than the Northern Ireland Government. British pressure on the Stormont administration now intensified. Wilson wrote to O'Neill on 19 November to express the British Government's disappointment that O'Neill and the Stormont Government had not been able to promise more immediate action on the matters discussed in London. He pointed out that the anxiety over the Londonderry disturbances had been but the culmination of concern that had existed for a long time on a number of issues. Wilson was pleased to hear of O'Neill's efforts to promote manifest fairness in housing allocation and of the subsequent decision of the Londonderry City Council to adopt the points system. In addition, Wilson had noted that his officials were meeting with their Northern Irish counterparts to discuss the Special Powers Act, and similar arrangements (as we have seen) were made in regard to the parliamentary commissioner. But, emphasised Wilson, this was only a beginning and 'we have a long way to go yet'.

It seemed to Wilson that the local government franchise, which was symptomatic of many of the present anxieties, represented a way forward towards reform, and 'we cannot regard the absence of firm proposals for action on this topic as satisfactory. We do not see the reform of the franchise as being so essentially linked with the reform of local government structure as to make it necessary to delay the former until the settlement of the latter.' What London wanted to see was a public pledge by the Northern Ireland Government to take action to bring the Northern Ireland local government franchise into line with that operating in Great Britain, with the necessary modifications relating to nationals of the Irish Republic. London wanted to see this pledge given at a very early date, but certainly within the six-months period within which Wilson understood O'Neill was likely to publish a white paper on local government reform. London also wanted to see a firm undertaking that the Northern Ireland Government would, by means of legislative or financial control exercise vigilance, ensure proper standards of housing allocation. Wilson once more hinted at the possible consequences of a failure to deliver on these reforms:

At our meeting I told you of the serious situation which would arise if we cannot have these pledges. As you know I have honoured the conventions that have hitherto governed our relationships. But we should have to have a fundamental re-appraisal of the situation, if these things are not dealt with.

I think we would both agree that it is infinitely more desirable that any legislation should proceed from Stormont. However this is a factor fundamental to democracy in local government and, particularly in view of the very generous financial contribution which we make for Northern Ireland, it is impossible for us to continue to defend a situation in which Parliament at Westminster retains supreme authority, but that authority is not brought to bear to ensure that all parts of the United Kingdom enjoy the same high standards in this respect.

Wilson warned that, if it were necessary for the British Government to resort to introducing legislation at Westminster, it would be wrong for the Northern Ireland Government to conclude that legislation would necessarily be limited to a reform of the local government franchise. It would be necessary to consider whether it should deal with other matters, and 'we should have to give a great deal more thought to whether we could continue our financial contribution at its present level'. Wilson had in mind the financing of the regional employment premium, the borrowing powers of the Northern Ireland Government, the special assistance grant and the fields of administration in which Northern Ireland expenditure was at a particularly high level: 'I have used plain language; I think you and your colleagues would want me to do so. You will want to consider what I have said with them with great care.'[19]

The Northern Ireland cabinet considered the letter the next day, 20 November. It was a day of mounting tension for, in Londonderry, Civil Rights demonstrators were preparing to defy another ban imposed by Craig. By now Craig's bans were becoming a farce. On 16 November four men were instructed to jump over police barriers in Derry as a symbolic defiance of an earlier ban. Fifteeen thousand people attended the banned march.[20] All meetings inside the walls of Derry had been banned but on 18 November the prohibition was broken several times following court cases brought against forty-seven people arising out of the 5 October disturbances. Fitt and Cooper were two of those who had been summonsed. Tensions remained high in the city.[21] There were minor clashes between Catholics and Protestants the next day.[22] The sacking of Craig once more became a rallying cry for Civil Rights leaders.[23]

So on 20 November at the cabinet's request the Inspector-General of the RUC outlined the situation in Londonderry as he and his senior officers saw it. They warned that it was logistically impossible to secure rigid enforcement of the ban on demonstrations with the city walls; that any statement of intention to enforce such a ban would not be helpful to the RUC; that further 'really firm' police action could lead to the most serious and prolonged disorder in Londonderry and elsewhere; and that it would be prudent to give early consideration to lifting the ban, particularly as moderates seemed to be in control of the Action Committee. The Inspector-General then made the general point that in his considered view, derived from long experience, bans should be used only in wholly exceptional conditions since they tended to create an atmosphere of defiance. The police had ample powers under the Common Law and the Public Order Act to deal with potentially riotous situations as they developed. It was much better that they should be allowed to exercise discretion and flexibility in coping with such situations. In response to a question from O'Neill the police stated that unless the heat could be taken out of events by political means the law and order situation could get completely out of control. This was clearly undermining Craig's position and he protested that if the ban were removed at this stage, elements hostile to the Civil Rights demonstrators might take the law into their own hands. The cabinet overruled him: the police advice that they simply could not enforce the ban could not be ignored. Ministers backed a suggestion from Faulkner that the Deputy Inspector-General and the County Inspector should go to Londonderry and explore, with moderate Civil Rights leaders, the prospect of securing a period of peace during which there would be no further demonstrations. The cabinet could then consider removing the ban after a period of peace had been demonstrated.[24]

This helped to reduce the immediate problem in Londonderry and allowed the Northern Ireland Government on 22 November to announce a five-point reform programme arising out of its discussions of Chichester-Clark's proposals. A new points system for the allocation of houses by local authorities was to be established, an ombudsman was to be appointed to investigate complaints, a development commission was to be appointed to take over the powers of Londonderry Corporation, the Special Powers Acts were to be abolished as soon as it was safe to do so and the company vote was to be ended. There was, however, no immediate decision on 'one man, one vote' in local government elections. Asked why the reforms were not introduced before people came onto the streets and rioting and bloodshed had resulted, O'Neill admitted: 'Perhaps they should have been. The point is that they have been brought in now.'

But the package did not appease the civil rights campaigners. John Hume, the school teacher who had emerged as an articulate and moderate voice, welcomed the points system for housing allocation, but said that there would be grave disappointment at the failure to introduce 'one man, one vote'. The Government, by refusing to grant 'one man, one vote', were, in other words, telling the people of Derry that they were not fit to rule or administer in their own city. This, said Hume, was a very serious matter. He had emerged as a substantial figure within the Civil Rights Movement in Derry. Together with Ivan Cooper he had formed the Derry Citizens' Action Committee (DCAC) in October from five local groups. The DCAC was committed to peaceful protest manifested in the form of marches or sit-ins. Eddie McAteer also criticised the Government for 'not grasping the nettle of one man-one vote'. While he realised that O'Neill had some difficulties to face in this regard, he warned: 'We will not rest until this, the simple background to normal democracy, is put into effect.' The *Irish News* editorial summed up the mood of Catholics: 'Too Little And Too Late.'[25] NICRA was even less impressed and almost rejected the entire package because the housing points system was left to local authorities to adopt, an ombudsman without power to investigate local authorities was useless in the Northern Ireland context, real local government reform would have entailed 'one man, one vote' and there was only a vague promise to repeal the Special Powers Acts. There was, however, a guarded welcome for the Londonderry Commission and the abolition of the company vote.[26]

If Catholics were unhappy with the reform package it at least bought O'Neill some time with Wilson. On 6 December O'Neill replied to Wilson. He explained that he and his colleagues had given long and anxious consideration to all the matters raised. In their discussions the Northern Ireland Government had regard not only to Wilson's views, but to its responsibility to restore, particularly in Londonderry, a more peaceful and harmonious atmosphere. Hence the decisions announced on 22 November which he outlined in detail to Wilson. As for the question of the franchise it went without saying that the Northern Ireland Government had considered this issue with particular care, bearing in mind the strong views which Wilson had expressed.

O'Neill, however, had to 'tell you that in asking us to make a pledge within six months to bring the local government franchise into line with that operating in Great Britain, you are urging a course of action which is not possible in political terms'. On several occasions clear and unambiguous statements had been made on behalf of the Northern Ireland Government to the effect that a review of the franchise would follow the re-shaping of local government. He and the Northern Ireland Government were convinced that a repudiation of these statements at this time would be widely regarded as a breach of faith; and indeed the view was widely held that so fundamental a change would require an electoral mandate. O'Neill hoped that this issue would not be allowed to get out of proportion. Although this was the slogan under which some people were demonstrating, the Northern Ireland Government was convinced that the real issues underlying the current agitation were predominantly social: Cardinal Conway, the Roman Catholic Primate, had emphasised the paramount importance of housing and employment, and this was also borne out by available results of public opinion polls. The franchise was primarily an issue appealing to political activists, but it was jobs and houses which most concerned the mass of the people. O'Neill stressed that, by the end of 1971, the Northern Ireland Government would propose to bring their re-shaping proposals into effect, and if—after considering the new structure of local government—they were to conclude that a change in the basis of franchise should be made, it could be implemented as the new areas came into being. O'Neill did not want Wilson to assume from this that a decision in principle had yet been taken; but the issue remained very much an open one, and the Northern Ireland Government would continue to give it the most careful consideration. In conclusion, O'Neill hoped Wilson would agree that the best means of achieving acceptable progress in Northern Ireland was through action by the Government and Parliament established there. The Northern Ireland

Government was willing, indeed anxious, to cope with the situation themselves in the context of political realities, and it would regard any fundamental re-appraisal of its constitution or financial relationship as a most serious step, likely to create more problems than it would solve.[27]

Wilson replied on 23 December when, having studied Stormont's proposed measures, he welcomed them whole-heartedly: 'It must be the hope of all of us that they will be speedily brought into effect in an atmosphere of peace and tranquillity.' But Wilson went on to write, 'It will not, however, come as any surprise to you that my colleagues and I are disappointed that you have not so far felt able to announce a policy of early introduction of universal adult suffrage in local government elections.' To the British Government this seemed to stand at the very heart of citizens' rights, and Wilson believed that the two Governments would have to discuss this again. He suggested sometime in the new year.[28] So it seemed that O'Neill had bought himself some more time. Wilson was clearly unwilling to force the issue—yet.

By the time of this exchange a dramatic change in the composition of the Stormont cabinet had occurred: the sacking, by O'Neill, of Craig. The background to this was a televised speech by O'Neill that became known as the 'Crossroads' speech. Soon after the announcement of the reform package attention had returned to the issue of law and order. In Armagh on 30 November the RUC were fully stretched keeping Civil Rights demonstrators and Paisley's supporters apart. With tensions rising, O'Neill appealed directly to the people of Northern Ireland for calm. This appeal was broadcast on television on 9 December. O'Neill warned that 'Ulster is at the crossroads', making clear his view that a Northern Ireland based upon the interests of any one section of the community, rather than upon the interests of all, could have no long-term future. He warned Protestants that Wilson had made it absolutely clear that if the Northern Ireland Government did not face up to its problems Westminster might act over Stormont's heads. O'Neill appealed for a swift end to the growing disorder throughout Northern Ireland, warning that 'as matters stand today, we are on the brink of chaos, where neighbour could be set against neighbour'. To the civil rights demonstrators O'Neill argued that the changes introduced were genuine and far-reaching, and that the Government was totally committed to them. If the Civil Rights campaigners were not entirely satisfied, O'Neill pleaded that Northern Ireland was a democracy, and he asked them to call their supporters off the streets so as to allow a favourable atmosphere for change to develop. Finally, O'Neill asked:

What kind of Ulster do you want? A happy and respected Province, in good standing with the rest of the United Kingdom? Or a place continually torn apart by riots and demonstrations, and regarded by the rest of Britain as a political outcast? . . . make your voice heard in whatever way you think best, so that we may know the views not of the few but of the many. For this is truly a time of decision, and in your silence all that we have built up could be lost.[29]

The speech elicited a favourable response from Eddie McAteer and Cardinal Conway while NICRA announced a suspension of marches until 11 January 1969. Then in a dramatic move O'Neill sacked Craig from the cabinet and replaced him with Captain William Long. Craig had added to, rather than try and help reduce, sectarian tension when on 28 November he made a speech at the Ulster Hall, repeated a week later, in which he displayed a lack of enthusiasm for the Government's ombudsman plan, and also criticised standards of democracy in countries where Catholics were in the majority. Craig stated that Ulster was facing a very difficult time, with 'all this nonsense centred around civil rights, and behind it all there is our old traditional enemy exploiting the situation'.[30] In December Craig declared: 'I would resist any effort by any Government in Great Britain . . . to interfere with proper jurisdiction of the Government of Northern Ireland.' Craig argued that Section 75 of the Government of Ireland Act, stating that the Westminster Parliament retained the supreme authority over all persons, matters and things in Ireland, was merely 'a reserve power to deal with an emergency situation', and he found it 'difficult to envisage any situation in which it could be exercised without the consent of the Government of Northern Ireland'.[31]

In the atmosphere pertaining after 5 October timing was everything: Craig might have said similar things before but he did not need to say such things now; heightening tensions was the last thing Northern Ireland needed at this point and Craig was well aware that the Government of which he was a member required this of him. O'Neill received substantial public support for dismissing his Minister. An 'I back O'Neill' campaign saw him receive over 150,000 telegrams and letters of support.[32] The Government tried to reduce tensions with what amounted to an unofficial amnesty to those being prosecuted for their part in disturbances: the Crown Counsel told Derry Court that it might take the view that prosecutions were not in the public interest.[33] O'Neill seemed to have found a corridor of goodwill amid the gloom of sectarian animosity. Perhaps no more than that. Unfortunately this was about to be blown away in the New Year.

A SHOCK FOR LONDON

In hindsight it might seem surprising, but the violence of October caught the Labour Government unprepared for the implications of what a greater intervention by Westminster might actually involve. The catalyst for the awakening came from an unlikely source: Eddie McAteer. He was received by Lord Stonham, Minister of State at the Home Office, in mid-November. McAteer had come to register his protest at the latest marching ban imposed by Craig. In the course of the interview McAteer pointed out that there had not been trouble between the Protestants and Catholics in Derry. The trouble had arisen between the Civil Rights marchers and the police. In this connection he was particularly concerned about a statement reported in the *Londonderry Sentinel* by a senior naval officer at the city's naval base, HMS *Sea Eagle*, that the Services would 'always be pleased to assist in any way with the maintenance of law and order in Northern Ireland'. McAteer wondered if it was fully understood in Britain that British naval personnel could be used in this sort of manner.[34]

It seemed that it was not, for McAteer's comments sent shockwaves through the Labour Government. No one had thought that British Service personnel might be involved in maintaining law and order in Northern Ireland. A note of the McAteer meeting was sent to No. 10 whereupon the Prime Minister asked for full consideration to be given to the question of whether or not British Service resources in Northern Ireland might have to be used to assist the civil authorities there, and in particular, whether British troops could be called out to assist with civil disorders. The Home Office suggested that the naval officer cited by McAteer might have been referring only to the assistance given by HMS *Sea Eagle* in providing temporary accommodation for Ulster police officers and sent a short note along these lines to Downing Street. Wilson's response was: 'Yes. But we must know where we stand. I am not so much concerned about what Stormont might ask, as what our reply would be. The Ministry of Defence must know the answer. I trust that, if it is the situation referred to by Mr. McAteer, the answer is no, and that the Ministry of Defence have made it clear to all relevant officers in Northern Ireland. The Home Office cannot leave the situation in this degree of uncertainty.' Wilson felt that the Ministry of Defence (MOD) should be given some guidance on the extent to which the armed forces in Northern Ireland should accept obligations to assist civil power.[35]

The answer from the MOD was not the one Wilson wanted to hear. K. T. Nash, Assistant Under-Secretary at the MOD, pointed out that while the Home Office unquestionably had a departmental responsibility for law and order in Great Britain, this would not extend to giving it the authority to prevent a provincial local council or police force, say in Birmingham, from exercising their Common Law right to call upon the military for help. The MOD could issue orders in due form to commanders-in-chief and others but could not properly order them to refuse a lawful demand for assistance in maintaining law and order. If the military were actually involved in Northern Ireland—in attempting to restore law and order—no doubt the Home and Defence Secretaries would advise the Prime Minister whether the military ought to be told to stop. But, pointed out Nash, they would all know that they would be 'breaking the law' if they did issue such orders, and that the 'lawyers and the Commons might even have an exciting time in due course preparing and debating an Act of Indemnity'.[36]

The Home Office were a bit more optimistic that London would be able to exercise greater control. Broadly speaking, it was the Common Law duty of the military authorities to come to the aid of the civil power if called upon by them to do so. In view of the long-standing IRA threat, the Home Office had no doubt that the Government of Northern Ireland—the civil power—already had arrangements with the senior military officer in the Province, the General Officer

Commanding Northern Ireland, for assistance if any particular situation demanded it. This would be with reference to the kind of threat likely to be presented by the IRA. However, it could not say that it was inconceivable that troops might be called upon to assist *in a civil disturbance totally unconnected with IRA activities*, although it felt confident that if any arrangements were currently in mind to this end, they should have been informed of them. Equally, the Home Office were confident that they should have a very early intimation in the very unlikely contingency of troops being called upon. They were reluctant to make any special inquiries at this juncture because inquiries of Stormont would cause a flutter there and an inquiry by the MOD would very likely produce the same result.[37]

The final confirmation came when Denis Healy, the Secretary of State for Defence, asked the most senior Services officer in the UK, the Chief of the Defence Staff (CDS), Marshal of the Royal Air Force Sir Charles Elworthy, for clarification of the legal position of British forces in Northern Ireland if they were called upon to give aid to the civil authorities there, and for information regarding safeguards so far as the MOD and the Services were concerned. The CDS replied that, as set out in the Manual of Military Law, Part II Section 5, under the Common Law it was the duty of every person to come to the assistance of the civil authorities to maintain law and order if called upon to do so. Military personnel were under no higher or lower obligation that any other citizens in this respect. The significance of their use lay in their greater power. In a situation of extreme necessity the civil authorities were entitled to request military assistance, but they should not do so unless the situation was, or was about to become, beyond civil control.

The law enabled reasonable force to be used according to the circumstances, but not more. When the military were employed in aid of the civil power it was the responsibility of the local military commander to decide what force was necessary to deal with the particular situation but he would be liable for prosecution in law if the force used was subsequently found to be excessive. If, on the other hand, the force he used was inadequate, it could be said he was failing in his duty. This law was the same in Northern Ireland. The reservation of control of the armed forces to the United Kingdom Parliament and Government did not affect the issue; the obligation derived from the Common Law. The CDS pointed out that in practice, a requisition for military assistance from the civil power should be given in writing (or at least confirmed in writing as soon as possible) and the appropriate military authority to whom the request was directed should, except in cases of great and sudden emergency which, in the opinion of the military commander, demanded immediate action, refer the request to the MOD and to the superior commander. All the above law was basically the same throughout the United Kingdom. However, because of the special problems associated with Northern Ireland, there was legislation—the Special Powers Acts—which was applicable only in Northern Ireland and which gave additional powers of arrest and search to troops when acting in aid of the civil authorities and if specifically authorised by the GOC NI. These powers, which could only become effective after the troops had been called out, allowed a member of Her Majesty's Forces, when so authorised, to:

a. Enter a house or building without a warrant.
b. Stop any vehicle on the public road and search it, and if necessary seize it.
c. Stop a person suspected of carrying firearms or documents, and search him; he may also seize the firearms or documents and arrest the person without a warrant.
d. Stop a person and make him show that his presence in Northern Ireland is not to the detriment of peace and preservation or maintenance of order in Northern Ireland.
e. Stop a person and order him to produce any information, article or document in his possession or control.

Healy had also asked, in reference to safeguards, what provision, consistent with political requirements and military effectiveness, could be made to ensure that proper consultation was always carried out between the GOC and the MOD before any British troops were committed to the maintenance of law and order in Northern Ireland. The CDS replied that in law there was nothing to compel a military commander at any level to seek permission before answering a request for military assistance in accordance with the terms of Queen's Regulations; indeed, he would be wrong to do so if the delay involved would be likely to bring about a worsening of the situation or prejudice the success of his intervention. The GOC and his subordinates had certain legal obligations which could not be inhibited or changed without a change in the law. It would not, therefore, be possible to ensure that consultation was *always* carried out *before* troops were committed in Northern Ireland. In extreme circumstances of urgency or gravity if a commander failed to act when the circumstances demanded it he would be acting in contravention of the law. However, in explaining the law relating to the duty of the soldier in case of riot or disturbance of the peace, the Manual of Military Law, whilst noting that a commander had the right and duty to act independently if circumstances so required, concluded that where a disturbance was grave enough to be beyond the power of the police to control it, it would be a matter of national concern. Therefore, pointed out the CDS, it would be most unlikely that a local military commander would be so cut off from superior command as to have to act on his own authority.

Bearing this in mind both the Army's senior officer, the Chief of the General Staff (GCS) and the Vice-Chief of the General Staff (VCGS) had taken steps to remind the GOC NI of the importance of referring, if possible, any request for military assistance to the MOD. The VCGS stressed in a signal to the CDS that, while appreciating the GOC's duty to act independently if the situation so required, it was believed that such a situation would be most unlikely. He stated that the MOD would expect to be consulted before the GOC acceded to any request. Another signal, from the CGS, made the point that before acceding to any request the GOC should refer to the MOD 'if humanly possible'. Therefore the CDS did not believe that, within the law, there was any other action the MOD could take on the question of consultation. In law, of course, the GOC was the sole judge of whether consultation was feasible. Indeed, even if he had referred the request to London, he might, if the gravity or urgency of the situation changed, have to act. If he failed to act under such circumstances he would be in contravention of the law; and if the MOD instructed the GOC to refuse a request for assistance the legality of such an instruction might be open to question. Under the law as it stood it was quite clear that the ultimate responsibility rested with the military commander concerned.

In reply to Healy's request regarding information on what instructions the MOD had issued to govern the use of military forces in Northern Ireland, the CDS replied that the Army Department had a general instruction on Internal Security (IS) in the United Kingdom which was issued to all GOCs. This instruction stated that the law made provision for certain situations in which troops might find themselves called upon to assist the civil authorities. These included situations of unlawful assembly, riot and insurrection.

The instruction stated that when a request for military assistance was received from the appropriate authority—as defined in Queen's Regulations in cases of immediate or pressing danger—the commander should take such action as he considered necessary, subsequently ensuring that the MOD was informed. In all other cases he was to inform the MOD and Command HQ immediately. The instruction drew the attention of all officers to the law and the procedures laid down in the Manual of Military Law and Queen's Regulations already referred to. In addition the GOC had also issued two recent instructions to the forces under his command. In an instruction to the Officers Commanding Regular Units he stated that while requests for military aid in Northern Ireland would normally be made to him by the Northern Ireland Government or by the Inspector-General of the RUC, exceptionally, in a local situation of extreme urgency, a District Inspector of the RUC might make a request to a local commander. He pointed out that the initial use of the military in aid to the civil power would be of critical importance and the consequences might be very grave. He therefore directed that a local request by a District Inspector, except in emergency, was to be referred to him for approval.

Here it seemed that the Army were one step ahead of the politicians and were already thinking of how the situation in Northern Ireland might develop: they were trying to avoid a premature deployment of troops to aid the civil power. More worryingly for the politicians the CDS considered it important to note that the RUC was an armed police force. Thus if the military were called out in aid to the civil power it seemed inevitable that they would also have to be armed. Although the commander was responsible for the degree of force used in the event, the situation with which he was likely to be faced was almost certain to need, if not the use of firearms, certainly the threat of their use. In sum the MOD believed that the military were required by law to assist in the maintenance of law and order in Northern Ireland, as elsewhere in the UK, if called on to do so by the civil power. They had instructed the GOC to consult the MOD, if humanly possible, before complying with any request for military assistance. With the law as it stood, the MOD did not believe that there were any further safeguards that could usefully be introduced concerning the use of the military aid of civil power in Northern Ireland. Finally, although not strictly related to the Secretary of State's questions, the CDS took the opportunity to make it quite clear that all military commanders at all levels were fully aware of the problems associated with giving aid to the civil power in the maintenance of law and order: 'It is probably the most unpopular and thankless duty a serviceman has and commanders would certainly be most loath to undertake this duty unless it was absolutely essential. However, they are also conscious of the most unpleasant consequences, political and social, as well as the loss of life which could ensue if there were a delay in taking action when the situation demanded it.'[38]

The final nail in the coffin that London might be able to avoid a military intervention was provided by the Government's law officers who confirmed the CDS's interpretation. The fact that the control of the armed forces was a subject reserved to the United Kingdom Parliament and Government while law and order was the responsibility of the Parliament and Government of Northern Ireland did not affect the soldier's common-law duties, though it did produce political problems. Healy was told that while he saw a dilemma in that the troops in Northern Ireland were responsible to him and through him to Parliament, 'in this respect you are helpless to control them because they are under an independent duty to assist in the maintenance of law and order'. The constitutional responsibility for the maintenance of law and order in Northern Ireland lay with the Government there and to this extent no question of 'consultation' could arise. If the Northern Ireland Government wished to discuss any matters in this field with the British Government, then the proper channel of communication was through the Home Secretary.[39]

So by the beginning of 1969, and with the possibility of intervention becoming ever more likely, it seemed prudent for London to begin military preparations since it was now clear that if the RUC failed to maintain law and order in Northern Ireland the Army would have to. In January the Defence Operations Staff began an examination of the problem of command and control for Internal Security operations covering aid to the civil power and ground defence in Northern Ireland. There was concern that, in the event of intervention, the GOC should not have to be responsible to more than one superior authority and that he should continue to report to the Army Department, and that the Chief of the General Staff should represent the Chief of the Defence Staff on the committee being formed in Whitehall to consider requests to the military for aid to the civil power in Northern Ireland. The Defence Operations Staff recommended that the GOC should have operational control over all forces of the three Services for the purposes of internal security covering aid to the civil power and ground defence. In carrying out this task the GOC would continue to be directly responsible to the Army Department at the MOD and the Army Department would keep the Chiefs of Staff Committee and the Central, Naval and Air Force Staffs fully informed of the situation in Northern Ireland.[40]

LONDON PREPARES FOR THE WORST

On 27 January 1969 Callaghan mentioned to Denis Healy that it was not beyond the bounds of possibility that O'Neill's Government could be replaced by a government led by Craig. Even worse a Craig government might ask for help from the military authorities in maintaining law and order. Callaghan supposed that in such circumstances the British Government might have to consider implementing direct rule in Northern Ireland—the suspension of the Northern Ireland Government and Parliament and the governing of the Province from London. Healy warned that this was not a possibility which could be considered on an ad hoc basis: the Government would have to be clear in advance what it would do if either a reactionary Stormont government were to ask London for military aid or if London were to attempt to impose direct rule on Northern Ireland. Callaghan agreed that contingency planning would have to be put in hand immediately.[41] The cabinet was informed the next day.[42]

The same day a meeting of Home Office and MOD officials convened to consider the defence aspects, both physical and legal, of a serious breakdown of law and order in Northern Ireland involving military assistance and leading to intervention by London. The importance of this assessment was the political consequences it had on the men who had to take the ultimate decision. Three broad kinds of situation leading up to intervention were envisaged: firstly, a single localised but very serious riot, involving intervention by troops and probably accompanied by loss of life (at this point it would be for the British Government to decide whether or not to assume direct responsibility for the government of the Province); secondly, a widespread and sustained threat to lives and property necessitating the presence of troops to maintain law and order on a continuing and long-term basis; and thirdly, a direct request from an extreme right-wing government in Northern Ireland for military assistance in putting down resistance in the form of direct action, for example the large-scale take-over of part of Londonderry by Civil Rights and Nationalist supporters who might well be armed with firearms.

As soon as the decision of the British Government to intervene was announced a 'twilight' period would begin, in which the Northern Ireland Government remained responsible for law and order pending the passage of legislation at Westminster, which might just conceivably be held up in Parliament, perhaps in the House of Lords, in which case the twilight period would be prolonged. Its authority might be completely undermined, and the GOC NI would use his troops to maintain law and order on the basis of their common-law duty, and independently of the civil authority if that were necessary. He was not in law under the duty to confirm the particular requests of the civil authority, only to the obligation laid down by the Common Law on his troops as soldiers and citizens. After the twilight period, when the United Kingdom Government had assumed responsibility for maintaining law and order, there would potentially be a double military problem: to maintain law and order and to maintain essential services as necessary. This would require planning of both military resources and of the legal powers that would need to be taken.[43]

Building on this the Chief of the Defence Staff, Sir Charles Elworthy, and Sir Philip Allen, the Permanent Under-Secretary at the Home Office, met at the MOD on 30 January. Allen did not think it practicable to consider running Northern Ireland from London. Even at the lower end of the intervention scale it was likely that, once the military became involved, they would have to continue to intervene further, and at the higher end of the scale this would apply not only to the military but to the Government in London. It would be only prudent to assume that the IRA would in some way cash in on the situation. At the lower end of the scale the military could expect to face any or all of the IRA 'problems', as well as riots, strikes on a large scale, illegal occupation of buildings, docks or airports and the taking over of sizeable areas on the lines of the Bogside. At the higher end of the scale Elworthy highlighted the possibility of dealing with active insurrection, disarming elements of the RUC/B-Specials, assuming the duties of the police force, imposing law and order and maintaining essential services on a country-wide basis, all of which added up to a very large operation.[44]

On the instructions of the Home Office the Parliamentary Counsel then prepared the first draft of a bill to make temporary provision for suspending the Parliament of Northern Ireland and vesting the executive power in the Governor to be exercised through such persons as he may designate as ministers.[45] The draft Northern Ireland (Emergency Provisions) Bill set out to 'Make temporary provision for suspending the Parliament of Northern Ireland and for the peace, order and good government of Northern Ireland, and for purpose connected therewith'. Clause 1 (1) stated that 'the Parliament of Northern Ireland shall stand dissolved'.[46] This meant direct rule from London. But when would it be implemented? Whitehall envisaged that there were three main situations which, if they occurred, might involve the imposition of direct rule. They were: (i) the resignation of Captain O'Neill, (ii) the use of the armed forces to restore order and (iii) the intervention of the British Parliament over the local government franchise. It was felt that, in a sense, all were subsumed in (i), since O'Neill had indicated (presumably to London) that he would resign in the event of (ii) and his resignation in the event of (iii) had to be regarded as highly probable. The Home Office expected any alternative government to be far to the right of O'Neill: it would hold out little hope of advance towards liberal policies and for that reason would engender disorders and perhaps large-scale communal strife which it would counter by repressive measures. If troops were used, except perhaps successfully in an isolated case, a situation might well arise in which the British Government had to assume full responsibility for administration in Northern Ireland. British ministers would be answerable at Westminster for what the troops did and it would no longer be tolerable to forego responsibility for the situation which rendered the use of the troops necessary. If the British Parliament enacted legislation relating to the local government franchise, the converse would apply. The legislation could engender disorders and the Westminster Parliament could hardly escape responsibility for maintaining order. An important question was whether any measures could be taken which fell short of the assumption of full executive power by London. It was very doubtful whether they could. In theory a limited reservation of power could be made, but where the power reserved was with, or directly affected, the maintenance of law and order, one would be dealing with one of the fundamental responsibilities of government. A government that had no responsibility for law and order was hardly a government at all. Apart from that it was hard to envisage a diarchy in the present transferred field.[47]

The next stage was, following consultations between the Director of Military Intelligence, the Assistant Under-Secretary to the General Staff and the Home Office, an assessment of five scenarios where actual intervention would be required. They covered in broad terms a whole range of possible situations, although not of equal probability.[48] The circumstances of Scenario 1 envisaged sporadic or minor civil disobedience and disturbances, very similar to situations that had occurred in Northern Ireland to date. In this example the primary aim of the GOC was for no intervention if possible. But if there were a request it should, if humanly possible, be referred to the MOD in London. If he were forced by circumstances to give military assistance, the GOC's aim was to restore law and order in the particular case in question as speedily as possible. However, if it was a request for the use of troops, and this was acceded to, then use of troops could lead to London deciding to intervene in Northern Ireland. In a post-election situation there were two possibilities: a liberal government returned, in which the situation remained as described above, or an illiberal government coming to power. In this case a problem would arise since this government, whose motives the British Government might suspect, could make a request for military assistance. It would then be necessary to see if there was any way in which this Northern Ireland government could be inhibited from making such a request. If not, then the only alternative would be for London to intervene politically in Northern Ireland. This would lead to one of a number of other scenarios.

Scenario 2 envisaged a serious but isolated riot. This incidence would not have arisen out of a deliberate plan but from emotions. The RUC, though armed, would be unable to control the situation because of the stage of violence reached or because police resources were over-extended; military assistance would therefore be requested. Again, if there had not been an election it was to be hoped that intervention could be avoided. If, however, an illiberal government had been returned, much would depend on the actual circumstances of the particular case, with possible political intervention from London. It could be expected that the IRA would take every opportunity to disrupt government and seize arms. It was also a possibility that the IRA might carry out ambushes and this would lead to a requirement for anti-IRA patrols on the border with Eire. Furthermore, it was likely that the reactions of the IRA and extreme militants, after the isolated incident had been quelled, were likely to change. An emotional reaction, to support their own 'kith and kin' and their own religious community, could set in, leading to a worsening situation.

The result of this could be Scenario 3, which envisaged serious riots on the pattern outlined in Scenario 2, but occurring or threatened or both in a number of places simultaneously across the country. Some six to ten towns might be involved. Riots could be caused by different factions in different places. Riots might well be of limited duration, possibly over two days at a weekend. This scenario could have arisen from Scenario 2, particularly if either the military had been used or civil police action had been extreme or thought to be so. It would be likely that firearms were in use and property was being destroyed. In this situation it was unlikely that the RUC would be able to contain such a situation without military assistance. With the police completely extended, law and order would be on the verge of breakdown. In such a situation either the Northern Ireland government would resort to the use of B-Specials or might request military assistance. In the circumstances described, the GOC's sole aim would be to restore law and order as speedily as possible, and be prepared to implement further military action that might be required. He would also have to be prepared to come under the authority of the Governor at short notice. The GOC would wish to have clear what additional legal powers would be available to deal with the circumstances described, for example the Special Powers Acts and what the legal status was if he was required to take 'preventative action'.

The RUC, it was assumed, would, as in previous scenarios, basically remain loyal. Some might quietly 'keep out of the way' and, locally, parts of the RUC might become ineffective with the general result being some reduced effectiveness. But it was feared that considerable numbers of the B-Specials, as individuals, some even possibly with arms, might actually join their kith and kin in demonstrations and rioting. Added to this there would be no doubt that militant extremists would be leaders of demonstrations, appealing to raw emotions, with some calling for further violence, revenge and avenging martyrs. In this they would be supported by the IRA which would ferment riots, possibly to take advantage of the situation to attack police stations and military installations. In this scenario, while it could be assumed that the majority of the population would remain relatively calm and likely to support any move to restore law and order the forces available to the GOC were unlikely to be sufficient. Almost certainly the British Government would have to intervene politically.

Scenario 4 envisaged a breakdown of law and order resulting from either an escalation of Scenario 3 and the British Government deciding to assume control in Northern Ireland, or a worsening of the situation described in Scenario 3 to equate to widespread rioting between various factions and/or communal conflict. The circumstances envisaged could involve:

a. Violence—including use of arms—between factions and communities. Destruction of property, burning, some looting, sacking of streets of opposing communities.
b. Citizens not taking part afraid to venture forth.
c. Essential services, supplies and communications out either by strike or because of labour that has remained at home or is involved in demonstrations/ violence.
d. IRA and militant nationalists on one side and Ulster volunteers and B Specials on the other—both sides in possession of arms and organised to greater or lesser degrees actively involved in violence.

Whatever government was in office in Northern Ireland it would have lost control and London would have decided to intervene and assume control. This scenario only considered a Northern Ireland government which acquiesced to London taking over control in Northern Ireland or the situation where in practice no Northern Ireland government was effective. London would govern through the Governor with an appointed executive council answerable to the Home Office in Westminster and making use, as far as possible, of Northern Ireland agencies such as the Civil Service and the RUC, who it was expected would generally do their duty. It was anticipated, however, that in the case of the B-Specials, London could see very considerable numbers, with or without arms, unorganised or organised, actively supporting the extremists and militants of their community with violence aimed primarily at the other community, and secondly, at London and even at her forces. Militant extremists and Nationalists, either without arms or with arms from IRA sources or caches, whether unorganised or organised, but certainly less organised than Protestants, would be taking active part in violence chiefly aimed at the other community. In addition to dealing with all these internal aspects it might also be necessary to close the border with Eire, possibly exercising control of entry into the country by sea and air, and in the worst possible case preventing interference, whether by government forces or otherwise, from Eire. All this could possibly require an infantry division in addition to the Northern Ireland garrison, with appropriate helicopter support.

Scenario 5 was the worst-case scenario. It envisaged circumstances in which in the British Government had decided to intervene politically in Northern Ireland and assume control but with the Northern Ireland government declining to quit office, opposing the take-over and then endeavouring to continue to exercise government as an illegal government. The British Government would be faced with deposing the illegal government and military forces might be required to assist in this operation. Clearly it would be impossible to have two governments—the British Government and an illegal Northern Ireland government—endeavouring to exercise power in Northern Ireland. Military assistance would be required to disarm and apprehend forces or elements actively supplying the illegal government and actively, and with violence, opposing London's assumption of power and British military forces. Here it was unknown what percentage of the RUC would remain loyal to and co-operate with the British Government. It could be expected, however, that very large numbers of the B-Specials, probably the majority, would actively support the illegal government. Protestant militants would actively support the illegal government. Opposing would be the IRA which would be expected to actively oppose both the British Government and its military forces and the illegal government and its 'forces'. It would endeavour to 'raise' the Nationalist-Catholic population to civil war. It would be likely to get considerable support. The military effort required would again be considerable, such as an infantry division reinforcing the Northern Ireland garrison.[49]

With these assessments before them the Chief of the General Staff and the GOC met with representatives of the Home Office to discuss the situation. While they doubted whether any group in Northern Ireland would be prepared to let the situation degenerate to a point at which Westminster would have no choice but to intervene, the consensus was that intervention might be inevitable if a state of virtual anarchy prevailed; but in whatever context it took place it would almost certainly provoke a worsening of the situation. Although it might initially be non-military in form intervention might provoke such bitterness that military intervention would be inevitable and the situation would resemble Scenario 5 in that large and responsible elements of the population, even if not the actual Northern Ireland government, would be hostile or obstructive.[50]

Suspend for one moment what we know eventually happened in Northern Ireland and put ourselves in the position of the ministers who had to take the final decisions on intervention in the Province. When Callaghan and Healy saw the scenarios produced by their officials it was little wonder that the Labour Government's policy became the avoidance of direct rule if this was at all possible: they were confronted with a potential quagmire from which it would be very difficult to withdraw. The outlook was grim. Now add the other problems with which the Labour Government was dealing. Given these maybe the Government should be given some credit for taking quite a firm line with Stormont: O'Neill was soon to be warned that the franchise would have to be altered or there would be British intervention. And London was still prepared to move to direct rule if all else failed. The question was whether the situation in Northern Ireland would give O'Neill time to produce a consensus to avoid this. But of course we can restore our hindsight to answer that one.

BURNTOLLET

By the time the above appreciations had been completed the situation in Northern Ireland had taken a turn for the worst. Burntollet has entered the history of the Troubles as yet another defining moment in Northern Ireland's descent into violence. It was here that student marchers were attacked by Protestant extremists. The result was that Northern Ireland was plunged into further communal disturbances. The idea for the march came from People's Democracy (PD), a radical student grouping which had its origins at the Queen's University, Belfast in October 1968. Prominent members were Michael Farrell, Bernadette Devlin and Kevin Boyle. PD was distinct from the Civil Rights Movement in that it was a student organisation, predominantly composed of young people, and with international links and influences. In contrast, NICRA was predominantly made up of branches in provincial towns which were rooted in traditional Nationalism and Republicanism. PD had affiliated with NICRA, but only as a tactical ploy. It had no constitution or recorded membership. At any meeting any person attending was entitled to speak and vote, with decisions at any meeting open to review at a subsequent meeting. There was no subscription or membership fee with funding coming from collections or well-wishers.

On 20 December PD announced that it was to undertake a four-day protest march from Belfast to Derry starting on 1 January 1969, breaking the marching truce announced after O'Neill sacked Craig. According to Bernadette Devlin, PD had been aware that the march could provoke confrontations with loyalists and the function of the march was to relaunch the Civil Rights organisation as a mass movement and to expose O'Neill, so as to 'pull the carpet off the floor to show the dirt that was under it'. In doing this Devlin was aware that 'we wouldn't finish the march without being molested'. Farrell was also well aware of the Protestant hostility that the march would arouse in the south Derry area through which the marchers would proceed. He believed the march would force the Northern Ireland Government either to confront the loyalists or to drop its pretensions about reform. The purpose of the march was to upset the status quo, with the result that the loyalists might back down, the Northern Ireland Government might fall, or the British Government might intervene in Northern Ireland's affairs, reopening the Irish question after fifty years. The march, according to Farrell, was based upon the Sema-Montgomery civil rights march in Alabama in

1966, 'which had exposed the racist thuggery of America's deep South and forced the US government into major reforms'. Farrell considered PD as not just a part of a civil rights movement, but as 'a revolutionary assembly'. Farrell had taken part in the Civil Rights agitation so as to radicalise the Catholic working class and to radicalise the civil rights demands themselves. Now Farrell wanted PD to 'complete the ideological development of the Catholic working class' and to 'develop concrete agitational work over housing and jobs to show the class interests of both Catholics and Protestants'.[51] Instead it heightened sectarian tensions with disastrous results.

It was decided that the march would start on 1 January, arriving in Londonderry on 4 January. There was the predictable opposition from Unionists but several Nationalist leaders, including McAteer, were also opposed to it, because of the violence it was expected to involve. Hume's organisation were also unenthusiastic, but they agreed to provide some sort of welcome for the marchers. NICRA, on the other hand, supported the march with a donation of £25. From the Ministry of Home Affairs, Captain Long tried to dissuade the organisers from their project but imposed no ban. The police had no definite threats of violence, although they expected it to develop at certain points.[52] So NICRA hailed the PD march as an apt beginning to the new year: 'the campaign will be renewed with even greater vigour and intensity in 1969'. PD were commended for resisting the subtle pressure of the new Minister of Home Affairs and the police 'whose forebodings are more likely to provoke tensions that lead to disorder than a peaceful march'. The Association dismissed as 'utter nonsense' the claims that the RUC's resources were being strained. This plea would fool no one: 'Police are never wanting on July 12, nor were they noticeably lacking on October 5.' NICRA added that it was the duty of the RUC to see that its full resources were used to ensure that the young marchers were not molested. Austin Currie also sent a message to the marchers on the eve of their trek: 'Hope your march will be both trouble-free and successful.'[53] He was unaware that, as far as the organisers were concerned, it couldn't be both.

The march encountered the opposition the organisers had hoped for from the start. On the first night about eighty marchers found themselves besieged for a time by militant Protestants in County Antrim. Six of the marchers slipped out of the hall and returned to Belfast where they contacted the Governor's private secretary in an attempt to secure more protection for the marchers the next day. They were told that Lord Grey, only recently appointed Governor, could not deal with the matter immediately. The PD delegation then contacted Downing Street in a dramatic bid to have British troops called out to protect the marchers. A police cordon had been thrown around the hall after a four-hour confrontation with loyalists on a bridge at the entrance to Antrim. Several fist fights were broken up by police.[54]

On 2 January scuffles broke out in the centre of Toomebridge as the marchers passed through the village. The marchers had earlier been foiled in their attempt to go through Randalstown by militant Protestants, and had arrived in Toomebridge in cars and mini-buses after being taken there through the side-roads by a police escort. Stones were thrown by a hostile crowd as the cavalcade of vehicles arrived in the village. As the marchers filed over the bridge at Toome and across the county boundary into Londonderry the procession sang the song 'Roddy McCorley'; a monument to Roddy McCorley had been shattered by an explosion at the bridge earlier in the day. A group of marchers carried a red banner written in Gaelic which represented the Queen's University Republican Club. At Randalstown the marchers were confronted by a large crowd of Protestants who carried a Union Jack and Ulster Flag. Workers in local factories joined them and kept their comrades at work informed of the progress of the procession.[55] Violence erupted again in Maghera as the marchers reached the half-way point in their journey. Police baton-charged crowds three times. At least four policemen and six civilians were treated for injuries. The marchers sent a telegram to Wilson asking him to intervene on the grounds that Stormont had lost control; Downing Street replied with a formal acknowledgment. Frank Gogarty, the NICRA press officer, claimed that the RUC now stood 'condemned as an inept force and one that is the willing tool of extreme Unionists. The events of the past few days have clearly proved the sectarian use of the RUC.' Gerry Fitt contacted the Home Office advising London that all the signs were that law and order had again broken down in Northern Ireland. Immediate intervention by the British Government was necessary. Either the police were now co-operating with the Paisleyites or were themselves being intimidated by the extremist Protestant thugs.[56] The accusations, however, were not all one way: Long accused some of the marchers of throwing pepper into the eyes of policemen. He pointed out that 'peaceful people do not go around carrying two to three ounces of pepper in their pockets, this must have been premeditated'.[57]

After the marchers left the turmoil of Maghera behind them they were welcomed as they arrived in Dungiven. By this stage some trouble had broken out in Derry. On the morning of 4 January the marchers assembled in Claudy where they met for an hour to consider whether the march should be called off. They were very tired, and although they were told that in Derry there were fears of communal violence they decided to march the last few miles to the city. At Cumber cross-roads they were warned by District Inspector Hood that there was a hostile crowd at Burntollet Bridge and that there was a risk of stone-throwing from the fields which sloped steeply down to the road beyond the bridge. The marchers decided to go forward. A party of police went in front of them. The marchers were told to keep well to the right-hand side of the road. At the bridge there were men with home-made weapons. The marchers in front were to some extent protected by the police presence. Those behind were not. Some at the end of the march broke away into the fields to the left and were attacked by individuals there. The casualties among the marchers were substantial, and several

were taken to hospital.[58] Major Ronald Bunting was prominent in the disturbances. Barry White, a journalist, described what he saw:

> It was a brisk, clear January morning as we headed down the road to
> Burntollet bridge but there was no one to appreciate the idyllic scene, with
> gentle hills leading to a tree-lined river and cows peacefully grazing on rough
> pasture. No one spared it a glance, for our eyes were drawn to the steeply-
> rising hillside to the right of the road, where already there were audible signs
> that the welcoming party was in position. A few students tried to start up 'We
> Shall Overcome' but soon lapsed into silence. Banners were furled, placards
> lowered . . . The few that had crash hats donned them a trifle guiltily and
> others pulled anorak hoods and scarves tightly over their heads . . . the . . . sky
> [was] almost black with missiles hurled from perfect range.
>
> A squad of police had the job of flushing out the ambushers from the
> hedges and field but they were hopelessly outnumbered. 'Put that down' I
> heard a few times as I made for the high ground but as soon as stones were
> knocked from hands there were others to pick them up.
>
> Not just pebbles either, but orange-sized rocks dumped in small heaps all
> over the field and some still in sacks. Bottles too were in good supply. Down
> the road it was like a mediaeval battle scene with the police vanguard pushing
> through against light opposition but the latter part of the march scattered into
> terrified, screaming clumps. The only escape was down to the river and, like
> foxes on the run, demonstrators threw themselves over the hedge and splashed
> across the knee-deep torrent.
>
> Scenting a noble victory, a Gannex-coated gent of a type usually described
> as 'respectable' urged the stone-throwers on to new endeavours. In the main
> they seemed to be farmers' sons, teenage and upwards, with the odd woman
> joining enthusiastically in the fray. It was a game that anybody could play, but
> the appearance of marshals with white armbands . . . suggested that there was
> considerable organisation behind it. 'Don't throw at the police' they cautioned
> as the accompanying convoy of police vans, packed with constables trundled
> past . . . The rout was almost complete . . . That was the infamous battle of
> Burntollet Bridge as I saw it, and what amazed me was that the march did not
> come to grief there and then. Some stragglers were rounded up by ambushers
> and 'worked over' with truncheons or flung in the river, but somehow or other
> they formed up again for the next battering.[59]

Some of the Protestant attackers were off-duty members of the B-Specials.
Burntollet effectively signalled the death of the B-Specials for if London were ever
forced to intervene one of the major casualties was likely to be the Ulster Special
Constabulary.

After Burntollet the marchers reassembled and made for Londonderry. The
three-and-a-half-day march ended in the Guildhall Square on the afternoon of 4

January. As the marchers, headed by forty police officers carrying shields and batons, reached their destination they were greeted by 5,000 supporters. In nearby Shipquay Street there was a build-up of several hundred Protestants who chanted 'Paisley, Paisley' and sang the National Anthem.[60] There was further violence. This occurred at Irish Street on the outskirts of Londonderry.[61] There followed several days of rioting in the city. Catholics in Derry accused the RUC of running amok—particularly in Lecky Road. The main complaint of residents there was that police had deliberately smashed downstairs windows in St Columb's Wells with their batons and that people inside had been assaulted. One of the housewives who claimed that a window in a house was smashed by a police baton was Mrs Sheila Tite, who was visiting relatives in Wellington Street. Her husband was serving with the US Army in Vietnam. She said: 'Early this morning I was sleeping in a bedroom downstairs at the front of the house when I heard a commotion outside. I pulled across the blind to look out and a policeman struck the window with his baton and broke the glass.' When Mrs Tite went out to remonstrate with the policeman he said to her: 'You Fenians will have no windows left before the night is over.' County Inspector David Corbett described the allegations that police were on the rampage as 'absolute nonsense'; the windows were probably broken when gangs of people were stoning policemen.[62] The Cameron Commission found differently. The police were in fact criticised by all sides. Allegations of inadequate protection by the RUC were made by Paisley's Ulster Constitution Defence Committee (UCDC). The Committee called for an inquiry into an attack on a Protestant meeting in the Guildhall. The UCDC alleged that the police were not instructed to give the meeting adequate protection and were ordered not to interfere with rioters hurling stones through the windows of the hall. Five policemen, it was alleged, were ordered not to interfere as Bunting's car was looted and burned.[63]

By 5 January, as a tentative truce between the police and the Catholic residents held sway, the DCAC held a meeting following police assurances that they would keep away from the area of the disturbances if there was no trouble. Plans for vigilante patrols were drawn up by Ivan Cooper who announced: 'We want nobody to enter the area . . . and nobody will enter it.' The meeting also arranged for all young people under eighteen in possession of any weapon such as sticks or iron bars to hand them in to the Action Committee. Hume told a gathering that no one could have any doubt now that the forces of law in the city were one-sided: this had been conclusively proved.[64] Fitt was also complaining bitterly about police behaviour; certain members of the RUC 'went completely berserk and wrecked almost every window in this small working-class area'. Unless the most stringent inquiry took place to root out those members of the RUC who took part in the affray, no one in Northern Ireland could any longer have confidence in the police force.[65] Makeshift barricades were also erected to keep the police out.

By 6 January things had deteriorated again and the Northern Ireland cabinet was informed by the Inspector-General that part of Londonderry was now being controlled by an 'organised and armed force'. He and his senior officers warned that considerable strength, possibly even involving the use of firearms, would be required to re-enter the area in the current atmosphere, and that thereafter it would represent a major and continuing policing problem. Accordingly it was their advice that other means of resolving the situation should first be attempted. The general view of the cabinet was that this situation could not be tolerated for more than a very brief period as there were grave dangers that others would take their cue from a failure to enforce police authority. They agreed, however, that in the short term the police had to use their own discretion in seeking the best method to solve the problem. Looking to the future, ministers considered the adequacy of current legislative powers and generally took the view that any review of the Public Order Act should include consideration of more stringent penalties, clearer powers to deal with counter-demonstrations and effective sanctions against those who participated in banned processions as well as the organisers. Herbie Kirk was the only minister to suggest—while having the greatest confidence in the police—an investigation by an outsider into the allegations against them rather than a domestic Northern Ireland inquiry. This would soon become a controversial issue and his colleagues set out the Government's stall by rejecting the idea. More immediately, consideration was given to the strength of the police force in the light of possible future developments. It was agreed that the regular force would have to be further supplemented both by a mobilisation of Special Constables and by a more extensive use of non-mobilised Specials on a patrol basis. As to the advisability of banning future marches, even taking into account the general view of the police that such bans were frequently unenforceable, there was considerable support for the proposition that, whatever the attitude to other types of demonstration, further marches lasting three or four days simply could not be tolerated.[66] When Long made the announcement on the Specials,[67] Currie immediately described the mobilisation as nothing short of provocation on the part of the Government. He could visualise situations where the Specials would behave in a worse way than the Black and Tans.[68]

As tempers cooled and the violent confrontations subsided—mainly because the police kept out of the barricaded areas—it was clear that community relations had been dealt a devastating blow. For example, a thirty-eight-year-old Derry Protestant worker was attacked as he left work in Lecky Road on 6 January. John Caldwell said the attack was completely unprovoked. The attack took place in the Bogside, now patrolled nightly by citizens' vigilante groups. His attackers hit him with sticks, fists and even their boots: 'The first thing I heard as I was leaving work was people running and someone calling to me "Are you Cresswell?" I turned round and said "No" and the next thing I knew I was hit with a fist.' Caldwell could not understand why he was attacked: 'I'm not even a member of any political organisation. I could probably understand if I had taken part in any of the attacks on civil rights marchers . . . But I'm not even interested in such things. I got a warning at dinner-time from a workmate, himself a Protestant, that I was a marked man, but I laughed it off as a joke.'[69] By 10 January at least five more Protestants—all young and including a seventeen-year-old girl—were attacked; all were scratched on the face with a sharp instrument.[70]

In Claudy, a village the PD march had passed through with a population of around 500 and roughly divided fifty–fifty between Catholics and Protestants, there was a level of bitterness described as the worst for over thirty years. Some Catholic businessmen in the town were being boycotted by Protestants. A publican and newsagent in the main street said: 'Ninety per cent of my business in the lounge comes from Protestants. Since the weekend strife this has gone. Their business has also disappeared from my newsagency.' A man who sheltered Civil Rights marchers *en route* to Derry had all his windows broken and received threats; and over one hundred Catholic girls from the local pyjama factory marched through the town and into the Protestant section at the Crescent singing Civil Rights songs. Their main aim, apparently, was to attack a garage owner who was alleged to have supplied weapons to Protestant extremists at Burntollet. There were all sorts of rumours circulating at the factory, including one that Protestant workers had been stabbed with scissors. Catholics, who recognised members of the B-Specials among their attackers at Burntollet, were consequently fearful once the Government announced the mobilisation of the USC.[71]

The barriers in the Bogside finally came down on 11 January following a decision from the DCAC to call off vigilante patrols because they felt that their point had now been powerfully made; but it warned: 'We will never allow a repetition of last Sunday morning . . . Our confidence in the forces of law and order was shattered when the ravage of people's homes took place in the early hours of Sunday morning.'[72] The tension in Derry appeared to be lifting—apart from the gable sign which proclaimed 'You are now entering Free Derry'—and with workmen repairing broken windows there were few signs left of the weekend trouble. The Housing Trust was prompt in starting repairs to houses and this seemed to have ended the threat of a rent strike. The feeling in the Bogside seemed to absolve local police from the trouble; it was the general opinion that any misbehaviour was by police drafted in from other areas. As an elderly man from Wellington Street said: 'We feel safe now as long as others stay out of it. We have made up our minds that they won't come here again. It wasn't the Derry police—you can't blame them and we don't mind them coming in.'[73] Clearly, though, there had been a sea change in opinion. Alongside the alienation between Protestants and Catholics (disastrous enough in its own right) there was the critical breakdown in relations between police—the embodiment of the state— and Catholics in Derry and crucially, in communal terms, with Catholics throughout Northern Ireland.

Almost as soon as the PD march had ended the blame game began. The police, said Eamonn McCann, had told the marchers at Comber that some opponents had gathered about 300 yards up the road and warned that some stones would be thrown. When the attack began the police had increased the pace of the march but not enough to get all the marchers through. The police to the left of the march had done nothing. McCann concluded that the 'only reasonable construction that can be placed on the sequence of events is that the march was led into an ambush. The police formation was such that the march was extremely vulnerable to an ambush.'[74] Bernadette Devlin was prepared to at least contemplate an alternative: that the ambush was the result of either a deliberate act by the police to lead marchers into a trap or a failure by them to reconnoitre the route properly.[75] In his first public comments O'Neill was understandably dismayed by the outcome of the march. He had some cause for this since it proved to be a turning point, and he watched all the goodwill generated by his sacking of Craig evaporate in the furnace of sectarian hatred. He described the PD march as a 'foolhardy and irresponsible undertaking'. At best, he thought, those who planned it were careless of the effects which it would have; at worst they embraced with enthusiasm the prospect of adverse publicity causing further damage to the interests of Northern Ireland as a whole. The Prime Minister pointed out that there were only 3,000 police officers in the whole of Ulster—that was one policeman to each 500 of the population. At times, one in six of the entire RUC were engaged in protecting the march. He also described some of the marchers and those who supported them in Londonderry as 'mere hooligans' ready to attack the police. Those who had, at various places, tried to impede the march using 'disgraceful violence' both to the marchers and the police had played into the hands of those who were encouraging the current agitation: had the march been treated with silent contempt and allowed to pass peacefully the entire affair would have made little mark and no further damage would have been made to the good name of Ulster. O'Neill believed that the only way to defeat the extremism of Republicans, radical socialists and anarchists was by the 'forces of moderation and not by the forces of some other form of extremism'. He recalled that it was the refusal of Catholics and Protestants to be provoked which defeated the last IRA campaign. Peaceful contempt would bring the marches to an end where violence would only tend to recruit further marchers. O'Neill finished with a stark warning:

Enough is enough. We have heard sufficient for now about civil rights: Let us hear about civic responsibility. For it is a short step from the throwing of paving stones to the laying of tombstones and I for one can think of no cause in Ulster to-day which will be advanced by the death of a single Ulsterman.[76]

Later he put it in more stark terms as he reflected bitterly: 'these youths are in fact stirring up religious feelings that were dying down . . . We had achieved peace before Christmas, the students broke the peace . . . If people had been sensible and had left these miserable, long-haired, bedraggled students alone, everything would have been alright.'[77]

Catholics, on the other hand, were clear in their view of where the blame lay. Farrell attacked the Prime Minister for devoting 'about 90 per cent' of his statement to attacking the march and 'about 10 per cent' to distaste at the manner in which opposition to the march was expressed.[78] The Derry Labour Party accused O'Neill of adopting the 'thick-headed' attitude of his Minister of Home Affairs: the result would be bloodshed in Derry, if not all over the North. If the Government deliberately provoked the police into the violence in Derry then Westminster should take over; if, on the other hand, the Government allowed this police violence to happen through sheer ineptitude then the same course of action was essential. O'Neill and his Government had created Paisleyism and they would not 'exterminate their monster because they cannot afford to'. The Prime Minister's 'liberal' views were now exposed as lies to mislead the people. He was exactly the same as Craig 'but with a much better disguise. The mask had slipped.' His bigotry was demonstrated by his threat to use the B-Specials: 'We warn him— this would lead directly to civil war.'[79] The DCAC condemned O'Neill's comments as 'disgraceful' and his attack on the marchers as 'indefensible' since, whether the Committee agreed with the march or not, they had preached and practised non-violence in the face of extreme and horrifying provocation. Furthermore, the Prime Minister's threat to mobilise the B-Specials was a 'threat to put uniforms on Paisleyites'. The DCAC had clear evidence that Specials were among the ambushers at Burntollet.[80]

In response, the RUC revealed that of the original fifty-seven officers who started out from Belfast to escort the PD march, thirty had been injured. The total number of police injured in Derry was seventy-four; one third of them had head injuries. At one point in the night a sword was thrust through the canvas cover of a police jeep. Another jeep had a long thin metal pole pushed through a canvas cover with such force that it went through the seat. Damage was estimated at £250,000.[81] The announcement that the RUC had begun an inquiry into police actions in Derry was dismissed by Fitt: it was an utter travesty to allow one police officer to act as judge and jury in an investigation of such importance to the whole of Northern Ireland. The outcome was a foregone conclusion. It was completely unrealistic to believe that a member of the RUC would condemn other members of the same force.[82] Coalisland Citizens Action Committee rejected 'as a monstrous lie' the charge that blame attached equally to both sides. Blame lay primarily with a 'weak and pathetic administration which has allowed this embryonic fascism to threaten all our liberties.' The time was now opportune for a campaign of civil disobedience.[83] Outrage was spread right across all anti-Unionists. Erskine Holmes of the NILP, who had been one of the marchers himself, believed that it was evident that O'Neill had reached the 'absolute limit in verbose empty comments' on events.[84] Harry Diamond of Republican Labour claimed that O'Neill's weekend comments had revealed his utter bankruptcy as Prime Minister: 'Black and Tanism is no substitute for social and political action.'[85] If there had been any hope of building a moderate middle ground before Burntollet it was gone now. And gone for good.

So, with the Catholic sense of outrage acute and, in view of the 'barbaric treatment' meted out to the marchers from Belfast, the Newry branch of PD decided that a Civil Rights march originally planned for Saturday 11 January, but then postponed as a gesture of goodwill, would take place after all.[86] This was probably the last thing Northern Ireland needed at this moment. But forced to deal with the situation the police concluded that the right course in the interests of peace would be to permit the proposed march to proceed, subject to re-routing which would exclude it from that portion of the proposed route where householders and shopkeepers were predominantly Protestant. In cabinet some ministers had asked whether it was wise to risk possible trouble for the sake of a comparatively minor re-routing, bearing in mind that those along the proposed route did not appear to be objecting to the march. It was decided, however, that this was a decision which could only be properly made by the police. The RUC were, on the positive side, able to report that tensions in Londonderry had eased to some extent. Detectives in plain clothes had been able to operate in the Bogside, and it was hoped that uniformed men could resume operations shortly. The regular city police had been able to enter the Creggan to serve summonses which had been accepted. However, the police warned that tension could rise again rapidly if there were serious trouble in Newry or elsewhere.[87] And there was trouble in Newry, although the disturbance which took place there differed substantially in origin from those which preceded and followed it.[88]

In Newry Catholic marchers turned violent for the first time. Lord Cameron's investigation found that the immediate causes of the disturbances in Newry were two-fold. First was the police decision to re-route the march after a threat of counter-demonstration. Newry was a Catholic town with good community relations, and many felt that it was objectionable to re-route at what appeared to be the behest of Major Bunting.[89] The other cause of violence lay in the 'ineptitude and confused motivation of the organisers'. The actions of the police in 'no way contributed to the disorders which occurred that night'.[90] Quite honestly, many Catholics were shocked that their co-religionists were to blame for the violence in Newry. While NICRA deplored the violence and destruction of property there it could not resist adding that the widely held suspicion was that the real culprits were not hot-headed youths but the people who were responsible for the maintenance of law and order. After the Belfast–Derry march the re-routing was equivalent to 'throwing a lighted match into a barrel of gunpowder'. It was not the Civil Rights Movement which was disgraced by the events in Newry but the Government which created the situation.[91] Fitt added that here was the occasion on which the Government finally capitulated to the forces of Bunting and Paisley. In an 'almost hysterical attempt' to justify police conduct at Burntollet and in Derry, the Government callously set out to 'sacrifice the people of the Nationalist town of Newry' to 'all the violence' they could find it possible to provoke. From the moment the cabinet had decided to re-route the march away from a 'non-existent Protestant area' it was evident that the Government, far from attempting to maintain peace, were only too happy to stand by and approve of any violence which might erupt. Fitt accused the police of 'silent approval' and standing by good humouredly while their tenders were being taken away to be burned. The Government was well aware that the eyes of the world were focused on these incidents and the police, far from taking any action to prevent what was happening, appeared to condone the burning of their vehicles.[92] Hume at least had the honesty to condemn without reservation the hooliganism and violence, some of it engineered, in Newry. People who engaged in that sort of activity could not consider themselves supporters of the Civil Rights Movement, he said. The violence was a salutary lesson to the movement that non-violent protest was the only effective protest.[93]

To be fair, after reflection, the Newry branch of PD admitted that most of the vandalism in the town was caused by 200 'irresponsibles'; they couldn't resist, however, blaming the police for failing to remove them before the march arrived at the RUC barricades.[94] Later Hume emphasised the greatest asset that the Civil Rights Movement ever had: 'We must be non-violent, even to the point of being smashed to the ground . . . Violence gets publicity and if we create it it is bad publicity.' He pointed out that when the Civil Rights Movement started it had no 'physical or political power, but when . . . the power of the spirit was risen, nothing could put it out'. If they continued to hold their heads high and march forward, despite the blows rained upon them, the view that would go out to the world was of innocent, quiet and peaceful people marching for their civil rights. This would bring the sympathy they needed.[95]

By now O'Neill was a worried man. He was aware that any more violence and there was a likely London intervention; but it might be possible to stave this off by appointing an inquiry into the disturbances. Yet the very fact that Catholics were demanding one seemed a good reason for Protestants to oppose one. Nevertheless O'Neill decided in favour of one and he told his cabinet so in mid-January. He had received a letter from the Irish Council of Churches calling upon the Government 'to institute a judicial and public inquiry into all the events and decisions which surround the present controversy'. O'Neill opened his case to his colleagues by expressing the view that at recent cabinet meetings the Government had tended to be preoccupied by the purely law-and-order aspects of the present situation. Their decision to reinforce the police was inevitable, but the Prime Minister did not think that the cabinet should delude themselves that so-called 'firm government' through the exercise of police power would provide any satisfactory answer to their problem. If the Government were to be forced to consider the ultimate remedy of seeking army support for the civil power, O'Neill had been left in no doubt by the Home Secretary that the British Government would refuse to give such help unconditionally. He therefore considered it essential that the Government continue to search for political as well as law-and-order solutions. Clearly no concession would satisfy those elements that were bent upon disruption as an end in itself. But the Government would take an enormous amount of steam out of the Civil Rights Movement if it 'demobilised' all its moderate support. It was in this context that O'Neill welcomed the suggestion of an inquiry of some kind.

He reminded his colleagues that such a step was amongst the proposals which Chichester-Clark had put forward in November. Even at that stage several members of the cabinet had seen some merit in it. Developments since that time convinced O'Neill that it was now essential. He asked: 'What have we to lose by such an inquiry? As things stand it is all too widely accepted throughout the United Kingdom that a sectarian Government, directing a partisan police force, is confronting a movement of idealists'. The complexities of the situation, and not least the involvement in Civil Rights of some extremely sinister elements, had not been successfully brought out. An inquiry might criticise some of the Government's actions or some of the actions of the police. But such criticism was being made in any event and in the case of the police had already led to a domestic inquiry whose results would be available before long. A wider inquiry could hardly fail to bring out in an objective way the real difficulties of the situation and the real aims of some of those involved. An inquiry into, amongst other issues, the aims of the Civil Rights Movement, might well conclude that on the question of the local government franchise the arguments for change were well founded. In setting up an inquiry the Government would have to face up to this possibility and to the implications of telling the UUP that such a change had to come.

O'Neill pointed out that the Government was committed to a review of the franchise once the pattern of their new local government structure had been established. He asked if any of his colleagues seriously imagined that the Government could conduct such a review and announce that it had decided to retain the present system. He did not believe this to be feasible at all. A review would involve stubborn political resistance to a change—which was in any case inevitable—and cause Northern Ireland immense damage. The Prime Minister knew full well that if and when the Government made this change, control in certain areas would be lost: 'But our loss of prestige, authority and standing since 5th October has already been catastrophic, and in my view the most cold-blooded appraisal of the situation shows that in resisting this molehill of reform we are allowing a mountain to fall upon us.' O'Neill reminded his colleagues that these were views which he had expressed consistently at numerous cabinet meetings in October and November. On 20 November, for instance, he had expressed fear 'that they might have a major fight to "sell" to their Party a "package" without the franchise, only to find that this omission made it unacceptable either to the Civil Rights campaign or Mr Wilson'; and on 21 November, after the cabinet had agreed to the five-point 'package', he was on record as having 'wondered whether the package, positive and concrete as it was, would be sufficient in the absence of a commitment to alter the local government franchise, to satisfy the United Kingdom Government or to restrain the Civil Rights marchers'.

It was now evident to O'Neill that 'we have achieved neither of these objectives'. He wanted his colleagues to understand very clearly that he was not opposed to the adoption of universal adult suffrage at local government elections; indeed, he believed it to be right in principle. He wanted it to be understood, therefore, that in endorsing the proposal for an inquiry he was asking all his colleagues to accept that a change of franchise might well be recommended and that it would be their duty to convince the UUP that this change must be made. O'Neill believed that the Government had to make this further attempt to restore confidence and to cope with the situation by political means. Any effort to impose a purely law-and-order solution was doomed to failure, and the implications could be disastrous. The Prime Minister had asked his colleagues immediately after the Londonderry disturbances to authorise some step to take the heat out of the situation; all that he had been authorised to do was to hold a housing conference. He then urged most strongly that the Government should take some positive proposals to Downing Street; but the decision was that they should go naked into the conference chamber. They had agreed on proposals which most of them knew in their hearts would not really meet the situation. Now, in this concept of an inquiry, O'Neill saw a very late, if not last, chance to deal with events before they disposed of them. But he was not prepared to preside indefinitely over a Government of which it would be said 'Too little, and too late'.[96]

In the ensuing discussion Chichester-Clark, Long, Fitzsimmons, Andrews and Ivor Neill supported the proposal while William Morgan, Minister for Health and Social Services, expressed concern about the effect which a commission might have upon police morale. Faulkner voiced anxiety on a number of grounds. This step, in his view, would be regarded as an abdication by the Government of responsibilities that were properly its own. Everyone knew that the franchise question was fundamental and in his opinion it would be more straightforward to tackle this issue head on. A commission could too easily develop into a fundamental, far-reaching and potentially highly embarrassing inquest into every aspect of Northern Ireland's affairs. Faulkner suggested that a more direct approach would be to agree as a cabinet to universal adult suffrage at local government elections and to tell the UUP that this was now their view. If this view was rejected the Government would, of course, have to resign. As he had indicated in October, he had never had the reservations on this issue which some members of the Party felt. Morgan agreed that the question of the franchise was the one major issue of contention now outstanding and that it would be better to tackle this directly.

The other ministers, however, did not share these views. They pointed out that the Civil Rights demonstrators had already declared other aims as well as a change in the franchise. An abrupt switch of policy in this respect would clearly be seen as action under duress; and moreover, action most unlikely to be acceptable to the UUP in view of the very recent pledges given to them. A 'considerable consensus' emerged that any breathing-space gained by the appointment of a commission should be used to press on as rapidly as possible with the re-structuring of local government and review of the franchise within the context of existing pledges.[97] With his cabinet's agreement—minus Faulkner and Morgan's dissension—O'Neill contacted Callaghan to make sure there would be no suggestion from London that, in announcing a commission, he was acting under pressure from Westminster. In particular, he was worried about the possibility of a Westminster debate on the Northern Ireland situation. Callaghan agreed that it would be preferable to defer a debate until the commission had completed their work, which was expected to be in three or four months' time.[98]

The Northern Ireland Government now advised the Governor to appoint a high-level and independent commission to inquire into and report upon the course of events leading to the violence of 5 October and to assess the composition and aims of those bodies involved in the current agitation and any incidents arising out of it.[99] In the light of this decision Long sought a strengthening of public order legislation.[100] This was approved by the cabinet[101] and it was announced that the Government would not tolerate any civil disorder or other disregard of the law. There would be a reinforcement and extension of existing legal powers with Parliament being asked to approve a number of amendments to the Public Order Act. This would include provisions to:

a. set out in further detail the principles to be followed by the Police in the directions they give to processions;
b. make it an offence not merely (as at present) to organise or assist in the organisation of a procession which has been banned or of which no notice has been given, but also to take part in any such procession;
c. make it clear that no counter procession or meeting will be allowed to interfere with a customary procession or one permitted by and complying with the directions of the Police;
d. make it an offence to hinder, molest, obstruct or act in a disorderly manner towards persons in a lawful procession;
e. require persons suspected of having an intention of acting as at (d) above to give their names and addresses to the Police;
f. make it an offence to organise, control, manage, train or take part in any association of persons which usurps the functions of the Police or the Armed Forces of the Crown, or is employed for the use or display of physical force in promoting any political object;

g. substantially increase certain existing penalties for offences under the Act of
    1951; and
h. otherwise strengthen or improve the law in this field.[102]

Nationalists, while opposing the new public order legislation, generally welcomed
the commission, which would be chaired by a Scottish judge, Lord Cameron. Fitt
said the inquiry was tantamount to a royal commission and recalled that, in his
Westminster maiden speech in 1966, he had called for one to inquire into the
operation of the Government of Ireland Act.[103] A potential flash-point was also
removed when Strabane Civil Rights Committee called off its march, planned for
18 January, to prevent the possibility of demonstrators being led into a
Government 'trap'. In response Bunting's Loyal Citizens of Ulster postponed a
motorcade which would have taken them through the town.[104]

    But there was resistance from the Unionist back benches. Harry West described
the decision to appoint the commission as 'high-handed', putting the Unionist
Party on trial without even discussing it with the Parliamentary Party. In his
opinion the Civil Rights Movement 'is a cloak for our traditional enemies who are
pressing not so much for reform and concessions as for control—and they will
not cease this agitation until they get it.'[105] Craig sought to put down a Parliamentary
motion seeking assurances that the Government would resist any attempted
interference on issues within the competence of Stormont—in particular he
meant the local government franchise.[106] He doubted that any reassurances on
policy from O'Neill would be enough: asked if the Prime Minister would have to
make way for a new leader, Craig replied: 'It seems to me we are moving in that
direction.' There was a feeling in the country that the Government, in appointing
the commission, had shown a lack of confidence in itself: 'There is a great deal of
annoyance over it.' While accepting that the public support for the Prime
Minister, after the dramatic 'Ulster at the Crossroads' speech, was a genuine desire
to have peace restored in the country, Craig felt that, after reflection, a large body
of public opinion realised there were 'serious damaging concessions' being made
by the Prime Minister.[107] Later Craig told a meeting of Unionists that the most
important of the basic principles of Unionism was 'Unity in our party'.[108]

    But this dissent was clearly survivable – until another crisis developed for
O'Neill. And this one was a bombshell. Faulkner suddenly announced his
resignation from the Government, citing the reasons he had expressed to the
cabinet. He was followed by Morgan who later complained that the cabinet had
only been made aware of the Prime Minister's intention to have an external
commission late on the day before the meeting to discuss it was called: the
decision was O'Neill's. It then became clear at the cabinet meeting, claimed
Morgan, that the likely outcome of the commission would be 'one man, one vote'.
It further became obvious to Morgan that the commission was merely a device to
bring about this measure because it was thought that to introduce it straight away

would provoke hostility among a considerable section of Unionist voters. Upon reflection, Morgan found it impossible to agree to such a move: 'Indeed, I strenuously resented any attempt to pass to an outside body the function of adjudicating upon our own affairs. I deeply resented . . . as I felt any decent Ulsterman would resent . . . the importation of outsiders to arbitrate on matters which it was perfectly within the ability and competence of the Ulster Parliament to determine.' It was even more distasteful to Morgan that the Prime Minister could bring himself to use such a device to introduce legislation and reform that he had not the courage to promote.[109] But it was Faulkner's resignation that was the damaging one: after O'Neill he was the most high-profile man in the cabinet and certainly the most dynamic. He later described it as a 'heart-breaking' decision. He delivered his resignation to the Prime Minister by hand, and according to his account, told O'Neill that if they both put it to the Party that 'one man, one vote' must be agreed they could succeed in persuading it to accept the reform. But O'Neill was convinced that the findings of the commission would be necessary to combine with 'the Westminster stick in order to beat his party into acceptance'.[110] This led to a bitter public exchange between O'Neill and Faulkner. The Prime Minister accused his former colleague of a lack of public support for his premiership going back to 1966.[111] The resignations were a godsend to O'Neill's critics and the Government was thrown into crisis once more.

Chapter 6 ∾

TOWARDS DISASTER:
NORTHERN IRELAND
FEBRUARY–AUGUST 1969

ULSTER AT THE CROSSROADS

The resignations of Faulkner and Morgan on their own were enough to raise once more the issue of O'Neill's premiership; they also acted as a catalyst for other disgruntled MPs to strike at the Prime Minister: less than twenty-four hours after the endorsement of his policies without a division in a Stormont debate, a group of 'rebels' struck unexpectedly with a statement calling for a change in the party leadership. On 29 January twelve backbenchers, including Craig, West, Boal, John Taylor and John Brooke, protested that the disunity in the Parliamentary Party and in the constituency associations had reached 'grave proportions' and, being 'dedicated to the belief' that the 'progressive policies' of the Unionist Party must be vigorously pursued by a united party, were satisfied that there must be a change in the leadership.[1] Craig described O'Neill as 'the greatest supporter of Mr Paisley'. Because of the lack of trust in O'Neill's leadership, those who looked to Unionism for their lead were now turning to the extremism that Paisley stood for. Craig suggested the Prime Minister visit the constituencies in order to get some sense of the strength of feeling in the country.[2]

As the rebel MPs met at a hotel in Portadown, Craig made it clear that they were not advocating a change of Government policy or the formation of a reactionary government: 'This is not a policy issue.' Craig suggested that John Andrews, the Leader of the Senate and son of a former Prime Minister, or William Morgan, 'are typical of the sort of men' who could replace O'Neill.[3] Another of the rebels, A. W. Anderson from Derry, also insisted that he accepted the five-point reform programme; the point of departure for him came when O'Neill said that he did not want a united Unionist Party but a united Ulster.[4] Explaining his actions Joe Burns stressed that his 'first thought was for the Party'. When he realised that 'nothing but nothing must be done which would split the Party' and that O'Neill could not, at any time, unite the Party 'the rest of it was easy' for him.[5] Together with the malcontents, Faulkner and Morgan, this 'Portadown Parliament' placed O'Neill in a precarious position with a significant number of the Parliamentary Party openly dissatisfied with his premiership.

The Prime Minister made a defiant reply declaring that while the rebels were claiming the issue was a change in leadership what they really wanted was a change in policy. But there would be no change of policy because he believed the present policies to be the correct ones. O'Neill declared that 'I intend to stand up and fight, together with those who have supported me in what I believe in. I will not back down. I will not trim my sails. I will do my duty.'[6] Almost immediately the cabinet and the officers of the UUC announced their support for the Prime Minister. From outside the Party all twenty-two ministers of the Presbyterian Church in Ireland added their approval.[7] Further evidence of support for O'Neill in the country included a declaration of support by 120 Church of Ireland clergy headed by four bishops. In Derry a petition was launched by local businessmen calling on Anderson to withdraw his name from the demand for a change of leader. Captain Ardill and Joe Burns, who had resigned as an assistant Government Whip, came under constituency pressure to withdraw from the campaign to oust O'Neill.[8] Burns received a narrow vote of no confidence in him from the executive of the North Down Unionist Association.[9] In Anderson's constituency opponents set up a caravan outside the Guildhall to collect signatures in an effort to force the MP to change his stance. A poster proclaimed: 'Support the Prime Minister. Anderson must go.'[10]

The Unionist Party made arrangements to call a meeting of the parliamentary grouping for 5 February. However, comments in the press by one of the rebels suggested that the dissidents were less concerned with decisions in the Parliamentary Party than with ridding themselves of O'Neill by any means; this allowed the Prime Minister and the cabinet to present the group's actions as a rejection of normal party procedures. The rebels' decision to hold their meeting to discuss tactics was the trigger for this: they had taken the debate outside the Parliamentary Party to the country and the cabinet decided that 'it is in the country that the answer must be taken'. O'Neill announced that the Governor had consented to dissolve the Northern Ireland Parliament with polling on 24 February.[11] Ten of the rebel MPs responded to the election announcement by calling for O'Neill's resignation in order to prevent a breaking up of the UUP. In a rebel 'manifesto' they crystallised their objections and ideas in four points: unity; strong, stable government; firm leadership and cabinet government; and 'realistic progressive policies for all'.[12] Austin Ardill criticised the Prime Minister for calling an election in which 'no one knows the issues at stake. The crisis is just a question of whether you vote for O'Neill or Unionism.' The leadership issue was a 'matter to be sorted out . . . behind closed doors. It is a family dispute, confined to the Unionist Party.'[13] O'Neill, in turn, responded to the criticism that he was disregarding the welfare of the Party by recalling that, in one of his books, Winston Churchill had made the following scathing reference to Stanley Baldwin: 'Baldwin confesses to putting party before country.' The Prime Minister believed that he owed his first duty to the country and to its constitution. The best way to protect that constitution, 'not just for our time but for generations to come', was to rally support from every section of Ulster. 'You cannot shout "Ulster is British" on [the] one hand and show a complete disregard for all British opinion on the other.' O'Neill believed that the logic of arguments such as Anderson's 'is that he wants to preserve an absolutely united party, even if it is bound to lead to a united Ireland. I say that I wanted a united Ulster so that it can stay in the United Kingdom.'[14]

The threat to O'Neill's position was not only from within the Unionist Party. Paisley sensed his moment had come. He decided to stand against O'Neill in his own constituency of Bannside. O'Neill came out fighting, lashing out at Paisley and his followers describing them as a 'collection of Canutes vainly trying to hold back the tide of the 20th century. They are political dinosaurs, suitable for relegation by the electorate to the natural history museum of politics.'[15] The Prime Minister felt that Paisley could 'not exist in any other part of the United Kingdom but Northern Ireland. He would be laughed out of court.' 'That is his tragedy.' More generally, O'Neill commented that Northern Ireland tended to have a 'fortress mentality'. There was a certain resistance to reform. But Catholics had to be made to feel that Northern Ireland was their home.[16] He warned that unless the Unionist Party attracted the support of Catholics the future of Northern Ireland was 'not too rosy'. O'Neill made particular reference to the fact that over fifty per cent of the children attending school belonged to the Catholic faith.[17] He argued that the threat to the Union took two forms. One was that, by failing to restore peace in Ulster, the work of fifty years could be ruined. The economic consequences of this could lead to a fall from a British standard of living to an Irish one. The other threat was the loss of 'our good name and good standing in Great Britain'. This too would be a calamity. 'Let us remember,' he argued, 'that the United Kingdom is a partnership in which we are a junior partner. Just as you cannot carry on a business partnership without a high regard between the partners, so you cannot carry on a successful constitutional partnership unless the partners trust and respect each other.'[18]

For Paisley and his Protestant Unionist supporters, O'Neill was just another Lundy—the Governor who had sought to betray Derry in the siege of 1688; at times it seemed that Paisley was unable to walk down the street for fear of tripping over 'Lundys' prepared to sell out Northern Ireland. In an election television broadcast, Paisley claimed that O'Neill had broken his word on the question of Northern Ireland's constitution: having said he would never meet a Southern leader, except when the South recognised Northern Ireland, he instead 'smuggled' Lemass into Stormont, a man who had taken part in the 1916 Rebellion and whose 'hands are stained with the blood of our kith and kin'. Paisley claimed O'Neill had a three-fold plan to destroy Northern Ireland, involving the breaking up of the Ulster Unionist Party (thereby setting candidate against candidate); then forming a coalition with the Nationalists; and finally establishing a United Ireland under pressure form Harold Wilson. Protestant Unionists, on the other hand, stood for the constitution and 'everything our fathers fought and died for'.[19] The most depressing aspect of the last accusation is that Paisley probably believed it to be true.

O'Neill felt he could dismiss such nonsense; a more pressing problem seemed to be how to attract Catholic votes. But any appeal to them was hindered by the fact that the Unionist Party manifesto only promised a 'consideration' of the local government voting system after methods of rebuilding the local authority structure had been decided.[20] The Unionist Party also scored a notable own goal when Louis Boyle, Young Unionist, Catholic and brother of NICRA's prominent activist Kevin, was rejected as the Party's candidate for South Down. A disheartened Boyle felt the Party had missed an opportunity in an election in which the Prime Minister would be heavily dependent on moderate Catholic support.[21] Catholics were even less likely to vote for the Unionist Party after the Minister for Home Affairs admitted that while the Party would ultimately welcome Catholic election candidates it 'was not just yet ready for this'. Asked why this was so, Long replied that over the years it had been an unfortunate fact that Catholics had not felt able to come out and openly support the Union and had not felt able to participate to any large extent in public life. But, pointed out Long, many Protestants were beginning to realise that there were loyal Catholics whom they could trust. He thought this would grow provided they could get back to the days of improving community relations before they were shattered by movements containing elements quite alien to the Catholic faith.[22]

When nominations closed on 13 February, 119 candidates under fourteen party labels had lodged papers. Seven were returned unopposed leaving 112 in the field. Of the seven new MPs declared elected, five were members of the Government. Of the forty-two official Unionist nominees selected by the Party's constituency associations (apart from O'Neill) twenty-seven were declared supporters of the Prime Minister, ten were opposed to his leadership of the Unionist Party and five had yet to state an unequivocal attitude. All ten official nominees who were critics of O'Neill were opposed by independent, or unofficial, pro-O'Neill Unionist candidates.[23] Thus some 'unofficial' Unionist candidates—those not selected by a constituency association—supported O'Neill while some 'official' Unionist Party candidates—selected by a constituency association—opposed O'Neill, and other 'official' Unionist Party candidates supported him. In a political system used to rigid choices this could be a little confusing for the Unionist electorate. So with his party imploding O'Neill made it clear that he was not giving his personal support to candidates who had attacked his leadership in the past—even if they had been nominated as official Unionist candidates. He declared: 'I cannot endorse men who have been progressive in public but reactionary in private. I do not back those who equivocate and hedge. I am unable to support Unionists who reject vital parts of the official election manifesto or whose deeds in the past are incompatible with its healing message.' O'Neill saw the election not as a potential split in the Unionist Party 'but as the potential triumph of a wider Unionism'. If there was any substance in opinion polls showing that this 'new Unionism' was favoured above all other groupings by all sections of the population 'then indeed we can lift our constitution to the heights on which it ought to stand—above politics and above contention'.

For the leader of a political party to decline to endorse a considerable number of his own candidates—selected by the legitimate selection process—was a monumental decision. How did O'Neill justify it? He did so by recalling how, at a December meeting called at his insistence, he had invited MPs to declare themselves honestly and openly. No member voted against him. Four MPs—McQuade, Hinds, West and Boal—abstained. Twenty-eight voted for O'Neill, including his current opponents Anderson, Taylor, Brooke, Dobson, Burns, Faulkner and Morgan. Craig had left the meeting by the time the vote was taken. This was the position until Faulkner and Morgan resigned. 'Then—and only then—was it apparent that there were members who when asked for an honest vote . . . very recently, had clearly not given it.' O'Neill observed that he was now told, from some quarters, that he must support these candidates in the name of Party unity: 'I cannot pretend that a man's nomination by a group of delegates absolves him of previous lack of loyalty and consistency. I will not be a party to the strange bargain of "Please support me, although of course I can't support you."'[24]

Understandably there was a sharp reaction from O'Neill's critics. Craig pointed out that it was declared Party policy for the Prime Minister and the officers of the UUC to support the official Unionist candidate. He accused O'Neill of distorting the facts. Craig was unable to understand what was meant by the Prime Minister's claim that some of the rebels did not support the Party's election manifesto: 'I do support this manifesto.' Even the Cameron Commission, 'although I disagreed with it as unnecessary, I nevertheless support it as part of Unionist policy'. Joe Burns felt vindicated: 'Some of us have always felt that the Prime Minister has not much use for the party. We are pleased he has now come out and made this clear.' There was now a situation where UUP headquarters was supporting official candidates while the Prime Minister was not.[25] While O'Neill almost seemed to revel in the split as an opportunity to establish his, and Unionism's, reformist credentials, it worried others in the Party, such as Faulkner. He believed that the Unionist Party was being split on class and social grounds. He was replying to what he described as a 'snide' attack on him by the Prime Minister. Earlier, O'Neill, when asked about a reference of Faulkner's relating to class tensions within Unionism, had said: 'Mr Faulkner is a master of fox hounds . . . I suggest that anybody who wants clarification should visit Mr Faulkner at his country estate in County Down.' Faulkner felt compelled to point out that: 'yes, I am a master of hounds—not fox hounds but harriers—and I am very proud of the fact . . . I don't own a country estate in County Down—or anywhere else for that matter. I live on an eight-acre holding and I am rather surprised because the Prime Minister has been to my home in the past.' For the first time in his political career, Faulkner was seeing evidence of a 'class war' in Northern Ireland. What disturbed him was the fear that it could wreck the Unionist Party if it developed.[26]

William Morgan also chipped in with a broadside against O'Neill. He said that the most sad and sorry thing was that the leader of the campaign that was vilifying decent men, who had devoted a significant part of their lives to serving the interests of Ulster, was the Prime Minister, a man of aristocratic lineage. O'Neill's family had enjoyed power and privilege for several hundred years. They could claim the friendship of landed gentry and call upon the support of the belted earls and feudal dukes. Morgan was not against this section of the community, but there was a limit and O'Neill's attitude seemed to be that it was only the like of such people who were competent leaders for the Province. This stung Robert Porter into action. Defending O'Neill, he complained that the word 'class' was being banded about in order to foster the impression that the Prime Minister was an 'unrepresentative aristocrat fighting a class battle with the help of a small group of dukes, earls, barons and landed gentry'. Just because a cause was supported by a duke it did not necessarily make it a ducal cause. People had little choice as to whose sons they would be and no doubt the fourteenth duke or fourteenth earl 'tries to make up his own mind as honestly about events as does the fourteenth Mr Morgan'.[27]

The election was proving a watershed, exploding the myth of the Unionist monolith. But the changes weren't limited to Protestant politics. Much to the surprise of Eamonn McCann, who was running in Derry, John Hume announced his candidature for Foyle on an Independent ticket. His victory would be the first step in his intellectual dominance of Northern Nationalism for the rest of the century. In 1969 Hume was seeking a mandate from the people to work for:

1. The formation of a new political movement based on social democratic principles, with open membership and elected executives to allow complete involvement of the people in the process of decision-making.
2. A movement that must provide what has been seriously lacking at Stormont —a strong energetic Opposition to Conservatism, proposing radical social and economic policies.
3. A movement that must be completely non-sectarian and committed to rooting out the fundamental evil in our society—sectarian division.
4. A movement that would be committed to the idea that the future of the North should be decided by its people and that there should be no change in its constitutional position without the consent of its people.

Hume added that what he fundamentally stood for was a just society in which Catholic, Protestant and dissenter could work together to build a new community, and base political action on political attitudes rather than use religion as a political weapon.[28] Hume explained that he had entered the fray because this was the most important election since the creation of Stormont (by which he meant the Northern Ireland Parliament of 1921 rather than the opening of Parliament Buildings in 1932) and, given his personal convictions, he believed it would have been moral cowardice on his part if he had stood apart. Those who said that with the Unionist Party tearing itself apart it was a wonderful opportunity for the opposition to unite had misunderstood what had happened in the past four months. They were only speaking of Catholic unity. Surely the lesson of the past fifty years was that Catholic unity was the quickest way to unite the Unionist Party, for the one fed the other. What was needed was a political unity against Unionism and Conservatism and an end to sectarianism.[29] Hume was particularly critical of the Nationalist Party. He believed that it had been clear for some time that it was disintegrating, with opposition emerging against it in all constituencies. Hume thought that this was an indictment of its leadership and its failure to weld people into a fighting parliamentary force. For a long time there was a growing frustration in anti-Unionist circles, especially among the young, and a need for a fresh approach.[30]

This did not impress McCann. He believed that Hume did not have any policies—his declaration of intent did not contain one single concrete statement beyond a vague appeal for goodwill, which might have been made by O'Neill or McAteer, who was also standing. For example, what did Hume mean by 'moderate' or 'left'? How did he suggest that jobs might be created? McCann dismissed Hume as a brilliantly successful leader of a non-political movement; but in this election it was policies and politics that mattered and only the Derry Labour Party offered this to the electorate of Foyle.[31] Elsewhere in the anti-Unionist community Eddie McGrady of the National Democratic Party (NDP) echoed the belief that Unionism had turned in upon itself and was in the process of self-destruction. For the first time, under the spotlight of world opinion, some Unionists were 'questioning their hardened attitudes, the causes and the remedies'. Reasonable people of all classes and creeds realised that a change must be made and an effective parliamentary opposition created. The new North would differ from the old because new men with new policies would have spoken out and made their voices heard.[32] In Belfast Central the battle was between the NDP candidate, Alderman John Brennan, and the Republican Labour Party candidate, Councillor Patrick Kennedy. Kennedy's platform rested upon the ultimate establishment of a thirty-two-county socialist republic, something he criticised the NDP for having no interest in at all. He described the NDP as essentially a 'green Tory party' without any defined policy regarding the unity of Ireland.[33]

Beyond the obvious sectarian divide a surprise development was the announcement that a new political grouping with Protestant and Catholic support had been formed to support O'Neill. Adopting the title of the New Ulster Movement (NUM) it appealed to moderate opinion, expecting to attract the support of those who had recently pledged support to O'Neill. The NUM described itself as a political movement rather than a political party, with two Protestants and one Catholic comprising its executive.[34] The NUM began to co-operate with another organisation, the Moderate Ulster Fund. Set up by a group of businessmen, the Fund also sought to provide promotional and logistical support to pro-O'Neill candidates.[35] To achieve these aims the NUM proposed taking the following steps:

a. To call on all moderates to take an active part in politics.
b. To support the progressive policies of the Prime Minister, Captain O'Neill. We are convinced that in the present circumstances only he has the courage and stature to implement the process of reform so necessary for Ulster's future.
c. To provide electoral support at the election for O'Neill candidates against extremists and where no O'Neill candidate is put forward, to sponsor candidates against extremists.[36]

The People's Democracy decided to field twelve candidates, with Bernadette Devlin standing against Chichester-Clark in South Derry and Michael Farrell against O'Neill in Bannside. In the main PD chose traditionally uncontested Unionist and Nationalist seats so as to give voters a 'real choice' for the first time. As far as they were concerned the election was about whether sectarianism was to be 'polite and covert'—the O'Neill approach—or paraded as something to be proud of—the approach of O'Neill's right-wing colleagues. PD's nine-point manifesto focused on a crash housing programme and direct state involvement in generating employment with a proposal for breaking up large estates: the land would be for co-operative farms farmed by small householders.[37] Farrell believed that the choice in the election was between civil rights and social justice on the one hand and reactionary Unionism on the other. It mattered little in practice whether the Unionism faced was the urbane and polished brand of O'Neill or the crude and vulgar one of Paisley; the end result would be the same.[38]

The main attention remained, however, the battle within Unionism. O'Neill was convinced that he could appeal across the sectarian divide. He was buoyed up by the results of an opinion poll which revealed that more than two-thirds of electors wanted him to continue as Prime Minister. He was the choice of sixty-eight per cent while only twelve per cent supported his nearest rival for the premiership, Faulkner. Other contenders were Craig (four per cent), Paisley (two per cent) and Morgan (one per cent). Significantly, O'Neill had the support of ninety-one per cent of Catholics compared to fifty-eight per cent of Protestants. The majority of all electors (sixty-two per cent) agreed with the principle of 'one man, one vote' including ninety-two per cent of Catholics but only forty-eight per cent of Protestants. Of the pro-O'Neill voters, sixty-one per cent approved of universal franchise and twenty-one per cent disapproved; among anti-O'Neillites thirty-eight per cent were in favour and forty-nine per cent against. About half (fifty-two per cent) of all electors were satisfied with the speed at which O'Neill had been implementing his reforms. Catholics were not particularly dissatisfied with the pace of change: fifty-seven per cent thought it 'about right'. But Protestants tended to think O'Neill had moved too quickly (twenty-one per cent) rather than too slowly (seventeen per cent).[39] It seemed O'Neill had reason to be optimistic, if Catholics voted for him as well as the pro-O'Neill Unionists.

Polling day was 24 February. There was a turnout of seventy-two per cent. Thirty-nine Unionists were returned of which twenty-four were 'official' Unionists and three 'unofficial' Unionists who supported O'Neill, while ten 'official' Unionists were opposed to O'Neill with two undecided. O'Neill's official Unionists took 31.1 per cent of the poll, and unofficial Unionist supporters 12.9 per cent, against the 12.9 per cent of anti-O'Neill official Unionists. Although it retained six seats the Nationalist Party began its journey into electoral oblivion as it lost three seats to pro-Civil Rights candidates, including Hume in Derry. In Belfast, Republican Labour returned two MPs (including Paddy Kennedy) as did the Northern Ireland Labour Party, its chairman, Paddy Devlin, defeating Harry Diamond.

But the big news was in the Prime Minister's constituency of Bannside where Paisley came within 1,414 votes of unseating O'Neill. After the result was declared Paisley was: 'delighted. This is a magnificent vote and I am going home a proud man.' He added: 'If I had had seven more days I would have won.' O'Neill, who was not in Ballymena for the result, spent the evening at Stormont Castle: he was fatigued and, at 8 p.m., was sitting down to his first meal of the day. Commenting on the Prime Minister's non-appearance, Paisley said 'it was very typical of the man'. Asked if he would have shaken hands with O'Neill, Paisley retorted: 'I wouldn't shake hands with a man who took the hand of Lemass.'[40] The result was seen as a personal setback for O'Neill. The Prime Minister reflected: 'I do not think there has been a massive Catholic vote. Although there was Catholic support after my last television broadcast, it does not seem to have translated itself to the polling booths to the same extent . . . It is there to some extent. They are prepared to write letters of support but they have not reached the stage of putting an "X" against your name.'[41] Some years later in his autobiography O'Neill could not hide his disappointment that more Catholics had not supported the pro-O'Neill candidates at the polls, and believed that had they done so a rejuvenated and reformed Unionist Party would have been returned to Stormont, and Catholics would have been given new heart to see that moderation actually paid off and produced results, while Protestant extremists would have seen that to win seats attention would have to be paid to moderate opinion.[42]

The Bannside result and the fact that the election didn't alter the overall composition of the Unionist Parliamentary Party did give the impression that O'Neill had suffered a notable setback. Certainly non-native—British—observers from the press thought so. But the results were a little more complex than they first seem. For example, O'Neill recognised the rural–urban divide in the pattern of the returns. Thus in Belfast he noted that pro-O'Neill candidates polled 58,000 votes against 41,000 for their opponents. Reflecting on the setbacks in rural areas he said: 'Probably more of the people in the country think of the past than do the people in the suburban areas.' He could also point to the fact that before the election he had fourteen opponents out of the Unionist grouping of thirty-five; now the figure was twelve out of thirty-five. So his majority was up two and, in addition, there were three pro-O'Neill MPs not yet in the Parliamentary Party. Still, this was not the decisive margin he had evidently been hoping for.

Yet in retrospect, given that the numbers of seats involved was relatively small and any variation would in itself be significant, the result wasn't all bad. There was even a positive case to be made for the result in Bannside: O'Neill pointed out, quite rightly, that this was the first time since the end of the War that the constituency had been contested. That 1945 contest—an independent Unionist against the official Unionist candidate—had produced a remarkably similar result: a majority of under 2,000 for the Unionist Party. The point here is that O'Neill had never faced a direct contest: he was always elected without a vote being necessary. Therefore it is virtually impossible to gauge the extent of O'Neill's support within Bannside, historically, because the 1969 contest was unique. For the Prime Minister the problem with the 1969 outcome was the expectations he seems to have placed on the margin of the outcome. He had lamented the lack of Catholic support for pro-O'Neill candidates, in particular the failure of significant numbers of Catholics to support O'Neill in Bannside. But in the gloom he missed the point. What was unusual about this election was the number of Catholics who did cross the sectarian divide to vote Unionist. It was the fact that this was not uniform that masked this change. As far as one could tell it seemed that the Catholic vote fell in one of two forms. Where there were three or more candidates in the field, as in Enniskillen and Mid-Armagh, Catholics seemed to have voted for the anti-Unionist. But in straight confrontations between pro- and anti-O'Neill contenders, as in Larne, South Tyrone and North Derry, a significant Catholic vote appeared to have swung behind the pro-O'Neill candidate. In Bannside this worked against O'Neill because it was a three-way contest including Michael Farrell; PD candidates polled well as did all those associated with Civil Rights, and Farrell was no different in securing the Catholic vote. But elsewhere in straight pro- and anti-O'Neill contests, Catholics supported the O'Neill Unionist. In a previously safe Unionist seat Craig had a majority of just 653 over the pro-O'Neill candidate, Hugh Wilson; Joe Burns scraped in by 115 after a recount. But in Enniskillen and East Down the pro-O'Neill candidates were bottom of the poll. In Clifton William Morgan was defeated by pro-O'Neill man Major Lloyd Hall-Thompson. Craig put his close call down to the Catholic vote. But even in solid Unionist areas such as Shankill, there was evidence of a split within the Protestant vote: Boal's majority was under 2,000; the unofficial

O'Neill candidate, Walsh, was pleased with the fact that he was only 1,839 votes behind.[43]

The significance of the 'Crossroads election' was that O'Neill did demonstrate that he could appeal across the sectarian divide—something no previous Unionist Prime Minister had ever done or shown a willingness to do—but only in certain circumstances would this translate into votes. Even if this Catholic vote for pro-Unionist candidates can be termed tactical it was, nevertheless, pretty revolutionary in the context of the trench warfare that had characterised Northern Ireland's electoral politics for decades. But on the surface nothing seemed to have changed much. On 28 February the Unionist Parliamentary Party gathered at Stormont to elect the leader of the Party. Ten of O'Neill's opponents staged a dramatic walk-out. Their departure followed the failure of a bid by the Prime Minister's critics to have a decision on the leadership deferred until after delegates from constituency associations had had an opportunity to express their views at the following week's meeting of the Party's Standing Committee. As he left Stormont John Taylor commented: 'The Prime Minister supported unofficial candidates and he is automatically ejected from the party leadership.' Craig did not join the walk-out; Faulkner had already returned home to his sick bed by the time of the walk-out. A short time later a vote on O'Neill's leadership resulted in twenty-three votes for the Prime Minister, one against and one abstention.[44] He was still Prime Minister—but for how long?

O'NEILL GOES

The short answer was: not for long. This naturally takes us to an assessment of the Labour Government's position because what would London's response be if O'Neill went? The Labour Government had watched the election campaign with interest—or, more accurately, apprehension, because an unfavourable result might actually entail their making a decision on Ulster. The assessments produced by the Home Office and Ministry of Defence (MOD) officials had made very unpleasant reading for senior ministers. Even so it was still a surprise that a meeting of Wilson, Stewart, Callaghan and Healy on 19 February saw the Home Secretary anxious for the General Officer Commanding not to keep his troops in barracks over the coming weekends unless he were specifically asked by the Northern Ireland Government to keep troops available at these times—presumably to reduce the chances of their being called on by the Northern Ireland Government to restore order.[45] These senior ministers became the cabinet committee on Northern Ireland known as MISC 238. Its core members were always the Prime Minister, the Home Secretary, the Defence Secretary and the Foreign and Commonwealth Secretary.

As London awaited the results from Northern Ireland, Callaghan produced a memorandum which set out his thoughts on the Northern Ireland situation. He had already focused on the possibility of applying financial pressure or sanctions on a reactionary or oppressive Stormont government as an attractive alternative to direct rule. But as he had explained to Wilson, the problem was that almost immediately he had found that the Home Office foresaw formidable handicaps attached to this as a means of achieving Westminster's object of securing acceptable policies in Northern Ireland: the danger was that London would hit at the very people it was seeking to help—the Catholics. The range and relative size of the Northern Ireland Government's expenditure was such that the only major items which would be affected by financial sanctions were social services. To attack those might alienate opinion and strengthen resistance.[46] So with his room for manoeuvre restricted Callaghan outlined to his colleagues his two principal objectives with regard to Northern Ireland and his overall interpretation of the problem. The British Government's objectives were:

(a) to ensure that the historic tensions and divisions in the community are resolved, and
(b) to ensure that political, economic and social conditions and institutions are of a standard acceptable by comparison with those in Great Britain.

These, he explained, were interdependent and advance towards one was conditional on advance towards the other: massive unemployment and poor housing in Londonderry and elsewhere had preserved and exacerbated old quarrels between politico-religious communities. As for the issue of the local government franchise, Callaghan warned that if O'Neill found himself unable to achieve it then London would have to intervene. And if the Government were forced to intervene by suspending the Northern Ireland constitution, its original objectives would remain but the healing of communal tensions would have received a grave setback. To secure those objectives in the advent of direct rule, London should aim during its intervention to win and retain the support of the mass of the people for a return to constitutional rule. It would be essential to reaffirm that the border was not in issue and that Unionists had nothing to fear on that score.

The second aim would be to reassure the Protestant majority that the advancement of the Catholic minority to equal status in local government, employment and housing would not threaten or destroy their standard of life or impair the liberties of the majority. A return to the 1920 constitution might entail the nomination, through the Governor and after discussion with the political parties, of a 'coalition' committee that would govern while arrangements were made for a general election and the recall of Stormont. If the emergency continued 'new constitutional arrangements' might be drawn up. The significance of these remarks was that if direct rule was imposed, a restoration of the 1920 settlement (devolution) remained the core aim—but not necessarily majority rule.

Callaghan considered that the possibility of bringing about Ulster's complete independence, which as a solution to the immediate problem of returning to

constitutional rule might have some appeal, but it would require profound
consideration and could be considered only in a context far different from the
present. It would be impossible until peaceful conditions had been firmly established for some time. The severance of financial and economic relationships
between Ulster and Great Britain would give independence little value and their
retention little meaning. Moreover, there could be substantial British interests at
stake in the fields of defence, agricultural produce, the massive industrial invest-
ment that had gone into Ulster and mineral and other rights in the Irish Sea.
Finally, the repercussions for Scotland and Wales of even discussing this
possibility—particularly with a royal commission on the constitution sitting—
would be profound.[47]

Fortunately, once the election results were in, Callaghan realised that he would
not have to make any immediate decisions. So when MISC 238 met on 26
February Callaghan was able to tell his colleagues that O'Neill's position in the
Unionist Party was marginally improved. He appeared to be determined to carry
on as Prime Minister and to have no intention of relinquishing his 'liberal
policies'. After hearing this the general feeling within MISC 238 was that it would
be unwise to press O'Neill into making an immediate announcement of further
measures to implement liberal policies. Instead, he was to be given the best
possible chance to consolidate his position, on the assumption that he would work
closely with London; it would also be prudent to accept his advice on the tactical
situation over the next few weeks. But indefinite delay would be unacceptable and
London could not retract its demand for 'one man, one vote'. It was also felt that
Northern Ireland's problems would not be solved solely by the continuance of
O'Neill as Prime Minister; the nerve of the present leadership might weaken or
law and order might break down. The aim was to keep O'Neill as Prime Minister,
but to keep him moving towards reform. It was particularly important that the
Queen's Speech at the opening of the new Stormont Parliament should not close
the door on further reforms. Yet if all else failed, Callaghan's colleagues were still
uneasy with the prospect of direct rule: while Callaghan was prepared to dismiss
the radical suggestion of independence for Northern Ireland other members of
MISC 238 were not. It was suggested that the threat of declaring Northern Ireland
independent might have a profound effect on the population there. Such a drastic
course of action was advanced on the basis that there would be enormous
difficulties in direct rule, particularly if it was imposed otherwise than at the
request of the Northern Ireland Government. MISC 238 decided that an inter-
departmental working party of officials would be set up to consider the various
possible forms of independence as an alternative to direct rule.[48]

As the officials began their assessment of the alternatives to direct rule, on the
following day the Home Secretary received a copy of the latest draft of the
Queen's Speech to be delivered at Stormont. He contacted O'Neill to highlight his
concerns. While he had expected there to be no reference to the reform of the

local government franchise in the speech, Callaghan reminded O'Neill that opinion in London regarded it as the 'touchstone of progress' and asked him how soon he thought he would be able to announce the reform. O'Neill replied that he was bound by his previous pronouncements and the Unionist Party manifesto to going no further than promising a review of the local government franchise when decisions had been taken over the structure of local government—he was not even in a position to implement any recommendation to reform the franchise that the Cameron Commission might make until these decisions were made. He had publicly said as much when he had been accused by Faulkner of abdicating authority in favour of the Cameron Commission. O'Neill asked Callaghan to understand that he had to carry his colleagues and indeed his Party with him. He had to face not only a meeting of the Parliamentary Unionist Party the next day, but also a meeting of the Standing Committee of the Unionist Party, which was to meet the following week and would elect a leader of the party. If he were not elected, he could at a pinch remain Prime Minister, but his power would be much weakened.

Callaghan's reply would not have eased O'Neill's difficulties. He told O'Neill that while he recognised his difficulties he thought it right to put on record the view of the British Government that the situation could not remain static; the momentum of progress had to be maintained and that the only satisfactory direction of progress was an early announcement of local government franchise reform. He did not expect O'Neill to announce the reform at once but he thought he would be likely to be in great trouble if he were not in a position to do so within the next few months, whether he introduced the reform in advance of decisions over the structure of the local government or accelerated the work of reaching those decisions. The conversation ended with Callaghan reassuring O'Neill that he did not expect an immediate reply, but O'Neill undertook to let Callaghan know as soon as he could when the review of the local government structure could be expected to be completed. After concluding their talk Callaghan reported back to Wilson. Callaghan thought that London could hardly do more in the circumstances than allow O'Neill to settle his new administration in before they approached him again. Clearly, this would be the dominant topic of their next meeting with him.[49] Wilson, however, was becoming impatient and wanted an early indication—perhaps by Easter—of what O'Neill had in mind.[50]

This represented a hardening of London's stance since O'Neill had previously been told that he had until June to indicate a move on 'one man, one vote'. So on 28 February Callaghan and O'Neill spoke once more on the telephone. They both made their positions clear. O'Neill's view was that at that moment he could give no indication of when a reform of the local government franchise could be announced. Callaghan therefore asked him for information about the prospect of accelerating the decision on local government reconstruction with which he linked the franchise. He left O'Neill to think on this but equally, as Callaghan told

Wilson, he made it clear that 'we shall expect to see him in London pretty shortly'. Callaghan thought that the best course was to let O'Neill surmount the hurdles he now faced over the leadership issue, and then at the meeting with him to concentrate on the particular issue of the local government franchise. Callaghan looked forward to a meeting around Easter.[51]

Back in Northern Ireland O'Neill now faced three major problems: the fall-out from the election and its effects on the Unionist Party, the threat of more violence and the increased pressure from London. It was the first two problems that combined to sweep O'Neill from office. At the state opening of Parliament O'Neill, after announcing that Sir Edmund Compton was to be Northern Ireland's first ombudsman, admitted that it would be less than frank of him if he did not confess that the results of the general election had been in some respects more indeterminate than he had hoped. Putting a brave face on the situation the Prime Minister claimed that modern and progressive policies had improved their position after the election result. Others had fallen back: 'The wind of change continues to blow especially in urban and sub-urban areas and in my view the future rests with those who are prepared to take risks to unite the country.'[52] In his cabinet reshuffle O'Neill brought Phelim O'Neill into the Government as Minister of Education, moving Fitzsimmons to Health, Porter from Health to Home Affairs, and Long from Home Affairs to Development.[53]

From the back benches the rebels could scent blood. Brooke declared that no MP worth his salt could be expected to commit himself to everlasting confidence in a Prime Minister.[54] He added that at Westminster the acceptance of party leadership had not always been followed by acceptance of the party line, but in Ulster this would be regarded as a heinous crime. At Westminster a vote by MPs against their party did not automatically produce a leadership crisis. Nor would it result in the vilification of a person's integrity. Brooke stated that his support for the Unionist Government in carrying out its policy would be active and constructive; but 'this in no way affects my view already expressed, that because of the obvious split in the Unionist Party, unity cannot be established under the present leader'. For 'confidence is a state of mind. And people who have expressed a lack of the confidence in a leader cannot be expected to do a somersault and change their minds just because they accept a majority verdict.' Confidence could not be regarded as an everlasting state: 'A vote of confidence on a specific issue at a specific point in time is not an eternal carte blanche.'[55]

Taylor warned that there were two things which could wreck Unionism—O'Neillism and Paisleyism. He accused the Prime Minister of breaking assurances and not giving MPs the opportunity to discuss things. For good measure Albert Anderson criticised O'Neill for visiting Cross Street in the Waterside during the election—'which is hardly a Unionist part at any time'.[56] The most vocal critic remained Craig who claimed that he had ceased to be a member of the Government because the Prime Minister was too ready to be intimidated by

Wilson. Craig pointed out that when Faulkner resigned he had charged the Government with dishonesty—a charge which had never been rebutted.[57] It was the attempts at 'appeasement' which had destroyed the confidence of so many people in the Unionist Party. This, Craig said, had led to a growing suspicion that the present leader of the Party lacked political judgment. The Unionist Party had to face up to the fact that, at the present time, it had massive disunity. Craig described O'Neill's conduct in the recent election as extraordinary: the leader of the Unionist Party had sponsored and maintained opponents to his own Party. If party members searched high and low in history they would not find any comparable situation. 'Many people who voted for so-called O'Neill candidates were, in fact, voting against the Unionist Party.' It seemed to Craig that it was impossible to see any progress being made unless there was a change of leader: 'I believe he [O'Neill] is a sincere and genuine Unionist and surely this requires of him to put his party first, because it is the party that serves the country, and it is only through the party that real service can be given.' There were, argued Craig, a number of alternatives for the leadership, all of them capable of 'healing the scars that have grown so deep in the last few months and the sooner it is done the better'.[58]

The split in the Unionist Party was there for all to see at the UUC meeting at the end of March. O'Neill warned delegates that the Party would get nowhere if one section was determined to triumph over another 'or if we are more interested in self-justification than in the needs of the party and the country'. He was prepared to admit that many 'of us, including myself, have made mistakes. Which of us has not? I only ask to have it accepted that in what I have done, right or wrong, I have always had the long term interests of Unionism and Ulster at heart.' He called on the Party to look to the future and not the past.[59] But the Party was looking to the future—one that seemed to have someone else in charge of it. In a vote O'Neill received 338 votes against 263, a majority of seventy-five in a poll of 601.[60] A raging crowd of 200 militant Protestants shook fists and shouted insults at O'Neill when he left by the back door of the Ulster Hall after the meeting. Some young women clutching umbrellas burst through the crowd and hammered the window of the Prime Minister's car. In contrast there were cheers and pats on the back for Craig and applause for Albert Anderson and John Taylor; Basil Kelly, the Attorney-General, went unrecognised by the crowd.[61]

From elsewhere within the Party a continuous source of trouble for O'Neill was the Young Unionists. The Prime Minister declined to perform the opening ceremony of their conference, informing Denis Rogan, Chairman of the Young Unionist Council, that this was because it refused to rescind a vote of no confidence in him.[62] Events at the conference would have confirmed to O'Neill that he was right to give it a miss: the Young Unionists' retort was to unfold a big civil-rights-type banner, stretching across a wall of their hotel, that stated 'We are Craig's people.' And for good measure they gave the man himself a number of standing ovations when the former Minster of Home Affairs told them that the party leadership would be 'sorted out' in a very short time. One speaker had to be scolded by Roy Bradford, the Government Chief Whip, for 'needless abuse' of the Prime Minister. And when there were accusations from the floor of 'weak Government', Bradford countered with a blistering condemnation of those who would 'rather use the boot than the head'. By fifty-three votes to seventeen the Young Unionists voted for the 'full use' of the Ulster Special Constabulary on all occasions of civil unrest and, by forty votes to one, they put the blame for unrest on 'weak and indecisive government'. In reply Bradford told them: 'Anybody who thinks the present unrest, the civil rights movement, the student ferment, and the revaluation of our ideas which is taking place all over the world, is, in Northern Ireland, caused by weak government is living in cloud-cuckoo land. You cannot have blind repression and you cannot baton down things of this nature. This talk of strong government implies that you get the Specials out, and that that solves every problem. "That way doth madness lie."'[63] It fell on deaf ears.

While all of this indicated the fragile state of the UUP, a far more dangerous situation was developing on the streets. The violence of October, November and January had altered things irrevocably: Pandora's Box was open. From January on, community relations deteriorated sharply. Prominent in this were Paisley and his supporters. On the eve of the state opening of Parliament Paisley announced that his latest campaign to oust O'Neill was only beginning. He told about 3,000 people at a Limavady rally that if O'Neill had not the manners to get out, the loyalists would put him out. Declaring that he would lead a march on Stormont, Paisley attacked Harold Wilson for saying that O'Neill was opposed by Fascists: 'Ulster Protestants resent being called Fascists.' Wilson, said Paisley, was longing for the day when Ireland would be united, and 'Who is going to unite the two parts of Ireland for him? Why, his friend, Capt. O'Neill.'[64] At a constituency meeting in Randalstown Orange Hall a familiar pattern re-emerged. About fifty people heckled and frequently shouted down O'Neill. Demonstrators, one of them carrying a large Union Jack across which 'No Surrender' was emblazoned, gathered outside the hall an hour before the Prime Minister arrived. The flag was carried into the hall by a young man and held aloft during the meeting. At the end of the meeting, after O'Neill was given a standing ovation by most of the 350-strong audience, a tomato was thrown towards the platform. It struck a reporter. There was foot-stamping and shouts of 'Up Paisley', 'What About Lemass?' and 'Traitor' during the Prime Minister's speech. O'Neill told the hecklers: 'People who just come here to shout rubbish must have very small brains indeed. I honestly think all you people who shout would far rather be employed under Paisley. You are only interested in sectarian bitterness.' Eggs were thrown at the Prime Minister as he left the hall.[65]

Such reactions towards the Prime Minister from Paisleyites were common-place. What was more worrying were the examples of community bitterness that were increasingly manifest. For example, scuffles broke out between PD demonstrators and loyalist counter-demonstrators in Armagh on 22 March.[66] Extra police were drafted into Maghera on the evening of 24 March, when an open-air meeting was held by NICRA to protest against the Public Order Bill. There were catcalls from about a hundred Protestants standing on the opposite side of the street from the meeting. At one stage the police parked two tenders between the opposing factions. At the close of the meeting the Protestant crowd who had earlier been singing 'The Sash' sang 'God Save the Queen'.[67] Such confrontations were becoming commonplace. When Paisley and Bunting lost their appeals against sentences of three months for taking part in an illegal assembly in Armagh on 30 November, their supporters now had two political martyrs to look to. It did not matter to them that the judge said both men had played at brinkmanship: 'Neither could leave these matters to the Government, the police, or even to the good sense of ordinary folk to sort matters out and neither has permitted the bitterness and agitation to lose impact.' He criticised them for failing to disperse their followers and said they could have taken a more active part in seeing that the confrontation between their followers and the civil rights procession was not built up.[68] The legacy of the rhetoric and street tactics espoused by Paisley and his supporters was soon apparent.

Trouble flared in Limavady after a Protestant crowd broke up a civil rights meeting in the town hall. The meeting ended in disorder after forty-five minutes. Later police had to help the key speaker, Ivan Cooper, to escape from the hall after a mob tried to attack him. Outside, where about 1,000 Protestants had gathered, a police Land-Rover was attacked and reporters intimidated. A strong force of police officers formed a cordon around Cooper. The protesters attacked the cordon amid cries of 'lynch him'. Reverend John Wylie, the Free Presbyterian minister, was cheered when he arrived. He addressed the gathering saying: 'Cooper should be in jail instead of Dr Paisley. The civil rights movement is another guise of the IRA.' Earlier, Peter Girr, Chairman of the North Derry Civil Rights Association, had been shouted down by the Protestant crowd. Two Union Jacks were draped over the front of the balcony and people there threw pennies at the platform. Eventually, after half an hour, Girr offered the microphone to one of the loyalists and one youth waving a Union Jack leapt onto the stage. He said: 'In 1688 there was no surrender and there will be no surrender now.'[69] There were scuffles at the Diamond in Londonderry on 29 March, when a Civil Rights procession of several thousand people made its way through the old walled part of the city. A small group of militant Protestants gathered at the war memorial, one of them wearing a crash helmet and waving a Union Jack. Some of the marchers broke past a cordon of stewards and police and a scuffle broke out in the centre of the war memorial where the man with the flag had retreated.[70] In Belfast more than a hundred people, including women and children, blocked the Shankill Road in protest against Paisley's jailing. One poster read: 'Protestants get O'Neill justice, but O'Neill will get God's justice.' After about twenty minutes the protesters broke up and the road was clear again—although it was understood that another road block would be set up later after the Grand National had finished on television.[71]

These tensions were manifest in the workplace as well. It was alleged that two Protestant workers at a Maydown engineering company had been forced to leave their work after threats from their Catholic workmates. At the factory there were twenty-five Protestants out of a total of 600 workers. The men had been warned that if they did not go home 'they would be carried home with arms broken and their ear burst'. Ivan Cooper pointed out that at least one of the men was responsible for trooping a flag up the centre aisle of a Civil Rights meeting.[72] One of the men concerned, Ivan Glendinning, recalled how a group of Catholic workers leaving after an earlier shift had gathered around his machine: 'They called me a Limavady Orange—and made remarks about Rev. Paisley. But I ignored them and went on working. About an hour later I was approached by two Roman Catholics in the factory with whom I am friendly. They advised me it would be better for my own safety that I should get out of the factory before the break and come back afterwards because other workers were planning to wreck my car and to attack me . . . I laughed at the idea at first but when I looked round I saw groups of workers standing watching me and I became afraid.'[73]

In an unscientific survey Alf McCreary of the *Belfast Telegraph* tried to ascertain the temperature on the streets by listening to 'ordinary' Protestants and Catholics. He found that the heat generated by recent Civil Rights marches had made everyday life 'a little more chilly' in Northern Ireland. Talking to people at random in Counties Tyrone and Londonderry, he found that the 'attractive tapestry' of community relations that was taking shape under O'Neill was 'beginning to fray rather badly'. Catholic and Protestant neighbours were not fighting and snubbing one another. The strain was more subtle. The prolonged violence was making them ask: 'Who is my neighbour?' and the uncertainty of events was making them retreat, ever so surely, into the familiar Orange and Green camps each with its own cosy interpretation of history. The Protestants, 'almost to a man', were certain that the Civil Rights Movement was a front for Republicanism. Any goodwill that was forthcoming last autumn had disappeared in the past winter of discontent. A Protestant professional in Derry said: 'A little civil rights is all right, but like manure too much of it becomes obnoxious.' He saw the Derry marches as the 'usual Saturday antagonistic march', a kind of counter-attraction to Derry City playing at Brandywell. Protestants pointed out that it was not very hard to find evidence of Republicans in the Civil Rights Movement. They gave as examples the carrying of a Republican banner in the PD march to Derry and the tearing down of a Union Jack in Armagh. A Paisleyite said: 'It may only be a piece of cloth but it is the flag of our country.' Down in the Bogside a publican told McCreary: 'Anything goes as long as it is against the establishment. Things will never be the same again. People now know that there is strength in force.' A Catholic businessman warned: 'There is a sense of frustration that people are not going to achieve anything and that Protestant militants are going to take over and "We are going to be ready for them."' Two days after this prediction Derry erupted once more.[74]

The rioting broke out on 17 April following a Government ban on a planned Civil Rights march from Burntollet to Derry. The march had been banned because of fears that a loyalist counter-demonstration would lead to violence. This was followed by a series of explosions that all but halted the supply of fresh water to Belfast. The first explosion was at the Silent Valley reservoir. This was followed by an explosion that wrecked Belfast's water supply from Lough Neagh early in the morning of 24 April. The explosion—which shattered an exposed four-foot diameter pipe at Clady, County Antrim—brought water restrictions to north Belfast. The whole of the city was now short of supplies following the blast at the Silent Valley reservoir, which had cut the domestic supplies in the south and east of the city to a muddy dribble. The Army were not on guard at the point of the explosion—the only point between Lough Neagh and the Hydepark reservoir on the fringe of Belfast at which the pipeline was exposed.[75]

Robert Porter, Minister of Home Affairs, declined to say that the explosions were the responsibility of the IRA but admitted they 'all fitted into a pattern'. There were, he said, splinter groups subscribing to the doctrines of the IRA but not necessarily accepting their disciplines. There was no evidence to suggest that an extreme Protestant element might be involved.[76] The Ulster Volunteer Force (UVF) denied—'As it is not the intention or the desire of our organisation to damage property of the Crown, or to antagonize or disturb the loyal subjects of Her Majesty'—that it had any part in the attacks.[77] This was a lie. It was the work of the UVF, designed to deliver a knock-out blow to O'Neill's premiership. O'Neill suspected that it might not be the IRA: Protestants, he thought, had better reasons for bringing about his departure from the political scene. With this in mind he told a senior police officer, while chatting, not to put it out of his mind that 'these explosions might be the work of extreme Protestants'. The police officer 'looked aghast' and his reply was to the effect that loyalists would never destroy their own country. O'Neill suggested that it might be worth their while blowing up the water supply to Belfast if the end result was to bring down a Prime Minister by making the people think that it was all the work of the IRA.[78]

The violent events of April had a profound affect on O'Neill: 'I felt that my time was running out and that I would, before I went, bring in "one man one vote" for local government elections.' In retrospect, O'Neill thought how odd it was that Protestant explosions may have hastened the introduction of this reform. Up to then it had been impossible for O'Neill to get cabinet agreement to this move.[79] But the mood within the Parliamentary Party had changed in the aftermath of the election, the rioting and the bombings: on 20 April, Roy Bradford (Minister for Commerce as well as doubling up as Chief Whip) informed the cabinet that, at a forthcoming meeting of the Parliamentary Party on 22 April, a group of MPs would be advocating acceptance of the principle of universal adult franchise. Now, after all the reticence of the past, the cabinet agreed that when this matter was raised it should be made clear that the Government would now favour an early declaration of acceptance of the principle of universal adult suffrage, to be implemented when the re-organised structure of local government came into being.[80]

Despite this it seemed, from Callaghan's perspective in London, that O'Neill seemed to waver at the last minute. But after speaking to O'Neill via telephone on the morning of 21 April and urging him to go ahead, the Prime Minister renewed his resolve and agreed to recommend implementation of the reform.[81] On the morning of 22 April, O'Neill and Porter intimated to their cabinet colleagues their intention of resigning from office if the Parliamentary Party failed to endorse an early announce-ment of the principle of universal adult suffrage. While they found support from most of the ministers, Chichester-Clark and Long, while making clear their unequivocal acceptance of the principle of universal suffrage, expressed doubt about the wisdom of making the declaration 'at the present time'; they were apprehensive that this concession would not merely fail to take the Civil Rights demonstrators off the streets but would have the potentially disastrous effect of stirring up massive resistance from militant Protestants. Both ministers agreed, however, that an assurance from London that troops would be available to assist the police in the preservation of law and order after the announcement on the franchise would greatly ease their fears.[82]

Cabinet ended around 8 p.m. Several ministers stayed behind at Stormont Castle for a talk and a drink. At 10 p.m. O'Neill received intelligence that Chichester-Clark had assured his colleagues that he would stick by them through a second day's Party meeting on the franchise. The following morning, 23 April, O'Neill was just driving off from Stormont Castle when he saw 'Jimmy' Chichester-Clark arriving in his official car: 'At first I waved, imagining that he was coming to see someone in the cabinet offices, but then I could see by the look on his face that he was a worried man. I jumped out and he explained that he must see me at once in my room. Pointing out that we had little time before the meeting started, we conversed standing up. "I just can't go through with it," he said. I reminded him that he had sat through yesterday's Party meeting and that the night before he had seemed relaxed and calm. "Well," he said, "I just can't go through with it." I asked whether he would abstain or absent himself from the Party meeting. "No," he replied, "I must vote against it."' Before the vote was taken that morning O'Neill announced that the Minister of Agriculture had resigned just before the meeting should any MPs be under any misapprehension. 'There was a low whistle of surprise.'[83] The Ulster Unionist Parliamentary Party then considered the motion recommending the acceptance of 'one man, one vote'. It was proposed by Porter and read: 'That this parliamentary party decides to adopt to the principle of universal adult franchise at the next local government elections and will seek the support of the standing committee for this decision.' But before it was voted on, an amendment was put forward by Sir George Clark and James Stronge, the MP for Mid-Armagh, calling for the issue to be put before the UUC. It was defeated by twenty-seven votes to twenty-two. The original motion accepting 'one man, one vote' was then passed by twenty-eight votes to twenty-two.[84]

'The hour is late . . . but we must make another attempt to set this country on a new course.' With these dramatic words O'Neill stood at the despatch box for the last time. As O'Neill announced to MPs his intention to secure the acceptance of the 'one man, one vote' principle, he coupled it with the message: 'I would not remain here for a moment longer for any purpose other than to make a final attempt to restore sanity to Ulster.' Speaking to a tense House of Commons he told of his sadness 'that the hand of one Ulsterman has been turned against another and that so many of our hopes and plans for the future have been put at risk'. But, he argued, those who spoke of civil war were using extravagant language, which he could not endorse. The Prime Minister was 'not one of those who would seek to condemn out of hand the movement of opinion we have seen over recent months. For myself, I accept that there are sincere people, seeking to express what they believe to be genuine grievances in a peaceful and orderly way. But now that movement seems to have created a monster it is unable to control.'

Coming to the franchise, O'Neill was determined to secure the acceptance of the principle of 'one man, one vote'. He was well aware that some Unionist MPs and those that they represented could not bring themselves to accept this principle. 'But I want to make it absolutely clear that I will either proceed with this reform or step down from the office which I hold.' O'Neill was strengthened in that resolve by the view that those directly responsible for the maintenance of law and order had themselves expressed to him that the terrible burdens which they were being asked to bear on behalf of everyone could only be alleviated by political means. He appealed to those on the opposition benches 'who have influence. Let us have a truce in our streets. You have my pledge that I will not stay in office if I am prevented from doing what needs to be done.' From the opposition benches Hume replied that the Civil Rights Movement fully accepted its responsibility and he hoped that this would be done by members of the movement at this time. But he warned they would continue to protest by non-violent means and to oppose measures that would seek to limit this policy of protest. He added, though, that in the present tense circumstances any action which took people onto the streets was bound to lead to violence and disturbance, and he hoped that no one would take people onto the streets because of this. Currie was more combative and openly sceptical: 'It has come to my attention recently that certain people in County Tyrone, being aware of the possibility of the introduction of one man one vote, have already started to manoeuvre and scheme in order to ensure that one man one vote will not produce majority rule.'[85] Already elements of the opposition were looking for a sell-out; nevertheless NICRA and PD called off street demonstrations. But they insisted this was not in response to the Government's concession of 'one man, one vote' but because of apprehension about further violence. This, however, did not mean an end to NICRA's demands. The remaining demands were: '1, One man one vote of equal value; 2, the extension of the ombudsman to local government; 3, legislation outlawing discrimination; 4, the repeal of the Special Powers Act and the withdrawal of the Public Order (Amendment) Bill; 5, the disbandment of the Specials.' The Executive warned that it would return to the streets when they decided it was necessary.[86]

O'Neill, however, could be pleased. He reflected that, with the entirely justifiable exception of the Special Powers Acts, his Government had now acted on all the points that Wilson had asked them to consider in November.[87] In London Callaghan told his cabinet colleagues that he considered O'Neill's securing of the five reforms a 'remarkable achievement'. He tempered this, however, with the gloomy conclusion that the implementation of 'one man, one vote' was unlikely to put an end to the violence, though it might result in separating the moderate members of NICRA from the hooligan elements. The problem was that although it was not possible to say who was responsible for the recent explosions it was known that the IRA was now dominated by a Communist element and that NICRA contained a 'mischievous fringe of extremists'. For the moment the leaders of the Civil Rights Movement were succeeding, though with difficulty, in maintaining their control. The actions of the extreme Protestant supporters of Paisley meant that O'Neill was exposed to attack from both sides. In Callaghan's opinion the root of the unrest seemed to lie in the growing contrast 'reminiscent of the situation in this country early in the century, between the relative prosperity of a section of the people and the continuing poverty of the majority'. For the present the best course seemed to be to support O'Neill while his programme of reform was implemented. Wilson offered support for this view and reassured the cabinet that O'Neill had undertaken that requests for military intervention would not be made except after consultation between the two governments—a major advance on the standard procedure that involved the calling-out of troops to assist the civil power. However, Wilson also feared that if it became necessary for the troops to intervene they would be thought to be doing so in order to maintain the 'Orange faction' in power. He left the cabinet in no doubt that the constitutional consequences of intervention might be very grave and once 'we were involved it would be very difficult to secure our withdrawal'.[88]

At this juncture it seemed, from London's perspective, that British intervention was more likely to occur with the fall of O'Neill rather than any immediate threat of communal disorder. Neither seemed imminent. On 25 April Callaghan even told MISC 238 that O'Neill's position as Prime Minister might not be as insecure as it appeared. Callaghan thought that it might be possible for O'Neill to remain Prime Minister even if he ceased to be leader of the Unionist Party. However, he was sure that if he did resign as Prime Minister the policy of the Northern Ireland Government would move further to the right. Callaghan believed that if O'Neill's position was seriously threatened by a breakdown of law and order, this would probably be due to Paisley's supporters and in such circumstances British troops should be used in support of O'Neill. If he resigned it would be necessary to invite his successor to London and ascertain what he proposed to do. It might then be appropriate to convene a round-table conference at Lancaster House including representatives of the Northern Ireland Government and other major Northern Ireland groups to examine the basic causes of the Troubles. This, thought Callaghan, would need very careful consideration but such a conference might be desirable even if O'Neill remained Prime Minister. Wilson wondered if it was possible that O'Neill, while remaining Prime Minister, might move further to the right, not on the main political issues but in other ways, for example by using the B-Specials against rioters. A further breakdown of law and order in Londonderry might result in the B-Specials being used for this purpose. It was also possible that O'Neill might say that he could not introduce 'one man, one vote' at once. In that event, Wilson suggested that consideration be given to legislating at Westminster under Section 75 of the Government of Ireland Act; this possibility could be mentioned to O'Neill, although he recognised that the use of Section 75 for this purpose might give rise to a serious reaction in Northern Ireland.[89]

Unknown to London, the British Government were going to have to face the reality of O'Neill's fall sooner rather than later, for the Prime Minister had already decided to resign from office. It was on the evening of 24 April that O'Neill reached his decision. Following a late-night sitting he decided to have a chat with Billy Fitzsimmons, one of the ministers whom he trusted most: 'I knew he would fight against any possibility of my giving up the premiership. And so it proved.' 'You are', said Fitzsimmons, 'trusted by the Catholics, and without you we shall go down to disaster.' However, under pressure he reluctantly admitted that if only one of O'Neill's supporters changed sides the latter's parliamentary majority would drop to one—'an impossible situation'. So 'What had started as a friendly chat ended by my being more and more insistent as he resisted my suggestions . . . my mind was made up.' The following day O'Neill invited Robert 'Bertie' Porter and the Attorney-General to lunch at Stormont House. Porter was against O'Neill resigning while the Attorney was 'more comprehending'. By the end of the meal 'they both agreed that I should be free to go if I wanted to'.[90]

By the afternoon of 27 April O'Neill's attention had turned to who would succeed him. Prior to announcing his resignation O'Neill had met with various friends in the cabinet at Stormont House. They felt, on balance, that the man they would best like to serve under would be Jack Andrews, the Leader of the Senate. Since Faulkner's resignation he had been No. 2 in the cabinet. Andrews, however, refused to let his name go forward. After this O'Neill told his friends that he could play no further part in picking a new leader: they would have to decide what to do next themselves; but that the more they delayed the less effect they would have on the ultimate decision. Later that evening O'Neill's friends in the cabinet rang him to say that a majority were now decided on Chichester-Clark; they hoped he would agree with the decision even though he had 'stabbed me in the back' (a reference to a comment made by O'Neill's daughter to the press). The following morning Brutus came to see his Caesar. Chichester-Clark was, 'I think', recalled O'Neill, 'genuinely upset that he had set all this in motion and in fact the worried look which I had seen on his face five days earlier when he had resigned . . . was not to leave it until he resigned as Prime Minister twenty-two months later. I don't think . . . that he had any idea what he was in for.'[91]

Not long afterwards the General Officer Commanding Northern Ireland (GOCNI), Sir Ian Harris, visited O'Neill at home to talk about the threat from the IRA; he found a depressed Prime Minister. The GOC told O'Neill that he was concerned about a meeting he had just had with Anthony Peacocke, Inspector-General of the RUC (since the new year), about possible IRA activity on the border. It appeared to the GOC that Peacocke had no positive information that the IRA were going to attack border police barracks and installations, but believed that this would happen because the IRA had stated that this was their plan if British troops were used in Ulster; as a result, he had strengthened all police barracks in the border areas. O'Neill replied that whilst he had no positive information he felt that the Inspector-General could be right because things were coming to a crunch and as the political situation would probably get worse it would only be right to assume that the IRA might take this opportunity to exploit it as much as possible.

At this point O'Neill revealed his depressed state to the GOC. He explained how he now only had a majority of two and that he might not be Prime Minister by the following weekend. He had a choice: to be thrown out or resign in a dignified way. He said that his policies had failed and although he had tried to bring the people together there was now more hatred between Protestants and Catholics than ever before and this was being exploited and encouraged by people for their own ends. It only needed 'something' to bring things to a flash-point: O'Neill thought it was important to plan for escalation. The GOC took this advice on board and, although the Northern Ireland garrison had recently acquired an extra battalion and there was no immediate need for any additional troops, he signalled the Director of Military Operations in Whitehall: 'I think it would be important to earmark another battalion just in case things should go sour quickly.'[92]

The day the GOC sent his signal to the MOD was 28 April. O'Neill resigned the same day. The following evening in a television broadcast, O'Neill reflected how: 'A few short weeks ago, you, the people of Ulster went to the polls. I called that election to afford you the chance to break out of the mould of sectarian politics once and for all.' He now realised that: 'In many places, old fears, old prejudices and old loyalties were too strong.'[93] His reforms had proved too much for many Protestants, and too little for many Catholics. Later, O'Neill reflected that Northern Ireland could have continued to enjoy a privileged position of being the only part of Ireland to enjoy a British standard of living: 'Instead, she chose to put all this at risk in the interests of maintaining a Protestant ascendancy that had ceased to have any meaning anywhere else in the United Kingdom.'[94] He, at least, got the dignified exit he was looking for.

A NEW PRIME MINISTER

There were now two choices for Prime Minister: Chichester-Clark (or 'Chi-Chi' as his wife liked to call him, after a giant panda in London Zoo) or Faulkner. Of the two Faulkner possessed by far the more dynamic personality. With his background in the family business he personified the commercial spirit of middle-class industry that Protestant and Catholic often associated Unionism with. Chichester-Clark, by contrast, represented another Unionist stereotype: that of the O'Neill aristocratic or 'Big House' tradition. Indeed O'Neill and Chichester-Clark were cousins but more in the aristocratic manner of ancient blood ties rather than with any contemporary intimacy. Like O'Neill, Chichester-Clark had been schooled in Eton and had gone on to serve in the Irish Guards during the War. In 1944 he was seriously wounded in Italy. After the war he entered politics and was returned for South Derry in 1960, making his way in government as Chief Whip and then Leader of the House of Commons before replacing Harry West as Minister of Agriculture in 1967. He now found himself with a chance of the premiership.

As London awaited the outcome of the leadership election, Callaghan's latest information, on 28 April, was that Faulkner had aroused so much opposition that he was unlikely to win the nomination. Opinion seemed to be crystallising in favour of Chichester-Clark. O'Neill informed Callaghan that he was unsure whether or not his supporters would make conditions about 'one man, one vote' before switching over to serve under Chichester-Clark who, it would seem, the former Prime Minster was supporting. O'Neill's own view was that, once his successor was appointed, he should be given time to appoint his cabinet and to discuss policies with them before pressure was brought to bear on him to come over to London for discussions.

Given this advice Callaghan believed that London had now to consider: (i) whether there was anything further they should do to meet the immediate situation, (ii) what line should be taken with the new Prime Minister about the timing of a discussion in London and (iii) what proposals London should have ready for such a discussion. On the first point, Callaghan thought it was difficult to assess whether there would be an increase in civil strife; but London could not ignore the possibility that the Paisleyites would take to the streets in celebration of O'Neill's downfall, and that the Civil Rights elements might counter this. It seemed necessary, at any rate, that the Secretary of State for Defence should now be authorised to order an additional army battalion to stand by. As for the second point, Callaghan feared that the new Prime Minister might well be reluctant to come to Westminster right at the start of his term of office, but he thought it right to press him to come fairly early anyway. As soon he was appointed 'we should remind him of the agreement that (save in the direst need) troops will be made available only on a request at Government level; and that he must not rely on British military support in maintaining policies which might arouse the antagonisms of large sections of the population'. Callaghan believed that the new Prime Minister was certain to be further to the right than O'Neill, but he was equally sure that it should remain London's policy to intervene as little as possible and to try to get the Northern Irish to solve their own problems. If London made its position clear at the outset this could be a means of preventing the new Government from veering too sharply to the right. As for (iii) there were a number of matters to be discussed with the new Prime Minister, including for example the ways and means in which confidence in the RUC could be strengthened and whether it would be appropriate to float with him the possibility of a round-table conference.[95]

By the time Callaghan could put these views to his colleagues in MISC 238 on 29 April, the latest indications he had were that support had swung away from Chichester-Clark and that Faulkner was more likely to be chosen. In Callaghan's view there would now be an uneasy lull with the chance—but no more—that if Faulkner were chosen as the new Prime Minister he would, by more adroit handling of the Unionist Party, be more successful in producing a stable government than O'Neill had. Much would depend on whether the Unionists loyal to O'Neill would be prepared to forgive his part in precipitating the crisis in their party. After hearing from Callaghan, MISC 238 agreed that London should not revise its policy on account of the resignation of O'Neill, but should wait to see what course the Northern Ireland Government followed under their new leadership, as O'Neill had suggested. However, as soon as the successor was chosen he would be reminded, in the terms that Callaghan proposed, of the arrangements and conditions for British military support; he would also be left in no doubt that, if he proposed to use troops in support of reactionary measures, London would have to consider the constitutional implications.[96]

Back in Northern Ireland the news of O'Neill's resignation delighted his Unionist opponents. Craig declared for Faulkner as the one man who had the qualities and capacity to reunite the Unionist Party.[97] He predicted an end to unrest in the Province if a strong united Unionist government was in place in Stormont; Craig was also willing to accept a cabinet position 'if it is for the good of the party' although the most important thing was to get the country back on its feet.[98] Harry West thought O'Neill's resignation 'the best thing he could do'. There was no hope of uniting the Party under O'Neill's leadership: 'He may talk of steering the country but his presentation of it was wrong.' William Morgan believed that reform could 'now go on quicker' under another leader. And that leader should be Faulkner.[99] And Eileen Paisley was delighted too: 'Thank God. Now I think Ulster will have a chance to settle down. We will see again the fair government of Lord Carson and Lord Brookeborough.'[100]

But first of all there had to be the small matter of an election. Under a new selection procedure, agreed by the Party in November 1967, a selection meeting had to be convened by the Chief Whip within seven days of the vacancy occurring. This meeting would select its own chairman who would be responsible for the conduct of a ballot for which candidates would have to be nominated in writing. The candidates themselves would have to signal their agreement to nomination either in writing or verbally at the selection meeting.[101] No longer would a leader 'emerge' from the men in 'grey suits'. Faulkner duly submitted two nomination papers, both signed by declared opponents of O'Neill: Dr Norman Laird and John Taylor; and Joe Burns and Harry West. Chichester-Clark's nomination paper, on the other hand, was signed by two firm supporters of O'Neill: Dr Robert Simpson and Herbie Kirk.[102] As if to confirm that O'Neill's fall had not been a question of resistance to reform, both candidates had exactly the same policies. Chichester-Clark declared that, if elected, his policies would be in broad terms similar to those of O'Neill.[103] Faulkner's position before O'Neill's resignation was that the Government had 'dishonestly' repealed the pledge in its manifesto not to review the local government franchise until the restructuring of local government was complete. 'The credibility of this Government has gone,' he had declared, calling for an administration which would represent different shades of opinion within the Party. But he emphasised that 'If I were asked to take part in an administration, I would not be prepared to serve in one which could be described as right-wing or hardline.' In fact he actually called for a speeding-up of the reforms announced in November. The Government should give absolute priority to reforming policies if it was to command respect from those who differed from it politically.[104] Following O'Neill's resignation Faulkner argued that, as far as the political situation inside the Unionist Party was concerned, 'it is clear that the present Government has lost credibility in handling this explosive situation'. If tension was to be lessened on both sides then reform had to be implemented in full 'in spirit as well as in the letter. Let it be made absolutely clear, by actions as well as words, that sectarianism is not equated with Unionism as our critics say, and that as a party we are quite aware that justice must be seen to be done.'[105] In essence then—particularly given the circumstances of O'Neill's resignation— there was little, if anything, between the two candidates: both were committed to reform.

With the vote imminent the feeling within the Unionist Parliamentary Party was that Chichester-Clark would win with a majority of five:[106] it turned out to be a lot closer than that. According to Belfast's bookmakers Faulkner was the favourite to become the next Prime Minister, but only just: Sean Graham, for example, had Faulkner at 4–6.[107] The bookies must have known something—after all one rarely encounters a poor bookmaker. The result was, indeed, a close-run thing. On 1 May 1969 Major James Chichester-Clark became the fifth Prime Minister of Northern Ireland. He beat Faulkner by seventeen votes to sixteen votes. Chichester-Clark had won by one vote and Faulkner had lost by one vote— the irony that it was Terence O'Neill's one vote probably wasn't lost on Faulkner.

'In a sense it seemed odd that I should vote for the man who had brought me down,' recalled O'Neill of his support for Chichester-Clark; but he consoled himself with the thought that his former Minister's actions 'had been due to worries and doubts in his very unpolitical mind'. O'Neill thought that, at Westminster, Chichester-Clark 'would have been one of the knights of the shires' although not a member of the right-wing Monday Club that was a characteristic of such Tory MPs. 'But in any event, I couldn't have brought myself to vote for the man who had been trying to bring me down for six years. It was as simple as that.'[108] O'Neill had the last laugh.

To unite the Party behind him the new premier brought Faulkner back into the cabinet as Minister of Development; Faulkner seems to have learnt his lesson as this would mark the beginning of a period of unquestionable loyalty, if not political devotion, on the part of the new Minister to his premier. Two other critics of O'Neill, John Taylor and John Brooke, both received junior Government posts (to the opposition's cry of disgust) in the Ministry of Home Affairs and Ministry of Commerce respectively. In a gesture to the community at large, and particularly those from the Catholic section of it, on 5 May the Northern Ireland cabinet agreed to recommend that the Governor exercise his prerogative to secure the release from prison of those serving sentences as a result of prosecutions arising from recent disturbances.[109] The next day Chichester-Clark announced the amnesty. He hoped that this would 'permit us to wipe the slate clean and look to the future. It is the earnest hope of the Government that all persons in the community will recognise that these decisions have been taken solely in the interests of restoring peace, and will respond to them in a spirit which acknowledges that all citizens share with their Government a responsibility to that end. Without such a spirit not only will disharmony persist but the economic progress of the country will be jeopardised.'[110] At cabinet the new Prime Minister made it clear that there would be no going back on any of the reforms promised.[111] NICRA reaffirmed that it would be easing up its campaign of agitation.

By 9 May Porter felt able to tell his colleagues that there were clear indications that, for the time being, the 'law and order' situation had improved. He felt that there was evidence on all sides of a degree of willingness to give the new administration a chance. Given this, it seemed perfectly clear to him that 'if we do not immediately seize the opportunity thus offered, and declare a positive intention to legislate at the earliest possible date in the appropriate fields, the breathing space we now enjoy will prove to be only temporary. Demonstrations and counter-demonstrations will begin again, and we shall find ourselves in a much less favourable position for introducing reforms than we are at present.' Accordingly Porter sought the approval of his cabinet colleagues to the immediate preparation of legislation providing for universal adult suffrage and the abolition of plural voting in local government, and strongly recommended a public announcement to this effect at the earliest possible date.[112] He also stressed the need for a decision before a bill on these matters from a Nationalist MP came before the House of Commons on 20 May.[113]

Porter got the decision he wanted so that when he, Chichester-Clark, Faulkner and Andrews travelled to Downing Street to meet with Wilson and Callaghan on the afternoon of 21 May, they were able to report rather more progress than London had expected. So much so, in fact, that Callaghan concluded that the change of government under Chichester-Clark's leadership appeared to have enabled him to embark on a progressive course that his predecessor had found impossible to follow; he also noted that Chichester-Clark had been much helped in this by Faulkner's active co-operation. The Northern Ireland team had been able to tell their British counterparts that legislation would be passed in the current parliamentary session providing for local government elections to be held on the basis of 'one man, one vote' and the local elections due in 1970 would be deferred until October 1971 so that they would be held on the new franchise. In 1970 a bill to reorganise local government and the local government franchise would be introduced to come into operation before the local government elections of 1971. These would be published in a white paper in the autumn. A crucial preliminary to this reform, which the Stormont delegation did not wish to make public yet since the proposal had not yet been endorsed by the Northern Ireland cabinet, was the appointment of an independent commission under a high court judge to determine the ward boundaries within the smaller number of new local authorities.

These proposals, as Callaghan later pointed out to his cabinet colleagues, would strike at the basis of the power of the Unionist Party in local government and there was likely to be strong opposition to them. The Northern Ireland delegation was also able to report that, in order to establish a system of allocation for local authority housing which was fair and could be seen to be fair, it proposed to issue to local authorities in the next month or so a model scheme based on the Scottish experience. It would be impracticable to compel the authorities to conform precisely to the scheme, but they accepted that they would be required to secure the British Government's approval to any alternative scheme they proposed. With the Parliamentary Commissioner for Administration for Northern Ireland taking up his duties as soon as the relevant bill received the royal assent, the Northern Ireland ministers also proposed the introduction of legislation to establish machinery to consider citizens' grievances against public authorities other than central government departments, including local authorities. The main purpose of this move was to tackle religious discrimination in employment.

Chichester-Clark's delegation then explained how an amendment of the Special Powers Acts had been impending when the attacks on vital installations were made. The Northern Ireland ministers appreciated the British Government's embarrassment vis-à-vis the Human Rights Convention and wished to remove the source of embarrassment as soon as possible, but considered that they could not forgo their powers under the Acts until the situation became calmer. They also pointed out that they had no wish to rely on British troops to guard vital installations, as they had been doing since the April bomb attacks, longer than was strictly necessary, but the numbers could not be significantly reduced in the present situation until the RUC had been strengthened. They proposed to conduct a special recruiting campaign in Catholic areas where the schools, if not the Church, might help, which would serve both to strengthen the RUC and to increase the proportion of Catholics in it. Overall Chichester-Clark's view was that the atmosphere in Northern Ireland was already better, although there was still tension below the surface which could produce fresh disorder at any moment. After the meeting Callaghan pronounced himself satisfied, concluding that Chichester-Clark and his colleagues had been able to give reasonable assurances on all the major points of concern to the two Governments.[114]

Despite this better-than-expected progress report some of Callaghan's colleagues remained concerned. While the Home Secretary had accepted that, in the last resort, British intervention would probably amount to direct rule, he found that it took some additional persuading to convince a few of the cabinet that a better alternative could not be found. There was a suggestion that the alternative might be some form of 'constitutional withdrawal'. It was pointed out that to put Northern Ireland in the position of an 'associated state' appeared impracticable. Full independence would not be acceptable to either of the main parties at Westminster. Disorder would grow, perhaps to the point of civil war, and the Irish Republic would be likely to intervene. To leave Northern Ireland to fend for itself in this situation could not be reconciled with Britain's legal responsibilities or with the defence of the United Kingdom. Full independence could not therefore be contemplated.[115] If, however, Callaghan thought this put the matter to rest he was wrong.

In early May, he explained to the cabinet that the British Government might be faced with a level of disorder amounting to insurrection which could mean that 'we might have to assume extreme powers' including special powers of arrest and search and the assumption by the GOC of direct responsibility for maintaining order including the power to try civilians by court martial. Not unnaturally this stark warning seems to have provoked some debate and a suggestion that the military garrison be withdrawn from Northern Ireland. But Callaghan dismissed this as unrealistic: if 'we had withdrawn troops, and law and order then broke down, we could not resist demands to send them back; and . . . we should be failing in our duty if we allowed blood to be spilt, the minority groups persecuted and buildings sacked while standing on the principle that we would not allow our troops to be used'. In Callaghan's view independence 'cannot be considered as a practical possibility; even if we could unilaterally change the national status of Northern Ireland, we should be abandoning the minority we are desiring to protect. Intervention by way of direct rule from Westminster might be forced upon us, particularly if the troops were committed to dealing with disorder, but I am sure that it is not a course we should consider adopting out of choice.'[116] But this still did not put an end to the matter.

On 7 May the cabinet invited the Defence Secretary, Denis Healy, to formally consider the possibility and implications of withdrawing troops from Northern Ireland before they had to be committed to the preservation of law and order. The reason for this was simple: the Northern Ireland garrison could not provide aid to the civil power in Northern Ireland if it was not in Northern Ireland in the first instance! It is important to note that what was being considered was military not political withdrawal. Healy reported back to MISC 238 in July. He argued that the United Kingdom Government could not absolve itself from its basic duties. Thus, while attempting to deal only with the military, economic and political consequences, Healy pointed out that whatever effect the withdrawal of all servicemen from Northern Ireland would have upon the legal obligation of the military to assist the civil power on request, it would not dispose of Britain's more fundamental, but potentially no less embarrassing, constitutional obligation to protect the border of Northern Ireland—'our only land frontier'—against violation; a contingency which was not as remote in Northern Ireland as it was elsewhere throughout the United Kingdom, and to maintain the integrity of Northern Ireland as a part of the United Kingdom: 'We have recognised that we cannot wash our hands of Northern Ireland's affairs. I do not think we can escape the conclusion that our responsibility for the integrity of the Province as part of the United Kingdom includes some responsibility for law and order. In theory this might be separate from the common law obligation of our troops; but I doubt whether their practical implications are really distinct.'

Indeed, if the Northern Ireland Government found itself unable to maintain order, or if it collapsed altogether, the troops would probably have to return. If lives were being lost and property destroyed on a large scale, or if democratic government in Northern Ireland had come to an end, both domestic and world opinion would compel the British Government to intervene directly, on whatever scale might be necessary. If, as was probable, this intervention could not be achieved without the use of troops, their task would be very much more difficult if they had severed the contacts which provided them with local intelligence, had lost their existing bases and were obliged to undertake what might amount to the invasion of a hostile country. Deployment would be slower and more difficult and intervention would probably have to be on a larger scale than if forces were already available on the ground. In short, Healy had concluded, after consultation with Callaghan, that the withdrawal of United Kingdom armed forces from Northern Ireland, although militarily feasible, would be a cumbersome and embarrassing operation.[117]

That put an end to any suggestion of a military withdrawal. But other possibilities such as financial sanctions were raised again. The question of the restriction or denial of funds to the Northern Ireland Exchequer was also shown to be, once and for all, a non-starter: legislation would be necessary if financial pressure were to have a substantial and immediate effect except as a warning to a reactionary government. Furthermore the legislation would be extremely controversial; the reduction of British subventions would force a departure from the principle of parity of services; and it could inflict serious damage on the economy of Northern Ireland.[118] Callaghan found it hard to escape the conclusion that financial sanctions would be ineffective as a deterrent or stimulus to the Northern Ireland Government, who could convincingly represent that they were hitting the minority 'we were trying to protect'. Given this there was no easy solution. Callaghan tried to illustrate to his colleagues the problem facing the Government and how it should deal with it. He explained that political thought in Northern Ireland since its inception had been divided between those who worked for a united Ireland and those who refused to be severed from the United Kingdom. The hardline Unionist line was engendered by fear of the minority. But if the minority could be persuaded to subscribe to the constitution of Northern Ireland and to work towards its prosperity, some part of this fear would be removed, although the Ulster Unionists would still want to cling to office. The British Government should encourage as far as it could the participation by Catholics in the institutions of government riot in Northern Ireland at every level, from which in some cases they had been deliberately excluded and in others they had deliberately excluded themselves. For instance, Callaghan wanted to see a drive to recruit Catholics into the regular ranks of the RUC where, theoretically, one third of the establishment was set aside for them. He also drew the cabinet's attention to the underlying point of existing British Government policy: that partition could not be ended without the consent of the people of Northern Ireland. It was his view that a united Ireland would be achieved 'only when North and South themselves voluntarily come together. And further, that this will not happen until the Northern Ireland Government are able to treat with the South from a position representing a united Province. That lies in the distant future.' The immediate need was to restore confidence. It might be that the new Northern Ireland Government would succeed. If it did not show signs of doing so it was up to the British Government to take whatever steps it could to encourage reconciliation.[119] The cabinet would just have to bite the bullet.

COUNTDOWN

As the marching season approached the Northern Ireland Government became increasingly worried. On 2 July Harold Black, the Northern Ireland Cabinet Secretary, wrote to the Home Office requesting authorisation for the RUC to be issued with Type S6 respirators and CS Riot Control Agent gas; this was less toxic than their current supplies of CN tear gas which were due for renewal. There was the added urgency that on 12 July nineteen separate demonstrations were planned throughout the Province, and feelings were likely to run high.[120] Black pointed out that in Londonderry on the evening of 19 April the police casualties amounted to almost 200 out of a total force of 600 men committed. Such a high casualty rate could not be accepted again.[121] Home Office officials informed Callaghan that they were in favour; they emphasised that the 'basic reason why we make this recommendation is that, if events get beyond the normal resources of the RUC, their possession of CS would provide an additional rung in the escalatory ladder short of opening fire or calling in the military'.[122] But Callaghan refused to authorise the issue of CS without the agreement of his colleagues in MISC 238. The contrast with the situation in the rest of the UK was stark: in Great Britain the police were under instructions that CS was not to be used in any circumstances for crowd control.[123] On 12 July 1969, however, serious rioting again broke out throughout Northern Ireland. So severe was it in Belfast that on 13 July Stormont's request for CS gas was urgently renewed by telephone. MISC 238 agreed to the Northern Ireland Government's request.[124] The ministers, however, turned down a further request from Stormont to use the flight of RAF Wessex helicopters stationed in the Province for the emergency transport of members of the RUC to trouble spots. They also turned down a request for the use of Sussex helicopters for crowd surveillance. Both decisions were on the grounds of provocation.[125]

By now it was becoming apparent that a new potential flash-point was coming into view: the Apprentice Boys of Derry's march on 12 August in which Protestants commemorated the relief of the city from James II's Catholic armies in 1689. Many within the Catholic community were displaying a tremendous bitterness towards the police after what were arguably—since it depends upon which date is regarded as the start of the conflict—the first deaths of the Troubles. Francis McCloskey, a sixty-seven-year-old Catholic, died after being fatally injured in the street when the police had carried out a baton charge against a crowd throwing stones at Dungiven Orange Hall on 13 July. He sustained serve head injuries and died the following day. He was buried with Republican honours. In Derry, Samuel Devenney, a forty-two-year-old Catholic, died of injuries on 16 July. He had been beaten by police and fatally injured as he stood at the front door of his home in William Street on 19 April. Other members of his family were injured in the incident. He was standing with a neighbour when police officers charged a group of young people several of whom ran into the Devenney home. The police, in pursuit, broke down the front door and batoned the family. Later a team of investigators from Scotland Yard were called in to investigate but were unable to break a 'conspiracy of silence' among members of the RUC. No charges were ever brought.[126] In Derry Catholic alienation from the police increased even further.

Now warnings about the potential problems with 12 August began to reach London. John Hume had expressed to Lord Stonham, Minister of State at the Home Office, the gravest apprehension over the prospects for the march. He had spoken of the loss, by the Catholic inhabitants of Derry, of respect for law and order in general and the RUC and the USC in particular. This opinion was echoed by Bernadette Devlin when she came to see Stonham on the same day.[127] Devlin had been elected to Westminster as MP for Mid-Ulster in a by-election in April and, in Callaghan's words, made 'the most eloquent maiden speech I had ever heard', although he also noted that 'it was wholly unconstructive and negative'. Nevertheless: 'Almost everyone else . . . including the British Press, were busy worshipping at the altar.'[128] From these sources it began to dawn on London that the moment of crisis might finally be approaching.

On 28 July Callaghan reported to the cabinet that it was as yet too soon for the Northern Ireland Government to make an authoritative appreciation of what was likely to happen on 12 August; but if Hume's fears were realised and rioting did break out again in Londonderry, with its becoming more serious than before, there was a danger that the police would lose control of the situation and the Northern Ireland Government would have to ask for military assistance to restore order. On the other hand, pointed out Callaghan, despite the setbacks of 12–15 July, there were some encouraging signs. Optimistically, he believed that the issues were no longer generally seen as the legitimate political grievances of a minority against an unheeding, repressive government. The Northern Ireland Government was now for the first time firmly committed to the removal of the main grievances and was taking steps to implement this. This fact was recognised by opinion on all sides, and leaders of all groups were showing an increasing readiness to join together in preventing the kind of violence that Londonderry and other towns had just experienced. Whether the more extreme factions would also co-operate remained to be seen. It was possible that the danger of organised violence on a large scale had to some extent receded, and that the greatest risk was of further hooliganism, which would be widely accepted as such. It was to be hoped that the police would be able to control such outbreaks. But the danger that they would be unable to do so, leading to the Northern Ireland Government's asking for military assistance, could not be underestimated.[129]

Thus with the British Government now fully aware of the potential gravity of the situation facing it, Wilson sought, and got on 31 July, authorisation from the cabinet for him, together with the Home Secretary, the Defence Secretary and, if available, the Foreign Secretary, to take any decision urgently required when other ministers could not be called together. This, along with Callaghan and Healy's recommendations agreeing to the use of CS gas by the RUC, was accepted by the cabinet.[130] Increasingly it seemed that the question was now not if Northern Ireland would experience further rioting but whether the disturbances would be so severe that troops would have to be deployed with all the consequences that entailed.

If so, this would fall on 39 Brigade,—the permanent Garrison Brigade for Northern Ireland. At the beginning of August it comprised the 1st Battalion The Royal Regiment of Wales, the 2nd Battalion The Queen's Regiment, the 1st Battalion The Prince of Wales Own Regiment and the 17/21 Lancers at Omagh. In

July the 1st Prince of Wales Own Regiment had been moved west to Magilligan, because of possible risks arising from the situation in Londonderry.[131] On the night of 2–3 August rioting broke out in Belfast once more. After the rioting ended Police Commissioner Wolseley, responsible for Belfast, recognised that his men were exhausted and had to be sent home to rest. The result was that, when trouble again broke out in the afternoon of the 3 August, there were very few policemen available. Wolseley contacted Lieutenant Colonel Fletcher, Commanding Officer of the 2nd Battalion The Queen's Regiment, who was based at Palace Barracks, Holywood. At 10 a.m. one company of the battalion was placed on two hours' notice from 4 p.m. onwards. Colonel Fletcher travelled to Wolseley's head-quarters at Castlereagh. At about 4.45 p.m. Wolseley told Fletcher that all police reserves had been committed and asked for his assistance. Fletcher replied that he would do all he could to help but that he would not deploy any of his soldiers without permission from higher authority. He communicated with Brigadier Dyball, Chief of Staff Northern Ireland at HQ Northern Ireland (HQNI) in Lisburn, who said that this was a political decision and confirmed that troops were not to be committed without the approval of higher authority.

During the afternoon Wolseley telephoned Anthony Peacocke, the Inspector-General, who with his deputy was attending a cabinet meeting called at 4 p.m. Wolseley told Peacocke that he had been in touch with the military. Wolseley and Bradley, the Deputy Commissioner, were both of the opinion that the situation was such that troops would have to be deployed on the ground in west Belfast. The Inspector-General did not, however, support Wolseley's request for army assistance: he did not think the representations made to him by the Commissioner warranted the taking of such a grave step. Quite apart from purely tactical considerations on the ground, the Inspector-General was aware of the possible constitutional consequences of calling in troops.[132] As a result of discussions between Peacocke, Robert Porter, Dyball and Harold Black, it was decided to bring in troops on a standby basis. In the event, at 5.50 p.m. a company of soldiers was ordered to the Commissioner's headquarters at Castlereagh. They arrived at about 6.35 p.m. by which time police reserves had been summoned from elsewhere in the Province and men from the local force had returned to duty. In the event, the RUC did not lose control of the situation.[133] But it had served as a warning to just how close the RUC had come to losing control.

In order to strengthen police manpower Peacocke proposed the raising of the number of Reserve Force platoons from eight to twelve by 'dilution' with Special Constabulary, at a ratio of 50:50 at constable level, under RUC officers.[134] The cabinet agreed[135] but rejected a proposal for the imposition of a curfew, even within a limited area, as being too difficult to enforce and administer, amid fears that it might even contribute to an exacerbation of feeling. Special Constables were deployed by Porter to guard threatened Catholic houses in Protestant areas, with Protestant houses in Catholic areas being protected by the RUC. This was designed to relieve the regular police and to demonstrate that the USC existed to help preserve law and order in the interests of all sections of the community. The cabinet authorised this in the light of the implications involved in any request for the assistance of the Army.[136]

In a further effort to prevent military intervention Porter was authorised by the cabinet on 3 August to interpret existing conditions applying to the use of CS gas in a less restrictive way, so that this could be used if other methods were inadequate.[137] This was not what had been agreed with London but anticipated a successful appeal from Chichester-Clark to Callaghan for such a relaxation on 4 August. Chichester-Clark explained to Callaghan how on 12–13 July—as in the earlier Londonderry disturbances of 19–20 April—it was clear that one of the objects of the rioters was to do injury to the police, as evidenced by their use of dangerous missiles such as petrol bombs, pieces of street gratings and potatoes with projecting nails, in addition to stones. There were also attempts on 12–13 July to lure the police into sections of streets over which petrol had been poured and one patrol had to fire warning shots to escape from the clutches of a mob in a cul-de-sac. With the next potentially difficult period on 12 August, Chichester-Clark and his colleagues were concerned if anything like the events of 12–13 July were to be repeated. 'Moreover,' said Chichester-Clark, 'the use of CS is a relatively humane way of coping with riot conditions—and could be said to be preferable to baton charges which leave the Police open to allegations of brutality. I may say that in order to satisfy himself that the effects of CS are not unduly severe, the Minister of Home Affairs has personally subjected himself to a concentration.'[138] The Home Office was in favour as was Callaghan,[139] so Wilson agreed.[140]

It was during this period that the Northern Ireland Government received what can only be described as a political bombshell from London that seemed to threaten their very existence. This had followed the cabinet meeting of 3 August when it seemed that Stormont might have to request the deployment of troops. Harold Black had spoken to Robin North in the Home Office to let him know, in fulfilment of the Northern Ireland Government's obligation to consult in advance on an inter-governmental basis, that they might be approaching the point when the Northern Ireland Government might have to seek help from the Army. At the same time the Northern Ireland Cabinet Secretary was told that in view of the serious constitutional consequences of the use of troops, which had been mentioned at the Downing Street inter-governmental meetings, it would be advisable for Northern Ireland to endure a quite considerable degree of disorder before invoking military assistance. At this point Black suggested that it was time Stormont knew precisely what these 'constitutional consequences' were. North replied that he hoped it would be possible to be more specific on this topic in the morning.

On the morning of 4 August, North telephoned Black to say he now had authority to spell out the constitutional aspects of the use of troops to maintain law and order in Northern Ireland. Her Majesty's Government had willingly acquiesced in the employment of troops for guarding key-points following damage by explosives to water mains but it had been made clear at the time that any extension of these duties to riot or crowd-control tasks would require prior discussion between the two governments. In the event of troops having to undertake these duties they could clearly not be placed under the orders of the Northern Ireland Government. It was, in addition, the Home Secretary's view that it would be necessary for Her Majesty's Government to consider whether drastic action involving legislation at Westminster might not have to be taken to provide for temporary direct rule from Whitehall. North went on to say that he was now able to tell Black that the previous evening the GOC had been informed that if, in fulfilment of his common-law responsibility to give aid to the civil power he decided to put troops on the streets, he might by that action be committing the United Kingdom Government to take over the Government of Northern Ireland. It was emphasised to Black that these views did not represent decisions which would necessarily be taken by Her Majesty's Government but indicated rather the kind of matter which would come under immediate consideration by the British cabinet once troops were employed on law and order functions. It was thought that Parliament would certainly have to be given an opportunity of debating the use of troops and for this purpose would have to be recalled if in recess.

A shocked Black felt it necessary to express 'my astonishment that such penal consequences could be in contemplation, that it had never occurred to us that the veiled hints at the Downing Street meetings about "review of the constitutional relationship" had ever meant more than the possible removal of responsibility for law and order—an extreme enough course in all conscience—and that our Ministers were bound to react vigorously against this attitude'. Black was dispatched by Chichester-Clark to see North and Sir Philip Allen in London the next day, 5 August. In a lengthy discussion at the Home Office, Black made it clear to Allen and North that it was extremely unwise and potentially dangerous to impose such constraints upon the Northern Ireland Government as they would delay a call for the intervention of troops up to and indeed beyond the last extremity; there could well be many situations in which limited intervention—limited that was in both numbers, time and area—could prevent escalation to the point of anarchy, by which time it might require much greater forces to restore order. Black argued that what the British Government were in fact saying to the Northern Ireland Government was that at the point where intervention was clearly needed they should pause and consider whether they were prepared to seek that intervention when one of the consequences would be their own demise.

Clearly in such a situation the Northern Ireland Government would be bound to consider every other course open to them, including the putting of armed Specials on the streets, with all the implications that that might carry for a deepening of the sectarian conflict and even for the possibility of an invasion from the Republic which the Home Office officials had pointed out might also be an unavoidable consequence. If disorders tended to continue and increase the Northern Ireland Government, in the absence of military intervention, would soon be called to explain why they were hesitating and they might have no option but to spell out the true situation, which would have to include an account of the very severe restrictions imposed upon their freedom of action by London in the use of CS smoke, in the use of the Special Constabulary, and in the constitutional consequences which could follow a request for army help.

Black emphasised that this situation was totally unacceptable to the Northern Ireland Government, whose Prime Minister would want immediate talks with the Home Secretary. He warned Allen and North that the United Kingdom authorities should consider the situation that might well arise if in fact they did decide to exercise direct rule from Whitehall. There would first of all be a frightening reaction by the Protestant community which could make anything that had happened up to now seem like child's play; a provisional government might be set up with extreme elements at its head and it was highly probable that wholesale sectarian strife would break out not only in the streets but also in the factories. The United Kingdom authorities should also consider what the reaction of responsible Catholic opinion would be; while it might in some quarters be favourable initially, it could not be other than appalled at the consequences.

Black felt that the action proposed by Her Majesty's Government was surely only proper in the case of a recalcitrant and intractable Government which was resisting desirable reforms. There was no ground for thinking that the present administration would wish to be other than entirely reasonable in taking any political course that might be open to them to ease the present situation; there could, of course, be no surrender to sectarian hooliganism, which was all that was afflicting the Northern Ireland scene at that moment. The present administration in Northern Ireland, far from being reactionary, had embarked upon every reform suggested to them by London and were completely committed to the implementation of these reforms.

Black left the British authorities in no doubt that in the Northern Ireland Government's view the suspension of a democratically elected government would lead to a major constitutional convulsion and the repercussions in terms of violence and civil strife would be very grave indeed. Then, attempting to find some area for compromise, Black explained that the course the Northern Ireland Government would most like to see would be a reversion to the normal arrangement, applicable in other parts of the Kingdom, of the Army being available for aid to the civil power in accordance with the accepted common-law doctrine governing this matter and without any political constraints of the kind already suggested.

He was told that British ministers would not be prepared to accept this. However, the Home Office officials indicated their readiness to put to the Home Secretary a proposal for the issue of a letter by him to the Northern Ireland Prime Minister in which he would outline the common-law position governing the intervention of the military in aid of the civil power, mentioning the recognition by Her Majesty's Government of the commendable attitude of the Northern Ireland Government in not wishing to call upon military help save in extreme necessity, then going on to indicate the readiness of Her Majesty's Government to respond to any request which the Government of Northern Ireland might make for the help of troops; the letter would conclude with a reference to the gravity of this step and the need to explain to the Westminster Parliament the circumstances under which it had been taken and would then say that it would be essential, once troops had taken part in peace-preservation functions, for the two governments to meet for an urgent and immediate examination of the situation and to assess what future course of action should be adopted. It was to be understood, of course, that in this joint consultation the possibility of a take-over by Westminster of the functions of the Northern Ireland Government could not be excluded. The Home Office officials agreed that the ultimate sanction which this would involve was a rather remote possibility in practical terms but they felt that their ministers would be bound to regard it as impossible to exclude from consideration.[141] When Chichester-Clark conveyed to his cabinet the information from London it was decided that he should seek an early meeting with Callaghan.[142]

But before this could be arranged it became apparent, to the Northern Ireland Government at least, from speculation in the national press that authoritative guidance had been given to journalists about the circumstances in which Northern Ireland could expect to be given military help.[143] In particular, the *Financial Times* reported on 6 August that: 'British troops would be used to restore law and order in Ulster only if the Northern Ireland Government first agreed to surrender its political authority to Westminster.'[144] As a result of this disclosure of considerations which, from Stormont's point of view, had been put to the Northern Ireland Government in the utmost confidentiality and which were liable, now that they had been brought out into the open, to become a matter of acute controversy, Chichester-Clark thought it necessary to speak on the telephone to the Home Secretary at the latter's farm in Kent.[145] As the two men talked Callaghan reminded Chichester-Clark that he should bear in mind that press reports did not determine British Government policy[146] and reassured him that the British Government had no intention or desire whatsoever to assume responsibility for Northern Ireland affairs. The only two situations in which this might arise were firstly, in the event that progress on the reforms discussed at previous Downing Street meetings was not satisfactory; and secondly, the continuing use of troops to control riot situations. On the question of the use of troops, Callaghan envisaged two alternative situations which might arise:

(a) a solitary occasion when troops would be used once to quell hooligans of any faction. Provided that this was only an isolated incident involving the use of troops he felt that nothing much would be called in question.

(b) In the case of continuing use of troops H.M.G. would undoubtedly feel that
they would have to control the circumstances of their use. He felt that it would
be difficult to separate the function of law and order, which H.M.G. might wish
to control, from other functions of the Northern Ireland Government and,
therefore, his personal view was that it was a case of taking over all Northern
Ireland's affairs or none. He would, however, instruct his officials to examine the
possibility of taking over the law and order function only.[147]

So while Callaghan accepted it was possible that the use of troops might be a
solitary occasion when short, sharp action would be sufficient to restore the
situation, he thought this seemed unlikely. The most likely situation would be
that there would be a continuing use of troops. And in the event of a continuing
use of troops the British Government would have to assume some sort of control
over the circumstances in which the troops were used. This would mean in some
senses assuming responsibility for Northern Ireland affairs as London could not
be left 'holding the baby' in respect of policies for which it had no responsibility.
It was inconceivable, and would not be tolerated by the British public, if there was
a continuing use of British troops without the Westminster Parliament's asserting
its authority. The Northern Ireland Government should assume that the intervention would be a case of 'all or nothing'.[148] However, Callaghan promised
Chichester-Clark that he would consult the Northern Ireland Government before
any drastic action of this kind was taken and that this would be done before he
went to Parliament for legislation. The conversation concluded with Callaghan
saying once again that the continuing use of British troops would almost certainly
mean that the Westminster Parliament would have to assert its authority.[149]

So alarmed were Chichester-Clark and his colleagues by this conversation that
the Prime Minister felt that he had to put clearly and unambiguously before the
Home Secretary the firm and unanimous view of the Northern Ireland cabinet's
attitude to a possible request for army assistance, which he did in writing the
same day. Chichester-Clark explained to Callaghan that not to do so would be to
risk a serious constitutional crisis with the gravest practical implications. In the
first place he stated the Stormont cabinet's attitude to the role of the Army. The
Prime Minister confessed with some irritation that his cabinet had read regular
press references to the use of 'British troops' as 'if we were some sort of external
territory. The British Army is our Army too. I and many Ulstermen have been
proud to serve in it. It never occurred to us that its role in relation to Northern
Ireland differed in any way from that role in relation to Great Britain.' He pointed
out that in any part of the United Kingdom unfortunate situations might arise—
and had arisen in the past—where law and order could not be maintained by
ordinary policing. Indeed, to maintain regular policing forces at a level to cope
with the most exceptional emergencies would represent an appalling burden on
the community. For that reason it was a well understood principle that the civil

power, when its ordinary resources were unable to cope with a situation in being or foreseen, had a right to call upon the assistance of the armed forces of the Crown.

The Northern Ireland Government had always appreciated that the control of troops in Northern Ireland had to rest—as indeed it did under the Government of Ireland Act—with Her Majesty's Government in the United Kingdom. Moreover, the Northern Ireland Government had always acknowledged that, since this was the case, the deployment of troops on any continuing basis would inevitably involve arrangements sufficient to satisfy UK ministers that troops were not being affected by situations which they could not influence or control. Accordingly the Northern Ireland Government always foresaw the possibility that London would seek methods by which it could feel confident of a proper voice in the 'law and order' field. This, explained Chichester-Clark, was what he and his colleagues thought Callaghan and Wilson had in mind in the various veiled references which they made to 'constitutional repercussions' and which the Northern Ireland Government believed could quite readily be agreed in the context of the normal co-operation between the two governments.

The Northern Ireland Government was therefore appalled—'I must not understate our reaction'—to learn that in the event of a deployment of troops, Westminster was proposing, albeit temporarily, a suspension of the Northern Ireland Government. This put Chichester-Clark's Government, and in particular his colleague the Minister of Home Affairs, in an impossible position. The grave decision as to whether the civil power could no longer cope with the situation ought surely to be made on law-and-order grounds and not on political ones. Yet the Northern Ireland Government could be faced with the unenviable decision as to whether to allow the situation to deteriorate or to seek military aid and thereby risk extinguishing representative institutions which they had built up and defended for nearly half a century. The Prime Minister assured the Home Secretary that in any event the Northern Ireland Government would not consider calling in the Army except in the gravest of circumstances; but should these grave circumstances arise,

Chichester-Clark did not think it right that the decision should be taken with a 'sword of Damocles hanging over our head'. Furthermore, Chichester-Clark could not see what justification there could be for adopting such an extreme course. Since the current difficulties had begun in October of the previous year, the Northern Ireland Government had met the Home Secretary and his colleagues in a 'most co-operative spirit, and in spite of all the formidable political obstacles standing in our way we have moved quite as far as you ever pressed us to do, and indeed further'. Moreover, the recent civil disturbances which led the Northern Ireland Government to contemplate the possibility of the need for troops were not of a political character at all. They were to some extent sectarian and to a lesser extent sheer hooliganism. Thus if London were to impose direct rule the Prime Minister warned Callaghan that he should be in no doubt that:

any move to replace a representative Government, freely and democratically elected as recently as February of this year, would be wholly unacceptable to the great majority of Ulster people. You would be taking on a very open-ended commitment, which would go far beyond what would be involved in ordinary aid to the civil power. I must make it clear that the people of Northern Ireland are as determined to have their own Government as the people of the South were from 1919 on; and you should seriously consider the history of how Dublin Castle tried to cope with Sinn Féin at that time.

As matters now stood, newspaper speculation about Westminster's intentions, which did not represent the Home Secretary's thinking as made known to him, could have the most unfortunate effect of encouraging further disorder on the part of those whose aim had always been to overthrow the Government of Northern Ireland. Anyone who sought that end and who read in the newspapers that use of the Army might involve suspension of that Government was surely going to redouble his efforts to escalate matters to a point where the police could no longer control the situation. In these circumstances it was Chichester-Clark's view that he and the Home Secretary should meet at a very early date to consider the entire situation.[150]

This letter made Callaghan pause and consider the consequences of direct rule. The evidence that he was retreating somewhat from a rapid take-over if troops were deployed can be seen in the hastily arranged inter-governmental meeting on the morning of 8 August at the Home Office. There Chichester-Clark and Porter met with Callaghan and Stonham. Callaghan asked the Stormont team what they considered was the role of the troops if they were called upon. When Chichester-Clark said that it would be a normal internal security role, Callaghan replied that troops had no 'normal internal security role'. Indeed, it seemed to Callaghan that the Northern Ireland Government seemed to contemplate the use of troops in a rather matter-of-fact way, with the troops being called in 'from time to time' to deal with 'day to day riots'. He strongly warned against thinking that troops might properly be called in except as a last resort in severely abnormal conditions. In practice troops had never been used in Great Britain in recent times. Nor was it right to call upon troops 'to get on with it' as though the maintenance of law and order was one of their normal functions. It was not: where there was disorder in overseas dependent territories the maintenance of law and order was the responsibility of strengthened police forces, and not of the troops. The deployment of British troops in Northern Ireland was dictated primarily by defence considerations and not in order that they might be available to help the civil power.

Chichester-Clark assured Callaghan that the Northern Ireland Government had never contemplated that the decision to call in troops would be taken lightly. Porter agreed that it was certainly a last resort, and was recognised to be a very grave step. What Chichester-Clark was trying to emphasise was that the suspension of the

Northern Ireland constitution would bring about the most serious reaction from a very wide section of moderate Protestant opinion. Any radical amendment of the Government of Ireland Act, and in particular the suspension of the Northern Ireland Parliament, would be regarded as a step in the direction of a merger with the Irish Republic. The law at present declared that there would be no change in Northern Ireland's position as part of the United Kingdom without the consent of the Northern Ireland Parliament; but if that Parliament disappeared one of the main safeguards against such a change would be thought to have been removed. He was not over-stating the position in saying that this would have dire results; the Protestant reaction would be massive and might be very violent indeed. At the very least there would be no co-operation with the troops; and he could foresee a situation in which the troops were subject to attack by the Protestant population of Northern Ireland. Porter added that the people of Northern Ireland regarded the 1920 Act as the foundation of their constitutional position. They would regard suspension as almost a betrayal of what they had been led to believe was the position.

Callaghan admitted that such a view of the implications of suspending the constitution had never occurred to him, but it was just not a realistic interpretation of London's intentions. He spoke for the whole of the cabinet in saying that such an intention—undermining Northern Ireland's position within the United Kingdom—was never in their minds. But he agreed that Chichester-Clark's forecast of the effect of suspension was an important consideration, and he would report it to his Prime Minister. Stonham said that he too was impressed by what the Northern Ireland ministers had said about this. Nevertheless, said Callaghan, Northern Ireland could not have it both ways. Chichester-Clark's letter had asserted that Northern Ireland was part of the United Kingdom and therefore entitled to call in British troops and at the same time that Northern Ireland was determined to have its own government. But the British public would not tolerate the use of British troops without the British Government being in control of the situation and the policies which might affect the position of the troops. He spoke for the whole cabinet in saying that although they had contingency plans they had no desire to assume greater responsibility for Northern Ireland affairs. It might be that the internal situation would be no better but the continuing use of troops would make political intervention inevitable.

When Porter acknowledged that Westminster was the sovereign authority but asked why, if the Northern Ireland Government acted responsibly in deciding under the Common Law to call in troops, they should then be removed from power, Callaghan explained that the continuing use of troops would presuppose a situation in which the Northern Ireland Government was unable to deal with the situation through the ordinary forces of law and order. A government which did not control law and order was not a government in the normal sense of the term. This was bound to have political and constitutional consequences. The Common

Law did not help at this point: it was concerned with the obligation on the military to help and not with the political consequences. Even if local magistrates in England were to find themselves in a situation in which they called in troops they would quickly find that the central government stepped in to control the situation. The same position would inevitably arise in Northern Ireland. The Northern Ireland Government was a government with devolved powers only. Although it was responsible for law and order, it did not have its own armed services, and therefore the use of troops inevitably brought in the United Kingdom Government. The troops were the agents of Westminster, and Westminster would be involved. The Northern Ireland ministers were right in saying that a Sword of Damocles hung over them. In a situation in which anarchy was developing and the military had to be moved in the Northern Ireland Government might lose its independence. The Minister of Home Affairs, who had the responsibility for law and order in Northern Ireland, was a politician, as the Prime Minister was, and they would inevitably have to have regard to the political consequences of calling in troops.

Chichester-Clark then suggested—he said this was for Porter's peace of mind as much as anything else—that it would greatly help to have some clarification of the sort of circumstances in which the use of troops would have fundamental constitutional consequences. Callaghan explained that there were many permutations of the detailed circumstances in which troops might come to be engaged, and he could not tie himself down to prescribe the consequences in advance. It was a question of political decisions to be taken at the time; it was not a matter of law. If the Northern Ireland Government wanted to suggest some clarification he would be ready to look at it but the general position was that if troops were used in Northern Ireland on any continuing basis the Northern Ireland Government could not remain in control of the situation. Chichester-Clark objected that he was also concerned about letting it be generally known that the use of troops would have grave constitutional consequences, which might encourage the extreme Civil Rights leaders to stir up further trouble in the hope of securing the removal of the Northern Ireland Government. Callaghan suggested that this possibility might also have a sobering effect on the Protestant extremists.

On a more positive note Callaghan was intrigued by Chichester-Clark's point in his letter that he thought it would be 'sufficient to satisfy United Kingdom ministers that troops were not being affected by situations which they could not influence or control'. Caught by surprise Chichester-Clark confessed that he had no detailed plan of how this might be arranged. He had assumed that the Home Secretary would lay down how he wanted it done; the Northern Ireland Government would co-operate completely. Porter then pointed out that, jurisprudentially, law and order was one of the fundamental, all-pervading functions of government, but he saw no difficulty about hiving off the law-and-order functions of the Northern Ireland Government and leaving the others alone. It would only mean someone else sitting in his seat as Minister of Home Affairs. Here Sir Philip Allen pointed out the practical difficulties of such a division of responsibilities. The United Kingdom Government, if responsible for law and order, could not divorce themselves from other policies of the Northern Ireland Government which had repercussions on law and order. It would be an odd government which was left at Stormont. Callaghan's view was that a straight division of functions was very difficult to envisage. The loyalty of the RUC would clearly have to be transferred to the United Kingdom Government (and he agreed with Chichester-Clark that this would itself cause difficulties which might lead to more troops having to be used). But the fundamental objection was that law and order sprang from the total policies of government and from people's reactions to those policies. If the United Kingdom Government were to take over law and order, they would inevitably have to take over the larger share of the total policies affecting Northern Ireland. Chichester-Clark accepted that the United Kingdom Government would want to control the purposes to which the troops were put, and would want a say in the general situation, as a decision of the Northern Ireland Government might result in the troops becoming further involved. But, because of the likely Protestant reaction, he hoped that a Northern Ireland government of some sort could remain in being, even if the United Kingdom Government took direct responsibility for law and order and exercised greater influence and control over other aspects of government than at present.

Callaghan now saw the force of Chichester-Clark's argument about retaining the Northern Ireland Government and Parliament: in the interests of all the people of Northern Ireland it was worthwhile considering whether alternative arrangements could be made. It appeared to Callaghan that Chichester-Clark was suggesting that the United Kingdom Government's ultimate sovereignty should be recognised but that the Northern Ireland Government should act as its agents over a wide field, for example agriculture. Chichester-Clark did not dissent from this way of putting it. It was then agreed that Allen and Harold Black should examine as quickly as possible whether it was practicable to devise a scheme whereby the Northern Ireland Government retained its functions outside the law and order field on an agency basis.

Towards the end of the discussion explanations began to emerge as to why there had been such confusion over the possible constitutional consequences. Callaghan asked how Porter could claim to have only heard about the constitutional consequences in the previous few days: Captain O'Neill had certainly taken the view that if troops were used on a continuing basis the Northern Ireland Government could not continue. Chichester-Clark explained that he had not supposed that the constitutional repercussions mentioned by Wilson at their meeting in May had meant the suspension of the Northern Ireland constitution. He had pressed O'Neill to clear the air about the consequences of calling in troops and had got the impression that the repercussions would be legislation at

Westminster on electoral law in Northern Ireland and financial sanctions. Callaghan agreed that the consequences had not been spelt out to Chichester-Clark personally. But he and Home Office officials were in no doubt that O'Neill knew them and had indeed almost volunteered that he realised what they were. It had been assumed that O'Neill had told the members of his Government, which at the time included Chichester-Clark and Porter. But apparently not. The meeting ended with a discussion of the Apprentice Boys march. Chichester-Clark explained that on the previous evening he had seen the organisers of the Londonderry parade. They were taking a responsible attitude and would that day meet the 'opposition' to see what agreement could be reached on the detailed arrangements, including the route of the march. It was perhaps the period immediately after the march which was the most dangerous. Even if there were legal powers to close the pubs it was doubtful whether this would help. Nor would it help to ban a march which was so popular and traditional. An extreme Protestant could readily organise a march in defiance of the ban with greater risk of disorder. Another source of potential trouble was the parade of the 'Hibernians' a few days later which could hardly be stopped if the Protestants were not stopped on 12 August. Stonham predicted that the greater danger would come from the march to be organised by Paisley at Newry later in the week while Callaghan wondered whether it would be worth considering if there were other demonstrations which might be extremely provocative and could be stopped. The Northern Ireland Government might well reach its decisions on the basis of whether they had the police strength to enforce a ban. His own declared policy after the violent anti-Vietnam-War demonstration in Grosvenor Square was to consider each case on its merits.[151] But it was clear from this that Callaghan was not advocating a banning of the march. Indeed, the Northern Ireland ministers could be well pleased with the outcome of a difficult meeting. Callaghan had taken Stormont's concerns relating to direct rule on board and was prepared to consider, at least, a diluted take-over which would preserve the Northern Ireland Government's existence. The rollback from a London take-over proved, in the long run, a controversial decision. All anyone could do now was wait and see what happened in Derry.

Chapter 7 ⌒

AUGUST
1969

THE BATTLE OF BOGSIDE: 12 AUGUST

For the police the July riots in Londonderry presented some disturbing features. They demonstrated that the police then available were unable either to prevent rioting or to end it once it had started. Their patrolling of the Bogside had been slight and occasional for many months: after the July riots it was almost non-existent. John Hume's subsequent remark that 'from 12 July the police themselves were publicly admitting that they were not policing a particular area, which was a public admission that law and order had broken down in a particular area' basically summed up the situation in Derry. When the July riots died away the ability to maintain public order in the city had slipped out of police control: peace depended not upon the will of lawfully constituted authority, but upon the whim of the youngsters of the Bogside. In Hume's opinion the situation in the city was out of control and trouble was inevitable on 12 August. In the opinion of the veteran Derry Republican, Sean Keenan: 'It did not matter who was to come into the Bogside, be it police, B-Specials or Apprentice Boys, Paisleyites, or whoever, we would defend ourselves against anybody coming in to attack us.' And NICRA's Michael Canavan commented that trouble could have started from 'maybe an innocent action of the police' or 'from somebody throwing a stone from the Civil Rights side'. It was 'the kind of situation where serious trouble could have started up from inconsequential events'.[1]

The first significant event was the Devenney funeral on 19 July, when some 30,000 people appeared on the streets to mourn his death and make their silent protest at what they believed to be the 'police brutality' which killed him. The next was the formation of the Derry Citizens' Defence Association (DCDA) on 20 July.[2] This body came to supersede the Derry Citizens' Action Committee (DCAC) which was by now in disarray, being unable to agree on what to do if there were an attack on the Bogside or on what, if any, stewarding arrangements to make for 12 August. The DCDA knew what it would do. Its objects were said to be first 'peace' and, failing peace, the 'defence' of the Bogside. Sean Keenan was to be its chairman: seven out of eight of its original committee were members of the James Connolly Republican Club, although later the committee was progressively broadened until in mid-August it was forty strong. The DCDA formed street committees, each under a chairman. It organised public meetings; five were held in various parts of the Bogside-Creggan area. Barricades, designed to keep unwanted strangers out of the Bogside, were planned and their locations determined. The use of firearms was ruled out but preparations to defend themselves with 'sticks, stones and the good old petrol bomb', in Keenan's words at a public meeting on 4 August, were put in hand.

In August a 'strident note' crept into the public utterances arising out of Derry. On 10 August at a meeting at Celtic Park, Eddie McAteer, in the course of an emotional speech, declared that: 'if this is, indeed, our hour of trial at hand, if we are to be beaten into the ground in this city as a helpless minority, then I pray to God that our watching brethren will not stand aside any longer'. These preparations and this language greatly increased tension. Further evidence was provided by the fact that a dairy delivering milk in bottles to the centre of the city got back very few empties on 10 August, and none on the 11th or the 12th. Whereas the emphasis of Hume's DCAC had been to maintain peace, the planning of the DCDA was directed to 'defence'. As Canavan later explained: 'It was absolutely essential in my opinion that preparations be made for defence . . . there was a very real danger in my opinion that, for whatever reason trouble would start, it would inevitably finish up in the Bogside.'

By 'defence' the DCDA in fact meant a fight to keep all comers (including the police) out of the Bogside. Their thinking was that sooner or later there would be disturbances which, as had happened before, notably in January, April and July, would end up in the Bogside; that in all probability this would happen on the 12th (for example there was the fear that 'Major Bunting would troop his colour in the Bogside') and that, when it did happen, the Bogside would fight. The leaders did nothing to dissuade their followers (amongst them the youths of the Bogside) from the view that the police were a partisan force opposed to them.[3]

With the tension so palpable in Derry the military authorities made their preparations. The 1st Prince of Wales Own Regiment was near Londonderry. One company of the Royal Regiment of Wales was in Omagh with the 17/21 Lancers. The total effective strength available for deployment in the Belfast area was five companies, which totalled, excluding one company in reserve at Holywood, about three hundred men. Once troops began to be committed a further battalion, the 3rd Light Infantry, was brought into Belfast. It arrived during the night of 15–16 August.[4] By that stage they were needed.

On the morning of 12 August members of the Apprentice Boys clubs assembled on the Mall Wall for their church parade. They went in procession to St Columb's Cathedral where at midday a service was held. After the service the clubs again assembled and at about 1 p.m. the procession through the city began. As the long column, three deep, with its bands and regalia moved through the streets, it 'evoked a sense of pride and triumph in Protestant hearts, but a feeling of irritation and frustration in some of the Catholics'. The youth of the Bogside were held back from the processional route by the presence of police and crush barriers. Before the procession a few Apprentice Boys tossed coins from the city walls towards small knots of people below. Nevertheless the procession was disciplined and orderly: its members, under the efficient control of their marshals, gave no provocation. At about 1.45 p.m. the head of the procession reached Waterloo Place, where some thirty police, wearing normal patrol dress, had taken up position. A metal crush barrier completely sealed off the entrance of Waterloo Street and William Street into Waterloo Place. Behind the barrier stood a crowd which, while 'fairly good-humoured', shouted abuse from time to time at the procession and the police. At 2.30 p.m. a handful of nails was flung across the barrier into the midst of the police. This was followed by stones. From this small beginning developed a riot which, enveloping the city for two days and nights, was not brought under control until the Army entered William Street at 5 p.m. on 14 August.

The stone-throwers, with a few exceptions, were young Bogsiders—teenagers or people in their early twenties. Almost as soon as the stoning of the police began, John Hume appeared at the barrier and, joined by Eddie McAteer and others, did his best with the Bogside crowd. But his success was only momentary. Very soon the young Bogsiders overwhelmed their stewards and set going a barrage of stones and bottles. A policeman fell unconscious, the first casualty of the riot: as he fell, there was a loud cheer from behind the barriers. At this moment the District Inspector ordered his men to put on their riot gear—helmets and shields. The procession cleared Waterloo Place at about 4 p.m., but not before the Bogsiders had increased their range to include it as a target for their stones. The supporters of the Apprentice Boys now became restless; a considerable crowd of them again gathered in Guildhall Square and began throwing stones. By 4.30 p.m. the Bogside crowd was swarming up to the barriers, out of control and attacking the police fiercely with stones and bottles.

From 2.30 until 5 p.m. the police had stood their ground in Waterloo Place, passively enduring a constant hail of missiles aimed at them from Waterloo Street and William Street. Though it was clear that some of the police threw some stones back, their conduct at this stage, viewed as a whole, won the praise of Hume. Yet the Bogside crowd became more and more violent. They attacked the crush barriers, pulling some of them away up William Street. The senior police officers, whose strategy had up to this time—5 p.m.—been one of static defence, feared an eruption into and beyond Waterloo Place; they therefore ordered a baton-charge. The crowd at once dispersed, some up Waterloo Street and some along William Street. In William Street the police, led by an armoured car, reached its junction with Chamberlain Street, where for the first time they came under heavy petrol-bomb attack. Despite their advance the police in William Street had now lost the power to control events. As District Inspector Slevin remarked, theirs was now 'a fight for survival'—well illustrated by the casualties sustained by his contingent of police for, when it returned the next day to County Down, out of a total of fifty-nine men forty-three had been injured.

By 5 p.m. a lightly constructed barricade which had been established by the Bogsiders in Little James Street, some twenty-five yards from its junction with William Street, was destroyed by a police armoured vehicle. The police advanced towards William Street, where they came under missile and petrol-bomb attack from a large crowd behind a barricade which had been built in Rossville Street near its junction with William Street. As the police moved forward, some civilians from the Protestant crowd in Great James Street accompanied them, throwing stones and using catapults. Some of these civilian stone-throwers were actively encouraged by individual policemen: it was also clear that some policemen were themselves throwing stones. At about 3.30 p.m. Sean Keenan had given the order to erect barricades.[5]

Shortly before 4 p.m. Bernadette Devlin arrived in Rossville Street and actively encouraged the building of barricades. One barricade in particular proved a formidable obstacle. By 7 p.m. a large crowd had built up behind the barricade and movement, even by vehicle, past it and up William Street was difficult and dangerous. District Inspector Hood, in charge of the Reserve Force, decided that it must be destroyed: 'If we got the barricade removed,' he said, 'we could push the rioters back up Rossville Street. This was meant to be simply a limited operation.' An armoured vehicle now attacked the barricade, and after six or seven attempts broke through. It was followed by a second armoured car, a number of Land-Rovers and perhaps as many as a hundred police on foot.[6] Head Constable Fleming, who led the police into the Bogside and then, under the pressure of heavy attack, brought them out in good order, was unaware of the Protestant civilian involvement in the movement of his force. But Sergeant Harris, who was on foot, saw them as the police fell back. After remarking that the police were not in sufficient numbers to remain in the Bogside, he saw, as he turned to go back, seventy to a hundred Protestant youths who must have followed the police in. They also ran back, and he saw them throwing stones.[7]

The whole of this incursion into the Bogside lasted no longer than some twenty minutes. The movement was observed by Father Mulvey. In Father Mulvey's opinion it was an event of profound significance. When asked what was its effect on the Bogside people he replied: 'I would say that it brushed aside any hope of moderation or any hope of restoring calm. In fact, there was a completely different attitude discernible from that at any previous disturbance that I had witnessed at close quarters. There was what I would call an apparently complete unanimity in opposition to the police force. In fact, then and later that night and over the next few days the determination was so unanimous that I would only regard it as a community in revolt rather than just a street disturbance or a riot.'[8]

Its effect on the course of the riot was to harden attitudes in the Bogside. The smashing of the barricade, the entry of the armoured cars and foot police, closely followed by Protestant civilians throwing stones, appeared to many as the physical embodiment of their worst fears. The fact that the police had in mind the limited tactical objective of relieving the pressure of rioters upon William Street and the fact that there was no concerted plan between police and Protestants were not evident to the people of the Bogside. They believed they were witnessing an attack on them by the police and Protestants. The effect of it in Father Mulvey's mind was typical: thereafter, there was 'complete unanimity in opposition to the police force' by 'a community in revolt'.

By 9 p.m. the situation was critical. Police numbers were being reduced by a fairly steady casualty rate. At a meeting of the head constables the unanimous view was expressed that it was now necessary to use CS gas. During the next two hours the riot grew more vicious. It was already the view of two senior police officers, DI McAtamney and DI Armstrong, that it was no longer a police but a military operation. When, therefore, the Deputy Inspector-General, Graham Shillington, arrived at about 11 p.m. at the Victoria Police Station, he learnt that there were serious misgivings as to the ability of the police to defend themselves, let alone to control or suppress the riot. On his way from Belfast he had heard over the car radio that the Minister for Home Affairs had authorised, if need be, the use of CS gas. Upon arrival he went to Sackville Street where he saw for himself how serious the situation was. Police, he observed, had actually pulled out exhausted, and were resting on the footpath: it was apparent to him that the police could not keep the crowds apart very much longer. He returned to the police station, spoke to the Minister on the telephone, and then instructed DI Hood first to give a loud-speaker warning and then to use the gas. CS gas was discharged.

The result was dramatic and immediate: Little James Street was cleared of rioters and police; the Bogsiders retreating into Rossville Street, the police into Sackville Street and the Protestants into Great James Street. Tactically the use of the gas was a success. But the rioters began once more to assemble in the early hours of 13 August: they threw stones sporadically from Rossville Street towards the police in William Street and Little James Street. The police therefore fired further cartridges and dropped grenades of the gas out of vehicles in the Rossville Street area with the result that by dawn, while the riot had become sporadic and far less intense than earlier, the area had become enveloped in a pall of gas, covering the streets and penetrating the houses. It was apparent to many that the gas was discharged not in the direction of Great James Street, where stood the Protestant crowd, but towards the Bogsiders in Rossville Street. While this was true, it reflected the real source of danger to the police. The Bogsiders were attacking the police; the Protestants were not.

One major incident of note was that, between 11 and 11.30 p.m., two men had suffered gunshot wounds in William Street: neither man was seriously hurt. Two bullets, which were removed from the injured men in the course of medical treatment, were subjected to expert examination and were found to be 9 mm bullets and appeared to have ricocheted. With one exception, there was no evidence of any civilian, Protestant or Catholic, carrying or using firearms during the Londonderry riots; on the other hand, some police were armed with Sterling sub-machine guns, which fired bullets of 9 mm calibre. These weapons were also on issue to Ulster Special Constabulary personnel.[9] The 'Battle of the Bogside' was well and truly under way.

13 AUGUST

At about 7 a.m. on 13 August the Deputy Inspector-General was again on the scene: he formed the opinion that army intervention would be required within twenty-four hours. He told the Inspector-General by telephone who set in motion the process necessary to ensure that the Army would be available if called upon.[10] Peacocke informed the Northern Ireland cabinet, which was meeting in emergency session, of the situation in Londonderry. Porter told his colleagues that County Inspectors had been authorised to call out Special Constabulary in support of the RUC in circumstances in which they considered it favourable to carry their normal arms. The cabinet agreed that if events escalated to a point at which the police had clearly lost control the assistance of the Army would have to be sought. This decision would be left to Porter who would consult, if possible, with his fellow members of the Cabinet Security Committee. The cabinet also discussed the desirability of dealing with leading agitators if solid evidence could be unearthed: the part being played by the IRA, and the possible control of supplies of petrol in the Bogside area. Significantly, the cabinet was now adamant that no contingency planning on the basis of a surrender of law and order powers to London would be acceptable in political terms. Any such planning would have to be in terms of effective liaison rather than any acceptance of a transfer of powers.[11]

In Dublin the events in Derry had also sent Jack Lynch's Irish Government into crisis. The cabinet convened at 11 a.m. Two of the most senior personalities in the Government, Neil Blaney, Minister for Agriculture and Fisheries and Kevin Boland, Minister for Local Government, favoured direct intervention in the North by the Irish Army. They argued that units could readily cross the border into areas such as Derry, Newry, Dungannon and south Armagh where there were Catholic majorities. There they could operate in a peace-keeping role; the British Government should be informed of this.

When the majority of the cabinet refused this request, Boland threatened to resign and stormed out of the meeting. He was only dissuaded from resigning on the grounds that any public split in the Government at this stage would have weakened the Government's position. In the event the Government ordered the Army to the border and set up field hospitals at various crossing-points to tend wounded from the North. In addition the first-line reserve of Army officers comprising some 2,000 men were called up.[12] At 3.40 p.m. Kevin Rush, at the London Embassy, was instructed by the Irish cabinet to 'convey immediately to British Government request that they arrange for the immediate cessation of police attacks on the people of Derry'. Stewart was not available but Lord Chalfont, Minister of State, was. At 4.50 p.m. further instructions were issued from the cabinet for the 'Ambassador in London to request the British Government to apply immediately to the United Nations for the urgent dispatch of peace-keeping force to the Six Counties of Northern Ireland, and to inform them that the Government have instructed the Irish Permanent Representative to the UN to inform the Secretary-General of the foregoing'. Rush, however, had departed for his meeting with Chalfont and only received the additional instructions just before going in to see the Minister. He conveyed both messages. Chalfont's response was that the matters raised were of concern to the Home Office rather than the Foreign Office; however, straight away he said that he could not at all accept that the police were attacking the people of Derry. As regarded the UN, Chalfont pointed out that since the matter was a British internal one it was not an appropriate matter to be raised in the UN. As the meeting ended Chalfont, escorting Rush to the door, indicated how concerned he was personally about the events in the North and he expressed the hope that they would improve very quickly. In New York the Irish Permanent Representative to the UN was instructed to inform the Secretary-General of the request to the British Government to apply for a UN peace-keeping force.[13]

That night the Taoiseach appeared on Irish television. His speech was the product of the cabinet's collective endeavours. Lynch said it was evident that the Stormont Government was no longer in control of the situation. Indeed, he argued that the present situation was the inevitable outcome of the policies pursued for decades by successive Stormont Governments. It was clear, stated Lynch, that the Irish Government 'can no longer stand by and see innocent people injured and perhaps worse'. Claiming that the RUC was no longer accepted as an impartial force and the deployment of the British Army would be unacceptable, the Irish Government requested the British Government to apply to the United Nations for the urgent despatch of a peace-keeping force to the six counties. Lynch announced that with so many injured, his Government had directed the Irish Army to establish field hospitals in County Donegal, adjacent to Derry, and at other points along the border. He concluded by saying that the re-unification of the national territory could provide the only permanent solution to the problem; it was the Irish Government's intention to request the British Government to enter into early negotiations with the Irish Government to review the present constitutional position of the six counties.[14]

Chichester-Clark attacked Lynch's speech as unnecessary and irresponsible, and 'not statesmanship but the effusions of a hostile propaganda'. The Prime Minister disputed the Taoiseach's claim that the police had attacked the people of

Londonderry, and reiterated that there would be no change in Northern Ireland's position as an integral part of the United Kingdom without its consent, 'and we do not consent, nor will we consent in the future'. Chichester-Clark claimed that the events in Northern Ireland were not the agitation of a minority seeking by lawful means the assertion of political rights, but the 'conspiracy of forces seeking to overthrow a Government democratically elected by a large majority'.[15] The Northern premier, who was just as mistaken as his Southern counterpart in identifying the causes of the disorders, was right to feel aggrieved. For while, from the Irish Government's perspective, Lynch's speech would be seen as statesmanlike, forcing the British to intervene, the truth was that the speech had a disastrous effect on the situation in the North, fanning the communal flames.

It was on 13 August that the rioting spread to other parts of the Province. There had already been disturbances in Coalisland, and now Belfast, which proved to be a powderkeg. Partly this was a consequence of a conscious decision by NICRA leaders to encourage others to distract RUC forces from Derry. Frank Gogarty, Chairman of NICRA, received telephone requests to organise diversions from Sean Keenan, Eamonn McCann and Bernadette Devlin. There was also a report to the Association from Kevin Agnew, a member of the Executive, who was present when CS gas was first used. These calls were received on the night of 12 August. On the morning of 13 August a special meeting of the NICRA Executive was called in Belfast with the intention of organising diversionary demonstrations. At 6 p.m. Chichester-Clark broadcast on television. During this speech he said, in relation to the Londonderry riots, 'We want peace not vengeance. If the rioters withdraw peacefully to their homes and observe the law no attempt will be made to exploit the situation.' The speech also announced that the Northern Ireland Parliament would be recalled for the following day and that the USC would be used to the full to relieve the regular police force for other duties. It also indicated that if necessary 'the civil power' would not shrink from summoning 'other aid'. The NICRA deputation saw this broadcast at Gogarty's house. Kevin Boyle, NICRA's press officer, and Paddy Devlin agreed that they detected in it some signs that a truce might be arranged. Devlin spoke to Chichester-Clark, who agreed that Devlin should talk to Bernadette Devlin. There was some difficulty in reaching her, however, but eventually a telephone discussion took place. However Miss Devlin said she could not give an assurance that the police would not be followed if they withdrew from the Bogside. The Prime Minister's proposal therefore came to nothing.

At 9 p.m. there was Lynch's broadcast. It was regarded as provocative in many Protestant and Unionist circles and as an encouragement by some Catholic activists. Paddy Kennedy MP, who was present on the Falls Road on 13 August, recalled 'So you had a situation, a very tense situation, here in Belfast and, because of the Derry situation, this tension was heightened on the Falls, in my opinion— and it is only my opinion—by the Taoiseach's speech of 13 August.' According to the journalist Max Hastings, 'It was the opinion of most observers at that time that it was as a direct consequence and immediately following Jack Lynch's television appearance that the attacks on Hastings Street police station and the events of Wednesday night began.'[16] The most dangerous situation was developing in Belfast.

On the night of 13 August rioting in the Ardoyne began with an attack by Catholic elements on policemen at the junction of Crumlin Road and Disraeli Street for which there was no provocation. The object of the attack was to occupy the attention of the police in the hope of drawing their forces away from the Bogside in Londonderry. There were two features of the night's disturbances. First, the riot was started by a few Catholics without warning and after a period of peace: their objective was to involve the police and so prevent reinforcements going to Londonderry. The second feature was the Protestant reaction. The Catholic tactic of stretching the police brought the Protestants on to the streets with the inevitable consequence of serious rioting.[17]

Late that evening Harold Wilson telephoned Callaghan to discuss the situation. By now he had heard the details of Lynch's speech which he thought 'really seemed to be putting the fat in the fire'.[18] The latest information which Callaghan had suggested that the situation was looking a little better and there had not yet been a formal request for troops. He had insisted that there would have to be a formal request from the Northern Ireland Government stating the reasons. When such a request was received it would be discussed with Roy Hattersley, Minister for Defence Administration (who was standing in for Healy while he was recovering from a minor operation). The Prime Minister would be consulted before a final decision was taken. Callaghan then referred to the statement which had been made earlier in the evening by Lynch. Chichester-Clark had already replied on behalf of the Northern Ireland Government but he thought that the British Government should make a proper statement also. The statement should respond to Lynch's suggestion of a United Nations peace-keeping force and should make it clear that Northern Ireland would not cease to be part of the United Kingdom without the consent of the Northern Ireland Parliament. Wilson agreed[19] and the Foreign Office issued a statement reaffirming previous British pledges and reiterating that the affairs of Northern Ireland were thus an internal matter for the United Kingdom.[20]

14 AUGUST

On the following day Sir Andrew Gilchrist, Her Britannic Majesty's Ambassador in Dublin, commented on Lynch's intervention: 'There is this to be said for Lynch: he warned us that when the pressure grew too great he would be compelled to string along with the Nationalist / Sinn Féin / IRA line.' Any recent hope that he would take preventive action against the IRA and so limit the scope of extremist intervention in the South had been dashed because 'Derry came too soon.' Lynch, having just achieved the 'leadership of Ireland', was not prepared to lose it to the extremists and had therefore taken his place at their head. Gilchrist believed that, to a limited and somewhat insincere extent, of course Lynch hoped to get away with a further round of shadow boxing. But he was on a slippery slope: 'our rejection of his main demands can in due course be used by the extremist to turn Irish opinion against ourselves instead of against the Stormont Government'. And Irish opinion, already much inflamed by 'one-sided' reporting of Northern events, would be hard to restrain when the moment came for restraining it. Gilchrist warned that Southern extremists would consider themselves entitled to use violence without incurring any more moral disapproval in Dublin than was accorded to the throwers of what were now 'in effect napalm bombs' in Derry.

With this in mind, Gilchrist thought that the officials in London dealing with Irish affairs might like to have on their desks the following extract from the leading article in the *Irish Times* of Tuesday 6 February 1940, when it appealed for clemency on behalf of the Coventry IRA murderers: 'The Irish are a dangerously emotional people. They are liable to condone any crime, however horrible, if it can be connected directly or remotely with a political motive.' All in all, warned Gilchrist, 'we are in for a fairly difficult time with the Irish, someone said to me last night that I would soon have as many friends in Ireland as I had in Indonesia. I doubt if it will be quite so bad as that, but if I were a fire insurance company I would not like to have the British Embassy on my books. (Fortunately, though highly inflammable, it isn't ours).'[21] He also recalled how several Irishmen, 'generally when in their cups or otherwise excited', had mentioned to him or in his presence the thought that to ensure proper ventilation of the Irish problem at the United Nations it might be desirable to create an international threat to peace by seizing some small town (preferably Catholic) in Northern Ireland by a bloodless *coup de main* and then defying by armed forces all British attempts to recapture it: television cameras would be assembled of course and urgent appeals made to the UN. Gilchrist doubted very much if the Irish Government would take part in any such operation in present circumstances, but the IRA quite certainly had the capability of carrying it out on its own.[22]

Meanwhile back in Londonderry the moment when troops would be committed was approaching. By now it was obvious to the senior police officers surveying the scene on the morning of 14 August that their men were too few and too tired to restore order in the face of Bogside resistance. Severe static rioting continued all day in the William Street/Rossville Street area and in the afternoon a serious disturbance developed in Bishop Street near the Fountain and Long Tower Street. The police did well to contain and limit these troubles but they knew that it was no longer possible for them to restore law and order to the Bogside or peace to the city. In the course of the day the USC were brought on to the streets.[23]

USC personnel were on duty in Bishop Street when the afternoon's rioting broke out. The sight of the hated B-Specials had its predictable effect on the Bogsiders: fear and anger.[24] Military intervention was inevitable. Across the Irish Sea, Callaghan flew from London to RAF St Mawgan in Cornwall where he updated Wilson who was holidaying there. A Group Captain was sent scurrying off for a map of Northern Ireland when the Prime Minister wanted to find out how far 'somewhere was from somewhere else'.[25] Callaghan had spoken to Chichester-Clark shortly before leaving the capital: the Northern Ireland Government were expecting more trouble that evening. Unaware of the evolving situation in Londonderry, the latest information Callaghan had was that the RUC were feeling happier about the situation since their mobility had been increased by the relief which the Special Constabulary were affording on their duties. On the other hand, the GOC, the recently appointed Lieutenant-General Sir Ian Freeland, had been advised that the police might not be able to handle adequately any further trouble that evening and that a request for troops from the Northern Ireland Government was likely. In Callaghan's view if such a request were received the British Government would have to accede. Once this happened he considered that the objective should be limited to the restoration of law and order in the limited area where this was necessary. It should then be the intention to withdraw the troops as soon as possible, leaving the maintenance of law and order to the police.

If it were found that it was not possible to hand back responsibility to the civil authorities quickly it would be necessary to consider what more formal administrative arrangements were required in this situation. He suggested that it might be possible to isolate Londonderry and to replace the RUC there with a new police force which it would be hoped would carry the confidence of both Protestants and Catholics and which could be made responsible to local commissioners drawn from both religious groups. It was important that the GOC should have clear orders on how the troops should go about their task. He also thought it important that there should be a police and possibly a civil servant liaison officer attached to the GOC. In order to have an independent assessment of the methods and activities of the RUC, Callaghan had suggested to Chichester-Clark that two police consultants should be sent to Northern Ireland for this purpose. He had not reacted unfavourably to this suggestion and Callaghan considered that the two officers should be sent out that evening if agreement could be reached. Callaghan envisaged that it might be necessary for him to go to Northern Ireland himself if it became clear that the troops were likely to be committed for an extended period. The Home Secretary emphasised to Wilson how, in his earlier contacts with Chichester-Clark, he had been impressed by what the latter had said about the likely reaction among Protestants of any decision by the United Kingdom Government to assume full responsibility for Northern Ireland affairs, and the possible effect of this on the standing and authority of the Northern Ireland Government. He had indicated to Chichester-Clark on the telephone that morning that he was considering possible proposals for a new type of delegated authority if the situation required this, though he had not spelt out to him the sort of ideas that were being examined by his officials. As alternatives to the full assumption of powers by Westminster, he was considering:

(i) an arrangement in which the Northern Ireland Parliament would remain in being in an advisory or consultative capacity;

(ii) arrangements under which the Northern Ireland Government would remain in being but the United Kingdom Government would assume certain specific functions in relation to the maintenance of law and order;

(iii) arrangements under which again the Northern Ireland Government would remain in being and would act as an agent for the United Kingdom Government in the maintenance of law and order.

Wilson's response was that, whatever the outcome of the immediate situation, it was important to avoid any appearance of using troops in the interests of one section of the community against those of another. There was a particular danger of this in a situation where the disruption was the result of the activities of a Catholic element. On the other hand it was clearly a matter for the UK Government if the Government of Northern Ireland were unable to maintain law and order.[26]

At 3.10 p.m. news of the changing situation in Londonderry began to filter through. Lord Stonham informed Callaghan he had just had a message from Harold Black stating that the situation in Londonderry had worsened. The RUC would probably be obliged to fall back to their main police station and possibly defend this with firearms. There was then the danger that the mob would be free to roam the town. It was feared that there would be widespread looting, arson and injury to persons. Under these circumstances Black wanted to alert the United Kingdom Government that a formal request for the use of troops might be made at any moment. Callaghan asked Stonham for an up-to-date assessment of the situation in Londonderry from the GOC and also to find out from Black what formal reasons the Northern Ireland Government would be giving for their request for the use of troops.

At 3.40 p.m. Stonham rang again. He said that he had consulted Roy Hattersley.[27] At his request Hattersley spoke to the GOC and asked him for a detailed account of how he would perform his task in Londonderry if he was instructed to act in support of the civil power. Freeland told Hattersley that he anticipated he would be called upon to act in this capacity before 1800 hours that day. The police station at Waterloo Place was the command centre of Londonderry: without it and its communications network law and order would completely break down in the town. Freeland told Hattersley that the 1st and 2nd Companies of the Battalion of the Prince of Wales Own, stationed at HMS *Sea Eagle*, would move in from their location just the other side of the town bridge. They would expect to do so before the police station was finally surrounded and therefore would not need to take positive action against the crowd. They would then throw a tight cordon around the police station, through which they would expect the exhausted officers of the RUC to withdraw; a third company would secure access from the police station to *Sea Eagle* over the town bridge; the fourth company would remain in reserve.

It was Freeland's hope that having held the police station by the use of troops, a rested and regrouped RUC could take whatever initiative was necessary to push back the crowd from the area immediately surrounding the police station. He accepted that it might not be possible for this action to be taken by the constabulary and it might fall to the lot of the troops. But this would, of course, change the nature of the operation from a defensive to an offensive role. The troops' initial actions would all be based on the use of their anti-riot weapons. Freeland warned, however, that it was conceivable, although highly unlikely, that the crowd would not be contained either by these methods or by the use of CS gas, which would be fired into the crowd both by troops on the ground and from helicopters overhead. In the altogether unlikely event of the troops facing the prospect of being overrun by the crowd, Freeland would regard it as his duty to instruct them to open fire. The crowd would of course first be warned it was the Army's intention to open fire, and if this extreme situation came about it would be contained in as limited a way as appeared necessary to achieve the objective. In no circumstances would British troops be asked to enter the Bogside.[28]

Hattersley had also been in touch with the officer commanding the troops located on the fringe of Londonderry who had reported that the rioters were now within 100 yards of the main police station; the RUC thought that they would be unable to hold out for longer than an hour or so. When Stonham spoke again to Black he stated the formal reasons given by the Northern Ireland Government for a call for troops:

(i)   the enforced withdrawal of the police to their police station;
(ii) the danger of occupation of the centre of the city by a riotous mob, with a prospect of looting, arson and injury to persons.

Black stressed that the Northern Ireland Government still hoped that it might be possible to avert a formal request for military intervention. They were seeking reinforcements from the B-Specials. However, it seemed very likely that the request would have to be made and Black hoped that his conversation with Stonham could be regarded as the consultation necessary between the Northern Ireland Government and the United Kingdom Government before a request for troops was made. Black asked that the GOC should be given permission to comply with a request for assistance by the Inspector-General, if such a request was made in Londonderry in the circumstances outlined. Accepting this, Callaghan told Stonham that the GOC could be given authority to comply with a request in these circumstances, but it should be made clear that the assistance was to be confined to the immediate situation in Londonderry.

Callaghan then told Stonham about certain actions which he wanted to be put in train. Firstly, he wanted to send across that night to Northern Ireland, if necessary in a Service plane, a policeman and a civilian to assist the GOC.

Secondly, Chichester-Clark should be warned that Callaghan would be pressing for senior police officers from Britain to be sent to Northern Ireland that night or the following morning. Thirdly, Stonham was to consult Hattersley on whether the GOC was clear about what he was expected to do in handling the situation in the Bogside. And finally, Callaghan inquired whether it had been arranged for him to see the editors of the leading newspapers that night. It was confirmed that the editors of all but two papers, *The Times* and *The Guardian*, would be available; *The Times* and *The Guardian* were sending their deputy editors. Callaghan then discussed with Stonham the timing of a statement about the use of troops. The conversation ended with Callaghan and Stonham agreeing that if the final decision to use troops was taken while he was in transit between St Mawgan and London, a message should be passed to the aircraft. Callaghan would issue a statement on his return to the Home Office.[29]

Callaghan reported his discussions to Wilson. The Prime Minister agreed that if a request for the assistance of troops was received then this should be met, though it should be made clear that they were being used only in the limited area for which they were requested and that this was intended as a short-term operation to restore law and order, and not to maintain it in the longer term. If the purpose was limited in this way Wilson did not consider the wider constitutional issue would arise immediately. If in the light of developments in the next few days their early withdrawal did not seem likely the position would have to be reviewed. In this connection further consideration would have to be given to relations with the Irish Republic whose attitude had so far been 'unhelpful'. In these circumstances a meeting of the cabinet might be necessary. Wilson agreed with Callaghan's proposal to send a police liaison officer, together with a member of the Home Office, to assist and advice the GOC. He also agreed with the proposal to dispatch two senior police consultants. Wilson was attracted by the suggestion of creating a separate police force in Londonderry. It would be necessary to consider carefully how this was presented publicly. If the Northern Ireland Government were allowed to take credit for the idea this could militate against the success of the proposal. Wilson suggested that consideration should be given to the possibility of encouraging some members of British police forces to volunteer for service in the new force.[30] After this Callaghan began his return journey to London. He had not been in the air for more than ten minutes when the navigator came into the cabin with a pencilled message scribbled on a signal pad. It stated that an official request for the use of troops had been made by the Northern Ireland Government. Callaghan immediately scribbled 'Permission granted' on the signal pad and handed it back to the navigator.[31]

Back in Whitehall, at 4 p.m. the Chiefs of Staff were making their own assessment of the situation. The Commanding Officer of the 1st Battalion The Prince of Wales Own Regiment had been ordered to make a military assessment of the situation. The Battalion had been placed at immediate readiness and the outlying company at Macgilligan Camp was on route to join the rest of the unit at HMS *Sea Eagle*. The GOC considered that intervention in either Belfast or Londonderry could well require a force of up to two battalions in each city. The GOC currently had only three battalions in 39 Brigade under his command. Since intervention in either city might well lead to a further requirement for intervention by troops in the other city almost immediately, the GOC could not meet such a requirement without reinforcement. The Chiefs believed it would be preferable that any such intervention by troops should not be on a piecemeal basis but should be in sufficient strength to:

a. show that really effective action was being taken
b. ensure that we would not be in a position to be physically rebuffed by the mob. It should be remembered that if only a small body of troops were employed it would be more tempting for the rioters to have a go at the military.
c. show that we are an independent force of law and order and non-partisan.

Therefore, the Chiefs suggested that it might be necessary to reinforce Northern Ireland with a further infantry brigade, which would comprise a Brigade HQ, three infantry battalions and supporting units and possibly an air-portable armoured car squadron as well. All these units would be required at short notice.[32]

By the time Sir Edward Peck of the Foreign Office turned up at 5 p.m. the GOC had reported to the Chiefs that the police were, at 1515 hours that afternoon, unable to hold the situation in Londonderry unless troops were brought in. The Vice-Chief of the General Staff reported that he had learnt that the Home Secretary had given the authority for the troops in Londonderry to be used for the specific task of safeguarding the police station and Waterloo Place. The Chiefs then considered whether they should increase the alert of the spearhead battalion —the reinforcements in Britain—and what they would, if called upon, send to Northern Ireland. The Chiefs understood that there was no authority so far for the use of troops outside the specific Londonderry operation. They feared, how-ever, that with the participation of the IRA the situation would deteriorate further elsewhere. Peck drew their attention to press reports about the mobilisation of the Irish Army and mentioned that he had spoken to Gilchrist in Dublin. Peck understood that any Irish Army moves were in connection with the installation of field hospitals along the border. Nevertheless he suggested that the Chiefs should not fail to take into account the strength of the Irish Army which amounted to some 7,000 men (but with no armour to speak of) when assessing the threat.[33]

In fact as Peck and the Chiefs were conducting their discussions the Northern Ireland Government had made their request for the assistance of troops. By 5 p.m., as the police in Derry were on the defensive in William Street, a sectarian riot was in progress in Bishop Street, and the Bogside was alive with rumours that the B-Specials were coming. At this moment a company of the 1st Battalion of the

Prince of Wales Own Regiment arrived in Waterloo Place under the command of Major Hanson. A barrier of wire was put across the roads leading into Waterloo Place, a gap being left through which the police withdrew from William Street. The Bogside crowd followed up to the wire, where Eddie McAteer parleyed with Hanson. He asked if the police could be moved out of sight and this was done. He asked for a fire engine to deal with the fires burning in William Street. A little later leading local figures such as Paddy Doherty, the Vice-Chairman of the DCDA and Michael Canavan together with the British Labour MP, Stanley Orme called on the Battalion Commanding Officer, Lieutenant Colonel Todd, at Victoria Barracks: the Colonel agreed to withdraw the police behind the Army lines, thereby modifying his original plan for a joint police-military operation. The Army now took over the police lines in Waterloo Place at Castle and Butcher Gates, and at about 7.15 p.m. at Bishop Street where the sectarian riot was dying away.[34]

In London it was announced that the British Government had agreed to the deployment of troops.[35] In Belfast at 7.30 p.m. Robert Porter and other members of the Cabinet Security Committee briefed the cabinet on the day's developments and likely future prospects. Concern was expressed about the exploitation of the situation by elements from the Republic. To counter this, the cabinet agreed in principle to the blowing-up or spiking of unapproved roads, should the Inspector-General feel this to be necessary, and authorised the use of powers of internment against known IRA agitators present in Northern Ireland. Chichester-Clark relayed the telephone conversation he had had with Callaghan that morning. While the cabinet accepted the presence of Callaghan's police officers as consultants, some concern was expressed that no damage should be caused to the morale of senior officers of the RUC. Callaghan had also suggested the possibility of raising a separate police force for Londonderry in the hope that substantial numbers of Catholics and perhaps some British police volunteers might join. The general impression of the cabinet was that this was impracticable.[36] Derry now had a quiet night. Whenever and wherever the soldiers appeared, rioting ended.[37]

BELFAST

Belfast did not have a quiet night. The violence in Belfast was essentially Protestant against Catholic with a rawness not seen anywhere else. In Belfast the situation came close to a complete breakdown of the civil power's ability to control the situation and the nearest Northern Ireland came to civil war. Why had events in Belfast proved so explosive? It is relatively easy to see how Catholics in Derry reacted the way they did; the causes can be traced back to their collapse in police confidence arising out of the events of January 1969. Belfast, however, had not experienced anything like this. The violence was clearly sectarian. It is possible to show how ethnic tensions can evolve to an explosive point, spurred on by events outside the immediate geographical area. Here we look at the microcosm of the areas bordering the Crumlin Road in Belfast as an example.

From a Catholic perspective, Father Columb O'Donnell, Rector of Holy Cross Church, Ardoyne, observed how confidence in the police had seemed to deteriorate after the Burntollet attack on marchers in January. O'Donnell felt that it wasn't because Catholics in Ardoyne agreed with the march but that they felt that when it had been approved there should have been proper protection for those taking part. It was clear that relations with Protestants were deteriorating as well. From early in 1969 O'Donnell found that several people who had in the past greeted him when they met him in the street now walked past in 'stony silence'. This type of thing increased as the year progressed. One of the district priests told him that tension in the area seemed to be growing. After incidents around the middle of May there was a lull for most of June. But by July the first Catholic families had started to move across the Crumlin Road from the Protestant areas. The police were told of the intimidation but because people there appeared not to receive any protection suspicion of the police increased. O'Donnell acknowledged that the threats were coming from outsiders; Protestants who tried to persuade their Catholic neighbours to stay were themselves threatened. On 12 July O'Donnell recalled that when the Orange parade was returning up the Crumlin Road the band started playing rather loudly as they passed the Catholic Church, grimacing as they did so, while a clergyman behind a banner took off his bowler hat and made a derisory gesture towards O'Donnell and the Church.[38]

And as the Reverend Father Ailbe Delaney, district parish priest for the Crumlin Road area, was walking along Hooker Street on 12 July, five police Land-Rovers entered the street from the Crumlin Road and turned up Butler Street. They were all moving very slowly. Delaney walked up Chatham Street and some time after that the Land-Rovers drove up there. 'Because they were going so slowly it seemed to annoy the people very much.' No one got out but some stones were thrown at the vehicles. Locals were of the view that the police were willing to lean particularly hard on them for any incident at all or even if an incident had not taken place. On two occasions Land-Rovers had followed people on to the footpaths after stones had been thrown. Delaney, Paddy Devlin and a third man spoke to District Inspector Montgomery and asked for the vehicles to be withdrawn. The DI told them that the Land-Rovers had been deployed because stones had been thrown at a Mrs Gilmore's house and assistance had been asked for. Montgomery had to send in what police he saw fit.[39]

There followed an incident at the Edenderry Arms as an Orange parade was passing by: a Tricolour was waved from the public house. Sergeant Thomas Gracey recalled that the police had tried to gain entry to the pub but found the doors barred; this was common practice at the Arms during Orange parades. The two men who were holding the flag up against the window seemed to be enjoying the whole incident. They were laughing. Not laughing, however, was the watching Protestant crowd which was incensed by the provocation. Some, with marchers, tried to break ranks but stewards held them back. Eventually the police broke down the doors and arrested the two men. Protestants had been angered by an incident on the night of 11 July, in which a woman who flew a Union Jack from her shop at the corner of Chatham Street had had it torn down. There had also been some damage to her house. This had the effect of bringing Protestant crowds to the Disraeli Street area. A situation now developed in which Protestant crowds gathered every night—this had not happened before. However, they did not try to enter into the nearby Hooker Street which was predominately Catholic. Mrs Elizabeth Gilmore, whose house at Chatham Street had been attacked, was described by Sergeant Gracey as a 'very excitable type of lady'. Frequently she made complaints regarding the views of people in the area which were opposed to her own. She would stand out in the street and shout at the top of her voice. When she displayed the Union Jack in July there was resentment in the area because conditions in the Province were worse than in previous years. John McKeague, a former member of the Ulster Protestant Volunteers (UPV), was seen quite frequently among the Protestant crowds gathering.[40]

One of the consequences of this tension was felt in nearby Hooker Street. Mrs Minnie Bailey, a Protestant and a widow, had lived for forty-seven years in Hooker Street until 1969. She was a daughter of Mrs Gilmore. Mrs Bailey recalled that, during the 1950s, there was a considerable increase in the number of Catholics in the street. Trouble for Protestants began in 1968 when there was the kicking of doors; after an incident at the Edenderry Arms in May, interference with Protestant homes became worse. 'I was terrorised and lived through hell,' claimed Bailey. On 11 July a crowd gathered outside her home chanting 'Burn Minnie Bailey out.' In a reference to the police they shouted: 'Shoot the black b——s.' On 26 July her mother's house was petrol-bombed and on 2 August a crowd again gathered outside her home: 'It terrorised me that much that I had to get out.' She left her home and went to live with her daughter. The following day, 3 August, the windows in her house were broken. Later, after she returned from hospital because of a slight heart condition which developed on 3 August, she found that her furniture had been thrown out on the street. By this time all Protestant families had left Hooker Street.[41]

This account was supported by others. Miss Dunville recalled that, before she left Hooker Street, crowds had gathered in the street shouting 'Ardoyne for the Fenians' and 'Get out you Orange . . .'. Intimidation got so bad she applied for a council house in another area. As the crowds gathered outside her home on the night of 2 August she and her seventy-four-year-old mother stayed upstairs in a bedroom. A Catholic neighbour asked her during the night not to leave the house but she told him she had no alternative. Dunville went to a Unionist MP about getting other accommodation but he could do nothing 'or didn't care'. Then she contacted Gerry Fitt about her plight; he lamented: 'Are they ever going to learn.' Later she met a woman who told her where she lived in Hooker Street. 'I said that's my mother's house.' And she said: 'It is very nice—I could not have picked a better one.'[42] In January 1969 there were twenty-four Protestants living in Hooker Street. By August there were none left. Although Father O'Donnell accepted there was some intimidation he thought this did not amount to organised intimidation: the situation arose from an atmosphere of intimidation on the opposite—Protestant—side of the Crumlin Road when 'panic was induced'. Some Protestant families were then advised by others on the opposite side of the Crumlin Road to leave their Hooker Street homes.[43]

That there was also intimidation of Catholics was undeniable. Anthony Dunham, a Catholic, lived among Protestants at Culmore Gardens off the Crumlin Road before he was forced to move out. On 2 August a crowd burned an off-licence in nearby Leopold Street and there were attacks on Catholic homes in Culmore Gardens. But he and his wife decided not to move out with their child because he thought they would be safe as they knew a lot of Protestants and had a lot of friends on the Shankill Road. Dunham recalled: 'I have lived among Protestants all my life—I have never lived among Roman Catholics. My wife did her shopping at the Shankill Road.' But then there was talk of trouble at the (Catholic) Unity Flats where it was claimed that a Protestant child had been injured. A woman said: 'They got our children, let's get theirs'; Dunham and his family got inside their house quickly. That night they lay on top of their bed with their clothes on in case anything should happen. They heard windows being broken and shouts from a crowd outside which was chanting 'Burn, burn, burn.' Next morning the Dunhams went to Mass and then to an uncle's house where they were warned of trouble in their home area. In Leopold Street Dunham saw a crowd and heard a shout of: 'There is one of the Fenian bastards now.' Stones were thrown at him. He and his uncle went to a police station and asked for protection so that they could reach his home but were told there was nothing the police could do for them.[44]

The rioting that occurred on 2–3 August had been bad. What had triggered Protestant anger had been an alleged attack on a Junior Orangeman parade as it passed the Unity Flats, populated predominately by Catholics. Catholics had protested at an incursion on their territory while rumours spread into surrounding Protestant areas that some of the children had been attacked. Belfast's Deputy Commissioner of Police, Samuel Bradley, had taken the decision not to re-route the Junior Orange parade on the way back, after trouble outside the Flats earlier, because 'there would have been serious opposition from the parents' and by re-routing he would have been creating additional flash-points. With the men at his disposal he felt he could not afford to divide them. If his men had been more widely spread he could not have prevented a Protestant attack on the Flats—if they had got in 'there would have been murder'. Bradley was aware that he wasn't 'dealing with children. You are dealing with hard ex-servicemen who know how to fight and can use themselves'. They fought with police for a period before eventually retreating, followed by Bradley and his men.

Bradley found the Protestant crowd gathered at the Flats in an ugly mood and policemen, including himself, were kicked. Three councillors, McCullagh, Kidd and Spence, borrowed his loudhailer and spoke to the crowd but they would not listen. Bradley decided against a baton charge—'It would have been a fatal mistake'—because the crowd would have broken into the Flats and the violence, he believed, would have escalated throughout the city. He also had to consider how to get the children in the parade away from the area because if any of them were injured there would have been serious trouble. Several times people in the Flats rushed onto the balcony and threw a bottle or a stone. When this happened the crowd below would throw stones over the police and break windows in the Flats. Some of the stones hit policemen. When the procession left people from other areas of the city arrived and joined the 'hard core' on Peter's Hill. There was a further attempt to invade the Flats when the parade got a little further down the road. By this stage Bradley had sufficient men to prevent anyone infiltrating the Flats area. There was also trouble inside the Flats. Bradley understood this to be part of a general pattern that, in an area where there was trouble, 'certain people' moved in and tried to 'stir it up' and turn the people against the police in an effort to create no-go areas. On the other hand, he also recognised that there was someone behind the Protestant crowd as well: 'This crowd did not just turn up— they were being led . . . there was some form of organisation behind it.'[45] Sergeant Samuel Johnston found that the Protestant crowd 'appeared to think police were sympathetic to them': they could not understand why the police were protecting the Flats and 'thought we should have let them have a go at the flats'. Johnston thought this was because 'it goes right back through history'.[46]

When the Reverend Martin Smyth, Minister of Alexandra Presbyterian Church in Belfast, went to the Shankill Road at about 11.30 in the evening, he saw people plundering shops. He succeeded in stopping a few people from looting. He found a feeling of tremendous agitation and confusion. The confusion stemmed from the conviction that the Junior Orange parade that morning had been attacked during a peaceful demonstration and the police had not punished the offenders. Smyth tried to explain to the people that even if this were true it was no excuse for what they were doing. He felt that the attack on the Unity Flats was unjustified even if allegations that a Tricolour was seen being waved from it were true; he also felt the Flats' inhabitants would have been justified in defending themselves.

By Sunday 3 August Bradley had been forced into leading about four baton charges up the Shankill when the viciousness of the crowd was directed against the police. Thirty-six officers were injured on this occasion. Peace returned to the Shankill after 100 Specials went on duty to prevent looting and Orangemen with regalia paraded on the road. In Bradley's opinion the 'murderous' intention of the Protestant crowd towards Unity Flats was not because the residents were Catholics but because of the reports of attacks on the Junior Orangemen: he considered the residents of the Shankill to be a quiet, respectable people 'unless they are incensed in some way'. In his opinion there was provocation on both sides, adding: 'My knowledge of the area is that it is the women who start the trouble.'[47]

The experience of Catholics at Unity Flats on 2 August was enough to alienate many of them from the police, as had happened in Derry. According to Catherine O'Rourke, when residents started throwing stones back at the Protestants the police in one of the courtyards of the Flats 'starting running mad'. O'Rourke claimed: 'The police wanted [to get at] the Catholic side.' From her perspective police made no attempt to disperse the crowd throwing stones at the Flats; this made the Catholics 'very, very angry'. O'Rourke described throwing herself, at one point, on top of her brother to prevent him being beaten by the police in one of the courtyards. Her brother, Emmanuel, who had served twelve years in The Royal Irish Fusiliers, had had nothing to do with any of the incidents and had been walking across the courtyard with his hands in his pockets, not even looking at what was happening, when he was set upon by the police. She claimed that the police attacked the people in the Flats who had defended themselves; if the police had intervened against the Protestant crowd who were throwing missiles and attacking the Flats, there would have been no trouble. But they did not do so.[48]

Yet one of the ironies of the negative opinions held by Catholics of the RUC and the Specials was that it was a member of the USC who thwarted an attack by Protestants on the Catholic area of the Crumlin Road on 2 August. Sergeant Anthony Owens received a message from Special Constable James Dunne that a crowd was moving from Unity Flats up the Crumlin Road. With other police, Owens rushed to the scene and heard a crowd of about a hundred and fifty approaching. The crowd was chanting 'We are the people' and 'Let's wreck the —— Popeheads.' Sergeant Owens assumed the crowd were going to launch an attack on the Hooker Street area and, although he had only a few men, he lined them across the Crumlin Road and drew batons. When the crowd came close by they threw stones, bottles and sticks at the police and then raced into side streets. The crowd later reassembled in Disraeli Street and by this time had swollen to between two and three hundred. Owens and his men, together with reinforcements numbering around twenty-five, formed a line across the mouth of the street. They reasoned with the crowd and eventually persuaded them to disperse but not before several missiles were thrown in the direction of Edenderry Arms at Hooker Street.[49] Unsurprisingly when the trouble had ended, bitterness ran deep in both communities. On 5 August the Reverend Donald Gilles, Minister of Agnes Street Presbyterian Church, received a telephone call from a colleague informing him that there was trouble threatening in the Crumlin Road. When he arrived at the junction of Disraeli and Ohio Streets at about 8.30 p.m., he found a gathering consisting mainly of young Protestants in a rather threatening mood. Gilles recognised very few of those present as being from the area and those he did recognise were only standing watching the group. Most of the people he saw came from other parts of the city such as the York and Shore Roads. The crowd eventually dispersed around 10 p.m., after a District Inspector warned them that if they did not do so the police would take action.[50]

So when the disturbances in Derry began on 12 August, Protestants and Catholics in the Crumlin Road area were at an ethnic fever pitch. Who started the trouble is an easy question: it was always the other side. There were no innocent or guilty parties to what happened in Belfast: all were culpable. The NICRA Executive, although committed to non-violence, must bear some responsibility with the call to divert police resources away from Derry. How could police be diverted other than by attacking them? Thus early in the evening of 13 August a car with a loudhailer toured the Unity Flats area calling people to a meeting at Divis Tower in support of the trouble in Derry. Both Springfield Road and Hastings Street RUC stations were later attacked by crowds which gathered near the Flats. There was also trouble in Hooker Street and police reinforcements were sent there.[51] Nineteen-year-old Robert Lannigan found that fellow Protestants had been angered by the Catholic attack from Hooker Street on the police. Lannigan saw one policemen hit on the eyebrow by a piece of iron grating. In the middle of the Crumlin Road another policeman lay, his clothes ablaze from a petrol bomb. A third constable was rolling over him trying to put the flames out and at the same time trying to protect himself from the mob who were still throwing things at him.[52]

The Reverend Donald Gilles saw a crowd of between 250 to 300 Protestants on the Disraeli Street side of the Crumlin Road. An ugly situation had arisen because of attacks which he understood had been made on three policemen. The crowd seemed to want to retaliate against what they believed might be a forthcoming attack on their homes. He and the other ministers did all they could to restrain the crowd and no action was taken.[53] But temperatures were running high. There were also deliberate gun attacks on the police: for Samuel Bradley, the RUC's Deputy Commissioner of Belfast, the significant moment of the trouble in the city came on the night of 13 August when police where fired on and grenades were thrown at them near Leeson Street. This happened when a platoon of the reserve force had gone to try and cut off a Catholic crowd moving down Leeson Street towards the Grosvenor Road. Bradley feared they might have crossed into territory which would be staunchly Protestant. Reports from Head Constable Ramsey, in charge of the party, told of how semi-automatic fire had been directed at police and one or two grenades had exploded. Bradley was 'shocked. I came to the conclusion immediately that the IRA were popping up their head and getting involved.' He made a request to use CS gas which was available to the reserve force but it was refused. Permission was not granted because the regulations for the use of gas did not apply.

Early in the morning of 14 August shots were fired at Springfield Road police station and a police patrol going to relieve it was ambushed by gunmen near the Falls Road. Bradley's strategy was 'to endeavour to keep people in their own area, not to become involved, and let them have their jollifications'. This latter point referred to bonfires in the Falls area on 14 August. But groups of people had broken away from these bonfires and carried out 'vicious' attacks on the police. There was also trouble at Hooker Street, Dover Street, Percy Street and Cupar Street. The general view among the police was that there was a plot by the IRA to take over an area of the city, hold it and then call for assistance from the country or across the border. There was no such plot, but that was difficult to explain to policemen who were coming under fire; Bradley: 'My view at that time was that this was not a riot. It was an armed uprising by the IRA, because I could not have, for the life of me, accepted that the ordinary people of the Falls Road could be armed with machine guns and take up vantage points.' He saw gun flashes from the top of maisonettes in Divis Street. It was either a Thompson sub-machine gun or a Bren gun. There were also reports about heavy machine-gun firing from St Comgall's school.[54] Intelligence reports reaching Belfast indicated that there would be incursions across the border by the IRA. It was also suggested that 'other people' convenient to the border would be making an attempt to cross. Then, in view of the intelligence reports, a decision was taken to have Shortland armoured cars fitted with machine guns. According to Bradley: 'The picture in Belfast that morning was pretty grim.' Other information suggested that the previous night's trouble was only to test the strength of the security forces and there was a warning that an isolated policeman could be shot.[55]

The Reverend Charles Sansom, Rector of St Mary's Parish Church, saw no reason for an 'onslaught' by Catholics from Hooker Street on Protestant streets on the opposite end of the Crumlin Road when trouble broke out on the night of 14 August. Petrol bombs, stones and other missiles where hurled by a crowd which emerged from Hooker Street; at this stage, claimed Sansom, there was no retaliation from Protestants. Sansom saw a man from Hooker Street firing a shotgun in broad daylight at about this time. Another man emerged from Disraeli Street, also with a shotgun, and fired in the air over the Hooker Street crowd. Sansom saw one of the Hooker Street crowd fall as 'if he was on the receiving end of something'. He was carried off by the others. Before the disturbances his parishioners had complained of their doors being kicked and windows broken. The effect of such incidents against Protestants was a hardening of attitudes among their co-religionists on the other side of the Crumlin Road. Sansom and other Protestant clergymen met a priest at Hooker Street who warned them not to enter it as it was 'seething'.[56]

William Trainor, a Catholic resident of the Crumlin Road, saw on 14 August what he described as a crowd of eighty to a hundred policemen and a smaller number of civilians come up the Crumlin Road in 'one large group'. About a quarter of the civilians had helmets and the same number armbands. The civilians sat down by Holy Cross Church and about one in three were carrying haversacks which they filled with broken stones and mineral bottles. After about twenty minutes both police and civilians moved into Butler Street. Trainor heard cries about Bernadette Devlin and shouts of: 'Come out you Fenian bastards and fight.' He did not know whether the calls came from the police, the civilians or both.[57] On the other hand, Thomas Passmore, who was a company director, Justice of the Peace and also Orange District Master of Belfast No. 1 District and a member of Duncairn Temperance Lodge No. 924, recalled that when the police baton-charged down Hooker Street on the night of 14 August they were 'totally unaware' that a group of Protestants were going to rush in behind them.[58]

Constable Martin Loney was one of the policemen involved in the baton charge down Hooker Street at about 11.30 p.m. after petrol bombs had rained down on the police. There was fierce fighting between police and civilians in Hooker Street and several policemen fell when struck by missiles. Some were also hit by petrol bombs and glass. The crowd was gradually driven down Hooker Street but the task of the police was made more difficult with the roadway a sea of flame and because of a barricade at the Chatham Street junction. At the junction, Loney and about twelve other policemen were pinned to the ground by a concentration of small arms fire coming from an entry. It appeared to be coming from a revolver or .22 rifle. When the firing stopped the police returned to the Crumlin Road. Loney recalled that on a number of occasions after police had contained Protestant crowds on the Disraeli Street side of the Crumlin Road they were subjected to 'completely unprovoked attacks' by people on the Hooker Street side. Shortly after midnight Constable Loney and other policemen went up the Crumlin Road towards Butler Street. A crowd came out of a street and started attacking policemen and their armoured vehicle with petrol bombs and missiles. After the Catholics had been driven back into the side streets there was suddenly the sound of machine-gun fire directed at the police from the direction of Butler Street. There were about six shots. Fire was returned by the police from a Browning machine gun mounted on the armoured car. The police were then forced to take cover after fire started from the Holy Cross Church grounds. To Constable Loney it sounded like rifle fire; it was returned by the police.[59] As far as Chief Inspector James Johnston was concerned an insurrection was taking place on the Falls Road by the night of 14–15 August. Johnston formed this view when he heard the firing of the RUC's Browning machine guns. It was inconceivable, he believed, that police would have fired these weapons unless there was an insurrection which the IRA were behind. Johnston considered it proper for police to use high-velocity rifles in a riot situation if this was the only weapon available for individual policemen.[60]

From a Protestant perspective, at about 10.30 in the morning, Robert Lannigan saw the sky lit up by petrol bombs thrown at the police by the Hooker Street crowd. The people of Disraeli Street believed that if the Catholic crowd beat the police they would then burn the Disraeli Street homes. The police were taking a real beating and the Protestants 'decided to give them a hand'.[61] By the evening the Edenderry Arms and a number of houses were burned. Reverend Gilles heard shooting. It seemed to come along Chief Street from the Crumlin Road. A group at the top of Ohio Street said the shooting came from the Holy Cross grounds. Protestants wanted to attack the Catholic church but he and a colleague persuaded them not to. One or two petrol bombs had been thrown at Holy Cross girls' school but no damage was done.[62] What seemed to have a dramatic impact on Protestant perceptions was Lynch's speech. Thomas Passmore had formed a group to go among Protestants to try and maintain the peace. He found a large Protestant crowd on the Crumlin Road. Television and radio reports of Lynch's speech, as well as talk of a movement of Irish troops, meant Protestants were under the impression that 'we were almost at war'. The Protestant crowd, at that time, were not disorderly. Then a Catholic crowd rushed from Hooker Street throwing petrol bombs and stones, directed mainly at the police across the Crumlin Road and Disraeli Street. 'Women were screaming and weeping,' recalled Passmore. Police baton-charged down Hooker Street and 'about 24 Protestants' followed them. 'These people were throwing petrol bombs and two of them were carrying crates which appeared to contain bombs.' In Passmore's opinion the Protestants who gathered associated the residents of Hooker Street with Lynch. Their feeling was that if Eire invaded Northern Ireland the people in Hooker Street would be more sympathetic 'towards them than towards us'.[63]

From a Catholic perspective things seemed different. Peter Toal, who lived in Butler Street, remembered that the first he and his neighbours felt that they were in danger of being burned out of their homes was on 14 and 15 August. From July Catholics had heard the mobs chanting on the other side of the road. 'Night after night we could hear chanting. It was like a war cry. We were anticipating that at any moment they would come in en masse and do their damage. At that time we believed we were not going to get any protection from the law. We felt it was hopeless to ask for any.' Toal praised two youths, who were going around the Hooker Street area firing off shotguns, for saving the district from being 'invaded'. He believed: 'It was a Godsend that there were some guns in the area that night. If there had not been we would have been wiped out.' He was also convinced that: 'All the shooting came into the area. It is there to be seen.'[64]

On 14 August Father Delaney was sure that policemen were involved in throwing petrol bombs. He was looking out from a house on the Crumlin Road near Butler Street after midnight, when he saw a crowd of civilians and a few policemen at the mouth of Butler Street. Stones and petrol bombs were being thrown by the crowd into the street; many of the civilians were wearing helmets and white armbands. Then Delaney saw a policeman turn away from Butler Street and crouch down and light a petrol bomb. A young man took it from him, walked a few steps, and threw the bomb into Butler Street. A short time later Delaney saw two men sheltering at the bottom of the steps up to the Holy Cross Church. One got up with a petrol bomb in his hand and, as he brought his arm back to throw it, the top appeared to come off. The petrol poured over the man and he was set on fire. Father Delaney thought, to the best of his knowledge, the man was uniformed and a member of the Special Constabulary. Others, however, who were with Delaney at the time, thought this man was a civilian.[65]

The effect of these events was to push Belfast to the point of a complete breakdown of civil authority. There had been an attempt by the state to prepare for the trouble: the reaction of the authorities to the disturbances of 13 August was to convince the heads of the RUC and the Government that they should expect very serious trouble on 14 August. The Belfast Deputy Commissioner of the RUC managed to arrange for a force of about four hundred police to be available for riot duty in Belfast on the evening of the 14th. It was also decided, in spite of the risks, that County Inspectors could if necessary use the USC for riot control.[66] But the scale of the disturbances, coupled with the police deployment in Derry, simply overwhelmed the RUC. And the violence in Belfast now spread. The first activity in the area was the gathering of Catholic crowds around bonfires in Divis Street and Lower Falls Road where, shortly before 7 p.m., there was some stoning of motor vehicles. At about 9 p.m. the crowd began breaking up paving stones and throwing petrol bombs at the houses in Divis Street to the east of Percy Street junction. These crowd movements along Divis Street were observed not only by the police in Hastings Street but by watching Protestants in Percy Street and Dover Street. The situation was explosive. Catholics moved up along their ends of Dover Street and Percy Street. Protestants were sensitive to any movement up these streets. Thus it needed only a movement of Catholics into Dover or Percy Streets or a thrust of Protestants down the same streets for there to develop, in the absence of police, an uncontrolled faction fight. Both these movements did in fact occur, and the result was an 'invasion' of Divis Street by Protestants, which ultimately led to Catholic gunfire intended to repel invaders and to much heavier police gunfire intended to silence Catholic gunmen. A boy and two young men were killed. There was also the complete loss of confidence by the Belfast Catholic community in the police force.[67]

On the morning of 15 August Sir Ian Freeland contacted the Ministry of Defence (MOD) to report that the situation in Belfast was 'bubbling' and could become very difficult. He therefore requested that at least part of the spearhead battalion should be moved in that day to join the garrison in Northern Ireland, and the more of it the better, with the balance to follow the next day. Roy Hattersley authorised this.[68] Wilson and Callaghan, who was back in London, spoke to each other by telephone at 11.10 a.m. Callaghan said it had been a bad night in Belfast. There was a report that one of those killed was a British soldier on leave from the Army who had been found on the roof with a machine gun beside him. Callaghan had also spoken to Chichester-Clark that morning. He sounded weary but was most grateful for the Government's assistance in agreeing to provide troops in Londonderry. The Northern Ireland cabinet was meeting at 12 noon and would probably decide then whether they wanted troops to be used in Belfast. Chichester-Clark had said that the situation in Belfast was very tense.

Callaghan told him to get some sleep as soon as possible and that there might be further political discussions between the Northern Ireland Government and Wilson. Wilson asked whether Callaghan thought that the Northern Ireland Government would request the use of troops in Belfast. Callaghan believed they would. Wilson commented that this could be a good thing and a stabilising influence on the situation. Callaghan agreed. Wilson presumed that London would respond straight away and agree to any request for the use of troops in Belfast on the same basis as for Londonderry. He thought that the sending of troops into Londonderry seemed to be going well and while Callaghan agreed he cautioned that it might be more difficult in the longer term.[69]

At the Northern Ireland cabinet's meeting at noon Peacocke, the Inspector-General, had outlined the situation which had developed in Belfast. Ministers bowed to the inevitable and decided that an immediate request should be made for the assistance of troops in the city. Porter reported that IRA agitators were being held and that an Appeals Tribunal was being constituted. What this meant—though no one seemed to notice because of other distractions—was that selective internment was being employed. The Army were continuing to assess what would be involved in blocking unapproved roads. The cabinet decided that this should be done if feasible, in view of the danger of infiltration. The possibility of a curfew in at least part of Belfast was considered, but doubts were expressed about the feasibility of enforcement; in any event, this would clearly depend on the views of the GOC once troops were deployed.[70] The Home Office received the request for troops at 12.15 p.m. Callaghan gave immediate approval. The troops entered Belfast in the early evening, throwing a cordon between Catholic and Protestant factions. Sporadic trouble continued into the next day.[71]

The disturbances had seen eight people killed; seven in Belfast. Herbert Roy, a twenty-six-year-old Protestant from west Belfast, was the first to die during the disturbances. He was shot by IRA gunmen while standing at the corner of the predominately Protestant Dover Street and the Catholic Divis Street. It was approximately 12.30 a.m. on 14 August when he was hit. Next to die was nine-year-old Patrick Rooney, a Catholic schoolboy. He was the first child to be killed in the Troubles. He died after being struck by a tracer bullet fired by the RUC as he lay in bed in his family's flat in Divis Tower. The shot was fired from a heavy Browning machine gun mounted on an RUC Shortland armoured car. There appeared to be no justification for the police's opening fire. Samuel McLarnon, a twenty-seven-year-old Catholic, was shot in the sitting room of his house at Herbert Street in the Ardoyne by policemen firing into the street sometime before 11 p.m. He was struck during what was later described as a 'catastrophic riot' between Catholics and Protestants. Michael Lynch, a twenty-eight-year-old Catholic from north Belfast, was hit by a police bullet as he crossed a street in Ardoyne. The RUC were returning fire at the time. In Armagh John Gallagher, a thirty-year-old Catholic, was shot by B-Specials in Cathedral Road in Armagh

City following a NICRA meeting. The Specials involved were from Tynan, a small village about twelve miles from Armagh. They became separated from their RUC commander as they arrived at the scene of rioting in Armagh. It would seem that the Specials panicked when confronted by the crowd. Most of them jumped out of their cars and fired. No orders were given to open fire. John Gallagher was shot in the back while two other men were injured. In the absence of the bullet which killed him no one was ever prosecuted for Gallagher's death.

Hugh McCabe, a twenty-year-old Catholic from west Belfast on leave from serving in the Queen's Royal Irish Hussars, was shot dead in disputed circumstances by police near his home at Whitehall Row in the Divis Flats complex. The RUC claimed the trooper was armed but witnesses said he was pulling a wounded man off a balcony when hit. The police were returning fire after coming under fire from the Flats. Gerald McAuley, a fifteen-year-old Catholic schoolboy, was shot by a loyalist gunman during fierce sectarian clashes in the Clonard district of the Falls. The clashes centred on the Clonard Monastery and the adjoining Bombay Street, which housed Catholics on the borderline between the Shankill and the Falls and became a symbol of how Catholics were burned out of their houses by Protestant mobs. McAuley was a member of the IRA's youth wing, the Fianna, and is considered the first Republican victim of the Troubles. David Linton, a forty-eight-year-old Protestant, was the last person to die. He had been fatally wounded on the 15th by Republicans at the corner of Palmer Street, where he lived, at its junction with the Crumlin Road.

The disturbances had left 745 people injured, 154 of them with gunshot wounds. Some 179 homes and other buildings were demolished, ninety-four other buildings were damaged and required major repair, and 323 needed minor repair. Around 1,800 families had moved home during the disturbances. Of these 1,500 were Catholic and 300 Protestant: 0.4 per cent of Protestant households and 5.3 per cent of Catholic households had been displaced. Of the premises damaged eighty-three per cent were occupied by Catholics. With the arrival of troops, 'peacelines', made up of corrugated iron and other materials, were erected across streets in parts of north and west Belfast.[72] Designed to be temporary they were to be become permanent features of Belfast's political and physical landscape.

Here we should take a raincheck from the prevailing high politics and turn our attention to the impact of the events of August 1969 on the mindset of Protestants and Catholics. For almost immediately a process that can only be described as mythmaking began. Protestants were the victims of an organised Republican conspiracy. Catholics were the victims of a pogrom that, if not instigated by the state, was conducted with the systematic compliance of it. Neither was true. But more importantly, large numbers of Protestants and Catholics believed them to be true. From this period on, sectarian interpretations of 'whose fault it was' were frozen to be unpacked and defrosted at various times over the next thirty years to explain the historical origins of the latest atrocity. So for Protestants the further confirmation of IRA involvement in the rioting and the Civil Rights Movement was provided from *Resistance*, a publication issued by the National Solidarity Committee from the *United Irishman* office in Dublin—basically the IRA. *Resistance* claimed that the 'real revolutionaries' in the North 'are those who established the united front of the Civil Rights movement and who have fought to keep it united and as well-led as possible, bearing always in mind that only the force of a united people can be strong enough to dislodge either Unionism and British imperialism from Ireland. Republicans have realised that by winning Civil Rights and thereby weakening the Unionist Party, the nationally-minded people would be in a much better position to push forward to ending partition and winning independence.' Dealing with the rioting in Belfast it mentioned a 'howling mob of armed bigots and Specials shooting indiscriminately and burning houses' and said that 'the only reply came from members of the Republican movement who defended the people as bravely as they had in Bogside, Derry, until they ran out of what weapons and ammunition they had'.[73] The irony of this statement was that, aided and abetted by a further statement, this time from the IRA leadership confirming involvement in the rioting, it annoyed many Belfast Catholics who dismissed these claims as hogwash and resented the Republican Movement for its failure to offer sufficient protection from Protestant mob attacks; but to Protestants it confirmed what they already knew.

A week after the deployment of troops, Paisley was warning that one-eighth of Belfast was still occupied by forces intent on overthrowing Northern Ireland's constitution. And he claimed that the IRA had set up a machine-gun post on sandbags in Devonshire Street off the Falls Road. Another unit of the IRA was active in Seaforde Street in east Belfast. Paisley also believed that Jack Lynch was going to create an international incident by taking over a part of Ulster— probably Newry.[74] John Taylor, the Parliamentary Secretary to the Ministry of Home Affairs, described the riots as having been started by 'anti-partitionists' with the encouragement of the Civil Rights Movement. While he condemned the 'vengeance' which Protestants had taken by destroying some houses he felt there was a ready explanation for this reaction because of the attacks from the Falls Road and the impression given by Lynch that the Irish Army was on its way to Belfast. He warned that it must be realised that more than one million of Ulster's citizens wished her to be British and that the tolerance of these people was being stretched to the limit by the behaviour of the anti-partitionist groups. Taylor believed that Gerry Fitt and others who denied Republican involvement in the disturbances had been completely discredited by the IRA's confirmation that it was active in Ulster.[75]

Fitt, however, summed up the belief of Catholics when he, in turn, claimed that members of the police, particularly the USC, had been involved in attacks upon Catholics. Austin Currie joined in with the claim that the forces of the state had been involved in attacks. The Unionist MP, John McQuade, and Belfast city councillor, Frank Quigley, jointly refuted Fitt's allegations. They dismissed Fitt and Currie's allegations as just another attempt to discredit the Government and pointed out that the IRA 'admitted they were actively involved' in the fighting. The constant target for Republican and Civil Rights propaganda was the USC 'who have given courageous service to the security of Northern Ireland'. The Specials had not entered Divis Street or the Falls Road, as was claimed, at any point. Their role was purely a defensive one. McQuade and Quigley pointed out that the first person shot was in fact a policeman, followed by Herbert Roy, a Protestant. At no time did the Specials lead the Ulster Volunteer Force (UVF) and armed Protestant extremists into any Catholic street. Some of the homeless Catholic families, they said, were not victims of Protestant threats but 'of the IRA clearance policy'. They left when it became evident that the IRA 'wanted the decks cleared of all Catholics to allow an all-out assault on the Protestant streets'. It was 'nauseating' for Protestant people who, having watched their Catholic neighbours being evicted, saw Republican helpers setting fire to their vacated homes, making them uninhabitable.[76] This was the view held by many Protestants; as a future paramilitary put it:

On the two nights before Bombay Street [was burned out by Protestants,] Catholics had attacked the Protestant lower Shankill. Then Herbert [Roy] was gunned down. All of that was orchestrated, it had been deliberate to provoke Protestants. Shooting Herbert was like throwing petrol onto a fire. . . . All we knew was our people had been attacked and they were living in fear and that they [Catholics/IRA] had started killing 'our' people. There were crowds of men facing each other . . . There was a young policeman there, a B-Special. He was saying, 'For God's sake lads keep well back. They [the Catholics] have guns.' We could hear a burst of automatic fire and the young officer turned around to look over at the Catholic side. The next thing I knew there was more shooting and he was shot right in front of me . . . a bullet . . . had gone . . . into his chest . . . I was trembling with emotion and anger and I just thought to myself over and over again, 'Right if that's what they fucking want, that's what they'll fucking get.' When I got back to the [Protestant] crowd everybody had heard about what had happened and they all felt exactly the same way as I did. First Herbert Roy and then a young B-Special gunned down in front of us. When we started moving down toward Bombay Street we noticed the removal lorries. The IRA were moving people out of Bombay Street, with removal lorries. It had all been planed. They [the IRA] had wanted us to invade Bombay Street, it was to be sacrificed in part of the wide strategy. But of course you didn't think like that at the time. Sometime afterwards, when I started to put two and two together it was obvious the gunmen, the lorries, all of that took planning. They [the IRA] were sacrificing Bombay Street and that part of the Falls Road so as they could take the role of 'defenders' of the oppressed 'Catholics'. The fact was that they had pushed us beyond any reasonable tolerance. They had attacked us, killed and shot 'our Protestants' and that young police officer, right before our eyes so it was absolutely inevitable that we [Protestants] would attack them.[77]

Protestants refused to accept that the police had been at fault in any way during the disturbances: in response to a Catholic correspondent who had written that on 12 August in Coalisland, she had witnessed riot police baton-charging a crowd of demonstrators and beating up a man without provocation, the Marquis of Hamilton, the Unionist MP for Fermanagh and South Tyrone, retorted that a 'whirlpool' of Republicanism existed in the town. Eight policemen had been injured in the disturbances: clearly these agitators were not interested in reform, 'not even in evolution but solely in revolution'. Did anyone, he asked, ever stop to think what police–public relations were like before all the marches? 'Did we suddenly become "thugs" overnight?' Prior to October 1968 there was seldom any criticism of the RUC's record of law enforcement. Lord Hamilton described himself as a moderate who had given full support to the Government's reform programme which would give to all British standards of democracy. But in return, 'cannot all law-abiding citizens demand the same standards of British behaviour from these anarchists and mini-gangsters? Do not human rights entail human duties to society?'[78]

At this point Cardinal Conway and five Northern Irish bishops responded to what they considered to be the inaccurate accounts of the violence in Belfast and issued a statement alleging that the Falls and Ardoyne were invaded by mobs equipped with machine guns and other firearms. They pointed out that a community which was virtually defenceless was swept by gunfire and streets of Catholic homes were systematically set on fire: 'We entirely reject the hypothesis that the origin of last week's tragedy was an armed insurrection.' They believed that a necessary precondition to any restoration of confidence on the part of the Catholic community had to be an open recognition of these facts. The Cardinal and the bishops finished with an appeal for 'all concerned to realize that among Catholics belief in the impartiality of the Ulster Special Constabulary is non-existent'.[79] The statement met with a sharp reaction from Government ministers and Protestant clergy. Roy Bradford said that to comment on and inflame the situation, as the Cardinal had done, with a specifically Roman Catholic and 'one-sided' version of what had taken place would only make things worse. No one denied there were excesses on both sides or that the Catholic homeless were more numerous than the Protestants but it must be clear to anyone that once the 'demon of sectarian violence' was released it was next to impossible to control. Furthermore, the statement overlooked one major fact. The shooting had started in Belfast when a call went out from the rioters in the Bogside to their sympathisers in Belfast and other centres to create a disturbance to draw off police from Londonderry. The spark which ignited Belfast was the direct result of this appeal. Chichester-Clark simply stated that 'no section of the community has a monopoly of either victims or the guilty'. Five Presbyterian ministers whose parishes included part of the border between the Shankill and Falls deplored the actions of the Cardinal and his bishops: in their view both the Shankill and the Falls were at fault.[80] Conway was unrepentant: 'the truth had to be told'.[81]

What had triggered the disturbances was tribal hatred. Lord Scarman's subsequent inquiry into the disorders found that although mistakes were made and certain individual officers acted wrongly on occasions, the general case of a partisan police force co-operating with Protestant mobs was found to be devoid of substance. Since most of the rioting developed from action on the streets started by Catholic crowds, the RUC were more often than not facing Catholics, who as a result came to feel that the police were always going for them, baton-charging them—never the 'other'. There had, however, been six occasions in the course of the disturbances when the police, by act or omission, were seriously at fault. This included a lack of firm direction in handling the Londonderry disturbances on 12 August, with the RUC incursion into the Bogside seen by the inhabitants there as a repetition of events in January and April, when the police had entered the Bogside, leading many, including moderates, to think that the police should be resisted; and the failure of the police to prevent Protestant mobs burning down Catholic homes in Belfast, on 14, 15 and 16 August.[82] Although there was undoubtedly an IRA influence at work in the DCDA in Londonderry, in the Ardoyne and Falls Roads areas of Belfast and in Newry these elements did not start the riots or plan them. Indeed the IRA was taken by surprise and did less than many of their supporters thought they should have done. While NICRA did not start any riots it did help to spread the disturbances on 13 August.

Protestant participation in the disorders was largely that of reaction to disturbances started by Catholics, though there were exceptions. Their reaction was particularly fierce in Belfast in mid-August, when it took the form of violent eruptions into Catholic areas—the Falls, Divis Street and Hooker Street. There was however, no Province-wide organisation sponsoring a policy of disturbance. The only centre where there was evidence of a Protestant organisation actively participating in the riots was Belfast, where the Shankill Defence Association, led by John McKeague—a particularly nasty piece of work—participated in disturbances on the Crumlin Road and in the Falls. Scarman found that Paisley's role in the events of August was similar to those of political leaders on the Catholic side, and he concluded that Paisley neither plotted nor organised the disorders, and there was no evidence that he was party to any of the acts of violence investigated; nevertheless Scarman argued that those who lived in a free country had to accept the powerful expression of views opposed to their own, and warned that Paisley's spoken words were 'often powerful and must have frequently appeared to some as provocative: his newspaper was such that its style and substance were likely to rouse the enthusiasm of his supporters and the fury of his opponents'.[83]

In short there 'was no plot to overthrow the Government or to mount an armed insurrection'. But while there was no conspiracy in the sense that this term was normally used, there was evidence that once the major riots had occurred in Londonderry, Belfast, Armagh and Dungannon, which were not deliberately started, they were continued by elements that found expression in bodies 'more or less' loosely organised, such as People's Democracy and the various local Defence Associations associated with NICRA and several action committees. However, the riots were a different matter, and neither the IRA nor any Protestant organisation nor anybody else planned a campaign of riots. They were communal disturbances arising from a complex political, social and economic situation. More often than not they arose from slight beginnings, but the communal tensions were such that, once begun, they could not be controlled. On one side people saw themselves, never the 'others', charged by a police force they regarded as partisan; on the other, police and people saw a violent challenge to the authority of the state. Their own interpretations of the events of 1968 and early 1969 had encouraged the belief among the minority that demonstrations did secure concessions, and that the police were their enemy and the main obstacle to a continuing programme of demonstrations, while the same events had convinced a large number of Protestants that a determined attempt, already gaining a measure of success, was being made to undermine the constitutional position of Northern Ireland within the United Kingdom. In so tense a situation it needed very little to set going a major disturbance.[84] By the time these findings became known in 1972, Northern Ireland had moved on to greater horrors and the events of August had entered into communal legend. It didn't really matter what the 'truth' surrounding the events of August 1969 were; what mattered was what both communities thought the 'truth' was.

AFTERMATH
The events in the North had a seismic impact on the body politic of the Irish Republic. On 15 August London's man in Dublin telegraphed the Foreign and Commonwealth Office that 'Our Union Jack (diplomatic version) now flying in honour of Princess Anne has been singled out for attention by protest marchers who are being addressed in an inflammatory manner. The following note has been handed in—"We demand the Union Jack be taken down immediately as it is an insult to the Irish people in view of the shooting of 6 people in the six counties by British armed personnel. From the people of Dublin. M. Smyth."' Sir Andrew Gilchrist warned that 'We must expect Belfast deaths to be exploited on a very large scale, and with considerable local effect and leverage.' The Embassy was getting 'ugly telephone calls, professedly from the IRA, about English dogs shooting Irish children, and threatening all sorts of things. No violence as yet.' The Ambassador's earlier concern as to the Embassy's inflammability seemed a

touch too prophetic as, later in the day, the protesters attacked his residence. A mob went into action with stones and 'we have lost some glass, most of it in my office'. At 2.10 p.m. an 'athletic young man shinned up a drainpipe' and tore down the flag, which was then ceremoniously burnt in the street. An Irish flag hoisted on a lamp-post gave an impression of flying on the Embassy. During the proceedings Michael O'Leary TD had come to see Gilchrist to try and persuade him to lower the Union Flag. Gilchrist told him he would gladly do so if the Irish authorities in the interests of law and order would make an official request. He could not induce them to do this so the Union Flag stayed up until torn down. The 'active section of the mob', though vicious, was not large, perhaps eighty-strong, but there were hundreds of inert onlookers. Several of the inciters spoke with Belfast accents and O'Leary confirmed that they included some who derived great prestige from having been 'out' in Belfast the night before. Some were said to be armed. The Gardaí put up a 'half-hearted performance'. Though roughly equal in numbers to the activists, they made no serious attempt to stop the stone-throwing or the burning of the flag: 'I take little pleasure in the outlook.'[85]

Inside the Irish Government Jack Lynch was feeling the pressure. He had to demonstrate that his Government was doing something constructive to relieve the situation in the North. Lynch issued a statement regretting that: 'Through last night's tragic loss of lives in Belfast and Armagh our worst fears have, unfortunately, now been realised.' He believed what was needed now, more than anything else, was a period of restraint so as to create an interim situation of non-violence during which every possible channel might be explored so as to arrive at an acceptable solution of the immediate problems and, eventually, to reach a permanent solution of the basic issues involved. The Irish Government were doing, and would continue to do, everything in their power towards this end. Lynch announced that the Minister for External Affairs, Dr Patrick Hillery, would be urging the British Government to agree to the deployment of a United Nations peace-keeping force or, as an alternative, to a joint Irish–British force in the North. The Minister would also press for the immediate withdrawal of the B-Specials. The Government had decided to authorise the mobilisation of the first line of the Defence Forces so as to ensure that they would be in readiness for participation in peace-keeping operations.[86]

In London Hillery met with Lord Chalfont, who was still temporarily in charge of the Foreign Office, and Lord Stonham, from the Home Office. The British rejected as 'without foundation' the Irish allegation that there had been police attacks on the people of Londonderry, reaffirmed that Northern Ireland was an integral part of the United Kingdom and 'that events there are consequently an internal matter'. In the circumstances the British did not regard a UN peace-keeping force as either necessary or appropriate.[87] With no satisfaction here, on the following day, 16 August, the Irish cabinet instructed Hillery to proceed immediately to New York, with a view to arranging to have the question of a UN peace-keeping force in the six counties raised with the Security Council at the earliest possible date.[88]

In London, as the dust settled, Callaghan and Wilson were taking stock of the situation. Callaghan observed that the presence of troops in Belfast had 'sterilised' one area of the city but the situation remained serious and there was, in his view, little hope that the troops could be withdrawn within a few days. In view of this, he considered that it was necessary for discussions to take place with ministerial colleagues about the longer-term situation. Callaghan had a report from Robert Mark, Deputy Commissioner of the Metropolitan Police and Douglas Osmond, Chief Constable of Hampshire, the senior police officers he had sent over from Britain. They were reasonably content about the operational position. They were impressed by the RUC regulars, who were effective though very tired. But the B-Specials in Belfast were a 'poor lot', many of whom were attracted to the force by the firearms. In their view the objective should be, in the longer term, to disband the B-Specials; but the regular police would feel that it was necessary to have something in their place before this was done. In the areas of the city which the troops had not sterilised the atmosphere was simmering, if not boiling.[89]

For the Northern Ireland Government the aftermath of the rioting was disconcerting: they were aware that they were losing the propaganda war. The cabinet expressed concern that the Government's policies and actions were being inaccurately or misleadingly reported, and that any suggestion of involvement by subversive organisations was being discounted.[90] The problem, as the Northern Ireland Government found to its frustration, was renewed criticism of the RUC and continuing hostility to the USC by the British and foreign press and leaders of the Roman Catholic community.[91] It was also clear to Chichester-Clark that, with the deployment of troops, the status quo was not an option.[92] Chichester-Clark saw a possible way forward when the Chief of Staff Northern Ireland suggested that the GOC should provide for a unified security command by assuming responsibility for all security operations including those units of the police engaged on security work, but leaving the Inspector-General in command of ordinary police activities. This appeared to offer an acceptable compromise but one only to be used to counter any definite proposals put forward by London.[93]

On 18 August Callaghan telephoned a glum Chichester-Clark. Callaghan told Chichester-Clark that he had heard back from Mark and Osmond. They had said that the leadership at the top of the RUC was poor and that Peacocke would have to be replaced. Callaghan did not have to push too hard—Chichester-Clark, like the Home Secretary, had reached the conclusion that public confidence in the police had ebbed away and that an inquiry into the RUC was needed. He had told Peacocke this but he had reacted unfavourably. Chichester-Clark feared that Peacocke might resign and if he did, this would be followed by mass resignations from the force. The Deputy Prime Minister, John Andrews, was out touring police stations to reassure officers that not all the world was against them. Reform of the police was becoming the key issue.

On the morning of 19 August Callaghan took Osmond to see Wilson in order for the Prime Minister to see how well-founded his concerns about the RUC were. Callaghan had found some of Osmond and Mark's findings very disturbing. Their first criticism was that the Minister of Home Affairs seemed totally dependent on the Inspector-General. He was the Minister's sole source of intelligence and professional advice, and the Minister seemed to take second place to him. They found the Inspector-General's office to be an informal meeting place for any minister or civil servant who cared to drop in. He clearly held a position of great authority. Osmond and Mark considered this a great weakness and were 'really rather horrified by it'. They felt that Peacocke's approach was sensationalist and that it was coupled with a very poor intelligence network. After an abortive IRA attempt to blow up Armagh police station he had deployed three armoured columns along the border, apparently in the belief that this was the right response. In contrast Osmond and Mark found the Deputy Inspector-General, Graham Shillington, a rational, unemotional, likeable person. The Commissioner for Belfast, Harold Wolseley, was desperately tired, a 'gentle and depressed' man. It was their view that the wrong men were in charge in Londonderry. The County Inspector was weak and ineffectual. He had been overwhelmed by the County Inspector in charge of traffic control who was pompous, dogmatic and self-important. However there was a useful District Inspector there and some excellent middle-ranking officers. 'The men feel they have done their best,' Mark and Osmond reported, 'and they are bewildered and angry at the reaction of the Press and the public. The ordinary policeman feels an injustice has been done to him. They have been on duty for long periods but there has been no real organization by the top-level command for proper reliefs or even for such ordinary domestic details as hot meals at night. All this should have been done and would have been done in an equivalent demonstration in Britain.'

Osmond and Mark were also very critical of the fact that police stations were bolted and barred. The police, they said, were on the defensive. Sentries had been armed with machine guns at the stations; there were large numbers of men sitting around in poor accommodation waiting for something to happen. One country station they visited was shuttered, bolted and barred and they had to bang on the shutters before one apprehensive policeman put his head around the door. 'Look we happen to be English policemen,' they said. 'Can we come in and see what you're doing?' Inside they found the station covered in litter and cigarette stubs and the vehicles and other equipment dirty. The men were just sitting there waiting for a non-existent attack to be made on them. Mark and Osmond went back three or four days later and found things in exactly the same disorganised and dirty state. They blamed the higher command for this. The public could not get near some stations, they said, because they were so heavily guarded. They said the force was obsessed with the belief that the rioting was the result of a deep IRA plot.

Mark and Osmond also said the police were in no way presented to the public as a safeguard or sign of stability. 'They are a force apart,' was how they put it. There was no real system for handling complaints against the police, who seemed to be a law unto themselves and more concerned with the military aspects of their work than with normal police duties. At the first hint of trouble normal police behaviour was suppressed and they became a paramilitary force; the police as a symbol of normality disappeared, only to reappear ready to meet force with force. As for the B-Specials, Mark and Osmond emphasised that it was not a special constabulary in the sense that those in Great Britain would understand the term. Its whole emphasis was on firearms training; it was not integrated with the RUC, it had its own chain of command, and it was seen as a Protestant reserve army. Mark and Osmond believed that in the present situation it could not be disbanded or disarmed unless something were put in its place, and they recommended that it should cease to be a special constabulary and become an openly military reserve with recruitment from all religions.[94] Sir Andrew Gilchrist's comment to the Foreign Office summed up what all this meant for the Specials: 'Even though it may be true that they are a fine body of men, the fact is that when a dog has an unacceptably bad name it must be hanged.'[95]

By now Callaghan had made his up his mind on how to proceed. He had decided against direct rule and told the cabinet that the British Government should aim to avoid the assumption of full responsibility for Northern Ireland affairs. The issue remained that London could not accept responsibility for maintaining law and order—which was in some ways what the presence of the troops meant—without also being held responsible for the factors in Northern Ireland life that caused disorder. The requirement, therefore, was that the British Government should be able to influence the Northern Ireland Government over a wide field of affairs. London should place a very senior official as its liaison officer with Chichester-Clark and another senior official and police officer with the Minister of Home Affairs. Their purpose would be to influence decisions of the Northern Ireland Government in accordance with instructions from London. The success of this approach would depend on the extent to which Northern Ireland ministers were prepared to co-operate in the general public interest of ending the emergency or whether their policies would continue to be bound by narrow party considerations.

He warned that the British Government 'must obviously be prepared for a more formal assumption of responsibility should the arrangement I have described above prove to be insufficient of itself'. But if London were justified in believing that there would be co-operation from a viable Northern Ireland Government, it would be right to see whether Westminster's intervention could be limited to assuming only such responsibility as was needed and leaving day-to-day administration to the Northern Ireland Government. If it was accepted that London should assume only a partial responsibility there were great advantages in not trying to lay down a new division of powers rigidly in a bill. Thus the

Parliament and Government of Northern Ireland would continue to exist and operate and this would be regarded as a guarantee that partition would not be ended against the wishes of the people of Northern Ireland. If legislation, for example in the field of housing allocation or police powers, were not enough, Westminster could assume executive responsibility over any topic such as the maintenance of public order, including the control of the RUC. There were serious practical problems in this approach, more serious perhaps even than those that arose from a total assumption of responsibility, but Callaghan believed it would be worth ascertaining from Chichester-Clark whether his Government would co-operate. If it would not, or if promises of co-operation became illusory, a total assumption of responsibility would be necessary.

The aim of the policies would be to 'restore confidence among the Roman Catholic minority without inflaming the Protestants beyond endurance'. Callaghan had hoped Chichester-Clark would be prepared to consider bringing into the government a number of non-Unionist members of the Northern Ireland Parliament—not necessarily Nationalists or Republicans who might not be prepared to serve, but members of the Northern Ireland Labour Party and those representing civil rights or other liberal interests. However, it now seemed that Chichester-Clark had 'disabled' himself from doing so by his press conference the previous day, ruling out a coalition. Summing up, Callaghan proposed:

  (i) we should insist on the B-Specials who are on the streets being withdrawn from the streets and disarmed;
 (ii) we should, if possible by agreement with Major Chichester-Clark send senior officials and a senior police officer (possibly led by a Minister) to represent United Kingdom policies to the Northern Ireland Government;
(iii) we should decide whether a limited Bill . . . would be a suitable instrument to hold in reserve and be likely to meet with co-operation from the Northern Ireland Government;
 (iv) we should find out what is in Major Chichester-Clark's mind in his public references to forming a 'broadly based government';
  (v) we should explore with Major Chichester-Clark other proposals such as one for a mixed community relations commission.[96]

Oliver Wright was one of the two senior civil servants which Callaghan had insisted should be sent to Belfast to represent the British Government there. Wright, Deputy Under-Secretary of State at the Foreign and Commonwealth Office, was appointed to Chichester-Clark's office while A. S. Baker, Assistant Secretary at the Home Office, went to the Ministry of Home Affairs. Wright, whose title would be 'United Kingdom Representative in Northern Ireland' and had until recently been British Ambassador to Denmark, was the key man.[97] He had a direct line to Callaghan and became his eyes and ears in Ulster.

THE DOWNING STREET DECLARATION

On the evening of 19 August Chichester-Clark, Faulkner, Andrews and Porter arrived at Downing Street. Sitting across the table from them were Wilson, Callaghan, Healy, Stewart and Stonham; also attending for part of the discussion was the Chief of the General Staff, General Sir Geoffrey Baker. Wilson began by inviting Chichester-Clark to give his impressions of the present situation. Chichester-Clark admitted that, following a campaign of vilification, the police force were now discredited among some sections of the community. It was necessary to consider how to restore civilian control over the areas in Belfast and Londonderry which had been affected by the rioting. He proposed that as a first step the GOC should take over control of all security operations in Northern Ireland, including control over the RUC and the USC. He understood that this proposal would be acceptable to General Freeland and he had established that Peacocke would fully support it. Healy asked whether Freeland's remit would extend to the command and administration of RUC and USC personnel, in so far as these matters affected the internal security operations for which he would be responsible; Chichester-Clark replied that this would be the case. Wilson then made the observation that, at present, it was generally accepted throughout Northern Ireland that British troops were impartial and were in no way involved in sectarian or other disputes. So long as this was the case, the troops would hold the confidence of all sections of the community; but he wondered whether Chichester-Clark's proposal would not soon lead to public hostility being diverted from the police to troops. It would be essential for the GOC to retain this responsibility only as a short-term measure until the RUC could be reorganised in such a way that it could command the confidence of the whole community. Healy explained that the GOC was of the opinion that immediate steps should be taken to restrict the deployment of B-Specials and to exercise central control over their arms. He asked whether the Northern Ireland Government intended that Freeland should be given authority to take such steps.

Chichester-Clark warned that the difficulties of disarming or disbanding the B-Specials should not be underestimated. To disarm them at this juncture would be highly inflammatory and, in view of the public threats from the IRA, it would undoubtedly lead to some citizens taking the law into their own hands. Wilson, however, noted that many responsible journalists in Britain had been highly critical of the activities of the Specials in Belfast. John Andrews replied that whatever might be said about events in Belfast, it should also be taken into account that the B-Specials had succeeded in maintaining law and order in provincial towns during the period when the RUC had been fully extended in Belfast and Londonderry. Healy, however, pointed out that the GOC was of the opinion that the B-Specials had used excessive force, including the use of arms, and had thus aggravated the problems faced by British forces in restoring law and order; Freeland considered that it would be necessary for him to exercise full control over their future use in internal security operations. Callaghan added that the B-Specials were not accustomed either to police or to military discipline, and were experienced only in the use of arms. While it might be possible to consider their deployment for guarding police barracks and other key points, he could not support their use for controlling crowds and riots. Moreover, tension in Northern Ireland would remain high so long as they were allowed to keep arms at home.

Chichester-Clark resisted. He felt that at present there was no doubt that the B-Specials themselves and people living in country areas would feel that their safety would be endangered if the USC were compelled to hand in their arms. At his meetings with community leaders in Northern Ireland the previous night the view had been generally taken that to disarm the B-Specials would invite a further breakdown of law and order and would undoubtedly lead to a resumption of violence. In response Wilson commented that the Northern Ireland Government, by proposing that the GOC should take control over internal security, were in effect inviting the British Government to take responsibility for the actions of the B-Specials and their consequences. In the very serious situation which Chichester-Clark had described it was essential to be clear about the authority that Freeland would be allowed to exercise over the use of B-Specials and over their arms. There would shortly be nearly 5,000 field troops deployed in Northern Ireland; public opinion would demand as a corollary that the B-Specials should be disarmed and possibly disbanded. Healy added that the GOC considered that the change in policy for the use of B-Specials in the current situation—and especially the decision to make no further use of them for crowd control or in riots—should be announced at the same time as it was made known that he would be made responsible for internal security in Northern Ireland. Chichester-Clark conceded that while he could accept an announcement that the B-Specials would not be used further for crowd and riot control, in the view of his Government any long-term measures to alter the normal role of the B-Specials should not be announced immediately, but should be introduced gradually and with the minimum of publicity.

Callaghan, however, thought that it was highly desirable that the Northern Ireland Government's intentions for standing down the B-Specials should be announced soon. As Wilson explained, the United Kingdom Government considered that the aim should be to withdraw British troops from internal security operations in Northern Ireland as soon as possible and in any case within a few weeks; and that the role, organisation and structure of the RUC should be investigated by means of an independent enquiry. The British police advisers who had visited Northern Ireland during the past week had formed the impression that the standards and approach of the RUC were different from those of the police in the remainder of the United Kingdom, and that the present command structure of the police forces left much to be desired. Wilson accepted that conditions in Northern Ireland were in many ways unique.

Faced with this insistence, and perhaps recalling that he had virtually conceded the point to Callaghan already, Chichester-Clark agreed to consider how such an enquiry might be carried out while the GOC remained responsible for internal security; such an enquiry would, however, probably lead to some resignations among senior officers in the RUC, and this would lower morale not only in the RUC but also in Northern Ireland at large. He agreed with Callaghan's suggestion that it would be appropriate for such an enquiry to be carried out by a police officer with experience in dependent territories as well as in Great Britain. Wilson emphasised that the aim should be to carry out the review as quickly as possible in order to hasten the day when British troops could be withdrawn from internal security duties. Callaghan then proposed that two senior officials from Whitehall be appointed in Belfast to advise both governments on matters as they developed, and also to undertake responsibilities on the spot as appropriate. Chichester-Clark thought that at first sight it appeared to have many advantages. Callaghan then enquired whether Chichester-Clark considered that there was any possibility of broadening the base of the Government in Northern Ireland. Chichester-Clark was adamant, however, that he saw no prospect of forming a coalition government since, with few exceptions, members of the opposition would not be working towards the same ends as the present Northern Ireland Government. Callaghan suggested that the Northern Ireland Government might widen its appeal to the electorate by appointing a minister for community relations, possibly supported by a commission on which all sections of the community would be represented. Chichester-Clark replied that his cabinet would be meeting the following day to discuss these and other suggestions.

During an adjournment the British ministers were joined by the Chief of the General Staff, Sir Geoffrey Baker, to consider Chichester-Clark's proposal that the GOC should assume operational control over the police forces in internal security duties. The fear remained that the proposal might increase the risk that British troops would become more closely identified with the Northern Ireland Government and police forces, thus aggravating the difficulties of securing a return to conditions of law and order and delaying the date when the British forces could be withdrawn from security duties. In the end, however, the British team concluded that the balance of advantage lay in proceeding with the proposal, provided that the Northern Ireland Government were prepared to agree to an independent enquiry into the role, structure and organisation of the civilian security forces, and provided that the GOC was given control over the deployment not only of the RUC but also of the B-Specials with, above all, central control over their arms. The rapid and progressive removal of the B-Specials from their present duties in the cities should also be a necessary condition of agreement. If these points were voluntarily accepted by the Northern Ireland Government, the requirements laid down by Callaghan and accepted by the cabinet earlier would in substance have been met. The Westminster Parliament would in any event remain responsible in the last resort for Northern Ireland.

It was felt that the proposal could not put London in a worse position so far as its responsibilities were concerned than it was in now, and it would give the UK

Government a measure of control and authority in Northern Ireland which had hitherto been lacking. The GOC himself was in favour of the proposal, and the Northern Ireland Government were well aware of his views; if there were any leakage, it would be difficult to defend its rejection if it were known to have been fully supported by the responsible officer on the spot. The British ministers accordingly decided that the proposal should be agreed to on the conditions outlined, and that provided the Northern Ireland Government were willing to accept an agreement on this basis, and a joint communiqué reflecting it, it would not be necessary to refer again to the cabinet. When the meeting resumed Wilson explained that the British Government attached particular importance to announcing that with the assumption of operational control by the GOC, the B-Specials would be progressively and rapidly relieved of their present temporary duties in the cities, and that the GOC should have discretion over the custody of their arms, subject to separate consideration of the situation in remote rural areas; they also attached importance to the appointment of a chief constable from Great Britain as Inspector-General of the RUC. Finally, Wilson proposed that a declaration should be issued concurrently with the communiqué which would indicate the principles which should guide the future actions of the two governments. The meeting adjourned at 9.45 p.m. and resumed, under the chairmanship of Stewart, at 10.30, in order to consider further drafts of the communiqué and declaration which were then approved. The meeting concluded at 10.45 p.m.[98]

The final communiqué agreed that the GOC Northern Ireland would with immediate effect assume overall responsibility for security operations. He would continue to be responsible to the MOD but would work closely with the Northern Ireland Government and the Inspector-General. For all security operations the GOC would have full control of the deployment and tasks of the RUC. For normal police duties outside the field of security the RUC would remain answerable to the Inspector-General who would be responsible to the Northern Ireland Government. The GOC was also to assume full command and control of the USC for all purposes including their organisation, deployment, tasks and arms. Their temporary employment by the Northern Ireland Government would end with Army deployment and the GOC's assumption of operational control. The question of USC arms would also fall within the GOC's discretion although consideration would be given to the defence of vital public service installations. An appeal was to be made for all members of the public to hand in unauthorised weapons under an amnesty. In order that British troops could be withdrawn from their internal security role at the earliest moment the two governments were to discuss the future of Northern Ireland's civilian security services which would take over when the troops withdrew. It was the intention of the Northern Ireland Government to set up an impartial investigation into the recent public disorders. The British Government proposed, and the Northern Ireland ministers had agreed, that two senior civil servants from London should be temporarily stationed with the Northern Ireland Government in Belfast to represent the increased concern which the British Government had necessarily acquired in Northern Ireland affairs through the commitment of troops.[99]

The declaration soon took on the title of the 'Downing Street Declaration'. It reaffirmed that every Northern Ireland citizen was entitled to the same equality of treatment and freedom from discrimination as elsewhere in the United Kingdom, and went on to state that the British Government had ultimate responsibility for the protection of those who lived in Northern Ireland when a breakdown of law and order had occurred. It was in this spirit that the British Government had responded to the requests of Northern Ireland's Government for military assistance. But troops would be withdrawn when law and order had been restored. The Northern Ireland Government had been informed that troops had been provided on a temporary basis in accordance with the United Kingdom's ultimate responsibility. The British Government welcomed the public acceptance by the Northern Ireland Government of the reforms which it had drawn up for implementation. In constitutional terms the crucial clauses stated:

1. The United Kingdom Government reaffirm that nothing which has happened in recent weeks in Northern Ireland derogates from the clear pledges made by successive United Kingdom Governments that Northern Ireland should not cease to be a part of the United Kingdom without the consent of the people of Northern Ireland or from the provision in Section 1 of the Ireland Act, 1949, that in no event will Northern Ireland or any part thereof cease to be part of the United Kingdom without the consent of the Parliament of Northern Ireland. The border is not an issue.
2. The United Kingdom Government again affirm that responsibility for affairs in Northern Ireland is entirely a matter of domestic jurisdiction. The United Kingdom Government will take full responsibility for asserting this principle in all international relationships.[100]

After the Stormont team returned to the Province, the Northern Ireland cabinet considered the communiqué and declaration the following day. In reality this was little more than a rubber-stamping exercise. Chichester-Clark told his colleagues that while the negotiations had proved difficult and long drawn-out nevertheless they had been conducted in a friendly atmosphere. He reassured them that reports that the transfer of the control of the police's security duties under the GOC's command foreshadowed the disarming and ultimately the disbanding of the Special Constabulary were incorrect. The Specials were to be withdrawn from riot control duties but would continue to be engaged in guarding key installations and on other security work. The deputation appreciated that in making this arrangement they were going beyond their specific brief from the cabinet but in the circumstances they considered that no other alternative was open to them: the approval of their colleagues for this action was now sought—and secured. Only Roy Bradford was prepared to state the truth which the rest of the cabinet seemed only too ready to deny: the transfer of the security duties of the police to the GOC represented a fundamental shift of power to Westminster.[101]

In the days following the Downing Street Declaration controversy over the future of the Special Constabulary dominated discussion in Northern Ireland. Harold Wilson had made a major contribution to the confusion when, in a televised interview during a break in the London talks, he had talked of the 'phasing out' of the Specials. The expression was being interpreted by some as meaning phasing-out of existence and by others as phasing-out of operational duties. Wilson had meant the latter; he hoped the MOD directive containing the GOC's orders would instruct him to phase out the Specials as fast as he could. As Callaghan saw it the position of the Specials was:

(i)   They should be off the streets in the cities within 48 hours.
(ii)   Their duties should be limited to the defence of key installations.
(iii) Their role in the country areas as a whole would be further considered.
(iv) There would be centralisation and control of their arms.
(v)   The Inquiry into the R.U.C would cover the role and future of the 'B' Specials.[102]

The discrepancies between what Wilson seemed to have said and what Chichester-Clark was telling Unionists back home led Harry West to warn that the loyalist people would not stand for the disbandment of the Specials: 'This is not acceptable in any shape or form.' West and Craig thought that such a prospect would lead to a demand for the Unionist Government to resign. Paisley claimed that Wilson had 'capitulated to the Hierarchy of the Roman Catholic Church to destroy at a stroke the Special Constabulary—Ulster loyalists' last line of defence. He has done exactly what the Civil Rights Association and the IRA wanted him to do. Ulster Protestants must now join themselves together as their father did in 1912.' From NICRA, Frank Gogarty pronounced himself totally dissatisfied with Wilson's statement: 'We still believe that the Stormont Government has no right to continue.' Bernadette Devlin, on the other hand, thought Wilson had 'given hope that now things are going to change for the better for the people of Ulster'. Ivan Cooper was prepared to use his influence to secure acceptance of British control of the security forces but he warned that this was an interim solution and in the long term he could only see that the RUC would have to be replaced by an impartial police force.[103]

The most important thing, however, seemed to be to calm Protestant nerves. After making it clear that there was no diminution of the Northern Ireland Government's powers, Faulkner stressed that there was 'absolutely no suggestion' that the Specials would be disbanded.[104] This and other reassurances seemed to do the trick. Backbench Unionist MPs gave their unanimous support to Chichester-Clark and the Government after the Downing Street talks. Craig, who had earlier called on the

Government to resign, decided, after hearing the premier's version of events, that he would give him his support. Craig said: 'It would seem that Mr Wilson was indulging in a lot of double talk. The Prime Minister gave an unambiguous explanation of what had taken place, and we gave him our full support.' He had been assured that the Specials would not be disbanded and that they would continue to be armed as and when they had to be.[105] On the ground the Shankill Defence Association threw its support behind the Declaration as well—although McKeague warned there must be no attempt to disband the USC. The Prime Minister was also surprisingly supported by Major Bunting who stated that Chichester-Clark was 'worthy of our support'.[106]

The immediate problem for London was to get the Specials out of public view, secure their arms and establish how the GOC's new role as Director of Operations would work out in practice.[107] The Home Secretary would be responsible for general policy on matters relating to Northern Ireland and relations between the United Kingdom Government and the Northern Ireland Government. The Defence Secretary had responsibility, within the framework of agreed policies, for all matters relating to security in Northern Ireland arising from the Directive to be given to the GOC, which would define his role and responsibilities. The direction of policy would continue to be carried out under the general supervision of the cabinet by MISC 238. The general authority given by the cabinet to the Prime Minister, Foreign Secretary, Home Secretary and Defence Secretary to take any decisions urgently required remained in force. At the official level a committee of senior officials would sit under the chairmanship of Sir Philip Allen to deal with general policy matters. The Home Office and MOD made arrangements for day-to-day consultation and co-ordination between themselves and with other interested departments. These arrangements were to be kept under regular review.[108] The Directive for the GOC informed Freeland that he was appointed Director of Operations in Northern Ireland and would, with immediate effect, assume overall responsibility for security operations. Security operations were defined as relating to internal and external security covering:

A. The execution of operations necessary to counter action (whether covert or overt) aimed at subverting the security of the state.
B. The action necessary for the protection of life and property in case of actual or apprehended civil commotion.

He was responsible to the MOD but would consult as appropriate with the Northern Ireland Government. In the event of any disagreement arising in this consultation process Freeland was instructed to at once refer the matter to the British Government. He was to keep his superiors fully informed on all major issues. He was also, if time permitted, to obtain guidance from the MOD on any matters which in his opinion or that of the British Government's representatives in Northern Ireland had wider political implications or which concerned any major redeployment of his forces. In terms of organisational matters, the GOC was empowered to set up, in consultation with the Northern Ireland Government and UK representatives in Northern Ireland, security committees and such other machinery as he considered necessary. Finally, he was reminded that any offences arising from subversion or civil commotion remained offences against the criminal law and were to be investigated and prosecuted by the police in the ordinary way.[109]

On 27 August Chichester-Clark announced the Government's intention to set up a tribunal into the riots. Mr Justice Scarman was to chair the tribunal. He was to be assisted by two Northern Irishmen, one Protestant and one Catholic, in his work: William Marshall, a businessman who had been called to the English Bar and George Lavery, a businessman who was a qualified solicitor.[110] Unlike the situation with the Cameron Commission, the Government enjoyed support for this measure from virtually all its backbenchers. Craig, for example, supported it although it was no substitute for 'strong government'.[111] The same day Callaghan arrived in Northern Ireland. He travelled with Lord Stonham, landing at Aldergrove in a camouflaged RAF Air Support Command plane. On the ground he was welcomed by Chichester-Clark, Lord Grey, the GOC and Oliver Wright. Callaghan declared: 'I am not here to dictate to the Northern Ireland Government.' He added: 'I am not here to solve your problems: It is up to you to decide if you can live together in freedom and without discrimination.' He would, however, put himself at their disposal.[112]

Callaghan was mobbed as he toured the Falls and received a hero's welcome in the Bogside; even the reception in Protestant districts was favourable. He also met with politicians from all sides, including Paisley, and visited troops, police and the B-Specials. After he met with the Northern Ireland cabinet a Home Office official said it was like watching a man play tennis against an opponent who never hit the ball back. 'He was right,' Callaghan later wrote. Callaghan pushed out ideas and suggestions throughout the session while the cabinet sat and listened, apparently accepting most of what he was saying with hardly any discussion. Callaghan thought his task at the cabinet meeting was 'to get to know them, reassure them, make them feel they had a role to play, that the situation was not as hopeless as they seemed to think it was, and that if only they would act quickly they would get results'. The first thing he discussed with the cabinet was the Cameron Report which was to be published shortly. Callaghan said that this would provide ammunition for more trouble and he asked the cabinet what they proposed to do. Chichester-Clark replied 'in the nicest possible way' that he hoped the lull they were now enjoying would lead not to more violence but to peace. He said it was very difficult to know what he and the Northern Ireland Government could do to reduce tension. They had no further reforms to suggest and they looked to time to heal the division. Callaghan was appalled, having come straight from the streets and seen the atmosphere there, and said that in his view the lull was temporary and they had only a short time to try to build something more permanent before disorder broke out again.

Porter then made a very helpful contribution. He said that if the Army would remain in control of the streets for the time being and the police were reorganised and rehabilitated in the minds of the minority, then peace could be restored. He hoped that the proposed enquiry into the police would lead to the creation of an English-type police force and that the RUC could drop its paramilitary role. Callaghan was attracted by this proposal because it was in line with his own thinking. He tried to soothe any ruffled feelings by explaining that the proposed inquiry was no reflection on the RUC but that after fifty years of existence its structure, like that of most other organisations of similar age, could well bear re-examination. Callaghan wanted to see the police as citizens in uniform, serving the whole community and not just part of it, and that as long as a significant minority of the community felt that the police did not serve them, the police could not function successfully. As for the B-Specials, the cabinet seemed somewhat reassured because some were beginning to hand in their arms without trouble. Freeland had indicated that there might be a role for them for some time ahead and that arms would be issued again if and when the men were needed to guard installations. Callaghan later wondered whether it was some tactical consideration that prompted Chichester-Clark to say they had no proposals for any further reforms, because he and his colleagues wanted him to make the running: 'But I think not. The cabinet were decent men entirely out of their depth. They were ready to go along with someone who had positive ideas.'

Among the flurry of suggestions Callaghan put that afternoon, the one that caused the greatest consternation was his proposal that there should be a single authority for the allocation and building of houses. They regarded the idea with 'near horror' both on political and administrative grounds, for of course it went to the heart of political patronage. But Callaghan pointed out to them that Northern Ireland's population was very little bigger than Birmingham's and that Birmingham's housing programme was centrally controlled, and so gradually brought them round to being willing to consider it. Callaghan asked them to consider this and other ideas and said they would talk about it when he met them again in two days' time. Chichester-Clark then explained that the cabinet were a little concerned about the visit Callaghan proposed to pay to the Bogside the following day. He would be asked when he got there to abolish Stormont and introduce a period of direct rule. Callaghan replied that he would say in the Bogside exactly what he had said to the cabinet: that there was no prospect of Her Majesty's Government's agreeing to abolish Stormont at that stage and that their aim was to work through the Northern Ireland Government, getting them to bring in some very necessary reforms. But he took the opportunity to inform the cabinet that London had contingency plans prepared should law and order break down completely and Stormont be incapable of functioning. Callaghan wanted them to understand that London was ready to use those powers although they would be very reluctant to do so:

Although I hope I did not show my feelings, I found it difficult to take seriously the idea that the Northern Ireland cabinet and Prime Minister bore any resemblance to what we in Britain understood by those offices. It was always in my mind that, by British standards, the Northern Ireland cabinet and Parliament was little more than an enlarged county council, with rather greater powers for raising taxes and spending money and with an unhealthy political control over the police. They took seriously the notion that the doctrine of collective responsibility must apply simply because they were called a cabinet . . .[113]

At midnight on 28 August Callaghan and his officials held a tactical conference. Neil Cairncross, the Under-Secretary at the Home Office, reported that while the Northern Ireland cabinet were likely to agree to consider Callaghan's proposed programme of reforms, they were showing an unwillingness to commit themselves to a specific examination of various items on the grounds that this might prove to be impractical and would savour of dictation from Westminster. Callaghan said this was not good enough: 'I was in no particular mood at that stage to be put off by a group of people who seemed to have no conception of how close they were to disaster.' Cairncross was instructed to find Harold Black—and drag him out of bed if necessary—and tell him that the Home Secretary was not satisfied. He would go public if the cabinet turned down the proposals. Callaghan recalled: 'I had a strong hand, for it would be the end of them if they did not fall into line . . . they would be absolutely on their own.'[114]

When Callaghan next met the cabinet Chichester-Clark announced the release of the detainees, and after a mutually agreeable exchange, they got down to business. Callaghan wanted the Northern Ireland Government to make certain propositions to him, including the setting up of a series of joint working parties to look into specific subjects: 'If they cared to put those propositions to me I could tell them straight away that the answer would be yes.' When Callaghan had finished the cabinet asked no questions. Chichester-Clark merely asked that the cabinet be allowed to consider Callaghan's statement on their own. And then 'after a very long hour of waiting' Callaghan and his team were told the cabinet were ready for them. Chichester-Clark 'began in his usual matter-of-fact way'. They had considered these matters and were ready to make the following proposals: first, Chichester-Clark would on his own responsibility appoint a minister of community relations; second, a series of working parties should be set up as requested.[115] A joint communiqué announced that the Northern Ireland Government agreed with Callaghan that the following fields were fundamental to the creation of confidence:

(i) Equality of opportunity for all in public employment, without regard to religious or political considerations.

(ii) Protection against the incitement of hatred against any citizen on the grounds of religious belief.

(iii) Guaranteed fairness in the allocation of public authority housing, with need, assessed by objective criteria, as the only relevant yardstick.

(iv) Effective means not only for the investigation of grievances against public bodies, but for their ultimate redress if conciliation and other procedures are ineffective.

(v) Proper representation of minorities, to be addressed at the elected levels of government by completely fair electoral laws, practices and boundaries, and at nominated or appointed levels by a recognition that such minorities have a right to an effective voice in affairs.

Accordingly the British and Northern Ireland Governments had set up joint working parties composed of officials from both administrations to examine the extent to which the Northern Ireland Government's present practice or pledged commitments adequately ensured:

(i) the fair allocation of houses by public authorities;

(ii) the avoidance of any discrimination in any form of public employment; and

(iii) the promotion of good community relations by methods including the prohibition of incitement to religious hatred.

The results of these investigations were to be reported to the Northern Ireland Government within a matter of weeks. Chichester-Clark agreed also to appoint a minister with special responsibility for community relations.[116] Callaghan was delighted that common sense had won. He disguised his elation as he made a few formal but friendly remarks welcoming their decision. Callaghan thought the cabinet saw the agreement as a way of preserving their own independence: 'Besides, what else could they do? They certainly had few if any ideas of their own. World opinion was against them. British troops were patrolling the streets. The police force had collapsed. They were dazed and at the end of their tether.'[117]

Chapter 8 ❧

COLD WAR: SEPTEMBER 1969–MAY 1970

ACROSS THE BARRICADES

In the absence of direct rule, London's man in Belfast was Oliver Wright. Three of the most influential men in Ulster were to be Englishmen: Sir Ian Freeland, Sir Arthur Young (who would soon replace Peacocke as RUC Inspector-General) and Wright. As the United Kingdom Representative to Northern Ireland (UKREP), Wright's instructions from Callaghan were to supply ideas for initiatives by the Stormont Government to heal divisions in the community, to warn that Government if they proposed action which the British Government would not approve and to inform the British Government of the situation in Northern Ireland generally. His position was based on the proposition that the problems of security which the British Government had taken special responsibility for by providing military assistance could not be isolated from the social policies of the Northern Ireland Government.[1] He could communicate London's views either on an individual basis or as part of a new forum: the Joint Security Committee (JSC). The JSC principals were the Prime Minister (Chichester-Clark), the Minister of Home Affairs (Porter), the UK Representative (Wright), the Chief Constable (Young) and the GOC (Freeland).[2]

His other key function was to reassure Catholics of the British Government's commitment to reform in Northern Ireland and to assess the state of feeling within that community. As part of this he accepted Cardinal Conway's invitation to dinner at his palace in Armagh. In the absence of a coherent opposition in Stormont the Cardinal was seen as the key source for assessing the mood of the Catholic community. When they met on 30 August 1969 the Cardinal expressed satisfaction at progress. On the general situation Wright explained to the Cardinal how, ten days before, he had been quietly 'washing the paintwork in my house' and repairing the 'depredations of three years of the tenants', when he had been summoned by the Home Secretary and sent to Belfast. As far as Wright could see, his qualifications were that he was on leave and therefore available, a 'gash hand' as 'we used to say in the Navy', and that he was unprejudiced by knowledge so far as Northern Ireland was concerned. But Wright admitted that he had found little in Belfast that he expected; least of all were Northern Ireland ministers as he had been led to believe. In his view they were not evil men bent on maintaining power at all costs. They were decent but bewildered men, out of their depth in the face of the magnitude of their problem. That was why they genuinely wanted help from the United Kingdom and that was why they had generally responded to the Home Secretary who had come in a spirit of elder-brotherliness with a totally non-partisan approach. Wright was convinced that not only did they want to do the right thing, they also wanted to be told what was the right thing to do.

The Cardinal commented that he had never analysed the situation in that way; it was an interesting view and might be right. He at any rate would act on the assumption that it might be right and use his influence to reconcile the two communities. It was 'now or never'. The two men parted with the Cardinal lending Wright his copy of *Whitehall Diary* by Thomas Jones and repeating his wish that they should keep closely in touch as the situation developed. Wright assured Conway that that was also his wish and that he was always at his disposal.[3]

But the Catholics were not the immediate concern. Wright identified this as the short-term survival of Chichester-Clark's Government. On the morning of 2 September, Chichester-Clark had met the Unionist backbenchers and party officers. This proved a difficult meeting and produced the following communiqué:

> The Parliamentary Party and executive officers of the Ulster Unionist Council fully support the Prime Minister and the Government in their efforts to establish stability in the community and call on all sections of the people to work together to play their part in building a new future for Northern Ireland.

Wright, in his Situation Report to Callaghan, observed that this committed the Party to supporting the Government but not specifically to the reform programme. Also agreed was that no one should go on television: this kept Craig silent, but it kept the Government silent as well. Since then Wright had spent a good deal of time and energy urging the Government, from the Prime Minister down, not only to agree to the reform programme, but to get out and sell it to the country. They agreed, but claimed that this was the close season for politics: the Prime Minister said that he had no meeting arranged until 20 September. They also said that until the barricades in Catholic areas of Belfast and Derry were down, campaigning would be counter-productive. Wright feared that they had, on present evidence, little stomach for this fight. This led Wright to rate the prospects of success as not above 50:50. He thought the possibility of failure was sufficiently strong for London not to put away contingency plans prepared for a 'greater degree of involvement in Northern Ireland'. Wright's recommendations were:

a) We should, for the time being, let the Northern Ireland Government play this their own way. Further overt pressure at present is likely to be counter-

productive. I will maintain pressure behind the scenes, but we should keep
open the possibility of a private adrenalin message from the Secretary of State
[Callaghan] to the Prime Minister of Northern Ireland ...

b) We should proceed as planned with the working groups, with condign
   publicity to keep people up to the mark.

c) We must be ready for trouble from the Protestant backlash and keep the rule
   book handy for more drastic measures of control. We are still on the knife
   edge.[4]

The continued existence of street barricades was becoming a test of the
Government's credibility in the eyes of the Protestant community: they had to be
removed if it was to demonstrate some degree of control over law and order. In
Belfast the Central Citizens' Defence Committee (CCDC), based mainly on the
Falls Road, co-ordinated the various west-Belfast defence and community groups
operating in Catholic areas. Its first chairman was Jim Sullivan, a leading IRA
figure; he was succeeded by Tom Conaty, a local businessman. It also brought
together local politicians such as Paddy Devlin and Paddy Kennedy and the local
priest, Canon Padraig Murphy, Dean of St Peters Pro-Cathedral.[5] In Londonderry
it was 'Free Derry' which symbolised the inability of the State's writ in parts of
Catholic Northern Ireland. On 22 August the Prime Minister assured a delegation
from the Middle Liberties Young Unionist Association in Londonderry that the
barricades would come down.[6] A group calling themselves the Londonderry
Citizens' Action Committee made representations to the Army, threatening to
erect similar obstructions at the entrances to the Protestant Fountain Street area.[7]
NICRA and the PD both declared that barricades were to stay; in NICRA's case
the Executive said this was because it could not make any sense of the Downing
Street communiqué and they wanted it made clear whether or not the British
Government was responsible for law and order and whether the USC were to be
disarmed and disbanded.[8] This was echoed by the Derry Citizens' Defence
Association (DCDA) which added the abolition of Stormont to the demands relating
to the Specials and the restriction of the RUC to 'ordinary' policing duties.[9]

   These groups were reflecting the attitude of ordinary Catholics. Mrs Catherine
Doagh, aged fifty-eight, was a Bogside resident. And a frightened one at that: 'I
can't sleep now,' she said. 'I'm sure if the barricades came down we would come
under attack.' Mrs Kathleen Quigley of Chamberlain Street, a mother of four,
explained: 'A lot of people, especially old, are frightened. The barricades give them
a sort of security. Most people feel that if they are removed, we will be attacked by
extreme Protestants who will make trips into the area. Residents are also worried
about the police, who obviously feel very bitter about what has happened. A lot of
people feel that if they are allowed back into the area, they will get their own
back.'[10] From the other side, the few Protestants living in the Bogside and Creggan
complained of being hindered by the DCDA's vigilante patrols. The vigilantes,

armed mainly with sticks and some with iron bars, patrolled the streets in the Creggan and Bogside by day and night on foot and by car. Protestant residents claimed they were stopped and questioned every time they came in or out. Many women would not go out at night because of the situation. But Paddy Doherty had nothing but praise for the 'peace corps'. They had about nine hundred acres to patrol and the population of both areas was around the 30,000 mark. The peace corps was divided up into seven different sections. This, pointed out Doherty, had prevented several burglaries.[11]

Yet fear existed on both sides. A new barricade was erected in Dover Street in Belfast on the evening of 28 August. It was hurriedly erected by Protestant residents on the Shankill Road side of the street because they feared trouble from a Catholic crowd at the corner of Dover Street and Divis Street. They were eventually dispersed by the Army.[12] After the BBC broadcast a statement on 1 September from a 'Captain Stevenson' of the UVF, claiming that its battalions were ready for action and new ones were being formed, a new barricade went up at the top of the New Lodge Road.[13]

With tensions still high, the Army moved in and removed two barricades on the morning of 2 September. Barricades were removed from Monagh Road and the intersection of the M1 motorway. This limited intervention was to keep the main routes in and out of Belfast open. At the Catholic Turf Lodge estate at the top of the Springfield Road, residents blocked the road in a human chain and alleged that the Army had been heavy-handed during the operation. The removal of the main barricade led to a strengthening of the barricades at entrances to side streets. Two new barricades went up in Protestant areas. One of the slogans read: 'When Bernadette takes hers down we will take ours down.'[14]

The Army's intention was to create a situation, as in Jamaica Street on the Glenard estate, whereby Catholic residents felt confident enough to remove their obstructions. In this instance it was so the troops could take over policing duties from the residents. Old-age pensioner John White, who had lived in the street for thirty-five years, explained: 'We don't need the barricades up, we have every confidence the troops will look after the situation.' Building labourer Charles Strain added: 'I agree the troops are doing a wonderful job. They patrol the road all the time and put men at the top of the street every night.' The feeling towards the troops in the area was summed up by mother-of-nine Mrs Mary Harrison: 'We can't do without the troops. They are doing all they can for us.'[15]

But on the evening of 4 September trouble flared in Belfast when crowds in the Donegall Road, Shankill Road and Newtownards Road erected barricades. At one stage troops threatened to use tear gas to disperse them.[16] The next day Chichester-Clark made an urgent plea to the people of Belfast for calm and a stop to barricade building. He could not believe that any responsible person could countenance any possibility of further violence and disorder. His call was supported by, among others, Craig, Paisley and Fitt.[17] But the pleas for peace went unheeded on the Newtownards Road where Paisley, for the second night in succession, was called out by the authorities to help calm the mobs, mainly of young people, who were roaming the streets looking for trouble. The crowd joined him in singing 'The Lord is my Shepherd' before beginning to disperse. Originally the crowd had been heading in the direction of a mixed Catholic/Protestant area around Seaforde Street. Police restrained Catholic men who had left their homes while clergymen—unsuccessfully—attempted to stop the crowd by linking arms across the Newtownards Road. At one point Brian Faulkner visited Protestant streets and then went behind Catholic barricades to discuss the situation and tell residents what the authorities were attempting to do.[18] Some improvement was evidenced with the removal of three barricades in Albert Street, a predominately Catholic street, following negotiations between Major General Dyball, Deputy Director of Operations and local representatives, including Father Murphy and Paddy Devlin. The Army were prepared to remove the barricades themselves if the residents refused.[19]

The optimism engendered by this move quickly dissipated as troops were then forced to use tear gas to break up a Protestant crowd during the first serious confrontation between rival factions in the city for three weeks. The trouble started after Catholics gathered at the Falls Road end of Percy Street and waved a Tricolour. Almost immediately hundreds of Protestants from the Shankill area poured into Percy Street as fifty troops formed a line to keep the two sides apart. It was as both crowds began to swell that the Army used tear gas. Police, as well as women and children, were affected by the gas. As news spread of the incident buses were hijacked to form new barricades elsewhere in Protestant areas.[20] Early the following morning a vigilante was shot dead in the Oldpark district of Belfast. He was Jack Todd, aged twenty-nine and a Protestant. Another man was hit in the heel.[21] As a result of the killing a number of Protestant families began to move their belongings out of their homes in Alloa Street, the scene of Todd's murder. The number of empty houses in the street now increased to around a dozen. One man said: 'I suppose for some people here the shooting was the last straw.'[22] From Westminster, Captain Orr criticised the progress made in restoring law and order by Freeland. Orr hoped the GOC understood 'that he is not in Ulster as some sort of impartial referee between the leaders of a rebellion and the forces of law. He is here in Ulster at the request of the civil authority and his clear duty was to restore the authority of the civil powers.' The Queen's writ must be made to run in every corner of Northern Ireland. The forces of law and order must prevail or parliamentary government had no meaning: 'We cannot go on in a society having areas where the law, as laid down by Parliament, does not in fact exist. Where people are setting up their own forms of law. It is a negation of Parliamentary government. It is intolerable and must be brought to an end as soon as possible.'[23]

This was the background to the problems facing the Northern Ireland Government. In Londonderry any suggestion that the security forces should take action against the barricades was vetoed by the local Commanding Officer and the RUC who had indicated to the Northern Ireland Government that their removal there should not be attempted by the use of either force or sanctions.[24] Now weekend tension and a damaging press report of Army negotiations with the IRA had changed the situation making it more difficult for the Government. The cabinet agreed that the military authorities should be pressed for a clear statement of their intentions with regard to the removal of barricades.[25]

On the evening of 9 September Chichester-Clark made a dramatic television address. He announced that all barricades were to be removed in all areas of Belfast and a 'Peace Line' was to be set up between Divis Street and the Shankill Road: the present situation in the city of Belfast could not be allowed to continue. Ordinary life was being paralysed. Irresponsible broadcasts from pirate radio stations were stirring up new hatreds and, above all, the many barricades were strangling the whole community. 'We cannot and we will not tolerate any further drift into anarchy. The elected Government is not going to surrender its authority to a mischief-making minority which had a minimum of real support.' Some people continued to justify the barricades on the grounds that they would remain until their demands had been met, but: 'The plain fact is that every demand—I repeat, every legitimate demand—is being met.' This did not mean appeasement or putting any of the constitution's fundamentals at stake. The Prime Minister considered demands that the forces of law and order—upon which the authority of any state rested—should be disbanded and that the Northern Ireland Government should step down or be suspended as 'absurd. To give them the slightest countenance would be to surrender to mob law.' Those making these 'foolish demands' were 'wasting their breath'. There was now an 'absolute guarantee' from the GOC to give the people behind the barricades protection. Chichester-Clark ended by putting a stark choice before the people of Northern Ireland: 'Bring the barricades down. Start tonight, or tomorrow, but start quickly. What do we want—more jobs, more houses or more funerals? That is the choice if we continue in this state. We have already had too many of the last already.'[26]

Oliver Wright was not impressed. He thought this gave the impression that the Northern Ireland Government was allowing the initiative to pass to its own supporters, who resented the agreement with the British Government, and so did nothing to restrain the 'wild men' on the Protestant right. In his despatch to London, Wright noted that the Prime Minister's statement, by giving the smack of firm government, succeeded in satisfying the Unionist majority and containing the Protestant backlash. Captain Long, the Minister of Education, described it to Wright as the finest speech by an Ulster Prime Minister ever. Unfortunately, by a breach of confidence on the part of the television authorities, the Prime Minister's speech was leaked, 'doubtless in a garbled and tendentious version', noted Wright, with the result that 'all hell broke loose' on the Catholic side. Instead of Wright being able to put Cardinal Conway in the picture in advance of the broadcast, virtually all the key Catholic churchmen were upset: he got a furious Father Murphy on the telephone, followed by an irate Bishop Philbin, followed by an angry Cardinal Conway. Father Murphy spoke of a 'declaration of war', Bishop Philbin demanded the cancellation of the Prime Minster's broadcast and the Cardinal registered a formal protest. Wright spent the next twenty-four hours trying to restore the situation. Two telephone calls to the Cardinal that evening, giving assurances—after consultation with Freeland—that the Army would pursue a policy of gradualness and provide massive protection, produced a much-subdued Father Murphy on the television that evening.[27]

On the morning of 10 September Wright met Conway at his palace to discuss the political situation. The Cardinal expressed a basic fear: the impression was growing among the Catholic community that people in Britain were losing interest in Northern Ireland. This would be disastrous, for if it were so the prospects for Northern Ireland would be very bad indeed. Wright at once assured the Cardinal that those who had this impression were totally mistaken. The facts, indeed, were quite the contrary. Britain was now probably involved in the affairs of Northern Ireland to a greater degree than at any time during the fifty years of its existence. Wright assured the Cardinal that these fears were groundless. The Cardinal, however, repeatedly impressed upon Wright the extreme uncertainty, and terror even, under which the Catholic community in Northern Ireland, and particularly in Belfast and Londonderry, were living. They had had no justice for fifty years. They did not trust the Northern Ireland Government, the Unionist Party or the Orange Order. They were desperate in their fear for their safety. The British authorities must understand how delicate the situation was. In reviewing his meeting with the Cardinal, Wright feared that there had been a crisis of confidence, but he hoped that the situation might in some measure have been retrieved. But 'Irish memories are long and this will not soon be forgotten.' Wright's efforts, however, seemed to have paid off when the Cardinal subsequently issued a statement which appeared in the *Belfast Telegraph* that evening:

'DO NOT OPPOSE SOLDIERS'—CONWAY
'Firstly , I sincerely hope the promise of massive military protection will be fulfilled—and will be seen to be fulfilled.
'Secondly, I am confident that the people in the barricaded areas will be truly wise and not allow themselves to be provoked into opposition to the military. Some people would dearly love to see conflict between the people and the military. Make sure they are disappointed.'[28]

In the afternoon Wright had the opportunity to inform Chichester-Clark at Stormont Castle in general terms of his visit to Armagh and discussed with him the Cardinal's proposal that a statement should be made that the Government would not use the Special Powers Act when the barricades were withdrawn. The

Prime Minister was sympathetic to this proposal and asked that it should be examined and a form of words submitted. At 4.30 p.m. a meeting was called, chaired by Porter, with Basil Kelly present, to discuss the possible form of words. At 5.15 p.m. a form of words was approved as follows: 'Fears have been expressed that on the removal of existing barricades, the Minister of Home Affairs may invoke the Special Powers Act to detain or intern those who have been involved in the erection or maintenance of barricades. The Minister has no such intention. Those persons against whom there is evidence of breaches of the Criminal Law will be liable, of course, to prosecution in the ordinary way.'[29]

Earlier in the day the Army had started setting up the Belfast Peace Line; no one probably thought that their successors would still be extending it thirty years later. Freeland announced that troops would start removing barricades throughout the city. Asked how the Army was going to tackle the task of removing them, Freeland said: 'It is not going to be a great military operation. We are not going to charge in and say to people we will shoot you if you don't remove the barriers, I hope we can get them down with co-operation. But we must be firm about it—the barricades must come down.' A wooden and barbed-wire obstacle was set up between the Falls and the Shankill—the first step towards the removal of the barricades. Freeland added that these new barriers would be 'a very temporary affair. We are not going to have a Berlin wall or anything like that in this city.' Earlier, Catholic councillors had agreed the path for the Peace Line after a meeting with the Lord Mayor and town clerk. It would start at Cupar Street on the Springfield Road and run along an irregular course between Protestant and Catholic areas to the Brown Street area. After the barrier had been erected there was to be a systematic removal of barricades on the edge of the city, moving inwards.[30] In fact, by the next day, the Army appeared to be marking time as plans to remove barricades from the periphery of Belfast proved unnecessary because of the voluntary response of people on the ground. More than twenty barricades were removed in this way during the night following the Prime Minister's broadcast.[31]

But this left others intact. With Chichester-Clark demanding the dismantling of these barricades a deputation of Catholics promptly flew to London to seek Callaghan's support for their retention. The party included three MPs, Paddy Kennedy, Paddy Devlin and Gerry Fitt, as well as Father Murphy and Tom Conaty. They were accompanied by Jim Sullivan, whom Callaghan knew to be a member of the IRA and whom he therefore refused to see; Sullivan waited in an ante-room. After a rather difficult five-hour meeting the participants agreed on a formula: that the local Army commander would first discuss the security situation with the people behind the barricades, that he would assess the requirements for military protection and how they could best be met and that the barricades would be removed either by the local people alone or with the help of the Army. After this agreement Callaghan gradually shifted his weight from reassuring the Catholics to showing understanding of the Protestants. He thought that the

Catholics now had adequate protection and that their fears were less necessary than they had been: 'They now seemed to be exploiting those fears and I felt that the Protestants had a case for saying that since the troops were available in sufficient numbers, there was no reason why the barricades should stay.'[32]

This was not enough for many members of the Northern Ireland cabinet who wanted to tie Freeland and the Army to a definite timetable for the removal of barricades. Chichester-Clark cautioned his colleagues that it would not be reasonable at this stage to seek to tie down the GOC although he agreed it was vital that continued progress on removal was seen to be made. Nevertheless, Fitzsimmons, the Minister of Health and Social Services, supported by other ministers, expressed concern at the general impression fostered not only by the turn of events but also by certain press reports that recent Government decisions emanated from Westminster rather than Stormont.[33] Wright reported to London that the Northern Ireland Government finally accepted that the formula in the Home Office communiqué was a fair compromise only on the grounds that it eased the public formulation of the Army's terms for removing the barricades as a return for a firm commitment on the part of the 'Wild Irishmen in Mr. Fitt's party' to help with dismantling the barricades. They feared, however, that the Army would be bound to keep its part of the bargain and doubted whether Fitt would keep his. At best, therefore, the meeting would assist the removal of the barricades at some slight, but containable, erosion of the authority of the Northern Ireland Government; at the worst, if Fitt double-crossed or procrastinated, the Northern Ireland Government might be unable to contain the Protestant backlash, and it might lose the capacity to control events. If that were to happen, Wright warned that they would be unable to sell to their supporters any recommendations relating to the reform of the police and might fail to carry their reform programme through Parliament. A lot was therefore at stake. Fitt's party had been out of contact for most of the day after the Callaghan meeting and had declined to meet Major General Dyball, Deputy Director of Operations, on 13 September, professing that they needed time to work on their followers. Wright's comment was: 'We shall see'.[34]

In fact many of the Belfast barricades came down—but not all. Instead, a decision that the barricades were to remain in twenty-three Catholic areas of the city—Ardoyne, Cormac Square, Clonard, Cavendish Street, Whiterock, Ballymurphy, Falls, Ballymacarrett, Unity Flats, Barrack Walk, New Lodge Road, Dock, North Queen Street, Turf Lodge, Divis Tower, St James, Rockmount Street, Iveagh, Hamill Street, La Salle and Beechmount—was taken at two weekend meetings of the Belfast Central Defence Committee. A statement from the CCDC—which claimed to speak for 75,000 Catholics—said delegates had made it known that an overwhelming majority of people wanted the barricades to remain until 'precise agreement is reached on adequate military protection'. It added that general discussions could not take place until the chairman of the CCDC had received a written undertaking, as requested, from Major General Dyball to the effect that the Special Powers Act would not be invoked against anyone at any time within the barricaded area. In addition to this the statement said that, as part of any future negotiations, the CCDC, in conjunction with local citizens' defence committees, outlined six demands. They wanted:

1. Disarming and disbanding of the Ulster Special Constabulary;
2. Disarming and reorganisation of the RUC;
3. Repeal of the Special Powers Act;
4. Amnesty for those who defended their homes during an attack on the Falls;
5. Implementation of the Civil Rights covenant;
6. Westminster legislation over the heads of Stormont in the event of the Northern Ireland Government's failure to implement the necessary reforms.[35]

Thus it was that on the afternoon of 15 September the issue of the barricades came to a head.[36] The Northern Ireland cabinet met to consider the statement. Chichester-Clark told his colleagues that he had been informed that Conaty and Father Murphy had stated that this did not give a true picture of the views of the majority of the people within the barricaded area. Their concern was rather for the extension to everyone within the barricades of the assurance given by Porter that the Special Powers Act would not be used against them. Callaghan was aware of this and had confirmed that the additional conditions could not be tolerated.

But this was no longer enough: the mood in the cabinet was for immediate action. It expressed the gravest fears about the situation which would arise if barricades were not removed at once; if bloodshed was to be avoided a strong Government statement—backed by Westminster—had to be issued rejecting the demands and making it clear that removal of barricades would go ahead quickly. Roy Bradford argued that in asking Callaghan for British Government support it should be made clear to him that unless such support was given, together with a guarantee of speedy implementation, ministers would have to give serious consideration to their own positions. Bradford had caught the mood of the meeting: he won the support of his colleagues and, having agreed the course of action to be pursued, the cabinet accordingly adjourned to allow a suitable statement to be drafted for agreement with the Home Secretary.[37]

As this drama was unfolding Wright and Freeland were in Downing Street having been recalled to London for a meeting with Wilson and Callaghan. Before going into a preliminary meeting with Callaghan, Wright received a message that Harold Black wished to have a word with him. Black told Wright about the CCDC statement. Wright informed the Home Secretary; he had already heard about the statement on the news. Callaghan telephoned Conaty and told him that the statement went far beyond the protection of the Catholic community as discussed with Fitt. This dealt with political matters which were quite clearly the concern of the elected representatives of the Northern Ireland people at Stormont and of the elected representatives of the British people at Westminster. There could be no question of negotiating on political matters with a body of people who had no political standing. Callaghan warned that the CCDC was near the knife-edge of disaster. Subsequently Conaty telephoned back to say that he was issuing the following statement to the local broadcasting stations in Northern Ireland:

> With regard to the earlier statement about the barricades in the Catholic areas of Belfast, the position is much more flexible than indicated. The London agreement was accepted. Already progress has been made in negotiation with the military authorities in some areas, the Central Committee indicated that each area was free to negotiate independently. It is likely that definite progress regarding removal of the barricades will be made very quickly.
>
> Mr. Conaty said that he had agreed the statement with Mr. Fitt, Mr. McSparran and Father Murphy. He added that the Bishop would be attending Mr. Conaty's meeting that evening.

At about 5.30 p.m. Wright was called out of the cabinet rooms to take another telephone call from Black who said that the Northern Ireland cabinet were at present in session and that he had been instructed by Chichester-Clark to speak to Wright in the following terms. There was unanimity in the Northern Ireland cabinet that there would have to be a strong statement from the Northern Ireland Government if it was to retain its credibility. They wished to issue a firm statement about the removal of the barricades, including a timetable. The Northern Ireland Government felt they had arrived at the crunch in the matter of the barricades and that unless there was a firm statement with a time limit, it could not be excluded that they had reached a situation where they would have no alternative but to tender their resignations. Wright at once said that he would convey the substance of his call to the meeting, which was being chaired by Wilson. Meanwhile Wright hoped that Black would persuade his Government not to issue such a statement until there had been consultation between the two Governments: it was essential in these circumstances that the two Governments should take counsel together and reach agreement on their future course of action. The Downing Street meeting finished at about 6.30 p.m. Just after this, Callaghan, with the authority of Wilson, telephoned Chichester-Clark to say that he thought the line the two Governments should take was:

a) that they should repudiate any political demands from behind the barricades: responsibility for legislation lay with the Northern Ireland Parliament and in the last resort with the Parliament at Westminster;

b) the two Governments should repeat that they were prepared to negotiate, but only about the conditions for ensuring the safety of the people behind the barricades, and reaffirm that the barricades would have to come down;

c) General Freeland would be returning immediately to Northern Ireland to discuss with the Northern Ireland Government the nature and manner of the removal of the barricades if the negotiations did not succeed. General Freeland was not authorised to negotiate on matters of politics; he had full authority to negotiate about anything concerning the safety and protection of the people behind the barricades.

Callaghan pointed out to Chichester-Clark that it would be most unwise to talk in terms of timetables and ultimata. It was difficult to foresee precisely what would be required. The two Governments could be faced with the position where they would have to conduct urban guerrilla warfare, a thing which the British Army had not done before. One would have to think in terms of the evacuation of women and children and so forth. Chichester-Clark appeared to take these points on board and to accept Callaghan's proposals for future action. Wright then returned with Freeland to Belfast where they arrived at 10 p.m.[38] Chichester-Clark reported back to his cabinet that he had spoken to Callaghan who had agreed to give his full support to the action proposed. The GOC would call in the morning to discuss the method of removal of barricades and Callaghan would, in a televised interview later in the evening, make it clear that he completely rejected the idea of political demands being brought in as a condition for removal.[39]

In the meantime Cardinal Conway had telephoned Wright's offices at about 7.30 p.m. Austin Wilson, Wright's No. 2, explained that he had not yet arrived back from his talks in London. Conway agreed to speak to him instead. He told Wilson that Father Murphy had been talking to him earlier in the day about the statement issued by the CCDC. This statement had been issued by a so-called press officer of the Committee but, in Murphy's view, it seriously misrepresented the mood of the meeting at which he had himself been present. In fact, according to Murphy, a much more flexible attitude had been adopted by the majority of those present and there was no question of general support for laying down specific political conditions as the only basis for negotiation with the Army. Murphy had appeared on one of the six o'clock news programmes and had expressed a much more moderate view than the one which had been given so much prominence earlier in the day. In short, the Cardinal's message was to the effect that he hoped that the authorities—by which he meant both the United Kingdom and Northern Ireland Governments—would not take that press statement at its face value.

Secondly, Cardinal Conway wanted Wilson to be aware that Bishop Philbin and Father Murphy were both going into the Falls Road area that evening, with his authority, in order to attempt what he described as 'a big push' in the struggle to get the Catholic barricades down. He was quite hopeful that, in the light of the flexible position which he was sure would be adopted by the majority of the people behind the barricades and in the light of the encouragement to remove the barricades that would be given by Philbin and Murphy, some real success might be achieved in the very near future. However, Conway was certain that the position in the Falls Road area that evening would be a very delicate one and he was therefore most anxious that nothing should be said or done, either in London or Belfast, which would mar the chances of achieving Catholic co-operation in the removal of the barricades. In particular he was anxious that no words should be spoken which could possibly be interpreted by Catholics as an ultimatum. Wilson assured Conway that he would pass this information on to the Home Secretary in London at once.

Later, at about 8 p.m., Wilson spoke to the Home Office's Private Office and he arranged for Callaghan to be made aware of Conway's intervention before he left the Home Office for the television studios. Wilson also telephoned Harold Black in order that the Northern Ireland Government should be equally aware of what Cardinal Conway had said. Having done both these things, Wilson spoke again to Conway largely in order to give him advance warning that Callaghan would be making a television broadcast later that evening. It was clear to Wilson from his previous conversation with him that Conway did not know definitely that anything of the kind was proposed. Wilson told him that he could not give him any definite information as to the terms in which the Home Secretary would speak. By this time, the Cardinal was already aware that the Northern Ireland Government intended to put out a statement of its own. He told Wilson that he intended to place on record his deep regret that such a statement was to be made at this particular time.[40]

When issued, the statement agreed by Belfast and London recalled that Chichester-Clark had already demanded that all barricades must be removed. The cabinet now reaffirmed this view without reservation and expressed disappointment that this 'reasonable demand' had not been complied with by all of those behind the barricades. As the democratically elected Government, the cabinet completely rejected any political demands of the nature specified by the Citizens' Defence Committee in their statement—demands which clearly could only properly be made through the normal parliamentary processes. The Northern Ireland Government restated that the security authorities would ensure adequate protection for all citizens wherever required after removal of the barricades. In these circumstances the Government insisted that the barricades come down. Ministers would be discussing with General Freeland the following morning the nature of the operations involved and the manner of dismantling the barricades. The Prime Minister had been in touch with the Home Secretary that evening and he had indicated his support for the attitude of the Northern Ireland Government in this matter.[41]

On his return to Belfast, Wright telephoned Black at about 11 p.m. in order to take the temperature at the Northern Ireland end. Black reported that while the cabinet had agreed the statement there had been considerable muttering and rumbling in some quarters about the absence of any reference to a timetable. In particular, Faulkner, and to some extent Bradford, felt that the statement had not gone far enough. Callaghan's subsequent appearance on television had tended to denigrate the Northern Ireland Government and reduce them to the status of puppets, and the question of some resignations at least was by no means excluded. Black had not heard or seen Conaty's alleged statement; when told of its content he agreed that it amounted to a very substantial retraction, but the important thing was to establish whether or not it had been made. Wright and Black agreed to compare notes again at 10 a.m. the following morning.[42]

The next day, 16 September, was, as Wright noted, 'Clearly, the day of crisis'. There was a meeting at 12 noon at Stormont Castle between the whole of the Northern Ireland cabinet on the one hand and Freeland and Wright on the other. Wright and Freeland found the Northern Ireland ministers in a rather sombre and belligerent mood to start with: they made it clear that action was needed on the barricades if they were to hold their own position with their own followers. When Freeland indicated his plans for the gradual removal of the barricades he was repeatedly asked to propose a timetable and a schedule; he repeatedly refused. Wright then gave an account of the Home Secretary's reaction to the noon statement of the Central Defence Committee of the previous day, of Callaghan's telephone call to Conaty and Conaty's subsequent reply. Wright read out the text of Conaty's reply to the cabinet and said that if this was accurate and represented the true situation inside the Central Committee, then it represented a very considerable back-tracking from the extreme political demands of the previous day. It might be too optimistic to say so, but on the best interpretation it might well mean that they should see movement very shortly. At about this moment, 12.30 p.m., news started coming in from the barricades. First one then another street agreement was reported; first one then another confirmation that barricades had actually been brought down. By 1 p.m. the news was coming in 'rather like election results'. The mood of the meeting changed markedly. The meeting broke up at 1.15 p.m.[43]

The Belfast barricades began coming down with virtually no opposition. Three infantry battalions—about 1,800 troops—were used in the Falls to provide protection and to assist the residents in dismantling the obstructions. A combined military–clerical diplomacy was conducted by Major General Dyball and Father Murphy who, together, conducted street-by-street negotiations with local residents. Bishop Philbin also toured the Falls urging people to remove the barricades. Residents were given leaflets signed by the Minister of Home Affairs promising adequate protection and guaranteeing immunity from action taken under the Special Powers Acts.[44] The Army erected their own barriers to replace the civilian ones. In Leeson Street, Army engineers installed corrugated iron barriers at the junction with the Grosvenor Road. These were to prevent traffic moving quickly into the street. At the Falls Road junction of the street heavy steel shuttering, which for six weeks had formed a barricade there, was converted into make-shift sentry boxes for the soldiers on guard duty.[45]

By now Wright was pretty certain that this crisis was over, but the 'patient is still in a post-operative state'. Wright believed that the crisis had passed, very largely due firstly to the Home Secretary's firmness in dealing, through Conaty, with the attempts at a double-cross by Messrs. Fitt and Co.—'double-cross is perhaps too strong a word; but they were certainly testing the Home Secretary to see how far they could push . . . without keeping their part of the bargain first'; secondly and within that context to General Freeland, who had handled the Northern Ireland Government with great tact and firmness; and finally to the people on the ground who actually gained the confidence of the people behind the barricades: General Dyball as the commander on the one hand and Father Murphy and his parishioners on the other. Bishop Philbin had put in a tactically important appearance in the Falls in the course of the day. Wright suspected that the whole Catholic operation was directed strategically, with great skill and wisdom, by Cardinal Conway.

The only people who made little or no contribution to this whole exercise were the Northern Ireland Government. They made a couple of firm broadcasts which had the effect of keeping their extremists in order and also, and perhaps just as important, warning London that things could not just be allowed to drift. But if the crisis was over, they had now to seize the political initiative: 'We have got the ball out of the scrum for them: they must now run hard for the line.'[46] Developing this theme Wright observed that 'Father Murphy had gained possession of the ball in the scrum, General Dyball, as scrum-half, had given him, Chichester-Clark, an excellent pass, he now had the ball and it was up to him to run for the line with it.' There was then some further elaboration of the metaphor. It was agreed that the ball was rather slippery: there was a back-row forward named Craig who was breaking rather swiftly from the scrum: and further away there loomed the figure of full-back Paisley. While Chichester-Clark took all this in very good part, it seemed to Wright to 'need a tremendous lot of voltage input to get the tiniest spark of output' from the Prime Minister.[47]

This was almost, but not quite, the end of the drama. In Derry the situation was a little more complicated: as the Belfast barricades were coming down the ones in the Bogside and Creggan were built higher. Sean Keenan said the decision had been made as a protest against Callaghan's call for their removal. According to Keenan the OC of the troops in Derry, Colonel Charles Millman, had assured the DCDA that he would do his best to honour the guarantee given by Brigadier Peter Leng, Commander of the 24th Infantry Brigade, that the barricades would not be removed until he had seen the findings of the inquiry into the RUC. But Millman stressed that he would have to abide by the orders given to him.[48] Paddy Doherty disagreed: he personally felt that the barriers should come down, but he suggested a white line might be painted on the roadway indicating the boundary of Free Derry. The Army had agreed that if this was done they would not cross the line unless invited to do so. No members of the RUC or Special Constabulary would be allowed in. Nor would the vigilantes be disbanded. Some force, said Doherty, was needed to maintain law and order until the inquiry reported. He added: 'If the . . . recommendations are not acceptable, the barricades could go up very quickly again.'[49] The Army, however, denied that it had agreed, either verbally or in writing, not to enter the Bogside when the barricades came down. The DCDA then declared that they would, after all, remove the barricades—but neither the police nor military would enter the Bogside. Military police could enter but only at the request of the DCDA watch committee. The DCDA denied that there was any real conflict between the Army and their statements.[50] After all-day negotiations on 18 September between the Army and the DCDA agreement was reached for the Derry barricades to come down. They largely reflected the terms set out by the DCDA earlier: no police or USC until after the inquiry reported and no military incursions without the invitation of the residents. As if to reinforce the opposition to the RUC a police car which ventured near the Little Diamond barricade was attacked with stones and petrol bombs hours after the announcement was made.[51]

Extra troops and police were drafted into Derry as the Army announced plans for a one-and-a-half-mile peace line separating the main Protestant and Catholic areas on the west side of the city. With the arrival of a company of the Grenadier Guards in support of the Queen's Regiment, troop levels in the city were up to just over 700 men.[52] The barricades now came down. Paddy Doherty explained to Eamonn Gallagher from the Republic's Ministry of External Affairs, who was on an intelligence-gathering mission to ascertain the mood of Northern Nationalists, how this was achieved. Gallagher was clearly impressed by Doherty. He reported that Doherty had made enormous strides in developing 'moderate and intelligent leadership'. Gallagher understood that about twelve of his committee were followers of Eamonn McCann or of the 'extreme IRA'. On all critical issues, however, they were out-voted by a total of seventeen moderates on whom Doherty could count. This enabled him to take initiatives on occasions which were not pleasing to the hard-liners, knowing that the committee as a whole would back him up: for example, when Doherty decided that it was necessary to take down the barricades in order, as he put it, to retain the initiative, he knew that he would have majority support, and all the rest including the 'negotiations' with the British Army representatives was just for show.[53]

CAMERON AND HUNT

The Cameron Report was published on 12 September 1969. It was, in some instances, a damning indictment of years of Unionist neglect. For the underlying causes of the disturbances of October 1968 it identified seven factors: a rising sense of injustice and grievance among large sections of the Catholic population in respect of the inadequacy of housing provision by certain local authorities; unfair methods of allocation of houses built and let by such authorities and the misuse in certain cases of discretionary powers of allocation of houses in order to perpetuate Unionist control of the local authority; complaints of discrimination in the making of local government appointments, at all levels but especially in the senior posts, to the prejudice of non-Unionists and especially Catholic members of the community, in some Unionist-controlled authorities; complaints in some cases of the deliberate manipulation of local government electoral boundaries; a growing and powerful sense of resentment and frustration among the Catholic population at failure to achieve either acceptance on the part of the Government of any need to investigate these complaints or to provide and enforce a remedy for them; resentment, particularly among Catholics, as to the existence of the USC as a partisan and paramilitary force exclusively recruited from Protestants; widespread resentment among Catholics at the continuance in force of regulations made under the Special Powers Act, and of the continued presence in the statute book of the Act itself; and fears and apprehensions among Protestants of a threat to Unionist domination and control of Government by an increase of Catholic population and powers, inflamed by the activities of the Ulster Constitution Defence Committee and the Ulster Protestant Volunteers.[54] Cameron observed 'that certain at least of the grievances fastened upon the Northern Ireland Civil Rights Association and its supporters'—such as those above—'were justified in fact is confirmed by decisions already taken by the Northern Ireland Government'.[55]

From London's perspective the impact of Cameron did not generate as much controversy as was originally feared: Callaghan thought his proposals of the previous month had partially defused the situation and that Chichester-Clark's critics had been silenced by the impartial nature of the Report.[56] This underestimated an undercurrent of Protestant discontent—they were basically being told that they were in the wrong. Protestants felt that Cameron failed to understand the relationship between Civil Rights and partition. For Catholics, on the other hand, it was vindication. Cameron marked, following the reforms conceded by Stormont under British pressure and then overt British intervention in the form of military deployment, another advance for Catholics. With Catholics feeling, on the whole, justified in their claims of discrimination, Cameron seemed to offer the chance of a fresh start. Cardinal Conway drew Oliver Wright's attention to paragraph 130 of the Report, the last sentence of which argued that the remedying of deeply held and justified grievances would be a 'major step towards healing the communal divisions which lie so close to the root of these disorders and towards promoting, not only a greater sense of unity within this community but also, as a probable consequence, an increased measure on all sides of loyal acceptance of the Constitution on Northern Ireland'. Conway thought that this sentence should be typed out and hung over the beds of all Northern Ireland ministers: it would do a lot more good than such texts as 'God is Love'. He agreed that the removal of legitimate grievances could bring about a totally new climate of co-operation in Northern Ireland.[57]

Yet Cameron was a difficult pill for the Unionist Government to swallow. It was not based on a comprehensive survey of practices in Northern Ireland's local authorities; rather it was a snapshot of the contentious. But it has to be said that Chichester-Clark and his ministers accepted its conclusions with magnanimity. While accepting the Report overall, Chichester-Clark did not accept it as an unqualified indictment of Unionist government down the years: the Commission had not been asked to survey the history of Northern Ireland or to give a judgment on the overall performance of the Government. Chichester-Clark denied absolutely that, in such things as the locating of new public developments or the promotion of industrial development, Unionist governments had been in the slightest degree influenced by sectarian or political considerations. However, while he could not accept that local government in general had been conducted on other than perfectly proper lines he also admitted that 'we must accept now, and I for one do accept, that some authorities in a number of instances have fallen below these high standards'. The Prime Minister agreed that 'it would have been well—and I say this frankly—if we had grasped this nettle some time ago'. Perhaps they had underestimated the effect which even isolated cases of injustices could have in a divided community. But what he now made clear was that 'we will not tolerate for the future, even in a trivial minority of cases, allocation based upon other criteria than a proper and objective method assessment of need'.

He appealed to the opposition to accept that 'fear and suspicion in this community of ours has never been one-sided. A fear which one does not share and may not understand can often seem absurd, but that does not make it seem less real.' The people the opposition represented would now again have the opportunity to play a full and constructive part in the public life of Northern Ireland. He said 'again' because he believed that it had never been the intention of the founding fathers of the state to debar Catholic citizens from a fuller part in affairs. If, later on, attitudes developed which were harmful to the cause of communal understanding was this not due in a very large part to a standing aside, a refusal of allegiance, a policy of public boycott? But now they had a chance of a fresh start which would only succeed if a basis of confidence was built up by experience at every level.[58]

Following Cameron, the next hurdle for Chichester-Clark was the Hunt Committee on policing. It had sat under the chairmanship of Lord Hunt (Chairman of the Home Office Parole Board and leader of the expedition which conquered Everest) with Sir James Robertson, the Chief Constable of Glasgow (appointed to reassure Protestants because he knew and was known in Northern Ireland)[59] and Robert Mark comprising the remainder of the Committee. The appointment of Mark was a key one. It was he, with Osmond, who had delivered the devastating assessment of the condition of the RUC to Callaghan in the aftermath of the August riots. Consequently the Hunt Report advocated the reforms suggested by the two policemen back in August. The Report's conclusions represented an assault on one of the key institutions of the Unionist community's sense of security. It was always likely to send tremors through that community. For the RUC and the Specials were, to the Ulster Protestant, the guardians of Ulster's security against a ruthless foe. There was a feeling abroad in that community that Westminster did not understand the nature of the threat or that the subsequent dismantling of a force—the Specials—with a detailed knowledge of their locality and the people therein, left a substantial gap in the security force's intelligence network.

It was on 5 October that Callaghan informed the British cabinet that he had now received a copy of John Hunt's report on the future of the RUC and the USC. The Home Secretary considered the security issues involved to be so sensitive that he presented an oral report rather than a memorandum to his colleagues. He also announced the results of the reports from the four joint working parties set up with the Northern Ireland Government. The working party on community relations, which also had advice from the Race Relations Board and Community Relations Commission, had produced three bills: one to establish a Commissioner for Complaints to investigate maladministration by local authorities and public boards, one to establish a Community Relations Commission on the model of Great Britain's and one to deal with incitement to religious hatred. This working party had also explored what to do about areas of discrimination outside the public sector, and had recommended prescribing anti-discrimination clauses in government contracts and seeking the co-operation of trade unions and employers to eliminate discrimination in private employment. Callaghan concluded that the working parties had done a thorough job and, assuming their recommendations were acceptable to the Northern Ireland Government, there was no other major issue he felt he needed to press. Effectively the Home Secretary was saying that all Catholic Civil Rights demands had been met.

The Home Secretary also reported to his colleagues that the working party on public employment had made a detailed review of measures which could be taken in the Northern Ireland Civil Service, local government and statutory bodies. Callaghan reminded his colleagues that the senior Civil Service was almost wholly Protestant for historical reasons: Catholics had not started coming into the Civil Service in any numbers until ten to fifteen years before. Northern Ireland officials did not accept that discrimination was practised in the Civil Service but acknowledged that there was thorough-going practice of discrimination in local authority recruitment and promotion especially among lower levels of staff. The working party's recommendations included the adoption of model codes of practice by local authorities and public boards which were to be made available to employees and applicants for employment, and the appointment of senior officials to supervise the application of the code at lower levels. They recommended an appeals machinery for both statutory bodies. This machinery would be within the purview of the Commissioner for Complaints and the powers of the Parliamentary Commissioner for Administration would be extended to Civil Service staffing.

The Northern Ireland Government had already set in hand arrangements to bring the machinery for Civil Service establishments' work more in line with Great Britain's, but the working party had also recommended using outside members on recruiting boards. Callaghan added that he had maintained close contact with the Northern Ireland Committee of the Irish Trades Union Congress and he proposed to find out what help they would be willing to give to ensure that appointments were made without regard to religion. The working party on housing allocation had examined the model allocation scheme—using a points system based on need—which the Northern Ireland Government had recommended to housing authorities during the summer and which was now being implemented by all but six of the sixty-five housing authorities in the Province. They endorsed the scheme as broadly satisfactory in achieving an impartial method of allocation. But this left the question of whether the Catholic minority would have sufficient confidence in those who administered the scheme and Callaghan had asked the British Government's representative on the working party to ensure that this received detailed consideration. Callaghan wanted to go further and intended to ask that responsibility for housing should be transferred to the Northern Ireland Housing Trust.[60] From this would come a central Northern Ireland House Executive for the allocation of all public housing in the Province and end once and for all allegations of discrimination in housing provision. By Northern Ireland standards, coupled with the O'Neill reforms and the forthcoming police reform, these would be revolutionary given the inability to deal with such grievances prior to the Troubles.

But the immediate hurdle to clear was the Hunt Report and when a draft of the Report was presented to the Northern Ireland cabinet, inevitable though its conclusions might be, it made uncomfortable reading. The cabinet was also was informed that Callaghan was now pushing for an Englishman—Sir Arthur Young, the Commissioner of Police for the City of London—to become the new Inspector-General. Peacocke would have to go. Some members of the cabinet preferred a Scottish rather than an English candidate. Age was also a factor: Young was 62 and it was thought a younger man could give a fair number of years' service before retirement. Faulkner grumbled about attempts by Callaghan to bounce the cabinet into a decision. He wanted a copper-bottomed guarantee from London of the provision of full security for the Province before accepting a civilianised police force. Faulkner was also concerned lest the term 'disbanded' appear in the draft with reference to the USC: this was inappropriate. If there was to be a part-time, locally recruited force drawing on the USC then the term 'disbandment' might involve a breach of faith. The cabinet agreed with both of Faulkner's points.[61]

Chichester-Clark took up these concerns with Callaghan on the telephone. The Home Secretary strongly recommended Young as the person best suited to succeed Peacocke should he, as Callaghan put it, 'retire'. Oliver Wright was wheeled in to reassure the cabinet on this issue. A compromise was reached with the cabinet agreeing that Young should be asked to come to Northern Ireland for an interview with Chichester-Clark and Porter. Further reassurance was obtained from Lord Hunt who met Chichester-Clark after he re-emphasised the cabinet's unease regarding references to the disbanding of the USC. Hunt agreed to delete the term from the final report.[62] The cabinet also wanted assurances that the Northern Ireland Government should control the size of the new force, have a voice in its arming and role and a veto on any proposal that it should be disbanded. In the end, however, the cabinet was aware that they could not insist on this.[63]

Chichester-Clark tried his luck anyway. Callaghan was not enthusiastic. He explained that the British cabinet had grave doubts about the very existence of an armed civilian force. It had come to accept it but only on the condition that if the British Government was responsible for creating it, it must also control it. In reply Chichester-Clark emphasised that if the Northern Ireland Government was to have no control at all over the proposed armed civilian force, reaction in Northern Ireland would be severe and he would be bound to disagree with the proposal. But Callaghan answered that if the force was to be on the MOD budget then control over the question of disbandment, if it should arise, must rest with the Westminster Parliament. The proposal was that the force should be recruited by the Army, be under its discipline and trained by it and that it should be available to assist the Army when needed. He could not accept—and nor would the British cabinet or Parliament—that control in the last resort could lie anywhere but with the British Government. Constitutionally one part of the United Kingdom could not be allowed to run its own army. Consultation between the two Governments was acceptable but responsibility must remain in Westminster. The creation of such a force was a special measure in itself requiring an amendment of the Army Act.

When Chichester-Clark remarked that the present problem would not have arisen if the USC remained, Callaghan replied that a substantial minority of the Northern Ireland public would not tolerate such a proposal. Chichester-Clark warned that if the Report were published unamended he would be bound to state that his Government disagreed with it.[64] Callaghan, however, was in no mood for further compromise: such an action by the Northern Ireland Government would give rise to a very serious constitutional situation and could call in question a number of things on which he and Chichester-Clark had agreed or were likely to agree. The British cabinet had gone as far as they could possibly go. He insisted that publication of the Report must proceed on the lines already planned. Callaghan had called Chichester-Clark's bluff. When told of the outcome the Northern Ireland cabinet consoled themselves they agreed to Callaghan's demands in the best long-term interests of Northern Ireland. All they could ask for were reassurances that the USC would be kept in existence until the new force had been created, with recruitment for the new force beginning immediately, and that sufficient guarantees provided for Northern Ireland's security.[65] It was the best they could get.

The Report itself—minus the odd deletion as requested—was published on 10 October. It proposed that the RUC immediately stop carrying arms on a routine basis in most areas. It rejected the adoption of a new name for the RUC on the grounds that this would be a 'blow to the morale' of many members of the force and would be unpopular with many of its supporters. However, other changes suggested included the adoption of a blue uniform instead of the current green as the symbol most likely to convince the public that the role of the force had been changed (this was never implemented). The Committee accepted that while there was general agreement on the continuing need for a reserve force to assist the regular police in times of emergency, all threats to the security of Northern Ireland from armed incursions and attacks 'are a military responsibility and should rest with the Government at Westminster'. This meant replacing the Specials. The Committee concluded: 'We know that to a man members of the USC are devoted to the cause of Ulster and that they and their forebears have done gallant service and we recognise the value of the anti-guerrilla patrols and armed guard duties they have carried out particularly in times of emergency. We consider, however, that the protection of the border and the State against armed attacks is not a role which should be undertaken by the police, whether they be regular or special.'

The Committee recommended that a locally recruited part-time force, under the control of the GOC, of about 4,000 should be raised as soon as possible. This new force, together with the police volunteer reserve, 'should replace the Ulster Special Constabulary'. The RUC 'should be relieved of all duties of a military nature' and its contribution to the security of the state should be limited to the gathering of intelligence, the protection of important persons and the enforcement of the relevant laws. On the basis of this recommendation it became necessary to improve the acceptability and effectiveness of the RUC in its new role. Accountability was unclear—the Minister for Home Affairs was responsible for law and order whereas the Inspector-General was responsible for operational control and the enforcement of the law, though not accountable to anyone for his operational policies. The relationship made it difficult to refute allegations of partiality. To remedy this the Committee proposed a Police Authority be set up which was representative of the community.

The Committee found the most striking difference between the RUC and mainland police forces to be that the former fulfilled a military as well as a civilian role and that in Northern Ireland the military role had been 'understandably' regarded as of first importance. But policing in a free society, concluded the Committee, depended on a wide measure of public approval and consent. This had never been obtained in the long term by military or paramilitary means. The present policy of the general issue and carrying of arms should be phased out. Automatic weapons, self-loading rifles and revolvers larger than a .38 calibre should no longer be part of the RUC's equipment. While not dismissing the IRA threat the Committee considered that a 'realistic assessment of the IRA to mount serious terrorist attacks would probably not rate it very high'. The greatest threat to order in Northern Ireland was much more likely to be sectarian strife stirred up by extremists on both sides.[66]

To coincide with the Report's publication Callaghan arrived in Belfast, accompanied by Lord Stonham, and attended a series of meetings with the Northern Ireland cabinet on 9 and 10 October. The Northern Ireland Government received their guarantees on security. They in turn 'accepted the principle of a civilianised and normally unarmed' RUC, that the Inspector-General should be responsible to a police authority which was representative of the community as a whole, in principle that the police should be relieved of all responsibility for prosecutions and that a system of independent public prosecutors should be adopted. The USC was to be replaced by two new forces: a volunteer reserve for routine police duties such as traffic control and a locally-recruited military force to protect key vital points and to guard against the threat of armed guerrilla-style attacks, commanded by the GOC. It was noticeable that the adoption of an unarmed police force was conditional upon the security situation throughout Northern Ireland and in particular areas. The new Inspector-General was to be Sir Arthur Young.[67] Peacocke had earlier 'resigned'.[68]

From Catholics the response to the Report was positive. Cardinal Conway welcomed the Report on the basis that what was now proposed was a 'new kind of police force and one which would prove much more attractive as a career to all sections of the community'. He anticipated that Catholics would be willing to join in considerable numbers. Austin Currie also favoured Catholic participation in the proposed new force; Ivan Cooper announced that he would 'certainly urge my supporters to join the new RUC'; while Hume acknowledged that the Report 'gives us a basis for a proper impartial civil police force'.[69] On this basis it seemed to offer the chance for a new departure in Catholic–police relations.

But the Report also provided ample Unionist ammunition for Chichester-Clark's opponents to attack his Government. Paisley described the Report as a 'complete and absolute sell-out to Republicans and the so-called civil rights movement' and warned that Protestants would resist it. It was part of a 'Socialist conspiracy to sell out Ulster so that when the time comes to hand over to the Republic there will be no opposition'. Direct rule would be better than 'this back-door method'.[70] Paisley remained a constant thorn in the Government's side. It was not long before he accused the Northern Ireland Government of planning to have him certified by psychiatrists: as a result of false reports about his health, which he alleged had been put out by the Government, some pressmen had gone to Purdysburn Hospital to see him. Purdysburn was a mental institution on the outskirts of Belfast.[71]

But Paisley, despite his paranoia, was articulating genuine fears and frustrations from within the Protestant community. John McQuade, Unionist MP for Woodvale, echoed these remarks when he demanded that the Government resign and call a general election. They had no mandate to 'change our police force'.[72] And from about this point on, Craig's speeches became more and more militant. He warned of civil war with Protestants and Catholics at each other's throats and predicted that Westminster would be 'loosing a river of blood' if it interfered in Ulster's constitution.[73] He refused to rule out the use of arms if Westminster was to suspend the Ulster Parliament and so remove the rights of the Northern Ireland people to decide their own political future.[74]

On the streets of Protestant Belfast anger with the Report erupted in violence. The most intense rioting was on and around the Shankill Road where three people were shot dead. A total of sixty-six people were injured, most of them by gunshot, in the fighting which began shortly before midnight on the Saturday night after the publication of Hunt and continued until dawn on Sunday morning. Two soldiers were seriously injured, fourteen more were slightly injured and three RUC officers were injured also.[75] Sixteen people were given jail sentences of between four months and a year for their parts in the riots.[76] The dead were Victor Arbuckle, aged twenty-nine, the first RUC officer to be killed in the Troubles; George Dickie, a twenty-five-year-old Protestant from west Belfast and Herbert Hawe, a thirty-two-year-old Protestant also from west Belfast. A member of the RUC's reserve, Arbuckle, who was from County Tyrone, was shot by the UVF. Dickie was killed apparently by the Army. He had a considerable amount of alcohol in his body and appeared to have been wandering about to see what was going on when he was hit possibly by a bullet which glanced off a wall above him. Hawe, a cousin of Dickie, was killed in a separate incident. The circumstances were disputed—the first of many to be so. The Army and police said shots were fired at a petrol bomber. A RUC sergeant said he saw a man in a white shirt throwing a petrol bomb. Another was firing shots from a revolver. An Army major gave instructions that the bomber was to be shot. A soldier leaned over the front of the police armoured vehicle and shot the bomber who was in the act of throwing a lighted petrol bomb. A civilian witness, however, said that he had not been throwing anything when shot. Hawe's family protested his innocence.[77]

The armed confrontation had been an intense affair. Twenty-one-year-old Private Shawn James, a marksman of the 3rd Battalion The Light Infantry, was later awarded the George Cross for spending more than four hours constantly exposed to fire in a bid to contain snipers. At one point his rifle butt was shot away and he reached calmly for another weapon. James was detailed as one of three marksmen for the difficult and dangerous task of identifying persons shooting or throwing petrol bombs at the soldiers and police and for neutralising the hostile fire under specific instruction. His CO, Lieutenant-Colonel John Patrick St Clair Ballenden MC, received the Order of the British Empire for directing and encouraging his troops, showing utter disregard for his own safety. Sergeant John Power was awarded the British Empire Medal for his actions during the riot.[78]

What the violence graphically illustrated was that the immediate problem was to reassure Protestants. Robert Porter put the disturbances down to a mistaken belief that the RUC and B-Specials had been 'sold down the river'. He emphasised that Specials were wanted in the new military force.[79] Chichester-Clark reassured Unionists that there was no 'sell-out' of the USC. They would, in future, have their name and organisation changed but there would be not one but two reserve forces to back up the police and the Army: 'I would have resigned at once if there had been any proposal to leave us naked to attack.' He emphasised that 'The Specials are not being disbanded.'[80] The USC's Staff Officer, Colonel Stephen Miskimmin, tried to give credence to the Prime Minister's claims in a letter to the force's 8,000 members telling them that the Hunt proposals merely meant a shift from one force to another.[81] But these efforts at reassurance were torpedoed from within the Government when John Taylor, the Parliamentary Secretary to the Ministry of Home Affairs, bluntly stated that it was quite clear that the Hunt Report was disbanding the Specials. 'I think it would be slightly dishonest to suggest otherwise.' He did, however, emphasise that the new force would be carrying out the same duties as the USC.[82]

Nevertheless, despite a general unease the Ulster Unionist Council backed the Government's reform package by 426 votes to eighty-nine against with fourteen abstentions.[83] But they, and the rest of the Party, did so with a heavy heart. Chichester-Clark lamented that many Unionist members had been reluctant to take part in parliamentary debates on reform.[84] When the Unionist Parliamentary Party gave its support to the reforms it did, in the words of one member, 'with about as much relish as they would take a dose of castor oil'. Only about half the MPs and Senators turned up to vote.[85]

Callaghan had been in Belfast when the violence erupted. When he travelled to Londonderry he got some idea of the different moods of the two communities. He smiled his way through the Bogside with Sir Arthur Young alongside him. The new Inspector-General announced that his motto was '"softly, softly" [a reference to the title of a popular cop show on TV]. I always keep that in front of me when considering how to handle a situation.' Callaghan received a cooler reception in the Protestant Fountain area. Someone in a crowd said: 'Here's the bugger that sold out Ulster.' Callaghan replied: 'We've given you a new and wonderful police force.' 'We already had the best police force in the world—what do we want another one for?' was the retort.[86]

By 15 October Wright was reporting to London that the political situation in Northern Ireland had taken a turn for the worse in the twenty-four hours following the Secretary of State's departure. Despite two nights of relative calm on the streets, the political situation was far from secure. They were now, as forecast, in the crisis of the reforms. Wright feared that the Northern Ireland Government might have under-estimated the determination of their own right wing to oppose reform and over-estimated their capacity to carry their supporters in the reforms to which they had, in good faith, put their signature. The Northern Ireland Government feared a chain reaction and sought to hold the situation by putting out yet another explanatory statement of what was intended for the B-Specials. This still left the matter of a police presence in the Falls and Bogside—or rather its continuing absence—unresolved. Wright reported to London that faced with the anger of their right-wing supporters, the Government had decided that they simply could not put up with this any longer and maintain their credibility as a Government. The decision of the Joint Security Committee was that Young should visit both the Falls and Bogside, together with the military commanders (the GOC in the case of Londonderry); that the people of both the Falls and the Bogside should be informed that police would accompany the military on joint patrols in both areas starting at the end of the week; that, to start with, the joint patrols would be in daylight only; and that an announcement to that effect would be made.

In Wright's account, at the hurriedly summoned meeting of the Joint Security Committee, Faulkner had warned: 'I shall resign this evening unless action is taken'; followed by Captain Long: 'I agree, I am only in this government to support Jimmy [Chichester-Clark]'; and by 'Beezer' Porter, who said, 'with his typical air of tortured anguish: "I am rapidly losing my self-respect."' Indeed, Young's trip to the Bogside increased rather than diminished the cabinet's sense of crisis once it found out that the Bogsiders were setting up new conditions and Sir Arthur was not thinking in terms of a re-entry into the Bogside before 19 October.[87] This was now coming to a head because, since the beginning of October, the Northern Ireland Government had been complaining that the absence of a police presence in the Bogside and the Falls had been responsible for a 'rising public resentment'.[88] This, of course, meant Protestant resentment.

However, once again, as with the crisis over the barricades, the tension fell away as the RUC, with Royal Military Police (RMP) support, re-entered the Falls and Bogside. This was always on the cards as the Northern Ireland Government was really pushing at an open door. On 8 October, with the agreement of the DCDA, two members of the RMP had entered the Bogside to take statements relating to an accidental death there on 29 August. They were escorted by Sean Keenan and Paddy Doherty.[89] A couple of days later Keenan announced that the DCDA was to dissolve in the hope that Callaghan and the Stormont Government would implement the just society they had promised. Military police and possibly troops would now have access.[90] This finally happened on 12 October. Groups of vigilantes applauded when the Redcaps entered the area. They were later accompanied by unarmed troops from the 2nd Battalion The Grenadier Guards.[91] Overall there was little resistance. In Belfast the CCDC's spokesman, Hugh Kennedy, welcomed an eventual phasing-out of the military and the phasing-in of an impartial unarmed police force.[92] Two policewomen and DI Frank Lagan were the first RUC officers to patrol back on the Falls. Jim Sullivan said he would never have welcomed the RUC under the old Inspector-General but now he believed they would bring normality again.[93] In the Bogside the return of the patrols was greeted with the following comments by local women: 'They're better in than out' and 'If they play fair, we'll play fair.'[94] It might be noted how two of those most favourable and optimistic towards the troops and looking towards the successful implementation of reform—Keenan and Sullivan—were IRA men.

Wright told London that the net result was that 'we have taken this fence in tolerably good order. But there are plenty more ahead.' Assessing the month's events Wright observed that 'Northern Ireland is, of course, Ireland; opinions and tempers and moods are therefore volatile. One hesitates to register and report a mood that may be evanescent.' But the one fairly constant factor in the equation was the pressure under which Northern Ireland ministers, and in particular the Prime Minister and the Minister of Home Affairs, had now been working for months, and the barely repressible desire of Faulkner to take control. Wright considered the pressure cumulative and beginning to take its toll. A television broadcast by Chichester-Clark showed him doing his level best, but the broadcast inevitably raised doubts as to whether or not his best was good enough. Already there was public discussion, encouraged by Craig and publicised by the Unionist *News Letter*, casting doubts upon the durability of the Chichester-Clark Government. Again there was talk about direct rule from Westminster. In these circumstances Wright believed that London still had no alternative but to pursue, for as long as it could, the present policies: to stick by the programme of reforms and to rely on the Northern Ireland Government as the instrument for putting them into effect. The Chichester-Clark Government was clearly in danger of losing both the desire and the will to govern. A few weeks of calm, as opposed to successful suppression of violence, might halt this erosion of confidence but 'I wouldn't like to bet on it. Success for our policy, with Chichester-Clark as the instrument, I regard as still being possible but not probable.'

As Wright saw it the key question was: 'what would we do if Chichester-Clark packs his hand in?' Much would depend on the circumstances in which he did it. At present there was a reasonably united cabinet, with a majority in its own Parliamentary Party and four and a half years to run. What London did not want was another general election in which, feared Wright, the Craigs and the Paisleys would most likely romp home. One man would be very ready to try and form a government and would have a fair chance of success: Brian Faulkner. But, warned Wright, he would be a pill for the moderates and Catholics to swallow and his bona fides had to be at least in question. Yet he was not without his virtues: committed as a member of the present Government to reform, a certain pragmatism, political abilities streets ahead of any competitor in sight and a passionate desire to be Prime Minister. Wright wondered: 'would he be preferable to the alternative: direct rule from Westminster? On the assumption that he is committed to reform and that we still prefer to govern Ulster at arm's length, I suppose the answer is: yes.' Meanwhile, Wright suggested that London's contingency plans should not merely be dusted off and looked at but prepared for urgent action if and when necessary. He warned that if the contingency plans were needed,

> we must hope for but should not assume a peaceful takeover of government responsibilities. Nor should we assume that control of the major towns will be all that is necessary. After seven weeks in Ulster I do not feel competent to form a judgement on the likelihood or otherwise of a countrywide rising at the grass-roots: all I can do is to report that many ordinary sensible people seem to assume that this will happen. They say they are not so much worried about the Belfast and Londonderry mobs as concerned with what will happen when the really rough boys from the countryside join them. I see reports in the newspapers that our forces in Germany are training in riot control: that comforts me a good deal, both the fact and the publicity for the fact. One can only echo in these circumstances the celebrated French dictum: '*Si vous voulez la paix, preparez la guerre*'.[95]

THE ULSTER DEFENCE REGIMENT

On 7 October the UK cabinet had decided to establish the new locally recruited part-time military force recommended by Hunt under the GOC's command. The inclusion of a large number of USC members provoked accusations from Catholics that the Northern Ireland Government was trying to create a new force of Specials. But the inclusion of USC members was a key part of the British Government's strategy. Denis Healy's proposals for the main features of the new force were intended, as far as was possible, to reconcile two conflicting aims. The first was to create a force which would include a substantial number of Catholics and 'members of other minority groups' who were reluctant to join the USC. The second was to ensure that enough people joined the force to enable it to begin a viable existence early in the next year. In practical terms this meant that, in the early months, it must attract a sufficient number of current USC personnel and members of the Protestant community in general. Failure to create a sufficiently large force might make it more difficult to disband the USC at an early date and could require London to maintain a larger permanent garrison than it could afford.

The force would be entirely military and therefore under the control of the GOC Northern Ireland who was responsible to Healy. The Northern Ireland Government had no constitutional relationship with the GOC in regard to the regular forces under his command, and there would be nothing in the legislation at Westminster to establish any formal relationship between them over the new force. They would be able to exercise influence only through consultative processes. The commander of the force would be a regular Army brigadier and there would be a regular Army major and a small regular staff at each battalion headquarters. Healy believed that the presence of this regular element would be a stabilising influence on the locally recruited members and would, through military training, help in shaping a disciplined and efficient force. Decisions to call out the force in whole or in part—or to stand it down—would be under the control of the GOC acting on the Secretary of State for Defence's behalf. The bill establishing the new force would specifically provide the Secretary of State with authority to designate officers empowered to call out the force, who would be officers of the regular forces not below the rank of major, and to prescribe conditions for the exercise of this power. The concurrent authority of the civil power would not be required.

To ensure that membership of the new force would be, and would be seen to be, open to all sections of the community, and eliminate local and sectarian bias, all applications to enlist would be considered and decided centrally at HQNI. The central board would naturally give due weight to the recommendation of the local force commander but would not regard it as conclusive for the acceptance or rejection of individual applications. These and other proposals in the white paper constituted a radical change from the existing arrangements and would ensure that the new force would not simply be the USC under a different guise. In exceptional circumstances it might be necessary to authorise some members of the force to keep arms and ammunition in their homes. On these occasions they would be subject to military law at all times, a measure unprecedented for a part-time force in peace. The actual size of the force would be determined in the light of experience but would not exceed 6,000 officers and men. This number was derived from calculation of the number of guards and patrols required for specific key points, installations and routes, the wide area requiring protection, and the need for relief for members of the force when on operational duty. It represented the maximum requirement which might arise in the next few years. In practice the force would be substantially smaller in the immediate future. Healy quickly realised that it was essential to quickly achieve a satisfactory strength if it was to be politically possible for the Northern Ireland Government to disband the USC. This could only be achieved by transfers from the USC. The appointment of influential county commandants of the USC as battalion commanders of the new force would encourage such transfers.[96]

What to call the new force would be almost as controversial as the inclusion of Specials. The Northern Ireland cabinet decided to push for the inclusion of the name 'Ulster' in the title of the force although, ironically, this was not an issue which they were prepared to press unduly.[97] They pointed out to the MOD that the claim to the title rested on its long acceptance in Crown forces' parlance, for example The Royal Ulster Rifles and The Ulster Division of the Royal Navy Volunteer Reserve. If the prefix 'Royal' was to be enjoyed in the future, as the Northern Ireland Government hoped it might be, the title 'The Royal Northern Ireland Defence Force' could prove rather cumbersome.[98] Eventually the Northern

Ireland Government settled on 'Ulster Defence Force'; Healy preferred to stick to 'Northern Ireland Defence force'.[99] It fell to Robert Porter to try and convince Roy Hattersley, Minister of Defence for Administration, of the justice of Stormont's case. Porter stressed that his Government felt strongly that the word 'Ulster' should be used and not 'Northern Ireland'. Hattersley replied that the latter was the correct description and was worried that if the word 'Ulster' were to be used, Roman Catholics would not join the new force. Porter, however, contested this adding for good measure that where this proved to be correct the person concerned would not be a suitable recruit in any event. The insistence on the use of 'Northern Ireland' would present presentational difficulties for the Northern Ireland Government as many people, quite unconnected with the Special Constabulary, felt that the constabulary in general were being made the scapegoats and that omission of 'Ulster' from the title would be taken as yet another example of the Government's alleged acceptance of criticism levelled at the constabulary. Hattersley undertook to put the point to his colleagues.[100]

It was thus explained to the British cabinet that the word 'Ulster' was geographically incorrect in that Northern Ireland comprised only six of the nine counties of the traditional Province of Ulster and that it carried associations which might arouse Catholic hostility to the new force. Against this it was pointed out that the police force was the Royal Ulster Constabulary and that the Northern Ireland Government attached importance to the concession, which was one of form and not of substance. After further discussion it was agreed that the force should be entitled 'The Ulster Defence Regiment' (UDR) and the white paper was amended accordingly.[101]

Much more controversial, in the short-term, was the decision to send 'application forms' for the new regiment to all members of the Specials. John Hume was angered that application forms were sent 'behind the backs of the British Government and the military authorities . . . in an attempt to reassure the Specials that the new force will be the Specials in another uniform'. The opposition, he warned, would fight this every inch of the way but would also avoid falling into the trap of encouraging Catholics to opt out of enlisting—as the Unionists obviously wanted them to do. In part Hume was replying to criticism of himself and Austin Currie from Eamonn McCann and Bernadette Devlin for 'giving support to an institution which can do nothing but harm'[102]—the UDR. The NICRA Executive had also joined in the criticism of the UDR declaring that the force should have been resisted from the outset. It was clear that a second 'B' force was to be established. If the Specials were welcome to join it why was the existing force being disbanded, they asked.[103]

The applications crisis proved to Hume that the Government was backtracking on the Hunt Report: the present Stormont Government was like previous Governments—unable to stand up to its right wing. Currie agreed: the Hunt Report did not say that Specials were to receive priority in the new force nor did it suggest that the county commandants should be its leaders. The sending out of application forms was an attempt to pack it with members of the 'totally discredited B-Specials'. He also accused Unionist MPs of telling constituents that Catholics would not be allowed into the force because most Catholics were disloyal. When challenged to name the MPs concerned he suggested John Taylor.[104] Currie declared: 'we have recognised their dirty little game': including the application form, an undue emphasis on the Oath of Allegiance for each new member and the tone of recruiting advertisements.[105] Bernadette Devlin, who was now a national figure at Westminster, told the House of Commons that Catholics would not join the UDR because of its name. Specials, on the other hand, would 'feel very much at home' in the UDR because its functions, like its title, had the 'smell of Unionist government' and 'junta politics'.[106]

The stance adopted by Hume and Currie angered Chichester-Clark. He wondered whether the opposition were really interested in the security of Northern Ireland. This, for him, was the nub of the matter. Where initially those associated with the Civil Rights Movement had welcomed the Hunt Report now Fitt was arranging 'panicky' meetings in London while NICRA claimed the white papers establishing the UDR and the part-time RUC Reserve departed from the Report. Chichester-Clark believed that it was 'absolute rubbish' to say that what had now emerged departed from the substance and the spirit of the Hunt Committee. The opposition had received what they wanted—the replacement of the USC—but they glossed over the argument for a defence force. Why was there any surprise over the encouragement of Specials to join the force? The Hunt Committee had spoken of giving all members of the community—and specifically mentioned the USC in this regard—the opportunity to serve the community. No one envisaged that all USC members would be thrown onto the scrap heap. The new forces could not get off the ground without a cadre of trained and experienced men. Those who had risen to political power and influence by constant talk of 'discrimination' now seemed to want to discriminate against loyal men who had served the North well. As for the USC, Chichester-Clark was not surprised that many were bound to regret its passing. It had been associated gloriously with Ulster's history since the earliest and most difficult days and if it had been in the most recent years virtually or entirely a Protestant force, that was no good reason to attack the men who had served in it. He believed that it was a contemptible conclusion on the part of the opposition that every Protestant was a sectarian bigot.[107]

The furore over the application forms was another headache the British Government did not need. While, publicly, Harold Wilson found 'nothing improper' with the advertisements,[108] Healy privately admitted that the application form business had been 'disastrous' to the public presentation of the UDR bill.[109] The problem had arisen from the GOC and the Inspector-General's need to know as soon as possible how many men would be available for duty after 1 January to meet the operational requirements for the UDR which was to replace the USC on 1 April 1970. The 'application form' was intended to provide an attitude survey. It had been drafted by a staff officer and the Ministry for Home Affairs, and

Freeland had not examined it in detail although it had been shown to him before issue. Both he and the MOD agreed that the form was inappropriate as an application form, but 'we had had no idea that it had been intended for use as such'. Similar newspaper advertisements had also come as a surprise to Freeland. General Dyball, Chief of Staff at HQNI, had been aware of the advertisements before publication but had mistakenly assumed that their issue had been agreed in principle in London. He had also assumed, mistakenly, that the Northern Ireland Government 'behaved in a normal manner'. The MOD decided that Stormont 'must not be allowed to make any more statements about the Ulster Defence Regiment without proper clearance'.[110] Porter was informed by Healy that all texts and announcements relating to the UDR had to be cleared by London first.[111]

The first Commanding Officer of the UDR was Brigadier Logan Scott-Bowden; with thirty years' active service in the Royal Engineers behind him he had won the DSO and the MC for swimming under the noses of the enemy to reconnoitre the Normandy beaches. He had three weeks' notice of his appointment; for security reasons he didn't even know what his new job was or where it would be: 'The last place I expected was Northern Ireland.' On 18 February 1970 a Protestant, Albert Richmond, and a Catholic, James McAree, stood side by side and took the Oath of Allegiance to the Queen as they were officially sworn in as the first members of the UDR. 'It seemed a good idea to join,' said McAree, a bookmaker's clerk. 'It will bring people of opposite religions together and I am sure it will be a moderate force both in persuasion and outlook.' Richmond had been in the British Army for six years and this was one of his reasons for joining. 'The other reason is that I feel very strongly about the recent disturbances.'[112] But like so much else, there was always controversy surrounding the composition of the UDR: Lawrence Cullen, one of the first Catholics to join, created a furore on television when asked what he would do if there was an armed invasion from the border; Cullen answered that it was a difficult question and it would be better to wait until that time came. When it was suggested that, after taking the Oath of Allegiance, surely Cullen would know what side he was on, he countered: 'I'm not that stupid; I know what side I am on ... I joined the UDR because it is a non-sectarian force and I want to protect the country against any attack—UVF or the IRA. That's the aim of the UDR. I am married and would like my children to grow up in a peaceful country.'[113]

This initial hesitancy sat uneasy among Protestants who could count on the unquestioning loyalty of every member of the Specials in such a scenario. Gerry Fitt, on the other hand, found that there was 'discontent and concern' about the high proportion of B-Specials applying to join the UDR in Tyrone, Fermanagh, Derry and Armagh. A situation was arising in which it was almost impossible for Catholics to join the regiment in those areas. There was also disquiet over the fact that there seemed to be an absence of Catholic officers.[114] But Protestants also complained: the Reverend John Brown, District Commandant of the USC in Londonderry, found that he had his application to join the UDR turned down.

The Army refused to disclose the reasons for their decision. Brown, a lecturer at Magee College, had declined to appear before the Cameron Commission, calling it 'ill-advised'.[115] In fact what had happened in this and other cases was that, back at the MOD, Healy had found that the only way to limit the political damage done by the application-form controversy was to give an assurance that the USC would play no part whatsoever in the recruiting process for the UDR. He was genuinely anxious to make sure that recruitment was open and fair. While there would be consultation with the RUC on Catholic applicants, Healy also wanted other checks, for example through the British intelligence structure, to ensure that the RUC Special Branch was not prejudicing the case against any Catholic applicant unnecessarily.

Healy decided not to accept, until their innocence had been proved, anyone who was believed to have been involved unlawfully in incidents such as the actions of the Tynan USC Platoon or anyone who could be identified as having played a part in the harassment of the Burntollet marchers. Healy was also concerned about the UDR taking on a number of the county and district commandants of the USC. But Freeland reassured him that the county commandants as a whole were 'not a bad bunch'—the big problem was the district commandants. These would be weeded out.[116] Brown was a district commander.

Just before the Specials were officially consigned to history on 30 April—the original date for their demise was moved back a month—a special service was held at the King's Hall, Balmoral, at which Chichester-Clark spoke. Craig also attended; he wore black ribbon on his lapel. 'I think it speaks for itself,' he said after the service.[117] London hoped these would only be teething troubles before the regiment became operational. But Catholics never quite trusted the Stormont Government over the UDR and Protestants never really forgave it over the USC.

CHICHESTER-CLARK'S TROUBLES: THE UNIONIST PARTY

A history of the opening years of the Troubles has to contain a history of the continuing implosions within the Unionist Party. That the governing party in Northern Ireland was in a semi-permanent crisis of leadership meant continuous instability as it reflected the agonies of the Unionist community in general. This is not an exaggeration as the Unionist Party was less a normal coherent party than a reflection of all sections of Protestant Ulster. Hence its instability. The problem with the UUP was that it was *too* democratic—it didn't actually exist in the normal sense of a centralised party. The Ulster Unionist Council was the decision-making body drawing together delegates from the constituency associations. The UUC met once a year, usually at the Ulster Hall in Belfast. Of the 1,000 delegates attending many were women: it was said that women were the backbone of Ulster Unionism. This was despite the fact that only one MP (Stormont and Westminster) was a woman and few made speeches at the Council meeting. But in fact, not only did they send six delegates from their exclusively female associations but many were also members of the main constituency associations in the Province. Pottinger was one of many Belfast constituencies with more than fifty per cent female representation on the Council: it had eleven out of thirteen delegates. All in all there were two women to every male delegate from the Belfast delegations.

Protestant organisations also had a special representation on the Council. The County Grand Lodges of Belfast were allotted the largest representation in this category—122 delegates. Adding the Apprentice Boys of Derry and the Orange Women meant that one-seventh of the Council delegates were *de facto* Protestants with a pledged support for the constitutional link with Britain. Then there were 120 positions reserved for 'distinguished persons' who were co-opted. The Willowfield Unionist Club, the Unionist Society and the Ulster Reform Club had the same or more delegates than constituency organisations. The Queen's University Unionist Voters' Association might be considered somewhat anachronistic since university seats were abolished years ago. For convenience sake the 'business of the council' was carried on by the Standing Committee, a smaller body of delegates who met quarterly. This was a whittled-down version of the Council— only 360 members—and whereas the Orange Order had a twelve per cent voice in the Council it had less than five per cent of the Committee. But Young Unionists, as well as MPs, Senators and Peers were allowed the same representation on both Council and Committee, which meant that while a small minority on the 1,000-strong Council they had a twenty-five per cent voice on the Committee—as much as all the constituency associations put together. The real hub were the fifty or so men and women who made up the Executive. Thirty-six of these were based on a territorial basis from and by the Standing Committee, including two Unionist Labour delegates, two Orange and two Young Unionist delegates. The rest were the officers of the Standing Committee and the Women's Unionist Council, as well as the Prime Minister, a representative of the Westminster MPs and the Chief Whip. They met once a month at the UUP headquarters in Glengall Street in Belfast.[118] It was in the councils of the associations, the Young Unionists, the UUC and the Standing Committee that members of the 'Party' fought each other.

The reforms had created disquiet within the Unionist Party—it was a hard pill to swallow to be told from outside that you and your system of government were flawed. Chichester-Clark was forced to deny suggestions that the Unionist Party had capitulated to the Civil Rights Movement and yielded to pressure from Westminster. He claimed that every reform on the statute book was there because 'we put it there. It was our decision.' They had been conceived at Stormont.[119] This was stretching it a bit of course but indicated Chichester-Clark's commitment to a new Unionism breaking links with the sectarian past. Yet despite the leadership's zeal for reform the Unionist Party remained in turmoil. The obvious reason for this would be dissatisfaction with reform—but it would appear to be a lot more complex than this.

For example, Chichester-Clark called for an investigation into events at Clifton Unionist Association which had resulted in the expulsion of seven of its leading members, including Major Lloyd Hall-Thompson, the sitting Stormont MP, in a row between 'right-wingers' and 'moderates' that had been out in the open since the 1969 election.[120] This was followed by the resignation of the Association's chairman and nineteen other members of the executive committee.[121] A few days later the former MP for the constituency and anti-O'Neillite, William Morgan, resigned, as did the president, William Irwin along with a vice-president of the Association.[122] The split in Clifton hinged on the 1969 general election row when the outgoing MP, Morgan, was forbidden by the High Court to describe himself as an official Unionist and was then defeated at the polls by Hall-Thompson, an unofficial Unionist. Since then Hall-Thompson had failed to secure the endorsement of the Clifton Association as an official Unionist MP. The internecine strife in the Clifton Association had been bubbling since 1966 when Morgan and the executive committee were asked, in a letter by John Ferguson, a rank-and-file member of the Association, to say unequivocally whether or not they supported the then Prime Minister, Terence O'Neill. From then on the right-wing had been at loggerheads with Ferguson and others who backed O'Neill.[123]

But just how one defined the differences in the Association was unclear: the last chairman, John Hutchinson, of the now inactive Clifton Young Unionist Association, noted that several of the seven recently expelled were instrumental in having their Young Unionist Association disaffiliated 'because of their opposition to Protestant extremism in the party'.[124] Yet John Beckett, as 'one who was born and reared' in Clifton Ward, disputed the commonly used terms of 'Right-wing' and 'Moderates' for the divisions in the Association. He suggested that the only thing which the 'moderates' could attack Morgan on was the claim demonstrated by their chanting of 'Bible thumper, Bible thumper!' during the 1969 candidate-ratification meeting. Beckett concluded: 'What a compliment to Mr Morgan that the only charge they could bring against him was that he was identified with those who belong to the Lord Jesus.' He suggested that in future instead of 'Right-wing' and 'Moderate' the proper terms should be 'Unionists' and 'O'Neillites'.[125] But those present and opposed to Morgan denied calling him a 'Bible thumper' pointing out that many belonged to his denomination: 'His religion was not in question. What annoyed us was that we felt he had "let down" his leader when he was most in need of support. It was a stab in the back.'[126] Beckett, however, rejected this suggesting instead that Morgan was loyal to his party all the way through and loyal to his leader for as long as he could remain so: 'In the name of logic and fair play how can anyone remain loyal to a leader who can support candidates set up in direct opposition to candidates chosen by the very party which that leader was supposed to lead?'[127] There was no mention in this dispute of the reforms since O'Neill had gone: the feuds in Clifton Ward were the result of the O'Neill era but they spilt over into the Chichester-Clark administration. It is probable that such divisions were repeated throughout the Party.

Another hangover from the O'Neill period had been, of course, the fall-out between the then premier and Harry West. One area of the reform package that was certain to rouse Unionists west of the Bann was the Government's commitment to restructuring local government. A new organisation, the West Ulster Unionist Council, was formed in January 1970 to represent Unionist interests in the west. It took over from the advisory committee representing constituency associations in Londonderry, Tyrone and Fermanagh, set up in 1969 to study the reshaping of local government. A spokesmen for the new body explained how 'Often when delegates from the west go to Belfast they find delegates from the east are not on the same wavelength.' The new body would enable the west to speak with one voice. The new Council was to have at least five hundred members.[128] The man who was going to be in its firing line was Faulkner, who brought forward proposals for restructuring local government and transferring the allocation of housing to a new central housing authority. This would, as Callaghan had recognised, break the power of Unionist patronage in the west.

Faulkner took up the task with zest: whatever criticism there could be made of Faulkner's past by his Nationalist/Catholic opponents, backtracking on reform does not stand up to close scrutiny. The UUP's Standing Committee was called to give Faulkner an opportunity of explaining his proposals to Unionist delegates. Following this, in January 1970, about a hundred Unionists met and challenged Faulkner's estimate that support in the Party as a whole for his proposals was around 2–1 in favour. The statement said that twenty-seven out of the thirty delegates who spoke at the Faulkner meeting were opposed to the Government's proposals. Particular exception was taken to the decision to set up the review body and establish a central housing authority without consultation with the Unionist people of the Province. Faulkner identified the opposition at the Standing Committee as coming mainly from the Tyrone, Fermanagh and Londonderry delegates. The statement criticising Faulkner was signed by an Enniskillen delegate.[129]

The challenge mounted by Fermanagh Unionists—Harry West's back yard— became still more evident as the veteran former MP for South Tyrone, W. F. McCoy, called for the Prime Minister to sack Faulkner.[130] Instead Chichester-Clark backed him, pointing out that these were cabinet decisions. At the same time the president of the Local Authorities of Northern Ireland, Councillor Hugh Brown of Belfast, said it was wrong to suggest that opposition to the Government's proposals came from only the west of the Province. He said that all local authorities were concerned.[131] Faulkner was clear, though, that the establishment of a central housing authority was a firm Government decision 'not to be reopened'.[132]

As tensions simmered throughout the Party some self-confessed moderates were under pressure. In late January 1970 it was announced that O'Neill and Richard Ferguson, a noted liberal Unionist, were to resign their seats at Stormont. O'Neill was to formally quit Northern Irish politics to spend much of his time in London where he was soon to be introduced to the House of Lords as Lord

O'Neill of Maine.[133] Ferguson, who said he was going for personal and medical reasons, wondered how much longer Chichester-Clark could hold the Party together: 'Mr John Taylor kicks the O'Neillites in the teeth and Major Chichester-Clark politely offers the service of his dentist to effect the repairs.' He gave Taylor a backhanded compliment with the observation that: 'I suppose every political Party must have its hatchet man—a man who expresses openly what the rest think privately but have not the guts to spit out.' At least you knew where you stood with Taylor, he reflected.

Ferguson recalled that, at the time of his election in 1968, he was pitchforked into a bitter Party dispute. Already a declared O'Neillite, 'I was imprudent enough in an election speech to declare my support for one man one vote in local government election.' He was told politely but firmly to drop it although he was informed that, off the record, O'Neill was delighted while Faulkner was rumoured to be bitterly antagonistic. On his very public resignation from the Orange Order, the issue which he thought eventually forced his resignation from public life, Ferguson believed that a majority of his South Antrim Unionist Association executive was opposed to his re-selection long before he actually resigned. His allegiance to O'Neill was, he believed, the real cause of his downfall. He concluded that the split between the pro- and anti-O'Neill factions was now even more obvious than before: Taylor wanted to eliminate the liberal element in the Party 'and he would win'. Party unity, Ferguson predicted, would be achieved between the centre and the right: 'Many of them would like to see Major Chichester-Clark and the Rev. Ian Paisley walking hand-in-hand up the drive to Stormont.' As to what would become of the liberals, Ferguson thought some of them would slump back into the arms of the Party; others would wash their hands of politics; but a small number would struggle on, determined never again to allow the management of their country to fall into the hands of those unanswerable to their criticism. Nevertheless the rift between these people and the 'official' Unionist Party was widening.[134]

In his resignation speech at Stormont, Ferguson made a plea for tolerance and an end to bitterness. He warned that those who opposed the integration of the two communities 'would, in the long run, destroy the State'. He absolved the Orange Order from any threats, intimidation or pressure in his decision to resign but, as a fourth generation Orangeman, while he never criticised the Order or its principles: 'I do believe most sincerely that the present relationship between the Orange Order and the Unionist Party is harmful to both organisations. It inhibits the Unionist Party from fully opening its ranks to Roman Catholics and it allows the Orange Order to be exploited for political purposes.'[135]

Ferguson's resignation once again opened the debate as to the relationship between the UUP and the Orange Order and the creation of a non-sectarian Unionism. This by its very nature went to the heart of what Unionism and the Unionist Party was—or should be. Roy Bradford, Minister of Commerce, urged the Orange Order to take the initiative in breaking the link with the UUP.[136] He wanted to see more Catholics 'freely active' in the Unionist Party and Catholic MPs on the Unionist back benches 'as soon as possible'. The Party, he said, ought to be all-embracing and totally non-denominational. Bradford believed that the majority of his Catholic fellow Ulstermen and women found left-wing extremism as much anathema as the 'right-wing brand'.[137] But for many this undermined the essentials of Unionism. Mrs Beryl Holland, of Bangor, was one who disagreed with Bradford:

> Speeches by various O'Neillite MPs who want the link with the Orange Order broken prove they are not Protestants and could not be even considered as loyal Unionists . . . attracting Roman Catholics into the Unionist Party . . . means breaking from the Orange Order, the backbone of Ulster, pushing the Union Jack under the carpet and having to omit the singing of the National Anthem before so-called British citizens would join the Unionist Party . . . A total surrender! . . . While the RC Church does not recognise the Constitution and is committed to the reunification of Ireland, Roman Catholics will infiltrate into the Unionist Party to break it up from within . . . The slogan for Ulster Loyalists still remains 'Not an inch! No Surrender!' . . . Ulster must have a Protestant Parliament for a Protestant community, still in the majority, and under a Protestant Queen.[138]

This Protestant Unionism, in its broadest sense, could always pop up its head in the most embarrassing of places: a blatantly anti-Catholic speech during a debate on community relations in April 1970 caused angry scenes at the UUP's annual conference after Harold Wesley, Chairman of the Grovefield branch of Willowfield Unionist Association, opposed a motion in favour of the Government's decision to set up a ministry of community relations. Wesley told the delegates: 'We are protesting against the Roman Catholic Church and its false doctrines. We will not accept the infallibility of the Pope or purgatory. We are standing against the Pope of Rome.' Sir George Clark, presiding at the conference, tried to inter-rupt Wesley, but he continued speaking. 'We are protesting against the Church of Rome,' repeated Wesley. Clark went to the microphone and tried to reason with Wesley. Finally, however, he asked him to resume his seat. Meanwhile many of the several hundred delegates stamped their feet angrily. One woman shouted: 'This is a Unionist meeting. It is not a religious meeting.' Wesley then left the platform. A large majority of the delegates backed the motion, proposed by the Reverend Desmond Mock of the Unionist Society, who told the meeting: 'The lie that all Roman Catholics wish to destroy Ulster must be put to rest. There are many Roman Catholics who are as loyal to Ulster as anyone here.'[139]

The Unionist Party was a reflection of the unionist community: a wide church. Hence the tensions. In fact dissatisfaction in the Party seemed to have no coherent source; rather it emanated from a variety of grievances. Faulkner was angered by how 'dissatisfaction about details has been allowed to swell irrationally into a blanket condemnation of, for example, the Government's policies on housing and local government'. He believed criticism in these fields had been founded on fears of what might be done in the future. There had been protests against nominated boards and bureaucratic machines: 'I would rather have constructive and comprehensive suggestions for the streamlining of local government than listen to vague apprehensions about the loss of democracy or argue within the context of petty prejudices.'[140]

James Kilfedder was labelled by some supporters of Chichester-Clark as intolerant for suggesting that Catholics should found their own pressure group within the Party; he denied this was an attempt to treat Catholics as 'second class' but was a genuine attempt to overcome their 'psychological' barrier to membership. Furthermore he 'wholeheartedly supported' the concept of a central housing authority, believed the system of local government had to be reshaped and supported a civilian role for the RUC. Indeed, 'I have never hesitated to speak out . . . for a progressive Ulster.'[141] As Craig emphasised, the so-called 'rebels' were not challenging the Government on its reform package but on the important decisions affecting security and the economy. He warned that 'Protestant' unionists were leaving the UUP because they had lost faith in it.[142] The Young Unionist Council, containing many future senior members of the UUP such as Reg Empey, Jim Rodgers and Denis Rogan, claimed that the crisis within the Party was precipitated by 'ambitious members' of the Government. It was not caused by a 'so-called right-wing plot' but those hoping that by causing disarray in Unionism they would gain political power. The 'YUs' thought it was 'deplorable' that Chichester-Clark had allowed this situation to develop.[143] Find one group within the UUP and you found another criticism of the leadership.

But none of this was by any means terminal for the Chichester-Clark leadership. As with the O'Neill reforms, internal Unionist Party critics of the Government complained but never sought—except with the disarming of the police—to reverse the decisions. Unrest within the Party increased and decreased according to the security situation. And 1970 witnessed more and more rioting in Belfast and Derry. The restoration of law and order on the streets, and how to accomplish this, became the core division among Unionists. When the disorders were coupled with a mysterious bombing campaign the issue of security became acute. The underlying reasons for the disturbances were a source of division as well.

Chichester-Clark did not apportion the blame to subversive forces. Instead he pointed out that Northern Ireland was, by virtually every index, the most underprivileged region of the UK in housing conditions. The Prime Minister drew the following conclusion: 'Who can reasonably doubt the disorders we have seen in Belfast and elsewhere are due in no small part to the social evils which stem from bad housing?' Whatever the difference, he argued, this was something which the Shankill shared with the Falls: it had to be the Government's aim to offer them, alike, 'something better, something which released them at long last from the chains of environment'.[144]

This was dismissed by his internal critics. Lack of housing and jobs was not entirely responsible for the difficulties in Ulster, concluded Harry West: 'We have in our community a lot of people who are determined to disrupt the constitution of this country.' And it didn't matter what they got from the state because 'they are hell bent on upsetting the constitution,' he added. In West's experience many street demonstrators actually came from new housing estates and this was why he was convinced that housing and jobs were not entirely responsible for the current troubles.[145] Craig believed it wrong to suggest that a traditional Unionist was someone who set out deliberately and with malice to repress any section of the community: those who were called 'hardliners' and 'right-wingers' were 'the people who carry the burden of thinking in progressive and imaginative terms for Unionism'.[146]

And by early 1970 it was the police and security that were the issues over which Chichester-Clark and his opponents clashed in Parliament as the Hunt reforms were implemented. In supporting these the Prime Minister admitted that there might, under extreme strain and pressure, have been those individuals who fell short of the highest standards. Policemen and soldiers were, nevertheless, human beings even though they wore a uniform. As a force the RUC had given splendid service. The policy was now to permit the RUC to concentrate upon a purely police role and to give the force all the human and other resources it needed to provide an exemplary service to the community.[147] These were hardly the words of a Prime Minister seeking to ratchet up the spectre of the enemy within or evidence of an administration dragging its feet over reform. Rather it was a sign of increasing, albeit fragile, confidence. The Minister of Home Affairs took up the enthusiasm for police reform in Stormont too. Porter told Parliament that while it could be argued that it was extravagant and unnecessary to set up a Police Authority simply to insulate the police from political controversy, the electrical analogy could be taken further: 'an insulator might look unnecessary to the casual observer, but it is vital where there is high tension'. Porter argued that previous proposals to restructure the administration of the police had foundered on the rock of its paramilitary role. It was Britain which had removed the obstacle by accepting practical responsibility for the defence of Northern Ireland. The circumstances in which the state had been conceived thrust a paramilitary role on the police force from its inception. That role tended to isolate the police from the life of the community and especially from those sections of the community who already tended to regard authority with suspicion. The Police Bill, incorporating the Hunt reforms, represented a landmark in the evolution of Northern Ireland.[148]

Such platitudes disgusted Craig and West who both abstained as the bill passed through Parliament. Craig dismissed the Government's judgment as faulty, claiming it had been 'hypnotised' by Hunt's talk of the RUC as a paramilitary force. It had never had such a role. He was alarmed that the role of the police was to be changed and disguised by completely false pretences. How could the RUC now operate against a local armed subversive organisation, he asked. The UDR did not seem a satisfactory approach to the problem. The Government had failed the police. It had given sops to the agitators in their midst.[149]

To demonstrate their dissent Craig and West led a backbench rebellion against the bill with a bid to give the Minister for Home Affairs more control over the Police Authority. They were joined by Norman Laird, John McQuade and Robert Mitchell. Their amendment was defeated on a thirty-seven to five vote.[150] This opened up the possibility of disciplinary action by the Parliamentary Party. What made this inevitable was a further act of defiance when the rebels made one last-ditch attempt to amend the bill. West proposed that arms should be maintained at all police stations instead of in central depots only. He claimed that police stations would have been taken over in cross-border attacks if arms had not been available in the past. These attacks were sudden and there would be no time for the UDR or the Army to be called in. Such attacks could reoccur. Porter replied that the police would be issued with arms when required. The aim was to keep the police above controversy and no longer the object of attack by enemies of the state. The existence of the UDR made such attacks less likely and having arms in every police station would be foreign to the concept of a civilian police force. The amendment was defeated by thirty-five votes to five. Later Craig claimed that the bill would not make one iota of difference to the attitude of 'subversive thugs' towards the police. The RUC and the B-Specials had been sacrificed for political expediency while they could have contained the recent challenge to the rule of law in Northern Ireland. The bill, he pointed out, did not in any way transform the role of the police away from that of a paramilitary force—they still had the responsibility to seek out criminals and those responsible for raids or using explosives.[151]

While this opposition to the Government was disquieting it was none the less manageable. There was no united Unionist opposition to Chichester-Clark either in or out of Parliament. The rebels and hardliners were just as likely to be attacked from outside the party. Cue Ian Paisley, who attacked West for attending a requiem mass before the funeral of the veteran Nationalist Cahir Healy. He recalled the rule under which an Orangeman should not, by his presence or by his action, 'support any Papist act of worship'. Paisley also attacked John Brooke— now inside the Government as a parliamentary secretary with responsibility for information—as a 'political somersaulter'. He told an audience in Portadown 'we are caught up in a conspiracy of lies: the Government is lying, the head of the police is deceiving the people, and, as for the Army authorities they are as great a bunch of liars as ever landed in this country'.[152] While Brooke was loathed by many Nationalists, Paisley had identified a weak link in any hardline image he might retain among Unionists: he was haunted by his remark in January 1969 that: 'If I am let down for one moment on that, it is over my dead body, and a hell of a lot of people in Portadown will be dead with me.' The 'that' in the sentence was taken to mean 'one man, one vote' although Brooke denied this: he said it related to the setting up of the Cameron Commission and to the Government's undertaking not to take a decision on the franchise until after the review of local government.[153] Several members of the Corcrain branch of the Central Armagh Unionist Association who claimed to have witnessed his comments disagreed: after hearing of Brooke's latest denial, the view was that 'he said it'.[154]

Despite the above Chichester-Clark felt confident enough, in March, if not to ignore the dissenters, to at least take them on. He used his speech at the annual meeting of the UUC to tell his opponents bluntly: 'Either come with us or go elsewhere.' The choice was between sensible, realistic and moderate government or the strong arm and the jackboot which could only lead to a sectarian bloodbath. He had tried to achieve party unity based on the assumption that most members would accept majority decisions and back up the Government. It was now clear to the Prime Minister that while a great majority of the Party were prepared to play their part there were others who wanted to have the luxury of remaining under the party umbrella yet continuing to fight against accepted party policies. Whenever majority decisions were taken the Party and Government had to be able to rely upon a loyal acceptance of those decisions by all. 'Not to put a tooth on it,' said the Prime Minister, 'for far too long our Party has been giving an impression of internal dissension and bickering. This simply cannot continue for if it does it will undermine in the public mind our whole creditability as a governing party.'[155] If Chichester-Clark thought he was now in a position to club the ball back over the critics' heads then he was soon to learn, once more, that each ball must be played on its merits. The patch of rough outside his off-stump was the by-elections caused by the resignations of O'Neill and Ferguson. From very early on it was clear that Paisley was going to have another crack at Bannside; in South Antrim it was the Reverend William Beattie who was going in to bat for the Protestant Unionists. Beattie's likely opponent was to be William Morgan who declared his support for Chichester-Clark—'I think he is doing a very difficult job very well'—and was upset at being unfairly labelled right-wing: 'This is publicity I don't deserve,' he concluded.[156] This may have been the occasion to stress his right-wing credentials. As the contest gathered momentum Paisley put six questions to Morgan:

1. Are you for or against the disarming and reorganisation of the RUC?
2. Are you prepared to say that you do not want the Ulster Special Constabulary disbanded or disarmed?
3. Can you guarantee that the Twelfth of July demonstrations will go on?
4. Where do you stand in law and order?
5. What are your views on local government?
6. Where do you stand on justice in the courts?[157]

This set out the areas that the Protestant Unionists were going to highlight in the forthcoming contests. They were certainly confident, particularly after Protestant Unionists successfully captured two vacant seats in Belfast City Council in Woodvale Ward in February. Paisley had warned that this election would not be fought solely on local issues, but also on the Government's failings: the disbanding of the B-Specials, local government reform and the handing over of the RUC to outside control as well as the continued 'IRA domination' of no-go areas in Belfast.[158] This approach appeared to have been successful. Both Protestant Unionists were triumphant on 4 February, although only 100 votes separated them from their UUP rivals. The victory doubled the number of Protestant Unionists on the Council. Paisley was clearly intoxicated by the emotion of victory as he declared afterwards: 'This is the beginning of the end of the O'Neill Government—or rather the Chichester-Clark Government. Anyway, it's the O'Neill thing.'[159]

All this was taking place against a deteriorating public order situation. While the Easter disturbances of 1970 had, for a short time at least, convinced the Irish Government that the Doomsday scenario they had long feared had arrived, for the British it initially represented just the latest in a long series of sectarian confrontations. In this latter view, as a Home Office memorandum explained, Easter was dominated by the celebrations of the Republicans provoking, as they always did, counter-demonstrations by the Unionists, and a build-up of tension between the communities both before and during the four-day holiday. There was sectarian trouble in Armagh during a UPV march led by Paisley, and in Londonderry when a Republican mob tried to remove a Union Jack from Victoria RUC Station. There were also sectarian confrontations in Lurgan. Nevertheless, until late on Tuesday 31 March, the Northern Ireland authorities had every reason to be pleased with the outcome. But then a Junior Orangeman's march led to sectarian disturbances. This was followed by a serious outbreak of trouble in the Springfield area of Belfast when a Catholic mob attacked troops. The fighting was renewed the following evening, 1 April. This followed action by the Army to prevent a confrontation of Catholics and Protestants; the Protestant mob was dispersed and the Catholics again turned on the Army. To bring the violence to an end the troops were forced to use tear gas and to charge the rioters. Few arrests were possible and the Army suffered fifty-four casualties. More fighting began in the same area during the nights of 1 and 2 April when the troops found it necessary to use CS gas before the rioters could be dispersed. The Home Office viewed these outbreaks of violence as all the more disappointing as there were grounds for believing that the Catholic minority was becoming more relaxed and less fearful of security dangers to themselves.[160]

On 3 April Ronnie Burroughs, the new UKREP, observed that a new pattern of violence had emerged during the disturbances, the causes of which were still obscure. But at least the early indications were that this was not an organised campaign but a spontaneous and irresponsible outburst against authority on the part of Catholic teenagers.[161] Further disturbances occurred in other areas of Belfast on 4 April during which a Protestant was shot by a Catholic. Worryingly, the Home Office now reported there was a growing belief in Northern Ireland that the recent disturbances were not spontaneous, although the outward appearance had been one of hooliganism. They were very different in nature from the demonstrations organised in support of demands for civil rights in 1969. The rioting had been so severe that, on 3 April, Freeland warned of a tougher line to be taken against rioters by the troops: in particular he said that petrol-bomb throwers were liable to be shot dead if they persisted in their activities after due warning. This was answered by a message purporting to come from the IRA, threatening that if one Irish life was lost as a result of the GOC's orders, members of the British Army would be shot on sight, where and when the opportunity arose. A statement was then issued, allegedly from the UVF, warning that a Roman Catholic would be shot for every soldier. There was more controversial comment from the GOC when he was interviewed on the BBC programme *Panorama* on 6 April: 'People are not working hard enough and fast enough to try and solve their problems while we are keeping the peace for them. Time will run out on them. And also the Army may not stay long enough or be allowed to stay long enough to solve the problems unless they get a move on.'[162] Together with an inability to subdue Catholic rioting, this placed more pressure on Chichester-Clark's Government.

The Stormont by-elections were now imminent. They proved a watershed in the fortunes of Chichester-Clark and his opponents. Bannside we have visited before; the 28,000 South Antrim electorate largely shared the relative prosperity of the greater Belfast area, with male unemployment running at half the Ulster average and plenty of new housing. Nearly two-thirds of the people lived in Lisburn, the only big town in the constituency, while many of its inhabitants worked in Belfast. Predominately Protestant, with a small Catholic minority mainly confined to the shores of Lough Neagh, it had returned three Unionist MPs since 1929.[163] William Morgan opened his campaign there asking not for 'blind loyalty' but warning that a rejection of official Unionist policies was to reject 'everything held dear by our forefathers'.[164] The UUP brought in its big hitters. Faulkner issued a message to electors in which he urged them not to be led astray by straight-out sectarian appeals: 'Think of the ultimate disastrous consequences of such a sterile policy.' His message followed the dramatic intervention of Lord Brookeborough who announced that he would go personally to Bannside to offer Dr Minford, the UUP candidate, his support. The UUP took out an advertisement to claim that the choice before the electors was to vote for anarchy and continued civil strife or for the official Unionist candidate and a policy of 'peace in our streets and prosperity for all'. Faulkner evoked the spirit of Carson: 'Division in the ranks was always the only fear of Carson and the great men of Unionism down the years.' It was always easy, he said, to voice carping criticism of the Government, particularly in difficult times, but it would be a different story if the critics had to handle by themselves some of the day-to-day problems of running the country: 'What a bleak, bitter and barren Ulster would be the result.'[165] Minford also echoed Carson and argued that a vote for Paisley was a vote for division: he had divided families, churches, Orange lodges and bands but he could not be allowed to divide the country in the eyes of Britain and the world. A vote for the UUP was a vote for British Ulster. Paisley, in his election address, never mentioned the word 'British'. 'Is he not proud of his British nationality?' Dr Minford asked. 'Has he forgotten that the British link is the foundation of our Constitution? Is he ashamed of that or does he think that Britain is ashamed of him?'[166]

Paisley, however, remained confident. He told a rally that the Government was trembling with fear. It was frightened that they would be exposed as never before on the floor of the House were he to be elected. Referring to Brookeborough's intervention, he suggested the former Prime Minister should have stayed away from a constituency about which he knew nothing at all. As for Minford's claim that if elected Paisley would leave Bannside to rot in the mud, the Reverend pointed out that a constituency 'cannot be left in the mud except it were first in the mud. Who put Bannside into the mud? Surely it was Capt. O'Neill who admitted that he had neglected the constituency.' What, said, Paisley, of the fact that no public body, neither the Housing Trust nor Ballymenna Rural Council, had built one house in Ahoghill for eighteen years? What of the Dreen housing estate in Cullybackey which had waited seventeen years for running water? It was a disgrace that in built-up areas in Bannside there were still dry closets. 'It is the Unionist Party that is responsible and it is from this deplorable condition that I want to salvage Bannside.'[167] Those were the local issues. As to the ones that crossed constituencies, Paisley claimed that Sir Arthur Young had ordered that all sporting rifles and shotguns in police stations were to be handed in and no member of the RUC was to be allowed a sporting weapon. He also claimed that no police officer was to be allowed to draw a baton or use it unless he was attacked by three or more people. Furthermore, every district inspector in Belfast who took part in recent troubles was to be demoted under a new officer rank coming into existence.[168] Much of this had a ring of truth—and it reinforced the image of a police force handicapped by political decisions.

Initially the UUP and the Government had themselves been confident of victory. But gradually the possibility of defeat became apparent. The Orange card was played in a final bid by the Government to achieve victory. It came in the shape of intervention by Captain Orr, the leader of the Order, who urged Orangemen to support Minford and Morgan, the only two Orangemen among the seven candidates in either by-election. Orr issued a statement saying that normally he did not expect the Order to intervene in elections but the issues were such that it was essential that the two UUP men should be supported to the full 'both for the protection of the Union and the furtherance of a just society'.[169] Nat Minford, a Parliamentary

Secretary and cousin of the UUP candidate, referred to a 'Protestant government for a Protestant people'.[170] If this intervention was designed to shore up the Protestant vote it also meant the loss of any moderate Catholic support. The UUP was caught between a rock and a hard place.

Beattie won in South Antrim. Paisley won in Bannside. Pat McHugh, the Labour candidate and a Catholic, polled 3,514 votes; Paisley secured 7,981 votes against Minford's 6,778 votes—a majority of 1,203. Paisley had turned around a 1,400-vote defeat to O'Neill in 1969.[171] He believed that the message from Bannside was clear: Chichester-Clark should quit; Ulster should have a Government that governs; and the rule of law and order should be fully applied with justice for all irrespective of creed or class. And he realised that he could not have won without divine intervention: 'You could not beat the Unionist Government without the help of the Lord.'[172]

The by-election results were a stunning blow to Chichester-Clark. Now Paisley had a platform in Stormont. Suddenly he was no longer just a street preacher. But it was not just from the 'right' that Chichester-Clark was losing support. Morgan blamed the New Ulster Movement's (NUM) intervention in the South Antrim contest for his defeat. He thought it surely wrong that he had been selected by a UUP committee that contained NUM members who then refused to shoulder their responsibility of supporting him: 'When they go further and put up a candidate of their own minority choice then the position is ridiculous.'[173]

Until now there had been an overlap between membership of the NUM and the Unionist Party. This changed in April 1970 with the launch of the Alliance Party of Northern Ireland. Its origins were in the New Ulster Movement. Many of its members—it claimed a membership of 7,000 in 1969—were to become active in the Alliance Party. The party itself was launched in April, and although its initial leadership was drawn from people previously unknown in politics, it gained support from a section of Unionists who had backed Terence O'Neill. It was committed to a non-sectarian society and attracted mainly middle-class Protestants and Catholics repelled by the naked sectarianism in Northern Irish society. It was also pro-Union unless a majority in Northern Ireland wanted to change the constitutional position.

But it also had another effect that Harry West quickly spotted: the Government was 'losing at both ends'. The Alliance Party was 'taking away the Liberals' and at the other end Paisley 'the hardliners'. The UUP 'sitting in the centre is being robbed'.[174] Craig saw the by-elections as a warning to the UUP that it was losing support in the constituencies. Traditional supporters the length and breadth of the country were disturbed by the policies to which the Government had committed itself without the support of the Party. What happened in Bannside and South Antrim could, he warned, happen in a lot of other constituencies.[175]

On 23 April Ronnie Burroughs noted in his despatch to London: 'We are going through a very sticky patch in Northern Ireland at the moment.' Certain constituents and associations in the Unionist Party had swung strongly to the right in the last few days, largely as a result of the by-elections. They were exerting considerable pressure on the Stormont Government. Three associations from the western counties were threatening to withdraw from the UUC unless the Prime Minister could convince them that he was taking a really strong line on the 'law and order' issue: 'By this they of course mean that it is high time a few Roman Catholics were clobbered.' Unfortunately the Prime Minister's nerve was far from good and in an interview with Burroughs the previous night Chichester-Clark had said that unless the GOC and the Inspector-General could give him some visible proofs that law and order was going to be demonstrated with a firmer hand than in the past, he would be obliged to resign within the next few days. London's immediate task was therefore to stiffen his resolve and prevent him throwing in his hand. Freeland was arranging for the UDR to undertake road checks in carefully selected areas that night in order that the 'windy' members of the Unionist Party should be able to see them operating as a credible alternative to the B-Specials.[176]

Some of the grassroot pressures on Chichester-Clark surfaced at the Ulster Unionist Council meeting held on 24 April. Chichester-Clark went on the offensive and told those who supported Paisley's Protestant Unionists to get out of the Unionist Party: 'There are people who want a double option. They want to remain in our Party, and try to suit candidates who suit their book. Then, if they don't succeed in this, they feel it is quite all right to go out and work for someone else who is opposing the duly nominated official candidate.' He considered this 'dishonest and dishonourable behaviour'.[177] Despite his demonstration of resolve, the Government narrowly survived a serious challenge to its authority when it won a majority of seventy-four on a motion which was regarded as one of confidence in its handling of recent events in Northern Ireland. After being told by the Prime Minister that if they passed the motion—critical of what was described as interference by Westminster in Ulster affairs—they would gravely embarrass the Government, the delegates voted 203 for the resolution and 277 against. The first vote on the motion, by a show of hands, was so close that a ballot was ordered. Put forward by Roy Garland, Vice-Chairman of Duncairn Young Unionists, the motion called on the Government to demonstrate clearly 'that they are masters in their own house' and to 'no longer tolerate interference from Westminster'. It said that the Government must not 'tolerate any semblance of government by a minority or from the streets' and it demanded 'that our democratically-elected Government begins to govern immediately with the fairness and firmness promised by our Prime Minister'.

Chichester-Clark departed from his prepared script in his response: 'Do not imagine that firm government means doing all the things that are talked about at Unionist meetings from time to time'. Firm government was about doing what was right and proper: 'That is the only sort of government you are going to get from me and my colleagues.' Less than half of the delegates rose to applaud him.

This was after they had heard Garland say: 'The Government has betrayed the B-Specials and the police. A Prime Minister speaking with two voices cannot lead Ulster.' Another Young Unionist, Frank Millar, said the frustration of the loyalist people at the actions of the Government had been demonstrated by the results of the recent by-elections. The reorganisation of the police force was nonsensical. The plans for the reorganisation of local government did nothing to dispel a strong suspicion that such a policy was not the workings of a Unionist Government. And the central housing authority was clearly a product of a Socialist Government and unacceptable to Unionists. The action of the Prime Minister in expelling five 'highly respectable' Unionists of the Parliamentary Party had been disgraceful. It was an action which only gave foundation to the belief 'that within this great party of ours has been the setting-up of a dictatorship'.

Chichester-Clark's response, in a militant anti-UDI speech, was: 'I do not seek to replace the Union Jack with an Ulster banner.' It was not that the Stormont Parliament should be a mere rubber stamp or that they should just take their orders from London; that would not be devolution, nor would it be democracy. But what the people of the United Kingdom had a perfect right to expect was that 'we should have some regard for their views, which did not represent interference by people who had nothing to do with us, but the views of our own fellow citizens'. The Prime Minister reassured Unionists that if any proposition was put to the Government which undermined their constitutional position they would reject it even if that rejection were to involve a major constitutional crisis with the UK Government.[178] A further resolution, disapproving of the Northern Ireland Government's decision to establish a central housing authority, was carried by 278 votes to 239 at the Council.[179] Phelim O'Neill summed up the Prime Minister's suspicions regarding the rebels when he came to the conclusion that the 'Craig-Paisley-West axis' were the 'apostles of UDI'.[180]

This completely missed the point. Later Roy Garland attacked Chichester-Clark's suggestion of dissident support for UDI as a 'myth' that was the 'deliberate creation' of the Prime Minister. The Government stood condemned before the conference because it had accepted a change 'in our conventional if not our constitutional relationship' with the UK Government. The resolution had objected only to interference from Westminster 'in matters clearly within the jurisdiction of Northern Ireland'. Westminster had no right to take from Northern Ireland those 'conventional rights' which it had enjoyed for half a century.[181] As West explained: he wasn't pushing for a new Prime Minister, merely the present one with different policies.[182]

By 28 April Burroughs, who had been optimistic when he had assumed his post some eight weeks before, had begun to realise the extent of the task before the British Government. He sent a more detailed assessment to Callaghan. He began by recalling that, when he first arrived, the prospects for a stable and just society seemed good. But behind hopeful developments lay deep-rooted instincts, which made mutual trust between the communities impossible, at least until several generations had passed. The most casual observer of the Northern Ireland scene could not avoid drawing parallels with the Southern States of America: the 'poor white' Protestant was convinced that if the Catholic minority was given an inch it would become 'uppity', and encroach on his entrenched though often minimal prerogatives. The Catholic reaction was self-evident. For the moment Burroughs saw that the principal dangers did not lie in the field of security but in the political arena and within the framework of the Unionist Party itself. This party lacked a common political ideology. It included both modern liberal and integrationist elements and people whose views could with difficulty be distinguished from those of Governor Wallace and Senator McCarthy in the United States. A reformist administration such as Chichester-Clark's was always threatened by a right-wing revolt. The tactics of the right-wing opposition were already becoming apparent. Like all demagogues of fascist or neo-fascist tendencies, Paisley was sliding to the left as power approached. Allied with demands for 'law and order'—these words had exactly the same connotation as they had in the mouths of Governor Wallace and Mayor Daly—he was beginning to champion the working man. It went without saying that the working men he had in mind were Protestants. Any administration which included people such as Craig would be unacceptable to the minority and would lead to a serious breakdown in law and order. Even a 'compromise candidate' such as Brooke could only rest on British bayonets. No amount of military force could prevent disorders and it was by no means fanciful to envisage civil war.

If, therefore, Chichester-Clark's administration were to be defeated, it would be necessary for Her Majesty's Government seriously to consider the suspension of the constitution and direct intervention by Westminster. But this itself would create or revive almost as many problems as it solved. Although it would go far towards guaranteeing the rights of the minority, Burroughs could not see the Republican Movement accepting without demur the reimposition of direct rule. On the other flank, the extremist Protestants against whom such a move would be aimed, would certainly fight, if only with gelignite and snipers' rifles in the dark. The UK Government's immediate task must therefore be to sustain the morale of the Prime Minister and his colleagues. He had above all to be encouraged not to hedge on the reform programme. He could not steal the clothes of the extremists by watering down his reforms, and he might well lose one or two of his adherents on the liberal wing of his party. His principal asset, thought Burroughs, was that he was regarded as a man of honour. If this reputation was tarnished he would not last long.[183]

As Ronnie Burroughs had realised, Chichester-Clark remained vulnerable to the slow attrition of violence on the streets; this would ultimately leave him exposed to the impact of more organised violence. The image of a Government unable to maintain order on the streets had become a widespread one within the Unionist community. There were constant complaints from the Unionist grassroots to the Unionist Government about the continuing disorder. Chichester-Clark, in turn, complained to Callaghan about the Army's inability to stem the rioting. After seeing a note of a Callaghan conversation with Chichester-Clark, Denis Healy explained to the Home Secretary the Army's policy regarding arrests. The law required the military commander on the spot to use the minimum force necessary for the execution of his immediate task, and that his was the personal responsibility of judging and if necessary justifying in law what that minimum was. It had to be recognised that the nature and location of the disturbances, in which lightly-clad and lightly-shod youths were able to dart in and out of a 'rabbit-warren' of houses and streets on a hit-and-run basis, did not lend itself easily to the making of arrests, particularly when soldiers were employed in what was essentially a police role. Consideration was being given by HQ Northern Ireland to the formation of groups of small and lightly-shod soldiers and to other possible tactics for dealing more effectively with this particular problem. Healy pointed out that the pursuit and arrest of hooligans of this type was not normally a military function. The function of the Army was essentially to prevent large-scale rioting, killing and destruction by bringing to bear resources which only the Army possessed. While it was accepted that in the short term Sir Arthur Young was building up the strength and morale of the RUC and gaining for it the confidence of a wider range of the community, the Army had to do a good many jobs for which the police should normally be better suited; but the police would never get back into business if the Army was expected as a matter of course to enforce the law as well as to keep the peace. Also there was probably not much advantage in making large numbers of arrests unless one could be reasonably confident that convictions could be sustained and exemplary sentences imposed. In this connection Healy noted that out of forty-seven persons who were arrested over the period 31 March to 4 April inclusive, sixteen were sentenced to imprisonment and five were fined; but eight had their cases dismissed, seven were given suspended sentences and eleven were bound over or given a conditional discharge. Deterrent punishment for a small number might well have had more effect than a large number of arrests which were dealt with leniently.[184]

In short there was little more the Army could do. And there was yet more Catholic rioting at the beginning of May.[185] A night of violence in the city's New Lodge Road area came to an end in the early hours of 10 May after five hours of bitter street fighting. The Army fired 125 gas canisters and 159 gas cartridges during the confrontation. Soldiers of the 1st Battalion King's Own Scottish Borderers and the 2nd and 3rd Battalions of The Queen's Regiment were subjected to a constant barrage of stones and bottles by a Catholic crowd which varied at different times from 150 to 400 people. One soldier was taken to hospital with a broken arm. Some families found it necessary to leave their homes because of the effect of the CS gas, particularly on their children. The trouble started shortly before midnight on North Queen Street, scene of a stoning incident that afternoon, after a bomb blast in nearby Dock Street. The blast, in the Regent Bar, was caused by four stove pipes which been filled with explosives and placed against the wall of the public house. Police and troops prevented rival Protestant and Catholic mobs clashing near the foot of Duncairn Gardens.[186]

The disturbances allowed Unionist Party dissidents to open another front in their attacks on the Government. The occasion was a law and order debate at Stormont. Craig moved a motion that the Minister of Home Affair's salary should be cut by £100—a parliamentary convention used to expression dissatisfaction with Government policy. Craig claimed that the 'no-go' areas were creating conditions for subversive organisations to carry on their activities with the intent to undermine the stability of the country and the ultimate aim of destroying the constitution. No one, he argued, in the light of the dramatic developments in the Republic, would question that the smuggling of arms boded ill for the future. It was an alarming prospect that arms were being provided for the minority against an imaginary attack. Craig feared the trouble would spread beyond Belfast and Londonderry. He believed that those behind the conspiracy deliberately intended this and might attempt to occupy and hold police stations, if not villages and towns. Even at this late hour the Government should reconsider reorganising the police. It was now obvious that it was inviting trouble by organising them on English lines.[187]

Paisley rowed in with more attacks on the Government. He complained of Government ineffectiveness in 'no go land' on the Falls Road and in the Bogside. He referred to the disparity in sentences meted out to civil rights people and Protestants. Searches in Protestant areas had taken place for harassment purposes. The claim of the Prime Minister and members of the Government, when they had gone around the country indicating that the police could go anywhere, was pure deception. He claimed that a directive from Freeland, late the previous year, indicated that only military police and their vehicles could go into certain areas. It was a ludicrous situation that the Prime Minister could go into country areas and say that the police could go anywhere when they could not. They were being dictated to by representatives of the IRA—vigilantes in the Catholic areas—and only went in after 'negotiations' had taken place. There seemed to be a conspiracy to hide the facts from the public.[188] West complained that, even at this stage, the Falls and the Bogside were not being policed effectively while the suspicion was that some of the arms in the South must have found their way North. The law and order situation was most disturbing and he summed up the basic problem that the disturbances meant for Chichester-Clark: 'A Government that is unable to govern the whole province must stand discredited in the eyes of the community in general.'[189]

Chapter 9

RESURRECTION: THE IRISH STATE AND ORIGINS OF THE REPUBLICAN WAR

FIANNA FÁIL AND THE EVOLUTION OF THE PROVISIONAL IRA 1969–70

The formation of the Provisional IRA in late 1969 to early 1970 is one of the defining episodes of the Troubles. How that came about is discussed in this chapter. But so too is how the Irish Government played a crucial role in its development. The relationship of the Irish Government to the Provisional IRA has proved to be one of the most controversial debates of the early part of the Troubles. It deserves some detailed scrutiny. But perhaps the premise is wrong: it is not so much the role played by the Irish Government in the formation of the Provisionals that merits scrutiny; rather its role in that organisation's evolution which calls for assessment. For it is, more than anything, what one might call the Irish Government's mindset in the aftermath of the August riots which is the key to understanding what is a quite extraordinary episode: an alliance between a government friendly to the United Kingdom with a subversive organisation dedicated to the ending of the British Government's presence in a part of the United Kingdom by the use of force. The role of the Irish Government in the evolution of the Provisional IRA was to provide it with life support after its birth by offering it money and political legitimacy. The Irish Government did not create the Provisionals, but it nurtured them. As far as the future stability of Northern Ireland was concerned it proved a colossal misjudgment. This was because it was the Provisional IRA that, more than any other single factor post-1969, transformed the nature of the Northern Ireland conflict from a tribal dispute into a cycle of sub-state and counter-state violence. It is in the actions of the Provisionals that we find the origins of the second Troubles—the war against the British state in Ireland.

Before we go any further it is necessary to assess, if such a thing is possible, the 'state of mind' that constituted the collective entity called the Government of Ireland in post-August 1969. The best way to describe this is: schizophrenic. At one level Jack Lynch's Fianna Fáil Government in Dublin sought to build bridges between South and North and to develop a working relationship between Ireland and Britain. But at another level the Irish Government prepared for military intervention in Northern Ireland in conjunction with the IRA. How did these two apparently contradictory policies come about?

The first point to bear in mind is the position of Lynch in his Government and the Fianna Fáil party. Lynch was a man regarded by senior and ambitious men within his own cabinet as having been a compromise candidate for his party's leadership. As such they regarded him as a short-term appointment. He was just keeping the Taoiseach's chair warm until the self-appointed rightful heirs to de Valera's legacy sat in it—men such as Neil Blaney, Minister for Agriculture and Charles Haughey, Minister for Finance. Furthermore some of them, such as Blaney, were at the forefront of upholding what they believed was the true Republican tradition. In the highly emotional atmosphere which existed in Ireland following the August riots, Lynch was under pressure to demonstrate that he was the sole spokesman for Republican Ireland. The best way to describe Dublin's attitude to British intervention in the North would be scepticism—as to whether the reforms hinted at in the Downing Street Declaration would be implemented. Dublin rejected the idea that Northern Ireland was a British domestic issue. The Irish Government declared that it 'does not concede in any way, and never will, Britain's right to exercise jurisdiction over any part of Irish territory'. The 'claim of the Irish nation to control the totality of Ireland has been asserted over centuries by successive generations of Irish men and women and it is one which will never be renounced'.[1]

Lynch added that while Callaghan had claimed that the border was not an issue it remained the Irish Government's conviction that the 'unnatural and unjustifiable' partition of Ireland was basic to the present unrest in the six counties and that no long-term, much less permanent, solution could be contemplated without having full regard to its existence. The presence of British troops and the placing of existing police forces under the command of a British GOC had brought a fundamental change in the constitutional status of the six counties, meaning that there could be no return to the status quo. The Taoiseach offered to discuss with the British intermediate steps towards the creation of a federal Ireland.[2]

Sir Andrew Gilchrist, after observing that the Taoiseach 'as usual conducts his political campaign not by diplomacy but by public statement', noted that he 'is explicitly addressing us'.[3] Thanks to a 'reliable British political writer' who had an off-the-record interview with the Taoiseach on 29 August, Gilchrist was able to piece together Dublin's policy (this account proved remarkably accurate). According to this source, Irish Government policy would continue to press the British Government to be consulted on Northern Ireland's affairs. Although a more positive line would be taken on non-acceptance of the border, it was the Irish intention to bring up the Northern Ireland problem in the General

Assembly of the United Nations. Lynch explained to the source that Ireland's present economic development was aimed towards parity with the standard of living in Northern Ireland, so that the Republic would have something to attract Northern citizens. At present the Republic could not compete with Westminster's subvention of £136 million. Lynch did, however, consider relations with the British Government to be excellent; he explained that his recent statements had been made under pressure from the 'young people's movement', the IRA, and from within the cabinet, Blaney and Kevin Boland, the Minister for Local Government: it was an act of faith that the border had to go sometime.

It was also true that the Taoiseach genuinely believed that the constitutional position of the six counties had been radically altered by recent events. It was now run by one British Lieutenant-General and two civil servants. The Stormont Government was discredited. The possible solution lay in a federal solution in which Westminster's powers would be transferred to Dublin. This would confirm that a Stormont authority was still required—Dublin did not want direct control over or interference in the Protestant tradition because 'we don't want the problem of Paisley'. When asked whether, if in due course a united Ireland were to come about, Ireland would consider a Commonwealth-type relationship with Britain, Lynch replied 'most certainly a relationship such as Britain and India'. However, when asked what would he do if Northern Ireland were to be handed to him 'on a plate', Lynch replied 'I would faint'.[4]

This led Gilchrist to conclude that Lynch and almost the 'whole orthodox Irish political establishment' regarded the prospect of an immediate and complete union of Ireland with genuine horror. In all their speeches about 'our people' they meant the Catholic Nationalist minority and they had no idea of how to attract or handle the Protestant Unionist majority: they quailed at the thought of Paisley browbeating them in the Dáil and they could not see how they could possibly cope with the economic problems involved in unification unless a pro-rata deficiency payment or transitory benefit from the British Government would be payable to the Irish Government for a number of years. The phrase which best summed this up was a 'golden handshake'.[5]

Gilchrist was right in seeing that the Irish Government was perplexed by two conceptual problems: could the events in the North be an opportunity to exploit with regard to Irish unity; and if they were, what on earth were they to do with those Protestants? The Tánaiste, Erskine Childers, cobbled together two memoranda to review policy regarding the unity of Ireland. It was done in haste; but that it needed to be demonstrated the long lack of strategic thinking towards the North. In the first paper Childers emphasised that the Government could not negotiate solely with the British. The need to get consent, even grudging consent, from the Unionist majority remained. Crucially, Childers presumed a tough control of the new IRA. He warned that their incursion from the South would spell disaster. The IRA could only destroy any reputation the Government had and discourage unity in the six counties.[6]

In his second paper Childers argued that if partition could only be ended by political action and not by force then anti-Unionist groups had to be separately or collectively exhorted to work on a long-term basis for an approach to unity. If a new Nationalist party emerged 'so much the better'. Childers estimated that 200,000 to 300,000 Unionists had to be won over—that is, persuaded of the merits of Irish unity—in purely electoral terms, to gain reunification; assuming all the anti-Unionists voted for unity[7] (it is perhaps worth noting that the Tánaiste was on good enough personal terms with Gilchrist to provide him with the gist of his arguments also).[8] Within the Department of External Affairs, Childers' efforts stimulated some debate. A paper produced by probably the most influential civil servant on Northern policy in the Department, Eamonn Gallagher, took as its primary assumption that there was no going back in the North to before 12 August; the Irish Government's thinking had to take account of what had changed. Noting that the Taoiseach's speech on 13 August had been 'brilliantly effective' in finally forcing Westminster to intervene directly in the North, Gallagher believed that the minority in the North remained Nationalist and attached to the objective of a united Ireland. For them the Civil Rights Movement was a means to this political end—and so far a decidedly successful one. The destruction of the Unionist pyramid of discrimination meant that the diversion into emigration of virtually all the natural increase in the minority population would become considerably less pronounced. As this became the case several consequences would begin to flow:

(a) the weight of the Nationalist minority will grow for purely demographic reasons;

(b) this translates into increasing political influence . . . the warping of political thought in the Unionist Party by their sheer success to date in preventing demographic change must necessarily change to face the new situation; while some elements of the Unionist right will remain incapable for the foreseeable future of responding to any such sharp change in perspective it can be anticipated that Unionist moderates will see the need to get out of a steadily more untenable dead end; their only credible alternative is an accommodation with Dublin; it seems reasonable to consider that this realisation of the gravity of their real position—incapable much longer of controlling effectively a growing and politicised minority, unable to count even on tacit outside support for a policy of overt discrimination as was the case for the past fifty years, squeezed from the Right by a monstrous bigotry of their own creation—will influence moderates to consider seriously such a possibility;

(d) even to begin to think in such terms will force Unionist moderates, in their own interest, to take early steps to suppress definitively the Orange disease. If they do not do this nothing is possible without bloodshed . . .;

(e) if the underlined alternative is adopted it will emerge as a live subject before the minority reaches near to 50% of the population. It will do this for the reason that Unionist moderates, having first isolated the irretrievable minority of diehards, will see it as their interest to make an arrangement acceptable to Dublin and the minority while they still have something to bargain with;

(f) consequently, the progression outlined above will be much swifter than demographic change and may become politically possible . . . [in] a matter of a decade or so . . .

Thus Gallagher could see unification being achieved within a relatively short timespan as moderate Unionists sought an accommodation with Dublin once they realised that their traditional method of holding power—combined with a shifting demographic balance—had been destroyed. He recommended that the Irish Government's policy should be to do everything suitable to hasten this process.[9]

The public face of Irish policy was played out on the international stage where Dublin launched an international propaganda campaign against partition that culminated in Ireland raising the matter at the UN: the aim of the latter, according to Dr Patrick Hillery, the Minister of External Affairs, was to affect British opinion with a view to bringing about talks on the situation in the North of Ireland between the Government of Ireland, the British Government and probably the Stormont Government.[10] Partition, while discussed at the UN was not put to a vote. The Irish attitude seemed to puzzle London: the Foreign and Commonwealth Office noted that despite the Irish 'insistence on raising the Northern Ireland problem in every conceivable forum even though to do so is almost certainly to neither their short or long term advantage . . . it seems that the Irish Government still regard their relations with us as excellent';[11] and even though the propaganda being disseminated was 'not strictly compatible with the friendly relations which Mr. Lynch continues to claim with H.M.G. they amount to direct criticism of H.M.G.'s policy in the internal affairs of the UK. But one must always make allowances in Ireland, and it might have been worse.' Despite these concerns, by September 1969 the Foreign Office could comfort itself with the knowledge that its latest report was showing that in the United States ('the most important audience') the Irish campaign was having relatively limited success.[12]

And it was this which allowed the British some flexibility in their response so that, in the end, from their point of view the events at the UN worked out to the satisfaction of both sides. Lynch, in Callaghan's view, 'was able to show his fellow countrymen that he had taken the matter to the Security Council and done as much as he could'.[13] Having released any pent-up frustration at the UN (regarding the unjustness of partition) Hillery returned to Dublin to think about future policy in relation to the North. The basic policy approach remained the reunification of Ireland by peaceful means through co-operation, agreement and consent between Irishmen; therefore, argued Hillery, care should be taken to 'avoid action leading to complete direct rule from Westminster which would make the North a closer integral part of the United Kingdom—unless of course Stormont should ultimately reject genuine reform'.[14]

At this point Lynch signalled in September the change of emphasis after the UN exercise. His speech in Tralee transformed the atmosphere of Anglo–Irish relations and reduced the tension between Dublin and Belfast, even producing a relatively moderate response from Chichester-Clark. Speaking at a dinner in honour of a former Fianna Fáil TD the Taoiseach stated: 'We were not seeking to overthrow by violence the Stormont Parliament, but rather to win the agreement of a sufficient number of people in the North to an acceptable form of re-unification.' He wanted to explain in clear and simple terms the basis of the Irish Government's thinking and policy. Lynch emphasised that the Irish Government had 'no intention of using force' but sought the reunification of the country by peaceful means:

> The unity we seek is not something forced but a free and genuine union of those living in Ireland based on mutual respect and tolerance and guaranteed by a form or forms of government ... Of its nature, this policy—of seeking unity through agreement in Ireland between Irishmen—is a long-term one ... Perseverance in winning the respect and confidence of those now opposed to unity must be sustained by good-will, patience, understanding and, at times, forbearance ... We are concerned that the grievances of so many of our fellow Irishmen and women be quickly remedied and their fears set at rest. We also have a legitimate concern regarding the disposition to be made by the British Government in relation to the future administration of Northern Ireland. Let me make it clear, too, that in seeking re-unification, our aim is not to extend the domination of Dublin. We have many times down the years expressed our willingness to seek a solution on federal lines and in my most recent statement I envisaged the possibility of intermediate stages in an approach to a final agreed solution.

After the Irish propaganda efforts around the world this was a clear shift in emphasis by the Irish Government back towards a policy of long-term rapprochement with Unionists. But Lynch also stressed that it was quite unreasonable for any Unionist to expect the Irish Government, or any future government, to abandon the belief and hope that Ireland should be reunited. It was unnecessary to repeat that the South sought reunification by peaceful means. It was also, for similar reasons, unreasonable and unnecessary to expect those living in the six counties who shared the desire for unity to renounce their deepest hopes. Against this he pointed out that Irish Nationalists had accepted, as a practical matter, the existence of a government in the North of Ireland exercising certain powers devolved on it by the British Parliament. They had had many fruitful contacts with that government in matters of mutual concern. He hoped that this co-operation between North and South would continue. Lynch concluded with a reference to the words of Lord Craigavon when he said: 'In this island, we cannot live always separated from one another. We are too small to be apart or for the border to be there for all time.'[15] This was the face of North–South detente. But in December Neil Blaney, the most powerful member of the cabinet alongside Charles Haughey and Lynch, made a speech in Letterkenny during the course of which he said:

> I believe, as do the vast majority, that the ideal way of ending partition is by peaceful means. But no one has the right to assert that force is irrevocably out. No political party or group at any time is entitled to predetermine the right of the Irish people to decide what course of action on this question may be justified in given circumstances.
>
> The Fianna Fáil Party has never taken a decision to rule out the use of force if the circumstances in the six counties in which the people who do not subscribe to the Unionist regime were under sustained and murderous assault, then, as the Taoiseach said on August 13th, we "cannot stand idly by".[16]

There was quite a reaction to this (although it should be noted that Lynch never actually said 'idly' in his 13 August broadcast). John Hume called it 'totally irresponsible' to talk of the use of force in the 'present uneasy situation'. He warned that an 'extremist breeds an extremist' and the speech would have the effect of hardening and uniting right-wing Unionist opinion. It had to be accepted that 800,000 Northern Protestants did not want a united Ireland.[17] Lynch's comment was to emphasise that Blaney 'knows and endorses Government policy on this issue'. The Government's policy was, and continued to be, the reunification of Ireland by peaceful means.[18] In his response to the controversy he had generated Blaney emphasised that he did not advocate that partition should be solved by force and that he had stated very specifically his belief in the idea of a peaceful solution. He had made his Letterkenny speech so that people would take notice of the fact that the reforms were not in fact going through as they had been promised.[19] In the Dáil Lynch denied that there was any cabinet conflict over Northern policy.[20] This was seen by some as a dressing-down of Blaney and a reassertion of the Taoiseach's authority. It was not. There was no division between Lynch and Blaney on this issue. Unknown to those outside the Government, the cabinet had embarked on a process in which Irish military forces might, in certain circumstances, intervene in Northern Ireland; it was also decided that they would co-operate in these military activities with the IRA. Blaney, far from dissenting from established Government policy, was at the heart of it. And so was Jack Lynch.

COURTSHIP

The background to this was on 16 August. On that day the Irish cabinet made two decisions with far-reaching consequences: to delegate to Charles Haughey, as

Minister for Finance, a sum of money to provide aid for the victims of the unrest in the six counties; and to establish machinery with the object of maintaining a permanent liaison with opinion in the six counties.[21] The same day the Government Information Bureau announced that Haughey 'will make funds available for the relief of victims of the disturbances in the six counties and he will have early consultations with the chairman of the Irish Red Cross'.[22] The Irish Red Cross would be the cover for the initial passing of money to the IRA.

Why this was deemed necessary can be seen by other events on the same day. At about 5.30 p.m. the Department of the Taoiseach received separate telephone calls from Ivan Cooper and Paddy Kennedy. Both said that the Catholic area of Ardoyne in Belfast was surrounded by Paisleyites and B-Specials and that the inhabitants were without any protection whatever. Unless British troops were moved in before nightfall, a massacre of the inhabitants of the area was inevitable.[23] It was claimed that B-Specials had been drinking and had begun to hand over their rifles to Paisleyites.[24] Shortly afterwards similar information was conveyed by Brendan Halligan, General Secretary of the Labour Party in Dublin, who had received the news from members of his party—two Deputies and two Senators—who were on a fact-finding mission in Belfast.[25] Their report was that the Ardoyne had been surrounded by Paisleyites who were at that moment moving in. There were no British troops in sight.[26] Lynch was immediately informed. He asked one of his senior civil servants, Hugh McCann of External Affairs, who was with him at the time, to convey the information to the Embassy in London. McCann telephoned Kevin Rush who contacted the Home Office 'who were most reluctant to listen to what he had to say, but agreed, under protest, to take the message' and then conveyed the information to the Foreign Office. Rush was given an assurance that his message would be conveyed without delay to Callaghan.[27]

In the evening three Northern politicians: Paddy Devlin, Paddy O'Hanlon and Paddy Kennedy, appeared at the Department of External Affairs seeking an interview with the Taoiseach, for the purpose of obtaining arms for Catholics in the Falls Road. Kennedy, who was the main spokesman, said that the B-Specials were on the loose in Belfast, that there was continuous sniping and that people were being shot down. More and more Catholics were being driven into the Falls Road area and were being forced further and further up in the Falls. Soon the whole Catholic population of Belfast would be concentrated in this area and they would be massacred. The men insisted that they could not return to the North until they had seen the Taoiseach. If Irish troops would not be sent in to the North, then the politicians wanted guns and they could not leave without definite answers. The situation of the Catholics in Belfast could not continue without protection. As regarded guns, nothing need be done openly or politically—a few hundred rifles could easily be "lost" and would not be missed.

They were told by an official, however, that the Taoiseach was not available for interview; he had heard of the worsening situation in Belfast and an appeal by

Bishop Philbin for British troops in the Ardoyne area and appropriate action had been taken through the Chargé d'Affaires in London. But the Northerners were so insistent on seeing the Taoiseach or getting answers to their questions about troops and guns that only an assurance that their message would be conveyed to the proper quarter temporarily appeased them. They insisted on returning to the Department in about three-quarters of an hour for the answers. The Taoiseach's Private Secretary was informed of the meeting and a general form of reply was agreed which Lynch approved with some modifications. When the three men returned at about 11.30 p.m. and asked if the Taoiseach was going to see them, they were told that their requests had been conveyed to the proper contact who again confirmed that the Taoiseach was not available for interview and that he might even be out of Dublin over the weekend. It was stated that the Government had taken all the action open to them and, indeed, it had now been confirmed that troops had entered Ardoyne and that the situation in Belfast was generally quiet. The request for troops or arms was a matter for the Government and perhaps even for the Dáil. It was stressed that this did not indicate any lack of concern by the Government. All three reacted vehemently to this response saying that it was a fob-off and an exasperating attitude. Devlin, who was more angry and emotional than the others, made for the door saying that he would see to it that he saw the Taoiseach before he left Dublin. He came back and muttered something abusive about the Government being responsible for deaths. All three then walked out of the Department, led by Devlin. In view of the probability that a further attempt might be made to contact the Taoiseach the guard was strengthened at his home.[28]

What this reveals is a snapshot of the information which the Irish Government, including the Taoiseach, was receiving about the situation in Northern Ireland. It was of a beleaguered and defenceless minority facing annihilation at the hands of Protestant mobs and a sectarian police force. This view was confirmed by a report from Irish intelligence sources in the North who reported the belief that the RUC, furious about the withdrawal of their comrades in Derry and anticipating the arrival of the British Army in Belfast within a matter of hours, 'decided to put a long term plan into immediate effect' which involved attacking the Falls Road.[29] Views such as this from intelligence-gathering exercises and the eye-witness evidence from Northern Nationalist representatives were taken at face value. It should be noted that these were genuinely held beliefs—the Catholic communities in Belfast and Derry really believed they had been the victims of a state-sponsored attack. But the significant factor is that the Irish Government believed these claims because it fitted into the traditional Nationalist interpretation of the sectarian Northern state and the relationship of sectarianism to the core beliefs of Unionist ideology.

The second significant cabinet decision which had long-term implications for the stability of Northern Ireland was to establish machinery with the object of

THE ORIGINS OF THE TROUBLES

maintaining 'a permanent liaison with opinion in the six counties'. This, in itself, need not have been a destabilising influence in relation to Northern Ireland. But how this machinery was put into use was. The key figure was Captain James Kelly of Irish Military Intelligence. By chance, when the August riots broke out in the North, Kelly was holidaying in Derry. He reported his impressions back to his superior, Colonel Michael Hefferon, in Dublin. Hefferon had been Director of Military Intelligence at Army Headquarters from October 1962. Kelly was already a member of the Intelligence Branch when Hefferon was appointed Director. Kelly reported any new information he received from the North directly to Hefferon. Due to the nature of his mission he was allowed a fair degree of freedom. He usually contacted Hefferon every second day either by telephone or personally. Hefferon was aware that during this period several approaches were made by Catholic residents in Northern Ireland to Irish Army personnel asking that arms and ammunition should be supplied to them for their defence. According to Hefferon the 'official view and my view' was that that could not be done under any circumstances.[30]

Kelly made his first report to Hefferon on 23 August. He made it clear that the Irish Government's stand had attracted widespread support even in extreme Republican circles where there was some evidence of a willingness to 'co-operate in achieving the unity ideal'. Kelly warned that interning the IRA would be a 'catastrophe'. Instead he recommended that all opinion in the Irish state be harnessed in a concerted drive towards achieving the goal of unification. Unfortunately, this would mean accepting the possibility of armed action of some sort as the ultimate solution. The only option open to the Government was to 'co-operate with the IRA and extreme republicanism generally' where they could be permitted 'to operate as covert nuisance squads generally in N.I., avoiding contact with British forces, and supported by a psychological campaign' from Dublin.[31] Hefferon instructed Kelly to maintain the contacts he had made in the North.[32]

Senior ministers took an interest in Military Intelligence's role in the North. Following the riots Hefferon attended a lunch given in McKee Barracks. Also attending were Haughey and James Gibbons, the Minister for Defence. Haughey stressed the importance of intelligence work in the North. He gave Hefferon an assurance that as far as his department was concerned funds would be made available if they should be required. What is significant here is how this seemed to by-pass the normal channel for procurement of Secret Service money which was from the Minister of Defence, on requisition, as required. Hefferon, for example, made a study of a communication system for transmission into Northern Ireland which was submitted as a report to Tom Fagan, the senior official in the Finance Ministry, for Haughey's information. Again this was unusual in that it seemed to by-pass Hefferon's own Minister to whom he was directly accountable. The project never materialised. Hefferon did, however, suggest to Fagan that financial assistance could be provided for the Civil Rights office in Monaghan in order to maintain the goodwill of the people there. £500 was provided in a cheque from Fagan. In October 1969 another £500 was provided by Fagan in response to a request from Captain Kelly, to cover the expenses of a conference he was organising on Defence and Aid. Hefferon had asked for these monies as a direct result of Haughey's offer to fund intelligence work made at the barracks lunch in 1969. Hefferon failed to inform Gibbons, his Minister, about the funding of the Civil Rights office and the conference.[33]

In September Kelly returned North with Seamus Brady, a journalist working on the Government's propaganda campaign.[34] Brady had been appointed to the propaganda unit on the instructions of the cabinet. Subsequently, he produced a detailed report on the Battle of the Bogside which was made available to each member of the cabinet.[35] Both Kelly and Brady were in regular contact with members of the IRA. They also introduced or arranged for senior members of the Government to meet with IRA members. While in Belfast Captain Kelly had made contact with John Kelly, a former IRA man who came from an old Republican family. John Kelly had been alienated by the leftward turn in Republican strategy but had now returned to the fold following the August disturbances. He told Captain Kelly that weapons were needed to defend Catholics in Belfast. John Kelly was then introduced by Brady to Neil Blaney; he in turn arranged for them to meet Haughey. The Minister for Finance agreed to finance Brady's idea of establishing a newspaper and even suggested its title—the *Voice of the North*.[36]

In November 1969 the establishment of the *Voice of the North* led to accusations from the Goulding leadership in the IRA that Fianna Fáil was attempting to take over the Civil Rights Movement. The direct financial involvement of the Irish Government was denied by Hugh Kennedy, formally the press officer for the Central Citizens' Defence Committee (CCDC) but now managing editor of the *Voice of the North*, who said that the paper was conceived by members of the CCDC who had become convinced of the necessity for a voice after Radio Free Belfast—a constant thorn in the Northern authorities' side—had been silenced by the British Army. Kennedy claimed that funds were donated by wealthy people in Belfast and by sympathetic organisations and individuals in the United States. He listed the names of the paper's directors as Aidan Corrigan, Sean Keenan, Tom Conaty, John Kelly, W. O'Hanlon and himself—a Republican 'in the tradition of Pearse and Tone, not de Valera'. A majority of the directors would later be associated with the Provisionals. Seamus Brady, Kennedy said, had only worked for the paper in a professional capacity as a journalist. Brady subsequently claimed that he had resigned from his position in the Government Information Bureau at about the time Corrigan asked him to co-operate in preparing his propagandist booklet *Eyewitness in Northern Ireland* for the press (which was then distributed around the world by the Irish Government). Brady was then 'invited' to assist in the organisation and production side of the *Voice*. The paper, pointed out Brady, existed by voluntary subscription. Having been born and bred in

Derry 'my sympathies in regard to the Republicans of the North have never been in question'.[37]

By now Blaney had become the main driving force inside the Government in terms of establishing links with the IRA. He was convinced that this was the final break-up of the six-county entity. In August he had wanted the Irish Army to go into the Bogside to protect the Catholics there. His colleague, Kevin Boland, recalled: 'We were prepared to give whatever assistance we could, whether it be effective or not, in the event of an all-out onslaught on the ghetto areas and isolated rural pockets taking place. Everybody believed that it was only a matter of time until it happened.' James Gibbons, as Minister of Defence, was instructed to consult with the Army authorities and report back on what could be done. He reported that the Army had neither the military nor the financial capacity to give any worthwhile assistance. Boland believed that Lynch was content to leave things at that. But Boland and others kept the pressure on to do something whether it was effective or not. Eventually the cabinet decided that authority would be delegated to Haughey and Gibbons to provide whatever assistance could be provided in the expected circumstances.[38]

Gibbons issued a directive to the General Staff of the Defence Forces to prepare an 'Estimate of the Situation' which assessed the Northern Ireland situation and the capabilities of the Defence Forces to provide 'more positive assistance' should the strife in Northern Ireland continue at the August level, or even deteriorate. The assessment indicated a very low standard of combat effectiveness and a critical situation in regard to personnel deficiencies and shortage of essential equipment which precluded action.[39] Specifically the General Staff looked at the feasibility of the Defence Forces' undertaking military combat or support operations in Northern Ireland, including the nature and implications of such operations. This was done through a two-sided war game that role-played an ongoing exercise—EX ARMAGEDDON—to 'study, plan and rehearse in detail the intervention of the Defence Forces in NORTHERN IRELAND in order to secure the safety of the minority population'.[40] The interim report of the Planning Board on Northern Ireland Operations was prepared in October 1969. It began by outlining the limitations facing it. This included the lack of a clearly defined political objective; the fact that, psychologically, the Defence Forces were oriented on defence (including 'offensive defensive operations'); that there was no precise knowledge available at that stage as to what the reaction of public opinion would be either North or South of the border to offensive action on the part of the Defence Forces in Northern Ireland; and that all situations visualised 'assume that military action would be taken unilaterally by the Defence Forces and would meet with hostility from Northern Ireland Security Forces'. Despite this, the political situations considered were:

a. Attacks on the Catholic minority by Protestant extremists with which the Northern Ireland Security Forces cannot cope (SITUATION A).

b. Conflict between the Catholic minority and the Northern Ireland Security Forces on Civil Rights issues (SITUATION B).

c. Conflict between Republican-Nationalist elements (possibly supported by illegal elements from South of the border) and the Northern Ireland Security Forces (SITUATION C).

d. Conflict between Protestant extremists and Northern Ireland Security Forces not directly involving the minority (SITUATION D).

As a basis for the development of feasible courses of action the first conclusion drawn was that the defence forces 'have NO capability of embarking on unilateral military operation, of any kind (either conventional or unconventional), from a firm base at home. This means, in effect, that were operations in any form to be launched into Northern Ireland we would be exposed to the threat of retaliatory punitive military action by United Kingdom forces on the Republic. Therefore any operations undertaken against Northern Ireland would be militarily unsound.' Furthermore, the Defence Forces 'have no capability to engage successfully in conventional offensive military operations against the security forces in Northern Ireland at unit or higher level'. While accepting the implications of this the Planning Board did, however, believe that conventional military operations on a small scale up to a maximum of company level, and 'unconventional operations', could be undertaken by the Defence Forces. This would require changes in the organisation, dispositions, training and motivation of the Defence Forces as they presently existed.

In addition to this the Defence Forces would also be capable of 'Organising and conducting military training in the Republic for nationalists living in Northern Ireland' and 'Supplying arms, ammunition and equipment in accordance with availability to nationalist elements in Northern Ireland'. This type of action would involve relatively minor planning and training problems. However, in the light of modern surveillance techniques available to the security forces in the North, 'guerrilla type operations in Northern Ireland would be difficult to conduct over a protracted period'. The key areas, politically, were Belfast, Derry, Strabane, Omagh, Enniskillen, Dungannon, Newry and Armagh. From the point of view of military operations Derry, Strabane, Enniskillen and Newry were most suitable by virtue of their proximity to the border. The majority of the more important vital installations in Northern Ireland such as Belfast Airport, television studios, the docks and main industries were located in the north-east corner, some distance from the border. Any military operations conducted against these should preferably be of the unconventional type.

The Planning Board warned that the adoption of a mission involving 'Active intervention in Northern Ireland' would demand an intensive intelligence effort oriented on the mission both before and during operations. This would involve the support of and co-operation with various movements in Northern Ireland such as Civil Rights and Republican groups and could also lead to co-operation with illegal groups in the Republic. These contacts 'would have serious political implications on the national and international scene. They could also pose serious problems in the aftermath, particularly where arms and equipment have been supplied.' Notwithstanding the implications of this it was considered that the support and assistance of a substantial part of the minority would be essential for success in defence force operations in Northern Ireland, although the fact that 'active intervention by us in the North, would expose the minority to retaliatory action and could limit the amount of overt assistance they would be prepared to give'. Whatever support was forthcoming it would be necessary to confine conventional operations to those areas where there was a Catholic/ Nationalist majority. In minority areas, particularly Belfast, only unconventional operations could be conducted.[41] The Planning Board warned that: 'Care would have to be exercised to ensure that training would not be given or weapons supplied to members of organisations whose motives would not be in the best interests of the State . . . The great danger in this course would be the loss of control by the Sate over the activities of personnel.' The State, through the Defence Forces, 'must maintain the maximum control of operations so that military activity will be in line with political objectives. The arming and training of an element which may not have the best interests of the State as their motive could seriously prejudice political aims.' Finally, the Board warned that 'Should the operation miscarry, the consequences could be very grave for the State and the people it is intended to assist.'[42]

Clearly then the Irish General Staff were warning against any Army intervention on military grounds. But the Defence Forces were also warning of the perils of intervention on a political level. This is the significance of the directive. It and the plan put forward are extraordinary documents. At one level the advice of the General Staff on military grounds was ignored by the politicians who were prepared to sacrifice the defence forces in the event of a 'Doomsday' situation: this was a one-way mission. At another level the military warned of the potential hazards of entering a pact with a subversive organisation: the long-term political aims of the Government and the IRA might be the same—the unification of Ireland—but only one wanted this done by peaceful means. Once the IRA were given guns it would be impossible to exercise control over what they did with them. But there is also a third factor that doesn't seem to have been considered by the politicians: that an 'incursion' into, and seizure of, UK territory by the army of a foreign power would be an act of war!

Instead, contacts relating to the arming of Northerners increased. Paddy Kennedy subsequently met with Lynch, Blaney and Boland. He found Lynch very reluctant to accede to a request for arms: he would have no control thereafter. Blaney, on the other hand, was anxious to provide whatever help he could. He felt that it might be necessary for guns to come into Belfast. Kennedy later saw Haughey and told him that Nationalists wanted guns: 'There was no secret about what we were asking,' he said. Jim Sullivan, Adjutant of the IRA's Belfast Brigade, travelled to Dublin for guns also. Sullivan was also chairman of the CCDC. The Defence Committees were dominated by the IRA. As John Kelly explained: 'They were, by and large, the same organization . . . remember that the only people who had any knowledge of arms were the IRA. There were no other people in Belfast on the Nationalist side who had a knowledge of guns and how to use them. So, naturally, they were the people who were looked to at this period for defence purposes.' In Dublin, Sullivan explained that arms were being sought for limited use: 'I pointed out that at no time would any weapons be used for an attack on any group of people in the North. They'd only be used in their defence.' On one visit he claimed that he was offered several hundred rifles which belonged to the FCA (the Irish Territorials)—which were put on the open market after the FCA was re-equipped with modern weapons. The offer appears to have been with-drawn when it became apparent that one of the other clients was a cover for Loyalist paramilitaries. The guns were to be stockpiled in case they would ever be needed in the North.[43] However, unknown to Sullivan, Captain Kelly was trying to steer the Government away from dealings with him. Kelly described Sullivan as a 'nut and a dangerous man' under the influence of the radical Left. He warned that, to date, arms and support 'seem to have got into the wrong hands' in Belfast. This situation had to be remedied. And the remedy was to finance John Kelly and his brother—also an IRA man—whose 'integrity' he underwrote.[44]

According to Captain Kelly, Dublin was selective in who they were prepared to supply weapons to. They did not want to hand money over to a group which wanted to overthrow them. They preferred the more traditional branch of Republicanism that was being offered by the emerging Provisional IRA. Such contacts had already begun by the end of August, when Blaney made contact with an IRA intermediary—before the General Staff Report. He was Francie Donnelly, a Northern IRA commander. The meeting took place along the shores of Malin Head in County Donegal. Donnelly recalled Blaney's making enquires about whether people would be prepared for the defence of the population if weapons were available for them. He wanted to know what amount of weapons would be needed without committing himself to saying that weapons were available. Blaney's recollection agreed with the thrust of Donnelly's account: 'It was my view that, since we, as a government through our army, were not prepared to provide protection for the people up there, then anything, including the procurement of arms for people to defend themselves, was on as far as I was concerned.' At this stage only money was offered as there were no guns available.

The follow-up to this meeting was when Captain Kelly called unannounced at Donnelly's farm. Donnelly recalled a long general discussion about the Northern situation and some questions from Kelly asking how Fianna Fáil would be accepted if the party were to set up branches in the North. Kelly wanted to know the position regarding arms, 'whether we had arms or not' and whether any were likely to be forthcoming. He then went on to ask about an IRA 'Northern Command' structure, although this was not the phrase actually used. Donnelly thought he was implying that there was too much control from Dublin headquarters and that it would be better if people in the North, who knew the situation better, would be willing to procure the necessary equipment for defence. Donnelly took this to imply a break from Dublin. In return there were suggestions—though this was not said directly —that, should the situation arise and should there be a Northern Command, supplies of weapons and possibly money would probably go directly to the North. Kelly's recollection emphasised that although he mentioned Fianna Fáil he was not interested in Fianna Fáil—it was just that the Government he worked for was a Fianna Fáil government. The point in raising this with Donnelly was that the IRA's Dublin leadership 'was seeking to overthrow the Dublin government [and] he would *ipso facto*, have to state that he didn't support that policy . . . I could not go back and say to my superiors, "You must support Francie Donnelly in Derry because this fella is a member of an organization that wants to overthrow you!" It's an unreal situation.' Kelly had paid his visit to Donnelly on 22 August, the same day that IRA dissidents in Belfast moved against the existing Goulding leadership in the city.

Large sums of money were now dispensed by Haughey. It is clear that a considerable proportion went to the IRA. Overall, between 29 August 1969 and 24 March 1970, the sum of £100,000 was made available from the Exchequer to provide aid for victims of the unrest in the North as grant in aid for the relief of distress in the North. Each of these payments was individually authorised, either orally or in writing, by Haughey. Because the Irish Red Cross Society was not permitted to operate in the North by its British equivalent alternative ways had to be found of getting the money into areas where it was needed. A body known as the Belfast Refugee Re-Establishment Committee approached Haughey for help. On his direction £20,000 was paid on 9 October to the Irish Red Cross Society which then transferred the money into the Committee's account in the Munster and Leinster Bank in Belfast. Other financial transactions were not so straight-forward. The same month Haughey suggested that the Irish Red Cross transfer £5,000 of its own funds to an account to be opened as 'The Belfast Fund for the Relief of Distress' at the Bank of Ireland in Clones, County Monaghan. Haughey instructed one of his officials to pay £10,000 to the Red Cross on the understanding it would be paid into the Clones account. The names of three prominent Northern Irish citizens, two of whom were Republican MPs at Stormont, were attached.

On 10 November, £2,500 in cash was drawn and used four days later to open another account at a Munster and Leinster Bank branch in Dublin under the pseudonym 'Anne O'Brien'. Also that day another £4,450 from Clones was used as a deposit at the same branch to open a second account under another fictitious name, 'George Dixon'. A third account—'Relief Committee for the Relief of Distress'—had already been put in place. This became the main working account, with Captain Kelly acting as the main intermediary between it and the three individuals authorised to make withdrawals under the pseudonyms 'John White', 'John Loughran' and 'Roger Murphy'. The account was topped up whenever Captain Kelly informed the Department for Finance that specific sums were required. These were transferred via the Irish Red Cross. Between 12 November 1969 and 9 April 1970, £59,000 of Government money was transferred. The change of location from Clones to Dublin was to bring the account nearer to the paymaster. The Public Accounts Committee which was subsequently set up to investigate what happened to the money could only tie down £20,000 to the Belfast Refugee Re-Establishment Committee and £9,000 to the signatories of the accounts as sums of money that were used for the purpose for which the payments were intended.

Finding out what happened to the rest of the money proved difficult. For example, the Public Accounts Committee found no corroborative documentary evidence that a sum of £31,150 was in fact used for the relief of distress. One of those to whom the cash was handed over and who did the carrying and distribution was IRA dissident John Kelly. He subsequently became a leading Provisional. In fact most of the money went to pay the men manning the barricades at roughly £30–50 a head. Billy McMillen, Belfast OC of the IRA, received the money from Kelly and distributed it. Money from the Irish Government was going into the hands of the IRA.[45] It is also clear that senior Government figures went beyond talking about the possibility of supplying arms to the IRA and were either involved or associated with attempts to supply arms to that group.

The first attempt to provide arms for the North involved John Kelly and Padraig Haughey, brother of Charles. The two travelled to London to arrange an arms deal. The money for the proposed shipment was to come from the 'George Dixon' account in Dublin. There was, however, a suspicion that the contact the Irishmen had made in London were British Secret Service on a spoiling operation. When Captain Kelly later intervened this particular avenue was abandoned.[46] In November Captain Kelly arranged for John Kelly and veteran Republican Sean Keenan to meet Blaney. They were to travel to the United States, according to John Kelly, 'on the express orders of Jim Kelly and Neil Blaney to ascertain how quickly arms would be available in New York from the Irish-American community'. In New York they met veterans of the Anglo–Irish War and the Civil War who were astonished that Kelly and Keenan were working with a Fianna Fáil government. Although no money was initially forthcoming for the procurement of arms, contacts were made which formed the basis of Northern Irish Aid which would later become a key fundraiser for the Provisionals.[47] Just a few days before Christmas, John Kelly came to see a leading IRA member, Sean MacStiofain, and told him about the arrangement to bring in arms, promising 'once they come in I will give them to you'. Soon afterwards, at a meeting arranged between John Kelly, Captain Kelly and Blaney, the Minister suggested that they look to the Continent instead of the US in order to speed up the process. John Kelly believed that this was a plan on Blaney's part to exercise more control over events rather than leaving it in the hands of the Irish Americans.[48]

The relationship between the IRA and the Government continued to develop. When Captain Kelly was later introduced to Haughey the latter was interested in the background of the various individuals who had been coming to Dublin to seek help from ministers. Haughey agreed to cover the Captain's expenses for a forthcoming meeting Kelly was having with members from the various defence committees—effectively, of course, the IRA—in Bailieborough, County Cavan. When Peter Berry, Secretary of the Department of Justice, found out about the proposed meeting he tried unsuccessfully to contact the Minister for Justice and Lynch. He did reach Haughey, however, who called to the hospital where Berry was staying for medical tests. Berry was reassured when Haughey did not appear unduly perturbed by the Bailieborough meeting. Eventually Berry was able to reach the Taoiseach who visited him in hospital on 17 October. The meeting had an element of farce. Berry, who was sedated, tried to explain the situation, but this proved unsuccessful for he had a tube going from one of his nostrils that was drawing fluid from his stomach. Lynch became exasperated with the situation declaring 'This is hopeless. I will get in touch with you again.' Berry, however, was certain—despite admitting to being 'a bit muzzy'—that he had told Lynch about Captain Kelly's Bailieborough meeting with known members of the IRA and the use of money for the purchase of arms.

Years later Lynch provided a different account: Berry, he claimed, made no mention of the alleged conspiracy although he did mention that, from time to time, a number of successful attempts to import arms had been made. However, a few days later Lynch questioned Gibbons about the Bailieborough meeting and Captain Kelly's involvement. Lynch told Gibbons that Berry was the source of his information. Gibbons claimed that he had passed on information relating to the questionable activities of certain members of the Government 'making contact with people they should not make contact with, certainly without the sanction of the government and the Taoiseach'. Berry later insisted: 'no person with a scrap of intelligence could doubt that the Taoiseach was made aware by me'. Yet Lynch did not make 'any more than a cursory inquiry' about the Bailieborough meeting.[49] Thus an extraordinary situation was allowed to develop, and the head of Government made little or no attempt to clarify the serious accusations levelled against some of his senior ministers. That is, of course, assuming he was disapproving of their actions. Put simply, the Irish state was participating actively in the resurrection of the IRA.

The Bailieborough meeting, held on 4–5 October, was a cover for the arming of a 'Northern Command'. Captain Kelly reported to his superior that the first priority of the Republicans gathered there was the acquisition of arms for defensive purposes. The second priority was that of training. This meant weapons training, intelligence training of selected men consisting of two from each of the six counties, demolition training and communications training. Republicans and the Irish Government were increasingly concerned with a potential 'Doomsday' situation in which the Northern minority faced massacre. In the final analysis the Irish Army would have to come to the rescue. Republicans saw themselves as holding areas such as Belfast, Derry, Coalisland and Dungannon, Armagh and Newry for a period. The Republicans were insistent that training, if agreed to, had to start immediately, otherwise 'events will overtake them'.[50] This led to the organisation of military training for Volunteers from Derry at Fort Dunree, a historical monument across the border in Donegal. Boland recalled that 'It was decided to give basic training to groups of individuals in what they call "military street fighting".'[51] Civilians from Derry were enrolled in the FCA and given firearms training until the press got wind of the story leading to the project's suspension. According to John Kelly, in the event of a Doomsday situation, the role of the IRA would have been that of a 'Trojan Horse, so to speak: the IRA would be the first line of defence in areas like Derry, Belfast and Newry. We would hold the line until such time as the Irish army got itself in position in Derry, in Newry and in Belfast. That was the crude outline of the strategy.' One of the crucial questions that was often discussed was how the Irish Army would get to Belfast. Belfast was the weak link. Republicans believed that the strategy was to get to Newry and 'then drive up the motorway to Belfast. We—the IRA—would hold the line in Belfast until such time as they arrived.' They believed that, however outlandish this plan seemed, it was the strategy that the Irish Government had worked out.[52] But the unattractive side of the plan was the dependency on external intervention. Many Republicans were impatient.

THE FORMATION OF THE PROVISIONAL IRA

The debate as to whether or not to set up a 'Northern Command' within the IRA was not one generated by the Irish Government or by any of its representatives such as Captain Kelly. It was an internally generated debate within the Republican Movement that, ultimately, led to a split in the IRA's ranks. This split, at the end of 1969, was an autonomous process driven by six-county dissidents who felt a sense of shame brought on by the failure of the IRA to defend the Catholic minority of Belfast during the August riots. Veteran Republicans involved in the struggle against the British, such as Joe Cahill—who had a death sentence commuted for his involvement in the murder of a RUC constable in the 1940s—and Jimmy Steele, knew that the IRA had been humiliated by the August riots. 'Walking down the road with Jimmy,' recalled Cahill, 'we were met by a group of people who actually spat on us. And they used what was to become a very familiar term at the time—and it was very, very insulting. They said, "IRA—I Ran Away". That was the reaction of the people to the IRA at the time. When I reported back to the IRA in August '69, one of the first tasks I was given was to organize a defence group in Ballymurphy. When I went into Ballymurphy, I was told to get out. I wasn't wanted. I was a member of the IRA. The IRA had deserted them. They didn't want us. "Get out!" they said. When Sean MacStiofain went up to Belfast, shortly after the riots, he was told that he was the only member of the Army Council acceptable from "down there"—Dublin—who was acceptable "up here"?[53]

On 24 August Republican veterans such as David O Conaill, Billy McKee, John Kelly, Joe Cahill, Leo Martin and Seamus Twomey together with (according to one account) a young Gerry Adams met in Andersonstown and decided to issue an ultimatum to the pro-Goulding IRA leadership in Belfast. They put it to the Belfast OC, Billy McMillen and Jim Sullivan, that unless Goulding and his three key supporters on the IRA's GHQ Staff in Dublin resigned they would break from the organisation. They claimed to have the support of the vast majority of Belfast Volunteers. McMillen and Sullivan agreed. A month later the dissidents burst in on a meeting of the Belfast Brigade Staff. McKee told them they had failed the Nationalist people. The dissidents were taking over as the existing IRA leadership. However, a compromise was reached. There was to be notional separation from Dublin; six of the dissidents were to be drafted onto the Belfast Brigade Staff and McMillen was to remain Brigade OC.[54] The tensions were such that Cahill recalled how Sullivan was 'fairly hot about it and wanted to know what the hell was going on'. He 'shook people's shoulders and demanded to know who was behind what he called a "mutiny"'. Sullivan was on the brink of provoking a shoot-out, stung by a taunt that one of the Companies he commanded was a group of 'pansies'. He shouted: 'You'll find out very shortly whether we are a "pansy" group or not. I'll have this block surrounded.' But McMillen intervened to calm things down suggesting the two groups sit down and talk. Because he was his OC, Sullivan agreed: 'You're the boss.'[55]

These tensions within the IRA had, at some point, to result in a final show-down. It was at an IRA Extraordinary Army Convention, held in Dublin in the middle of December 1969, that matters finally came to a head. Here we can see the other factor in the split: a dissatisfaction with the leftist influence within the Republican Movement since the mid-1960s. Those dissatisfied by the Republican Movement's policy in the North and its leftist politics, led by Sean MacStiofain, Ruairi O Bradaigh and David O Conaill, decided that if the incumbent leadership secured a majority at the Convention, reducing the IRA to what they considered a 'cog in a Marxist political machine', then they would regroup and reorganise the Republican Movement. At the Convention there were two critical resolutions from the Goulding leadership: that the IRA should enter a 'National Liberation Front' (NLF), in close connection with organisations of the 'radical left'; and that the Republican Movement should end its policy of parliamentary abstention from the Dáil, London and Stormont Parliaments. It was the second proposal that presented, for traditionalists like MacStiofain, the clear-cut issue of whether to choose between accepting the institutions of partition or upholding the basic Republican principle of Ireland's right to national unity. But MacStiofain and his supporters also opposed anything to do with 'communist organisations' on the basis of their 'ineffectiveness, their reactionary foot-dragging on the national question and their opposition to armed struggle. We opposed the extreme socialism of the revisionists because we believed that its aim was a Marxist dictatorship, which would be no more acceptable to us than British imperialism or Free State capitalism. We believed that every country must travel its own road to the kind of socialism that suits it best.'[56] As far as MacStiofain and his supporters were concerned this was the final proof of the poisonous influence that the influx of left-wing intellectuals was having on the Movement.

The meeting was packed with Goulding's supporters. The NLF motion was passed. So was the ending-of-abstention motion. MacStiofain left with his supporters at the end of the proceedings. He headed north to inform the absent dissidents. In Belfast Billy McKee was appalled. Recognising the Irish Government delegitimised every action taken by the IRA: the taking of a life by a Volunteer became murder. MacStiofain called a special Army Convention to give standing to those who had just split from Goulding.[57] It pledged its allegiance to the thirty-two-county Irish Republic proclaimed at Easter 1916, and established by Dáil Eireann in 1919. A Provisional Executive and a Provisional Army Council of seven were then elected, the term 'Provisional' referring to the claim that the original Extraordinary Army Convention in Dublin had been improperly convened and the decisions taken by it were therefore not irrevocable.[58] MacStiofain became the Provisional IRA's first Chief of Staff.[59]

On 28 December 1969 the Provisional Army Council announced that in view of the decision by a majority of the delegates at an 'unrepresentative' Convention of the IRA to recognise the British six-county and twenty-six-county Parliaments, the minority of the delegates at the Convention, together with those delegates denied admission and the representatives of areas—including Belfast—that had already withdrawn allegiance from Army control, reassembled in their own Convention, repudiated the compromising decision and reaffirmed the fundamental Republican position: 'We declare our allegiance to the 32-County Republic proclaimed at Easter 1916, established by the first Dáil Eireann in 1919, overthrown by force of arms in 1922 and suppressed to this day by the existing British imposed Six County and 26 County partition states.' Already, it was claimed, a majority of Army Units, individual Volunteers and Republicans generally, had given their allegiance to the Provisional Army Council elected by the new Convention and had rejected the 'new compromising leadership'. The adoption of the compromising policy was the logical outcome of an 'obsession' in recent years with parliamentary politics and the consequent undermining of the basic military role of the IRA. The failure to provide the maximum defence possible to 'our people' in Belfast and in other parts of the six counties against the 'forces of British Imperialism' in August was ample evidence of this neglect. The Provisional Army Council called on the Irish people at home and in exile for increased support towards defending their people in the North and the eventual achievement of the full political, social, economic and cultural freedom of Ireland.[60]

The formal severance of the Republican Movement was completed on 11 January 1970 when Sinn Féin delegates met for their Ard Fheis in Dublin. The ending of abstentionism was passed by a majority, although not by the two-thirds required to make it binding under the party's constitution. MacStiofain seized a microphone and declared his allegiance to the Provisional Army Council.[61] A Provisional Caretaker Executive of Sinn Féin followed its IRA alter ego in reiterating that, since its foundation in 1905, Sinn Féin had consistently denied the British Parliament's right to rule in Ireland. Similarly, Provisional Sinn Féin refused to recognise the two 'partition parliaments' in Dublin and Belfast forced on the Irish people. Provisional Sinn Féin's alternative was the 1919 all-Ireland Republican Dáil, and it remained the task of Provisional Sinn Féin to lead the Irish people away from the 'British' six- and twenty-six-county Parliaments, and back towards the re-assembly of the thirty-two-county Dáil which would then legislate for and rule all Ireland.[62] From this point there were two IRAs—Goulding's Official IRA (nicknamed the 'Stickies' after their supporters' habit of sticking their Easter lilies on their lapels) and MacStiofain's Provisional IRA—matched by two parallel Sinn Féins—Official Sinn Féin and Provisional Sinn Féin.

The Officials were bitter over what they thought were the false allegations levelled against them. As he reflected on the split, Goulding identified three reasons for it. The first was that there was a 'certain section of the Republican Movement who come from middle-class families'. Their real interest in the Movement and in Irish freedom was a sentimental one: a traditional rather than an ideological or socialist one. They were involved in the Movement in most cases simply because their fathers or grandfathers were involved in the Tan War or the Fenian Movement. A lot of these people, believed Goulding, welcomed socialist policies and were willing to make all the sacrifices: to sacrifice their privileges and their class position in the interests of the majority of the people of Ireland. There was a section, however, who were not. This section provided the leadership for the split.

The second reason involved another group who were good revolutionaries and good socialists but who disagreed with parliamentary participation because they felt that the Movement, in entering into any of these institutions, was going to deteriorate from a revolutionary organisation into a reformist organisation. They feared that it would become part and parcel of the establishment by being engaged in the institutions of the establishment. This was their objection and this was an honest objection. A section of these, however, merely for the reason that abstentionism had been a principle of Republicanism, held rigidly to that as a principle because it had always been a tenet of their faith—not for ideological reasons—and broke away. The third section included those who had been 'misled into believing that our concentration on the political and agitationary aspects of revolution was responsible for a lack of armed strength when this was needed for defence in the North'. They were led to believe that the Army [IRA] had gone altogether 'political' and did not intend to fight.

Goulding explained the apparent failure to defend Catholic areas in the North: he pointed out that when the 1956–62 guerrilla campaign in the six counties finished, because of the efficiency of the security forces there and because of the lack of support for the IRA among the ordinary people, the actual fighting was dying down anyway. The IRA was unable to sustain it, to keep it going and certainly were unable to expand it. As the fight in the six counties got weaker so also did the financial support from America. When the leadership finally decided that it would have to end the campaign 'our position from the point of view of military material was very bad. We had practically no ammunition left, we had very few arms because of our losses in both the Six and the Twenty six counties. Our finance at the time the campaign finished amounted to about £12. We couldn't adequately defend the people in the North.'

This was not for the want of trying. In 1964 Goulding had gone to America where he spent three or four weeks with the Clann na Gael, the traditional source of Irish-American support for the IRA. He was constantly pointing out to them why he needed support and emphasising the changes in the IRA's policy and the reasons for them. The reaction he got was that they could not support the IRA financially unless there was some form of revolutionary activity, particularly military activity, actually going on in Ireland. Exiles would support activity, but they would not help to prepare for it. Irishmen whom they would ask for money in the Bronx or in Boston would say: 'What is the IRA doing anyway? Their military campaign is over. All they'll do with the money is live a soft life.' Given this it seemed logical to the IRA leadership to go ahead with its leftward agitationary campaign. Maybe the Americans would see that as real revolutionary 'activity'. If not, the IRA was committed to going ahead with it anyway to develop the revolutionary potential in Ireland. Goulding was not saying the Republican Movement did not need the money. 'We did—to start the education programmes, to finance new publicity and publications, to employ lecturers. We'd have taken money from anyone. But we didn't get the support we needed from America.' In the Constitution of the Clann na Gael it stated that they would support the people in Ireland who were working for the freedom of Ireland, but they would only support those that were using force alone. Those two words: 'force alone' meant that they would not support political or agitationary activities in Ireland. Goulding, however, persuaded them to change this so that the revolutionary movement in Ireland could use any means to attain the freedom of Ireland.

After this whatever support did come was diverted into the Civil Rights Movement, instead of coming to the IRA. 'So, we were broke. We hadn't got the wherewithal to buy arms. We were in no position, either in England, in the North or in the South to get arms by military means. Further, because we had decided that the agitationary policies should develop in a political way—in a militant but peaceful way—any arms raids or military activities would obstruct the development of those political and agitationary tactics. We were in a cleft stick. We couldn't be militarily active because we hadn't got the resources and we hadn't conditioned the people for military activities. We knew from all our discussions, decisions and the conclusions that we had come to, that military activity alone couldn't make the revolution. We would first of all have to get the support of the people for military activity. We had to start at the beginning, we had to start with our economic resistance campaign and our political activities from scratch.'

Goulding pointed out that no arms were used in the Bogside by the police when they attacked the people who had barricaded themselves in there. If the IRA had introduced arms into the conflict in the Bogside it would have given the police the excuse to use arms and their potential concentration of arms would have been far greater than the IRA's. It would have been irresponsible for the IRA to have used arms, since a like retaliation by the police would have caused enormous casualties. In Belfast it was a different kettle of fish. There the police and the B-Specials were spearheading the armed elements of the right-wing mob of the Unionist Party. They came in and they used arms first. They attacked with guns. They shot people dead. They attacked schools and houses. The only defence was an armed defence. There the IRA leadership did not provide any *extra* arms. Their policy had always been to maintain local units of the Republican Army in all areas in Ireland and to see that they had what arms were available. There was a small number of arms available in Belfast. These arms were used, and 'used to very good effect', by members of the IRA in the defence of other areas. Extra arms were not sent to Belfast because: 'We didn't think that the police would come in and deliberately shoot up people in the Falls Road area. We felt that the best way for people to engage the police and B-Specials was the way that things had developed in the Bogside. We had a very small amount of arms in . . . our GHQ dumps—a very small amount indeed.'

It was believed that if, prior to 12 August, they had sent these into Belfast, into Derry, into Newry or elsewhere, there might not have been any real fighting in the areas into which they sent these precious arms. This would mean that the IRA leadership would not be able to take them out of that area again and put them where they were really needed. The leadership also felt that dividing these up among different areas would not make an appreciable difference to any one area. The only way that the leadership could see that it might effectively intervene was to arm sections of the IRA from the South using the arms that it had in the GHQ reserve and using whatever arms were in the possession of the local units all over the South of Ireland. It instructed all the local units to bring any arms they had to central dumps. It mobilised people from different areas and formed a number of Active Service Units which were billeted in border areas. The leadership did not use them because, by that time, there were numbers of people in different areas behind barricades. The leadership knew that they had not got the proper means for defence. The British Army was coming in and forming a kind of 'peace' line between the Protestant and Catholic areas. The leadership believed that any outbreak of fighting on the border would do one thing: it would draw the British Army to the border; it would deprive those areas of defence. It would also give the justification needed for the Unionist Government and their right-wing elements such as the RUC, the B-Specials and UVF to commence attacking again and this time with greater effectiveness and claim on justification. Finally, Goulding emphasised that the Republican Movement under his stewardship had not adopted Marxist policies and had not rejected the right to engage in armed struggle:

> We're not Reds. We are not dictated to, nor is our policy made by any outside force. Our policies are policies that have developed because of our own investigations of the situation in Ireland; our policies are a direct development of our historical analysis of the situation in Ireland. What we want to establish in Ireland is the ownership of Ireland.
>
> This idea has been advocated by Pearse, by Connolly, by Mitchell, Lawlor, Emmet and by Tone. Our policy is in the developing tradition of these thinkers. They re-thought the principles in each generation in the light of the problems that beset them in their times. Our time has its own needs and its own demands . . . So, this is our interpretation of their ideas. We believe that now is the opportune time to implement them.[63]

This defence was rejected by the new Provisional leadership. And here it is important to note that, at leadership level, the split was not as simple as some people have suggested—between Neanderthal traditionalists and leftists. Rory O Bradaigh and his supporters regarded Goulding's re-examination of the Movement— its structure and its policies, following on the calling-off of the resistance campaign to British rule in 1962—as a 'very good thing'. The social and economic side of the Movement had been neglected, and there was a definite need to give the Movement a social and economic dimension, as well as the national, political and cultural ones. For that reason, the Movement took part in drawing up the headings for a social and economic programme. The committees which took on various aspects of this programme developed them, brought them back to the Sinn Féin Ard Chomhairle and finalised them. This was the process which went on up to 1966, with which O Bradaigh and his supporters were in agreement. They agreed entirely with the idea of an economic resistance movement; of resistance to the foreign take-over of Irish national assets, of the land of Ireland, of the retail distribution, of the factories and shops. O Bradaigh did not wish the Provisionals to be seen purely as a physical force movement concerned only with the removal of British troops from Irish soil. It should be seen as a movement fighting on many fronts—on the military, on the social, economic, political and cultural fronts, and seeking in turn all these objectives. With regard to social matters, the Provisionals wished to see a co-operative form of ownership. These were based on an idea called Comhar na gComhairsan, or Neighbours' Co-operation, which was developed in the 1920s and 30s in the Republican Movement, and which was broadcast over the IRA radio in 1939.

But there was a combination of specific reasons for the split. As the Provisionals listed these reasons, O Bradaigh made a key theological point: that it was the Goulding wing which had left the IRA and that they were not entitled to claim the title of IRA at all. There were five specific reasons for the split. As a Provisional Army Council representative stated, the first point of difference, 'and a very big one', was the deliberate attempt to undermine and run down the military wing of the Republican Movement—the Army. This began to happen as far back as early 1964 when 'certain reactionary instructions' were issued to the different Units throughout the country: a cut-back on training parades, a restricted recruitment, a reduction in the number of training camps to be held and an obvious lack of interest in the acquisition of arms. All of this led directly to the decline of the IRA and led also directly to the disaster of August 1969.

The second point concerned the different attitudes to the various parliaments that claimed jurisdiction in Ireland. Goulding's attitude was one of participation, and participation, as far as the Provisionals were concerned, involved recognition. As O Bradaigh emphasised, this involved the whole question of what a revolutionary movement and the Republican Movement were and where they came from— before one could even consider where they were going. The Army Council representative listed the third point as the Goulding leadership's determination to set up a National Liberation Front with what was then the Irish Worker's Party, now the Communist Party; and their determination to co-operate, regardless of the consequences, with other Marxist organisations. This was not in the interests of the Irish people or the Republican Movement: 'We feel that Marxism has no place in Ireland, that our Socialism must be based on, first of all, the Proclamation of 1916. It must be based on Irish tradition; it must be based on Christian principles . . . we feel . . . that close co-operation with these Marxist organisations would not help us achieve the objectives of the Republican Movement.'

The fourth point was the abolition of Stormont. The Provisionals believed the abolition of Stormont would be a major step forward towards the achievement of the National Aim: 'We do not regard Stormont as an Irish institution. It's just a puppet-Parliament, and obviously, its abolition would mean the destruction of the Unionist power-base. They would have no source from which to dole out their powers or their privileges. Its abolition would bring about a direct confrontation between the Irish people, particularly the people in the North, and the British occupying power. That this buffer of Stormont, which, after all, it just gives this—tá mé ag smaoineamh as Gaeilge anois—this appearance of democracy in the North, we felt that with that gone, it's obviously a very significant step forward towards the achievement of National Aims. We just can't see why any Irish person, who regards himself as Nationalist or Republican, should be concerned with retaining Stormont.' O Bradaigh added: 'I don't think it should be thought that we want direct British rule as a solution.'

The fifth point concerned the internal methods in use in the Republican Movement: 'We feel there is evidence to show, that for six or seven years now, there has been an infiltration and an attempted takeover of the Republican Movement. This consisted of bringing people who would be called intellectuals (certainly very able and competent people) into the Republican Movement from the British Communist Party, the Connolly Association in England, and the Irish Worker's Party here. They were positioned in places of influence; in Head Office; in HQ Staff; in the Ard Comhairle.' O Bradaigh explained how, following on this, came the squeezing out of whole sections of the Movement, for instance, the Cumann na mBan women's organisation, the entire North Kerry Comhairle Cheantair, involving 250 members and thirteen cumainn, the expulsion of people like Jimmy Steele of Belfast and Sean Keenan of Derry. There was also the pushing forward of others of 'mature years' who had never displayed any interest whatsoever in the Movement, nor indeed, had ever bought Republican journals or subscribed to the Prisoners' Dependents' Fund. But they invariably had a background in extreme Socialist organisations. They were brought in, and they were quickly promoted to positions of influence, and the whole tone and direction of these people acted as a pressure group within the Movement. They encouraged each other and pushed each other forward. The policy seemed to be 'handed down from the top, they were master-minded, one could say, and they were handed down, and, if one might use the term, they were imposed on the movement, rather than the result of membership-participation'. The Army Council representative added that it also became evident that there were two standards of discipline, that the people who accepted these new policies, within reason, could do more or less what they liked. Where they did overstep the mark altogether, such disciplinary action as was taken against them was 'ridiculously lenient'.[64]

This was the background to the ideological and policy divisions that led to the split of 1969–70. The split was engineered by Dublin. But elements of the Irish state nurtured the Provisionals. After the split MacStiofain confirmed that the money from the Irish Government changed direction: 'Before the split, the money was going to somebody who was active in the Goulding wing of the movement. The money was stopped altogether for a few weeks. When it resumed again it went to somebody who was working with us. That was the way it worked out. The money in Belfast for the Defence Committee was distributed by a person who was one of our leading members.'[65] Like the Irish Government, MacStiofain believed that the most urgent task facing Republicans was to provide all possible assistance to 'our people' in the North, left defenceless against the violence of 'sectarian bigots'. But there was a sting in the tail: the Irish people, he warned, would never be free until British rule was overthrown and the 'free Gaelic Republic of all Ireland' was established. And he reminded Republicans that the 'Irish Republic was proclaimed by the only way possible—by force of arms—and only by force of arms can the Republic we seek be established'.[66] And it is at this point that one can see the fatal flaw in the Irish Government's policy towards the Provisionals. They could not control the Provos for they had their own agenda. It was a dangerous game to play. And it was about to blow up in Lynch's face.

THE ARMS CRISIS

Senior cabinet ministers and members of Irish Military Intelligence now became embroiled in attempts to import arms and transfer them to the Provisionals. Captain Kelly had been arguing for a time that the Northerners should go down to Dublin and ask for the Irish Government's support and secure co-operation for the protection of Catholic areas. Eventually, in January 1970, the Northerners agreed to this in principle. On his own admission, Kelly was offering advice rather than limiting his role to intelligence-gathering, without any explicit authorisation from Dublin. He did not think, as others were to allege, that he had gone beyond his instructions: for example, in discussion with Gibbons, Kelly found it difficult to define the phrase 'an Intelligence operation'. He defined the training which had been given to people from the Bogside in the use of firearms for their own defence as an 'intelligence operation'. Everything that was related to the six counties was intelligence. This was in case the Irish Army became involved in the situation. Therefore it was necessary to find out what the situation was there and contingency plans had to be made. Kelly argued that one prepared for these contingency plans by getting information and by finding out what the people in the area of potential operations intended doing, what they were doing and what they would do.[67]

So in mid-January Kelly saw Colonel Hefferon, Director of Military Intelligence, and told him that the defence committees were without arms and were determined to purchase arms to defend the Catholic population in the event of Protestant extremists trying to 'wipe them out'. The defence committees had requested Kelly to help and the impression Hefferon had was that it was 'technical assistance' they needed in the purchase. Hefferon pointed out to Kelly that he could not, as a serving Army officer, become involved in the purchase of guns and that, if he wished to become involved, he would have to resign from the Army. Hefferon did not, however, see any necessity for him to become involved. But Kelly felt that he would be acting dishonourably if he did not assist the Catholics in the North. Hefferon advised Kelly that he should look into the interests of his family and career and return to see him some time the following week. At the end of January Kelly returned and informed Hefferon that he was determined to retire from the Army.[68]

In early February 1970 Paddy Doherty and Sean Keenan—a Provo himself—met with Blaney who told them how some of the obsolete .303 rifles that were being discarded by the Irish Army had almost fallen into the hands of loyalists. Blaney suggested that if the weapons could have been supplied to the loyalists so easily there was no reason why they should not be provided for the Nationalist population. He was thinking of a scheme to get Haughey to supply defence committees with the money to buy the arms. Blaney summoned Haughey to the meeting. Gibbons was also invited. They were all exercised by the attempt of the Protestant extremists to accumulate arms. With the setting up of gun clubs by ex-Specials in the North and the knowledge that there were around 100,000 guns in the North—overwhelmingly in Protestant hands as legally-held firearms—they feared that another 'pogrom against the Catholic population' was on the cards. According to Doherty's account Haughey then made what can only be described as an astonishing statement to Blaney and Gibbons: 'Let's take the North . . . We should not apologise for what is our right.' Gibbons, however, pointed out that this just was not possible—the Army was 3,500 under establishment figures. A recruitment drive was underway and he was also preparing for a 'Doomsday' situation in the North. However, if the fears being expressed became a reality 'we will have to become involved'.

Blaney decided that the Northern men should put their case to Lynch—but Haughey would have to telephone the Taoiseach because 'I can't stand the man.' Haughey phoned Lynch there and then making an appointment for Keenan and Doherty to meet him the following morning. Doherty decided that the best approach would be to ask that the weapons be held near to the border by the Irish Army—he thought close to Derry—so that 'we can be quickly armed in the event of an attack and play the rest by ear'. Blaney suggested that the men should try and get some kind of commitment from Lynch and should press for the rifles which were being discarded to be given to the defence associations. If he would not agree to this then they should ask for gas masks: 'That's the least he can do.'

The next morning Doherty and Keenan travelled with Billy Kelly, both a spokesman for the Defence Association in Belfast and a member of the Provisional IRA; he was also John Kelly's brother. Thus the Taoiseach was meeting with a three-man delegation which included two Provisionals. When they met Lynch, Keenan urged him to be prepared for the inevitable confrontation. Doherty suggested that guns were not necessary. Keenan added that weapons should be stored so as to be accessible for ready distribution near the border in County Donegal. At this point, Billy Kelly waded in: he demanded guns to protect the Nationalist population of Belfast. Doherty watched the Taoiseach flinch; he tried to calm Kelly down and returned to the situation in Derry which was much more manageable. Doherty asked Lynch for gas masks. Lynch replied: 'Gas masks I can give you . . . but guns I will have to think about.' The Taoiseach then turned his attention to partition and shocked his visitors by suggesting that a speedy end to the problem was out of the question: 'If we were given a gift of Northern Ireland tomorrow, we could not accept it,' he said. This was because of the financial subvention being provided by Britain for social services. At the present rate of economic growth this might be possible in a decade. Although Doherty was despondent on leaving the Taoiseach's office he was surprised to find that

Keenan and Kelly were jubilant. They thought that Lynch had given them a commitment to provide weapons. 'We blew it,' Doherty told them. 'That man has no intention of getting involved in Northern Ireland.'[69]

But the Irish Government was preparing to intervene in Northern Ireland if need be. On 6 February 1970 the cabinet formally instructed the Minister for Defence to order the Chief of Staff to prepare and train the Army for incursions into Northern Ireland 'if and when such a cause became necessary' and to have respirators, arms and ammunition made ready for the Northern minority to protect themselves. Gibbons explained to the Chief of Staff and the Director of Intelligence that the Taoiseach and other ministers had met delegations from the North. At these meetings there were urgent demands for respirators, weapons and ammunition, 'the provision of which the Government agreed as and when necessary'. Accordingly, the Chief of Staff was instructed to put truck-loads of these items at readiness so that they could be available in a matter of hours if required. The Minister asked the Chief of Staff the nature of the most critical deficiencies of the defence forces, to which the Chief of Staff replied: manpower, armoured fighting vehicles and transport! Gibbons then instructed the Chief of Staff to hold himself in readiness to discuss estimates with Haughey. A military study of the directive was undertaken and the Chief of Staff arranged a meeting with the Minister on 13 February to seek clarification as follows:

1. The military assumed that incursions would only be mandated in circumstances where there would be a complete breakdown of law in N Ireland.
    The Minister confirmed that such a situation was what was envisaged.
2. The military assumed that the sole objective of the incursions would be the protection of the lives and property of the minority.
    The Minister confirmed that such was envisaged.
3. The military requested information regarding the Government's diplomatic representations before incursions would be mounted.
    The Minister did not consider that such representations would be made.
4. The Chief of Staff queried if the Government intended in the circumstances of incursions:
    (a) to declare a state of emergency
    (b) to introduce the National Security Bill
    (c) to introduce a form of compulsory military service.
    The Minister thought that the Government would declare a state of emergency.
5. In view of the absolute necessity to ensure secrecy in contingency planning, the Chief of Staff enquired how much information had been given to the Northern delegations of the Government's intentions.
    The Minister indicated that the Northern delegations had not been informed of the directive to the defence forces.

On 18 February the equipment to be handed over was assembled in Dublin and Athlone. It consisted of 500 rifles, 3,000 respirators, 80,000 rounds of .303 ammunition and 99,000 rounds of 9 mm ammunition.[70]

If, in a Doomsday situation, these arms were to be transferred to the North they would meet a well organised recipient for, by Easter, the Provisionals had grown so quickly that they were obliged to reorganise. At this time they operated at three levels. At the bottom were the local defence committees which were vigilantes who acted as early warning systems against loyalist incursions. Above them were the Auxiliary IRA composed of men whose job was to defend those of their own areas most likely from Protestant attack. Above them was the full-time IRA unit or company modelled on the British Army's structure. Now the Provisionals expanded from one Belfast battalion to three each with its own complement of companies.[71] What makes all the co-operation of Dublin with the Provisionals so controversial is that any arms transferred to them might, in the beginning, be used for defensive purposes; but thereafter they could be used for offensive operations. Early in January 1970 the Provisional Army Council had already met to decide military policy for the reorganised movement. The aim was, in time, to launch an all-out offensive action against the 'British occupation system'.[72] In providing financial and (attempted) military support elements of the Irish Government and Military Intelligence were helping to start a war.

In Easter of 1970 the Irish Government thought the foretold Doomsday situation had arrived. Rioting broke out in Derry, Armagh and Belfast. The most severe was in Belfast where Catholics from the Ballymurphy estate confronted first Protestants and then the British Army. A Military Intelligence file records how, on 2 April, Gibbons rang the Chief of Staff from Naas. He indicated that he had received information from Blaney that attacks on the minority were planned and that the British security forces would be withdrawn and accordingly would not afford protection for the minority. The Minister felt that material stored in Dublin should be moved forward. That night 500 rifles, 80,000 rounds of ammunition and 3,000 respirators were stored in Dundalk military barracks. Military Intelligence subsequently ascertained that the information provided by Blaney was without foundation. On 4 April 350 rifles were returned to stores in Dublin because of storage problems in Dundalk. Following intelligence reports of a possible raid by subversive elements on Dundalk military barracks the balance of 150 rifles and 80,000 rounds of ammunition were also returned to Dublin.[73]

Captain Kelly, who was abroad at the time of the riots, had been asked to return in order to distribute the rifles in the North. The consignment had been loaded in such haste that the next morning gas masks littered the road to Dundalk. Blaney, asked years later if the arms would have gone to the Provisionals, commented: 'Probably, probably, very probably.' When asked if they would have gone to the Officials he was a little more forthcoming: 'No way.'[74] Meanwhile the Chief of Staff had proceeded to form a small select planning board to prepare contingency plans to implement the Government's directive for an incursion into Northern Ireland. As we have seen, a preliminary study had indicated the very low standard of combat efficiency for the tasks which might arise. A new paper prepared on 6 April was presented to Gibbons and Haughey.[75] It updated the assessment of the defence forces' military capabilities for an incursion. It assumed that the purpose of the operations by the defence forces in Northern Ireland would be directed solely towards the protection of the lives and property of the minority. It was accepted that incursions would be opposed by force. An estimate of forces available to the British made uncomfortable reading:

Table 1 Forces available to Northern Ireland

British Military Forces	Strength
Eight infantry battalions	5,000 combat troops
Two armoured car sqadrons	1,000 support troops
One battalion Territorial Army Volunteer Reserve and support troops	3,000
Ulster Defence Regiment (ceiling 5,000)	4,000
Police	
Royal Ulster Constabulary (unarmed but trained in the use of arms and arms available)	3,500
Ulster Special Constabulary over and above those inducted in the Ulster Defence Regiment	5,000
Total	21,500

On the other hand the strength of the Irish Defence Forces in permanent service was 8,860. This figure, however, included the Air Corps, the Naval Service, troops overseas and service elements such as the Observer Corps, Medical Corps, Ordnance Corps, Supply and Transport Corps and Cadets, Apprentices, Band Boys and recruits in training. Excluding these elements there would not be more than 2,500 line troops available to be mustered, organised into units and trained to undertake incursions. Furthermore over 1,700 serving personnel were over the age of forty years and a high proportion of these would be unfit for front-line combat duties: a total of 560 personnel were unfit for combat duty. The assessment indicated that the armed opposition likely to be encountered by incursions into Northern Ireland was vastly superior in strength, organisation, combat training and equipment to those elements of the Defence Forces which could be mustered for such operations. The superiority in equipment was most critical in armoured cars, armoured personnel carriers (APCs) and offensive air support which could immobilise Irish forces. The General Staff felt that 'the Government should be made aware of the disastrous consequences which would follow if such operations were mounted on the basis of present strength and status of supply'.[76]

Despite these warnings it remained the Irish Government's policy to implement an incursion into Northern Ireland in a Doomsday situation. In June the Taoiseach confirmed Gibbons' outlining of Government policy to the military as part of a briefing for the new Minister of Defence. In a meeting with Lynch, An Ceann Foirne explained to the new Minister the context in which military policy towards Northern Ireland was examined: in view of the Government's policy to reunify the national territory by 'peaceful means' no military studies had been undertaken nor had any plans been prepared, even on a contingency basis, for military action in Northern Ireland prior to August 1969. The term 'incursion' had been used in order to convey that 'cross border activity' was not intended as an invasion but rather as a 'short temporary stay' to carry out a mercy mission and return.

The Chief of Staff indicated that an incursion into Newry, although close to the border, was considered as the extreme limit of incursion capability at the defence forces' present strength and status of supply. Some 800 troops would be necessary for such an incursion, the stay might have to be limited to some twenty-four hours at most and 'considerable casualties could be anticipated'. Lynch confirmed that it was the policy of the Government that force 'would NOT be used as a means to reintegrate the national territory' and recounted the various means used by Hillery to bring the matter before the UN, including the deployment of a UN peace-keeping force which would include Irish troops. The Taoiseach explained that he had given considerable thought to the possibility that Irish troops could work in conjunction with British troops in the event that a situation arose in the future in which British troops would be unable to defend the minority. He confirmed that any incursion would not be preceded by political or diplomatic representations.[77] The significance of this briefing is that it took place in June, following the controversy over the arms-smuggling operation described below and the sacking of two senior ministers—the gravest internal crisis that the Irish state had faced since the Civil War. The Irish Government's policy remained that of military intervention in the North in a Doomsday situation even after the arms crisis.

The trouble with playing with fire is that one can get burnt. Jack Lynch got burnt in mid-1970 when the clandestine intrigue surrounding Northern policy burst into the public gaze. The reason Captain Kelly had to be ordered back to Ireland during the Ballymurphy disturbances in early April was because he was in Europe with the Provisionals' John Kelly buying guns. The money he had used—£32,500—had come from the 'George Dixon' account in Dublin.[78] By this stage he had already visited Germany on a number of occasions to purchase a variety of weapons including machine guns, grenades, rifles and pistols as well as flak jackets and ammunition. It was initially planned to ship the arms from Antwerp on the

City of Dublin which set sail on 19 March and docked in Dublin six days later. Haughey instructed customs to authorise entry of the cargo without inspecting it. Captain Kelly and John Kelly were at Dublin docks with a lorry to take the arms to a hiding place. The weapons, however, had not been loaded in Antwerp because the papers for them were not in order.

Captain Kelly made a further trip to the Continent and brought Albert Luykx, a businessman of Belgian origin, along to act as an interpreter. The arms consignment consisted of 200 machine guns, eighty-four light machine guns, fifty general-purpose machine guns, fifty rifles, 200 grenades, 200 pistols and 250,000 rounds of ammunition—which hardly seemed defensive weapons. The plan was to fly the consignment into Dublin Airport. But Special Branch were also aware of the shipment and planned to intercept it on arrival. Haughey was tipped off that the importation was compromised. He contacted Peter Berry who confirmed that the Department of Justice knew. Haughey asked if the consignment could be let through on a guarantee that it would go direct to the North. Berry said 'No'. Haughey thought this was 'a bad decision'. Haughey called the operation off.[79]

According to Gibbons the first intimation of gun-running that he recalled was Hefferon's suggestion that an application for leave by Captain Kelly to visit his sister in Frankfurt might be used as an opportunity to vet guns; Hefferon also pointed out to the Defence Minister that Kelly did in fact have a sister in Frankfurt and that the proposed visit might well be bona fide. Gibbons assumed that if guns were involved these would be for 'some groups' in Northern Ireland.[80] When Gibbons asked Haughey if he knew anything about a 'gun-project' he replied that he did not, that his views on it were the same as Gibbons and that any action would have to be taken by the Government collectively.[81] Gibbons had raised the matter because it was becoming apparent to him that such a project was underway. Kelly had already told him in early April of an abortive attempt to send in arms by sea. Blaney also mentioned the incident to Gibbons around the same time. Soon afterwards Blaney sounded Gibbons out on his willingness to permit the importation of arms by use of his office of Minister of Defence.[82]

Although Blaney spoke somewhat obliquely, Gibbons clearly understood that what Blaney was conveying was that he knew the Minister of Defence could authorise the customs-free importation of arms and was inquiring if there were any circumstances in which he would consider issuing this authority irregularly: if arms were brought in with the authorisation of the Minister of Defence then they would be deemed a legal importation; if not the importation would be illegal. Gibbons told Blaney that he would not consider it under any circumstances. Blaney said 'You wouldn't?'; Gibbons replied 'No.' Blaney seemed angry and disappointed. By now Gibbons knew from the Minister for Justice that his Department had had Captain Kelly under surveillance for a considerable time. Gibbons was worried about certain of 'our colleagues' in the cabinet and mentioned his intention of 'having a chat' with the Taoiseach. This was also in early April. Gibbons claimed that Military Intelligence was 'very dissatisfied' with Captain Kelly's performance and failure to report over long periods.[83] What Gibbons was probably referring to was the fact that Hefferon had just retired as Director of Military Intelligence on 1 April and was replaced by Colonel Delaney who unexpectedly found himself in the midst of a political earthquake. Delaney took a radically different approach from that of his predecessor to the actions of Captain Kelly.

A second attempt to import arms came to Gibbons' attention when the Department of Defence was contacted on 17 April by Dublin Airport about a supposed consignment of arms for the Irish Army. Gibbons' Department immediately contacted the Department of Justice. Gibbons spoke to Delaney on 20 April and asked him to prepare a report for the Taoiseach. The new Director asked for a couple of days to collect all the available data.[84] That same day Gibbons spoke to Haughey and told him of the news from Dublin Airport. Haughey commented: 'The dogs on the street are barking it.' Gibbons asked Haughey if he could stop the operation. He replied 'I will stop it for a month.' The ability to delay the operation implies that Haughey was involved. Gibbons pleaded: 'For God's sake stop it altogether.' Gibbons added jokingly: 'Are these guns yours or Blaney's?' Haughey jokingly replied 'There [sic] mine.'[85]

On 22 April Gibbons spoke again to Delaney who, in the meantime, had been building a picture of some of the detail behind Captain Kelly's activities.[86] As far as the new Director of Military Intelligence was concerned Kelly was a rogue officer (whereas Kelly believed he was faithfully implementing Government policy). Delaney had little idea of what Kelly's activities had been in Northern Ireland, since he had not been briefed by his predecessor and was struggling to put the pieces together. As a picture emerged An tAire was briefed that Kelly had connected with Nationalist and Republican elements in Northern Ireland acting as a field liaison officer and as a 'link man' for these groups, and that he had reported directly to Colonel Hefferon with very little contact with the Security Sub-Section, from October 1969. His activities had also brought him into contact with IRA leaders and he had openly promised money for the purchase of arms. From late November 1969 it seemed that he ceased to have any contact with the Security Sub-Section. No reports from him were on record in the Intelligence Security Sub-Section. The 'Comdt Kelly' who had come to notice as seeking a licence to import tons of 'goods'—arms—had been identified as Captain Kelly and 'it is apparent that this is an attempt to import arms illegally for subversive groups on both sides of the border'. The conclusions reached were that:

> The purchase of arms in this fashion has grave implications for military and State Security. Weapons should be purchased only for the forces of the State and NOT for illegal underground groups ... The giving of arms to untrained people is a most serious matter. John HUME expressed the view that such

action would be 'suicide' . . . If illegal groups get arms in this fashion they are as likely to use them against our forces as they are against the BRITISH and so we are jeopardising our forces' safety . . . It may be surmised that the import of arms in this way will mean that they cannot be traced back but this is just not so. If any of these weapons are subsequently captured it will be possible to trace their origins . . . It is emphasised strongly that the weapons should be seized at point of entry . . . KELLY's own activities give cause for disquiet. He has been operating openly as a G 2 (Int) Officer and is well known on both sides of the border as such. He has made no apparent effort to conceal his identity. This is utterly irresponsible and must seriously compromise the activities of the Intelligence Section . . . His open consorting with illegal groups is also a serious Security matter, particularly as he is well informed on all activities and connections of the Intelligence Service here. Other agencies, such as the Gardaí, could be compromised also . . . It must be accepted that BRITISH Intelligence, now operating in a big way in NORTHERN IRELAND, will get on to it. They have their international links with European Security Agencies and CIA so the likelihood of this activity going undetected is small. As well as the Intelligence implication, there is the political reaction of the BRITISH Government to be considered . . . These arms will eventually end up in IRA hands thus constituting a threat to Army SECURITY, which is the direct responsibility of the Minister For Defence, Int Security, the Chief of Staff and the General Staff.[87]

An tAire agreed with the recommendation that Kelly should leave Military Intelligence immediately and suggested switching him to an infantry appointment for a few months until he could get a job outside the Army. He also agreed that: 'a. Arms could be turned against us', 'b. Untrained people in NORTHERN IRELAND should not get arms' and 'c. BRITISH Intelligence and CIA could know.'[88]

The accusations that Kelly was a loose cannon relate as much to the inept supervision he was given by Hefferon. Despite being Director of Intelligence and Kelly's superior, Hefferon did not ask Kelly directly about any financial transaction he carried out between the Northerners and Haughey. As far as he was concerned the operation of other accounts was a matter between Kelly and Haughey. On two occasions Hefferon did inform Gibbons that Kelly was operating outside the state's jurisdiction—that is in Northern Ireland—and drawing money for services rendered outside the states jurisdiction. This was most unusual. But as he was not told to stop these activities Hefferon felt that it was not his job to do so. Crucially, for Hefferon, the incursion directive of February 1970 'possibly put a different complexion on matters than had been the case previously'. Hefferon subsequently rejected the claim suggested at the Committee on Public Accounts that it seemed that Captain Kelly was the Director of Intelligence and that Colonel Hefferon the junior officer: 'At the time this trouble boiled up we had to set up a sizable operation for us and recruit from the very small peacetime staff which was geared for purely military intelligence. We were faced with the situation where there was an involvement of some kind in Northern Ireland, where our troops were within a few miles of the border and in which we had tremendous problems, not alone in the north but in the south also and even in Dublin where we had a situation of some thousands of people clamouring outside gates of a barracks asking for weapons. It was a state of high public excitement.'[89]

On 23 April Gibbons met Blaney in his office at the latter's request. Hefferon, who was no longer in post, and Captain Kelly were present when he arrived. There was a conversation about the breakdown of a project to bring guns into Dublin Airport and the means by which the situation could be handled. Blaney did most of the talking. He said that the operation had been halted and felt that since there was no delivery there 'could be no big row about it'. This confirmed Gibbons' earlier suspicions regarding Blaney. On 24 April Gibbons submitted his own verbal report and a written one from Delaney to Lynch. At the end of the month Kelly submitted his resignation from the Army. Gibbons sent for him and asked him if he had any remarks to make; Kelly replied that he had not and Gibbons signed his resignation.[90]

By this stage Lynch had already been informed by Peter Berry about the arms plot. Berry had been worried that his Minister for Justice, Michael Moran, was not passing on information to the Taoiseach. Moran had a serious drink problem and it was impacting seriously on his ability to carry out his ministerial duties. Berry decided to force Lynch's hand. He went to see President de Valera who told him to see Lynch. This he did. The Taoiseach instructed Berry to have the whole matter investigated. On 22 April Lynch had decided to interview Blaney and Haughey. However, Haughey had been hospitalised that morning, apparently due to a riding accident, although controversy surrounded the authenticity of this story with more colourful rumours alleging the Minister for Finance was beaten up by a jealous husband. Either way the Minister for Finance was in a serious condition and Haughey's doctor refused Lynch access to his patient. There were also problems with Moran. There were calls for his resignation following a drunken outburst at a public reception. On 29 April Lynch interviewed Blaney who denied everything and refused to resign. Haughey, still in hospital, also denied involvement.[91]

But if Lynch hoped the matter was finished his hand was forced when the Leader of the Opposition, Liam Cosgrave, received an anonymous note simply signed 'Garda' and stating: 'a plot to bring in arms from Germany worth £80,000 for the North under the guise of the Department of Defence has been discovered. Those involved are a Captain Kelly, Intelligence Officer, Colonel Hefferon, Director of Intelligence. See that this scandal is not hushed up.' The note also referred to Blaney and Haughey. On 1 May Lynch was approached by Cosgrave. Cosgrave told Lynch of the note. The Taoiseach issued a statement announcing that he had already been informed of a plot to unlawfully import arms. *Prima facie* these reports involved two members of the Government—Blaney and Haughey—whom Lynch had interviewed.[92] At 2.50 a.m. Lynch confirmed the resignation of Blaney and Haughey 'because I am satisfied that they do not subscribe fully to government policy in relation to the present situation in the six counties as stated by me at the Fianna Fáil ard fheis'.[93] Kevin Boland also resigned in support of his colleagues and in protest at the Taoiseach's handling of the affair.

It fell to an outsider, the new British Ambassador, John Peck, to capture the enormity of the crisis: it was, he told London, 'one of the more momentous events in the history of the Republic'. Just how deep the crisis was could be illustrated by transposing the crisis to the government of any country one cared to mention: the Prime Minister had dismissed two of his party strong-men for suspected illegal activities and handed the papers over to the Attorney-General. As a result they were arrested on criminal charges. Another powerful minister resigned in sympathy and made public his hostility to the Prime Minister over a fundamental and highly inflammable issue of foreign policy in which he considered the arrested ministers to have been right. No such thing had ever happened before in the history of the Irish Republic and 'it would be sensational in any country'.[94]

Where then did this leave Lynch's Northern policy and, indeed, his position as Taoiseach? In the short term the matter was resolved when, in October, Haughey, Captain Kelly, John Kelly and Albert Luykx were put on trial for the second time after a first trial was halted by the judge. They were charged with the illegal importation of arms. The charges against Blaney were dropped. In a sensational verdict all four were acquitted. The jury decided in less than half an hour that the attempted arms importation was not illegal because it had been authorised by the Minister of Defence.[95] In the longer term Blaney, Boland and Haughey remained a constant threat to the Taoiseach's position.

But part of what had been sown by Dublin in 1969–70 was now about to be reaped in the North. In January 1970 a defining moment occurred in the history of the Troubles: the Provisional Army Council met to decide military policy for the reorganised movement. With the summer marching season of 1970 as the most likely flashpoint, the Provisional IRA determined that the most urgent priority would be area defence against loyalists and the British Army. All energies would be devoted to providing material, financial and training assistance for Northern units. As soon as it became feasible and practical, the Provisionals would move from a purely defensive position into a phase of 'combined defence and retaliation'. After a sufficient period of preparation, when the movement was considered strong enough and the circumstances ripe, it would go into the third phase, launching an all-out offensive action against the 'British occupation system'.[96] By the end of January 1970 the Provisionals had a Belfast Brigade that was structured into Battalion and Company levels. The Belfast Staff had Billy McKee as OC with Seamus Twomey as his Adjutant. Leo Martin became Intelligence

Officer; Sean McNally, Quartermaster; Tom O'Donnell, Finance Officer; Sean Murphy, Training Officer; with Albert Price controlling the Auxiliaries. They divided the city into three battalion areas.

The First Battalion area stretched from the Upper Falls and extended north to cover the Ballymurphy estate and west Andersonstown. The Second Battalion operated in the Lower Falls, Clonard and the Divis Flats. The Third Battalion covered Ardyone and the Boyne to the north, the New Lodge and Unity Flats and the Short Strand/Ballymacarrett just over the bridges on the fringe of Protestant east Belfast. McKee was regarded as a disciplinarian by his men; single and a devout Catholic, he attended Mass daily. Twomey was born in Marchioness Street in 1919. He joined the Movement's youth wing, Fianna Éireann, in 1936 and the IRA in 1937. Twomey was interned during the Second World War.[97] Jimmy Steele was in charge of publicity. Born in 1907, Steele joined na Fianna Éireann at a very early age. After the Treaty split he was first arrested in 1923; his first term of penal servitude came in 1936; more prison terms followed in 1940 and 1943.[98] Steele—at the time of his death in August 1970 he had risen to the rank of Lieutenant-General within the IRA—set up *Republican News*, the Provisionals' mouthpiece. Tom O'Donnell was a fifties man from the Short Strand. Born in July 1932 he joined the Republican Movement in 1950 at the age of eighteen. He was interned in 1957. In 1969, when a defence association was set up in the Short Strand, he and another local man, Jimmy George, were arrested in England for attempting to procure arms. After six months in Brixton Prison the charges were dropped and they returned to Belfast where O'Donnell joined the new Provisional Staff. Another leading figure at this time, who played a key role in the re-organisation of the Movement, was Frank Card—Proinsias MacAirt. Another internee of the forties he assisted Steele in the foundation of *Republican News*, later becoming editor.[99]

With a return to traditional values, Republicans who had dropped out rejoined. Martin Meehan, a future senior IRA commander in Belfast, disgusted by the failure of August, was assured by Billy McKee that the first priority would be the protection of Nationalist areas. While there was not going to be an immediate offensive against the British Army the intention was there: McKee said 'these things take time. People have to be trained. People have to be motivated. People have to be equipped. All this won't happen overnight.' Meehan rejoined.[100] Another Volunteer, Brendan Hughes, recalled that the 'only objective I ever heard in the early days was to get the Brits out of Ireland. I remember sitting in Proinsias McAirt's house which was the hub of Republican activity at the time, and I recall Billy McKee saying that this is our opportunity now with the Brits on the streets, this is what we wanted, open confrontation with the army. Get the Brits out through armed resistance, engage them in armed conflict and send them back across the water with their tanks and guns. That was the Republican objective.'[101] It was as simple as that: on the sectarian embers of the 1969 violence was poured the inflammable liquid that was violent Republicanism. A small

group of unrepresentative members made the decision to attack the British Army
—the personification of the cancer they believed was at the heart of Ireland's
problems. It was this single decision that transformed the relations between the
Army and the Catholic community. The Army's role was transformed from
peacekeeping to peacemaking by the actions of the Provisional IRA. Nothing
would be the same again. The original Troubles that erupted in 1968—Protestant
against Catholic—were the basic essence of the conflict in Northern Ireland; it
now evolved into a second phase—a second Troubles. The tragedy was that the
basic division in Ireland was distorted into a conflict between the Republican
Movement and the British state. It set hopes of a rapprochement between North
and South, Unionist and Nationalist, Protestant, Catholic and dissenter back
decades. It was not the British state that stood in the way of unity. For nearly
thirty years the IRA fought the wrong war.

CONCLUSION

What's in a word? In Northern Ireland quite a lot, the most obvious being 'Londonderry'/'Derry': used often but not exclusively to denote whether one is Protestant or Catholic. In order to comprehend the origins of the Troubles that broke out in the late 1960s it is necessary to understand that there were two completely different worldviews contained within Unionism and Nationalism: for example, as ordinary working class folk in the districts of Belfast or Derry, or as farmers in rural Fermanagh, the people of Northern Ireland would have a myriad of similar experiences that everyday life would throw up; but as Unionists and Nationalists, though they inhabited the same geographical space, their communal psychologies were light years apart. Language is a crucial clue to this. Unionists lived in 'Ulster'; Nationalists in the 'Six Counties' (although, interestingly, Catholics' use of 'Ulster' to denote Northern Ireland was more widespread at this time than it has become since). Unionists lived in the United Kingdom of Great Britain and Northern Ireland; Nationalists in Ireland. Unionists tended to be Protestants; Nationalists tended to be Catholics. Unionists described themselves as 'British'; Nationalists described themselves as 'Irish'. These were more than just words. They denoted completely different perceptions of the political, social and cultural world that constituted Northern Ireland in the 1960s. And yet men and women were not born Protestants or Catholics, Unionists or Nationalists, British or Irish. They were moulded into these identities by their families, their schools and even their sports.

For Unionists, Northern Ireland was Protestant Ulster. It was the Protestant part of Ireland reflecting Protestant values. Ulster was also British, loyal to the Crown and proud of its place in the Commonwealth. Eire—Unionists felt that the very name evoked an artificial redefinition of Irishness while they remained proud of Ireland's centuries-long association with the Crown and Empire—was regarded as a cold place for Protestants when viewed from the North. Republicanism seemed a denial of all Irish associations the Ulster Protestants held dear to them. Gaelicisation re-emphasised this. Dublin did not even respect the Ulster Protestant identity and instead claimed Northern Ireland as part of the national territory: Northern Protestants were defined as Irish only and Northern Ireland was deemed by the Irish Constitution to be not a part of the United Kingdom but a part of Eire. It was not, believed Unionists, they who were the partitionists: it was Nationalists who had artificially partitioned the natural geographical entity of the British Isles. The Roman Catholic Church was also considered to hold sway in the Republic. It was considered by Ulster Protestants as more than a religious organisation: the insistence that the offspring of mixed religious marriages be brought up as Catholics was decimating the Southern Protestant population as far as the latters' Northern brethren were concerned. This was the fate they knew awaited them in a united Ireland.

Protestants may have been a majority in Northern Ireland but the statelet was built on fragile foundations. More than a third of its population was Roman Catholic and, broadly, wanted unification with the South. This minority regarded themselves as part of an Irish nation whose origins stretched back centuries. But Unionists could not perceive that the Irish nation did not recognise and, therefore, halt at the border between the British state and the Irish state. Parts of the Irish nation existed in substantial numbers within that part of the United Kingdom in Ireland: Northern Nationalists. The Irish nation existed within Northern Ireland because large numbers of people there brought it into existence. This was a psychological experience on a communal scale. The symbols of the Protestant state, however, were British: the Union flag; royal toasts; the British national anthem played on formal occasions. The Tricolour was effectively, albeit not officially, banned on the grounds that it could annoy enough Protestants to create a breach of the peace. All of this might not matter if Catholics were a minority on a scale similar to that of Protestants in the Republic; but they were not. The cultural dominance of British and Protestant symbols—the marching season an obvious example, where 'traditional' incursions into Catholic territory would not be accepted were the roles reversed—being the most obvious example.

This was the political environment into which Terence O'Neill came to the leadership of the Ulster Unionist Party and the premiership of Northern Ireland in 1963. O'Neill signalled a new departure with an emphasis on modernisation in the economic field and an attempt to improve community relations. He might be criticised for upsetting the sectarian status quo by first, misunderstanding just how entrenched sectarianism was within the Unionist Party (possessing, as he did, a cosmopolitan background and being more at home in London than Antrim) and second, by raising Catholic expectations that could not be fulfilled. The first charge does not really stand up: quite the opposite in fact. O'Neill appeared quite aware of the obstacles he faced from the Unionist grassroots; beyond cosmetic gestures to the Catholic minority he steadfastly avoided upsetting the power basis of Unionism, by reforming or suggesting a reform of local government. It was only with the Crossroads election of 1969 that he appealed over the heads of the Party to the electorate. That his cosmetic approach to community relations provoked so much discontent says much about the nature of the Unionist Party.

While it is true that he initiated this new departure it is also true that Northern Ireland could no longer remain aloof from contemporary Britain; and the situation was going to be an issue there if Labour were returned to power—as they were in 1964. What, then, was O'Neill's strategy for improving community relations? Did he even have one? The short answer is: sort of. O'Neill looked to the long-term erosion of Northern Ireland's communal difficulties. He hoped that, with the economic benefits of British citizenship, Catholic hostility to the state might lapse into acquiescence and ultimately support for it. Time would be the great healer. He did not move to heal long-standing sores such as the local government franchise because this was never his intention—until London began to apply pressure. As discontent grew he warned against both Protestants' and Catholics' pushing their demands too hard for this could lead to the unleashing of primal forces that could not be contained. O'Neill was criticised for his limited approach; against this, however, it can also be pointed out that he was proved right about the violence sectarianism might unleash. His moderate approach produced a sharp reaction in some Unionist quarters. His lack of movement on reform produced the Civil Rights Movement and demonstrations on the streets. He was caught between a rock and a hard place. O'Neill was accused of selling out 'traditional Unionism' by visiting a few Catholic schools. This is the hub of the matter. Northern Ireland oozed Protestantism in its official life; the attitude taken by many Protestants was that Northern Ireland was for the Protestants and the rest of the island could look after the Catholics and their Nationalism.

Yet O'Neill felt confident enough to challenge some of the assumptions that Unionism equated with Protestantism because he believed that Northern Ireland no longer faced the same constitutional threat as it did in the past. And, logically, he was right: Northern Ireland, after fifty years of self-government, and after the IRA had just been defeated, was more secure than it had ever been. The proof of this was the policy of détente between Irishmen followed by Sean Lemass: this represented a realisation on the part of the Irish state of this reality; and by Northern Catholics who, faced with the apparent permanence of Stormont, increasingly sought to work within the system. They had no alternative. This allowed O'Neill to emphasise how dangerous it was for Northern Ireland's position within the Union to rely forever on a Protestant majority. Catholics had to be brought into the fold if the long-term future of the Union was to be secured. But this was a long-term project and he—and Unionism—were running out of time, for constitutional security did not mean that Stormont was free from scrutiny in Great Britain.

Unfortunately for O'Neill, prominent figures within Unionism saw any potential British intervention as either bluff or a concern with partition. It was neither. When it became clear to O'Neill that stalling London on reform was no longer a viable option his position was undermined by key colleagues. Faulkner did not believe that the British would dare to intervene; he was wrong. Craig took the view that a quasi-federal relationship existed between London and Stormont; he was wrong. To many Unionists any interference from London marked the start of the slippery slope towards a united Ireland; they were wrong. It is true that many within the Labour Party did have sympathies with the ultimate goal of a united Ireland—probably Wilson and, according to his memoirs, Callaghan. But the Labour Government was bound by the 1949 Ireland Act: the consent principle.

This was non-negotiable. The Labour Government was determined to honour it. It would be for the Northern Ireland Parliament to decide its constitutional future; but the granting of this fundamental right to Stormont by Westminster did not mean the latter could not dictate, if need be, to the former on non-constitutional issues. The over-confidence of key members of the Northern Ireland Cabinet, such as Faulkner and Craig, in this matter made O'Neill's room for manoeuvre very difficult, although Faulkner, when it came to the crunch, was willing to lead from the front with regard to the reform of the local government franchise. Craig was the problem on this issue, leading opposition to any immediate reform, not because he was opposed to reform—he accepted this was necessary—but because of the commitments he had given to the Party that there would be no alteration in the current Parliament. Adding to O'Neill's problems were his rift with West, another key personality, and Faulkner's barely concealed ambition to become Prime Minister. So at the top the Unionist Party was divided about strategic relations with London and along personalities. If that was not unstable enough—which it was—the Party was also facing increasing tensions at the grassroots. Discontent had been bubbling for a considerable time among border Unionists convinced of the deliberate neglect of the west, and throughout the Party with claims that the Government was dictatorial in the manner in which it decided and implemented policy.

It was also unfortunate for O'Neill that his premiership coincided with a fashion in some Protestant quarters for ecumenicalism. It was the perception that traditional religious values were being diluted that gave impetus to Ian Paisley's political career. The United Kingdom was, in theory if not in practice, a Protestant state. But Protestantism as a living denomination had survived, and would continue to, in Northern Ireland, unlike Great Britain, because of a key difference: proportionately Northern Ireland had a lot of Roman Catholics while Great Britain did not. The rhetoric of anti-Catholicism became just that in Britain as secularisation and class politics evolved from the early twentieth century. Back in Northern Ireland the fiftieth anniversary of the Easter Rising also contributed to the view that the Unionist Government was going soft on traditional Unionist values: displays of such disloyalty to Britain were regarded as a direct challenge to the British ethos of the statelet. In the context of 1966, and the centrality of symbols and parades, this was unacceptable to many Unionists. There was a sense that such manifestations of disloyalty would not have been tolerated under earlier governments; O'Neill was thus seen as an appeaser.

Paisley gave voice to these concerns. His power came from his oratory. It is only when one hears the power and emotion in that voice that one can comprehend how he stirred emotions in some. It wasn't what Paisley said—for he did not advocate violence, rather he warned of it—but how he said it. Its effect on many people was extraordinary in the way that only religious fervour can be; when the topics were political, and delivered in this manner, those concerned with the political threat from the combined forces of Romanism and Nationalism found that the effect upon them was electrifying. But with such power comes great responsibility. Paisley's flirtation with private armies was irresponsible to say the least. If Paisley did not know of the illegal activities of some of the members of his political organisations then he should have realised the potential for danger. That is the difference between a statesman and a rabble-rouser. Yet the rabble-rousing reflected the fears genuinely held by Paisley and his supporters. He was not a prophet in the wilderness on these issues. Paisley represented a widespread concern within Ulster Protestantism with the ecumenical movement. But, not to put too fine a point on it, Paisley's interpretation of what O'Neill was up to was intellectually incontinent: his claim that O'Neill was engaged in a plot with Harold Wilson and Jack Lynch to destroy the Unionist Party and bring about a united Ireland was nonsense. But, alarmingly, this is what he and many of his supporters seemed to believe. It also reveals the level of paranoia within some sections of Protestant Unionism. Even worse, from a Unionist perspective, it was incredibly short-sighted. To ensure the long-term stability of Northern Ireland within the Union it was necessary to engage with Catholics. Paradoxically, what gave Paisley his platform alienated many other Unionists who were sympathetic to his core views. Paisley was prominent but in electoral terms, marginal, although a significant minority agreed with him.

But Paisley had a disproportionate impact on Unionist politics: this was because one of the major contributions to political instability in Northern Ireland was, as we have seen, institutional—the Ulster Unionist Party. The problem with the Unionist Party was that it was too broad a church and too democratic, and party activists are not always reflective of the wider electorate. Power lay at the grassroots with the Unionist Associations, not with the Party HQ in Glengall Street. In fact there was no such thing as the Unionist Party as such, rather a collection of Unionist Associations that came together in gatherings such as the Standing Committee and the UUC. And it was this devolution of power that made for a fractious relationship with a modernising and reforming leadership, for it is arguable that more real power lay with the Unionist Associations than with the Unionist Government. The allocation of scarce local resources, such as council housing and jobs, was in the power of Unionist controlled councils, not Stormont. In the west in particular, gerrymandered councils had a vested interest in resisting reform. Stormont was reluctant to intervene for this would produce opposition from Unionist local authorities and create problems with local associations. This meant that only outside pressure was likely to push Unionist leaders to reform the system. And London was reluctant to intervene, at least initially. But when O'Neill, and after him Chichester-Clark, did embrace reform, the institutional problem of the Unionist Party manifested itself. The Unionist Party functioned best when there was no challenge to the established order: that Northern Ireland was the Protestant Ulster of Craigavon and Brookeborough. As soon as the question of how Catholics might be included within the system, and the Party, was raised, the problems started, as it revealed how ingrained anti-Catholicism was in the DNA of the Party. This question, and whether Catholics could be integrated into the public life of Northern Ireland, revealed a fault-line based upon integrationist and exclusivist Unionism that had largely remained hidden as long as the issue was kept under wraps: basically between pluralism and bigotry. Often the image portrayed of Unionism is one of sectarianism. This is unfair as the events of the 1960s showed that pluralist Unionism (and Protestantism) was alive and kicking. But it is also true that the self-image of many Unionists who equate Unionism with Protestantism is that they are non-sectarian: this is an illusion, for to exclude a whole group on the basis of religion is bigotry.

The turbulence within the Unionist Party, and Protestant society generally, might have remained within the ambit of the curious but for the fact that Catholics were no longer prepared to sit back and accept their second-class status. It was this, combined with the inability of the UUP to react decisively in the face of British pressure, that created the crisis. At the heart of Catholic grievances were two factors: discrimination and partition. Catholics were discriminated against by the Unionist state. This is clear despite the denial of many Unionists at the time and since. Catholics were discriminated against in terms of public and private employment, at local government level and in housing. Against this it has to be said that Catholics were not discriminated against to the extent that they claimed to be. The issue of discrimination is complicated. In terms of evidence discrimination in regional policy does not bare close scrutiny; nor do claims relating to the new city and the new university. Employment is different: while it is impossible not to discount educational, social and cultural differences between Protestants and Catholics as a factor that worked against the latter, perhaps the crucial factor is the ethos of the state—it was a Protestant state for a Protestant people. The statements of Unionist politicians and other prominent figures clearly encouraged a policy of Protestant employing Protestant: even O'Neill had once advertised for a Protestant housekeeper. Against this it has to be said that some Catholics did exactly the same—discriminated against Protestants in employment.

But the greatest manifestation of Protestant patronage was in local government: this was where gerrymandering and the allocation of resources became so controversial. Gerrymandering was a clear-cut example of discrimination against Nationalists. Londonderry made claims to the contrary quite farcical. The resulting control of local councils and, therefore, the allocation of many jobs in local government was another clear-cut example of discrimination. The allocation of council housing—the motor of civil disobedience—is more complex. It was clear that some Unionist-controlled councils, particularly in the west, allocated council houses to Protestants only; others were fairer in their allocations but placed the Catholic allocations in particular 'Nationalist' wards to preserve the gerry-mandered nature of the local political dispensation. Yet it was not discrimination in the sense that Catholics were denied a fair allocation of housing: Unionist councils knew that the Housing Trust would ensure Catholics did not miss out. Overall, Catholics appear to have had a fair allocation of housing. In this sense they were not denied a fair allocation of houses within the Unionist state. But it was discriminatory in the sense that the principle that public housing should be allocated on a fair and equitable basis by public authorities was disregarded. In this sense it was wrong and indefensible. And it gave Catholics a manifest focus for complaint: it was difficult for slum-dwelling Catholics who were waiting to be rehoused to be told they were not being discriminated against—the Housing Trust would see you right—when some Unionist councils blatantly gave public housing to Protestants only (in Armagh, for example, the system worked 'fairly' and both sides were content, as a 'gentleman's agreement' operated whereby Protestant councillors nominated Protestants for council houses and Catholic councillors nominated Catholics; both Protestants and Catholics therefore got council housing but in the 'correct' wards).

So Catholics were discriminated against. But did this did mean that they were oppressed. To claim that they were devalues the term and the experience of the oppressed the world over. Core political and socio-economic rights and religious freedoms were not denied them. But Catholics, as long as a majority-rule system persisted that was based on a Protestant ethnic Unionism, were always going to be discontented and feel disadvantaged. For this to change and not involve the ultimate end of majority rule would have needed the emergence of a non-sectarian civic Unionism.

The rationale for discrimination was based on the claim that all Catholics were Nationalists and vice versa; it seems some Unionists thought a Catholic and his or her descendants were almost genetically programmed to be disloyal. The adherents of 'traditional' Unionism even excluded Catholics who had fought for Britain in both world wars, even though some of these 'loyalists' had bravely stayed at home. Survey data, however, revealed that far more Catholics were likely to have Unionist sympathies than Protestants were likely to have Nationalist sympathies. In this sense the failure to try and attract more Catholics towards Unionism was an own goal. But Nationalism was not the only fear: floating not far beneath the surface of many Protestant perceptions of Catholics was the ancient fear that the latter were completely dominated by their Church. The Roman Catholic Church was seen as an international organisation that tried to control its flock from the cradle to the grave. This was, to be honest, an accurate depiction and herein lay the religious dimension to the conflict. The fear of Roman Catholicism formed a core element of Unionism. For many Unionists this is what defined Unionism and what it meant to be British—the United Kingdom was a Protestant state and the Crown was Protestant. This Unionism crossed all Protestant denominations and was far more than evangelical Protestantism: it represented a world view based on a core theological doctrine—the rejection of the over-arching dominance of a self-proclaimed infallible individual attempting to control millions of people's consciences. This interpretation applied as much to members of the Episcopalian Church in Ireland, who had no overall individual in charge, as to the nonhierarchical Presbyterians. There was nothing comparable on the Catholic side: Nationalism did not have, as a key component, the factor of Catholic doctrine in opposition to Protestantism. Nevertheless Nationalism, despite a pluralist ideology, had a *de facto* Catholic ethnic identity. In the end, the dearth of a strategic vision within Unionism and an ability to see beyond the Giant's Causeway and the changes occurring across the Irish Sea cruelly illustrate the intellectual limits of political dinosaurs such as Brookeborough: the noble Viscount did a disservice to his people and Province in not using his twenty years in power to soften the polarisation in his beloved Ulster. In the sense that 'only Nixon could go to China', only someone like Brookeborough could achieve this; but this required a strategic vision, not tunnel vision. And into the category of political dinosaurs can be placed Paisley and all those Unionists outside and within the UUP who resisted change, however small. In trying to resist any change to the ethos of a Protestant state they were laying the foundations for it to be swept away.

What set this in motion was the Civil Rights Movement. It was perceived by many Protestants as a Republican plot to overthrow the state. It was. But this is not the same as its being a Republican cover organisation. The Civil Rights Movement was a loose coalition dominated by moderate Catholics. Republicans were in a minority. Civil Rights was a narrow window of opportunity in which Catholics might have been seduced into reformism rather than remaining forever complaining about the injustice of partition. But this would have taken a generation and would also have required a corresponding assertion of O'Neill's civic Unionism over Protestant Unionists who remained anally retentive over anything Catholic. The Nationalism and Republicanism that came to dominate Catholic politics, once the IRA insurgency began in earnest, does not mean that Civil Rights was about partition in 1968–9. Catholics were, on the whole, Nationalists. But, by the beginning of 1970, Catholics and their representatives still had to work within the confines of Stormont and the reality that majority rule would be around for a long time to come. Before the deterioration in relations between the British Army and the Catholic community the latter remained flexible in its outlook. The limited Catholic support for O'Neill candidates in the Crossroads election demonstrated this.

This brings us to the Civil Rights campaign itself. The decision by Catholic leaders to take politics onto the streets had momentous consequences. The criticism that can be levelled at them is that they had no idea of the subterranean forces they might unleash. This reflected a fundamental misunderstanding of the Northern Ireland situation that was common to Catholics whether they were Nationalists of the constitutional or the armed-struggle variety. O'Neill, in retrospect, was proved correct: the only way to ease the communal split was by the long and slow evolution of improved community relations in a peaceful atmosphere. Against this, Catholics were clearly second-class citizens and this was unacceptable in the United Kingdom in the second half of the twentieth century. The frustration of many Catholics—though not by any means the majority, who seemed satisfied with the pace of the improvement in community relations—was driven by the Catholic political elite, particularly Austin Currie and Gerry Fitt. While they pontificated to British politicians about the latter's ignorance of the North, the unpalatable truth is that they were equally ignorant—ignorant in the sense that, certain in the correctness of their interpretation of the Northern Ireland problem, they in fact had little comprehension of the deeper cause of division in the North. There was a good reason for this: an understanding of the core problem would have destroyed their entire worldview. Thus a core underlying cause of the outbreak of the Troubles was Irish Nationalism.

The core Nationalist belief was that geographical Ireland equated with the political Irish nation; Ulster Protestant opposition to a united Ireland was explained thus: Unionism was based upon ascendancy over Catholics; nothing less than the sectarian monopoly of political and economic power. This belief seems to have been universal among Nationalists. If this ascendancy could be broken, if there was genuine equality between Protestant and Catholic in Ireland—Wolfe Tone's ideal—then the whole edifice of Unionism would collapse because its *raison d'être*—privilege—would disappear. It had after all been created by British imperialism and an artificial state carved out for Protestants to continue Britain's old colonial policy of divide and rule. But what if this interpretation were wrong? What if the entire basis of the Nationalist case—Ireland a nation—had a massive ideological black hole at its centre?

The fundamental problem with which Irish Nationalism has never come to terms is the claim that Unionists were British. This went far beyond the legal status of being British subjects in a British state or a British 'tradition'. Unionists lived and breathed their sense of Britishness. Their whole way of life, their symbols, their historical memory made them feel British. Unionists have possessed a *consciousness* of being part of a historic British national community. The argument that the Britons in Great Britain might think of Ulster Protestants—if they thought of them at all—as being Irish rather than British does not dilute the perception on the part of Unionists that they are British: only if they were faced with expulsion from the UK were they ever likely to have to reappraise their sense of belonging. And, it should be remembered, to be Scots and British—a dual identity—was not the same as that which the English possessed: a fused identity of Englishness and Britishness that saw Great Britain as Greater England; Britishness was multifaceted and not monolithic. The vast majority of Northern Ireland's Protestants did not feel part of an Irish nation as defined by a narrow Gaelic, Republican and Catholic ethos that was the independent Irish state. They felt British *and* Irish, or Ulster-British or just British. The British presence in Ireland was not just the British state. It was the members of the British nation who lived in that part of the British state.

It is easy to identify Protestant bigotry; Catholic bigotry is less obvious, for bigotry seems more respectable when it is called 'Nationalism': an ideology, in the modern world, that confers greater political legitimacy rather than a commitment to a particular religious belief. However, it is only a matter of degree in terms of bigotry between someone who dismisses another's religious belief and someone who dismisses another's national identity. Somehow Paisleyite religious fundamentalism seemed antiquarian while Irish Nationalism did not. In fact both were mirror images of the other. Both required an unquestioning belief in the sacred: one, God; the other, the Nation. Both were as transcendental as the other. Both required faith. There are no such natural entities as 'nations'. They are psychological constructs created by peoples in their own image. The only reliable definition of a national community is the consciousness of a people that they constitute a nation. And in Ireland the Protestants of the North-east corner did not regard themselves as part of the Irish Nation as defined by the Catholics of the island. Nationalists and Unionists may have had a common language—English, whatever the Irish Constitution might say—but they inhabited different mental worlds in terms of history and culture. The year 1966 and its anniversaries summed this up like no other: 1916 was, for Nationalists, the Easter Rising and a blow struck for Irish freedom against British imperialism; for Unionists, 1916 was the Battle of the Somme and blood sacrifice for King and Country, while the Rising was a foul act of betrayal. On such interpretations of history were some men prepared to kill. For all Nationalist claims that British interference in Ireland had artificially divided the Irish nation the truth was that, whatever its historical origins, it is people who make a nation, for it is the collective consciousness of a people—a psychological condition—that makes a nation a social and political reality. And in Ireland there were two collective national consciousnesses: one Irish and one British. There were two nations inhabiting the geographical entity of Ireland and God didn't put them there: people did. A nation cannot exist without a people's being conscious that they are a nation or part of one. And in Northern Ireland, Ulster Protestants were part of a British nation because they believed themselves to be and they willed it into existence. Nationalists were willing to give Ulster Protestants everything they wanted—except what they really wanted, which was to remain part of the British state and retain their sense of Britishness. The Nationalist failure to recognise this is their core contribution to the origins of the Troubles because their whole interpretation of the division in Ireland, and why Unionists discriminated against Catholics, was built on a denial of a political reality. Ireland may be a geographical entity but it is not naturally one political unit. In political terms it would be unnatural not to have a border within the island. It was just drawn in the wrong place.

Now, while a united Ireland might be the goal of all Nationalists and most Catholics this did not mean that what became the Civil Rights Movement was based solely on Nationalism. This was one of the crucial reasons it was so successful. It was not like the Anti-Partition League of the 1950s. It was not that organisations such as the Campaign for Social Justice were evidence of a new Catholic middle class that was significant: it was that the CSJ was concerned with reform within

Northern Ireland and not partition. This was why the CSJ had more of an impact among Labour backbenchers and the Liberal leadership than all the years of huffing and puffing by the Nationalist Party. For the other crucial element was that there was a receptive audience at Westminster. Had Nationalism rather than reform been the appeal of the CSJ the likely response in Britain would have been negative. The most important aspect of this was not the Campaign for Democracy in Ulster, although its role was crucial in raising the issue within the Labour Party, but that there was a receptive Prime Minister in the form of Harold Wilson.

It has been suggested that had Wilson's Government intervened earlier in Northern Ireland or introduced direct rule years before it did, then the tragedy of the Troubles might have been prevented. First of all we need to banish what we know about the events of the next three decades. It was not obvious to the Labour Government or to many others in the mid-1960s that violence in Ulster was inevitable. Confronted with mounting economic and political problems at home and abroad it would have been madness for Wilson to go looking for trouble in Ireland, the political graveyard of many a British politician. Yet Wilson's policy towards Ulster was not passive: he was the most interventionist British Prime Minister in Ireland since Lloyd George. Criticisms of Wilson and his Government miss this elemental point. Pressure on O'Neill was subtle but real. That Wilson remained interventionist is clear when one remembers that he continued to take an interest in Northern Ireland after he had secured a large parliamentary majority in 1966 and the CDU was not as much a factor in his calculations as it had been when he had a small majority. And in August 1969 it was not clear that direct rule would have prevented decades of violence: the key factor in the next few months was the actions of the Provisional IRA. For Wilson and Callaghan to impose direct rule on Chichester-Clark's Government when it was committed to reform would have been to invite a violent Protestant reaction; the political and security situation in 1969 was far different than that in 1972. The key problem with Stormont would always be that Catholics were excluded from power, as Callaghan recognised, for he was in favour of a coalition or power-sharing type arrangement; but in the context of 1969 this would have been unacceptable to Protestants. A lot more pain would have to be endured by that community before it would consider it.

When it came the Civil Rights campaign on the streets was the result of a basic breakdown of trust among some Catholics with regard to O'Neill. Yet reform was on the cards, starting with an overhaul of local government, including the franchise; and any reform of local government would involve the resetting of electoral boundaries by an independent tribunal. Electoral boundaries, not the local government franchise, were the real source of Unionist local power. And this would break that power. But Civil Rights leaders could not know this as the Stormont cabinet feared revealing it because of the probable reaction in the Unionist Party. And so the tragedy unfolded. Taking to the streets was always risky given the historic reaction to communal encroachments on territory by one group or another. Yet why should Catholics not protest over their perceived grievances? It was a fundamental British right to march peacefully, and NICRA was committed to peaceful demonstrations; even civil disobedience, such as squatting, while illegal was non-violent. In this way such protests were legitimate tactics.

But what politics on the streets unleashed were subterranean, elemental forces—the core of the division in Northern Ireland: ethnic division. This was the driving force of the conflict. Leaders could not control it. It is sometimes difficult to understand the sheer emotional power generated by group identity. Many readers may think they are immune to such forces; the truth is that most are not: it is only in certain circumstances that the unseen influences—school, family, cultural reference points (as simple a reference point as whether a post box is painted red in Belfast and green in Dublin) socialise and politicise the individual. These identities only become active at certain times. Marches and counter-marches triggered these identities across Northern Ireland in 1968–9. Catholics may have been right to protest against discrimination in these terms but Northern Ireland was not like the rest of the United Kingdom. As Catholics penetrated into areas that were regarded by Protestants as 'theirs' an emotional reaction occurred. Protestants saw IRA stewards accompanying the marchers, they saw the Nationalist slogans carried by Catholic crowds and heard the Nationalist songs they sang; they perceived a Republican conspiracy and, as NICRA associated itself with the demonstrations, moderate Protestant support for it melted away. It may be that Civil Rights was, in McCann's memorable phrase, about getting at the Prods, but getting at Prods could be about Civil Rights within the six counties as much as about partition. But NICRA was naïve in the extreme to believe that Protestants had not read of a civil rights movement as the IRA's idea (they had, in the *Belfast Telegraph*); that Republicans on its platforms would only confirm this; and, perhaps the dumbest decision of all, allowing IRA Volunteers to act as stewards on marches, as if that was what they were experts at. Perceptions were everything in Northern Ireland and the role of Republicans in the organisation proved crucial in undermining moderate Protestant support for it.

Individual decisions also made significant contributions to the outbreak of violence and then to the scale of the breakdown in community relations. The decision of Bill Craig to ban the 5 October march appears a major blunder. Craig proved a disastrous Minister of Home Affairs for Unionism, though he proved a good one as far as Nationalists were concerned. In his defence the information he had received relating to IRA activities indicated how they planned to use agitation to create popular support for an insurgency; and it should not be forgotten that, despite Provo claims to the contrary, there is no evidence that the Goulding leadership ever abandoned a commitment to armed struggle. Craig saw NICRA as a cover for the IRA and a plot to overthrow the state. But instead of trying to take the sting out of the demonstrations he turned them into a major trial of strength with the Government. The RUC's senior officers, it should not be forgotten, contributed to this with their recommendation that the 5 October march be banned; a view they did not take with subsequent marches. Craig's misjudgments accelerated British intervention—the very thing he sought to avoid (or more accurately did not believe would happen). Indeed, his inability to reverse a decision once he had taken it was evident from his days at the Ministry of Development. He demonstrated this inflexibility after 5 October when he refused to budge, in cabinet, on the local government franchise: this was the time to concede.

The other major responsibility lies with some of the marchers and the police. NICRA wanted no confrontation. It was committed to a peaceful demonstration. The left-wing organisers of the Derry march, on the other hand, deliberately played with fire by planning a march that traversed Protestant areas; they wanted confrontation and had no plans to control the march. The police, caught unawares on the day, over-reacted and used their batons indiscriminately. The subsequent behaviour of some officers was enough to destroy any confidence the majority of the Catholic population of Derry had in the police. Yet this was not planned or premeditated. The plan to provoke confrontation was. The left-wing agitators of Derry might protest about the oppressive nature of the Orange state but it was they who unleashed the forces of sectarian violence. The potential was always there and might have been released anyway, but they started the chain reaction. The poor discipline of the RUC made the situation even worse. Communal polarisation became acute. But it did not necessarily have to deteriorate further, for the results were not all negative. London intervened. Pressure on the Unionist Government increased. Craig was sacked by O'Neill. There was a window of opportunity. Calm was needed. The Civil Rights Movement held back. Enter Peoples Democracy.

The decision by the leaders of this revolutionary student movement to engage in another march in January 1969 proved they had a feebler grasp of the politics of Northern Ireland than any other group of people in the Province. It was criminal in the sense that they deliberately sought to provoke Protestant reaction by penetrating Protestant territory—and they succeeded. And they were helped, of course, by Paisley's supporters who attacked the marchers: while it was the marchers who walked into a physical trap it was the Paisleyites who walked into a political trap. Instead, as O'Neill had hoped, of leaving the marchers alone they guaranteed that their beloved Specials were on borrowed time. Instead of blaming Chichester-Clark for the demise of that 'fine body of men' it was the Paisleyites and the off-duty Specials who took part in the Burntollet attack that discredited the USC in the eyes of London. Burntollet and its aftermath had a devastating impact. It was the turning point. It had the opposite effect than that of uniting the Protestant and Catholic members of the working class: it exacerbated sectarian bitterness to a hitherto unprecedented scale. The only ones suffering from a false consciousness were the leaders of PD. Sectarianism, not class politics, was the natural division in Northern Ireland. Indeed one might argue that the natural state of pre-partition Ireland, defined in terms of the organic growth of communal relationships and identities, was sectarian; so while Northern Ireland retained that pre-partition state, the Republic of Ireland was artificially insulated (few Protestants and their views to have to accommodate any more) so over time what was once artificial itself became 'natural'.

As the middle ground melted away in early 1969, O'Neill took a gamble; it proved his undoing. In the Crossroads election O'Neill put his country before his Party—and split the UUP even more. This merely confirmed to his opponents within the Unionist Party that he was unsuitable to lead their great institution. Other factors, such as his aloofness, his inability to communicate with backbenchers, his lack of a common touch, all contributed to his difficulties within the Party. It is important to remember that the 'rebels' such as Craig were not opposed to reform or seeking to reverse the measures already introduced. They accepted party policy once it had been decided. O'Neill knew the game was up when he did not receive the decisive mandate he was seeking from the electorate. This, and Paisley's coming within 2000 votes of him in Bannside, gave the election the appearance of a defeat for O'Neill. It was, in the sense that he set the bar too high in what would be regarded as a victory. But it should be recalled that Paisley's challenge only produced a similar result to the one previous occasion that Bannside was contested by more than one Unionist; conditions when Paisley won Bannside in 1970 were very different to those in 1969. And Craig, it should also be remembered, came very close to being unseated. Unionism was split. Yet Catholics had voted in unprecedented numbers for pro-O'Neill Unionists: an extraordinary achievement in the sterile sectarian landscape of Northern Ireland. It has not happened since.

The Northern Ireland that Chichester-Clark inherited was one that was on the brink of disaster. By August 1969 there had been a complete Catholic breakdown of confidence in the police. This was a new development: despite Republican claims to the contrary, the RUC had been a tolerated rather than an accepted force even though they were overwhelmingly Protestant and a symbol of the Unionist state. But the behaviour of a number of police officers in Derry in October 1968 and January 1969 began the process of alienation. This was accentuated with police brutality as shown in the death of Samuel Devenney. After these events Catholics in Belfast as well as Derry perceived the police as unacceptable and agents of state repression. This was what was at the heart of the Battle of the Bogside. A community was now in revolt. The events that followed in Belfast were pure tribal warfare. Catholics sought to relieve the pressure on Catholics whom they had never, or were never likely, to meet. This was the tribal bond. Protestants responded similarly as 'their' police were attacked. There were no state-authorised or co-ordinated attacks on Catholics. And there was no IRA conspiracy to overthrow the state. Yet in the heat of battle, realities were replaced by such perceptions, which then entered the respective communal mythologies.

The crisis was, of course, not limited to Northern Ireland. It was Jack Lynch's misfortune that the outbreak of violence in the North occurred on his watch as

Taoiseach. In the end, though, the arms crisis made him. When he became Taoiseach the prospect of violence in the six counties seemed remote. North–South relations were better than they had ever been. Lynch continued the policy of détente initiated by his predecessor, Sean Lemass. This was the only policy that could conceivably bring about a united Ireland in the long term. Even if one accepts that Ulster Protestants were not part of the Irish nation this did not mean that an Irish nation containing Ulster Protestants, and separate from Britain, had not existed in the past and might not re-emerge one day in the distant future; nations, after all, are not eternal or fixed in time but evolve and retreat through time. The key point was that the Lemass-Lynch strategy was for Irishmen, South and North, to work together and build trust between the two parts. This, it was believed, would break down the barriers of distrust in the North towards the South. But this strategy, rather like O'Neill's attempt to woo Northern Catholics away from Nationalism, could only work in the absence of violence. Once violence broke out in the North the actions of Lynch's Government from August 1969 to mid-1970, when they became public during the arms crisis, convinced many Unionists that the old enemy could not be trusted: with regard to the South many Unionists thought it best, once more, to trust in God and keep their powder dry.

The decisive role in the evolution of the Troubles played by the Irish Government came after the outbreak of communal division in August 1969. More than one of Lynch's cabinet colleagues saw themselves as more qualified for the top job, and more in the mantle of the giants who preceded Lynch: the very names de Valera and Lemass give some idea of why others saw the unassuming Taoiseach from Cork as a temporary incumbent as Taoiseach. This in itself was not unusual in normal internal party politics. But the crisis of August 1969 was not normal. It raised fundamental issues about the nature of Republicanism in the South. Under tremendous pressure from heavyweights such as Blaney, it is easy to see how Lynch acquiesced in a dangerous new Northern policy. But it would be unfair to suggest that he did this merely because of his internal position within Fianna Fáil. The entire Government was convinced that there had been an orchestrated attack by the Protestant state on the Northern minority. This mistaken view was compounded by the poor intelligence reports that were delivered to Dublin confirming this. The choice of personnel for this task was, to say the least, unfortunate—in particular Captain Kelly. Lynch and his Government, nevertheless, did not deviate from their long-term policy of unity by consent. In terms of Anglo–Irish relations, despite the international propaganda campaign that baffled the British, coming as it did from a friendly neighbour, one thing is clear: Dublin, whatever the sins of past British governments, did not view the current London Government as anything but fair. This view, to a limited degree, was later applied to the Chichester-Clark Government after initial doubts as to its sincerity: this in itself is a significant fact—that Dublin believed the reform package would end discrimination in the six counties.

Lynch and his colleagues believed that they were better placed to understand the six counties than their neighbours across the Irish Sea. At one level this was inevitable and Lynch was no more responsible for the socialisation process that made him an Irish Nationalist than were O'Neill and Chichester-Clark for the forces that shaped them into Ulster Unionists. But like a recovering alcoholic as the drinks trolley rolls by, the Irish Government—in particular the Ministry of External Affairs and civil servants such as Eamonn Gallagher—could not resist the opportunity to see the crisis in the North as a policy opportunity to further Nationalist aims for a united Ireland. This in itself could be destabilising. What springs forth from the Dublin documents is the centrality of the goal of Irish unity. The point here is that such gifted men—politicians and civil servants— never sought to question their Nationalist fundamentalism. This is a key to understanding the origins of the Troubles: faith overcomes logic. In their own way the Dublin establishment was every bit as driven by the transcendental as were the evangelical Protestants in the North they looked down upon. But at certain times this unchallenged view could have serious consequences: the speech made by Lynch on 13 August is one example. It was regarded in Dublin governmental circles as statesmanlike and crucial in securing British intervention. It certainly did contribute to that, but only because it sent the Protestants in Belfast, fearing an Irish invasion, into a frenzy and encouraged Catholics to hope for Irish intervention. Lynch did more to produce a near civil war in one television speech than all Paisley's rantings in six years. And it was the product of an ignorance of the true reality of the Northern Ireland Question.

And never were the inadequacies of this interpretation of the Northern problem more cruelly exposed than with the events leading up to the arms crisis. Lynch has had a relatively good press given the pressures of holding his Government and Party together during and after the August crisis. Considering that one of the key players was Charles Haughey this is perhaps unsurprising, given the passions he arouses in commentators. But the arms crisis revealed the fault line in Irish politics towards the North. Both the major parties of the South, and the state itself, were born of violence. The martyrs of 1916 had as much of a mandate as the Provisional IRA in 1970. And the arms crisis revealed that a subversive organisation was perceived by Dublin to have a level of legitimacy in the North—as potential defenders of the Northern minority—that it would never have been granted in the Republic. The fact is that the Provisional IRA was nurtured and encouraged, through financial assistance, by elements of the Irish Government. This money sustained the organisation at a crucial time. This is not to say that the Provos would not otherwise have evolved as they did. But Dublin's assistance made sure they survived and made it certain that they would have the basis for growth. And all this was based on an intelligence fiasco of tragic proportions. If Lynch was unaware of these activities then Blaney and Haughey were running a government within a Government. If Lynch did not know that arms were to be imported with a view to transferring them North then this was either because he chose not to know or he was incompetent: the fact is that, after the cabinet authorised Haughey to make funds available for relief in the North, he should have made it his business to know exactly where the money was going; but instead he seems to have let Blaney and Haughey run the whole operation without reference to him.

Almost as extraordinary, if not more so, was the Government's preparation for a 'Doomsday' scenario. Here the Irish state was engaged with a subversive organisation to seize the territory of a friendly power. Lynch was clearly aware of this as it was based on a cabinet decision. Given the intelligence the Government had received, and was likely to receive in an explosive situation similar to that of August 1969, little confidence can be placed in the hope that Dublin would interpret correctly what was going on in the North. Instead of protecting Catholics it would have enraged Protestant passions to such an extent that it would probably have precipitated a massacre rather than prevented one and it would probably have diverted British forces from protecting the minority on the basis that they could not sit idly by while a foreign army marched into the United Kingdom unannounced. And any doubt of the Protestant reaction needs only to be referenced against Lynch's speech of 13 August. The idea that Blaney seemed to have that he was pulling the strings of the Provisionals was a gross error of judgment. The Provos were quite capable of acting independently with their own agenda as they were about to demonstrate. No one seems to have realised that an incursion into British territory—whatever the Irish Constitution said about its being Irish territory—would be akin to an act of war.

By the beginning of 1970, Northern Ireland was a bitterly polarised community. The events of August had left a bitter legacy. British troops could not be withdrawn because of the collapse in the RUC's morale, the poor quality of their higher command and their continued unacceptability to the Catholic population. Craig, West and Paisley appeared not to have noticed this and believed that a return of the police to front-line duties would solve Northern Ireland's security problems. It would not, because the police were incapable of such duties. There continued to be sporadic disorders that only the Army, in the absence of the police, could cope with. Partly this was associated with a collapse in respect for civil authority. Alongside this there was the central continuing lack of a consensus on how Northern Ireland should be governed—indeed whether it should even exist at all. But none of this made the next thirty years of violence inevitable: despite the breakdown in authority and periodic street disorders, the British Army was more than capable of containing outbursts of sectarian animosity.

Furthermore, a radical set of reforms—almost revolutionary in a Northern Ireland context—was being set in place: an unarmed civilianised police force was to be introduced, the RUC were to be relieved of responsibility for public prosecutions, the B-Specials had been disbanded, a central housing authority was to remove from local councils the power to allocate houses, a Ministry of Community Relations was established, a Commissioner for Complaints was to investigate individual grievances in local government and public bodies and universal adult suffrage was introduced in local elections. Catholics had clearly emerged as the victors; they might still be denied power at the centre of government but it was the Protestants who were punch-drunk from London's intervention. The reforms, from a Catholic perspective, may not have been perfect but there was no reason why further reforms might not be contemplated over the long term: no Unionist Government could any longer ignore the anxieties of Catholics, at least not while Westminster cast a wistful eye over events in Ulster and had their man there, in the form of the UKREP, to convey British concerns and effectively to veto any policies repugnant to it. The Joint Security Committee, with Sir Ian Freeland and Sir Arthur Young on it, as well as the UKREP, confirmed that security policy would be subject to similar tests. All this would, of course, mean Catholics operating within the confines of majority rule as a reconstitution of Stormont was not on the agenda as long as there was a Unionist Government willing to carry out the reforms. In London there was a Government that was clearly in sympathy with the plight of Catholics rather than with the Protestants. But as significant was Chichester-Clark's Unionist Government: many criticisms might justly be levelled at previous administrations regarding their sectarian attitudes towards the minority—but not in this case. Cynics might doubt such a conversion on the road to Damascus but here was a Unionist Government led by a Prime Minister who was committed to the principle of reform and committed to the enactment of reform. And finally, relations between the British Army and the Catholic population were relatively good. The old Civil Rights Movement may have served its purpose but civil rights and reform was not yet dead. They soon would be.

Reform and any chances of remedying inequalities between the two com-munities—real or imagined—were to be frozen for the next couple of decades. As a result a generation's progress was lost. Perhaps the violence of 1969 was inevitable: tribal warfare in a tribal society. But the evolution of the Troubles into a war that would last for a generation was not. The single most disastrous decision that produced the next two and a half decades of conflict was the decision of the Provisional IRA's Army Council in January 1970 to begin a war—their war—against the British state. There was no moral justification for this decision. It was not a campaign against a totalitarian state: forget the injustices that were to follow—internment or Bloody Sunday—for in January 1970 there were Governments in London and Belfast committed in word and deed to remedying the grievances of a discriminated-against minority. The Provisional IRA's war was not about civil rights. Subsequent claims relating to this are self-satisfying justifications for the next two decades of killing. The Provisionals' war was about national rights. And whether or not Ireland had been unjustly partitioned, this was not a morally acceptable reason for a small group of men with no mandate, except from the dead of past generations who could no longer express an opinion, to condemn future generations. And it was a small group of men: here we should separate the guilty men, such as MacStiofain, O Bradaigh, O Connell, McKee and those lower down the food chain but equally willing to take up the fight, such as the Martin Meehans and the Gerry Adamses, from those drawn into the armed struggle by state violence in 1971–2 and thereafter. Other Nationalists held their desire for a united sovereign Ireland just as dearly as did these men. But borders, they recognised, could not be altered by force. This was the cardinal principle that governed international law from Munich onwards. The only morally defensible case for armed struggle would be in a situation in which Catholics had been denied legitimate avenues for protest—and even in the examples of the Craigavon and Brookeborough regimes such a justification would be hard to make. In 1970 no such justification could be made. From that decision of the Army Council in 1970, civil rights for Catholics was a side issue as the British state reacted to the Provos' insurgency. The Cassandras of the Protestant right were self-satisfyingly proved right in their predictions that Civil Rights was a cover for the overthrow of the state. The Republicans were to be self-satisfyingly proved right in their claim that the state could not be reformed—but it was they, not the British or Unionist Governments, who made it so. In the meantime if the people of Northern Ireland thought the worst was over they were soon to find out that the worst was yet to come.

NOTES

Introduction (PAGES IX–XIII)

1. T. J. Campbell, *Fifty Years of Ulster: 1890–1940*, Belfast 1941, 278.
2. Ibid. 223–6.
3. PRONI CAB 9B/13/1 Minstry of Home Affairs Memorandum, (8/3/23).
4. Patrick Buckland, *The Factory of Grievances: Devolved Government in Northern Ireland 1921–39*, Dublin 1979, 243–5.
5. Northern Ireland House of Commons debates Volume XVI, Col. 1090, (24/4/34).
6. Ireland Act 1949 Clause 1 (1) B.
7. Thomas Hennessey, *A History of Northern Ireland 1920–1997*, Basingstoke 1997, 99–109.
8. Michael Farrell, *Northern Ireland the Orange State*, London 1976, 90.

Chapter 1. Protestant Ulster (PAGES 1–35)

1. PRONI CAB 9R/196/1 Death of Pope John Memorandum, 12 June 1963.
2. PRONI CAB 9R/196/1 Prime Minister to The Most Rev. William Conway.
3. *Belfast Telegraph*, 2 May 1964.
4. *Belfast Telegraph*, 28 June 1965.
5. *Belfast Telegraph*, 30 January 1964.
6. *Belfast Telegraph*, 6 February 1964.
7. *Belfast Telegraph*, 17 March 1964.
8. *Belfast Telegraph*, 24 April 1964.
9. *Belfast Telegraph*, 24 April 1964.
10. *Belfast Telegraph*, 24 April 1964.
11. *Belfast Telegraph*, 13 May 1964.
12. *Belfast Telegraph*, 27 April 1964.
13. *Belfast Telegraph*, 17 August 1964.
14. *Belfast Telegraph*, 4 October 1965.
15. *Belfast Telegraph*, 13 October 1965.
16. *Belfast Telegraph*, 13 January 1966.
17. *Belfast Telegraph*, 10 April 1964.
18. *Belfast Telegraph*, 21 April 1964.
19. *Belfast Telegraph*, 12 May 1964.
20. *Belfast Telegraph*, 13 May 1964.
21. *Belfast Telegraph*, 4 June 1964.
22. *Belfast Telegraph*, 5 June 1964.
23. *Belfast Telegraph*, 11 June 1964.
24. *Belfast Telegraph*, 9 June 1965.
25. *Belfast Telegraph*, 9 June 1965.
26. *Belfast Telegraph*, 14 June 1965.
27. *Belfast Telegraph*, 14 May 1964.
28. *Belfast Telegraph*, 12 August 1964.
29. *Belfast Telegraph*, 24 April 1964.
30. *Belfast Telegraph*, 5 May 1964.

31. *Belfast Telegraph*, 16 March 1967.
32. *Belfast Telegraph*, 6 February 1967.
33. *Belfast Telegraph*, 2 February 1967.
34. *Belfast Telegraph*, 3 February 1967.
35. *Belfast Telegraph*, 3 February 1967.
36. *Belfast Telegraph*, 4 February 1967.
37. *Belfast Telegraph*, 6 February 1967.
38. *Belfast Telegraph*, 9 February 1967.
39. *Belfast Telegraph*, 11 March 1967.
40. *Belfast Telegraph*, 17 April 1967.
41. *Belfast Telegraph*, 25 October 1967.
42. *Belfast Telegraph*, 1 November 1967.
43. *Belfast Telegraph*, 18 June 1965.
44. *Belfast Telegraph*, 21 June 1965.
45. *Belfast Telegraph*, 22 June 1965.
46. *Belfast Telegraph*, 20 September 1966.
47. *Belfast Telegraph*, 29 August 1964.
48. *Irish News*, 1 July 1967.
49. *Irish News*, 3 July 1967.
50. *Irish News*, 20 July 1967.
51. *Irish News*, 31 July 1967.
52. *News Letter*, 13 June 1968.
53. *Irish News*, 13 June 1968.
54. *Belfast Telegraph*, 13 June 1968.
55. *Irish News*, 13 June 1968.
56. *Belfast Telegraph*, 13 June 1968.
57. *News Letter*, 15 June 1968.
58. *Belfast Telegraph*, 14 June 1968.
59. *Belfast Telegraph*, 10 June 1965.
60. *Irish News*, 11 June 1966.
61. *Belfast Telegraph*, 25 April 1964.
62. *Belfast Telegraph*, 12 May 1964.
63. *Belfast Telegraph*, 13 May 1964.
64. *Belfast Telegraph*, 13 May 1964.
65. *Belfast Telegraph*, 6 October 1966.
66. *Belfast Telegraph*, 6 October 1966.
67. *Belfast Telegraph*, 25 April 1964.
68. *Belfast Telegraph*, 6 October 1966.
69. *Belfast Telegraph*, 8 December 1967.
70. *Belfast Telegraph*, 13 December 1967.
71. *Belfast Telegraph*, 12 May 1964.
72. *Belfast Telegraph*, 5 May 1964.
73. *Belfast Telegraph*, 12 August 1965.
74. *Belfast Telegraph*, 24 November 1966.
75. *Belfast Telegraph*, 3 January 1966.
76. *Belfast Telegraph*, 10 January 1966.
77. *Belfast Telegraph*, 17 January 1966.
78. *Belfast Telegraph*, 17 January 1966.
79. *Belfast Telegraph*, 25 January 1966.
80. *Belfast Telegraph*, 8 February 1966.

81. *Belfast Telegraph*, 8 November 1966.
82. *Belfast Telegraph*, 13 November 1966.
83. *Belfast Telegraph*, 2 November 1966.
84. *Belfast Telegraph*, 11 November 1966 ES letter.
85. *Belfast Telegraph*, 16 November 1966.
86. *Belfast Telegraph*, 15 December 1966.
87. *Belfast Telegraph*, 22 January 1966.
88. *Irish News*, 10 May 1967.
89. *Irish News*, 5 May 1967.
90. *Irish News*, 6 May 1967.
91. *Irish News*, 10 May 1967.
92. *Belfast Telegraph*, 30 July 1963.
93. *Belfast Telegraph*, 12 September 1963.
94. *Belfast Telegraph*, 16 September 1963.
95. *Belfast Telegraph*, 15 October 1963.
96. *Belfast Telegraph*, 17 October 1963.
97. *Belfast Telegraph*, 17 October 1963.
98. *Belfast Telegraph*, 18 October 1963.
99. *Belfast Telegraph*, 19 October 1963.
100. *Belfast Telegraph*, 20 November 1963.
101. *Belfast Telegraph*, 18 March 1964.
102. *Belfast Telegraph*, 25 March 1964.
103. *Belfast Telegraph*, 18 November 1964.
104. *Belfast Telegraph*, 19 March 1964.
105. Terence O'Neill, *The Autobiography of Terence O'Neill*, London 1972, 68–70.
106. Ibid. 72.
107. *Belfast Telegraph*, 16 January 1965.
108. *Belfast Telegraph*, 15 January 1965.
109. *Belfast Telegraph*, 14 January 1965.
110. *Belfast Telegraph*, 15 January 1965.
111. *Belfast Telegraph*, 26 January 1965.
112. *Belfast Telegraph*, 24 November 1964.
113. *Belfast Telegraph*, 15 January 1965.
114. *Belfast Telegraph*, 4 February 1965.
115. *Belfast Telegraph*, 16 January 1965.
116. *Belfast Telegraph*, 19 February 1965.
117. *Belfast Telegraph*, 20 February 1965.
118. *Belfast Telegraph*, 19 January 1965.
119. *Belfast Telegraph*, 16 January 1965.
120. *Belfast Telegraph*, 5 February 1965.
121. *Belfast Telegraph*, 15 January 1965.
122. *Belfast Telegraph*, 22 January 1965.
123. *Belfast Telegraph*, 23 January 1965.
124. *Belfast Telegraph*, 1 February 1965.
125. *Belfast Telegraph*, 4 February 1965.
126. *Belfast Telegraph*, 9 February 1965.
127. *Belfast Telegraph*, 10 February 1965.
128. *Belfast Telegraph*, 12 February 1965.
129. *Belfast Telegraph*, 10 March 1965.
130. *Belfast Telegraph*, 10 March 1965.

131. *Belfast Telegraph*, 12 March 1965.
132. *Belfast Telegraph*, 26 February 1965.
133. *Belfast Telegraph*, 21 June 1965.
134. *Belfast Telegraph*, 2 March 1965.
135. *Belfast Telegraph*, 18 February 1965.
136. *Belfast Telegraph*, 18 March 1965.
137. *Belfast Telegraph*, 26 February 1965.
138. O'Neill, *Autobiography*, 76.
139. *Belfast Telegraph*, 8 December 1967.

Chapter 2. O'Neill and the Enemy Within: the Unionist Party (PAGES 36–66)

1. John Whyte, 'How Much Discrimination Was There Under the Unionist Regime 1921–68?', in *Contemporary Irish Studies*, ed. Tom Gallagher and James O'Connell, Manchester 1983, 18–22.
2. *Belfast Telegraph*, 11 May 1965.
3. *Belfast Telegraph*, 16 November 1963.
4. *Belfast Telegraph*, 11 December 1963.
5. *Belfast Telegraph*, 23 September 1963.
6. *Belfast Telegraph*, 9 May 1964.
7. *Belfast Telegraph*, 7 May 1965.
8. *Belfast Telegraph*, 8 May 1965.
9. *Belfast Telegraph*, 7 May 1965.
10. *Belfast Telegraph*, 8 May 1965.
11. *Belfast Telegraph*, 12 May 1965.
12. *Belfast Telegraph*, 27 May 1965.
13. *Belfast Telegraph*, 28 May 1965.
14. *Belfast Telegraph*, 1 June 1965.
15. *Belfast Telegraph*, 25 May 1965.
16. *Belfast Telegraph*, 25 May 1965.
17. *Belfast Telegraph*, 18 May 1965.
18. *Belfast Telegraph*, 20 May 1965.
19. *Belfast Telegraph*, 5 June 1965.
20. *Belfast Telegraph*, 14 August 1964.
21. *Belfast Telegraph*, 14 August 1964.
22. *Belfast Telegraph*, 1 May 1965.
23. *Belfast Telegraph*, 21 June 1965.
24. *Belfast Telegraph*, 25 May 1965.
25. *Belfast Telegraph*, 13 October 1965.
26. *Belfast Telegraph*, 11 October 1966.
27. *Belfast Telegraph*, 11 June 1965.
28. *Belfast Telegraph*, 18 November 1965.
29. *Belfast Telegraph*, 3 December 1965.
30. *Belfast Telegraph*, 23 November 1965.
31. *Belfast Telegraph*, 24 November 1965.
32. *Belfast Telegraph*, 24 November 1965.
33. *Belfast Telegraph*, 26 November 1965.
34. *Belfast Telegraph*, 26 November 1965.
35. *Belfast Telegraph*, 15 February 1966.
36. *Belfast Telegraph*, 16 February 1966.
37. *Belfast Telegraph*, 21 February 1966.

38. *Belfast Telegraph*, 17 February 1966.
39. *Belfast Telegraph*, 21 February 1966.
40. *Belfast Telegraph*, 22 February 1966.
41. *Belfast Telegraph*, 25 February 1966.
42. *Belfast Telegraph*, 1 March 1966.
43. *Belfast Telegraph*, 2 March 1966.
44. *Belfast Telegraph*, 16 March 1966.
45. *Belfast Telegraph*, 17 March 1966.
46. *Belfast Telegraph*, 19 March 1966.
47. *Belfast Telegraph*, 21 March 1966.
48. *Belfast Telegraph*, 25 March 1966.
49. *Belfast Telegraph*, 22 March 1966.
50. *Belfast Telegraph*, 31 March 1966.
51. *Belfast Telegraph*, 1 April 1966.
52. *Irish News*, 1 April 1966.
53. *Belfast Telegraph*, 11 May 1966.
54. *Disturbances in Northern Ireland: Report of the Cameron Commission*, Cmnd.532, Belfast 1969, 118–19.
55. *Belfast Telegraph*, 1 March 1966.
56. *Belfast Telegraph*, 25 February 1966.
57. *Belfast Telegraph*, 25 February 1966.
58. *Belfast Telegraph*, 2 March 1966.
59. *Belfast Telegraph*, 8 March 1966.
60. *Belfast Telegraph*, 15 March 1966.
61. *Belfast Telegraph*, 4 February 1966.
62. *Belfast Telegraph*, 4 April 1966.
63. *Belfast Telegraph*, 7 February 1966.
64. *Belfast Telegraph*, 21 February 1966.
65. *Belfast Telegraph*, 28 February 1966 Ulsterman letter.
66. *Belfast Telegraph*, 28 February 1966.
67. *Belfast Telegraph*, 7 April 1966.
68. *Belfast Telegraph*, 7 April 1966.
69. *Belfast Telegraph*, 7 April 1966.
70. Farrell, *Northern Ireland the Orange State*, 235.
71. *Irish News*, 8 June 1966.
72. *Irish News*, 9 June 1966.
73. *Irish News*, 16 June 1966.
74. *Irish News*, 16 June 1966.
75. Peter Taylor, *Loyalists*, London 1999, 32–3.
76. Ibid. 30–31.
77. Ibid. 36–9.
78. Roy Garland, *Gusty Spence*, Belfast 2001, 5–6.
79. Ibid. 12–13.
80. Ibid. 15.
81. Ibid. 21.
82. Ibid. 31–32.
83. Ibid. 48–53.
84. Ibid. 56.
85. Taylor, *Loyalists*, 41–4.
86. *Irish News*, 29 June 1966.

87. *Irish News*, 30 June 1966.
88. *Belfast Telegraph*, 12 December 1967.
89. *Belfast Telegraph*, 21 September 1966.
90. *Belfast Telegraph*, 23 September 1966.
91. *Belfast Telegraph*, 24 September 1966.
92. *Belfast Telegraph*, 24 September 1966.
93. *Belfast Telegraph*, 26 September 1966.
94. *Belfast Telegraph*, 26 September 1966.
95. *Belfast Telegraph*, 26 September 1966.
96. *Belfast Telegraph*, 26 September 1966.
97. *Belfast Telegraph*, 27 September 1966.
98. *Belfast Telegraph*, 28 September 1966.
99. *Belfast Telegraph*, 28 September 1966.
100. *Belfast Telegraph*, 28 September 1966.
101. *Belfast Telegraph*, 28 September 1966.
102. *Belfast Telegraph*, 28 September 1966.
103. *Belfast Telegraph*, 28 September 1966.
104. *Belfast Telegraph*, 8 October 1966.
105. *Belfast Telegraph*, 11 October 1966.
106. *Belfast Telegraph*, 26 September 1966.
107. *Belfast Telegraph*, 28 September 1966.
108. *Belfast Telegraph*, 26 April 1967.
109. *Belfast Telegraph*, 26 April 1967.
110. *Belfast Telegraph*, 3 May 1967.
111. *Belfast Telegraph*, 2 May 1967.
112. *Irish News*, 3 May 1967.
113. *Irish News*, 3 May 1967.
114. *Irish News*, 29 April 1967.
115. *Irish News*, 1 May 1967.
116. *Belfast Telegraph*, 3 May 1967.
117. *Belfast Telegraph*, 3 May 1967.

Chapter 3. Catholic in the Six Counties (PAGES 67–106)
1. John Whyte, *Interpreting Northern Ireland*, Oxford 1990, 55–6.
2. Ibid. 59.
3. Ibid. 13.
4. David Smith and Gerald Chambers, *Inequality in Northern Ireland*, Oxford 1991, 19–20.
5. Ibid. 8–10.
6. Ibid. 13.
7. Ibid. 300–301.
8. *Belfast Telegraph*, 16 January 1964.
9. *Belfast Telegraph*, 25 January 1964.
10. Richard Rose, *Governing Without Consensus: An Irish Perspective*, London 1971, 300.
11. *Belfast Telegraph*, 7 February 1964.
12. *Belfast Telegraph*, 27 May 1966.
13. *Belfast Telegraph*, 2 June 1966.
14. *Belfast Telegraph*, 11 November 1966.
15. *Belfast Telegraph*, 3 November 1967.
16. Whyte, *Interpreting Northern Ireland*, 18–22.
17. Smith and Chambers, *Inequality in Northern Ireland*, 17.

18. Whyte, *Interpreting Northern Ireland*, 18–22.

19. Smith and Chambers, *Inequality in Northern Ireland*, 21.

20. *Belfast Telegraph*, 19 November 1963.

21. *Belfast Telegraph*, 19 November 1963.

22. *Belfast Telegraph*, 3 December 1963.

23. *Belfast Telegraph*, 4 December 1963.

24. *Belfast Telegraph*, 8 January 1964.

25. *Belfast Telegraph*, 25 November 1964.

26. *Belfast Telegraph*, 26 November 1964.

27. *Belfast Telegraph*, 27 November 1964.

28. *Belfast Telegraph*, 2 November 1967.

29. *Belfast Telegraph*, 2 November 1967.

30. *Irish News*, 27 December 1967.

31. O'Neill, *Autobiography*, 44.

32. Ibid. 47.

33. *Belfast Telegraph*, 21 October 1963.

34. *Belfast Telegraph*, 1 October 1963.

35. *Belfast Telegraph*, 7 October 1963.

36. *Belfast Telegraph*, 7 October 1963.

37. *Belfast Telegraph*, 16 October 1963.

38. *Belfast Telegraph*, 29 October 1963.

39. *Belfast Telegraph*, 9 March 1964.

40. *Belfast Telegraph*, 3 March 1964.

41. *Belfast Telegraph*, 13 March 1964.

42. *Belfast Telegraph*, 19 March 1964.

43. *Belfast Telegraph*, 3 April 1964.

44. *Belfast Telegraph*, 4 April 1964.

45. *Belfast Telegraph*, 2 May 1964.

46. *Belfast Telegraph*, 8 May 1964.

47. *Belfast Telegraph*, 20 November 1963.

48. *Belfast Telegraph*, 11 December 1963.

49. *Belfast Telegraph*, 11 December 1963.

50. *Belfast Telegraph*, 10 March 1964.

51. *Belfast Telegraph*, 11 March 1964.

52. *Belfast Telegraph*, 31 January 1964.

53. *Belfast Telegraph*, 17 January 1964.

54. *Belfast Telegraph*, 29 January 1964.

55. *Belfast Telegraph*, 7 February 1964.

56. *Belfast Telegraph*, 8 December 1964.

57. *Belfast Telegraph*, 9 December 1964.

58. *Belfast Telegraph*, 6 May 1964.

59. *Belfast Telegraph*, 13 May 1964.

60. *Belfast Telegraph*, 11 December 1964.

61. *Belfast Telegraph*, 29 April 1964.

62. *Belfast Telegraph*, 16 June 1964.

63. *Belfast Telegraph*, 11 June 1964.

64. *Belfast Telegraph*, 14 January 1965.

65. Michael Kennedy, *Division and Consensus. The Politics of Cross-Border Relations in Ireland 1925–1969*, Dublin 2000, 236–7.

66. *Belfast Telegraph*, 26 January 1965.

NOTES FROM PAGES 88–113

67. *Belfast Telegraph*, 3 February 1965.
68. *Belfast Telegraph*, 13 March 1965.
69. *Belfast Telegraph*, 15 June 1965.
70. *Belfast Telegraph*, 17 June 1965.
71. *Belfast Telegraph*, 19 October 1965.
72. *Belfast Telegraph*, 27 January 1966.
73. *Irish News*, 25 May 1967.
74. *Irish News*, 5 June 1967.
75. *Irish News*, 6 June 1967.
76. *Belfast Telegraph*, 3 August 1964.
77. *Belfast Telegraph*, 12 May 1964.
78. *Irish News*, 18 December 1967.
79. *Belfast Telegraph*, 13 November 1964.
80. *Belfast Telegraph*, 14 November 1964.
81. *Irish News*, 14 June 1967.
82. *Irish News*, 9 April 1966.
83. *Belfast Telegraph*, 9 April 1966.
84. *Belfast Telegraph*, 8 December 1967.
85. *Belfast Telegraph*, 23 June 1965.
86. *Belfast Telegraph*, 17 March 1966.
87. *Belfast Telegraph*, 15 August 1964.
88. *Belfast Telegraph*, 23 June 1965.
89. Paddy Doherty, *Paddy Bogside*, Cork 2001, 12.
90. Ibid. 14–15.
91. Ibid. 23.
92. Ibid. 32–3.
93. Rose, *Governing Without Consensus*, 300–301.
94. Ibid. 363–4.
95. NAI 98/6/495 *Review of Unlawful and Allied Organisations*, December 1 1964 to November 21 1966.
96. Bob Purdy, *Politics in the Streets: The Origins of the Civil Rights Movement in Northern Ireland*, Belfast 1990, 128.

Chapter 4. The Gathering Storm (PAGES 107–144)

1. *Irish News*, 30 April 1966.
2. PRONI HO 5/189.
3. PRONI HO 5/189 Why Justice Can Not be Done: The Douglas Home Correspondence.
4. PRONI HO5/189 Gregory to Longford, 18 November 1964.
5. PRONI HO 5/188 McCluskey to Thomas.
6. PRONI HO 5/188 Wilson to McCluskey, September 1964.
7. *Belfast Telegraph*, 4 May 1965.
8. *Belfast Telegraph*, 6 May 1965.
9. *Belfast Telegraph*, 6 May 1965.
10. *Belfast Telegraph*, 7 May 1965.
11. *Irish News*, 6 April 1966.
12. *CDU Newsletter* 1 (November 1966).
13. *Belfast Telegraph*, 3 June 1965.
14. *Belfast Telegraph*, 3 June 1965.
15. *Irish News*, 30 April 1966.
16. *Belfast Telegraph*, 23 May 1966.

17. *Irish News*, 23 May 1966.

18. *Irish News*, 27 May 1966.

19. NAUK PREM 13/2266, 8 June 1966.

20. NAUK PREM 13/2266, 5 August 1966.

21. NAUK PREM 13/2266, 12 January 1967.

22. *Irish News*, 3 January 1967.

23. *Irish News*, 6 January 1967.

24. *Irish News*, 13 January 1967.

25. *Irish News*, 14 January 1967.

26. *Belfast Telegraph*, 7 March 1967.

27. *Irish News*, 9 March 1967.

28. *Irish News*, 17 March 1967.

29. *Belfast Telegraph*, 17 March 1967.

30. *Irish News*, 17 March 1967.

31. *Irish News*, 18 March 1967.

32. *Irish News*, 20 March 1967.

33. *Irish News*, 21 March 1967.

34. *Belfast Telegraph*, 23 March 1967.

35. *Irish News*, 9 March 1967.

36. *Belfast Telegraph*, 8 March 1967.

37. *Belfast Telegraph*, 8 March 1967.

38. *Irish News*, 28 March 1967.

39. *Irish News*, 3 April 1967.

40. *Irish News*, 8 April 1967.

41. *Irish News*, 17 April 1967.

42. *Irish News*, 21 April 1967.

43. *Irish News*, 26 April 1967.

44. *Irish News*, 25 April 1967.

45. *Belfast Telegraph*, 24 April 1967.

46. *Irish News*, 25 April 1967.

47. *Irish News*, 26 April 1967.

48. *Irish News*, 28 April 1967.

49. *Belfast Telegraph*, 20 March 1967.

50. *Belfast Telegraph*, 24 March 1967.

51. *Irish News*, 1 May 1967.

52. *Irish News*, 1 July 1967.

53. *Irish News*, 15 June 1967.

54. *Irish News*, 31 July 1967.

55. *Irish News*, 29 August; 12 September 1967.

56. *Irish News*, 23 September 1967.

57. *Irish News*, 12 October 1967.

58. *Irish News*, 13 October 1967.

59. *Irish News*, 18 October 1967.

60. *Irish News*, 30 October 1967.

61. *Irish News*, 31 October 1967.

62. *Irish News*, 1 November 1967.

63. *Irish News*, 2 November 1967.

64. *Irish News*, 25 September 1967.

65. *Irish News*, 7 October 1967.

66. *Irish News*, 31 October 1967.

67. James Callaghan, *A House Divided. The Dilemma of Northern Ireland*, London 1973, 2.
68. *News Letter*, 7 June 1968.
69. *Irish News*, 7 June 1968.
70. *Belfast Telegraph*, 7 June 1968.
71. *Belfast Telegraph*, 7 June 1968.
72. Callaghan, *A House Divided*, 1.
73. Hennessey, *A History of Northern Ireland 1920–1996*, 137.
74. *Irish News*, 13 September 1967.
75. *Irish News*, 9 October 1967.
76. *Irish News*, 19 October 1967.
77. *Irish News*, 24 October 1967.
78. *Irish News*, 4 November 1967.
79. *Belfast Telegraph*, 14 October 1967.
80. *Belfast Telegraph*, 19 October 1967.
81. *Belfast Telegraph*, 21 October 1967.
82. *Irish News*, 18 June 1968.
83. *Irish News*, 19 June 1968.
84. *Belfast Telegraph*, 17 June 1968.
85. *Irish News*, 19 June 1968.
86. *Belfast Telegraph*, 19 June 1968.
87. *Belfast Telegraph*, 19 June 1968.
88. *Irish News*, 19 June 1968.
89. *Belfast Telegraph*,.
90. *Irish News*, 21 June 1968.
91. *Belfast Telegraph*, 21 June 1968.
92. *Belfast Telegraph*, 22 June 1968.
93. *Irish News*, 24 June 1968.
94. *Belfast Telegraph*, 24 June 1968.
95. *Irish News*, 24 June 1968.
96. *Belfast Telegraph*, 24 June 1968.
97. *Irish News*, 24 June 1968.
98. *News Letter*, 26 June 1968.
99. *Belfast Telegraph*, 28 June 1968.
100. Cameron, paras. 29–34.
101. Ibid. paras. 38–42.
102. *Irish News*, 4 October 1968.
103. Cameron, para. 44.
104. Ibid. para. 43.
105. *Irish News*, 3 October 1968.
106. *Irish News*, 3 October 1968.
107. *Irish News*, 4 October 1968.
108. Cameron, para. 45.
109. Ibid. paras. 48–55.
110. *Irish News*, 7 October 1968.
111. Austin Currie, *All Hell Will Break Loose*, Dublin 2004, 9–10.

Chapter 5. London Intervenes: British Policy and Westminster–Stormont Relations October 1968–February 1969 (PAGES 145–189)

1. NAUK PRO PREM 13/2841/74674 notes for the Record, 7 October 1968.
2. NAUK PRO PREM 13/2841 Cubbon note, 7 October 1968.

3. PRONI CAB/4/1406/2 Memorandum by the Prime Minister, 14 October 1968.

4. PRONI CAB/4/1407/11 Cabinet Conclusions, 15 October 1968 10.45 a.m.

5. PRONI CAB/4/1409/11 Cabinet Conclusions, 23 October 1968 10 a.m.

6. PRONI CAB/4/1410/24 Cabinet Conclusions, 24 October 1968 11.15 a.m.

7. PRONI CAB/4/1412/12 Memorandum by the Prime Minister, 28 October 1968.

8. PRONI CAB/4/1412/23 Cabinet Conclusions, 31 October 1968 at 11 a.m.

9. NAUK PRO PREM 13/2847 Note of a Meeting held at Downing Street, 4 November 1968.

10. PRONI CAB/4/1415/11 Cabinet Conclusions, 15 November 1968 at 2.30 p.m.

11. PRONI CAB/4/1416/11 Cabinet Conclusions, 18 November 1968 at 2.30 p.m.

12. PRONI CAB/4/1415/11 Cabinet Conclusions, 15 November 1968 at 2.30 p.m.

13. PRONI CAB/4/1416/11 Cabinet Conclusions, 18 November 1968 at 2.30 p.m.

14. PRONI CAB/4/1415/11 Cabinet Conclusions, 15 November 1968 at 2.30 p.m.

15. PRONI CAB/4/1416/11 Cabinet Conclusions, 18 November 1968 at 2.30 p.m.

16. PRONI CAB/4/1415/11 Cabinet Conclusions, 15 November 1968 at 2.30 p.m.

17. PRONI CAB/4/1419/15 Meeting at the Home Office, 19 November 1968.

18. PRONI CAB/4/1415/11 Cabinet Conclusions, 15 November 1968 at 2.30 p.m.

19. NAUK PRO PREM 13/2841 Prime Minister's Personal Message Serial No. T287/68: Wilson to O'Neill, 19 November 1968.

20. *Irish News*, 18 November 1968.

21. *Irish News*, 19 November 1968.

22. *Irish News*, 20 November 1968.

23. *Irish News*, 21 November 1968.

24. PRONI CAB/4/1420 Cabinet Conclusions, 20 November 1968.

25. *Irish News*, 22 November 1968.

26. *Irish News*, 25 November 1968.

27. NAUK PRO PREM 13/2841 Prime Minister's Personal Message Serial No. T302/68: O'Neill to Wilson, 6 December 1968.

28. NAUK PRO PREM 13/2841 Prime Minister's Personal Message Serial No. T316/68 Wilson to O'Neill, 23 December 1968.

29. Terence O'Neill, *Ulster at the Crossroads*, London 1969, 140–46.

30. *Belfast Telegraph*, 16 December 1968.

31. *Belfast News Letter*, 1 January 1969.

32. Paul Bew and Gordon Gillespie, *Northern Ireland: A Chronology of the Troubles 1968–1993*, Dublin 1993, 10.

33. *Irish News*, 17 December 1968.

34. NAUK PRO PREM 13/2841/74674.

35. NAUK PRO PREM 13/2841 Note from the Private Secretary at the Home Office, Brian Cubbon, 19 November 1968.

36. NAUK PRO DEFE 25/257-13 Military Aid to the Civil Power in Northern Ireland, 5 December 1968.

37. NAUK PRO PREM 13/2841 Northern Ireland.

38. NAUK PRO PREM 13/2841 Military Aid to the Civil Power in Northern Ireland: Chief of the Defence Staff to the Secretary of State for Defence, 12 December 1968.

39. NAUK PRO PREM 13/2841 Military Aid to the Civil Authority in Northern Ireland: Secretary of State for Defence, 13 December 1968.

40. NAUK PRO DEFE 25/257 Chiefs of Staff Committee Defence Operations Staff. Northern Ireland Internal Security Higher Chain of Command; Draft Note by the Defence Operations Staff, 15 January 1969.

41. NAUK PRO DEFE 25/257 Military Aid to Civil Power in Northern Ireland, 27 January 1969.

42. NAUK PRO CAB 128/44/CC 6, 69, 30 January 1969.

43. NAUK PRO DEFE 25/257 Note of a Meeting held at 10.30 a.m. on Tuesday 28 January 1969 at the Home Office.

44. NAUK PRO DEFE 25/257 Minute of a Meeting held at 3 p.m. on Thursday 30 January 1969 in the Ministry of Defence, 30 January 1969.

45. NAUK PRO DEFE 25/257, 9 February 1969.

46. NAUK PRO PREM 13/2844 Top Secret Northern Ireland, Emergency Provisions, Draft of a Bill.

47. NAUK PRO DEFE 25/257 Emergency Provisions in respect of Northern Ireland nd.

48. NAUK PRO DEFE 25/257, 9 February 1969.

49. NAUK PRO DEFE 25/257, February 1969.

50. NAUK PRO DEFE 25/257 Chief of the General Staff, 9 February 1969.

51. Purdy, *Politics in the Streets*, 216–17.

52. *Irish News*, 2 January 1968.

53. *Irish News*, 1 January 1969.

54. *Irish News*, 2 January 1969.

55. *Belfast Telegraph*, 2 January 1969.

56. *Irish News*, 3 January 1969.

57. *Belfast Telegraph*, 4 January 1969.

58. *Violence and Disturbance in Northern Ireland* Cmd 566 1972, hereafter Scarman, 97–8.

59. *Belfast Telegraph*, 6 January 1969.

60. *Belfast Telegraph*, 4 January 1969.

61. Scarman, 100.

62. *Belfast Telegraph*, 6 January 1969.

63. *Belfast Telegraph*, 7 January 1969.

64. *Irish News*, 6 January 1969.

65. *Irish News*, 6 January 1969.

66. PRONI CAB/4/1425/12 Cabinet Conclusions, 6 January 1969 2.30 p.m.

67. *Irish News*, 7 January 1969.

68. *Irish News*, 8 January 1969.

69. *Belfast Telegraph*, 7 January 1969.

70. *Belfast Telegraph*, 11 January 1969.

71. *Belfast Telegraph*, 8 January 1969.

72. *Belfast Telegraph*, 11 January 1969.

73. *Belfast Telegraph*, 13 January 1969.

74. *Irish News*, 6 January 1969.

75. *Belfast Telegraph*, 6 January 1969.

76. *Irish News*, 6 January 1969.

77. *Belfast Telegraph*, 21 January 1969.

78. *Irish News*, 6 January 1969.

79. *Irish News*, 7 January 1969.

80. *Irish News*, 7 January 1969.

81. *Irish News*, 6 January 1969.

82. *Irish News*, 8 January 1969.

83. *Irish News*, 7 January 1969.

84. *Irish News*, 7 January 1969.

85. *Irish News*, 7 January 1969.

86. *Irish News*, 7 January 1969.

87. PRONI CAB/4/1426/12 Cabinet Conclusions, 10 January 1969 10.30 at a.m.

88. Scarman, 102.

89. Cameron, para. 117.

90. Ibid. para. 120.

91. *Irish News*, 13 January 1969.

92. *Irish News*, 13 January 1969.

93. *Irish News*, 13 January 1969.

94. *Irish News*, 15 January 1969.

95. *Belfast Telegraph*, 22 January 1969.

96. PRONI CAB/4/1427/12 The Political Situation Memorandum by the Prime Minister, 14 January 1969.

97. PRONI CAB/4/1427/24 Cabinet Conclusions, 15 January 1969 at 10.00 a.m.

98. NAUK PRO CAB 128/44/5, 1, 69C, 23 January 1969.

99. *Irish News*, 16 January 1969.

100. PRONI CAB/4/1427/9 Memorandum for the Cabinet by the Minister of Home Affairs on Proposed Amendments to the Public Order Act, Northern Ireland, 1951, 10 January 1969.

101. PRONI CAB/4/1427/24 Cabinet Conclusions, 15 January 1969.

102. *Irish News*, 16 January 1969.

103. *Irish News*, 16 January 1969.

104. *Irish News*, 17 January 1969.

105. *Belfast Telegraph*, 16 January 1969.

106. *Belfast Telegraph*, 17 January 1969.

107. *Belfast Telegraph*, 20 January 1969.

108. *Belfast Telegraph*, 22 January 1969.

109. *Irish News*, 18 January 1969.

110. Brian Faulkner, *Memoirs of a Statesman*, London 1978, 51–2.

111. *Belfast Telegraph*, 25 January 1969.

Chapter 6. Towards Disaster: Northern Ireland February–August 1969 (PAGES 190–236)

1. *Irish News*, 30 January 1969.

2. *Belfast Telegraph*, 1 February 1969.

3. *Belfast Telegraph*, 3 February 1969.

4. *Belfast Telegraph*, 1 February 1969.

5. *Belfast Telegraph*, 3 February 1969.

6. *Irish News*, 30 January 1969.

7. *Irish News*, 1 February 1969.

8. *Belfast Telegraph*, 1 February 1969.

9. *Belfast Telegraph*, 3 February 1969.

10. *Belfast Telegraph*, 3 February 1969.

11. *Irish News*, 4 February 1969.

12. *Belfast Telegraph*, 4 February 1969.

13. *Belfast Telegraph*, 4 February 1969.

14. *Belfast Telegraph*, 7 February 1969.

15. *Irish News*, 13 February 1969.

16. *Irish News*, 7 February 1969.

17. *Irish News*, 18 February 1969.

18. *Irish News*, 11 February 1969.

19. *Protestant Telegraph*, 22 February 1969.

20. *Irish News*, 15 February 1969.

21. *Irish News*, 12 February 1969.

22. *Irish News*, 20 February 1969.

23. *Belfast Telegraph*, 13 February 1969.

24. *Belfast Telegraph*, 20 February 1969.

25. *Belfast Telegraph*, 20 February 1969.

NOTES FROM PAGES 195–208

26. *Irish News*, 15 February 1969.
27. *Irish News*, 18 February 1969.
28. *Irish News*, 7 February 1969.
29. *Irish News*, 11 February 1969.
30. *Belfast Telegraph*, 14 February 1969.
31. *Irish News*, 10 February 1969.
32. *Irish News*, 12 February 1969.
33. *Irish News*, 12 February 1969.
34. *Irish News*, 7 February 1969.
35. *Irish News*, 8 February 1969.
36. *Irish News*, 7 February 1969.
37. *Irish News*, 10 February 1969.
38. *Irish News*, 11 February 1969.
39. *Belfast Telegraph*, 13 February 1969.
40. *Belfast Telegraph*, 25 February 1969.
41. *Belfast Telegraph*, 25 February 1969.
42. O'Neill, *Autobiography*, 121.
43. *Belfast Telegraph*, 25 February 1969.
44. *Belfast Telegraph*, 28 February 1969.
45. NAUK PRO DEFE 25/257, 19 February 1969.
46. NAUK PRO DEFE 25/257, Callaghan to Wilson.
47. NAUK PRO CAB/130/416/19 MISC 238(69) 1st Meeting Northern Ireland Political Appreciation. Memorandum by the Secretary of State for the Home Department, 24 February 1969.
48. NAUK PRO CAB/130/416/17 MISC 238(69) 1st Meeting Cabinet; Minutes of a Meeting held in the Prime Minister's Room, House of Commons on Wednesday 26 February 1969, at 6 p.m.
49. NAUK PRO DEFE 25/257 Callaghan to Wilson, 27 February 1969.
50. NAUK PRO DEFE 25/257, 28 February 1969.
51. NAUK PRO DEFE 25/302 Callaghan to Wilson, 28 February 1969.
52. *Belfast Telegraph*, 4 March 1969.
53. *Belfast Telegraph*, 12 March 1969.
54. *Belfast Telegraph*, 4 March 1969.
55. *Belfast Telegraph*, 12 March 1969.
56. *Belfast Telegraph*, 26 March 1969.
57. *Belfast Telegraph*, 21 March 1969.
58. *Belfast Telegraph*, 12 April 1969.
59. *Belfast Telegraph*, 31 March 1969.
60. *Belfast Telegraph*, 31 March 1969.
61. *Belfast Telegraph*, 31 March 1969.
62. *Belfast Telegraph*, 11 April 1969.
63. *Belfast Telegraph*, 12 April 1969.
64. *Belfast Telegraph*, 4 March 1969.
65. *Belfast Telegraph*, 25 March 1969.
66. *Belfast Telegraph*, 14 April 1969.
67. *Belfast Telegraph*, 25 March 1969.
68. *Belfast Telegraph*, 26 March 1969.
69. *Belfast Telegraph*, 27 March 1969.
70. *Belfast Telegraph*, 29 March 1969.
71. *Belfast Telegraph*, 29 March 1969.
72. *Belfast Telegraph*, 4 April 1969.
73. *Belfast Telegraph*, 5 April 1969.

74. *Belfast Telegraph*, 22 April 1969.

75. *Belfast Telegraph*, 24 April 1969.

76. *Belfast Telegraph*, 24 April 1969.

77. *Belfast Telegraph*, 25 April 1969.

78. O'Neill, *Autobiography*, 123.

79. Ibid. 124.

80. PRONI CAB/4/1435/13 Cabinet Conclusions, 20 April 1969 4.30 p.m.

81. NAUK PRO CAB/130/416/18: MISC 238(69) 2nd Meeting; Minutes of a Meeting held in the Prime Minister's Room, House of Commons on Monday 21 April 1969 at 2.45 p.m.

82. PRONI CAB/4/1437/11 Cabinet Conclusions, 22 April 1969 6.40 p.m.

83. O'Neill, *Autobiography*, 124–5.

84. *Belfast Telegraph*, 23 April 1969.

85. *Belfast Telegraph*, 24 April 1969.

86. *Belfast Telegraph*, 24 April 1969.

87. PRONI CAB/4/1439/11 Cabinet Conclusions, 25 April 1969 4.30 p.m.

88. NAUK PRO CAB 128/44 CC 19, (69), 24 April 1969.

89. NAUK PRO CAB/130/416/18 MISC 238(69) 3rd Meeting. Minutes of a Meeting held at 10 Downing Street on Friday, 25 April 1969 at 9.30 a.m.

90. O'Neill, *Autobiography*, 126.

91. Ibid. 126–7.

92. NAUK PRO DEFE 25/272 GOCNI to DMO, 28 April 1969.

93. O'Neill, *Ulster at the Crossroads*, 200.

94. O'Neill, *Autobiography*, 139.

95. NAUK PRO CAB/130/416/17 MISC 238(69) 3 Northern Ireland: Resignation of Captain O'Neill. Memorandum by the Secretary of State for the Home Department, 28 April 1969.

96. NAUK PRO CAB/130/416/19 MISC 238(69) 4th Meeting Northern Ireland Minutes of a Meeting held at 10 Downing Street on Tuesday 29 April, 1969 at 10.30 a.m.

97. *Belfast Telegraph*, 30 April 1969.

98. *Belfast Telegraph*, 29 April 1969.

99. *Belfast Telegraph*, 29 April 1969.

100. *Belfast Telegraph*, 29 April 1969.

101. *Belfast Telegraph*, 28 April 1969.

102. *Belfast Telegraph*, 30 April 1969.

103. *Belfast Telegraph*, 30 April 1969.

104. *Belfast Telegraph*, 26 April 1969.

105. *Belfast Telegraph*, 28 April 1969.

106. O'Neill, *Autobiography*, 128.

107. *Belfast Telegraph*, 30 April 1969.

108. O'Neill, *Autobiography*, 128–9.

109. PRONI CAB/4/1440/13 Cabinet Conclusions, 5 May 1969 3 p.m.

110. PRONI CAB/4/1441/13 Cabinet Conclusions, 6 May 1969 11.30 a.m.

111. PRONI CAB/4/1441/13 Cabinet Conclusions, 6 May 1969 11.30 a.m.

112. PRONI CAB/4/1443/6 Memorandum for the Cabinet by the Minister for Home Affairs on Local Government Franchise, 9 May 1969.

113. PRONI CAB/4/1443/23 Cabinet Conclusions, 15 May 1969 10 a.m.

114. NAUK PRO CAB 128/44 CC 24, (69), 22 May 1969.

115. NAUK PRO CAB/130/416/19 MISC 238(69) 4th Meeting Northern Ireland Minutes of a Meeting held at 10 Downing Street on Tuesday 29 April, 1969 at 10.30 a.m.

116. NAUK PRO CAB 129/141C(69) 45 Northern Ireland: Memorandum by the Secretary of State for the Home Department, 5 May 1969.

117. NAUK PRO CAB/130/416/17 MISC 238(69) 5, 14 July 1969 Northern Ireland: Memorandum by the Secretary of State for Defence.

118. NAUK PRO CAB/130/416/17 MISC 238(69) 5 14 July 1969 Annex B Withdrawal for United Kingdom Subventions to Northern Ireland.

119. NAUK PRO CAB 129/141C(69) 45 Northern Ireland: Memorandum by the Secretary of State for the Home Department, 5 May 1969.

120. NAUK PRO DEFE 24/655 Northern Ireland, 8 July 1969.

121. NAUK PRO DEFE 24/655, 2 July 1969.

122. NAUK PRO DEFE 24/655 Northern Ireland, 8 July 1969.

123. NAUK PRO CAB 129/144 C(69) 107 Northern Ireland: Memorandum by the Minister of Defence for Administration, 28 July 1969.

124. NAUK PRO CAB/130/416/18 MISC 238(69) 6th Meeting Northern Ireland: Minutes of a Meeting held in the Prime Minister's Room, House of Commons on Tuesday, 15 July, 1969 at 5 p.m.

125. NAUK PRO CAB 129/144 C(69) 107 Northern Ireland: Memorandum by the Minister of Defence for Administration, 28 July 1969.

126. David McKittrick, Seamus Kelters, Brian Feeney and Chris Thornton, *Lost Lives: The Stories of the Men, Women and Children Who Died as a Result of the Northern Ireland Troubles*, Edinburgh 1999, 32.

127. NAUK PRO CAB 129/144 C(69) 108 Northern Ireland: Memorandum by the Secretary of State for the Home Department, 28 July 1969.

128. Callaghan, *A House Divided*, 14.

129. NAUK PRO CAB 129/144 C(69) 108 Northern Ireland: Memorandum by the Secretary of State for the Home Department, 28 July 1969.

130. NAUK PRO CAB 128/44 CC 39(69), 31 July 1969.

131. Scarman, 19.1.

132. Ibid. 19.3–19.4.

133. Ibid. 19.6.

134. PRONI CAB/4/1455/1 Cabinet Conclusions, 3 August 1969 4 p.m.

135. PRONI CAB/4/1456/1 Cabinet Conclusions, 4 August 1969 4 p.m.

136. PRONI CAB/4/1457/1 Cabinet Conclusions, 5 August 1969 4 p.m.

137. PRONI CAB/4/1455/1 Cabinet Conclusions, 3 August 1969 4 p.m.

138. NAUK PRO DEFE 24/655 Chichester-Clark to Callaghan, 4 August 1969.

139. NAUK PRO FCO 33/765 Cubbon to Gregson, 7 August 1969.

140. NAUK PRO FCO 33/765 Gregson to Cubbon, 8 August 1969.

141. PRONI CAB/4/1458/13 Discussion on Possible Use of Troops in Aid of the Civil Power Arising out of Disturbances in Belfast on 2–3 August 1969, 7 August 1969.

142. PRONI CAB/4/1457/1 Cabinet Conclusions, 5 August 1969 4 p.m.

143. PRONI CAB/4/1458/13 Discussion on Possible Use of Troops in Aid of the Civil Power Arising out of Disturbances in Belfast on 2–3 August 1969, 7 August 1969.

144. Scarman, 20.3.

145. PRONI CAB/4/1458/13 Discussion on Possible Use of Troops in Aid of the Civil Power Arising out of Disturbances in Belfast on 2–3 August 1969, 7 August 1969.

146. NAUK PRO FCO 33/765 Cubbon to Gregson, 6 August 1969.

147. PRONI CAB/4/1458/14 Notes on Telephone Conversations with Home Secretary on Wednesday 6 August.

148. NAUK PRO FCO 33/765 Cubbon to Gregson, 6 August 1969.
149. PRONI CAB/4/1458/14 Notes on Telephone Conversations with Home Secretary on Wednesday August 6th.
150. NAUK PRO FCO 33/765 Chichester-Clark to Callaghan, 6 August 1969.
151. NAUK PRO CAB 164/1577 Meeting at the Home Office, 8 August 1969.

Chapter 7. August 1969 (PAGES 237–285)
1. Scarman, 10.4–10.5.
2. Ibid. 10.9.
3. Ibid. 10.11–10.14.
4. Ibid. 19.2.
5. Ibid. 11.4–11.15.
6. Ibid. 11.16–11.20.
7. Ibid. 11.23.
8. Ibid. 11.25.
9. Ibid. 11.29–11.34.
10. Ibid. 12.1.
11. PRONI CAB/4/1459/12 Cabinet Conclusions, 13 August 1969 Noon.
12. Seamus Brady, *Arms and the Men*, Wicklow 1971, 34–7.
13. NAI 2000/5/38 Note, 13 August.
14. Scarman, Volume 2, 44.
15. Ibid. 36–7.
16. Scarman, 13.1–13.9.
17. Ibid. 17.9–17.10.
18. Callaghan, *A House Divided*, 39.
19. PRO PREM 13/2844 Note for the Record, 2, 14 August 1969.
20. NAUK PRO PREM 13/2844 To Dublin. Telegram No. 87, 14 August 1969.
21. NAUK PRO PREM 13/2844 Mr Lynch's Intervention, 14 August 1969.
22. NAUK PRO PREM 13/2844 Telegram No. 175, 14 August 1969.
23. Scarman, 12.25.
24. Ibid. 12.27–12.28.
25. Callaghan, *A House Divided*, 41.
26. NAUK PRO PREM 13/2844 Note of a meeting held at R.A.F. St. Mawgan on Thursday 14 August 1969.
27. NAUK PRO PREM 13/2844 Note for the Record, 14 August 1969.
28. NAUK PRO DEFE 24/655 Hattersley to Callaghan, 14 August 1969.
29. NAUK PRO PREM 13/2844 Note for the Record, 14 August 1969.
30. NAUK PRO PREM 13/2844 Note of a meeting held at R.A.F. St. Mawgan on Thursday 14 August 1969.
31. Callaghan, *A House Divided*, 41–2.
32. NAUK PRO FCO 33/765 Draft Submission to Minister, A, 14 August 1969.
33. NAUK PRO FCO 33/765 Ireland, 14 August 1969.
34. Scarman, 12.30–12.31.
35. NAUK PRO PREM 13/2844 Northern Ireland statement released 14 August 1969.
36. PRONI CAB/4/1460/12 Cabinet Conclusions, 14 August 1969 7.30 p.m.
37. Scarman, 12.30–12.31.
38. *Belfast Telegraph*, 3 March 1970.
39. *Belfast Telegraph*, 26 February 1970.
40. *Belfast Telegraph*, 2 March 1970.
41. *Belfast Telegraph*, 6 March 1970.

42. *Belfast Telegraph*, 6 March 1970.
43. *Belfast Telegraph*, 4 March 1970.
44. *Belfast Telegraph*, 6 March 1970.
45. *Belfast Telegraph*, 26 February 1970.
46. *Belfast Telegraph*, 26 February 1970.
47. *Belfast Telegraph*, 26 February 1970.
48. *Belfast Telegraph*, 24 February 1970.
49. *Belfast Telegraph*, 4 March 1970.
50. *Belfast Telegraph*, 19 March 1970.
51. *Belfast Telegraph*, 20 October 1970.
52. *Belfast Telegraph*, 19 March 1970.
53. *Belfast Telegraph*, 20 March 1970.
54. *Belfast Telegraph*, 20 October 1970.
55. *Belfast Telegraph*, 20 October 1970.
56. *Belfast Telegraph*, 3 March 1970.
57. *Belfast Telegraph*, 6 March 1970.
58. *Belfast Telegraph*, 6 March 1970.
59. *Belfast Telegraph*, 5 March 1970.
60. *Belfast Telegraph*, 19 October 1970.
61. *Belfast Telegraph*, 19 March 1970.
62. *Belfast Telegraph*, 20 March 1970.
63. *Belfast Telegraph*, 5 March 1970.
64. *Belfast Telegraph*, 16 March 1970.
65. *Belfast Telegraph*, 20 March 1970.
66. Scarman, 18.50.
67. Ibid. 21.4–21.6.
68. NAUK PRO PREM 13/2844 Note for the Record, 2, 15 August 1969.
69. NAUK PRO PREM 13/2844 Note of Telephone Conversation between The Prime Minister and The Home Secretary on Friday 15 August 15 at 11.10 a.m.
70. PRONI CAB/4/1461/12 Cabinet Conclusions, 15 August 1969 Noon.
71. Callaghan, *A House Divided*, 49–51.
72. McKittrick, *Lost Lives*, 33–41.
73. *Belfast Telegraph*, 21 August 1969.
74. *Belfast Telegraph*, 22 August 1969.
75. *Belfast Telegraph*, 22 August 1969.
76. *Belfast Telegraph*, 22 August 1969.
77. Colin Crawford, *Inside the UDA. Volunteers and Violence*, London 2003, 53–4.
78. *Belfast Telegraph*, 22 August 1969.
79. *Belfast Telegraph*, 25 August 1969.
80. *Belfast Telegraph*, 25 August 1969.
81. *Belfast Telegraph*, 28 August 1969.
82. Scarman, 15–17.
83. Ibid. 10–14.
84. Ibid. 11.
85. NAUK PRO PREM 13/2844 Telegram No. 182, 15 August 1969.
86. NAUK PRO PREM 13/2844 Telegram No. 185, Taoiseach's Statement 15 August 1969.
87. NAI 2000/5/38 Aide Memoire, 15 August 1969.
88. NAI 200/6/58 Item 1 Cabinet Minutes, 16 August 1969, Situation in Six Counties.
89. NAUK PRO PREM 13/2844 Note of a Telephone Discussion which took place between the Prime Minister and the Home Secretary at 10.40 a.m. on Sunday 16 August 1969.

90. PRONI CAB/4/1462/11 Cabinet Conclusions, 16 August 1969 2.15 p.m.

91. PRONI CAB/4/1463/12, 18 August 1969 2 m.

92. PRONI CAB/4/1462/11 Cabinet Conclusions, 16 August 1969 2.15 p.m.

93. PRONI CAB/4/1464/12 Cabinet Conclusions, 19 August 1969.

94. Callaghan, *A House Divided*, 55–8.

95. NAUK PRO PREM 13/2844 Immediate Dublin to Foreign and Commonwealth Office Telegram Number 198 Secret Irish Affairs, 18 August 1969.

96. NAUK PRO PREM 13/2844 Northern Ireland. Memorandum by the Secretary of State for the Home Department, 19 August 1969.

97. NAUK PRO PREM 13/2844 Press Notice, 22 August 1969.

98. NAUK PRO PREM 13/2844 Note of a Meeting held at 10 Downing Street, SW1 on Tuesday 19 August 1969 at 5 p.m.

99. NAUK PRO CAB 129/144 C, (69) 112, 20 August 1969: Communiqué of 19 August 1969.

100. NAUK PRO CAB 129/144 C, (69) 112, 20 August 1969: Communiqué of 19 August 1969.

101. PRONI CAB/4/1465/14 Cabinet Conclusions, 20 August 1969 2.30 p.m.

102. NAUK PRO PREM 13/2844 Note of Telephone Conversation between the Prime Minister and the Home Secretary on Wednesday 20 August at 10.45 p.m.

103. *Belfast Telegraph*, 20 August 1969.

104. *Belfast Telegraph*, 20 August 1969.

105. *Belfast Telegraph*, 21 August 1969.

106. *Belfast Telegraph*, 22 August 1969.

107. NAUK PRO PREM 13/2844 Note of Telephone Conversation between the Prime Minister and the Defence Secretary at 11.05 p.m. on Wednesday 20 August 1969.

108. NAUK PRO FCO 33/767 Hooper to Allen, 4 September 1969.

109. NAUK PRO PREM 13/2844 Directive for General Officer Commanding Northern Ireland.

110. *Belfast Telegraph*, 27 August 1969.

111. *Belfast Telegraph*, 28 August 1969.

112. *Belfast Telegraph*, 27 August 1969.

113. Callaghan, *A House Divided*, 72–8.

114. Ibid. 89–90.

115. Ibid. 94–5.

116. NAUK PRO CAB 129/144 C(69) 114 Northern Ireland: Note by the Secretary of the Cabinet, 2 September 1969 re Communiqué 29 August 1969.

117. Callaghan, *A House Divided*, 95–6.

Chapter 8. Cold War: September 1969–May 1970 (PAGES 286–336)

1. NAUK PRO CAB 164/1577, 20 August 1969.

2. BSI AW27 Statement of Sir Oliver Wright.

3. NAUK PRO FCO 33/767 Office of the United Kingdom Representative in Northern Ireland, 4 September 1969; Record of a Conversation with Cardinal Conway.

4. NAUK PRO FCO 33/767 Office of the United Kingdom Representative in Northern Ireland: Situation Report, 4 September 1969.

5. W.D. Flackes and Sydney Elliot, *Northern Ireland A Political Directory 1968–88*, Belfast 1989, 54.

6. *Belfast Telegraph*, 23 August 1969.

7. *Belfast Telegraph*, 26 August 1969.

8. *Belfast Telegraph*, 21 August 1969.

9. *Belfast Telegraph*, 21 August 1969.

10. *Belfast Telegraph*, 27 August 1969.

11. *Belfast Telegraph*, 29 August 1969.

12. *Belfast Telegraph*, 29 August 1969.

13. *Belfast Telegraph*, 2 September 1969.
14. *Belfast Telegraph*, 4 September 1969.
15. *Belfast Telegraph*, 5 September 1969.
16. *Belfast Telegraph*, 5 September 1969.
17. *Belfast Telegraph*, 5 September 1969.
18. *Belfast Telegraph*, 5 September 1969.
19. *Belfast Telegraph*, 6 September 1969.
20. *Belfast Telegraph*, 8 September 1969.
21. *Belfast Telegraph*, 8 September 1969.
22. *Belfast Telegraph*, 9 September 1969.
23. *Belfast Telegraph*, 9 September 1969.
24. PRONI CAB/4/1472/16 Cabinet Conclusions, 4 September 1969 10.30 a.m.
25. PRONI CAB/4/1473/12, 8 September 1969 2.30 p.m.
26. *Belfast Telegraph*, 10 September 1969.
27. NAUK PRO FCO 33/767 Office of the United Kingdom Representative in Northern Ireland: Narrative of Events, 29 August–14 September 1969; 14 September 1969.
28. NAUK PRO FCO 33/767 Office of the United Kingdom Representative in Northern Ireland 10 September 1969. Record of a Conversation with Cardinal Conway.
29. NAUK PRO FCO 33/767 Office of the United Kingdom Representative in Northern Ireland: Narrative of Events 29 August–14 September 1969, 14 September 1969.
30. *Belfast Telegraph*, 10 September 1969.
31. *Belfast Telegraph*, 11 September 1969.
32. Callaghan, *A House Divided*, 103–104.
33. PRONI CAB/4/1474/13 Cabinet Conclusions, 12 September 1969.
34. NAUK PRO FCO 33/767 Office of the United Kingdom Representative in Northern Ireland: Narrative of Events, 29 August–14 September 1969, 14 September 1969.
35. *Belfast Telegraph*, 15 September 1969.
36. NAUK PRO FCO 33/767 Office of the United Kingdom Representative in Northern Ireland: Narrative of Events, 15 September 1969.
37. PRONI CAB/4/1475/13 Cabinet Conclusions, 15 September 1969 4.30 p.m.
38. NAUK PRO FCO 33/767 Office of the United Kingdom Representative in Northern Ireland: Narrative of Events, Monday 15 September 1969.
39. PRONI CAB/4/1475/13 Cabinet Conclusions, 15 September 1969 4.30 p.m.
40. NAUK PRO FCO 33/767 Office of the United Kingdom Representative in Northern Ireland, 16 September 1969: Record of a Conversation with Cardinal Conway, 15 September 1969.
41. PRONI CAB/4/1475/13 Northern Ireland Government Statement, 15 September 1969.
42. NAUK PRO FCO 33/767 Office of the United Kingdom Representative in Northern Ireland: Narrative of Events Monday, 15 September 1969.
43. NAUK PRO FCO 33/767 Office of the United Kingdom Representative in Northern Ireland, 17 September 1969: Narrative of Events, Tuesday 16 September 1969.
44. *Belfast Telegraph*, 16 September 1969.
45. *Belfast Telegraph*, 20 September 1969.
46. NAUK PRO FCO 33/767 Office of the United Kingdom Representative in Northern Ireland 17 September 1969: Narrative of Events, Tuesday 16 September 1969.
47. NAUK PRO FCO 33/767 Office of the United Kingdom Representative in Northern Ireland, 17 September 1969.
48. *Belfast Telegraph*, 16 September 1969.
49. *Belfast Telegraph*, 17 September 1969.
50. *Belfast Telegraph*, 19 September 1969.
51. *Belfast Telegraph*, 19 September 1969.

52. *Belfast Telegraph*, 25 September 1969.
53. NAI 2000/6/660 Ronan to Gallagher, September 1969.
54. Cameron, para. 229.
55. Ibid. para. 142.
56. Callaghan, *A House Divided*, 105.
57. NAUK PRO FCO 33/767 Office of the United Kingdom Representative in Northern Ireland: Record of a Conversation with Cardinal Conway, 19 September 1969.
58. *Irish Times*, 1 October 1969.
59. Callaghan, *A House Divided*, 67.
60. NAUK PRO CAB 129/145 C, (69) 131 Northern Ireland: Memorandum by the Secretary of State for the Home Department, 5 October 1969.
61. PRONI CAB/4/1479/13 Cabinet Conclusions, 6 October 1969 11.30 a.m.
62. PRONI CAB/4/1480/13 Cabinet Conclusions, 7 October 1969 11 a.m.
63. PRONI CAB/4/1481/13 7 October 1969 at 4 p.m.
64. NAUK PRO CAB 164/1577 Note for the Record, 8 October 1969.
65. PRONI CAB/4/1482/13, 7 October 1969 at 8 p.m.
66. *Irish Times*, 11 October 1969.
67. NAUK PRO CAB 164/1577 Communiqué, 10 October 1969.
68. *Irish Times*, 11 October 1969.
69. *Irish Times*, 11 October 1969.
70. *Irish Times*, 11 October 1969.
71. *Irish Times*, 5 November 1969.
72. *Irish Times*, 11 October 1969.
73. *Irish Times*, 17 October 1969.
74. *Irish Times*, 2 October 1969.
75. *Irish Times*, 13 October 1969.
76. *Irish Times*, 14 October 1969.
77. McKittrick, *Lost Lives*, 42–3.
78. *Belfast Telegraph*, 25 February 1970.
79. *Irish Times*, 13 October 1969.
80. *Irish Times*, 14 October 1969.
81. *Irish Times*, 15 October 1969.
82. *Irish Times*, 18 October 1969.
83. *Irish Times*, 25 October 1969.
84. *Irish Times*, 4 November 1969.
85. *Irish Times*, 14 November 1969.
86. *Irish Times*, 13 October 1969.
87. NAUK PRO FCO 33/769 Office of the United Kingdom Representative in Northern Ireland: Wright to NF Cairncross, Home Office, 15 October 1969.
88. PRONI CAB/4/1478/32 Cabinet Conclusions, 2 October 1969 10.30 a.m.
89. *Irish Times*, 9 October 1969.
90. *Irish Times*, 11 October 1969.
91. *Irish Times*, 13 October 1969.
92. *Irish Times*, 16 October 1969.
93. *Irish Times*, 18 October 1969.
94. *Irish Times*, 18 October 1969.
95. NAUK PRO FCO 33/769 Office of the United Kingdom Representative in Northern Ireland: Wright to NF Cairncross, Home Office, 15 October 1969.
96. NAUK PRO CAB 129/145 C, 69, 150 The New Defence Force for Northern Ireland, 3 November 1969.

97. PRONI CAB/4/1478/28, 6 November 1969.
98. PRONI CAB/4/1478/14 Draft White Paper on the Proposed Defence Force.
99. NAUK PRO CAB 129/145 C, (69) 150 New Defence Force for Northern Ireland. Memorandum by the Secretary of State for Defence, 4 November 1969.
100. PRONI CAB/4/1490.
101. NAUK PRO CAB 128/44 CC 53(69) 6 November 1969.
102. *Irish Times*, 16 November 1969.
103. *Irish Times*, 16 November 1969.
104. *Irish Times*, 19 November 1969.
105. *Irish Times*, 2 December 1969.
106. *Irish Times*, 2 December 1969.
107. *Irish Times*, 20 November 1969.
108. *Irish Times*, 19 November 1969.
109. NAUK PRO DEFE 13/758, 27 November 1969.
110. NAUK PRO DEFE 13/758 Note for the record of a conversation between Minister, A, and GOC Northern Ireland on 27 November, 1969 Ulster Defence Regiment – 'Application Forms' and Advertisements.
111. NAUK PRO DEFE 13/758 Healy to Porter, 1 December 1969.
112. *Belfast Telegraph*, 18 February 1970.
113. *Belfast Telegraph*, 10 March 1970 Cullen letter.
114. *Belfast Telegraph*, 5 March 1970.
115. *Belfast Telegraph*, 27 February 1970.
116. NAUK PRO DEFE 13/758, 27 November 1969.
117. *Belfast Telegraph*, 23 March 1970.
118. *Belfast Telegraph*, 12 March 1970.
119. *Belfast Telegraph*, 5 January 1970.
120. *Belfast Telegraph*, 13 January 1970.
121. *Belfast Telegraph*, 14 January 1970.
122. *Belfast Telegraph*, 16 January 1970.
123. *Belfast Telegraph*, 15 January 1970.
124. *Belfast Telegraph*, 16 January 1970 Hutchinson letter.
125. *Belfast Telegraph*, 16 January 1970 Beckett letter.
126. *Belfast Telegraph*, 20 January 1970.
127. *Belfast Telegraph*, 23 January 1970 Beckett letter.
128. *Belfast Telegraph*, 14 January 1970.
129. *Belfast Telegraph*, 17 January 1970.
130. *Belfast Telegraph*, 19 January 1970.
131. *Belfast Telegraph*, 21 January 1970.
132. *Belfast Telegraph*, 22 January 1970.
133. *Belfast Telegraph*, 23 January 1970.
134. *Belfast Telegraph*, 21 January 1970.
135. *Belfast Telegraph*, 27 January 1970.
136. *Belfast Telegraph*, 11 February 1970.
137. *Belfast Telegraph*, 31 January 1970.
138. *Belfast Telegraph*, 21 February 1970.
139. *Belfast Telegraph*, 24 April 1970.
140. *Belfast Telegraph*, 18 March 1970.
141. *Belfast Telegraph*, 16 March 1970.
142. *Belfast Telegraph*, 18 March 1970.
143. *Belfast Telegraph*, 23 March 1970.

144. *Irish News*, 11 February 1970.
145. *Belfast Telegraph*, 14 February 1970.
146. *Belfast Telegraph*, 14 February 1970 .
147. *Irish News*, 11 February 1970.
148. *Irish News*, 19 February 1970.
149. *Irish News*, 20 February 1970.
150. *Irish News*, 27 February 1970.
151. *Irish News*, 4 March 1970.
152. *Irish News*, 2 March 1970.
153. *Belfast Telegraph*, 12 February 1970.
154. *Belfast Telegraph*, 27 February 1970.
155. *Irish News*, 7 March 1970.
156. *Belfast Telegraph*, 10 February 1970.
157. *Belfast Telegraph*, 11 February 1970.
158. *Belfast Telegraph*, 19 January 1970.
159. *Belfast Telegraph*, 5 February 1970.
160. NAUK PRO FCO 33/1075 Northern Ireland: Political Summary for the Period 25 March–1 April 1970. Memorandum by the Home Office, 3 April 1970.
161. PRO FCO 33/1075 The Events of Easter 1970 in Northern Ireland, 3 April 1970.
162. NAUK PRO FCO 33/1075 Northern Ireland: Political Summary for the Period 2–9 April 1970. Memorandum by the Home Office, 10 April 1970.
163. *Belfast Telegraph*, 14 April 1970.
164. *Belfast Telegraph*, 14 April 1970.
165. *Belfast Telegraph*, 14 April 1970.
166. *Belfast Telegraph*, 14 April 1970 .
167. *Belfast Telegraph*, 15 April 1970.
168. *Belfast Telegraph*, 16 April 1970.
169. *Belfast Telegraph*, 16 April 1970.
170. *Belfast Telegraph*, 17 April 1970.
171. *Belfast Telegraph*, 17 April 1970.
172. *Belfast Telegraph*, 17 April 1070.
173. *Belfast Telegraph*, 23 April 1970.
174. *Belfast Telegraph*, 22 May 1970.
175. *Belfast Telegraph*, 17 April 1970.
176. NAUK PRO FCO 33/1075 Office of the United Kingdom Representative in Northern Ireland, 23 April 1970.
177. *Belfast Telegraph*, 23 April 1970.
178. *Belfast Telegraph*, 24 April 1970.
179. NAUK PRO FCO 33/1075 Northern Ireland: Political Summary for the Period 24–30 April 1970, Memorandum by the Home Office, 1 May 1970.
180. *Belfast Telegraph*, 1 May 1970.
181. *Belfast Telegraph*, 29 April 1970 Garland letter.
182. *Belfast Telegraph*, 8 May 1970.
183. NAUK PRO FCO 33/1075 Office of the United Kingdom Representative in Northern Ireland: Burroughs to Callaghan, 28 April 1970.
184. NAUK PRO DEFE 24/655 Note to Home Secretary, 15 May 1970.
185. *Irish News*, 2 May 1970.
186. *Belfast Telegraph*, 11 May 1970.
187. *Irish News*, 21 May 1970.
188. *Irish News*, 21 May 1970.
189. *Belfast Telegraph*, 22 May 1970.

Chapter 9. Resurrection: the Irish State and Origins of the Republican War (PAGES 337–376)

1. NAI 2000/6/658 Government Information Bureau, 21 August 1969.
2. NAI 2000/6/658, 28 August 1969.
3. NAUK PRO FCO 33/758/74674 Telegram No.237 Gilchrist to FCO, 29 August 1969.
4. NAUK PRO FCO 33/758/74674 Telegram No.273 Gilchrist to FCO, 1 September 1969.
5. NAUK PRO FCO 33/758/74674 Telegram No.237 Gilchrist to FCO, 29 August 1969.
6. NAI 200/6/659 Notes on the Present Northern Situation, 26 August 1969.
7. NAI 200/6/59 Summary on New Unity Programme, 4 September 1969.
8. UKNA PRO FCO 33/758 Telegram No.250 British Embassy, Dublin to FCO, 5 September 1969.
9. NAI 2000/5/12 Policy As An End, 10 September 1969.
10. NAI 2000/6/660 Meeting of Dr Hillery, Minister for External Affairs, with Press Officers September 16 1969 at the Irish United Nations Mission, New York.
11. NAUK PRO FCO 33/767 Cabinet 4 September 1969 Northern Ireland (C (69) 114).
12. NAUK PRO FCO 33/758 HT Morgan to Sir Edward Peck, 8 September 1969.
13. Callaghan, *A House Divided*, 52–3.
14. NAI 2000/6/657 Memorandum for the Information of the Government. Policy in Relation to Northern Ireland, 28 Samhain 1969.
15. *Sunday Press*, 21 September 1969.
16. *Irish Times*, 12 December 1969.
17. *Irish Times*, 10 December 1969.
18. *Irish Times*, 12 December 1969.
19. *Irish Times*, 15 December 1969.
20. *Irish Times*, 17 December 1969.
21. NAI 200/6/58 Item 1 Cabinet Minutes 16 August 1969 Situation in Six Counties.
22. NAI 2001/61/1 Answers Given by Mr James Gibbons, Minister for Agriculture to the Understated Questions on 8 June 1970.
23. NAI 2000/6/658 Roinn An Taoiseach Note, 18 August 1969.
24. NAI 2000/6/658 Memorandum, 19 August 1969.
25. NAI 2000/6/658 Roinn An Taoiseach Note, 18 August 1969.
26. NAI 2000/6/658 Memorandum, 19 August 1969.
27. NAI 2000/6/658 Roinn An Taoiseach Note,18 August 1969.
28. NAI 2000/6/658 Visit of Northern Ireland M.P.s, 18 August 1969.
29. NAI 2000/6/660 Memorandum re Visit to Six Counties.
30. NAI 2000/61/1 Statement of Colonel Michael Hefferon, 30 May 1970.
31. Justin O'Brien, *The Arms Trial*, Dublin 2000, 58–60.
32. NAI 2000/61/1 Statement of Colonel Michael Hefferon, 30 May 1970.
33. NAI 2000/61/1 Further Statement of Colonel Michael Hefferon, 31 May 1970.
34. T. Ryle Dwyer, *Nice Fellow: A Biography of Jack Lynch*, Cork 2001, 195.
35. *Irish Times*, 6 August 1971.
36. Dwyer, *Nice Fellow*, 195.
37. *Irish Times*, 5 November 1969.
38. Peter Taylor, *States of Terror: Democracy and Political Violence*, London 1993, 130.
39. NAI Military Intelligence File: Situation in Northern Ireland.
40. NAI SCS 29 Oifig an Chinn Fóirne. 27u Meán Fómhair, 1969 Interim Report of Planning Board on Northern Ireland Operations.
41. NAI Military Intelligence File: Recommendations of Planning Board, 13 October 1969.
42. Taylor, *States of Terror*, 130–37.
43. O'Brien, *The Arms Trial*, 58–60.
44. Taylor, *States of Terror*, 138–139.
45. O'Brien, *The Arms Trial*, 84–85.

46. Ibid. 87–90.
47. Ibid. 94.
48. Dwyer, *Nice Fellow*, 195–201.
49. O'Brien, *The Arms Trial*, 69–70.
50. Taylor, *States of Terror*, 130.
51. Ibid. 143.
52. Ibid. 129.
53. Peter Taylor, *Provos: The IRA and Sinn Féin*, London 1997, 60–62.
54. Taylor, *States of Terror*, 137–8.
55. Sean MacStiofain, *Revolutionary in Ireland*, Farnbourgh 1974, 133–8.
56. Taylor, *Provos*, 66–7.
57. MacStiofain, *Revolutionary in Ireland*, 133–8.
58. Taylor, *Provos*, 66–67.
59. *An Phoblacht*, Feabhra 1970.
60. Taylor, *Provos*, 66–7.
61. *An Phoblacht*, Feabhra 1970.
62. NAUK PRO FCO 33/1197 This Week extract 1.
63. NAUK PRO FCO 33/1197 This Week extract 2.
64. Taylor, *States of Terror*, 142.
65. *An Phoblacht*, Aibreán 1970.
66. *Irish Times*, 6 August 1971.
67. NAI 2000/61/1 Statement of Colonel Michael Hefferon, 30 May 1970.
68. Dwyer, *Nice Fellow*, 209–13.
69. NAI Military Intelligence File: Situation in Northern Ireland.
70. Ed Maloney, *A Secret History of the IRA*, London 2002, 87.
71. MacStiofain, *Revolutionary in Ireland*, 145–6.
72. NA Military Intelligence File: Situation in Northern Ireland.
73. Taylor, *States of Terror*, 144.
74. NAI Military Intelligence File: Situation in Northern Ireland.
75. NAI Military Intelligence Files SCS 18/1 Memorandum: Military Commitments and Requirements, 6 April 1970.
76. NAI Military Intelligence Operations File 4: Meeting with An Taoiseach Tuesday 9 June 1970.
77. Taylor, *States of Terror*, 144.
78. Dwyer, *Nice Fellow*, 214–5.
79. NA 2001/61/1 Answers Given by Mr James Gibbons, Minister for Agriculture to the Understated Questions on 8 June 1970.
80. NAI 2001/61/1 James Gibbons Statement, 28 May 1970.
81. NAI 2001/61/1 Answers Given by Mr James Gibbons, Minister for Agriculture to the Understated Questions on 8 June 1970.
82. NA 2001/61/1 James Gibbons Statement, 28 May 1970.
83. NA 2001/61/1 James Gibbons Statement, 28 May 1970.
84. NA 2001/61/1 Answers Given by Mr James Gibbons, Minister for Agriculture to the Understated Questions on 8 June 1970.
85. NA 2001/61/1 James Gibbons Statement, 28 May 1970.
86. NAI Military Intelligence File: Verbal Briefing for An tAire, 22 April 1970.
87. NAI Military Intelligence File: Verbal Briefing for An Ceann Foirne, 23 April 1970.
88. *Irish Times*, 28 January 1971.
89. NAI 2001/61/1 Answers Given by Mr James Gibbons, Minister for Agriculture to the Understated Questions on 8 June 1970.
90. Dwyer, *Nice Fellow*, 213–19.

91. Taylor, *States of Terror*, 145.
92. Dwyer, *Nice Fellow*, 224.
93. NAUK PRO DEFE 25/273 Political Relations Between the Government of the Republic of Ireland and Northern Ireland, 3 July 1970.
94. Taylor, *States of Terror*, 145.
95. NAUK PRO PREM 15/476 Meeting between PM & Taoiseach in New York, 21 October 1970.
96. MacStiofain, *Revolutionary in Ireland*, 145–6.
97. Raymond J. Quinn, *A Rebel Voice: A History of Belfast Republicanism 1925–1972*, Belfast 1999, 155–7.
98. *Irish News*, 12 August 1970.
99. Quinn, *A Rebel Voice*, 157.
100. Ibid. 63–4
101. Kevin Bean and Mark Hayes, eds, *Republican Voices*, Monaghan 2001, 50.

BIBLIOGRAPHY

PRIMARY SOURCES

National Archives of the United Kingdom: Public Record Office, NAUK PRO.
CAB   Cabinet Office
PREM Prime Minister's Office
DEFE Ministry of Defence
FCO   Foreign and Commonwealth Office

Public Record Office of Northern Ireland, PRONI.
CAB   Cabinet Records
HO   Ministry of Home Affairs

National Archives of Ireland, NAI.
Department of the Taoiseach
Department of Foreign Affairs
Military Intelligence Files

Bloody Sunday Inquiry, BSI.
Witness Statements

Official reports
Disturbances in Northern Ireland: Report of the Cameron Commission Cmnd 532, Belfast 1969.
Violence and Disturbance in Northern Ireland Cmnd 566, Belfast 1972.

Periodicals and newspapers
An Phoblacht
Belfast Telegraph
CDU Newsletter
News Letter
Irish News
Irish Times

Memoirs and autobiographies
— Bloomfield, Ken, *Stormont in Crisis: A Memoir*, Belfast 1994.
— Brady, Seamus, *Arms and the Men*, Wicklow 1971.
— Callaghan, James, *A House Divided: The Dilemma of Northern Ireland*, London 1973.
— Campbell, T. J., *Fifty Years of Ulster: 1890–1940*, Belfast 1941.
— Currie, Austin, *All Hell Will Break Loose*, Dublin 2004.
— Devlin, Bernadette, *The Price of My Soul*, London 1969.

— Devlin, Paddy, *The Fall of the N.I. Executive*, Belfast 1975.
— Devlin, Paddy, *Straight Left: An Autobiography*, Belfast 1993.
— Doherty, Paddy, *Paddy Bogside*, Cork 2001.
— Faulkner, Brian, *Memoirs of a Statesman*, London 1978.
— FitzGerald, Garret, *All in a Life*, Dublin 1991.
— MacStiofain, Sean, *Revolutionary in Ireland*, Farnborough 1974.
— McCann, Eamon, *War in an Irish Town*, London 1980.
— O'Neill, Terence, *The Autobiography of Terence O'Neill*, London 1972.
— Shea, Patrick, *Voices and the Sound of Drums: An Irish Autobiography*, Belfast 1981.
— Wilson, Harold, *The Labour Government 1964–1970: A Personal Record*, London 1971.

Books, articles and chapters
— Adams, Gerry, *The Politics of Irish Freedom*, Dublin 1986.
— Adams, Gerry, *Free Ireland: Towards a Lasting Peace*, Dublin 1995.
— Adamson, Ian, *The Identity of Ulster*, Belfast 1982.
— Anderson, Don, *14 May Days: The Inside Story of the Loyalist Strike of 1974*, Dublin 1994.
— Arthur, Paul, *The People's Democracy 1968–73*, Belfast 1974.
— Arthur, Paul, *Government and Politics of Northern Ireland*, Essex 1980.
— Arthur, Paul and Keith Jeffrey, *Northern Ireland since 1968*, Oxford 1988.
— Aughey, Arthur, *Under Siege: Ulster Unionism and the Anglo–Irish Agreement*, Belfast 1989.
— Aughey, Arthur, 'Unionism and Self-Determination' in Patrick J. Roche and Brian Barton, eds,
    The Northern Ireland Question: Myth and Reality, Aldershot 1991.
— Bardon, Jonathan, *A History of Ulster*, Belfast 1992.
— Barritt, D. P. and Charles F. Carter, *The Northern Ireland Problem: A Study in Group Relations*,
    Oxford 1962.
— Barton, Brian, *Brookeborough: The Making of a Prime Minister*, Belfast 1988.
— Barton, Brian, *Northern Ireland in the Second World War*, Belfast 1995.
— Barzilay, David, *The British Army in Ulster*, I, Belfast 1973.
— Bell, Desmond, *Acts of Union: Youth Culture and Sectarianism in Northern Ireland*, London 1990.
— Bell, J. Bowyer, *The Secret Army: The IRA 1916–1979*, Dublin 1979.
— Bell, J. Bowyer, *The Irish Troubles: A Generation of Violence 1967–1992*, Dublin 1993.
— Beresford, David, *Ten Men Dead: The Story of the 1981 Irish Hunger Strike*, London 1987.
— Bew, Paul, *Conflict and Conciliation in Ireland 1890–1910: Parnellites and Radical Agrarians*,
    Oxford 1987.
— Bew, Paul, Peter Gibbon and Henry Patterson, *Northern Ireland: Political Forces and Social
    Classes 1921–1994*, London 1995.
— Bew, Paul, Kenneth Darwin and Gordon Gillespie, *Passion and Prejudice: Nationalist–Unionist
    Conflict in Ulster in the 1930s and the Foundation of the Irish Association*, Belfast 1993.
— Bew, Paul and Gordon Gillespie, *Northern Ireland: A Chronology of the Troubles 1968–1993*,
    Dublin 1993.
— Bew, Paul and Gordon Gillespie, *The Northern Ireland Peace Process 1993–1996: A Chronology*,
    London 1996.
— Bew, Paul, Henry Patterson and Paul Teague, *Northern Ireland: Between War and Peace: The
    Political Future of Northern Ireland*, London 1997.
— Birrell, Derek and Alan Murie, *Policy and Government in Northern Ireland: Lessons of
    Devolution*, Dublin 1980.
— Bishop, Patrick and Eamon Mallie, *The Provisional IRA*, London 1987.
— Bowman, John, *De Valera and the Ulster Question 1917–1973*, Oxford 1982.
— Boyce, D. G., 'British Conservative Opinion, the Ulster Question and the Partition of Ireland,
    1912–1921', *Irish Historical Studies* XVII/65 (1970).

— Boyce, D. G., 'British Opinion, Ireland and the War', *Historical Journal* XVII/3 (1974).
— Boyce, D. G. and John Stubbs, 'F. S. Oliver, Lord Shelbourne and Federalism', *Journal of Imperial and Commonwealth History* V (1976).
— Boyce, D. G., *Nationalism in Ireland*, London 1982.
— Boyce, D. G., *The Irish Question and British Politics 1868–1986*, London 1988.
— Boyce, D. G., ed., *The Revolution in Ireland 1879–1923*, London 1988.
— Boyce, D. G., 'Edward Carson and Irish Unionism' in Ciaran Brady, ed., *Worsted in the Game: Losers in Irish History*, Dublin 1989.
— Boyce, D. G., *Nineteenth-Century Ireland: The Search for Stability*, Dublin 1991.
— Boyce, D. G., R. Eccleshall and V. Geoghegan, eds, *Political Thought in Ireland since the Seventeenth Century*, London 1993.
— Boyd, Andrew, *Brian Faulkner and the Crisis of Ulster Unionism*, Kerry 1972.
— Boyle, Kevin and Tom Hadden, *Ireland: A Positive Proposal*, Harmondsworth 1985.
— Boyle, Kevin and Tom Hadden, *Northern Ireland: the Choice*, London 1994.
— Brewer, John D. with Kathleen Magee, *Inside the RUC: Routine Policing in a Divided Society*, Oxford 1991.
— Brooke, Peter, *Ulster Presbyterianism: The Historical Perspective 1610–1970*, Dublin 1987.
— Bruce, Steve, *God Save Ulster! The Religion and Politics of Paisleyism*, Oxford 1986.
— Bruce, Steve, *The Red Hand: Protestant Paramilitaries in Northern Ireland*, Oxford 1992.
— Bruce, Steve, 'Loyalists in Northern Ireland: Further Thoughts on "Pro-State Terror"', *Terrorism and Political Violence*, V/4 (Winter 1993), 262–3.
— Bruce, Steve, *The Edge of the Union: The Ulster Loyalist Political Vision*, Oxford 1994.
— Bruce, Steve and Fiona Alderdice, 'Religious Belief and Behaviour' in Peter Stringer and Gillian Robinson, eds, *Social Attitudes in Northern Ireland: The Third Report 1992–1993*, Belfast 1993.
— Bryson, Lucy and Clem McCartney, *Clashing Symbols? A report on the use of flags, anthems and other national symbols in Northern Ireland*, Belfast 1994.
— Buckland, Patrick, *Irish Unionism, I: The Anglo-Irish and the New Ireland 1885–1922*, Dublin 1972.
— Buckland, Patrick, *Irish Unionism, II: Ulster Unionism and the Origins of Northern Ireland 1886–1922*, Dublin 1973.
— Buckland, Patrick, *Irish Unionism 1885–1923: A Documentary History*, Belfast 1973.
— Buckland, Patrick, *The Factory of Grievances: Devolved Government in Northern Ireland 1921–39*, Dublin 1979.
— Buckland, Patrick, *James Craig, Lord Craigavon*, Dublin 1980.
— Buckland, Patrick, *A History of Northern Ireland*, Dublin 1981.
— Budge, Ian and Cornelius O'Leary, *Belfast: Approach to Crisis: A Study of Belfast Politics 1613–1970*, London 1973.
— Burton, Frank, *The Politics of Legitimacy: Struggles in a Belfast Community*, London 1978.
— Campbell, Brian, Laurence McKeown and Felim O'Hagan, eds, *Nor Meekly Serve My Time: The H-Block Struggle 1976–1981*, Belfast 1994.
— Campbell, Colm, *Emergency Law in Ireland 1918–1925*, Oxford 1994.
— Cash, John D., *Identity, Ideology and Conflict: The Structuration of Politics in Northern Ireland*, Cambridge 1996.
— Cathcart, Rex, *The Most Contrary Region: The BBC in Northern Ireland 1924–1984*, Belfast 1984.
— Coldrey, B.M., *Faith and Fatherland: The Christian Brothers and the Development of Irish Nationalism 1838–1921*, Dublin 1988.
— Connolly, Michael, *Politics and Policy Making in Northern Ireland*, London 1990.
— Connolly, Michael and Andrew Erridge, 'Central Government in Northern Ireland' in M. E. H. Connolly and S. Loughlin, eds, *Public Policy in Northern Ireland: Adoption or Adaption?*, Belfast and Coleraine 1990.

— Coogan, Tim Pat, *The IRA*, London 1970.

— Coogan, Tim Pat, *Michael Collins: A Biography*, London 1990.

— Coogan, Tim Pat, *De Valera: Long Fellow, Long Shadow*, London 1993.

— Coogan, Tim Pat, *The Troubles: Ireland's Ordeal 1966–1995 and the Search for Peace*, London 1995.

— Cormack, R. J. and R. D. Osborne, eds, *Religion, Education and Employment: Aspects of Equal Opportunity in Northern Ireland*, Belfast 1983.

— Cormack, R. J. and R. D. Osborne, eds, *Discrimination and Public Policy in Northern Ireland*, Oxford 1991.

— Cormack, R. J. and R. D. Osborne, 'The evolution of a Catholic middle class' in *New Perspectives on the Northern Ireland Conflict*, Aldershot 1994, 67–76.

— Cormack, R. J. and Robert Osborne, 'Education in Northern Ireland: The Struggle for Equality' in Patrick Clancy, Sheelagh Drudy, Kathleen Lynch and Liam O'Dowd, eds, *Irish Society: Sociological Perspectives*, Dublin 1995.

— Coulter, Colin, 'The Character of Unionism', *Irish Political Studies*, IX (1994), 1–24.

— Crawford, Colin, *Inside the UDA: Volunteers and Violence*, London 2003.

— Crawford, Robert G., *Loyal to King Billy: A Portrait of the Ulster Protestants*, Dublin 1987.

— Crozier, Maurna, ed., *Cultural Traditions in Northern Ireland: Varieties of Irishness*, Belfast 1989.

— Crozier, Maurna, ed., *Cultural Traditions in Northern Ireland: Varieties of Britishness*, Belfast 1990.

— Crozier, Maurna, ed., *Cultural Traditions in Northern Ireland: All Europeans Now?*, Belfast 1991.

— Cunningham, Michael J., *British Government Policy in Northern Ireland 1969–89: Its Nature and Execution*, Manchester 1991.

— Curran, Frank, *Derry: Countdown to Disaster*, Dublin 1986.

— Cusack, Jim and Max Taylor, 'The Resurgence of a Terrorist Organization: Part 1: The UDA, a Case Study', *Terrorism and Political Violence* V/3 (Autumn 1993).

— Daly, Cathal, *The Price of Peace*, Belfast 1991.

— Darby, John, *Northern Ireland: The Background to the Conflict*, Belfast 1983.

— Darby, John, *Intimidation and the Control of Conflict*, Dublin 1986.

— Darby, John, 'Legitimate Targets: a control on violence?' in Adrian Guelke, ed., *New Perspectives on the Northern Ireland Conflict*, Aldershot 1994.

— Davis, Richard, *Arthur Griffith and Non-Violent Sinn Fein*, Tralee 1974.

— de Baroid, Ciaran, *Ballymurphy and the Irish War*, Dublin 1989.

— Duggan, John P., *A History of the Irish Army*, Dublin 1991.

— Dunlop, John, *A Precarious Belonging: Presbyterians and the Conflict in Ireland*, Belfast 1995.

— Dunn, Seamus and Valerie Morgan, *Protestant Alienation in Northern Ireland: A Preliminary Survey*, Coleraine 1994.

— Dunn, Seamus and Thomas Hennessey, 'Ireland' in T. G. Fraser and Seamus Dunn, eds, *Europe and Ethnicity: World War One and Contemporary Ethnic Conflict*, London 1996.

— Dwyer, T. Ryle, *Eamon de Valera*, Dublin 1980.

— Eames, Robin, *Chains to be Broken: A Personal Reflection on Northern Ireland and Its People*, London 1992.

— Edwards, Ruth Dudley, *Patrick Pearse: The Triumph of Failure*, Dublin 1977.

— English, Richard, *Armed Struggle: A History of the IRA*, London 2003.

— English, Richard and Graham Walker, *Unionism in Modern Ireland: New Perspectives on Politics and Culture*, Dublin 1996.

— Ervine, St John, *Craigavon, Ulsterman*, London 1949.

— Eversley, David, *Religion and Employment in Northern Ireland*, London 1989.

— Farrell, Brian, *The Founding of Dáil Eireann: Parliament and Nation-Building*, Dublin 1971.

— Farrell, Michael, *Northern Ireland: The Orange State*, London 1976.

— Farrell, Michael, *Arming the Protestants: The Formation of the Ulster Special Constabulary and the Royal Ulster Constabulary 1920–27*, London 1983.
— Fisk, Robert, *In Time of War: Ireland, Ulster and the Price of Neutrality*, London 1985.
— Flackes, W. D. and Sydney Elliott, *Northern Ireland: A Political Directory 1968–88*, Belfast 1989.
— Follis, Brian, *A State Under Siege: The Establishment of Northern Ireland 1920–1925*, Oxford 1995.
— Forester, Margaret, *Michael Collins: The Lost Leader*, London 1971.
— Forum for Peace and Reconciliation, *Paths to a Political Settlement in Ireland: Policy Papers Submitted to the Forum for Peace and Reconciliation*, Belfast 1995.
— Foster, R. F., *Modern Ireland 1600–1972*, London 1988.
— Fulton, John, *The Tragedy of Belief Politics and Religion in Northern Ireland*, Oxford 1991.
— Gailey, Andrew, ed., *Crying in the Wilderness: Jack Sayers: A Liberal Editor in Ulster 1939–69*, Belfast 1995.
— Gallagher, Anthony M., 'The Approach of Government: Community Relations and Equity' in Seamus Dunn, ed., *Facets of the Conflict in Northern Ireland*, London 1995.
— Gallagher, Eric and Stanley Worrall, *Christians in Ulster 1968–1980*, Oxford 1982.
— Gallagher, Frank, *The Indivisible Island*, London 1957.
— Gallagher, John F. and Jerry L. de Gregory, *Violence in Northern Ireland: Understanding Protestant Perspectives*, Dublin 1985.
— Garvin, Tom, *The Evolution of Irish Nationalist Politics*, Dublin 1981.
— Garvin, Tom, *Nationalist Revolutionaries in Ireland 1858–1928*, Oxford 1987.
— Gearty, Conor, *Terror*, London 1991.
— Garland, Roy, *Gusty Spence*, Belfast 2001.
— Gibbon, Peter, *The Origins of Ulster Unionism: The Formation of Popular Protestant Politics and Ideology in Nineteenth-Century Ireland*, Manchester 1975.
— Gordon, David, *The O'Neill Years: Unionist Politics 1963–1969*, Belfast 1989.
— Guelke, Adrian, *Northern Ireland: The International Perspective*, Dublin 1988.
— Guelke, Adrian, 'Paramilitaries, Republicans and Loyalists' in Seamus Dunn, ed., *Facets of the Conflict in Northern Ireland*, London 1995.
— Hadfield, Bridgid, *The Constitution of Northern Ireland*, Belfast 1989.
— Hadfield, Bridgid, 'Legislating for Northern Ireland at Westminster' in M. E. H. Connolly and S. Loughlin, eds, *Public Policy in Northern Ireland: Adoption or Adaption?*, Belfast and Coleraine 1990.
— Hadfield, Bridgid, *Northern Ireland: Politics and the Constitution*, Milton Keynes 1992.
— Hadfield, Bridgid, 'The Belfast Agreement, Sovereignty and the State of the Union', *Public Law*, Winter 1998.
— Hamill, Desmond, *Pig in the Middle: The Army in Northern Ireland 1969–1985*, London 1985.
— Hamilton, Andrew and Linda Moore, 'Policing a Divided Society' in Seamus Dunn, ed., *Facets of the Conflict in Northern Ireland*, London 1995.
— Hand, Geoffrey J., *Report of the Irish Boundary Commission 1925*, Dublin 1969.
— Harbinson, John E., *The Ulster Unionist Party 1882–1973: Its Development and Organisation*, Belfast 1973.
— Harkness, David, *Northern Ireland since 1920*, Dublin 1983.
— Harris, Mary, *The Catholic Church and the Foundation of the Northern Irish State*, Cork 1993.
— Harris, Rosemary, *Prejudice and Tolerance in Ulster: A Study of Neighbours and Strangers in a Border Community*, Manchester 1972.
— Harrison, Richard T., 'Industrial Development in Northern Ireland – The Industrial Development Board' in M. E. H. Connolly and S. Loughlin, eds, *Public Policy in Northern Ireland: Adoption or Adaption?*, Belfast and Coleraine 1990.
— Hempton, David and Myrtle Hill, *Evangelical Protestantism in Ulster Society 1740–1890*, London 1992.

— Hennessey, Peter, *Whitehall*, New York 1989.
— Hennessey, Thomas, 'Ulster Unionist Territorial and National Identities 1886–1893: province, island, kingdom and empire', *Irish Political Studies*, VIII (1993).
— Hennessey, Thomas, *A History of Northern Ireland 1920–1996*, Dublin 1997.
— Hennessey, Thomas, *Dividing Ireland: World War One and Partition*, London 1998.
— Hennessey, Thomas, *The Northern Ireland Peace Process: Ending the Troubles?*, Dublin 2000.
— Heskin, Ken, *Northern Ireland: A Psychological Analysis*, Dublin 1980.
— Hickey, John, *Religion and the Northern Ireland Problem*, Dublin 1984.
— Hogan, Gerald and Clive Walker, *Political Violence and the Law in Ireland*, Manchester 1989.
— Holland, Jack and Henry McDonald, *INLA: Deadly Divisions*, Dublin 1994.
— Holt, E., *Protest in Arms: The Irish Troubles 1916–1923*, London 1963.
— Howell, David, *A Lost Left: Three Studies in Socialism and Nationalism*, Manchester 1986.
— Hume, John, *Personal Views: Politics, Peace and Reconciliation in Ireland*, Dublin 1996.
— Hutchinson, John, *The Dynamics of Cultural Nationalism: The Gaelic Revival and the Creation of the Irish Nation State*, London 1987.
— Hyde, H. Montgomery, *Carson: The Life of Lord Carson of Duncairn*, London 1953.
— Jackson, Alvin, *The Ulster Party: Irish Unionists in the House of Commons 1884–1911*, Oxford 1989.
— Jackson, Alvin, 'Unionist Myths 1912–1985', *Past and Present* 136 (August 1992), 164–85.
— Jackson, Alvin, *Sir Edward Carson*, Dundalk 1993.
— Jackson, Alvin, 'Irish Unionism, 1905–21' in Peter Collins, ed., *Nationalism and Unionism: Conflict in Ireland 1885–1921*, Belfast 1994.
— Jackson, Alvin, *Ireland 1798–1998*, Oxford 1999.
— Jackson, Alvin, *Home Rule: An Irish History 1800–2000*, London 2003.
— Jalland, Patricia, *The Liberals and Ireland: The Ulster Question in British Politics to 1914*, Brighton 1980.
— Kee, Robert, *The Green Flag*, London 1972.
— Keena, Colm, *A Biography of Gerry Adams*, Dublin 1990.
— Kelly, Henry, *How Stormont Fell*, Dublin 1972.
— Kendle, John, *Ireland and the Federal Solution: The Debate over the United Kingdom Constitution 1870–1921*, Kingston 1989.
— Kennedy, Dennis, *The Widening Gulf: Northern Attitudes to the Independent Irish State 1919–1949*, Belfast 1988.
— Kennedy, Michael, *Division and Consensus: The Politics of Cross-Border Relations in Ireland 1925–1969*, Dublin 2000.
— Kennedy-Pipe, Caroline, *The Origins of the Present Troubles in Northern Ireland*, Essex 1997.
— Keogh, Dermot, *Twentieth-Century Ireland: Nation and State*, Dublin 1994.
— Knox, Colin, 'Local Government in Northern Ireland – Adoption or Adaption?' in M. E. H. Connolly and S. Loughlin, eds., *Public Policy in Northern Ireland: Adoption or Adaption?*, Belfast and Coleraine 1990, 35–8.
— Laffan, Michael, *The Partition of Ireland 1911–1925*, Dundalk 1983.
— Lawlor, Sheila, *Britain and Ireland 1914–23*, Dublin 1983.
— Lawrence, R. J., *The Government of Northern Ireland*, Oxford 1965.
— Lee, J. J., *Ireland 1912–1985: Politics and Society*, Cambridge 1989.
— Longford, Lord and Anne McHardy, *Ulster*, London 1981.
— Longley, Edna, 'The Rising, the Somme and Irish Memory' in Mairin Ni Dhonnchadha and Theo Dorgan, eds, *Revising the Rising*, Derry 1991.
— Loughlin, James, *Gladstone, Home Rule and the Ulster Question 1882–93*, Dublin 1986.
— Loughlin, James, *Ulster Unionism and British National Identity since 1885*, London 1995.
— Lyons, F. S. L., *Ireland since the Famine*, London 1973.

— McAllister, Ian, *The Northern Ireland Social Democratic and Labour Party: Political Opposition in a Divided Society*, London 1977.

— McAuley, James W., *The Politics of Identity: A Loyalist Community in Belfast*, Aldershot 1994.

— McCabe, Ian, *A Diplomatic History of Ireland 1948–49: The Republic, the Commonwealth and NATO*, Dublin 1991.

— McElroy, Gerald, *The Catholic Church and the Northern Ireland Crisis 1969–86*, Dublin 1991.

— McGarry, John and Brendan O'Leary, eds, *The Future of Northern Ireland*, Oxford 1990.

— McGarry, John and Brendan O'Leary, *Explaining Northern Ireland: Broken Images*, Oxford 1995.

— McGuire, Maria, *To Take Arms: A Year in the Provisional IRA*, London 1973.

— McIntyre, Anthony, 'Modern Irish Republicanism: The Product of British State Strategies', *Irish Political Studies* X, 1995.

— McKeown, Ciaran, *The Passion of Peace*, Belfast 1984.

— McMahon, Deirdre, *Republicans and Imperialists: Anglo–Irish Relations in the 1930s*, Yale 1984.

— Mallie, Eamon and David McKittrick, *The Fight for Peace: The Secret Story Behind the Irish Peace Process*, London 1996.

— Mansergh, Nicholas, *The Unresolved Question: The Anglo–Irish Settlement and its Undoing 1912–72*, Yale 1991.

— Marjoribanks, Edward and Ian Colvin, *The Life of Lord Carson*, 3 Volumes, London 1932–4.

— Miller, David, *Queen's Rebels: Ulster Loyalism in Historical Perspective*, Dublin 1978.

— Mitchell, George J., *Making Peace*, London 1999.

— Moloney, Ed and Andy Pollock, *Paisley*, Dublin 1986.

— Moxon-Browne, Edward, *Nation, Class and Creed in Northern Ireland*, Aldershot 1983.

— Mulholland, Marc, *Northern Ireland at the Crossroads: Ulster Unionism in the O'Neill Years 1960–9*, Basingstoke 2000.

— Murphy, Brian P., *Patrick Pearse and the Lost Republican Ideal*, Dublin 1991.

— Murphy, Richard, 'Faction in the Conservative Party and the Home Rule Crisis 1912–14', *History* Vol. 711986 No. 232.

— Murray, Dominic, *Worlds Apart: Segregated Schools in Northern Ireland*, Belfast 1985.

— Murray, Raymond, *The SAS in Ireland*, Dublin 1990.

— Nelson, Sarah, *Ulster Uncertain Defenders: Loyalists and the Northern Ireland Conflict*, Belfast 1984.

— O'Brien, Brendan, *The Long War: The IRA and Sinn Fein 1985 to Today*, Dublin 1993.

— O'Brien, Justin, *The Arms Trial*, Dublin 2000.

— O'Connor, Fionnuala, *In Search of a State: Catholics in Northern Ireland*, Belfast 1993.

— O Dochartaigh, Niall, *From Civil Rights to Armalites: Derry and the Birth of the Irish Troubles*, Cork 1997.

— O'Dowd, Liam, Bill Rolston and Mike Tomlinson, *Northern Ireland: Between Civil Rights and Civil War*, London 1980.

— O'Dowd, Liam, 'Development or Dependency? State, Economy and Society in Northern Ireland' in Patrick Clancy, Sheelagh Drudy, Kathleen Lynch and Liam O'Dowd, eds, *Irish Society: Sociological Perspectives*, Dublin 1995.

— O'Halloran, Clare, *Partition and the Limits of Irish Nationalism*, Dublin 1987.

— O'Leary, Brendan and John McGarry, *The Politics of Antagonism: Understanding Northern Ireland*, London 1993.

— O'Malley, Padraig, *The Uncivil Wars: Ireland Today*, Belfast 1983.

— O'Malley, Padraig, *Biting at the Grave: The Irish Hunger Strikes and the Politics of Despair*, Belfast 1990.

— O'Malley, Padraig, *Northern Ireland: Questions of Nuance*, Belfast 1990.

— O'Neill, Terence, *Ulster at the Crossroads*, London 1969.

— Patterson, Henry, *Class Conflict and Sectarianism: The Protestant Working Class and the Belfast Labour Movement 1868–1920*, Belfast 1980.

— Patterson, Henry, *The Politics of Illusion: Republicanism and Socialism in Modern Ireland*, London 1989.

— Patterson, Henry, *Ireland since 1939*, Oxford 2002.

— Phoenix, Eamon, 'Northern Nationalists, Ulster Unionists and the Development of Partition 1900–1921' in Peter Collins, ed., *Nationalism and Unionism: Conflict in Ireland 1885–1921*, Belfast 1994.

— Phoenix, Eamon, *Northern Nationalism: Nationalist Politics, Partition and the Catholic Minority in Northern Ireland 1890–1940*, Belfast 1994.

— Pollack, Andy, ed., *A Citizens' Inquiry: The Opsahl Report on Northern Ireland*, Dublin 1993.

— Purdy, Ann, *Molyneaux: The Long View*, Belfast 1989.

— Purdy, Bob, *Politics in the Streets: The Origins of the Civil Rights Movement in Northern Ireland*, Belfast 1990.

— Quinn, Raymond, *A Rebel Voice. A History of Belfast Republicanism 1925–1972*, Belfast 1999.

— Rea, Desmond, ed., *Political Co-operation in Divided Societies: A Series of Papers Relevant to the Conflict in Northern Ireland*, Dublin 1982.

— Rolston, Bill, ed., *The Media and Northern Ireland: Covering the Troubles*, London 1991.

— Rose, Peter, *How the Troubles Came to Northern Ireland*, Basingstoke 1997.

— Rose, Richard, *Governing Without Consensus: An Irish Perspective*, London 1971.

— Rowan, Brian, *Behind the Lines: The Story of the IRA and Loyalist Ceasefires*, Belfast 1995.

— Rowthorn, Bob and Naomi Wayne, *Northern Ireland: The Political Economy of Conflict*, Cambridge 1988.

— Ruane, Joseph and Jennifer Todd, *The Dynamics of Conflict in Northern Ireland: Power, Conflict and Emancipation*, Cambridge 1996.

— Ryder, Chris, *The RUC: A Force Under Fire*, London 1989.

— Ryder, Chris, *The Ulster Defence Regiment: An Instrument of Peace?*, London 1991.

— Ryder, Chris, *The Fateful Split: Catholics and the Royal Ulster Constabulary*, London 2004.

— Scoular, Clive, *James Chichester-Clark, Prime Minister of Northern Ireland*, Killyleagh 2000.

— Smith, Alan, 'Education and the Conflict in Northern Ireland' in Seamus Dunn, ed., *Facets of the Conflict in Northern Ireland*, London 1995.

— Smith, Alan and Alan Robinson, *Education for Mutual Understanding: The Initial Statutory Years*, Coleraine 1996.

— Smith, David and Gerald Chambers, *Inequality in Northern Ireland*, Oxford 1991.

— Smith, M. L. R., *Fighting for Ireland: The Military Strategy of the Irish Republican Movement*, London 1995.

— Smyth, Clifford, *Ian Paisley: Voice of Protestant Ulster*, Edinburgh 1987.

— Stewart, A. T. Q., *The Ulster Crisis: Resistance to Home Rule 1912–14*, London 1967.

— Stewart, A. T. Q., *The Narrow Ground: The Roots of Conflict in Ulster*, London 1977.

— Stewart, A. T. Q., *Edward Carson*, Dublin 1981.

— Stringer, Peter and Gillian Robinson, eds, *Social Attitudes in Northern Ireland*, Belfast 1991.

— Stringer, Peter and Gillian Robinson, eds, *Social Attitudes in Northern Ireland: The Second Report*, Belfast 1992.

— Stringer, Peter and Gillian Robinson, eds, *Social Attitudes in Northern Ireland: The Third Report*, Belfast 1993.

— Taylor, Peter, *States of Terror: Democracy and Political Violence*, London 1993.

— Taylor, Peter, *Provos: The IRA and Sinn Fein*, London 1997.

— Taylor, Peter, *Loyalists*, London 1999.

— Taylor, Peter, *Brits: The War Against the IRA*, London 2001.

— Tools, Kevin, *Rebel Hearts: Journeys within the IRA's Soul*, London 1995.

— Townshend, Charles, ed., *Consensus in Ireland*, Oxford 1983.

— Townshend, Charles, *Political Violence in Ireland: Government and Resistance since 1848*, Oxford 1983.

— Travers, Pauric, *Settlements and Divisions: Ireland 1870–1922*, Dublin 1988.

— Urban, Mark, *Big Boys' Rules: The Secret Struggle Against the IRA*, London 1992.

— Walker, B. M., *Ulster Politics: The Formative Years 1868–86*, Belfast 1989.

— Walker, Graham, *The Politics of Frustration: Harry Midgley and the Failure of Labour in Northern Ireland*, Manchester 1985.

— Walker, Graham, *A History of the Ulster Unionist Party: Protest, Pragmatism and Pessimism*, Manchester 2004.

— Walsh, Pat, *From Civil Rights to National War: Northern Ireland Catholic Politics 1964–74*, Belfast 1989.

— Walsh, Pat, *Irish Republicanism and Socialism: The Politics of the Movement 1905 to 1994*, Belfast 1994.

— Ward, Margaret, *Unmanageable Revolutionaries: Women and Irish Nationalism*, London 1983.

— White, Barry, *John Hume: Statesman of the Troubles*, Belfast 1984.

— Whyte, J. H., *Church and State in Modern Ireland 1923–1979*, Dublin 1979.

— Whyte, J. H., 'How much discrimination was there under the unionist regime 1921–1968?' in Tom Gallagher and James O'Connell, eds, *Contemporary Irish Studies*, Manchester 1983.

— Whyte, John, *Interpreting Northern Ireland*, Oxford 1990.

— Wichert, Sabine, *Northern Ireland since 1945*, Essex 1991.

— Wilson, Derick and Jerry Tyrrell, 'Institutions for Conciliation and Mediation' in Seamus Dunn, ed., *Facets of the Conflict in Northern Ireland*, London 1995.

— Wilson, Tom, *Ulster: Conflict and Consent*, Oxford 1989.

— Wright, Frank, *Northern Ireland: A Comparative Analysis*, Dublin 1987.

INDEX

Adams, Gerry, 356, 395
Agnew, Kevin, 135, 244
Aiken, Frank, 88
Allen, John, 21
Allen, Sir Philip, 169, 227–8, 235
Alliance Party of Northern Ireland, 331
Ancient Order of Hibernians, 93, 236
Anderson, Albert W., 91, 190, 191, 192, 194, 204, 205
Andrews, John, 40, 149, 186, 190, 213, 219, 271, 275
Anglican Church, 3–4, 10
Apprentice Boys of Derry, 137, 138, 319
    march (1969), 223–4, 236, 238–9
Arbuckle, Victor, 309
Archer, Peter, 119
Ardill, Austin, 60, 61, 191
Armagh, 272, 367
    B-Specials shoot Catholic, 263–4
    civil rights demonstrations, 161, 269
    housing, 383
    UPV march, 328
arms smuggling, 336, 353–4, 364–7, 369–74, 391, 392–3
    arms trial, 374
    Dublin shipment, 370
    overview, 391, 392–3
Armstrong, District-Inspector, 241
Association of Loyal Orangewomen of Ireland, 12
Aunger, Edmund, 67
Austin, Campbell, 38, 39

Bacon, Alice, 114
Bailey, Minnie, 254
Baker, A.S., 274
Baker, Sir Geoffrey, 275–8
Ballenden, Lt-Colonel John Patrick St Clair, 309
Ballie, J.O., 120

Ballymena, bowling controversy, 11
Barnhill, J.E.N., 69–70
barricades, 288–301
    CCDC demands for dismantling, 294–5, 297, 298
Bateman, Cecil, 83
Bateson, Larry, 97
Beattie, Emily, 133, 134
Beattie, Jack, 47
Beattie, Revd William, 327, 331
Beckett, John, 320
Beggs, R.J., 11
Belfast
    barricades, 288–300
    peace lines, 264, 291, 293, 361
    protest against Paisley jailing, 207–8
    Provisional IRA reorganised, 374–6
    riots (1969), 223, 225, 244–5, 252–69, 290, 309, 344–5, 390
        British Army, 263, 290, 309, 335–6
        B-Specials, 225–6, 257, 262, 265–6, 344
        build-up, 252–5
        deaths and casualties, 263–4, 309
        flashpoint (Unity Flats), 255–7
        impact of, 264–85
        inquiry proposed, 278–9, 282
        IRA, 259, 263, 265, 266–7, 268, 329, 360
        Lynch speech inflames, 244–5, 261, 392
        response by British Government, 262–3, 271–85
        RUC, 225, 253–62, 263–4, 266–9, 309
        Scarman inquiry, 268–9, 282
    riots (1970), 328–9, 335–6, 367
    sectarianism, 252–5
    UVF disrupt water supply, 209
    vigilantes, 290, 336
Belfast Refugee Re-Establishment Committee, 352, 353
Belfast Telegraph, 5, 208, 292, 388

Belfast Trades Council, 129
Belfast Wolfe Tone Society, 129
Benedict XV, Pope, 51
Benner, Frank, 80
Benson Report (1963), 36, 37
Bergin, Lorcan, 98
Berry, Peter, 354, 370, 373
bigotry, 382, 385–6
Black, Harold, 222–3, 284
    barricades and, 295–6, 298–9
    troop deployment and, 225, 226–9, 235,
    248, 249
Black Institution, 13
Blaney, Neil, 33, 242, 338, 339, 391
    arms-running, 347, 350, 351, 353–4, 364–5,
    367, 370–1, 373–4, 392–3
    arms trial, 374
    IRA and, 347, 348, 351, 364–5
    Irish intervention speech, 343
Bleakley, David, 37
Blitz (1941), 55
Boal, Desmond, 21, 29–30, 31, 32, 34, 87, 199
    rebels against O'Neill, 190, 194
Boland, Kevin, 242, 339, 348, 350, 374
Boundary Commission, 115
Boyd, Tom, 31, 44
Boyle, Kevin, 174, 244
Boyle, Louis, 20, 193
Bradford, Roy, 44, 62, 206, 209–10, 267, 280,
295, 299, 322–3
Bradley, Samuel, 225, 255–7, 258–9
Brady, Oliver, 72
Brady, Rory, 96, 97, 98
Brady, Seamus, 347–8
Brady, Thomas, 97
Brennan, John, 196
British Army, 89–90, 394
    battalions, 224–5, 238, 248, 250–2, 300, 309,
    311, 335
    Belfast riots, 263, 290, 309, 335–6
        put on stand-by, 225, 262
    bravery awards, 309
    Derry riots, 238, 251–2, 311–12
        deployment lead-up, 246–51, 262
    dismantles barricades, 299, 300–1
    impartiality claim, 275

policy regarding arrests, 335
Royal Military Police, 311–12
strength of (1970), 368
39 Brigade, 224–5, 251
see also military involvement issue
British Government
    Belfast riots and, 262–3, 271–85
    Cameron Report and, 302
    Chichester Clark government fragility,
    334–5
    Derry riots and, 245, 246–52
    direct rule issue, 116, 121, 145, 148, 201–3,
    212–13, 379, 387
        military intervention and, 226–36
        moves towards, 168–74
        overview, 387
        power of intervention, 108–10, 151
        reluctance to intervene, 111, 112, 127–9,
        139, 173–4, 381, 387
    Downing Street Declaration (1969), 275–80
        crucial clauses, 279
    Hunt Report, 303–10
    inter-governmental meeting (1968), 151–5
    inter-governmental meeting (1969), 219–20
    military involvement issue, 162–8, 200, 213,
    220–1, 225, 246–52
        direct rule and, 226–36
        troops requested and deployed, 250,
        251–2, 262–3
    MISC 238 committee, 200, 202, 212, 216, 281
    objectives (1969), 200–2
    O'Neill's leadership fragility, 200, 202–4,
    210, 212–13
    sanctions threat, 146–7, 149–50, 155, 200–1,
    221–2
    UKREP, 286, 328, 394
British Legion, 90
British Society of Labour Lawyers, 119
Brockway, Fenner, 85
Brockway, Lord, 112
Brooke, Capt John, 87, 190, 194, 204, 218, 326–7,
334
Brookeborough, Lord, xiii, 19, 29, 32, 38, 45, 47,
52, 59, 78, 329, 395
    political dinosaur, 384
Brown, George, 110

Brown, Hugh, 321
Brown, Revd John, 317–18
Bryson, W.F., 75
B-Specials (Ulster Special Constabulary)
  Armagh, 263–4
  Belfast riots (1969), 225–6, 257, 262, 265–6, 344
  at Burntollet, 177, 179, 180, 182, 389
  Callaghan proposals, 274, 280
  Cameron Report on, 302
  criticised by British police, 271, 273
  Derry riots (1969), 242, 244, 246
  disbanded, 307, 310, 318, 393
  Hunt Report, 304, 305–7, 308, 310, 311
  Irish Government calls for withdrawal, 270
  military planning scenarios and, 171, 172, 173, 213, 228
  restrictions on deployment, 275–81, 283
    Wilson proposals, 276, 278, 280, 281
  strength of (1970), 368
  UDR recruitment, 313, 314, 315–18
Buchanan, Alan, Bishop of Clogher, 8
Bunting, Major Ronald, 177, 183–4, 188, 207, 238, 281
Burns, Joseph, 91, 190, 191, 194, 199, 217
Burntollet, 174–83, 209, 253
Burroughs, Ronnie, 328, 331–2, 333–4

Cahill, Joe, 355–6
Cairncross, Neil, 284
Caldwell, John, 179–80
Caledon, 130–1, 133–4
  legacy of, 143–4
Callaghan, James, 110, 145, 187, 335, 379
  Belfast riots (1969), 262–3, 271–2
    barricades, 293, 295–7, 298–9, 300
    decides against direct rule, 273–4
  on Bernadette Devlin, 224
  B-Specials proposals, 274
  Cameron Report and, 302
  on Craig-led government, 168
  Derry riots (1969), 224, 245, 249–50, 251, 252
    considers troops deployment, 246–8
  direct rule issue, 168, 273–4, 379, 387
  discrimination measures, 283–5
  Downing Street Declaration (1969), 275–7

Hunt Report, 304–7, 308
inter-governmental meeting (1968), 151–5
inter-governmental meeting (1969), 219–20
  on Lynch, 341
  military intervention scenarios and, 173, 229–36
  military withdrawal discussed, 220–1
  on NICRA, 212
  objectives (1969), 200–2, 222
  O'Neill's leadership fragility, 202–4, 210, 212–13
  O'Neill's succession and, 215–16
  rejects sanctions, 222
  RUC, CS gas issue, 223, 224, 226
  RUC, suggests replacing, 247, 250, 252, 283
  visits Northern Ireland, 282–5, 310
  workload as Home Secretary, 128–9
  Wright and, 286, 287
Cameron Report, 68, 73–4, 138, 139, 140, 141, 142, 178, 183, 188, 203, 282
  findings and impact of, 301–3
Campaign for Democracy in Ulster (CDU), 111–12, 119, 387
Campaign for Social Justice (CSJ), 68, 72, 111, 112, 116, 129, 136
  overview, 386–7
  policy, 107–8, 109
Campbell, J.J., 80–1, 82–4
Canavan, Michael, 237, 252
Card, Frank, 375
Carson, Lord Edward, 17, 45, 329
Carson, Edward (jnr), 45, 46–7, 48
Carson, James, 77, 78
Carter, Dennis and Barritt, Charles, 81
Catholic Church, 86–7, 94–5, 383–4
  anger over Chichester-Clark barricades speech, 292
  Belfast riots reaction, 267–8
  ecumenical movement, 3–9
  Lisburn Road church building plan, 20–1
  Protestant perceptions, 383
  in Republic of Ireland, 9, 377–8
Catholics, 377–8, 382–3, 388
  discrimination see discrimination
  family planning and size, 82

Catholics (*cont.*)
    grievances, 382–3
        Cameron Report, 301–2
        Hunt Report and, 308
        impact of Belfast riots, 264–5
    intolerance of, 11–12
    language and perception, 377
    Nationalism and, 92–5, 377
    O'Neill's liberalism, 1–2, 3, 4–5, 17, 78–9, 82–4, 95, 131, 378–80, 381, 384
    O'Neill's popularity, 107
    oppression, 383
    RUC, loss of confidence in, 253, 255, 262, 269, 275, 389, 390
    Ulster Unionist Party and, 17–22, 193, 323, 324, 384
        1969 election, 198, 199–200, 390
    Unionist symbols and, 89–91
    urged to co-operate, 79–84
Central Citizens' Defence Committee (CCDC), 288, 347, 351
    demands for dismantling barricades, 294–5, 297, 298
Chalfont, Lord, 243, 270
Chichester-Clark, Major James, 22, 39–40, 59, 61–2, 66, 210, 381, 387, 390
    background, 215
    Belfast riots and, 262–3, 268, 271, 273, 274
        barricades and, 289, 291–3, 294, 295, 296–7, 298, 300
        inquiry, 282
    B-Specials and Hunt Report, 305–7, 310, 325
    Callaghan visit, 282–5
    Cameron Report and, 302, 303
    criticised, 218, 308, 312, 319–22, 324–5, 327, 331
        no-confidence motion, 332–3
    declares amnesty, 218
    Derry riots and, 243–4, 245, 247, 250, 252
    Downing Street Declaration (1969), 275–7, 279, 280–1
    elected Prime Minister, 217–18
        lead-up, 213–14, 215, 216, 217
    election (1970), 329, 331
    Faulkner loyal to, 218, 321
    fragility of government, 312–13, 334–5

    inter-governmental meeting (1969), 219–20
    Joint Security Committee, 286
    Lynch and, 243–4, 342
    Paisley calls for resignation, 331
    proposals package (1968), 150, 155–7, 159–60, 185, 186
    resignation threat, 332
    RUC, use of CS gas, 226
    troop deployment and direct rule issue, 227–36
    UDR and, 316
    on underprivileged state of NI, 324–5
Chichester-Clark, Robin, 39, 48
Chief of the Defence Staff (CDS), 164–8
Childers, Erskine, 33, 339–40
Church of Ireland
    Easter Rising Commemoration (1966), 50
    ecumenical movement, 3–10
    support for O'Neill, 191
Church of Ireland Gazette, 18
Churchill, Winston, 191
City of Dublin (ship), 370
Civil Authorities (Special Powers) Act 1922, xi–xii, 67, 117, 118, 119, 132, 145, 295
    Cameron Report on, 302
    military involvement, 164
    reform discussed, 153–4, 219–20
civil disobedience advocated, 130, 135, 384–5
civil rights movement, 93–4, 129, 174–5
    demonstrations, 135–43, 174–84, 207, 208–9
    IRA and, 105–6, 153, 265
        presence at demonstrations, 135, 137, 139, 388
    leaders underestimate consequences, 143–4, 384–5, 388
    overview, 384–5, 386–8
    see also Northern Ireland Civil Rights Association
Civil Service, discrimination in, 68–9, 86, 122
    Hunt Report, 305
Clady, 209
Clann na Gael, 359
Clark, Sir George, 10, 19, 33, 52, 211, 323
Claudy, 176, 180
Clifton Unionist Association, 320

Coalisland Citizens Action Committee, 182

Coalisland demonstrations, 135–7, 138, 267

Cole, Robert, 129

Coleraine, 42, 36, 38–9

Comber, 181

Comhar na gComhairsan, 362

Committee on Inter-Church Relations, 6

Communist Party, 129, 362, 363

Community Relations Commission, 304, 323, 394

Compton, Sir Edmund, 156, 204

Conaty, Tom, 288, 293, 295–6, 299, 300, 347

Congregational Church, 7

Connellan, Joseph, 86, 93, 113

Conway, Cardinal William, 2, 9, 160, 162

    Belfast riots and, 267–8, 297–8, 300

        Wright meetings, 286–7, 291–2

    Cameron Report and, 302–3

    Hunt Report and, 308

Cooper, Ivan, 139, 158, 159, 178, 207, 208, 280, 308, 344

Cooper, Robert, 33, 84

Copcutt, Geoffrey, 41

Corbett, County Inspector David, 178

Corrigan, Aidan, 347

Cosgrave, Liam, 373

Cosgrave, W.T., 28

Costello, Séamus, 96, 97

Coughlan, Anthony, 105

Craig, Sir James, xiii (Lord Craigavon), 17, 28, 343, 395

Craig, William, 19, 33, 59, 62, 114, 146, 287, 289, 300, 331, 393

    arms smuggling and, 336

    bans Derry demonstrations, 138, 158–9, 388–9

    bans Easter parade and Republican Clubs, 117–19, 125

    on British Government interference, 121, 379

    on B-Specials disbandment, 318

    on commission proposals, 188

    on community relations, 82, 83

    Downing Street Declaration response, 280–1, 282

    election (1969), 199

    franchise reform proposals, 148–51

    Hunt Report and, 324, 325–6

    inter-governmental meeting (1968), 151–5

    militancy increases, 309, 334

    O'Neill resignation, 216

    overview, 380, 388–9

    railway closures, 37–8, 41

    rebels against O'Neill, 190, 194, 197, 200, 204–5, 380, 390

    rebels over Police Bill, 326

    sacked from Cabinet, 161, 162

Craigavon, 36, 40–1

Craigavon, Lord (Sir James Craig), xiii, 17, 28, 343, 395

Cramsie, Colonel Henry, 13

Cullen, Lawrence, 317

Cumann na mBan, 125, 363

curfew rejected, 225, 263

Curran, Edmund, 20

Currie, Austin, 14, 109–10, 118, 126, 211, 265, 308

    Burntollet and, 175, 179

    civil disobedience advocacy, 135, 385

    Coalisland demonstration, 135–6, 143–4

    Derry demonstration (1968), 140

    expelled from Commons chamber, 134

    housing discrimination and, 129–34

        squatting, 133–4

    on O'Neill, 131–3

    questions wisdom of his actions, 143–4

    UDR and, 315–16

Cyril Lord Carpets Ltd, 70

Dawson, Patrick, 98

DCAC see Derry Citizens' Action Committee

DCDA see Derry Citizens' Defence Association

Delaney, Colonel, 371–2, 373

Delaney, Revd Fr Ailbe, 253, 261–2

Derry

    Apprentice Boys, 137, 138, 223–4, 236, 238–9

    barricades, 288–9, 290–1, 300–1

    Burntollet march, 174–83, 389

    civil rights march (1968), 137–43, 388–9

        discussed at inter-governmental meeting, 154–5

    civil rights marches (1969), 207, 208–9, 223

    commission proposed, 156–7, 159

Derry (*cont.*)
  Craig ban on marches, 138, 158–9, 388–9
  gerrymandering, 72–3, 382
  housing protests, 134–5, 137
  naval base closed, 36
  peace line, 301
  regional development neglected, 36–42
  riots (1969, Battle of Bogside), 237–52, 389, 390
    British Army, 238, 246–52, 262, 311–12
    B-Specials, 242, 244, 246
    IRA, 246, 360
    lead-up, 223–4, 236
    Catholics killed, 223
    RUC, 223, 237, 239–42, 248, 268, 388–9
  riots (1970), 328–9, 367
  Royal Military Police, 311–12
  RUC policy, 158–9, 291, 388–9
  university claim, 36, 38–40
  vigilantes, 288–9, 301, 311, 336
Derry Citizens' Action Committee (DCAC), 159, 237, 238
  Burntollet and, 178, 180, 182
Derry Citizens' Defence Association (DCDA), 288–9, 300–1, 311
  formation and objectives, 237–8
Derry Corporation, 88–9, 130, 137, 159, 160, 382
Derry Housing Action Committee (DHAC), 134–5, 137
Derry Labour Party, 182, 196
Derry Trades Council, 70
Devenney, Samuel, 223, 237, 390
Devlin, Bernadette, 174, 181, 197
  Battle of Bogside, 240, 244
  Callaghan on, 224
  Downing Street Declaration response, 280
  elected MP, 224
  UDR and, 315, 316
Devlin, Jim and Gertie, 143
Devlin, Paddy, 138–9, 198, 244, 253, 288, 290, 293
  requests arms, 344–5
DHAC (Derry Housing Action Committee), 134–5, 137
Diamond, Harry, 13, 65, 77, 88, 182–3, 198

Dickie, George, 309
Diminution of Discord Bill, 85
direct rule, 116, 121, 145, 148, 201–3, 212–13, 379, 387
  military intervention and, 226–36
  moves towards, 168–74
  overview, 387
  power of intervention, 108–10, 151
  reluctance to intervene, 111, 112, 127–9, 139, 173–4, 381, 387
discrimination, 67–78, 84–8, 382–3
  Callaghan proposals, 283–5
  Cameron Report on, 302
  CDU policy and, 111–12
  Currie and, 129–34
  employment, 67–72, 77, 86, 87, 122, 132
  gerrymandering, 72–3, 107–8, 381
  housing, 72, 73–8, 85, 86, 129–31, 393–4
    reform to system discussed, 152–3, 154, 156, 160, 219, 283
    squatting and evictions, 130–1, 133–4
  Hunt Report, 304, 305
  investigation (1965), 14–15
  Nationalist Party policy and, 84–6, 112–13
  O'Neill defends status quo, 121–4
  overview, 382–3, 394
  regional policy, 36–42, 67, 74–5, 321
  Times article on, 120
  Unionist denials, 86, 115, 120, 126
Doagh, Catherine, 288
Dobson (MP), 194
Doherty, Noel, 53, 54
Doherty, Paddy, 94–5, 252, 289, 300–1, 311, 364–6
Donnelly, Francie, 351–2
Douglas, William, 80
Douglas-Home, Sir Alec, 85, 108
Downing Street Declaration (1969), 275–80, 288, 338
  crucial clauses, 279
Doyle, Liam, 56
Drennan, J.C., 89
Drennan, Margaret, 12
Driver, Frank, 96
Dublin
  British embassy attacked, 269–70

Nelson's Pillar blown up, 50
see also Irish Government
Duffy, Peter, 98
Dungannon, 269
civil rights march (1968), 135–7, 138
legacy of, 143–4
gerrymandering, 107–8
housing discrimination, 130–1
squatting and evictions, 133–4
Dunham, Anthony, 255
Dunne, Special Constable James, 257
Dunville, Miss, 254–5
Dyball, General, 225, 290, 294, 295, 299, 300, 317

Eakin, John, 94–5
Easter Rising Commemoration (1966), 49–52, 55, 117–18, 380, 386
ecumenical movement, 3–10, 80–1, 380, 381
Edenberry Arms (Belfast), 253–4, 257, 260
Edinburgh, Duke of, 145
education system, 84, 113
Elder, Nelson, 18
election (1966), 47–9
election (1969), 193–200, 204, 320, 378, 384, 390
elections (1970), 327–8, 329–31
electoral boundaries *see* gerrymandering
electricity, cross-border scheme, 33
Elizabeth II, Queen, 45, 114
Elliott, George, 74–5
Elworthy, Sir Charles, 164, 169
Empey, Reg, 324
employment discrimination, 67–72, 77, 86, 87, 122, 132
Cameron Report, 302
Hunt Report, 305
overview, 382
Enniskillen, 42
housing discrimination, 74–7
Episcopalian Church, 383
Erskine, Lord, 28, 45, 46, 88
Erwin, Robert, 20
ethnic division, 388
Evangelical Protestant Society, 7, 11, 31
Ewing, Elizabeth, 33
Eyewitness in Northern Ireland, 347

Fagan, Tom, 346–7
Fair, Revd J.A., 11
Farrell, Michael, 174–5, 182, 197, 199
Faulkner, Brian, 46, 80, 83, 114, 146, 200, 275
barricades and, 290, 299
B-Specials disbandment and, 305, 311
on changes in NI, 124–5
Chichester-Clark loyalty, 218, 321
denies discrimination, 86
election (1970), 329–30
franchise reform proposals, 148–51, 186–7
inter-governmental meeting (1968), 151–5
inter-governmental meeting (1969), 219
North–South co-operation, 32–3
on O'Neill, 194–5, 322
Orange Order and, 13, 14
overview, 379, 380
Prime Minister bid, 215, 216, 217–18, 380
rebels against O'Neill, 59, 60, 62–3, 194, 197
regional development, 42, 321
resignation, 188, 189, 190, 194, 205
UUP and, 194, 323–4
criticised by Standing Committee, 321
Wright considers for Prime Minister, 312
FCA (Irish Territorials), 351, 355
Fenian Rising commemoration (1967), 117, 122
Fennell, Desmond, 69
Ferguson, John, 320
Ferguson, Richard, 321–2, 327
Fianna Éireann, 264, 375
Fianna Fáil, 337–8, 343, 352, 353, 391
Financial Times, 229
Fitt, Gerry, 22, 44, 72, 92, 126, 188
advocates demonstrations, 130, 385
barricades, 289, 293, 294, 295–6, 300
Belfast riots and, 254
B-Specials, 265–6
Burntollet and, 176, 178, 182
Catholic co-operation debate, 81
Coalisland demonstration, 135
Derry demonstration (1968), 138–9, 140, 158
election (1966), 47, 48, 111
Labour Party and, 111, 112, 113, 117, 119–20, 138–9
Newry march and, 183–4

Fitt, Gerry (*cont.*)
    O'Neill on, 133
    Orange Order and, 13–14
    Republican Clubs ban and, 118, 125
    UDR and, 316, 317
Fitzpatrick, Thomas, 45
Fitzsimmons, William, 62, 77, 87, 134, 186, 204, 213, 294
Flags and Emblems (Display) Act (NI) 1954, xii
Fleming, Head Constable, 240
Fletcher, Lt Colonel, 225
Foley, Denis, 97
franchise reform proposals, 148–52, 156, 157–8, 160, 186–7, 203, 210–12, 219
Freeland, Lt-General Sir Ian
    barricades and, 292, 293, 294, 295, 297, 298, 299, 300
    Belfast riots and, 262, 283, 329, 336
    B-Specials and, 275, 276
    criticised by Orr, 290
    Derry riots and, 247, 248–9
    security operations responsibility, 275, 281–2, 286, 394
    UDR and, 317, 318, 332

Gallagher, Eamonn, 301, 340–1, 392
Gallagher, Revd Eric, 10
Gallagher, John, 263, 264
Garland, Roy, 332, 333
Garland, Seán, 96, 97, 100, 102
Garron Tower, 80
George, Jimmy, 375
gerrymandering, 72–3, 107–8, 381
    Cameron Report, 302
    overview, 382
Gibbons, James, 346, 347, 348, 354, 364, 365, 366, 367, 368, 369, 370–3
Gibson, Edward, 33
Gifford, Lord, 119
Gilchrist, Sir Andrew, 245–6, 251, 269–70, 273, 338–9, 340
Gill, Thomas, 97, 104
Gilles, Revd Donald, 257–8, 260
Gilmore, Elizabeth, 253, 254
Girr, Peter, 207
Glendinning, Ivan, 208

Glover, Major, 39, 69–70
Gogarty, Frank, 176, 244, 280
Goodfellow family, 133–4
Gormley, Patrick, 30, 38–9, 48, 80, 90
Gormley, Thomas, 89
Gould, Matilda, 55
Goulding, Cathal, 96, 97, 347, 352, 356, 357, 362, 388
    defends IRA actions, 358–61
Government of Ireland Act 1920, x–xi, 17, 84, 108–9, 113, 116, 121, 162
Gracey, Sgt Thomas, 253, 254
Graham, Sean, 217
Grey, Lord, 175, 282
Grimond, Joe, 85
Grogan, Laurence, 97

Halligan, Brendan, 344
Hall-Thompson, Major Lloyd, 199, 320
Hamill, John, 37
Hamilton, Lord, 267
Hanson, Major, 252
Harris, Sergeant, 240
Harris, Sir Ian, 214
Harrison, Mary, 289
Hastings, Revd Edwin, 8
Hastings, Max, 245
Hattersley, Roy, 245, 248–9, 250, 262
    UDR and, 315
Haughey, Charles, 33, 338, 343
    arms funding, 343–4, 346–7, 348, 350–1, 352–3
    arms smuggling, 353–4, 365, 371, 373–4, 392–3
        Dublin shipment, 370
    arms trial, 374
    NI incursion plans, 366, 368
Haughey, Padraig, 353
Hawe, Herbert, 309
Hayes, Patrick, 98
health services, employment in, 132
Healy, Cahir, 74, 75, 326
Healy, Denis, 224, 245
    Army policy on arrests, 335
    Downing Street Declaration (1969), 275, 276

military intervention, 164, 165, 166, 167, 168, 173, 200
    withdrawal implications, 221
  UDR and, 313–14, 315, 316–17, 318
Heatley, Fred, 135
Hefferon, Colonel Michael, 346–7, 364, 370, 371–3
Hegarty, James, 89
Henry, J.D., 11
Herdman, E.T.R., 37
Hillery, Dr Patrick, 270–1, 341–2, 369
Hinds (MP), 194
Holland, Beryl, 323
Holmes, Erskine, 182
Home Office (UK), 127–8
Homeless Citizens' League, 107
Honourable The Irish Society, 89
Hood, District Inspector, 176, 240, 241
housing discrimination, 72, 73–8, 85, 86, 129–31, 393–4
  Cameron Report, 302
  Hunt Report, 305
  overview, 382–3
  reform to system discussed, 152–3, 154, 156, 160, 219
    Callaghan proposal, 283
  squatting and evictions, 130–1, 133–4
Housing Trust, 73, 74, 75, 76, 85, 305, 382–3
Hughes, Brendan, 375
Human Rights Convention, 145, 154, 219
Hume, John, 120, 139, 308
  arms crisis, 371–2
  Blaney speech and, 343
  Burntollet and, 175, 178
  Chichester-Clark proposals and, 159
  on civil rights movement, 184, 211
  Derry riots (1969) and, 223–4, 237, 239
  election (1969), 198
    manifesto, 195–6
  growing influence, 159, 195
  Nationalist Party criticism, 196
  on RUC, 237, 239
  UDR and, 315–16
Hunt Report, 303–10, 315, 316
  recommendations, 304–5
  responses, 308–10, 325–6
Hutchinson, John, 320

IRA see Irish Republican Army
Irish Church Association, 10
Irish Council of Churches, 10, 184
Irish Government
  arms funding, 343–7, 350–5
  arms requested, 344–5, 346, 350–1
  arms smuggling, 353–4, 364–7, 369–74, 391
    Dublin shipment, 370
    overview, 391, 392–3
  arms trial, 374
  attitude to British intervention, 338, 339
  Belfast riots and, 269–71, 337
    misinformation, 344–5
  Derry riots and, 242–6, 251, 261, 337
  Downing Street Declaration response, 338
  IRA and, 337–8, 339, 346, 348, 392–3
    engineers IRA split, 363
    funding of IRA, 343–7, 350–5, 392–3
    method of funding, 352–3
    see also arms smuggling
  Irish Constitution, x, 22
  military action considered, 343, 348–50, 366, 368–9
    directive, 366, 368
    Irish Army, 365, 366
    overview, 393
    scenarios, 348–50
    strength of opposition, 368–9
  North–South relations (Lemass government), 22–35, 379
    Lemass visits NI, 28–32, 33–5
  North–South relations (Lynch government), 337–55, 391
  overview, 390–3
  Planning Board on Northern Ireland Operations, 348–50
  UN suggested as peace-keepers, 243, 245, 270–1, 339, 341, 369
  unification of Ireland issue, 338–43
    Lynch speech, 342–3
Irish Red Cross, 344, 352–3
Irish Republican Army (IRA), 95–106, 119, 153, 214, 384
  Belfast riots, 263, 265, 266–7, 268, 329, 360
    RUC suspect plot, 259
  Border Campaign, 2, 95, 359

Irish Republican Army (*cont.*)
British Army planning scenarios, 171, 172, 173
civil rights movement and, 105–6, 153, 265
presence at demonstrations, 135, 137, 139, 388
Derry riots and, 246, 360
finances and funding, 359–60
internments, 252, 263
Irish Government and, 337–8, 339, 346, 348, 392–3
engineers IRA split, 363
funding of IRA, 343–7, 350–5, 392–3
method of funding, 352–3
see also arms smuggling
personnel and structure (1966), 95–99
policy altered (1966), 99–106
Dept of Political Education, 103–5
Economic Resistance theory, 99–101
Provisional IRA, 355–76, 392–3, 394–5
formed, 337, 355–64
naming of, 357
offensive against British Army, 374–6
policy, 357–8, 367, 374–6
reorganised, 367, 374–5
smuggling of arms, 364–7, 369–74, 392–3
reprisal warning (1970), 329
sectarian attacks (pre-Troubles), 42–3, 46
split (1969–70), 355–64
training of 'Northern Command', 354–5
transforms nature of conflict, 337, 376, 394–5
Irish Times, 246
Irish Workers' Party, 362, 363
Irwin, William, 320

James, Private Shawn, 309
James Connolly Republican Club, 238
Jenkins, Roy, 113, 114, 125, 126, 127
Jenkins, William, 15, 41
John XXIII, Pope, 2, 15
Johnston, Chief Inspector James, 260
Johnston, Roy, 97, 103–5
Johnston, Sgt Samuel, 256
Johnston, William, 56

Joint Security Committee (JSC), 286, 311, 394
Jones, E.W., 43

Kee, Robert, 86
Keenan, Sean, 237–8, 240, 244, 300, 311, 347, 363
arms running, 353, 364–6
Kelly, Andrew, 56
Kelly, Basil, 44, 148, 150, 205, 293
Kelly, Billy, 365–6
Kelly, Jack, 77
Kelly, Captain James, 346, 347, 351–4, 355, 364, 367, 369–73, 374, 391
Kelly, John, 347, 351, 353–4, 355, 356, 369–70, 374
Kennedy, Dennis, 43–4, 75–7
Kennedy, Hugh, 311, 347
Kennedy, Patrick, 196, 198, 244, 288, 293
requests arms, 344–5, 350–1
Kerr, Annie, 143
Kidd, Councillor, 256
Kilfedder, James, 30, 47, 48, 324
Kirk, Herbie, 148, 149, 179, 217
Kreuter, Franz, 12

Labour Party (UK), 378, 379–80
Fitt and, 111, 112, 113, 117, 119–20, 138–9
MPs at Derry demonstration, 143
objectives (1969), 200–2
see also British Government
Lady of Lourdes Intermediate School, 4
Lagan, DI Frank, 311
Lagan bridge controversy, 45
Laird, Dr Norman D., 41, 217, 326
language and perception, 377
Lannigan, Robert, 258, 260
Lavery, George, 282
Law, Edward, 12
Lemass, Sean, 23–35, 48, 88, 107, 131–2, 192, 379, 391
Leng, Brigadier Peter, 300
Lennon, James, 93
Leppington, Richard, 56
Liberal Party, 125, 126
Liddle, Lt Colonel, 30, 32
Lilley, Roy, 83
Limavady, 207
Linton, David, 264

Lloyd George, David, 94
local government, 86, 115–16, 122, 382
    Cameron Report on, 302
    reform proposals, 148–52, 156, 157, 158, 203,
    219
Lockwood Report (1965), 36, 38–40, 41, 84, 122
Londonderry see Derry
Londonderry Citizens' Action Committee, 288
Loney, Constable Martin, 260
Long, Capt William, 62, 91, 162, 186, 187, 193,
204, 210, 291, 311
    Burntollet and, 175, 176, 179
Loyal Citizens of Ulster, 188
Lurgan, 328
    housing policy, 77–8
Luykx, Albert, 370, 374
Lynch, Jack, 33, 35, 151, 337–45, 390–3
    arms crisis, 354, 364, 365–6, 369, 370, 373–4,
    391, 392–3
        arms requested, 344–5, 348, 350
    Belfast riots reaction, 270
        misinformation, 344–5
    Callaghan on, 341
    compromise as Taoiseach, 338, 391
    Derry riots reaction, 242–6
    inflames riots, 244–5, 261, 392
    NI incursion plans, 366, 369
    Northern policy, 337–45, 390–3
    overview, 390–3
    Paisley on, 265
    unification of Ireland issue, 338–43
        unification speech, 342–3
Lynch, Michael, 263

MacAirt, Proinsias, 375
McAree, James, 317
McAtamney, District-Inspector, 241
McAteer, Eddie, 31, 39, 42, 72
    on British Government intervention, 128
    Burntollet and, 175
    Chichester-Clark proposals and, 159
    Coalisland demonstration, 135
    Derry demonstration (1968), 138, 139, 140
    Derry riots (1969), 238, 239, 252
    housing evictions, 134
    military involvement issue, 162–3

Nationalist Party co-operation, 19, 80,
88–9, 92–3, 113
    O'Neill and, 85, 88, 92, 116, 119, 120
        'Crossroads' speech, 162
    Orange Order and, 13, 84
    on Unionist denial of discrimination, 126
    Unionist symbols and, 90–1
McAteer, Hugh, 119
McAuley, Gerald, 264
McBride, Ronnie, 80
McCabe, Hugh, 264
McCann, Eamonn, 137, 140, 181, 195, 244, 301,
315, 388
    on Hume, 196
McCann, Hugh, 344
McCann, Joe (IRA), 43
McCann, Joe (NDP), 134
McCelland, David, 69
McClean, Hugh, 56, 57
McCloskey, Francis, 223
McCluskey, Conn, 107, 136
McCluskey, John, 98
McCluskey, Patricia, 107, 108, 109, 112, 116, 127,
135
McConnell, Brian, 52, 62, 84, 85–6, 109–10
McConnell, Revd G.B.G., 14
McConville, H.P., 77
McCoy, W.F., 321
McCreary, Alf, 208
McCullagh, Councillor, 256
McGill, Patrick, 89
McGirl, John J., 98
McGrady, Eddie, 196
McGuigan, Brian, 82–4
MaGuire, E.D., 70–1
McGurran, Malachy, 97
McHugh, Pat, 331
McKeague, John, 254, 268, 281
McKee, Billy, 356, 357, 374, 375, 395
McKee, Sir Cecil, 15–16, 45
McKenna, Brian and Matthew, 133
McKnight, Billy, 98
McLarnon, Samuel, 263
McLaughlin, Thomas, 81–2
McMillen, Billy, 353, 356
McNally, Sean, 375

McQuade, John, 13–14, 194, 265–6, 308–9, 326

McQuaid, Elizabeth, 133

McQuaid, John Charles, Archbishop of Dublin, 9

MacStiofain, Sean, 353, 356–7, 358, 363–4, 395

Magee University College, 39

Maghera, 176, 207

Magowan, Sam, 15–16, 62

Malley, Jim, 28

Malvern Arms (Belfast), 56–7

Manual of Military Law, 164–5, 166

Margaret, Princess, 89

Margaret Craig Memorial Women's Lodge, 12

Mark, Robert, 271, 272–3, 303–4

marriages, mixed, 4, 7, 8, 15, 94, 378

Marshall, William, 282

Martin, Alfred, 17

Martin, Leo, 56, 356, 374–5

Mater Hospital, 156

Matthew Report (1964), 36, 40

Matthews, Francis, 93

Maydown engineering company, 208

Meade, Michael A., 96

Meehan, Martin, 375, 395

Melaugh, Eamonn, 137

Mercier, Ven. John, 10

Methodist Church, 3–4, 6–7, 10

Middle Liberties Young Unionist Association, 137, 288

military involvement issue, 162–8, 200, 213, 225
    in Derry, 246–51, 262
    direct rule and, 226–36
    planning and scenarios, 168–73, 229–36
    requested by NI Government, 250
    withdrawal suggestion, 220–1
    see also British Army

Millar, Frank, 333

Miller, Maurice, 120

Millman, Colonel Charles, 300

Mills, Stratton, 16, 47, 110

Minford, Dr, 329, 330–1

Minford, Nat, 13, 19, 31, 91, 330–1

Ministry of Defence (MOD), 163–73, 200, 317

Miskimmin, Colonel Stephen, 310

Mitchell, Robert, 326

Mitchell, Thomas (IRA), 97

Mitchell, Tom (MP), 48

mixed marriages, 4, 7, 8, 15, 94, 378

Mock, Revd Desmond, 323

Moderate Ulster Fund, 197

Montgomery, District-Inspector, 253

Moody, W.S., 41

Moore, Revd E.J., 10

Moore, R.N.L., 69

Moorman, John, Bishop of Ripon, 10

Moran, Michael, 373

Morgan, William, 65, 74–5, 85, 186, 187
    Clifton Unionist Association, 320
    election (1969), 199, 320
    elections (1970), 327–8, 329, 330, 331
    O'Neill rebellion, 190, 194, 195, 197
    O'Neill resignation, 216
    Paisley challenge, 327–8
    resignation, 188–9, 190, 194

Morrison, J.D., 21

Mulcahy, Patrick, 98

Mulvey, Father, 240–1

Murphy, Fr Joseph, 90

Murphy, Canon Padraig, 288, 290, 292, 293, 295, 296, 297–8, 299, 300

Murphy, Sean, 375

Murray, Philip, 99

Nash, K.T., 163

national anthem, 90

National Council for Civil Liberties (NCCL), 119

National Democratic Party, 44, 134, 196

National Farmers Association (NFA), 105

National Liberation Front (NLF), 356, 362

Nationalism, 92–5, 384
    bigotry and, 385–6
    language and perception, 377
    overview, 377–8, 385–6
    views on Unionists, 385

Nationalist Party, 19, 111, 387
    civil disobedience advocacy, 135
    decline of, 198
    discrimination reform policy, 84–6, 112–13
    Hume criticism, 196
    official opposition role, 88–9, 113

Neighbours' Co-operation, 362

Neill, Ivan, 79, 148, 149, 150, 186
Nelson, Revd Robert, 10
New Ulster Movement (NUM), 196–7, 331
Newe, Gerald B., 79–80, 81
Newry
    civil rights march (1968), 183–4
    Paisley organises march (1969), 236
News, Hugh, 77
News Letter, 312
NICRA *see* Northern Ireland Civil Rights
Association
Nixon, Robert, 38–40, 77, 86
Nolan, Liam, 97
North, Robin, 226–9
Northern Ireland Civil Rights Association
(NICRA), 129, 183, 218, 389
    Belfast riots (1969), 258, 268, 269
    Chichester-Clark proposals and, 159–60
    civil disobedience campaign, 135
    demonstrations, 135–44, 207, 208–9
        called off, 162, 211–12
    Derry riots (1969), 244, 389
    Downing Street Declaration response, 280,
    288
    Dungannon evictions and, 134
    objectives, 129
    People's Democracy and, 174, 175
    Protestant views on, 129, 136, 208, 388
    UDR and, 315, 316
    Unionist support for, 129
Northern Ireland (Emergency Provisions) Bill
1969, 169
Northern Ireland Labour Party (NILP), 119
    election (1965, Stormont), 42, 44
    election (1966), 47, 48
    election (1969), 198
Northern Irish Aid, 353
North–South relations (O'Neill–Lemass),
22–35, 379
    opinion poll (1967), 35
North–South relations (Chichester-Clark–
Lynch), 337–55, 391

O Bradaigh, Ruairi, 356, 361–3, 395
O'Callaghan, Eugene, Bishop of Clogher, 75
O Conaill, David, 356, 395

O'Connor, Joe, 99
O'Connor, Rory, 32
O'Donnell, Fr Columb, 253, 255
O'Donnell, Tom, 375
O'Hagan, Right Revd Dean, 78
O'Hagan, J.B., 98
O'Hanlon, Paddy, 344–5, 347
O'Leary, Matt, 135
O'Leary, Michael, 270
Oliver, Neill, 20
Omagh, 42
ombudsman proposals, 85–6, 114, 151–2, 153,
154, 156
    Compton appointed, 204
O'Neill, Phelim, 13, 14, 37, 87, 204, 333
O'Neill, Capt Terence, 378–80
    background, xiii, 378
    Burntollet and, 181–3
        aftermath, 184–8
    Catholic bridge-building, 1–2, 3, 4–5, 17,
    78–9, 82–4, 95, 131, 378–80, 381, 384
    Catholic popularity, 107
    Catholics and UUP, 17–18, 20, 21–2
    Chichester-Clark proposals, 159, 160–1, 185
    Craig sacking, 161, 162
    'Crossroads' speech, 161–2
    Currie on, 131–3
    defends status quo, 121–4
    Derry riot, memorandum, 146–8
    direct rule moves, 169–70
    on discrimination, 115, 120
    election (1965), 42–4
    election (1966), 48–9
    election (1969), 193–5, 197–200, 204, 378,
    384, 390
    on Faulkner, 194
    Faulkner's resignation, 189
    on Fitt, 133
    franchise reform proposals, 148–51
    inquiry call welcomed, 185–8
    IRA attacks feared, 214
    leadership challenged, 59–63, 65–6, 190–5,
    200, 204–6, 320, 321
    Lemass visit, 28–32, 33–5, 48, 88, 107, 131–2,
    192, 379
    McAteer and, 85, 92, 116

O'Neill, Capt Terence (cont.)
  moderation, 378–9
  North–South relations, 22–35, 379
    constitutional recognition, 24, 25
  opinion poll on (1966), 58–9
  overview, 378–80
  on Paisley, 192
  Paisley critical of, 15, 29, 34–5, 44–5, 46,
    52–3, 192–3, 198, 206, 381
  persona, 43
  police protection, 152
  on Protestant explosions, 209
  regional development, 37, 38, 40, 41–2
  resigns as Prime Minister, 214–15, 216
    build-up to, 200, 202–14
    decision to, 213
    discusses successor, 213–14, 215
    votes for successor, 217–18
  resigns Stormont seat, 321–2, 327
  troop deployment issue, 235–6
  'Ulster Community' address, 91–2
  Unionist Party opposition, 56, 59–63, 65–6,
    107, 190–2
  on UVF killings, 57–8
  West dismissal, 63–5
  Wilson talks, 113–16, 151–5
  Young Unionists critical of, 205–6
Orange Order
  ecumenism and reaffirmation services,
    10–11
  expels Phelim O'Neill, 13, 14
  Lemass visit and, 28, 33
  marches, 253, 255–6, 328
  McAteer proposes barring from LAs, 84
  Orangewomen, 12, 319
  political influence, 12–14, 319, 322–3
    intervenes in election, 330–1
O'Reilly, James, 85–6, 112
Orme, Stanley, 120, 252
O'Rourke, Catherine, 257
O'Rourke, Emmanuel, 257
Orr, Capt L.P.S., 18, 47, 84, 110, 120, 290,
330
Osmond, Douglas, 271, 272–3, 303–4
O'Toole, Terence S., 98
Owens, Sgt Anthony, 257

Paisley, Eileen, 15, 16, 216
Paisley, Revd Ian, 380–1, 384, 386
  Armagh march (1970), 328
  Belfast riots and, 265, 268–9
    called to calm mob, 290
  Brooke criticism, 326–7
  B-Special redeployment and, 280
  Burntollet and, 178
  by-election (1964), 15–16
  Chichester-Clark criticism, 331, 336
  Coalisland demonstration, 135
  condones discriminatory practices, 72
  Easter Rising Commemoration (1966),
    50–1, 52
  ecumenical movement, 3–6, 380, 381
  election (1966), 48
  election (1969), 192, 197, 198, 390
  elections (1970), 327–8, 330, 331
  Hunt Report and, 308
  influence, 53, 114, 334, 380–1
  jailed, 16–17, 207
  Lemass visit and, 28–9
  on Lynch, 265
  media and, 5
  mental health questioned, 308
  Morgan challenged, 327–8
  Newry march (1969), 236
  O'Neill criticism, 15, 29, 34–5, 44–5, 46,
    52–3, 192–3, 198, 206, 381
  opinion poll on (1966), 58–9
  oratory, 54, 268, 380
  overview, 380–1, 386
    political dinosaur, 384
  provocation, 53–4, 268–9, 381
  religious fundamentalism, 386
  'traditional Unionism', 2
  UCDC and, 46, 49, 58
  Unionists turn to, 190, 380–1
  UPV and, 49, 54, 328
  UVF and, 57–8
  Wilson criticism, 206, 280
Paisley, Revd J.K., 11
paramilitary revivals, 49–50, 54–8, 95–106,
  355–64, 374–6, 384, 394–5
parliamentary commissioner proposals, 85–6,
  114, 151–2, 153, 154

partition, x–xi, 2, 23, 25–6, 382
  and unification issue, 338–43
Passmore, Thomas, 260, 261
Patterson, Revd Carlisle, 6
Paul VI, Pope, 5, 10
peace lines, 264, 291, 293, 301, 361
Peacocke, Inspector-General Anthony, 214, 225, 242, 263, 275
  criticised by British police, 271, 272
  replaced, 305–6, 308
Peacocke, Very Revd C.I., 10
Peck, Sir Edward, 251
Peck, John, 374
People's Democracy (PD), 206–7, 211, 288
  Burntollet march, 174–83, 389
  election (1969), 197, 199
  formed, 143, 174
  Newry march, 183–4
Philbin, William, Bishop of Down and Connor, 22, 70–1, 72, 82, 292, 297–8, 299, 300, 345
pluralism, 382
Police Authority, 307, 325–6
Porter, Norman, 7–8, 11, 31
Porter, Robert, 20, 66, 195, 204, 209, 210, 213, 218–19, 275
  Belfast riots and, 263, 293, 310
  Derry riots and, 242, 252
  Hunt Report and, 306, 311, 325, 326
  Joint Security Committee, 286
  troops deployment, 225–6, 232–3, 234, 235, 283
  UDR and, 315, 317
Porter, Revd W.W., 7
Pounder, Rafton, 121
Power, Sgt John, 309
Poyntz, George, 98
Presbyterian Church, 3–4, 6, 7, 14, 191, 384
Price, Albert, 375
Pringle, Peter, 98
prisoner releases, 218
proportional representation, xii
Protestant Telegraph, 5, 15
Protestants, 1–17, 377–8, 385
  Cameron Report and, 302–3
  civil rights movement and, 136, 208, 388

ecumenical movement, 3–10
  fears, 2–3, 383
  Hunt Report and, 308–10, 325–6
  impact of Belfast riots, 264–5
  intolerance of Catholics, 11–12
  language and perception, 377
  symbols, 89–91, 378
Provisional IRA, 355–76, 392–3
  formed, 337, 355–64
  naming of, 357
  offensive against British Army, 374–6
  policy, 357–8, 367, 374–6
  reorganised, 367, 374–5
  smuggling of arms, 364–7, 369–74, 392–3
  transforms nature of conflict, 337, 376, 394–5
Public Order Act 1951, 117
  amendment proposals, 187–8

Queen's University, 143, 174
Queen's University Conservative and Unionist Association, 20, 129
Queen's University Unionist Voters' Association, 319
Quigley, Frank, 266
Quigley, Kathleen, 288
Quinn, B., 97
Quinn, Seamus, 70

Race Relations Act, 109–10, 112
Race Relations Board, 304
Radio Free Belfast, 347
railway closures, 36, 37, 41
Ramsey, Dr, Archbishop of Canterbury, 4
Ramsey, Head Constable, 258
Randalstown, 176
Rankin, William, 41
regional development, 36–42, 67, 74–5, 321
Republic of Ireland
  British embassy attacked, 269–70
  Constitution, x, 22, 377
  Easter Rising Commemoration (1966), 50
  IRA personnel and structure, 95–9, 103–5
  Nelson's Pillar blown up, 50
  Protestant/Catholic population, 2–3, 8–9, 377–8

Republic of Ireland (*cont.*)
   Unionist views on, 377–8
   see also Irish Government
Republican Clubs, 105, 129
   banned, 117–19, 125
Republican Labour Party, 47, 48, 182, 196, 198
Republican News, 375
Resistance (publication), 265
Revels, Stanley, 87
Richard, Ivor, 119
Richmond, Albert, 317
Robertson, Sir James, 303
Rodgers, Jim, 324
Rodgers, Robert, 15
Rogan, Denis, 205, 324
Rooney, Patrick, 263
Rose, Paul, 111, 112, 120, 121, 123
Rose, Richard, 68, 69, 74, 95
Roy, Herbert, 263, 266
Royal Military Police (RMP), 311–12
Royal Ulster Constabulary (RUC)
   Belfast riots (1969), 225, 253–4, 255–62, 266–9, 309
     Catholics killed, 263–4
     IRA plot suspected, 259
     policeman killed, 309
   Burntollet march, 176–9, 181
   Catholic recruitment campaign (1969), 220, 222
   Catholics lose confidence in, 253, 255, 262, 269, 275, 389, 390
   'conspiracy of silence', 223
   criticised by British police, 271–3, 303–4
   CS gas issued, 222–3, 224, 226, 228, 241, 249
   Derry marches (1968), 140–3, 154–5, 178–9, 388–9
   Derry policy, 158–9, 291, 388–9
   Derry riots (1969), 237, 239–42, 248, 268
     casualties, 223, 239, 240
     Catholics killed, 223
     CS gas used, 241
     guns used, 241–2
   disarmed, 307–8, 330, 393
   GOC control over, 275–81
   Hume on, 237, 239
   Hunt Report, 303–4, 307–8, 310, 325–6

   IRA attacks feared, 214
   new police force suggested, 247, 250, 252, 283
   Newry march and, 183, 184
   RAF helicopter request denied, 223
   reform called for, 271–3, 283
   reformed, 307–8, 325–6, 393
   'Riot Police' (Reserve Force), 140, 141
   sectarianism, 176
   strength of (1970), 368
Royal Ulster Rifles, 55
Royal Victoria Hospital, 5
RUC *see* Royal Ulster Constabulary
Rush, Kevin, 243, 344
Ryan, John, 143

St Angelo Airport, 63–4
St Anne's Cathedral, Belfast, 10
Sansom, Revd Charles, 259
Scarman, Lord, 268–9, 282
Scott, Walter, 60–1, 86
Scott, W.H., 130–1
Scott-Bowden, Brigadier Logan, 317
Scullion, John Patrick, 56, 57
Sea Eagle, HMS, 162–3, 248, 251
Sean McGaughey Club, 125
sectarianism, 389–90
   attacks (1965–6), 42–3, 45–6, 56–7
   build-up of tensions (Belfast, 1969), 252–5
   impact of Belfast riots, 264–5
   in RUC, 176
Shankhill Defence Association, 268, 281
Shea, Patrick, 68, 69
Shillington, Deputy Inspector-General Graham, 241, 242, 272
Silent Valley reservoir, 209
Silkin, Samuel, 119
Simpson, Robert, 62, 217
Sinclair, Betty, 137, 140
Sinclair, Marjorie, 34
Sinn Féin, 117, 361
   flag in office removed, 53
   split, 358
Sirocco Engineering Works, 70–2
Slevin, District Inspector, 240
Smith, Harold, 16

Smyth, M., 269
Smyth, Revd Martin, 7, 256
Soskice, Sir Frank, 109
Special Powers Act *see* Civil Authorities Act
Spence, Councillor, 256
Spence, Gusty, 54–7
squatting and evictions, 130–1, 133–4
Steele, Jimmy, 355, 363, 375
Stephenson, Seán, 96, 97
Stevenson, Captain (UVF), 289
Stewart (Labour Party), 200, 243, 275, 278
Stewart, Revd John, 7
Stewart, Senator, 136
Stonham, Lord, 127–8, 162, 223–4, 232–3, 236, 248–50, 270, 275, 282, 308
Stormont election (1965), 42–4
Stormont '66 Committee, 62, 65
Strabane, 42
Strabane Civil Rights Committee, 188
Strain, Charles, 289
Stronge, James, 211
Sullivan, Jim, 288, 293, 311–12, 351, 356
symbols, Unionist, 89–91, 378

Taylor, John, 44, 72, 120, 136, 217, 316
    Belfast riots and, 265
    B-Specials and Hunt Report, 310
    Chichester-Clark criticism, 218
    Dungannon housing discrimination, 133, 134
    'hatchet man', 322
    rebels against O'Neill, 60, 61, 190, 194, 200, 204, 205
Thant, U, 5
Thicknesse, Brigadier, 50
Thornberry, Cedric, 119
Thorpe, Jeremy, 125, 126
Times, The, 120, 250
Tite, Sheila, 178
Toal, Peter, 261
Todd, Jack, 290
Todd, Lt-Colonel, 252
Toomebridge, 175–6
'traditional Unionism', 2, 4, 325, 383
Trainor, William, 259–60
Trinity College, Dublin, 9
Twomey, Seamus, 356, 374, 375

Ulster Constitution Defence Committee (UCDC), 46, 49, 51, 58, 178, 302
Ulster Defence Regiment (UDR), 313–18, 326, 332
    B-Specials recruited, 313, 314, 315–18
    formation and organisation, 312–18
    naming of, 314–15
    strength of (1970), 368
Ulster Liberal Party, 129
Ulster Protestant Volunteers (UPV), 49, 54, 136, 254, 302, 328
Ulster Reform Club, 319
Ulster Special Constabulary *see* B-Specials
Ulster Unionist Council (UUC), 39, 310, 318–19, 332, 381
Ulster Unionist Party (UUP), 36–66, 318–34, 390
    Cameron Report and, 303
    Catholics and, 17–22, 193, 323, 324
        election (1969), 198, 199–200
    Chichester-Clark criticism, 308, 312, 319–22, 324–5, 327
        no-confidence motion, 332–3
    denies discrimination, 86, 115
    dissension in, 59–63, 107, 188–9, 190–5, 204–6, 318–34, 380, 390
        continued instability, 318, 378, 381–2
    election (1964), 15–16
    election (1965), 42–4
    election (1966), 47–9
    election (1969), 193–5, 197–200, 320, 378, 390
    elections (1970), 327–8, 329–31
        polarisation following, 331–2
    Hunt Report and, 310, 325–6
        backbench rebellion, 326
    ideology, lack of common, 334
    Lemass visit, reaction to, 29–32, 33–4
    O'Neill leadership challenges, 59–63, 65–6, 190–5, 204–6
    O'Neill's successor elected, 215–18
    Orange Order and, 12–14, 319, 322–3, 330–1
    overview, 381–2
    regional development, 36–42, 321
    Thorpe attack and, 126
    Ulster Unionist Council, 39, 310, 318–19, 332, 381

Ulster Unionist Party (*cont.*)
  at Westminster, 110, 111, 116
  women in, 318–19
  Wright meeting, 287
Ulster Volunteer Force (UVF)
  Belfast riots and, 266, 289
  declares war on IRA, 56–7
  Paisley and, 57–8
  re-formed (1966), 49–50, 54–8
  reprisal warning (1970), 329
  wrecks Belfast water supply, 209
Unionism
  language and perception, 377
  Nationalist views on, 385
  1916 symbolism, 386
  opinion poll (1967), 17
  overview, 377–8, 385, 386
  symbols, 89–91, 378
  traditional Unionism, 2, 4, 325, 383
Unionist Society, 319, 323
United Irishman, 265
United Nations, 5
  suggested as peace-keepers, 243, 245,
    270–1, 339, 341, 369
United States
  civil rights movement, 174–5
  IRA funding, 359
USC *see* B-Specials
UUC *see* Ulster Unionist Council
UUP *see* Ulster Unionist Party
UVF *see* Ulster Volunteer Force

Vatican, Fascist links, 5
Victoria Unionist Association, 21
vigilantes, 288–9, 290, 301, 311, 336, 367
Voice of the North, 347

Wakehurst, Lord, 89
Wallace, Sir Martin, 15
Walsh (UUP), 200
Ward, Peter, 56–7
Warnock, Edmond, 32, 59–60
Watson, Mrs Thomas, 12
Wesley, Harold, 323
West, Harry, 33, 188, 217, 325, 331, 333
  B-Special disbandment and, 280

O'Neill dismisses, 63–5
O'Neill resignation and, 216
rebels against O'Neill, 190, 194, 321
rebels over Police Bill, 326
West, Victor, 63
West Ulster Unionist Council, 321
Whitaker, Ken, 28
White, Barry, 177
White, John, 289
Williams, William E., 98
Williamson, Robert, 57
Willowfield Unionist Association, 319, 323
Wilson, Austin, 297–8
Wilson, Harold, 85, 109–11, 113–17, 176, 379, 387
  Belfast riots and, 262–3, 271–2
    barricades, 295, 296
  B-Special deployment changes, 276, 278,
    280, 281
  Catholic sympathies, 379
    discrimination concern, 121
  Chichester-Clark proposals, 160–1
  Chichester-Clark talks, 219
  Derry riots and, 245, 247–8, 250
  Downing Street Declaration, 275–81
  military involvement issue, 163, 231
  O'Neill talks, 113–16, 145
    inter-governmental meeting (1968),
      151–5
  overview, 387
  Paisley critical of, 206, 280
  pressure on NI Government, 155, 157–8,
    161, 379, 387
  pressure to intervene, 143, 145, 146, 212
  reluctance to intervene, 112, 113, 127, 387
  RUC, use of CS gas, 226
  UDR and, 316
  UUP and, 110–11
Wilson, Hugh, 199
Wilton, Claude, 43
Wolfe Tone Society, 105, 129
Wolseley, Harold, 225, 272
Women's Orange Order, 12, 319
World Council of Churches, 3–4, 6–7
Wright, Oliver, 274, 282, 286–8, 302, 306, 310–11
  analyses and recommendations, 287–8,
    312–13

barricades and, 291–3, 294, 295–6, 298–9, 300
Cardinal Conway meetings, 286–7, 292
on Chichester-Clark and Faulkner, 312–13
role of, 286
Wylie, Revd John, 4, 48, 207
Wyse, Bonaparte, 68

Young, Sir Arthur, 286, 305–6, 308, 330, 335, 394
visits Bogside, 310, 311
Young Socialists Alliance, 140–1
Young Unionists, 33–4, 37, 129, 137, 319
crisis in UUP, 324, 332, 333
critical of O'Neill, 205–6